D0438233

Coming of Age

OTHER BOOKS BY STUDS TERKEL

American Dreams: Lost and Found

Division Street: America

Giants of Jazz

The "Good War": An Oral History of World War II

The Great Divide: Second Thoughts on the American Dream

Hard Times: An Oral History of the Great Depression

*Race: How Blacks and Whites Think and Feel
About the American Obsession*

Talking to Myself: A Memoir of My Times

*Working: People Talk About What They Do All Day
and How They Feel About What They Do*

Coming *of* Age

The Story of Our Century by
Those Who've Lived It

STUDS TERKEL

The New Press · New York

© 1995 by Studs Terkel

All rights reserved.
No part of this book may be reproduced in any form
without written permission from the publisher.

Library of Congress Cataloging-in-Publication Data
Terkel, Studs, 1912–
    Coming of age: the story of our century by those who've lived it /
    Studs Terkel.
      p.   cm.
    ISBN 1-56584-284-7
    1. Aged—United States—Interviews. 2. Aged—United
States—Attitudes. 3. Social participation—United States—
Case studies. 4. Self-actualization (Psychology) in old age—
United States—Case studies. I. Title.
HG1064.U5T44   1995
305.26'0973—dc20   95-3806
                                        CIP

Published in the United States by The New Press, New York
Distributed by W. W. Norton & Company, Inc., New York

Established in 1990 as a major alternative to the large,
commercial publishing houses, The New Press is the first full-scale
nonprofit American book publisher outside of the
university presses. The Press is operated editorially in the public
interest, rather than for private gain; it is committed to
publishing in innovative ways works of educational, cultural,
and community value that, despite their intellectual merits, might
not normally be commercially viable. The New Press's
editorial offices are located at the City University of New York.

Book design by Charles Nix

Production management by Kim Waymer
Printed in the United States of America

95 96 97 98   9 8 7 6 5 4 3 2

*To those old ones who still
do battle with dragons*

When I'm an old woman I shall wear purple
With a red hat which doesn't go, and doesn't suit me.
And I shall spend my pension on brandy and summer gloves
And satin sandals, and say we've no money for butter.
I shall sit down on the pavement when I'm tired
And gobble up samples in shops and press alarm bells
And run my stick along public railings
And make up for the sobriety of my youth.
I shall go out in my slippers in the rain
And pick the flowers in other people's gardens
And learn to spit.

JENNY JOSEPH

Earth every day is clumsier. Stairs are stumbly;
Keys slip from fingers; floors are down too far.
Games show their age; balls bobble, thumbs are fumbly.
Mallets? They've turned flamingoes—there you are!
Worse: mirrors once full-bodied, rose and gold,
Show withering apparitions. Old! They're old!

JOHN FREDERICK NIMS

Sometimes when the fights begin,
I think I'll let the dragons win,
But then again, perhaps I won't,
Because they're dragons, and I don't.

A. A. MILNE

Contents

Acknowledgments
and
Apologies

As usual, a salute to my scouts—friends, acquaintances, and passing strangers—who were generous with tips and telltale anecdotes. Among them, in alphabetical order, are: James Achenbach, Michael Anania, Bill Ayers, Emily Barker, Jack Beatty, Ann Bernays, Kevin T. Berrill, Earl Bourdon (embattled to the end), Joe Brisben, Quinn Brisben, Bernice Buresh, Richard Carbray, Susan Corbett, Alex Coutts, Andrew Davis, Moe Foner, Tom Fox, Carole Gallagher, Thula Hampton, Randy Hecht, Elma Holder, Gary Johnson, Tony Judge, Jamie Kalvin, Kathy Kelly, Jeff Kisselgoff, Paul Kleyman, Lucy Kroll, Marie Kuda, Jim McFarland, Eric Marcus, Jill Nelson, Leroy Pearlman, Nelson Peery, Jack Price, Eric Reuther, Renault Robinson, Susan Rossen, Ed Sadlowski, Howard Saffold, Ralph Schoeneman, Harley G. Sellkregg, and Robert Wyatt.

To my colleagues at WFMT for winking at absenteeism far beyond my due, especially Norm Pellegrini, Lois Baum, and Linda Lewis, a tip of the hat. For transcribing my higgledy-piggledy tapes to print, in the elegant tradition of the late Cathy Zmuda, my gratitude to Sydney Lewis, Tammey Kikta, and Lucy Bukowski.

To Dawn Davis of The New Press for her thoughtful suggestions; to Jodie Patterson for keeping track of my maddening changes of heart and mind; and to Don McMahon for his assiduous copy editing—my thanks. And, of course, a bow to my editor and publisher, Andrè Schiffrin, who has always been there, for this work as well as for my previous adventures of like nature.

Lastly, my apologies to the elders not appearing in this book who had offered me their precious time, energies, and vibrance. Their stories were no less exhilarating and revealing than those that are present in these pages. As in the case of the director of a play, faced with the choice of equally splendid actors, mine were judgment calls. Omitting these storytellers was the toughest part of my job.

Introduction

> *"I am of the opinion that my life belongs to the whole commu-*
> *nity and as long as I live, it is my privilege to do for it what I*
> *can. I want to be thoroughly used up when I die, for the harder I*
> *work, the more I live. I rejoice in life for its own sake. Life is no*
> *brief candle for me. It is sort of a splendid torch which I have got*
> *hold of for a moment and I want to make it burn as brightly as*
> *possible before handing it on to future generations."*

Was George Bernard Shaw touching ninety when he wrote that? Or
eighty? Or seventy? The odds are his red whiskers had already
turned white. I know this was so with the seventy-five-year-old
storekeeper whose domain had become the center of the ghost
town, somewhere in the hills and hollers of eastern Kentucky.
"There's no way a man can slow down. I owe it to the people of this
community. There's no end to the battle. The last flicker of my life
will be against something that I don't think has to be."

Astonishingly, though the town is still up against it, among the
many wretched enclaves of the strip-mined region, it refuses to die.
The ghost has assumed flesh and is once again alive and kicking.
Thanks in no small way to this man's obdurate nature. He had never
met Shaw, nor, I'm fairly certain, had he ever read any of his stuff,
yet the two subscribe to the same tenet.

I have chosen him, along with sixty-nine other graying contemporaries of like nature as the protagonists of this work. A few will be
found here of another bent, perhaps, who nonetheless share his life
span and hang on as obstinately as he.

The choice—seventy as the minimum age for admission to this
circle—is not an arbitrary one. In our century, the scriptural three
score and ten as the allotted earthly portion has been considerably
extended, thanks to advances in medicine and—mixed blessing—
technology. There is a note of exquisite irony here.

It is not technology per se that the grayheads in these pages challenge, though there are a couple of Luddites in the crowd. It is the purpose toward which it has so often been put. Among the grievances aired: the promiscuous use of the machine; the loss of the personal touch; the vanishing skills of the hand; the competitive edge rather than the cooperative center; the corporate credo as all-encompassing truth; the sound bite as instant wisdom; trivia as substance; and the denigration of language. Wright Morris, some thirty years ago, pinpointed the dilemma: "We're in the world of communications more and more, though we're in communication less and less."

I talk into the telephone these days as hopefully, though uncertainly, as my brother once talked to horses. He was a small-time follower of the races, who, at the corner bookie shop, listening to the wire, desperately urged on his long shots. Of course, they also ran. It was a precious moment, Lord, when one of them delivered. (O rare Morvich!)*

So it is with me and the telephone: Will I reach my party? In the dear, dead days almost beyond recall, a human voice responded. Today, in metallic speech, seemingly human, you are offered a choice of numbers from one to, say, six. If you are lucky, or if God is with you, you might connect—that is, if you remember who it was you called.

The Atlanta airport is as modern as they come. As you leave the gate, there are trains that transport you to the concourse of your choice. As you enter one, the voice you hear, unlike the old-time train caller's, is robotic. It, rather than he or she, offers destinations. The blessed moment for me, as I and fellow passengers entered in dead silence, was when a late-arriving couple desperately parted the pneumatic doors and made it inside. The voice, without missing a beat, intoned: "Because of late entry, there is a thirty-second delay." So much for the tardy miscreants. All eyes turned toward the guilty two. They quailed. Having had a couple of drinks, I called out, "George Orwell, your time has come and gone." Silence. I quailed. As any fool can plainly see, we have made remarkable technological advances.

There was a moment of saving grace in the presence of a baby, seated in the lap of its Hispanic mother. Having overcome my momentary guilt, I addressed the infant: "What is your considered opinion of all this?" The child broke into a wide FDR grin. "There is still hope," I cried triumphantly, despite the ensuing silence. Then came sobriety and a cold morning.

Chalk this up as the crotchet of an octogenarian, singularly suspi-

---

*A runty little colt who won the Kentucky Derby in 1922. My brother had a two-dollar bet on him. It was one of his life's memorable moments.

cious of machines of any sort. It may have been one of my kindred spirits at the turn of the century, who, spotting a stranded motorist, shouted gleefully, "Get yourself a horse!"

It may have been an old man's arrogance in interpreting a baby's smile. The baby, much as Buckminster Fuller's grandchild, may have been attuned to the sound of the 727 long before it heard the song of the lark. The one song, the machine's, has become natural; the other, the bird's, has become exotic. Perhaps that's why old environmentalists sound so querulous.

Yet it was a ninety-year-old composer, who, at a concert of Stockhausen's electronic works, shouted "Bravo!" He had, sixty years before, in Vienna, cheered the revolutionary music of Webern, as others threw eggs. As I remained seated, bewildered by what sounded like static, he called out, "You'll see, my friend, one day you'll see." A young couple, seated nearby, holding hands, murmured, "They're playing our song." At least, I so imagined.

It evoked the memory of another concert, at a London watering hole, attended by serious, hardly audible young people. A tape of John Cage's sounds and silences filled the room, wall-to-wall with listeners enraptured. Standing. My calves were killing me. Bad circulation.

Life certainly does not begin at seventy, God knows, what with the ineluctable infirmities ruefully cited by our heroes. "I'm on my third pacemaker," says the eighty-year-old invalid, "and it's often out of rhythm and I use only half my heart. It takes down my spirits considerably." Yet her spirits soar, as she, in her sick bed, recalls her twenty-three-year-old self as the firebrand of the 1937 Flint sit-down strike. She is atop that sound truck once more. "I can't become cynical. I still hope we'll see a decent society, for cryin' out loud." A deep sigh. "I better take that pill now."

The Mexican American, doyen of his community, is philosophical as he responds to his buddy, who grieves on seeing him hobble with his cane. "It beats not walking at all." The widow of our century's preeminent cultural critic laments her husband's last years. "He was living half the way, obstreperous, incontinent, who had lived with such dignity." She bangs her fist on her walker. "This glorification of old age is a great mistake." Yet none of them will accept the status of Beckett's gaffers and crones. No trash can finale for these embattled ones. Their sphere is still Out There.

This work is not so much a gathering of individuals, survivors leading passionate lives, as it is about enclaves, helter-skelter, with these singular beings as metaphor as well as flesh. "Maybe there are people talking and thinking as we are now," says the African American painter. "I feel as long as there's one person or two aware of our capacity to feel, think, and remember, we're on pretty sound ground." He adds tentatively, "I hope so."

During my occasional appearances in small towns as well as large cities—Dallas among them—there is always an individual or a couple, or an eccentric or town troublemaker, or a small group of gentle folk, who hang around after the formalities to unburden themselves. There is a recurrent refrain: What's happened to history? What's happened to imagination? It is these people the painter had in mind.

In Edwardsville, Indiana, home of Wabash College and General Lew Wallace, author of *Ben Hur*, an elderly woman, scion of the town's pioneer family, speaks softly, almost in a whisper, during the wine-and-cheese reception: "It is lonely here, thinking as I do. Remembering." It is she the painter had in mind.

Remembrance is the attribute that most distinguishes them. They are, in a sense, living repositories of our past, our history. Unfortunately, life's attrition is rapidly diminishing them in number; thus, the underlying note of desperation in the making of this book. Five I had hoped to visit died within a month of one another. At least three who appear in this book have since died. For that matter, I shall be eighty-three, if my luck holds out, at the time of this book's publication.

Naturally, the young are in the thoughts of these elders. Constantly. Though I had anticipated the touch of the curmudgeon, it was far less forthcoming than I had expected. There was sharp commentary, but the recurrent refrain was one of mourning. "I feel sorry for my grandchildren," says a pioneer public relations man. He adds, "I have no faith in my contemporaries." A West Coast philanthropist, a once-upon-a-time southern belle, provides a coda: "We must do something to merit their respect."

What is inescapable, a reflection offered by all the protagonists, is the innocence of the youngbloods when it comes to the past. And their lack of interest. There are the usual exceptions: the raggle-taggle marching kids so often maligned and ridiculed. "Most kids are frighteningly ignorant. They have no sense of history. What's worse, they don't think it matters." This from a woman who herself had been so much a part of our unwritten history.

The storekeeper remembers "the young lady student, she never heard of Roosevelt." Yet others saunter into his place seeking out his knowledge. The embattled old environmentalist counters, "Their history has been stolen from them." Among his most devoted colleagues are the young.

The actress regards her student-aspirants with guarded optimism. "Until five years ago, I thought they were all slobs. There was a kind of cynicism, an arrogance. In the last few years, I've sensed a change. There seems to be a new purpose in young people. Maybe, I don't know..."

The sparrow of a woman, touching ninety-four, says, "I think the young today are much more honest than we were. They see things as they are. I would not want to be young now. They're having a hell of a time. Often, they annoy me, almost knocking me down with their bikes and roller skates. Yet they help me across the street. They always come through, every single one."

A retired admiral who founded a whistle-blowing contingent of ex-officers which monitors the Pentagon is disturbed. "I lecture in colleges and high schools, the pick of the crop. It's obvious their attention is not on anything except their personal lives. I don't want to be an old curmudgeon who suggests that us older guys had a better world. We didn't. But this is unlike anything when I was in school." The elderly Jesuit suggests, "What they need is a national cause."

There appeared to be a couple of national causes in the '60s: civil rights and the Vietnam War. For all its excesses, well advertised by the media, many of the young engaged themselves in matters outside their personal lives. The ensuing decades of two conservative presidents succeeded in revising, rather than conserving, the story of that tumultuous time.

On a popular Sunday morning round-table program, two of its regular participants savaged a guest who, we were told, was an emblem of the '60s. The two, one labeled conservative, the other, liberal (an egregious case of lingo-promiscuity), had a high old time with the hapless visitor. They were somewhat more self-righteous than the Katzenjammer Kids, but equaled them in light-heartedness and mischief. Joan Nestle put it succinctly. "The '60s is the favorite target of people who take delight in the failure of dreams." It is, I'm afraid, the sign of something else: a national Alzheimer's disease.

It is ironic that so many old ones in this book, though forgetful of many personal things, remember that decade as they had actually observed it. "I worry because I usually forget things, like where I put my shoes," says the Georgia widow who had been active in civil rights. "My daughter said, 'Mama, yes, deaf you are. Blind, yes, you are. But, Mama, you're not senile. You still think and remember important things.'"

The eighty-three-year-old woman, a stockbroker, laughs. "In some ways I'm better than I was thirty-five years ago when I broke in. My memory isn't so good on unimportant things: Where did I put my glasses? Where did I leave my keys? But if a customer asks me, 'Do you remember what I paid for my IBM stock?,' I remember right off the bat. I remember the birth dates of people I love." In the remembrance of these elders may be a slender reed of hope. It is not upon them that a lobotomy has been performed, though you may find, especially among the golf-cart set, a self-imposed amnesia.

More than in any other sphere, it is the young's attitude toward the world of labor that most alarms the old trade union veteran. "The younger generation's outlook is shaped by the media, which draws a blank on labor matters. It's a rare newspaper that has a labor reporter these days."

At the very moment of this writing, a bitter strike is being waged in Decatur, Illinois, against a company owned by a British conglomerate. Most of the men and women on strike have lived in this town all their lives. Five minutes ago, I reran a homemade videotape: The city's police, helmeted, in full riot gear, are spraying the seated strikers with pepper gas. As the screams are heard, almost to a breaking point, I hold a stopwatch: ten and a half minutes.

I scanned both our local papers and several of our most respected journals: not one reference to the encounter. In 1937, when Chicago police attacked a gathering of steel workers, it made national headlines.

Each day, I sort out parts of the newspaper. I come across the Business section. Of course. I read about markets, mergers, LBOs, dividends, downsizing (read: *layoffs*) and related money matters. In an occasional spirit of whimsy, I look for the Labor section. It's my private joke. There ain't no such animal.

No wonder I had that contretemps with the young couple as we waited for our morning bus: I, with my haphazard bundle of papers; he, with the *Wall Street Journal* neatly under arm; she, with the latest *Vanity Fair*. We nodded toward one another, as we've done daily for at least a year. This time, I spoke. "I see where Labor Day is approaching." (It was a few days before that once-celebrated holiday.) The response was a cool, dead-blank stare. They turned away. I was hurt. Perversity got the best of me.

"That's the day," I insisted, "working people paraded down State Street by the thousands, honoring their unions." I was unable to stop; a soap box speech was in the making. With a clipped response worthy of Noel Coward, he cut off the old bum. "We *loathe* unions." Apparently, he spoke for both.

Instantly, I was the Ancient Mariner, fixing him with glittering eye. (Fortuitously, the bus was late.) "How many hours a day do you work?" It was something of a non sequitur. Caught off guard, he replied, "Eight hours." I had him. "How come you don't work fourteen hours? Your great-grandfather did." He was pinned against the mail box. He looked about, as for a passing patrol car. The devil had me on the hip. "Know why you work eight hours instead of fourteen? Some guys got hanged in 1886. Fighting for the eight-hour day—for *you*." It was a reference to the Haymarket Affair in Chicago, so long, long, long ago. "They were union men." The young woman tugged at the sleeve of her stricken young man and, as the bus finally came, they scurried onto it. I never saw them again.

Often I think of them and feel ashamed of myself. How could I thus abuse them, this sweet-looking, all-American young pair? They had never done me any harm. Yet why do I, like Huck Finn on the raft, feel so good when I think about it?

The labor advocate is even more critical of his peers: several, comrades in old battles. "Some of my generation has been elevated into the middle class, thanks to our fights to improve living standards. They have forgotten."

The economist, on the sunny side of eighty-six, sees further irony. "One of the reasons liberals have been marginalized is that government, through social security, through one benefit and another, has made many people comfortable, contented, and conservative. Where would Bob Dole be today were it not for the farm program and agricultural price supports?"

In the neatest trick of the century, big government the benefactor has been transmogrified into Big Guv'ment the bête noire. An old dissenter adds his touch to the tale: "Government today is most hated by those it's most helped." The old, old woman is less burdened by her Parkinson's than by her impotent rage: "They tell us what to think, the big ones up there. Don't they own everything—the TV, the radio, papers, the whatnot?" Her dark humor undiminished, she croaks: "Glory, glory, hallelujah, His truth goes marching on." Perhaps it's the mission of these old ones, vestigial remainders of a throbbing, embattled past, to question this chorus and remind us what the song was all about.

"History is bunk," Henry Ford once proclaimed. At the moment, he has the mark of a prophet. With our past become so irrelevant, with yesterday's fevered communiqué as archaic as a pharaonic news flash, is it any wonder that the young feel so disdainful of their elders? If it's a matter of competition (*competitive*, the fighting adjective that pervades all discourse on education, health, and business), it's "Out of my way, you old geezer. One side or a leg off!"

The retired CEO has seen it all. "There's a new breed now. In the old days, to become top man of a company, you had to be in your fifties and sixties. Today you've got twenty-nine-year-old CEOs. When I started out in the jungle, you were a baby at forty-five. Yet people are still vigorous at seventy, seventy-five. That's the catch."

The senior partner of one of Chicago's oldest and most prestigious law firms was retired after thirty-three years. It was mandatory: he was seventy-three. It was tradition. What was untraditional was his loss of pension. A disastrous merger had taken place without his consent or advice. He sued the partners and lost in federal court. The judge, a young alumnus of the law school the plaintiff had attended years before, said, in effect: "Those are the chances you take, Pops."

A pioneer television producer, a founder of the Chicago school,* is easy about it. "Naah, nobody wants lunch with me. Why should they? It's like spending time with your grandfather. You can't make a buck that way. Today's shows wouldn't have worked in our time. They're too hard, too cruel."

A successful comedy writer of the '60s and '70s has few offers of work these days. Though he is well-off in residuals, he's even richer in anecdotes. An agent was warned by a young executive: "Don't you dare send me any more over forty." A regular writer for Jack Benny pleaded with his daughter as they entered the office of a kid executive: "Please don't mention Jack Benny's name. He'll think I'm ninety years old."

The coming of age is regarded in some quarters as something of an affliction. For several years, a hand lotion commercial extolled its salubrious effect in freeing the elderly from "those ugly age freckles." A hair formula advertises, with considerable pride, the transforming of natural gray hair to ersatz black. The delighted wife, appraising her suddenly brunet spouse, announces to the world that he looks so much better. If further evidence were needed to prove that love is blind, this will do. The subtext is obvious: he may hold on to his job a bit longer.

Do schoolchildren still recite "John Anderson, My Jo John"? It was in all those *Most-Beloved Poems* readers: Robert Burns's endearing toast to gray locks, wrinkles, love, and beauty. How can they stifle their childish giggles, having been daily attuned to the message of Grecian Hair Formula?

George Bernard Shaw, as a drama critic, saw Europe's two most celebrated actresses at work, and aging: Sarah Bernhardt, mistress of makeup, and Eleanora Duse, who had no use for cosmetics. He said, "I prefer the Italian. Her wrinkles are her credentials of humanity."

Joe Matthews told me of his father's funeral. The old man was ninety. Joe, a minister, was asked by the family to say a few words.

---

* "TV, Chicago style" is a phrase coined by John Crosby, television's preeminent critic in the '50s. He was referring to a free and easy, improvisational approach.

"I hadn't seen my father in years. I wanted one last look at him. In the funeral parlor, the night before, I looked into the casket and saw a kewpie doll! All rouged and powdered. I asked the undertaker for a basin of hot water, soap, and a towel. The guy was indignant. 'Your father looks perfectly wonderful.' I said, 'The hell he does. This is not my father.' Unless he gave me the stuff, I'd carry the body out myself. After two hours of washing off the guck, the old man's face caved in and all those wrinkles appeared. Those wrinkles we put there, my ten brothers, sisters, and mother. Those wrinkles told us that he had lived and so did we. At long last, I saw my father."

What most disturbs the painter is the young's obsession with the computer. "I am not averse to technology. But when a student can do a portrait by computer, without having laid a finger on brush, canvas, or paper, he's proud. 'My hand never touched it.' He can do that portrait in one day: no breathing felt, no blinking, no air around you, no space. Hammer? Chisel? They don't want to be accused of succumbing to this human thing: touch. Distance is a plus."

"The laying on of hands," says the doctor, "has been the most wonderful experience of my life. The house call, which may be coming back, became the hostage of high tech. Just as it's changed the nature of the practice, it has affected medical students. If you ask a doctor in training, 'How's Mrs. Smith doing?,' he'll instinctively go to the computer and punch out the latest lab test. 'Did she have a good night's sleep? Is that pain in her chest different?' 'Oh, I didn't check that.' Distant? You bet."

Yet the young scholar of avant-garde comic books points out the computer's liberating attributes: freeing us from drudge work for the more creative life. He's probably right, though I, a relic of another time, am somewhat bewildered by the new lingo. It is as arcane to me as Aramaic. "Hardware" does not concern hammer and nails and wrench, but something else. "Software" is altogether something apart from bedspread, pillowcases, and Turkish towels. My abysmal ignorance of the new technology has probably colored these introductory pages. I am, to put it baldly, a high-tech Philistine.

I envy the ninety-five-year-old sparrow who delights in her word processor and laser printer. "It's easy as pie," she says. I have just learned the mysteries of an electric *typewriter*, though it has in no way improved my hunt-and-peckery. It has, of this moment, gone on the blink. (Time out. It is a few hours later. The man has come and fixed it. "Nothing wrong with it. You pounded it too hard and bent the key slightly. There are some cigar ashes in the machine. The ribbon is stuck—I don't know how you did it." It was easy.)

After thirty-odd years with one tape recorder or another, German Uher or Japanese Sony, I encounter trouble—court it, some would say. My ineptitude is ecumenical. Pressing the wrong button, I have lost (erased or failed to record) Michael Redgrave, Peter Hall, Martha Graham, Jacques Tati and almost succeeded in making Bertrand Russell disappear. You might say I'm a magician of sorts. Did Cagliostro ever make philosophers vanish?

These maladventures have nothing to do with age or oncoming dotage. It has been thus from the very beginning. My encounters with elevator doors need not be gone into. I have kicked at them on more than one occasion and there has always been a response. They close. Perhaps I'm a closet Luddite and my hostility, at times, bursts forth. So there is no point in my ever considering a computer or its next of kin.

The elderly lawyer finds his daily work far less demanding today than in pre-high-tech times. "We had to rely on the drudgery of recopying old documents. Today we photocopy. We have instant communication by fax. All of which makes the practice far more enjoyable than it used to be."

The investment banker remembers when "I used to sit with a spreadsheet, doing comparisons of statistics, ours and all the other companies. You'd be absolutely bleary-eyed. It was terrible work. Today it's easy: machines. I don't understand them. I don't want to. Too little time. The young ones know all about them. They're in, I'm out."

The carpenter agrees that technology has made his work easier, though he observes wistfully that "very few carpenters can file their own saws today. They don't need to. Hand saws are out." (It is the disappearance of the hand tool—and thus the loss of the human touch—that the painter mourned.)

There is a deeper grievance the carpenter feels. With technology putting so many skilled craftsmen out of work, why not a shorter work week, say thirty hours? "More jobs and more time for creative leisure."

The retired printer says amen to that. "You can't stop progress, but don't tell me there's no way that replaced workers can't share in all these savings. It was their skills and muscle and pride that kept all this going all these years. Now our skills have been turned into binary numbers."

There is another matter that disturbs this voluble man: the disappearance of talk in the workplace. "Today the composing room is as silent as the editorial room. Have you been over at the city desk of any of the papers lately? It used to be so wild and romantic. Now it's dead. Like the composing room."

The irrepressible press agent, the last of his species, remembers his glory days as a familiar in the city room. "I'm in my shirt sleeves at the typewriter, flailing away with two fingers. I *belonged* there. If you tried that today, seven security guards would escort you out. Anyway, I couldn't work their computers."

On the desks of young reporters in the city room, as on the desks of young traders at the brokerage house, is the ubiquitous IT, through whose windows they stare, in the manner of voyeurs. Each is in a private world, close by colleagues, yet planets away. It is solipsism en masse.

Though silence pervades where once there was a human sound, conversely, noise overwhelms where once there was quiet. There was a time when a long-established Chicago restaurant had as its hallmark: No Orchestral Din. A quiet conversation could take place across the table and the patrons could actually hear one another. The place has long since been shuttered.

Several years ago, a friend of mine, a singer, concluded his concert. A half dozen of us adjourned to a nearby restaurant. It was about eleven at night. We were the only patrons. The canned Muzak was so loud we had difficulty hearing one another, though we shared the same table. We asked the hostess if she could turn it off or at least lower the volume. She declined. The simple truth: she could do nothing. It was remotely controlled.

When talk, where it matters, is discouraged, and quiet, where it matters, is also discouraged, is it any wonder that the speech of the young has been affected. "They talk in short, curt sentences," says the high school teacher, "in phrases that are vague and often not to the point. It is their sound bite. And on the bus, with plugs in their ears, they're sitting next to you, but not near you."

The bus I take each morning affords me a window seat. The old ones are among the first to board. As we head downtown, it is no longer the Geriatric Special; the young ad people, traders, lawyers, secretaries crowd into it. For the most part, they are standing; the crones and gaffers, seated. My vantage point is a good one. I need hardly turn my head to see all my fellow passengers, especially the young standees.

Having nothing better to do, I study the young faces and, in passing, a wrinkled one or two. I stare almost to the point of rudeness; perhaps it's to attract their attention. I'm doing this more frequently than ever before—to make sure that I understand what is happening. I find what is happening somewhat troubling.

I am directly in their line of vision; they can't miss me. For a fleeting instant, Brooke looks down at me; Jason looks down at me. I, with the unblinking stare of a baby, await their recognition of my being—a something. Look, an old boy, a nut, a dirty old man, a retired lawyer, a landlord—a something. Not a flicker, not a millisecond blink of the eye. They look past the space I occupy and turn back to their casual, coded conversation. I am the invisible man, post-Ellison.

To make certain that my finding is not simply a matter of bruised ego, I peer several aisles forward and see the back of gray heads turned upward toward the standing young. I see the same piece of theater enacted; eyeless eyes passing through gray space, and becoming a touch alive as they turn languorously toward one another.

As for the old ones on the bus, they, having little else to do, sneak a peek, a squint at the young, in the manner of squirrels. They occasionally look at one another, too. They, in contrast to the new ones, recognize the presence of others, for better or worse.

Yet on the same bus, a doddering passenger is frequently offered a seat by a young one. Perhaps that's why the old environmental battler, aware of all sorts of contradictions, considers himself "fortunate to be working with young people. That's the big reason I haven't burned out. I keep getting recharged by these kids."

"There is no rule of thumb," muses an old nonstop peace advocate. He passes out leaflets as frequently as he breathes; it's a matter of reflex. "The attitudes of the conductors on the trains I ride differ so much. Some were rough; some were wonderful. Same leaflets, same me, gray ponytail and everything."

The experience of a celebrated agitator is more personal. "My father was a right-winger, a real Horatio Alger hero. Yet he always defended people others looked down upon. When a waitress spilled something on my mother's new dress, he said it was his fault. Always. He was against almost every stand I took. But at his deathbed, I told him, 'Dad, you were my inspiration. I was following your example.' You simply can't prejudge people anymore."

So it is with retirement, too. When do you step down? Does the calendar decide when a person has had it? Is age of retirement a testament written in stone? To a spot welder at an auto plant, whose daily chore is mind-numbing, retirement after thirty years is devoutly to be wished. (Assuming, of course, an adequate pension.) To an old teacher in love with the job, it may be a disaster.

To me, at eighty-two, my job at the radio microphone, continuing or hanging up my gloves, is a matter of personal decision. Am I as skilled as I may have been when I began at the station forty-two years ago? I may be better in some ways, though not as adventurous as I once was. Do I enjoy the job as I once did, or is the law of diminishing delight taking effect? Energy or the loss of it may be the deciding actor. If only I had the wisdom and honesty of Lotte Lehmann.

One Sunday afternoon, at the end of her regular Town Hall concert, Mme. Lehmann, the nonpareil of our century's lieder singers, announced her retirement as of that moment. To her devoted, stunned audience crying out "No! No! No!" she gently responded, "Yes! Yes! Yes!" She graciously explained that, though her voice to others remained unblemished, *she* knew it was not so. She reminded them of her most celebrated role, the Marschallin in *Der Rosenkavalier.* "Remember the mirror scene? When she looked into the mirror and saw her first wrinkle, she decided to give up her young lover. I have learned from her, this wise, beautiful woman."

The aging CEO may see retirement as an end to power, yet the retired social worker may see her job-goodbye as the beginning of a new sort of power. He says: "When you suddenly leave the jungle, the phone stops ringing. You want to have lunch with old friends, but they're busy, working. I'm not in demand anymore. I'm seeking company rather than being sought." She says, "People who have had power, when they become powerless, are really tragic. We just allow ourselves to be conditioned by a society that tells us we've lost it, whether we really have or not. We accept premature death. When you inject something *live* into it, kick up your heels, you're exhilarated. You count."

Maggie Kuhn was recalling the moment she was declared redundant at sixty-five. She took to heart the lyric of Kris Kristofferson: "Freedom's just another word for nothin' left to lose"—and the Gray Panthers came into being. At eighty-eight, frail and faltering, she's still at it.

The Nebraska farmer, eighty, and the Kentucky storekeeper, seventy-five, still breathe fire, as keepers of the flame. Says the farmer: "If I could get ten active people, well organized, well informed, in each county, I could come pretty close to running this state." Says the storekeeper: "A handful in the beginning saved this country. They did the fightin'. While three quarters of 'em, by God, watched it. You never give up, because a handful can win."

Though the embattled spirit of the elderly suffuses this work, it is the sense of mortality, among the nonbelievers as well as the devout, that most colors their thoughts. As time is running out, their own and the century's, there is a consensus: We've had a pretty good run of it. Personally. As for their dreams of the world, there is a sense of loss. Their mourning is not so much for themselves as for those who follow. Their own passing is passed off casually, often with a touch of humor. "I would like to spend my day in a class at MIT, absorbing knowledge, says the eighty-five-year-old woman. "They can take me out in a body bag after that." (Among the Georgia Sea Islanders, the thought is put to song: "Throw me anywhere, Lord, in that old field...")

The printer, having a beer: "As time is running out, I want to win the lottery, buy three ships, man them with American Indians, and send them over to discover Italy."

The Iowa gadfly: "Mozart is my entrance into the sublime. At my service, let there be wine, cheese, and Mozart."

The radio bard, whose father lived to be 110, wants his obituary short: "At the age of 124, he was killed in a duel with a jealous lover. His gun jammed."

The sparrow sums up the light-hearted farewells: "Listen, since I got to be this age, I've got it made. No matter what happens next, I'm still ahead of the game."

Yet, the gay adieus do conceal a reluctance of these vital folk to cross the lonesome valley—not just yet. There are several, in despair, who would just as soon not greet the year 2000. Others insist on getting things in order before the long voyage, so, in the words of the venerable judge, "when I kick the bucket, I'll have everything filed." The ninety-nine-year-old child of slaves, considering her forthcoming hundredth birthday celebration: "I'd just as soon have a good dinner and let it go at that."

There are always second thoughts and regrets. The most frequent show of grief is toward the fate of their own children. The deaths, whether by auto accident, suicide, AIDS, war, or alcohol, they have, for much of their lives, taken unto themselves. Few are more rueful and moving than the dread of guilt felt by the Flint firebrand of '37, who gave so much of herself to the community. "Maybe I should have spent more time with the two wonderful kids I lost. Killed by a speeding taxi. Oh, my God, sometimes you think...they had such a short life." She offers a consoling coda: "Yet if I hadn't gone through all these experiences, I couldn't be the same person." Nor does she know how many others' children she may have saved from that dark and hollow bound.

It is she and her sixty-nine other colleagues in this work to whom the old battler pays tribute: "Think of what's stored in an eighty-, ninety-year-old mind. Just marvel at it. You see faces of people, places you've been to, images in your head. You've got a file nobody else has. *There'll be nobody like you ever again.* Make the most of every molecule you've got, as long as you've got a second to go. That's your charge."

Prologue: Whose Garden Was This?

David Brower, 79
SAN FRANCISCO, CALIFORNIA

A leading apostle of the modern environmental movement. His fervor, as well as his vigor, is apparent. His young companions are obviously fond of him and get a kick out of his perorations and spirit of bonhomie.

What do I think about age? I think I've learned to accept it. I never expected to get this old. With no effort on my part, I'm now about to be eighty and an elder. I find a certain freedom in this.

I was in Prescott, Arizona, for the first day of the Dave Foreman* trial and I spoke out. The Earth Firsters were on the griddle. They'd been infiltrated by the FBI, some of them, and coaxed to do a certain act of violence on behalf of the earth—to try to knock down some power towers in Arizona. That was entrapment. I was at the trial with about two hundred others. Old as I was, I took on the FBI, who had infiltrated the audience. I said, "You should investigate those who are tearing the earth apart rather than those who are trying to save it. I invite the FBI to join our organization."

If I'm on the telephone and I know my line is tapped, I'll interrupt my conversation and say, "I have the following message for you eavesdroppers: For God's sake, we don't need you to entrap us. We need you to join us." There's never any response on the other end. [*Laughs.*]

At my age, they can't do much to hurt me. I have a new freedom. They can't change my career, I've got it made. If I go to jail or am executed, it doesn't matter—though I'd rather stick around. I'd rather be out of jail than in, but not at the expense of this newfound freedom.

Young people don't have this liberty. They've got years ahead of them, families, need for income. They can't alienate themselves too

---

*A founder of Earth First!

much from the system. I say to people my age, "You have this freedom. Please use it. You've had a role in whatever's happened to the earth, and it hasn't been that good. You now have a role in doing something about it. If you're going to die, make sure your boots are on. There are so many of us. More and more of us.

"You're not going to be around that much longer and you know it. Get into the fight, it gets your juices flowing. Maybe like me, you'll have a double martini because you're not sure you'll be around to order the next one. [*He is, at this moment, having one.*] Or maybe you hate phone mail and you're not sure you'll be around to answer all your calls.

"You should be impatient with the slow pace of reform. You should resent having been put out to pasture, because no other species ever does that. You should fight against being put on the fringe of the herd. There is so much potential, you have so much to offer. There is so much information stored in you. At eighty, I've got this important file in my head. I'm not always able to find exactly what I want when I want it, but I can do so much better with my mind than with what's on paper. I haven't reached for a single note, have I?

"Think of what's stored in an eighty- or a ninety-year-old mind. Just marvel at it. Think of these visual images stored in your head—your own videotapes. You can see the faces of people you've met throughout your life. You remember the places you've been to. If you're a concert pianist, where the hell did you store all those notes and in what order are they supposed to come, at what volume, at what pace? It's not going to be there much longer. Let's get with it.

"You've got to get out this information, this knowledge, because you've got something to pass on. You've got a file that nobody else has. *There'll be nobody like you ever again.* Make the most of every molecule you've got as long as you've got a second to go. That's the charge. That is your assignment."

I was forced out of the Sierra Club staff in 1969. I was just a kid of fifty-seven. Russell Train, who is the finest Republican conservationist—a contradiction in terms—we've ever had, said to John McPhee, "Thank God for David Brower because he makes it so easy for the rest of us to be reasonable." I enjoyed that. Eight years later, I retorted, "Thank God for Russ Train because he makes it so easy for the rest of us to be outrageous."

I don't like to reason with the people who are determined to get rid of what makes us possible: the realists. Richard Barnett says that we march toward annihilation under the banner of realism.

It's fun to rock the boat—particularly if you become unreasonable—because within five years or so, your heresy becomes old hat. Maybe I started something that was worth starting. I've had a lot of delights. I didn't know where I was going, but I was going somewhere.

I wish that Earth Firsters were unnecessary, but they *are* necessary. After I left the Sierra Club, I founded Friends of the Earth to make the Sierra Club look reasonable. Now we need an organization that will make Dave Foreman look reasonable.

One night, as we were closing a bar in Ann Arbor, I said, "Hey, Dave, there's already an organization that makes you look reasonable: Earth Last. It's got a big membership—the Fortune 500. What they're doing to the earth makes what you're doing look more reasonable than anything else going on."

Everybody else says you're bad, you're getting in the way of everything, you're costing jobs, you're nasty, get lost. I've been called "cantankerous," "abrasive," a "troublemaker." All true. It all adds up to being really reasonable—keeping the life support system alive. We all use it. We're trashing it and we should cut that out. This isn't what's getting across, so I say that the people who are trashing the earth's life support system are the unreasonables, the bad guys. We're trying to say, "The earth is not a bad place, people are not that bad, life is not that bad."

We have to have a sense of the future. The only thing that is real is Now. The Nows to come are going to be as real for the people living in the next year, the next century, the next millennium as the Now of this moment. The indigenous people were thinking seven generations ahead. They were too conservative. They didn't know the capability of the human species to damage their stamping ground the way we do. So we have to think further ahead. What is the earth going to be like a thousand years from now? What do we do with the nuclear stuff? What do we do for the new child or the new fawn or the new baby seal pup that's born a thousand years from now, so that it opens its eyes on a beautiful, livable planet? I don't know your answer. I have a pretty good idea of my answer.

This is no time to relax. They say you've reached the retirement age, but if you're this old, damn well, there's no real reason to retire and to be put on the shelf and forget what you've spent all this time learning. If you were in an indigenous culture, you would be an elder, and admitted, even required, to advise. And you'd be heeded. Don't demand that they pay that much attention to you. But just, hey, give us a little attention.

The old ones should try very hard not to be boring, not to talk endlessly, which I do constantly. In most other cultures—say, Native American—older women have a great deal of power. They determine who the chief will be. This is something we've got to learn again. It doesn't take very long to fertilize an egg, but it takes quite a while to mature that egg until it's ready to emerge and become an individual—and to help that individual into maturity. Decisions should be predominantly made by the people who do the nurturing, not by those who pass by quickly at the inception.

I'm leery of the feminists who say, "We cannot allow you to quote Robinson Jeffers's "Man apart." It should be "person apart" or "people apart." The poet in him required one syllable. If they would worry less about nouns and pronouns and worry more about getting their rights back, we'd all be better off.

Of course, there are changes necessary in our vocabulary. When I went over some of my early writings, I was embarrassed. I was using "man," "his," "son," "father" all the way through. I can understand women being tired of that by now. Those changes were easy to make.

My wife appreciates the need. We were both editors at the University of California Press. She never forgot how abrupt I was with her. She was already working there. I passed her by and went to the guy instead. I was paid more than she was even though she'd been there for some time. That was fifty years ago, 1941, and she still remembers. Annoyed as she justifiably is, she says, "Feminists should be concentrating not on sisterhood but on being human beings, and maybe men will catch on." I'd like that as a goal, women's rights rather than watching the pronouns.

Women. Youth. Old age. All are connected in my mind. And memory. I remember when I was a battalion intelligence officer in World War II, in northern Italy. We were the mountain troops, the ski troops. Our first battle was in the Northern Apennines. The next, across the Po River valley. Our third took us into the Alps, as the war ended.

We were passing through these little old towns. The houses weren't big but all the generations were there. The old weren't put out to pasture. They were our best means of communication. They were what civilization is about: human history, work, generations. Old ones, grandparents, even great-grandparents, talked to the little ones, and fascinated them. It was the oral tradition, generation after generation. Instead of watching television, the child listened to the old one, learning his history of dreams and wonder.

Our young haven't lost their history, it was taken from them. We've stuffed them into a procrustean bed. Remember him? Procustes? If the guest didn't fit, he'd cut him or stretch him. That's what we're doing to our young, making them fit.

Here is a child, born with a sense of wonder, ready to admire and love what is seen and experienced. We say, "Watch it now, a little bit less, cool it, cool it," until this extraordinary sense of wonder is reduced to nothing.

I'm very fortunate to be working with young people. That's a big reason I haven't burned out. I keep getting recharged by these people. They're somebody to pass the torch on to. You don't hold on to it, that's no good. You have to pass it on.

In the Sierra Club, what bothered me was seeing the average age rising each year. There wasn't an influx of young ones. I work with a new group, Earth Island, which has a lot of younger people. You can't grow old as an organization without losing your effectiveness. You need that flow.

If the old person can't listen anymore, he perpetuates the errors of his ancestors. You don't need him. You need to say, "All right, Grandpa, when did you last change your mind about anything? When did you last get a new idea? Can I help you change your mind while you help me change mine? Considering that what has governed your behavior through your lifetime has gotten this world into one hell of a mess, have you got something new going on in your head?" That's what we need, your experience. That's what corporate boards should be about.

I like to collect rocks. The history of the earth is there. Finer forms are in the quarry than ever Michelangelo evoked. I think it's a quote from somewhere. As an old person, when I look at young people it charges me. Here, in effect, is a quarry. Something within this stone can be shaped. It's in somebody's imagination.

A student I once had at Stanford, where I taught for one quarter, told the class she had planted a garden, and one day they saw the seeds had sprouted and the first shoots were appearing and they applauded. They experienced a sense of wonder. It hadn't been squelched out of them yet. They were enjoying something that we all are forgetting how to enjoy: how the world works and the beauty of it. It still moves me. That's why I'm constantly challenging Operation Squelch.

My oldest son says I'm going through the "gee whiz" phase. But it is a sense of wonder. I know I'm not so young anymore, but I'm trying to get my damn knee to work better so I can get back to my rock climbing. I've got to lose some weight and get the right shoes. Listen, I'm not going to go very high.

For the next decade—what am I saying?—for the next century, we've got to put together what we so carelessly tore apart with so little concern for those who were gonna follow us. This sounds preachy and that's exactly what it is. I'm a preacher and I make no apologies. You've got to sound off. The older you are, the freer you are, as long as you last.

Part I

Chapter One

The Big Boys

Jack Culberg, 79
Chicago, Illinois

The corporation is a jungle. It's exciting. You're thrown in on your own and you're constantly battling to survive. When you learn to survive, the game is to become the conqueror, the leader.
—Larry Ross (pseudonym for Jack Culberg), *Working*, 1970

He is now a corporate consultant. Over the years, he has served as CEO of several conglomerates.

We're a new generation. When we grew up anybody fifty or sixty was considered old. I remember as a young boy, thirteen, fourteen, attending the twenty-fifth wedding anniversary of my mother and father. Everybody was dancing and singing and having a wonderful time. I remember saying to myself: "What are they so happy about? They're on the verge of dying." They were maybe fifty-five.

There's a new breed now. I'm going to be seventy-nine in July and I don't for a second consider myself old. I still play a good game of golf, and I exercise and swim and am active in business. There are many corporations out there that feel you're old and should be out of it, no matter how you look or feel. You have to quit at sixty-five or seventy. You can't be on the board. I don't feel that way at all. I'm still involved. I don't feel any older than them in any way. I feel I have more vitality than those who call me an old man. You turn around and want to know who the hell they're talking about.

What I said about the corporate jungle twenty-five years ago still goes. I've been in it ever since 1942. When you suddenly leave it, life is pretty empty. I was sixty-five, the age people are supposed to retire. I started to miss it quite a bit. The phone stops ringing. The king is dead. You start wanting to have lunch with old friends. At the beginning, they're nice to you, but then you realize that they're busy, they're working. They've got a job to do and just don't have the time to talk to anybody where it doesn't involve their business. I could be nasty and say, "Unless they can make a buck out of it"—but I won't. [*Chuckles.*] You hesitate to call them.*

You get involved in so-called charity work. I did a lot of consulting for not-for-profit organizations. It was encouraging for a while, but the people who run that world are a different breed. They're social workers who've become managers. The great curse of business is amateurs running things. They can't make it. It's amazing how much money is foolishly wasted in charitable organizations.

But Jobs for Youth is something else. It's a sensational group. It takes dropouts from high school, ages seventeen to twenty-one. We train them, get them a diploma, counseling, and jobs. We place eight hundred to nine hundred a year. I'm still on the board.

As for the corporate jungle, it's even worse today. The circle of power is becoming smaller and smaller with fewer and fewer dominant people in control. IBM can lay off fifty thousand, or General Motors. They're not talking about blue-collar workers necessarily. They're talking about middle management who aspire to become CEOs. Today lots more people are fired or forced to retire before they reach the 50 percent mark on the way to the top. The jungle has become worse. You can smell the insecurity and fear all over the place. And the people who lose those jobs have nowhere else to go.

Most big corporations suggest early retirement. It isn't as much pension as you'd get if you lived out the entire thing. You take it. A genteel form of being fired.†

Of course, you're more afraid now than when we last met, twenty-five years ago. If you lost your job then, there were many more opportunities to find another. Today there are fewer companies. I'm talking about middle management and up. Let's say you're the manager of a company division and they're merged or bought out. They cut down on the bureaucrats and you're fired. Where do you go? A lot of them are taking lesser jobs.

---

* It was Gaylord Freeman's last year as chairman of the board of the First National Bank of Chicago. A successor had already been chosen. "As soon as Bob was designated as my successor, it was inevitable that people say, 'Gale Freeman's a nice guy, but Bob's the fella we should be talking to.' I find now that every couple of weeks I have a free luncheon engagement. Where will I have lunch? I had a magnificent dining room here. I'll go to a club. I won't be in demand. I'll be seeking company rather than being sought."

—From *American Dreams: Lost and Found,* 1980

† A neighbor of mine, an executive of a large consulting firm, had just touched fifty-five. It was suggested—astonishing him—that he accept early retirement. There had been no forewarning at all; he had been expecting a promotion. "They made me an offer I couldn't refuse," he deadpanned. "They had a younger guy in the wings, for about half my salary and none of my benefits…"

Most of these people live on their investments or whatever they saved up. The interest rate is so low, they're having great difficulty. Let's say you have a million dollars saved. In the old days, it was an astronomical amount of money. If you're getting an interest of 3 percent, that's $30,000 a year. You can't live on that. So you have to go into the principal. It's very uneasy now. In the old days, it didn't mean a hell of a lot because nobody lived that long. The longer the life span, the more the insecurity—for the great majority.

I happen to be one of the lucky ones. When I retired at the age of sixty-five, I thought I had enough money to live comfortably. If things hadn't happened for me during my retirement, I'd have a rough time now. With retirement, I started doing some consulting. I wasn't satisfied just playing golf or spending winters in Florida. I was too involved in the business world because it was exciting. It had been my whole life.

So I started dabbling around. The LBO* swing came in. One of the top men in the business is someone I've known for years. I found some businesses for him. For at least nine years, I've been involved with these companies. I'm still the chairman of one. In the last seven, eight years, I've made myself an awful lot of money—I was able to work three to four days a week and have a ball. Now I spend maybe two days a month. I still have a hand in. I have a fax machine at home and daily reports, but I'm not in active management.

Because you're a top businessman, you don't stop being a human being. Human frailties exist in the corporate world as they do outside. The top executive is the loneliest guy in the world because he can't talk confidentially to the board of directors. They expect him to be strong and know everything. They don't want a guy that's doubtful or weak. He can't talk to the people working for him because he's got a guy who'll say yes to anything he says and the other guy wants his job. So he doesn't have anybody to talk to. So he becomes insecure and makes the decisions covering his ass.

The board of directors will never take the blame. They're heads of big corporations and don't have time to spend on this particular one. It's more or less a social thing.

With fewer companies, the tension is at its greatest in fifty years. There's a joke that someday there will be one manufacturing and one retailing concern. The retailer will say to the manufacturer, "I don't like your line." And the business dies. There used to be a business saying: "Eighty-twenty." Eighty percent of your volume comes from 20 percent of your customers. Eighty percent of the work is done by 20 percent of the workers. Today I think it's changed to ninety-five–five. Today, Wal-Mart, K-Mart, Target, Service

---

* Leveraged buy-out.

Merchandise. People aren't buying less. There are as many places to buy, but they're controlled by fewer people.

Youngsters are coming up now and want a crack at the big jobs. In the old days, to become president of a company, top man, you had to be in your fifties and sixties. Today, you've got CEOs that are thirty-seven years old, twenty-nine. When I started out in the jungle, you were considered a baby at forty-one.

Also, there's a new way of doing business. A lot of older people didn't keep up with the modern ways. It's difficult, too, because computers are running the world. Yet people are still vigorous at seventy, seventy-five.

Ageism is a tremendous problem today. Investment bankers will tell you they're very uncomfortable with old people running anything. Business analysts don't give a good rating if a seventy-five-year-old guy is running the company. What the hell, he's going to die any minute, a change in management, an upset. It starts getting dangerous at sixty, sixty-five.

A guy was saying the other day, "You people on Medicare are making it awful tough. The costs are unbelievable." There is that feeling: taxes wouldn't be so high if it weren't for the old geezers.

As for me, if I didn't work, I'd deteriorate and die. My doctor tells me to keep active, keep your brain going, keep your body going. Some people my age have hobbies—painting, gardening. That keeps them alive. Unfortunately, I'm not one of these. I love golf, I love swimming, but that doesn't stimulate the mind. I need something else.

Power, age, greed. These are human qualities. They don't disappear when you become a CEO. Having the telephone constantly ring, all the perks, people catering to you, asking your opinions, asking you on boards. It's very flattering and ego-building. Many of the top executives start to believe their publicity and think they walk on water. Many of the business failures today are the result of top executives feeling that they walk with God.

People of my age are a lost generation. What's left for him to do if he's not creating? Every businessman feels he's doing something creative. What the hell are you alive for? It's nice being a great father and a great grandfather—but they're a different generation, your kids, no matter how close you are to them. I don't know what's to be done.

We're living longer and we're cursed with such things as Alzheimer's, heart attacks, and strokes. That's the great fear with us. But if you're busy running a business, you don't sit around and think about your sicknesses. You have this big struggle not to deteriorate. When you create and contribute, you feel marvelous.

One of the nice things at this age is the luxurious morning. Before, you had to get up, get out, get going. Now, I can lay around, read the paper, *Wall Street Journal*, trade magazines, take my time with breakfast, go over the mail. Then I talk on the phone, spend time with my investment counselor. If it's a nice day, play golf or find someone to have lunch with. I'll take long walks, walk the treadmill, swim at about four o'clock, and then I'm ready for dinner. [*Pauses.*] It sounds pretty dull.

Yeah, I get a little bored. The pain of being unneeded and unwanted is uncomfortable at every stage. There are some guys who are unneeded 100 percent of the day. That would drive me absolutely insane. There are some guys who play golf in the morning, play cards in the afternoon, go out for dinner at night, spend the summers here and winters in Florida or Palm Springs, do the same things there. I don't know how they live.

When you're CEO, people are always after you. [*Snaps his fingers.*] What are we gonna do here? What are we gonna do there? What do you think about this guy? That guy? Mr. Culberg, so-and-so called and wants to have lunch with you at two o'clock. You're being wanted always. That ties in with being needed. That's a massive human desire.

When you're a CEO, my goodness, you're at the office at eight o'clock. You have meetings going on, correspondence, phone, this guy calls you, that guy calls you, planning for a board meeting, people problems, manufacturing problems. And they need somebody for a final decision.

Your social circle has diminished by the deaths. Mostly what's left of your social world are the widows. [*Chuckles.*] You read the obituaries by habit now.*

As for politics, I've become a cynical old man. I don't believe in miracles anymore. I don't believe anybody walks on water. It's kind of a hopeless feeling. There's a lot to be done, but I don't think it can ever be done because the people will never allow it. I don't think the human species has changed since it was created. The horrors of centuries ago are still happening today. What have we learned? The human failing. And the CEO is no different than the rest of us.

In my opinion, the world is in a worse mess than it's ever been. I know it's been said of every generation, but this time it's really true. I wasn't this cynical when I was younger. I thought we were helping save the world. I have no regrets for those feelings.

---

* "I wake up in the morning and dust off my wits,
I grab the newspaper and read the obits.
If I'm not there, I know I'm not dead,
So I have a good breakfast and go back to bed."

—From a turn-of-the-century parlor song

I envy the young their rage but not their future. I think they're in for some rough times. You see it in their daily lives. A small percentage of young executives will hit the top and make far more money than we did. But there will be far less opportunities for the majority. The great middle class is going to be less and less. There will be extreme wealth and extreme poverty. I hope I'm completely wrong. I'd be the happiest guy in the world, even if I'm not around.

Personally, I look forward to some years of health, and when my time comes, to go immediately.

Wallace Rasmussen, 80

NASHVILLE, TENNESSEE

In 1967, when he was appointed senior vice-president, Beatrice Foods was worth $4.3 billion. In 1975, when he was retired as president and chief executive officer, the company was worth $7.8 billion. He won the Horatio Alger Award in 1978.

Big-boned and heavy-set, with calloused hands, he has the appearance of the archetypal workingman in Sunday clothes.

"I'm just a country boy. Born in Nebraska and came up right through the Great Depression...I'm convinced it will repeat itself when it's time, and probably it'll be good for the country. It will be hard on people who never experienced doing without, but it's amazing what you can get along without. You don't have it, so you begin to spend more time with your family. There's a way in history, a way in nature, of always bringing people back down to earth."

—*In* American Dreams: Lost and Found, 1980

What I did today? I have a friend who bought an old plantation around here. He said, "I need somebody to bulldoze my fence rows and clean it up." I said, "I'll do it if you pay me the going rate." I'll give it to the exchange program I have started at Belmont University. It's here in Nashville. I enjoy doing it. Today I took down an old cottonwood tree that had died many years ago but was still standing. It was at least fourteen foot in circumference. Heavy work, but good for me.

I think I was born with some mechanical sense—and nothing else, maybe. As a child, if something broke down, well, I fixed it. My mother would say, "Wallace can fix anything." When I started working for the company, I was nineteen, and when they give me the job, and somethin' broke, instead of having someone come in to work on it, I fixed it myself. You just gradually work yourself into fixing anything.

When I was twenty-two, I was asked to go to Vincennes, Indiana, to install a piece of equipment because nobody else could do it. I had never seen that piece of equipment in my life, but the chief engineer said, "Do it." So I did it. When it started running, they said, "Stay down here and work with us." It was the biggest milk plant in the country. I became chief engineer.

Everybody working for me was fifty-five, sixty, old men in those days. Then, during the war, I went on the road and kept sixteen plants running. I became CEO by the mere fact that whenever I had the opportunity to learn something different, I did. Many times they come into our headquarters and say, "We can't get this done. We have to have a new piece of equipment." I'd say, "Tell me about it. Don't give me that stuff. I know what's wrong with it." And I would tell them. One of the board members said, "We thought we were electing a plumber to the president and we got a statesman."

I've been active all my life and still am. I just bought myself an Apple 450 computer. I'm teaching myself how to operate it. It's the only way I can keep my mind as active as it should be. Somebody said, "Don't you hate to get old?" I say, "Hell, no. I'm having more fun, because now I can do what I please, and what pleases me I do." I say what I want to say. If they don't like it, they say, "Oh, don't pay any attention to him, he's senile." Naturally, I don't pay any attention to them. I operate a big farm and I've been very active on boards.

I often disagree with the CEO of a company. Sometimes in a nice way, sometimes not too nice. When they ask me to go on boards, I say, "You know I'm going to speak my piece." They say, "That's why we want you." I was on this one board and they were doing some funny things with the bookkeeping. This other board member and I said we have to investigate. We found out that one employee had taken over $3 million. Some people around town say, "Don't get into a battle with Rasmussen, because you ain't gonna win."

I can't lose. It's not my nature. If I think it's not gonna work out right, I get myself out of it, because I'm not gonna be attached to a losing situation. Take this student exchange program I started at Belmont University. When they named it the Rasmussen Student Exchange Program, I said, "If you're going to call it by my name, I do not stand for failures. Now you have to go out and raise money, because I'm not gonna live forever. It needs to be self-sustaining. I'll pay half the fund-raiser's salary for a year and you've got to go on from there, because once you put my name on that, it must not fail."

Before I got to be head of Beatrice, we'd had contests between divisions on profits and sales. I won all the time. When I beat the eastern division, the guy had to pull me down—at a sales meeting—in a Buster Brown suit, on a little red wagon, with a crown on my head. They had to cut out these contests. I never lost at any time. I'd bust my butt to keep from losing.

I had the ability to get people to work for me, because I'd give them credit all the time. If the person you were working for was not successful, you had to step over him. They weren't doing what should be done—or what *I* thought should be done.

I've been called ruthless, of course. That didn't bother me because I was doing my job. My job was to do the best I could for the company and for the people working for me. To protect their jobs. That is lost today—too many CEOs today run the company for their own enjoyment.

Almost immediately after I stepped down as CEO, I developed a power base on the board of a bank here. I was chairman of the executive committee. I was instrumental in saving the bank by getting rid of the CEO and putting in another who made it very successful. Wielding power is part of my nature. I was born that way.

I'm always the first one off a plane because you don't have to worry about running into people. You look straight ahead and they just part because they think you don't see them. There's a lot of things you can do in this world. I try different things.

In these thirteen years since I've retired, I've seen the greatest transfer of wealth from a lot of people to a few. Mergers, unfriendly takeovers, LBOs (leveraged buy-outs). It happened to Beatrice. I sent a note in 1981 to the man who succeeded me as CEO. He was not my choice. I said, "In five years, this company will not be in existence." I saw the way they were handling people. You can't mistreat them and get them to work the way they should. It happened. The CEO was spending money on himself like a drunken sailor. It's now out of existence. It was LBO'd.

The new guys who take over these companies can't even read a balance sheet. I saw what the merger mania did to Beatrice. They sell all its assets, cut out people, and do away with research and development. That's what's built this country, research and development. No new products coming along. Terrible. Corporate America is in debt, high debt.

There's been an upheaval in middle-class American jobs. You need a strong middle-class person with an eight-, nine-year-old child to know he's gonna be able to send him to college when he's ready to go. But that's not how it is now.

I think it will swing and come back, but it will be small companies that will develop and do it—small businesses and entrepreneurs. I hope our system doesn't get so powerful that these small enterprises can't exist.

During the '80s, corporate America was allowed to do anything, without the SEC and the FTC getting on you.* Until then, we were pretty well regulated. I don't know what happened, except that greed took over, started it and ended it.

I don't see the Great Depression happening again. But it's getting worse between the haves and the have-nots. And it's different. The racial tension is deeper today than it's been for years. Just last week, I took two ladies out to dinner, one white and one black, both

---

* The Securities and Exchange Commission and the Federal Trade Commission.

intelligent. The waitress, a nice white girl, nicely put the food on the table for me and the white lady and just slid it across to the black lady. She said it happens to her and her friends all the time. It happened to be a restaurant which I'm on the board of, and I'll talk to them about it.

I'm supporting black students in college and white. Some of the whites say to me, "We have five black students, but do you think we can sit down and talk with them? No." And that's a fine university, hard to get into. So things are a lot better in some ways, but that undercurrent is really something.

If we had the Great Depression today, we'd have a revolution. What's making the racial tension deeper is the invasion of Asians and others. Cubans, who are hard workers, take jobs that these other people think they're entitled to.

Oh sure, full employment would help. Idleness causes trouble. The worst thing that happened was when they raised the age limit before you could work. Now what the hell can a young man or woman do? Nothing. They can't get a job. They're out there, getting in trouble. When I was coming up, I started when I was but eight, nine years old. On a Nebraska farm, fifty cents a day. It didn't hurt me.

I'm not opposed to the minimum wage, but I'm opposed to setting an age level. I think a child of fourteen can work on time and all her disciplines necessary for a job. They have to learn these things while they're young. By the time they're seventeen, eighteen, they're pretty well gone down the road.

Do I worry about growing old? I don't worry about a damn thing. Why should I worry? The things you worry about never happen. Someday, maybe, if I fall on my face, I can say, "Well, I did my job."

My health is good. I have two artificial hips and some arthritis, but anybody who can stay on a bulldozer for six hours, he's got to be in pretty good shape, I don't care how old he is. I'm going back on it tomorrow because I gotta get this job done before it rains. And I need to earn: for every twenty-five hundred dollars I earn, I can send another student overseas.

There are a lot of good young people. There was a young country girl working here when my wife got sick. She was a kind person with skills in caring for people. But her language wasn't too good, a white girl. I sent her to nursing school and she's doing fine. If she wants a role model, there's a female doctor here in Nashville. The first black surgeon in the South. I helped her get the Horatio Alger Award this year. She's seventy-five. I think they're going to make a miniseries of her life. I guess I still have some influence.

It's been a good life, but if I have any regrets, I wasn't the best husband in the world. I was short on that, but I was one of the best damn providers. She was a good wife for that kind of deal because she left me alone. One time, I almost left her in Tulsa, Oklahoma. I was getting on the plane and the guy says, "Don't you have your wife with you?" I said, "Oh, my God, she's sitting back there in the hotel!" [*Laughs.*] Yeah, *there's* something I could have done better. I don't look back and say, "Oh, gee." You can't undo it, so why worry about it?

When I was the plant superintendent here in Nashville, I used to fight the unions. I found out later I could get along with them, and I did. I would stand up for what I thought was right, and I would do what was right for them. I never really had any problem. I settled some strikes that our labor relations people didn't know what the hell to do about. Because I knew the people. Later on, I realized the necessity for unions, because, in so many cases, labor was abused.

Yeah, I'd say I mellowed maybe, I don't know. You couldn't get anybody around here to say I've mellowed. I don't mind being regarded as a tough customer. It keeps people away from you that you don't want to be bothered with. I am what I am. I began as a kid working with machines and my hands and I'm still at it, touching eighty. Once a child, twice a child, but only a man once.

Paul Miller, 74

NEW YORK CITY

He lives on a farm in Plainfield, New Jersey.

He was president of First Boston, a highly respected investment banking house, for fifteen years. He retired from that office seventeen years ago, at the age of fifty-seven. "I stayed on and did some work there. They manufactured a title for me: senior adviser." [Chuckles softly.]

We are seated in his well-appointed office on the thirty-first floor of a Manhattan commercial building. "They were nice enough to give me this office, though it's rather badly located from the point of view of everything else." It is at the end of a long, narrow aisle. Seated in glass enclosures along the corridor are scores of young men peering intently at the windows of their computers. The eerie silence and their unwavering stares offer the impression of a voyeurs' collective.

These young guys are all internal auditors. They are First Boston employees, but I don't know them. I doubt whether any of them know me. I've been out of business for fifteen years and a lot of these people haven't been here that long.

I don't want to say this building is a dumping ground, but it's an area we used when we had to expand. The former chairman of the firm, a contemporary of mine, who retired last year, has an office down the corner. He doesn't come in much. We built this place and sold it to the Japanese, who've rented it out.

When this outfit was six hundred people, I knew everybody and they knew me. Now that it's five-thousand employees, there's no occasion for them to know me, particularly since I have no official function. My acquaintance is with the management of the firm and the corporate finance types, all of whom are in the other building. These people do say hello. They probably ask each other, "Who's that guy?" [*Chuckles, as he does frequently.*]

I'm a forty-six-year employee of this place. When World War II was over, after college and the army, they offered me a job, provided I started the next day. I had no other offers so I decided to get in out of the rain. That was February of '46. I was twenty-six.

My interest was horses, playing polo, and doing nothing else. I never owned a horse [*Laughs.*] The ROTC* at Princeton had horses given to them by some old graduate. I was given three of these for myself for three years, which was pretty good.

---

* Reserve Officers' Training Corps.

I had no idea what investment banking was. I had wished to go to medical school, but my father couldn't afford it. When the war was over, I felt too old to take pre-medical courses. I really didn't know what I wanted to do. And nobody offered me anything else.

I'm not working these days, I'm loafing. I wanted to get out as president, have another fellow serve. There were too many other duties that go with the presidency, administrative stuff. Nothing to do with investment banking. I was still active in handling clients, until two years ago when I really stopped.

There's been a great deal of change in our business right along. It just keeps on changing. That's one of the fascinations of this business. You're always in over your head. I am. [*Chuckles.*] You don't know what you're talking about because it's always a brand new subject and you got to figure it out. That's always been true in corporate finance.

Nearly every time somebody invents a new kind of security, it turns out that somebody thought of it a long time ago. So it's not really new. Only the scale has changed. The transactions are much larger and the markets are more liquid. There was virtually no international element in the late '40s. We did the first financing for Japan and ran into a great deal of resistance at the time. Nowadays, it's just routine.

Until the beginning of this year, I sat on an investment banking committee through which every deal of the company had to be cleared. Although I didn't head it, I had enough rank, so I had some considerable influence. And it was, for me, a way of keeping up with what was going on. I've stopped doing that just because it was good for the company. They said, in effect, "We'd like you to get off this committee now." And I did.

Why was it good for the company? Probably because when I said something, everybody listened. [*Chuckles.*] They figured they ought to be making their own decisions. Among other things, I was the oldest employee, except for the lady who sits right there, my secretary. Did age play a role? Probably. I didn't like it personally, but I think it was a very good move. I don't think they ought to let people like me—or you go on. [*Multiple chuckles.*]

And I'm not being ironic. No, I'm not. I'm certainly less up-to-date than I used to be on the changes taking place in the market. It's important to keep up-to-date. I'm also lazier than I used to be. You have to know who is merging with who, et cetera. And what's happening to other investment firms as they change stature.

It's always been typical of young men to want to get ahead and not be meddled with by old-fashioned fuddy-duddies like you and me. I'm accepting that it's right. I think it's exactly as it should be.

This is a corporate entity that has to carry on. Who was that Chicago guy that got carried out of his plant? Sewell Avery.* You don't want that to go on.

I'm not sought out by most people anymore. I don't know why. [*Chuckles.*] But that suits me. I'm not particularly hurt, no. I guess it's because I was relatively young when I was made president of First Boston. I was in my middle forties and my peers were in their sixties. I lost touch with them when they retired and I kept on going. It's just a natural progression. I have no particular friends in the business anymore. They've all been retired.

Are you as detached as you sound?

I damn well better be. I don't know what I'd do about it if I weren't. I'm not aware of my ego being hurt, not consciously. I think it's the right thing that happened. I've always been quite an organization man. I have a loyalty to the company.

One thing I don't like about young men these days is they don't seem to have an organizational loyalty. They're all very self-oriented. They change jobs easily, without any looking back, and skip around to different companies. I don't like that. I've always had a loyalty to whatever the corporate entity was as a whole.

The trouble is they make so goddamned much money, you can't count it. Most of the managing directors of First Boston make more money than I ever made as president. That's true of the whole Street.† They're way overpaid for the contribution that they make to the United States. I'd much rather see that kind of money going to surgeons or teachers, but not investment bankers. And they all think they're underpaid.

I'd like to see these young people go through a severe business contraction and realize that it isn't a simple business where everybody ought to get paid three quarters of a million dollars a year for showing up. They're very bright and very well trained. We train people and other firms steal them from us. But I do think being self-centered is the basis, really, of the capitalistic system.

I'm generally optimistic. It may sound trite, but I think we always look at each event as a crisis and most of them turn out to be not very important. I think the system will evolve. There may be a lot of second=rate people coming to the fore, but the pendulum swings back and forth.

---

* Sewall Avery, head of Montgomery Ward, was carried out, hands defiantly folded, by a couple of federal marshals, for refusing to abide by some New Deal regulations.

† I.e., Wall Street.

I think our current administration is perfectly frightful. Personally, professionally, every way. The previous twelve years were not perfect, but they were a lot better than the present. Yes, I classify myself as a conservative. I was completely unconscious of what was going on during the New Deal days, but I was very conscious of my father being in a state of continuous turmoil. He was anti-Roosevelt. Very. [*Chuckles.*]

I feel the same way about big government. This business has been severely regulated, and it needs to be. At first, I thought that was terrible, but now I think it needs to be. There are some very second-rate people in this business. If you give them an inch, they'll take the atoms off your eyelids. There are three or four very high-grade firms in this business, of which I'd like to think we're one. But there are a whole bunch of not very attractive, not very ethical firms in the securities business, and they need to be regulated.

The SEC, as much as you get annoyed at them in our business, is probably one of the best regulatory agencies in the government. The people there know what they're doing. Yes, I know it came out of Roosevelt's New Deal, but so did a lot of agencies that are no good at all. We have a lot of self-regulation in this business.

I'd like to feel there's some way we could improve the ethical consciousness of businessmen generally. I have a tendency to err on the assumption that they're ethical, that they're telling you the truth and dealing honestly, and I keep finding that a lot of them aren't. At the moment, the trend is bad. I won't say it's disastrous or that we're going to hell in a hack. But there seems to be less dealing in an ethical fashion.

As for advances in technology, computers and such, I don't understand most. They're necessary to understand, and the younger people, educated in them, use them actively. I don't want to. I haven't much time to just take time off and understand these machines. Other people can do that.

I can remember when I used to sit with a spreadsheet, doing comparisons of all the statistics relating to a company and how its bonds were compared with others. You'd look up everything about every one of those companies and put it on that sheet and you'd be absolutely bleary-eyed. That was terrible work. There's a lot less of that today because they've got machines.

In this business, a lot of our people are subject to burn-out. They work very long, hard hours. If they're traders, they're incredibly pressured. If they're investment bankers, they're traveling all over the world. They're usually dealing with what they think are weighty questions, full of uncertainties. Most people get pretty tired of that. I did. But I had this organizational loyalty, for whatever it's worth.

What's my day like now? My day isn't figured out. If I don't want to come in, I don't come in. I'm in just about two days a week. My day at home is worrying about what I'm going to occupy myself with. I do a lot of reading. I have a place that takes a great deal of maintenance. And a body that's deteriorating to the point where I can't do much of that.

I spent my life being pretty busy, so I didn't do any retirement planning. I haven't figured out yet what I ought to be doing, except maybe dying. That might not be a bad idea. My health is just fine, except for what you'd consider normal age problems. I have spinal stenosis and I get very stiff and I hurt. Arthritic all over the place. My hands are starting to go. I used to have very strong hands. And my breathing is bad.

What do I look forward to? I'm confused about that. I keep putting the question off, so I read books and watch television and wish I could get out and do something around the place. On a tractor or on a manure spreader or some damn thing.

Oh, I suppose I'd like to be remembered for having made some contribution, but I'm not sure what. I don't think I'll be remembered for much. It's too late for that. I don't think I've made any contribution worth remembering. [*Chuckles.*] A number of people around the farm may think I did, but *I* don't. Oh, I don't think I have a low self-esteem. But I don't have a high one, either. [*Chuckles.*]

Did I feel any resentment when I was removed from that committee? Hell, no. I figured I overstayed my welcome. Very few people stay beyond sixty-five and I'm seventy-four, for God's sake. They're all thrown out and they retire. They were nice enough to give me this nice office, even at seventy-four.

CHAPTER TWO

The Money Tree

Estelle Strongin, 82
NEW YORK CITY

She is a stockbroker at Smith, Barney. "They call us financial consultants these days." On her desk is the ubiquitous computer, constantly flashing the latest communiqués from the front: the Exchange. At the contiguous desk, facing her, is her daughter, Anne; she, too, is a broker. "She's my partner. We've worked together for twenty-five years. My husband used to say it was because of her angelic disposition." [Laughs.]

She is trim, modishly dressed. Her age comes as a stunning surprise.

My husband was an old-fashioned kind of doctor. He loved medicine and devoted himself to it totally. During the depression, when he started practice, he was charging three dollars a house call. In his sixties, he was still making house calls when nobody else did, and never raised his fees. He didn't care about money. But in those days, working day and night, he accumulated quite a bit. Since he was interested only in medicine and his patients, I had to become the investor of family funds. One of the advantages of this society is that, along with its disadvantages, money can work for you instead of you always working for it.

This was in the late '40s and into the '50s. I had asked a friend to handle some money for me and, unfortunately, it didn't work out too well. So I decided to read the financial section of the paper and make some decisions myself. Economics was the *furthest* thing from my mind. I was a French major in school.

Our two children were old enough to go to school, so I had a lot of free time and too much energy just to meet the girls for lunch. I did a lot of civic work, tapped for one committee after another. It became a full-time occupation. On the board of one such association was a well-known stock person. I noticed that everything he did on the finance committee worked out very well for us. So I decided to get in on the inside and find out how this is done.

I applied for a job at Shearson, and I believe I was the second woman stockbroker in New York. This was 1959. My husband was not happy about it. I had been dabbling in sculpture at the time and he thought I should develop my talents in that field. He said, "As a stockbroker, you'll make more money, but we don't need any more."

Some of our friends were shocked. "Her husband is a successful doctor. Why is she working?" In those days, many women didn't work if they didn't have to. "If she did anything, why didn't she open an art gallery?" Our social set looked down on stockbrokers—vulgar, vulgar, vulgar. [*Laughs.*]

As I began to read the papers, I realized this wasn't just economics and arithmetic. This was *everything:* psychology, science, discovery, politics, population trends. Consider what the Southwest has become, from backwater to a lively industrial region. And it all impinges on Wall Street. When President Roosevelt announced in 1944 that "[w]e're going to build five thousand war planes," you rushed out and bought Lockheed. [*Laughs.*] As a good stockbroker, you can capitalize on all this. That's what I liked about this work. It's not a highly specialized matter. One of my neighbors is a marine biologist who studies the eyeballs of an almost-extinct fish. This encompasses our whole civilization. You have to know what's going on everywhere. I have to be aware of what's going on in medicine because it impacts the pharmaceutical industry. I read professional journals, the *Times*, the *Washington Post*, *The Nation*, everything I can get my hands on.

I used to have a much bigger office than this, but a lot of my clients have died. As people get older, they lose interest in making money. All they want to do is conserve what they have. Older people are not as adventurous, less interested in taking chances. This has not overtaken me. I'm the swinger; Anne is the more conservative one.

But I have to adjust to customers. They began to just want bonds. As far as I'm concerned, a bond is a four-letter word. [*Laughs.*] It is a pledge by a company or a country to pay you a guaranteed interest and return your original investment at the end of ten, twenty, or thirty years. In the meantime, your money has eroded because of inflation, even at three percent! At the end of thirty years, you've lost 90 percent of your purchasing power. Nobody cares. They want the same money back. Safety. They don't figure on inflation. In stocks, there are no guarantees.

You think I'm a gambler? [*Laughs.*] I have to work on you. That's not gambling, that's a calculated risk. A gambler will bet that the next person entering this room will have blue eyes instead of brown.

There's no intellectual challenge. With a calculated risk, you can intellectualize your reasons for doing what you're about to do.

There's a terrible emotional involvement. You can't escape it if you have any conscience. Nobody wants to purposely lose money for anybody else. If something goes wrong in the industry, or if the product is technologically outmoded, or if, on rare occasions, the management is dishonest, there are risks. But you can protect your clients by diversification. That's my style. You hedge your bets. If you have ten or twelve stocks in your portfolio and lightning hits one company, the other eleven will carry you over.

You don't stay in business five years if you keep losing money for people. [*Laughs.*] I *never* would have believed I'd be doing this work for thirty-five years. Never. When I started, my husband laid down the law. "You may not do business with any doctors on the hospital staff. Nor with any relatives or good friends." So it was a hard beginning. I was lucky at the very start. During one of my cold calls—calling someone you don't know—I met a man who subsequently become a Wall Street legend: Bob Wilson. He started with $15,000 and retired with $200 million. This was long before he was rich and famous. Somehow he felt that I was not the normal broker who calls to solicit business. He had written in to ask for some research, and I was following up on it. He thought I was unusual. With a little luck, I gave him good advice and I became his regular broker. We became good friends and he was very helpful to me in my career.

The editor of *Ms.* magazine, whom I knew, asked me to write a piece about breaking into men's areas of expertise, because it would encourage other women to become brokers. I wrote about the help I had received from all the men at Shearson. I had no difficulties. They didn't publish it. [*Laughs.*]

Today, perhaps 30 percent of the brokers are women. When the younger ones ask me about the early hard times I had, I tell them I didn't. They don't believe me. A lot of them tell me they are still encountering condescension and no help at all. Sink or swim: you're on your own. Maybe it's the climate, I don't know. I expected to be treated well. Maybe they don't expect it.

In these thirty-five years, I've encountered a lot of attrition among my customers because of age. Lots of death and lots of apathy. I've had a lot of illnesses myself: a major heart attack, two cancers, chemotherapy, X-ray therapy. I've had everything under the sun. One of my friends was astonished. "Are you going back to work after all this? Don't you know that your job now is *survival?*" A lot of my contemporaries feel that's their only job.

Do I feel that way? Oh, God, no! [*Laughs.*] Just surviving isn't enough. It's a form of death. It's giving up. Everybody has a different kind of energy, I guess. I always had a lot of it. I came to work during chemotherapy. That goes back thirteen years. The heart, about eight years ago. Survival is more than just eating and breathing. It's being involved with life.

I can't say I'm as good as I was thirty-five years ago. In some ways I'm better. I find that my memory isn't as good in unimportant things—Where did I put my glasses? Where did I leave my keys?—but if a customer asks me, "Do you remember what I paid for my IBM?," I remember that right off the bat. [*Laughs.*] I remember the birthdays of the people I love. I remember what Norman Thomas* said years ago—anything that has some meaning for me.

My father admired Emma Goldman, the anarchist. [*Laughs.*] I still have great feelings about injustice in the world.

My work probably has affected the way I think. In studying companies and the problems they face, I think I've modified some of my political thinking. There are problems on all sides. I think I'm an easier person to live with, though nobody lives with me at the moment. My husband died four years ago. I think I've lost some of the intolerance of youth, demanding perfection of other people, as well as of myself. I'm much more tolerant of other people's failings as well as of my own. I think age brings you that. Of course, there's always the danger of becoming crotchety, too.

My children are very lucky that I have this job. What a pain in the neck I'd be if I didn't work. [*Laughs.*] I get to work at 9:30 A.M. and leave at 8:00 P.M. I constantly monitor my stocks, because nothing is a lifetime commitment when you buy. You have to also watch for reasons to sell it.

There's that IBM computer up there. [*She had casually glanced at it, in answering a caller: "You know the market is down sixteen."*] It's right up there, all the stocks I monitor: Apple Computer, Charter Medical, Oppenheimer Capital, UIS, Pfizer, IBM. This machine tells me who's got what and when they bought it, what they paid for it, what the profit is and the unrealized loss, if there is one. A blue-collar worker is at his machine and I'm at mine. I do this five days a week and I'm involved with it over the weekend, too, watching financial programs on TV.

I try to socialize quite a bit, but my horizons have shrunk because many of my old friends have either died or moved away. They find life in New York too difficult, too expensive, or just lose interest. I try to have younger friends because they're willing to go out at night. Old ladies are not that eager and I understand why. I was mugged on Park Avenue at 9:30 P.M. about two weeks ago. [*Laughs.*]

---

* The perennial Socialist candidate for president.

I feel sorry for the young people today. I think we've had the best of it, our generation. And our children may have the last of the best. I am very, very sad about my grandchildren. Look how long we've been trying to perfect democracy and look what's happening all over the world: people killing one another. For what? The same killing the same.

It was ever thus, right? What's going to change? I'm frightened for the kids. Many of them are terrific, but they're going to miss something I enjoyed. I just wanted New York to be a wonderful place for my children to grow up.

As for growing old, I don't mind that at all. I loved every age, except adolescence. I can't remember being too happy then. I loved the twenties, being young and romantic. When I got married and had children, oh, nothing could be better than this. In my thirties, a little more mature, I didn't mind my waistline thickening. The forties I loved, and I didn't mind being fifty. Even the sixties, even with my illnesses, I found life exciting.

When I was studying sculpture, I found I was never happy alone in my studio. I was always in a hurry to get it done quickly. My ideas were always ahead of my execution. I discovered I needed the stimulus of people. That's why retiring is out of the question. I find there are rewards to every age, and the inevitability of death doesn't bother me, as long as I keep postponing it. [*Laughs.*]

Katherine "Kit" Tremaine, 87

Santa Barbara, California

A telephone conversation, long distance. Hers is the tone of a young woman, with intimations of an easy life, easy ways, an easy southern accent, and an easy laugh. Yet, there is a fervor to her speech.

"God was good to me. I have naturally curly hair, blue eyes, and I have all my teeth, too. How much more could I ask?"

Among her philanthropies, she is the angel of the Santa Barbara Independent, *a popular alternative weekly.*

I don't get around much anymore. At the moment, I'm lying on the bed. I hardly leave it. My health is not too bad, but I'm not too crazy about it either. My knees are bad. I use a walker. My heart is bad. The doctor told me three or four years ago that I should have a valve replacement. I'd had a knee replacement just a few years before that. So I said, "No. One replacement is enough for me." [*Chuckles.*]

People come here to see me and, amazingly, I've made some new and exciting friends lately. I've been described as a woman who'd gone from being a socialite to a socialist to a spiritual seeker.

I was born under a money tree. All I've had to do all my life is to shake it gently to have that golden shower come down. It isn't so much so anymore, because it's mainly dependent on oil and gas, which aren't doing too well lately.

I was born into a wealthy family in New Orleans. My grandfather came from Alabama after the Civil War to seek his fortune. He got a job on the railroad, started to buy up swamp land, and eventually became the lumber baron of Louisiana. Had mills all over the state. It was he who started the family fortune and I'm one of the inheritors. The ripple effect of money never stops. It just goes out and out and out.

I have no idea how he'd feel about the uses I've made of that money, although I think I'm a lot like him. He had a very strong social conscience and I do, too. My father was a sick man who never did much of anything. He went to the racetrack in the afternoon. I did, too, as far as that goes. [*Chuckles.*] I watched him go downhill all his life.

You might say I was a southern belle. Back in 1926, when I was eighteen, I was Rex's Queen at the Mardi Gras. I went to a day school in New Orleans, boarding schools in Lake Placid and Miami, and to Miss Bennett's on the Hudson, a well-known girl's school.

I married when I was nineteen. We had one child, a son. After seven years, I divorced him to marry my second husband, who lived west. I've been here ever since. His father was an executive vice-president of General Electric. They had this huge, marvelous spread in Arizona.

But I always had this burning desire to work. I had this feeling that I had to justify my existence, to leave something behind me, to do something that was of value to the world. I have no idea what made me think this way. It may have been that little black boy, Henry.

We lived in an old Victorian house that I hated. Dark velvet curtains and dark, terrible furniture. It had servant's quarters. One day, the cook asked my mother if she could bring her little grandson in from the country so he could go to school in New Orleans. I was about seven or eight. So was Henry. He was never allowed to go to the front part of the house. He couldn't do this, he couldn't do that. Every time I asked my mother why, I never got an answer that satisfied me. I realized, as that small child, there was something not right with the world. It changed my life and set me on the path I've been on ever since. You might say Henry made me a socialist then and there.

I was desperately unhappy during a great many years of my life. I hated the life I led. I thought I'd been born to the wrong family. I didn't want to just go to parties. I wanted to do something. I felt ashamed of my role.

My mother was a charmer, absolutely delightful and very intelligent. She should never have had me, because my brother was the sun, the moon, and the stars as far as she was concerned. My mother always put me down. She'd say things in front of me: "She's very pretty, isn't she? But she's really not very bright." I adored my mother until she made it clear she wasn't worthy of it. When I told her I was going to divorce and remarry, she said, "Of course, you'll do nothing of the kind. Come upstairs with me and we'll discuss it." As if I were ten years old. I realized then, she had no understanding of anything. She was a charming southern belle, but totally insensitive. When I was given an honorary doctorate some years ago, my first thought was "That would show her, wouldn't it?" After she died, I began to write about her—I've published several books—and began to understand her.

My second husband was an alcoholic. So was my first husband. So was my brother. So were two of my children. My elder daughter died of alcoholism a few years back. It's been a menace to me all my life. It's only by the grace of God that I don't have those demons.

I was always seeking something outside. I finally found it when I left my second husband after thirty years. I was in my early sixties.

It was a big move. I got into my car and headed down our long drive-way, down to my little beach house. I thought to myself, "I've done it!" Suddenly this tremendous feeling of joy rose up in me. I began to realize that the world was full of people just like me. I didn't have to go around with my dukes up, defending myself because I wasn't a conservative Republican. All my family, of course, were.

During the Vietnam War, I stood on the sidewalk in front of the Santa Barbara Art Museum for seven years, from twelve to one, demonstrating. At the time, I was one of the trustees of the museum. For several years, I chaired the acquisitions committee. My fellow trustees would walk by and avert their eyes.

It was a marvelous feeling to do what I wanted to do. At night, I'd walk down to the edge of the water of the beautiful Pacific, look up at the sky, and think it's all mine, to do with as I want. Everything is my universe. It was pure joy.

I became active when I was still married. My husband would say, "If we were at war, you could be branded a traitor." Of course, we were at war, Vietnam. I was the only maverick among family and friends. I've always had a reputation for plain speaking and express-ing my opinion.

At a dinner dance at the Valley Club, some guy would come up to me and say, "I thought you'd be here. I saw your car with the McGovern sticker on it. Knew it had to be you." One night, I said to one of these men, "Why does it threaten you that I feel this way? I don't care who you vote for. Why do you care who I vote for?" Oh, I enjoyed this. I'd get out of my Mercedes and there was always some bumper sticker, anti-nukes, peace, civil rights. Another time, toward the end of the dance, a woman came up to me, drunk. "Oh, how's my pretty little communist friend?" I said, "What did you say?" "I said, 'How's my Democratic friend?'" I said, "That's not what you said. You know what I'm going to do? I'm taking you to court and sueing you for defamation of character." She really thought I was going to. [*Laughs.*] Of course I didn't intend to, but that was one time I let my temper go. Often I was called a commu-nist. My ex-husband did, too. I was attacked so often for my quote-unquote communist beliefs that I was on my guard. Now I don't have to be. I have new friends, whom I like, and I meet more all the time. I no longer worry about what others may say.

At eighty-seven, my days are busy enough. My secretary comes two mornings a week. We have a lot of business stuff to get through. I confer with my accountant frequently. There are all sorts of requests for money. I have the Sunflower Foundation. I like to spend my money on hands-on things, having to do with environ-ment, ecology, sometimes a book. And, of course, the *Santa Barbara*

Independent. There is nothing I want in material things, so I have to do something with my money. I give it away.

I started the homeless movement in Santa Barbara. I used to take my dog down walking on the beach in the mornings and I'd see these guys coming out of what we call the Jungle, an undeveloped lot. I'd see them patting their clothes and smoothing their hair down before walking into town to get something to eat. I always made it a point to make eye contact with them and say, "Good morning." An expression of astonishment would always come over their faces: somebody was speaking to them. The hardest thing, one of them told me, was people not meeting their eyes. We want them to be invisible. I'd go there and sit.

I must say I startled the respectables. I did it on purpose, just for that reason. A few years ago, the mayor told me that I owe the city of Santa Barbara a public apology—"Because you brought Mitch Snyder out here," she said. He started the homeless movement in Washington, D.C.

Homelessness has been criminalized in our city. It's a crime to sleep in public. They can't lie on the beach, they can't lie on the lawns, they can't set in a doorway. They've been opening the armory for a few hours on cold, rainy nights. The rest of the time, they go where they can. I funded a survey on the homeless in Santa Barbara and that's how the movement started.

People around here think I'm nutty. But I'm in a good position. Aside from being a radical thinker, I'm a rich woman. That's very, very helpful. I can say and do things others can't do, because of my money. If I didn't have the dough, they'd look at me as worse than a flake. But I do find all kinds of allies. I don't go around with my fists up all the time. We made a video, *Wisdom of the Elders:* old people telling of their lives. The president of the chamber of commerce wrote me a letter saying: "You've really hit on something. This is the first time your generation is speaking in words understood by the generation that will follow."

People are always coming to see me. A visitor from China. A professor who heads the Peace Foundation here. Lots of people. They tell me things. I tell them things. By two o'clock, I'm usually exhausted.

My work from this bed is like being in business: all sorts of things to tend to. Papers from my accountant, things to do with my own estate. I read. I have a lap computer that I no longer have the energy to use. We're just bombarded with an overload of information nowadays. My mail is so depressing, I can't bear to look at it most of the time. I just pick and choose. On way or another, time just flies.

I hardly see anybody from my past life, though there are a few old grade school classmates from my New Orleans days with whom I'm still in touch. I have care-givers, who stay with me until the time's up and somebody else comes. They're people of harmony and intelligence. My best friends.

She appears to be tiring. We resume the conversation the following day.

Someone is here all the time, in case I have another heart attack. I had a small one a few years ago. It creates a certain degree of anxiety, because we live in a high fire range. It's a high risk area. I've lived with risk all my life. Life really isn't any good without it. If you don't take that risk, you're static, you're going backward. If it may sometimes not be the right thing to do, change it. Do it. We didn't come here to sit around and suck our thumbs.

One young man said of our foundation: "I'm very grateful to you people for doing this, because you help us understand our grandparents. We had no idea you were so interesting." I really have a great admiration for the young. I'm half envious of them, too, because they're going to see so many things you and I never will. I don't feel they have too much respect for older people. Maybe they shouldn't. We have to do something to merit their respect. I said to some of them the other day: "I've lived in a fantastic century. There's never been anything like it in the history of the world. You are the ones who've really got it made. You live not only in the Space Age, but you've also got the tremendous world underseas that we've just begun to explore. You're the people who are really going to find out."

Would you like to see the year 2000?

Kind of. I wish I could, but my body's worn out and I'm ready to go. That force up in the sky, She—you probably refer to it as He—

I refer to it as hermaphroditic.

—I guess She's not ready for me because if She were, I wouldn't be here, I'd be there. I have a channeler, Indira, who transmits thoughts to me of people who have already died. They speak through her. We used to call such a person a medium. About ten days after my daughter Diana died, Verna said, "Today we will talk about the one you call daughter, the one who just came over to our side."

Who's Verna? I thought Indira was the channeler?

Indira is the spirit who speaks through Verna, a country girl raised in Iowa. Verna always had this feeling she knew what people were thinking and what they were going to say. She assumed everybody had this gift. She studied, meditated, worked on developing the power to channel, and it happened.

She told me about a conversation Diana and I had the day she died. There was no question about it. There was such a conversation. Diana died of alcohol and valium. She had a very stormy life.

I was talking to Katie, my other daughter, about it. She's Diana's younger sister. All her life, she's had a feeling of hostility toward me. We've had a breakthrough in the last three months. I spoke to Indira about it. I said, "Did Katie came into this life with a chip on her shoulder about me?" She said, "Yes. It stems back to a life in Greece eons ago. You were the mother of a family with no money. You sent Katie out to earn money." I gather she meant as a prostitute.

I believe we've had many, many former lives. I think we're in this life, preparing ourselves to go as far along our spiritual path as we can. There are things we won't accomplish in this life, but we'll come back and do it again.

Did grief over Diana's death play a role in your belief?

It isn't like that at all. I've always believed in reincarnation. I've been ready for death for years. I feel that when we go there, wherever *there* is, we'll be attending a university of higher learning. We'll be learning. We'll be learning things we can't even formulate now. We're so limited by our finite minds.

I'm not a bit religious. I grew up an Episcopalian, but I left that years ago. I don't go to any church, but I consider myself a spiritual person.

All in all, I've had a lot of fun and some heartbreaks. When Diana died, I had a sense of despair. We had so many good times together, laughed and enjoyed each other's company. I'd been talking to her son, Thomas, the very morning she died. He's about thirty-five, has three charming children, so I'm a great-grandmother. I said, "It wouldn't surprise me either." That was the very day she died.

I expected Diana to die but I didn't expect John to die. He was my lover. I was seventy-something when he came into my life. He was about sixty. He was a socioanthropologist. We met on a Hopi reservation in New Mexico. We fell in love. It lasted too short a time. He drowned in a hot tub. He was an alcoholic. I knew it, but I didn't want to know it. It hit me in the solar plexus. I couldn't eat, couldn't do anything. He was my life, at that point.

Shortly after he died, I began to realize that it had to end this way.

We were at the peak of our passion for each other, and you know that doesn't really last. I'm old enough to know that. With John's death, everybody who knew him began to grow and expand and reach out. It was as if he *had* to do it. As Indira says, we're all here for a purpose.

I'm ready to go and, in a way, I'm looking forward to it. There's nothing to keep me here. I feel I got my message out, and I think I've done what I was sent here to do. I think we're all sent here to do something.

I don't want to be remembered as the rich lady who lived on the hill. [*Laughs.*] I read something Aldous Huxley said when he was asked what he would have changed about his life if he could. He said, "I'd have been kinder to people." That's the epitaph I'd like. I've often thought I should have been kinder, could have been kinder to my two husbands. I wasn't. I want to be buried in the Sonoran desert. Somebody will have to hire a little jet and fly my ashes over there. I'd love that.

W. H. "Ping" Ferry, 85

SCARSDALE, NEW YORK

"It became my custom at age sixty to write a self-appraisal every five years, to remind my children what their old man was all about. The first one I wrote, on December 17, 1970, says:

'Male, white, born Detroit, Michigan, December 17, 1910; Dartmouth, 1932. Self-employed. American populist. Bird watcher, beach walker, rubberneck. Frequent depressions, along with warm pleasure brought on by sky, books, flowers, conversation, music. Pacifist, underproof Christian. Harassed relentlessly by conscience, probably in need of analysis. (Bored equally by polls, liberals, television, administrators, technophiliacs, editors. Easily slighted.) Each year less gregarious. Given to effectiveness. Daydreams of escape to serene precincts. Dislike of authority. Intolerant of rock, J. Edgar Hoover, unpunctuality, Los Angeles, false-speaking philanthropoids, noise in all its forms. Unperturbed by feminists, reds, homosexuality, pornography. Perturbed by ravaged land, plight of aged, and insensitivity of the rich. Finds claims of blacks, Chicanos, Indians, young people, wild and emotional and 90 percent correct. View of man's chances to survive, dim. One result: less writing and public shouting, heavier dependence on U.S. mails, much solitary walking.'"

My father was a smart mick and a hard worker. I don't think he went beyond eighth grade. A good Irish center-cut Catholic. He went to work for Packard as a bookkeeper in 1908, and taught himself. He rose to become president of the Packard Motor Car Company in the '50s. He refused to take more than fifty thousand dollars a year. He believed that's all he was worth and that the money out of the dividends should go to the people who owned the place. He believed firmly in free enterprise. We lived in Grosse Point, among the rich and privileged.

My mother was a schoolteacher, a starchy Episcopalian. I was the first of two boys. We went to public school and the Episcopalian church, though I attended a Jesuit high school. That's why I'm great in Latin. At Dartmouth, I thought of becoming an Episcopalian minister. In my senior year, I attended the Union Theological Seminary. But no, not for me.

I have no idea what made me think the way I do. I have lived a life of unalloyed good luck. I've never had the proper human portion of grief.

Everybody is entitled to some grief. My health at this age is perfectly fine, though I broke my neck once. It almost killed me, but it didn't.

When I got out of Dartmouth, I got a job at Choate School, to help with football and Latin. John Kennedy and his brother Joe were students there. I was their house master. I think their old man, who was ambitious for his kids, didn't want it to be said they were raised by priests and nuns, so he sent them to this Episcopalian school. I was fired from that job for being drunk and disorderly.

I drifted around, worked in a steel mill as a third helper at the open hearth. I got into some newspaper work in Detroit. Sort of floundering, my parents thought. One year, at the *Detroit Times*, I was sent down to Indianapolis to do a color story on the 500 auto race. I didn't think it was a very good piece, but it caught the eye of Eddie Rickenbacker, who had taken over Eastern Airlines and was looking for a publicity man. He owned the raceway, too. This was '36.

The job lasted about eight months, a long time for me. Rickenbacker was a hard man to work for, so I quit. With eight hundred dollars in my pocket, I went down to Puerto Rico, where I met my first wife, a ballet dancer from Toronto. We got married and went to live in New Hampshire, where I got a job on the *Manchester Union-Leader*. This was in '37, before Bill Loeb, the malignant one, took over.

I quit that and became a consultant for the International Labor Office (ILO) in Montreal. That's when I got an offer from Sidney Hillman.* He said, "We've just organized the CIO Political Action Committee (CIO-PAC). I want you to do publicity for us." I got $10,000 a year. After Roosevelt was reelected, I quit PAC and went to work for Earl Newsome & Company, one of the most prestigious public relations outfits in the country. They had Standard Oil, American Locomotive, Ford, as clients. It was a dreamy job and I made lots of money. I was there for a long time.

I think one of the reasons Newsome hired me was that my father was a friend of Edsel Ford. My job was primarily dealing with the public conduct of the Ford Motor Company. It was probably the best known trade name in America. But it had all sorts of public relations problems because it was run by a cranky, anti-Semitic old man. He hired Harry Bennett, a thug, to terrify the workers, and Bill Cameron, to edit Ford's anti-Semitic rag, the *Dearborn Independent*.

By the time I came on the scene, still working for Newsome, only eight people owned the entire Ford Company, all members of the family. There was a big tax squabble. That's how the Ford Founda-

---

* Head of the Amalgamated Clothing Workers of America. He became a close adviser to President Roosevelt in labor matters. His presence and influence prompted FDR's antagonists to coin the popular phrase "Clear it with Sidney."

tion came into being. Otherwise, the inheritance tax would have wiped out the company. Eventually, the foundation owned 84 percent of the company, about two billion dollars, when I got there. It's about six or seven billion today. There was so much dough, and so much publicity, that Henry II, the old man's grandson, now president of the company, hired Paul Hoffman to head the foundation. Hoffman, a former head of Studebaker, had just finished a couple of years in Europe, running the Marshall Plan.

Hoffman had two conditions. It had to be run from Pasadena and he wanted Bob Hutchins as his associate director. Bob was just quitting the University of Chicago. Some of the Ford people were edgy, because Hutchins spoke about everything, abolishing football at the university, letting loose at the rich and the haughty. I'd never met Hutchins before, but we came together and liked each other right away. I had by this time become public relations consultant for the foundation.

Hoffman was paying less and less attention, because he had become interested in Eisenhower's presidential campaign. So Hutchins was really running it. We were in the headlines because we were getting rid of enormous sums: funds for the advancement of education. There were five of these funds set up, with about thirty million dollars each. The publicity was good and bad, but with the advent of McCarthyism, it became mostly bad. There were Congressional investigations. Old Henry Ford would have turned over in his grave. I was right in the middle of it and enjoying it all.

We had to do something about McCarthyism, which was a running sore across the land. So the Fund for the Republic was set up, an invention of Hutchins and mine. We thought it best to be outside the foundation's province. The board of the Ford Company was leery, because they worried about McCarthy. The fund's projects were fighting censorship and the blacklist. Hutchins was under much attack, and the people were being frightened to pieces, especially by J. Edgar Hoover.

The TV stations refused to accept our programs. We said we'd pay for everything, but they wouldn't take our money. We were not having the effect we had hoped for. We wanted to explore all this nonsense called McCarthyism and the loyalty oaths. We couldn't get through.

The fund had about five million dollars left at the end of four years. This was about 1956. We were somehow missing the boat. So we set up the Center for the Study of Democratic Institutions. It was sort of a monastic affair, in which dialogue about the deeper issues was the idea. We had a couple of international conferences, one in Geneva and one in New York. *Pacem in Terris* was one. Did we have any effect? I don't know. If you want to affect people, go buy a shoe store. You can tell at once whether you make money or not.

I guess I was something of a lightning rod for the center, to the discomfort of some. It was usually on issues dear to the hearts of America. Say, capital punishment. I suggested that schoolchildren be sent to watch executions. Why not? How else are they going to learn?

The way to deal with war was somewhat on the same line. This was at the height of the Cold War. I suggested that the president of the United States and the premier of the Soviet Union agree to take fifty of their own country's children, nine to eleven, and just before war was declared, personally go out and kill all fifty of these kids. Why not? It's worth a try. Nobody accepted the idea, as far as I know.

All my life, I've been something of a smart ass, I suppose. I caused quite a controversy in '65 or '66, when I said that integration was a loser, a pious fraud. Neither black nor white people really wanted it. What the black people want are the same rights as the whites. I thought we had something good going with affirmative action, but it's been pretty well diluted. We have to look at race in fresh ways, something pluralistic. Long after you and I are planted, race will still be the number one issue.

I was part of something called the Committee of the Triple Revolution. It's obvious that technology is outrunning our capacity to contain it. It's beyond ideology. We don't have the vocabulary to describe what's happening to our dehumanized culture.

Look what's happening to colleges. At Dartmouth, my alma mater, they got a bequest of fifty million dollars to build a new library. I'm sure it's going to look more like a shopping mall than a library. It's going to be full of mainframes, the apparatus at the heart of computer activity. By the time this thing is finished, a young man or woman can walk into a room in his or her freshman year, and never emerge until four years later to get the degree. He can go to all his classes by computer. He can get his grub brought in by computer. He will never have to emerge.*

I was trying to mount a challenge to the use of this fifty million dollars. I put this to members of my class. I keep in touch. What happens to books, to teachers, to the liberal arts? Only one or two of my classmates showed the slightest interest. They said: "Oh, that's all bogeyman stuff. Forget it. You've got to keep up with things."

---

* "The average college student in 2050 will not have to leave home to earn a degree," predicts Dr. Arthur Levine, president of Columbia University Teachers College. "If you can do those things from your desk, why do you need a physical plant called a college?" he asked.

—*Chicago Sun-Times*, November 7, 1994

I had something to say all the time. We encouraged everybody on the center staff to do this. I was called to make a speech in Seattle, to pinch hit for someone. This was in '56. It was my famous—or infamous—J. Edgar Hoover speech, in which I called him an ineffectual fly swatter. It's the first time anybody had ever spoken of Hoover that way in public. There were about two, three hundred editorials attacking me and the center. It was the ultimate heresy. Elmo Roper, who was a chairman of our board at that time, called me in and said, "As far as I can see, you've got the dimmest future of anybody. I can't imagine anyone as unemployable as you." From then on, I just depended on luck.

I went into business for myself. I worked for three or four foundations of liberal disposition. One was the DJB Foundation, a small one set up by Dan Bernstein, whom I knew slightly. He died, and it became his wife's foundation. Carol is now my wife. My first wife had died some years before.

I have a very large correspondence with dozens of people. We are still in the philanthropy business and trying to get rid of the dough as fast as we can. We do it all ourselves. We're interested in people who can't get help anywhere else: prisoners and poor people. It's to prolong hope.

Do *I* have hope? Look at any newspaper now. Until about fifteen years ago, I often said to myself, "I hope I live long enough to see how all this is going to turn out." I was curious, because I thought there was some hope. I'm not curious anymore. I don't want to live that long. I think civilization is on the skids for good. We still have the capabilities of blowing up the world and we're not going to give up our nukes. Sooner or later, we'll use them. Absolutely.

I have never felt very optimistic about things. It may just be a fault in my nature. I should have a nicer view, but look around and what do you see? As for living to the year 2000, I don't much care. I feel sorry for my grandchildren. I don't have too much faith in my contemporaries. Look at my Dartmouth classmates. The ranks of my old allies are getting thinner...

Damned if I know why I work so hard, but I can't quit. I think I'm constantly trying to pay back. I owe somebody something. How will I ever pay back for all this good fortune that's been my lot in life? My conscience is gnawing the hell out of me. Where do I pay, for Christ's sake?

There's something I feel good about. I haven't been too bad a Nostradamus. Some of the things I've advocated are back on the center of the table. Have I made a mark? Yup. But I couldn't tell you on whom.

CHAPTER THREE

The Learning Tree

Rochelle Lee, 71
EVANSTON, ILLINOIS

For twenty-one years, she had been a librarian in Chicago public schools. At her retirement party in 1988, parents of the students she had served set up the Rochelle Lee Fund to Make Reading a Part of Children's Lives. It is voluntary.

"Any teacher can apply for an award. The teachers select the books because they presumably know their kids. They are required to spend eight hours in our workshops. We are asking the teachers to become learners. If you don't know what's in a book, you can't be enthusiastic—and neither will the children.

"The books can be about anything: stories, mythology, social studies, science, African American life, math. We found that math concepts in story form can reach children who otherwise would be lost.

"We are now in ninety-nine Chicago public schools, covering four districts. Next month, we're going to fund 240 teachers."

I worked at Arnold, a junior high school, and, after it was phased out, at Oscar Mayer, an elementary school. There, we had the only open library in our city's public schools. Kids were free to come in at any time. They were not programmed. The school libraries in Chicago were set up to relieve the teachers for their preparation periods. The children were generally led in by the gym teacher. Our library was open before and after school and during lunchtime. All day.

Oscar Mayer was in a middle-class neighborhood, but we bused in kids from the South Side: African American, Hispanic. We had a mixture of all socioeconomic classes. As of today, 73.4 percent of Chicago schoolchildren can't read up to the national average. These same kids came to love our library.

I grew up during the depression. In those days, you were going to be either a nurse or a teacher. I'd always wanted to be a teacher. In the mid-'40s, I taught sixth grade for a couple of years in a suburban school. Then my husband returned from the air corps. You know what happened when the "boys" came back. The woman stopped work and raised her family. We had a couple of daughters.

After several years of volunteer work—League of Women Voters and all that—I went back to school. In the '60s, I got my master's degree in political science at the University of Chicago.

One day, I came across a double-page ad in which the Chicago Board of Education was exhorting people to substitute teach if you had any kind of degree. I thought I could do that one or two days a week.

I was sent to the inner city: a tough junior high school, Arnold. The kids were African American, Hispanic, some Gypsies. We had everything. A very few middle-class kids. There were three security officers at the school at all times.

At first, I was a little bit afraid of going as a substitute. My daughters pleaded with me not to do it. "Mom, kids take such advantage, they're just waiting for the substitute." They spoke from their suburban school experience. I saw this as a challenge.

I remember when the supervisor asked me if I'd go to Arnold. I didn't know why they asked me that question. I was naive. I said, "Of course I'll go." Just the day before, there had been a riot at Waller High. It had been the first such outbreak in Chicago public high schools. This was '67. They threw food and dishes all over the lunchroom. Since then, Chicago high schools have used paper plates. I heard swear words I'd never heard before. Waller was just across the street from Arnold. We used their facilities. Substitutes who knew the system refused to go. What did I know? "You'd better have magic tricks," they warned me.

The first day I got there, the school was surrounded by a sea of blue. All these police cars were patrolling the school. I didn't know where I was. I had never before seen a police officer at a school. The police didn't know how to handle it. It was on the front page of the newspapers.

I did have a magic trick: a little shopping bag full of books. In the afternoon, I was asked to take over a seventh-grade class. The teacher had an emergency at home. When I got there, all the kids were in the hall and the janitors were in the room. A kid had thrown a chair at the window and broke it. They were busy cleaning up the broken glass. The kids were all excited, shouting. I didn't know what to do, so I said, "I'm going to read you a story." There was a sudden hush. They were stunned. "A story?!" [*Laughs.*] I had some gang kids there. For some reason, they listened as I read. They loved it. So we talked about it.

Somehow, they related the story to their lives. The next day, I came back and read and read. We talked and talked. It was a real challenge. They started telling me of their experiences, of their family life. My uncle did this. My auntie did that. Oh, I loved these kids. They were so warm. And absolutely mesmerized by the stories.

When I got home, my daughters had their faces plastered to the window, waiting for me. They were worried I wouldn't come home. [*Laughs.*] I hadn't planned on going back, but the following week I got a call from the principal. She said, "I have a petition from the children asking you to come back. I've never gotten that for a substitute." I didn't do anything special. All I did was read to the kids. These children had no books in their lives and had never been read to. Many of them couldn't read. This may have been the first time in their lives. They were hungry for stories.

The principal asked me if I would take over the school library. I love books, but I'd never had a library course in my life. She said it didn't matter: "Just get the kids reading." I took on the job. The first thing I noticed is that grades are given for library. It bothered me.

"How many kids do I see during the week?" I asked.

"You see every child in the school." she said. "Nine hundred fifty."

"How often do I see them?"

"Once a week."

"If I see 950 kids eight or nine times during the year, what's the purpose of the grade?"

She was stunned. "Oh, it's on the list."

I said, "I'll give it a fling. But I will never, ever give a child a grade in library. My job is to turn kids on to reading, I can't think of a better way to turn them off than to give a grade."

In my twenty-one years, I was the one librarian who never gave a grade.

When I first got there, there wasn't even one book per child. Half the books could have been tossed out, they were so bad. "How can you expect me to run a library without books?" The principal suggested I write to the Division of Libraries. Letters went back and forth. I found no help there at all. I lost track of the frustrating exchanges, there were so many.

I suggested we buy paperbacks. They are less forbidding, less like textbooks than hardbacks. No soap. Finally, I said to the principal, "If I raise the money myself, can I buy paperbacks?" She said, "If you raise your own money, I don't care what you buy." So I got the kids and their families involved. We had taffy apple sales, bake sales, auctions.

I knew Herb Fried, president of Charles Levy, the large paperback distributor. He said, "I wouldn't give a wooden nickel to Chicago public schools." He had saturated a dozen classrooms with books, he said, "and I never received a single report from any of the teachers, not even a thank-you note." I said, "You're not giving books to the schools. You're giving them to deprived kids." He finally said, "I'll make a deal. If you raise the money to buy books here, I'll match every penny." We raised the money and the books rolled in by the hundreds.

I had the kids write thank you notes. I realized at once that not only could they not read, they couldn't write. We worked and worked on those letters and Herb was overwhelmed. He *loved* them. He started sending in huge cases of books, whatever kind I wanted: almanacs, magazines. He let me pick them all.

One day, his secretary called. It was confidential. "This whole company is tied up with thank you notes. Mr. Fried has them plastered on all the bulletin boards, in the lunchroom, everywhere. We have to read every darn one to pick out the choice for the cover of our annual report. I'll send you all the books you need, if you promise to never again send us a thank you note." [*Laughs.*]

S. E. Hinton's *The Outsiders* was one of their favorites. She was seventeen when she wrote it. It's in the first person. That was '68, '69. It's about street gangs. What the kids don't get at home or anywhere else, they get in the gangs: the nurturing and the loyalty. You cannot believe how that book hooked the students.

They loved *Oliver Twist*, too. I was always successful with Dickens because London was Chicago a hundred years ago. Mark Twain didn't go over that well, because it was mostly about rural life. Dickens wrote of the city, and these were city kids. They were crazy about him.

At my retirement party in '88, some of the kids, now in their mid-thirties, came back to talk about those days. They reminisced about climbing through the window at Arnold "to hear Mrs. Lee read." I'm not a good reader. They couldn't come through the door because they had been suspended. They had been with the Latin Kings and other tough gangs. One of them came from California on his own.

I would read to each class and get to know them, so I could match the book to their interests. I was reading every night. One of the most important things a teacher can do is to read aloud to kids. It gives them access to language and literature they can't get on their own.

I remember one guy who had never read a book. He wrote me years later and said how embarrassed he always felt. Here he was in seventh grade and was just reading a Dr. Seuss book. It was his very first one and he loved it.

A former student in California asked if the fund could send him fifty dollars worth of paperbacks on Martin Luther King. He said he learned about Dr. King through paperbacks in our library. He had a group of African American kids he was mentoring, and he wanted to teach them the same way he had learned about it. At the end of his letter was a P.S.: "Would you please send your picture along with the books?" I wondered why. He replied: "They love the stories, but the one thing they don't believe is that I learned about Martin Luther King Jr. from a white woman." We just don't know what effect we have on people's lives.

They loved that library because that's where they were nurtured and felt at home. I was there at eight in the morning and would stay as long as anyone needed me. We had no library classes. Kids came in as though it were the public library. Volunteer parents were at the desk and I'd stand nearby. "If you don't like this book," I'd say, "I'll help you find something else."

I got sick in '88. That's why I retired. It was at that great retirement party that the fund was born. We have seventy-six hours of workshops for the teachers: how to read aloud, how to discuss a book, how to assess kids. We don't subscribe to the standardized tests, those Iowa and California skill tests. No way. Most of these were really written for middle-class kids. That shouldn't be the only way to assess students. In our workshops, nobody stands and lectures. They learn by doing.

These days, we have all sorts of computers, but there's no substitute for reading. My husband, an electrical engineer, who taught at Purdue, loves computers, but he says, "I don't know what my life would be without reading. Unless a child can read, the computer is nothing but fun and games." What good is a word processor if somebody can't read? First you get to read, then you get to write. I feel computers in schools have often been grossly misused as shortcuts for reading. How do you shortcut the joy of discovering something for yourself?

I'm working now harder than ever. I go down almost every day. I have less energy now and feel I have to slow down a bit. There are some minor heart problems, and the body is making more demands. [*Laughs.*] But we have to make a commitment to the next generation. In the ideal world, we'd get to the parents prenatally, so when a child is born, he'd have a language that would give him an even chance at life. The only thing we know how to do is to get the teachers to give that child the gift of reading. Hopefully, it will go on beyond my lifetime.

Timuel Black, 74

CHICAGO, ILLINOIS

He was a Chicago schoolteacher for forty years.

"We came to Chicago when I was six months old, toward the end of the 1919 race riots. In those days, black folk were not welcome east of Cottage Grove, unless they worked for white families. Most of my childhood was spent between Thirty-first Street on the north to Sixty-seventh Street on the south, and between west of Cottage Grove to the Rock Island railroad tracks. It was known as the Black Belt.

"We were moving south as often as we could, because that's where new housing opened up. My mother wanted good schools for her children, and that's where the white kids were. Of course, there were restrictive covenants in these neighborhoods. In 1947, they were outlawed by the Supreme Court. Whites simply moved out. I don't remember any violence during that time.

"There were some very good buys for blacks, because the whites were so anxious to get out. Our new neighborhood was nice and quiet, a contrast to the old ones, where families were packed one on top of the other.

"In 1943, I was drafted into the army. I was in the Quartermaster Corps. I was in the first contingent that entered Paris during its liberation. I'll never forget the exhilaration, the exuberance of the French people. As bedraggled as we were, all these people were paying tribute not only to us, the American soldiers, but to the idea of freedom. The other high moment was the trip to Washington for the march in 1963. The feeling was the same in both experiences: high hopes.

"With the Brown v. Board of Education *decision in 1954 and the 1965 Voting Rights Act, there appeared to be a change in the behavior of the nation. Today..."*

I became a teacher in 1952. Before that, I had been a social case worker in the children's division. This was shortly after World War II. I dealt with troubled young men and women, helping them get back on track. It was hard work, though satisfying. We could see some results, but it was painful. I decided to go into education and hopefully touch some lives.

My first teaching job was in Gary, Indiana, at Roosevelt High School. I taught social studies. It was all black. Many of the black teachers were highly trained, with Ph.D.'s. For them, Roosevelt was a haven, because they couldn't find jobs elsewhere, despite their training. Two of them went on to become college presidents:

one, at Morgan State University in Maryland, and the other, at Jackson State College in Mississippi.

There was much hope. The steel industry was booming in Gary. Most of the people lived in family-owned homes. There was little rental property. Let's face it, there was a class division in the neighborhood. Some were considered less socially acceptable than others. I was in the middle because I didn't respect class differences among people who were already déclassé. So I accepted all the children as equals. The principal, an absolute dictator, was hostile to my style of teaching. He made life very uncomfortable for me, so, after three years, I came to Chicago.

I took over the classes of my favorite teacher, the late Miss Mary Herring, at DuSable High School: civics and history. I was in my middle thirties, full of vim and vigor. I was teaching the children of my former classmates. Though many had moved outside this Black Belt, a lot would return because of old friendships, and sent their kids to DuSable. It was easy, knowing the parents of so many of my students. I had no discipline problems ever, because the kids were highly motivated. Many went on to Harvard, Princeton, the University of Chicago.

Unfortunately, the administration felt that I didn't know my place. A case in point: A student teacher from the University of Chicago was working under me. He happened to be white. The kids were puzzled by a black man giving a white man instructions and the white man accepting enthusiastically. [*Chuckles.*] They asked him and he said, "Oh, sure, Mr. Black is my boss." These children had never seen a black person in charge of a white. They were simply thrilled. The principal didn't like the idea at all, so she called the university.

She saw these kids as graduating into menial jobs and didn't like the ideas that I was getting them to believe. The previous principal, Miss Carlson, had pushed the academics. Even though our 1954 basketball team thrilled the whole state, she preached the doctrine of academic excellence as well. The general atmosphere of the school had been high.

Because of differences with the principal, I went to Farragut High School on the West Side. It was a Bohemian neighborhood at the time. I was invited to come by the principal, Mr. McBride. I was the first certified black teacher they ever had. This was 1958.

The reason I was invited was the growing conflict between white and black students. The blacks, mostly from the South, had just arrived. One of them had been bludgeoned to death at the nearby corner by a bunch of white kids. Tensions were very high. By this time, I had a fairly decent reputation in race relations. So the principal offered me any class I wanted.

Remember the time. The civil rights movement is on the move. Dr. King is known. The Supreme Court decision is the law of the land. Malcolm X has arrived. The Black Muslims are on the scene. There was a great deal of unrest.

I've a hunch the students in my classes, overwhelmingly white, thought: "Well, well, here's a black man. We'll soon fix him." I didn't worry about it, because I considered them all my students, white or black. Very soon, they realized that I was serious and knew my business. So they toed the line. After my first year, I was honored in the schools' yearbook as "My Most Interesting Teacher."

Now I had offers from a lot of Chicago high schools. I chose Hyde Park. They had a tracking system there. It was identified with so-called ability, but actually with race. The black and the Hispanic kids were in the lower tracks, while the whites, regardless of accomplishment or lack of it, were in the middle or super tracks. Black middle-class kids were in that league, too.

I told the principal I would accept the job but at least two of my five classes would have students from the lower track.

One of the students in my freshman class of 1964 was Jeff Fort.* He had natural leadership ability. Hyde Park, at the time, was somewhat snobbish toward poor kids in general and poor black kids in particular. They were constantly trying to get rid of these "undesirables." Jeff Fort was one of those. He conformed to a number of us teachers, black and white. But there were a good number of other teachers who wanted him and the others out.

Lyndon Johnson, who had just been elected, called a civil rights conference in Washington. I was asked to participate. I went there on a Wednesday, and when I returned on Monday, the "undesirables" were gone.

I went around the corner to the poolroom where they hung out, to try to encourage them to come back to school. They said, "Mr. Black, they don't want us there." I would say this was the beginning of what has now become a violent street gang. There had been gangs earlier, but not nearly as well organized and as violent as this one. I remember the stages it went through: Blackstone Rangers into P-Stone Nation into El Rukns.

I am almost certain that we would have been able to improve on Jeff Fort's academic skills and that he would have graduated a different person, a participating, productive citizen. What we did was to put this talent out on the street, undernourished academically, and on a destructive path.

I became so frustrated that I quit schoolteaching. I became a

* He later became the leader of Chicago's most notorious street gang, the El Rukns, and is now in prison.

member of the National Teacher Corps. My job was to instruct prospective teachers in the art of working in troubled, urban schools. Many of these teachers-to-be were anti–Vietnam War protestors, and this program afforded them an exemption from armed service. These were guys from Harvard and Yale, who later went south to some of the black colleges.

Things were changing. The old junior colleges were looking for black administrators as well as teachers. I had all the qualifications to do either. My name was put up for many of these positions, but the trouble was I had been in too many campaigns challenging the status quo. My name was put up for the presidency of Malcolm X College and then withdrawn. I was in and out as dean of Wright College. Friends throughout the city came to my side—black, white, Jewish, Catholic Protestant—but it did no good. No reasons were given.

I had tenure, so I decided to go back to the classroom. I chose Loop College. Its name has since been changed to Harold Washington College.

The city college system had, at the time, the retirement age of seventy. It was revoked when a court ruled that you could not retire a teacher as long as that person was able to do his job satisfactorily. I had already had my fill, and it was not with any great sadness that I retired from the city college system on December 31, 1988.

I have more time now to do what I was interested in doing anyhow—being active in the political areas of black and liberal life. I still teach a course at Roosevelt University once a week. And I'm trying to do some writing.

My day is very full. The phone rings constantly. People believe I have nothing but time now, so they ask to borrow some of it. To speak to this or that group, attend one meeting or another. My vacation is when I'm out of town, and away from the telephone.

I was in the march on Washington this past weekend.* I went in memory of my son, who passed recently, and, of course, to see how it compared with the first one. I was pleasantly surprised, although the numbers were relatively small. There were quite a number of young people. They were asking: How do we transfer the knowledge of our generation to theirs? They call it "passing the torch."

At this point, the young do not feel as optimistic as we did. There's a different look on their faces, much more grim and serious. They seem to be searching for answers. They would like us to pass on our experiences, but they also want to find their own answers, by their

---

* August 1993. The march commemorated the thirtieth anniversary of the 1963 civil rights march. For further discussion, see Esther Thompson's interview in chapter 13, "Health."

own methods. They want the support of their fathers and mothers, but they do not want the sort of control that they fear would stop them from doing what they ought to do. There was a feeling of commonality, but no sense of organization. The issues were clearer in '63: End segregation, Jim Crow, and every form of discrimination.

It was much less exciting than the earlier march, but more contemplative. The young looked at older people as having done the best they could—but it wasn't enough. Naturally, I was among those older people. And don't think I didn't feel it.

It was very, very, very hot, ninety-two degrees throughout. I walked all over, around the mall, and up to the Lincoln Memorial, and stood from about 10:30 A.M. to 2:30 P.M. So I guess my health is still pretty good. Thirty years ago, I didn't think about it. Now, I was exhaustedly aware of it.

Considering my age and all, I'm doing fairly well. I had a cataract operation, and my memory may not be as great as it was, but it's still there.

I'm still able to teach that class at Roosevelt. It's an introduction to African American studies, through forms of music: singing, dancing, orchestrating. I use recordings and video cassettes of Duke Ellington, Louis Armstrong, and Quincy Jones, as well as Kathleen Battle and Jessye Norman.

My class fills up. Usually there are too many students—whites, Asians, and South Americans, too. It's fascinating to discover what these young people are thinking. In many ways, they're hardly in touch with the generation that preceded them, their parents and grandparents. There's a sense of loneliness that transcends race. They're looking for answers, but are not prepared to take the long view. They're impatient and sometimes act out that impatience because they don't believe the forces in control will give up anything.

I get a kid from Chile who is as exasperated as a kid from the South Side of Chicago. Kids from the Far East, from almost any place, talk about the growing reduction of opportunities in their own countries. And it's immediate gratification they desire.

When I look at their basic skills, reading, writing, and even in conversation, they're much more limited than they were when I first started teaching. The sound bite. They talk in short, curt sentences. They write, even if legibly, in phrases that are short, vague, and often not to the point. They are not prepared to do the hard Jimmy Higgins work to get where they want to go.* There's a trend. Not all kids are like that, but—I could almost document it. This is one of the concerns of most college professors.

---

* Upton Sinclair's novel *Jimmy Higgins* is about the world of labor. Its protagonist is the man who did all the hard, necessary, unglamorous work, though he seldom got recognition for it.

You ride public transportation and you'll see a lot of young people with plugs in their ears, listening to something. Certainly they can't listen to you if they're listening to that. They're sitting next to you, but they're not near you. The breakdown of communications between the generations is profound and scary.

As for reading—voluntary reading—it's distressing. When I was a young teacher, a kid would come up and say, "Mr. Black, have you read...?" I hardly ever hear that anymore

From my experience with the peasantry in Gary [*chuckles*], to the immigrant in Farragut, to the more sophisticated at DuSable or Hyde Park, I've observed these children's access to sources of information, uncensored, that neither my children nor I ever had. They have not been prepared to ask questions about these sources, so voluminous, so exciting. So they're unable to articulate their feelings.

They have to have noise. It's a fix, hardly different from dope. They seem unable to spend private time by themselves without noise. You can't carry on a conversation because they're not looking at you, not listening to you. To be heard, you have to shout.

It transcends race. The children of this generation, white as well as black, can hardly hope to live better than their parents, even if they're in the so-called middle class. At the very bottom, about a third of African Americans, they're in dire straits. Perhaps more than any other group, they are exposed to commercial television, which tells them they ought to have all these good material things. With the breakdown in the family, in education, and in religion, these young are left with no hope, so necessary for people to move forward. But the impoverished young are more inclined to act out their frustrations. A kid growing up in an impoverished community is not certain about tomorrow. The uncertainty causes him to seek status immediately. Status may come with outtalking, outdoing, outfighting the other person.

Status comes to a young girl, who doesn't know what the world is like, by having a baby at fourteen. Freeing herself up, so she can become socially "as grown" as her mother, who may be twenty-seven or something. The status of the boy who impregnates her comes from being able to brag that he is the father of a child—without understanding the responsibilities that go along with it.

Think of the insecurity of a youngster coming out of a household where there's been no love, who has already been made responsible for giving love. Now it carries through into at least two generations. If I were teaching today, my students might be some of the great-grandchildren of students I had forty years ago. It just happens that most of the kids I taught forty years ago are in the mainstream of American life.

With the removal of a spiritual center to which children can refer, we see the decline of mainstream churches and the growth of fundamentalism. Given the insecurities, it could be the basis of a kind of fascism. I remember reading about the wandering youth going through Germany. Many of these youngsters became storm troopers. This may be generalizing, but I see the possibility of a strong, charismatic leader, in an insecure society, focusing in on minorities.

The kids in the Washington march may be the cream of the crop, but they bore the same characteristics of alienation and loneliness and a distrust of the past generation. They challenged their elders: You didn't get the job done; if you had, we wouldn't feel this way.

My look at tomorrow? I'm a perennial pessimist-optimist, a walking contradiction. I look at the worst so I can warn people how to go about the best. I think the task of young people is much more difficult than ours was. But I think they'll find answers and solutions. My generation's responsibility is to offer them moral support and advice, hoping they'll accept it.

The job will be a lot tougher than in the days when I was growing up. My mother or my father would say, "We've come this far by faith and we'll move further by faith." We didn't have to have concrete proof. We had faith. These kids are demanding concrete proof because their faith has been destroyed. To a great extent, the restoration of that faith is in the work of the church. I see it happening in my neighborhood, with young people taking part. The church has always played an important role in black life. I see it happening, and I think the white youngsters are hungry, too.

Tomorrow? I have to look at my calendar. I'm attending a meeting about the school crisis. Let's see, I think I have to be at a couple of other gatherings, too. I may do some more writing...Oh, yes, I enjoy every day.

Aki Kurose, approaching 70
SEATTLE, WASHINGTON

She is a Nisei, born and raised in Seattle.

As a sixteen-year-old, shortly after World War II was declared, she and her family, among scores of thousands of Japanese Americans, were arrested and sent off to internment camps.

"Horse stalls and pigpens were converted to shelters for many of us. Our family of six was assigned to one room. They gave us burlap bags. We were told to stuff straw in them and they would be our mattresses...There were machine-gun towers in parking lot. The guns were aimed inside, at us. People would drive around in cars, calling us names. You'd feel like an animal in the zoo.

"Everything was so surreal. The assignment one teacher in camp gave us was: 'Write why you are proud to be an American.' [Laughs softly.] We had to salute the flag every day and sing the national anthem."

Around 1965, I was a Head Start volunteer. I got turned on to working with young people, so after my children were raised, I went back to school. I got my master's degree in early childhood education when I was fifty-six years old.

I started teaching in the early '70s and have been doing so ever since. I teach six-year-olds, first grade. I've taught kindergarten and preschool, as well. I teach mathematics, science, and peace.

How does one teach peace? Well, I immediately say to them, "If you're not at peace with yourself, with your neighbor, with your community, you can't really learn very much. We have to get rid of all this garbage, this angry, competitive feeling. Then we'll all get along."

We'd go outside and do these exercises in the morning to invigorate ourselves. We pretend that we're taking all the anger out of our bodies, getting rid of our anxieties and throwing them all into outer space. We're not polluting the space, because what we're throwing out is just being disintegrated. So we talk about environment that way also.

I tell them: When you're in school, no one is going to be sent to the principal, and nobody's going to be turned bad. If something unpleasant happens, we're going to resolve our own conflicts. When trouble may start, I tell them to stop, rest awhile, let's talk things over, because we need a cooling-off period. What happens in our classroom has to be a win-win situation for everybody. We don't have a winner and a loser.

Under no circumstances will they be punished. I tell them that making a mistake is the most natural thing to do. Everybody makes mistakes. The thing to do is to learn from our mistakes. The more mistakes you make, the more you're learning, so don't worry about that.

At my school, they didn't quite know what to do about me. The principal called me and said we were to attend a community meeting. I said, "Fine. Are the other teachers coming, too?" He said, "No. I'm going to forewarn you. This is in a doctor's very beautiful home. You'll be meeting with parents and you must be prepared to tell them how you're going to teach their privileged children."

When I walked in, there were forty parents already seated. They had met an hour before, getting all their questions organized. They immediately wanted to know where I had been educated. I told them I had been to the University of Washington and was just about to get my master's degree.

They wanted to know if their children would pick up my Japanese accent. I told them, "I'm sorry, but this is a Seattle public school accent. I was born in this city." They were so very anxious and worried. "You've been teaching poor children all these years. How will you deal with our children, who have had lots of preschool and are very advanced? Can you meet the challenge of these children?" I said I could meet the challenge of any child. "It's the challenge of the parents that may be more difficult." They were quite shocked. [*Laughs softly.*] Two parents monitored my classroom every day for a month.

Here is a very affluent neighborhood of ambitious parents who don't know quite what to do with this Asian woman who is so outspoken. After a month of monitoring, they decided that I could teach. Eventually, these parents became more supportive of me than the staff did. They were the ones who recommended me for the Teacher for Excellence Award. Some of their attitudes were at first condescending, but that changed and it was wonderful.

The staff had a very hard time of it when I first came there. Remember, I had displaced a white teacher, who was transferred to the central area. They were naturally feeling sorry for the other woman and said, in so many words, that it wasn't fair that I should get all the breaks because I was of the minority. They felt it was a real privilege for me to come here to teach white children. Referring to my old school, they'd say, "Oooh, how did you stand it?" I said I loved it down there. I said, "Actually, I feel it's an inconvenience for me to come here. At the old place, I could walk to school. Now I have to drive all the way out there."

One teacher asked me, "Who are you?"

"I'm Aki Kurose."

"Well, you know what I mean."

"No, I'm not sure, though I suspect I know what you mean."

"*What* are you?"

"Oh, I'm a teacher."

Finally, she said, "Well, where do you come from?"

"Oh. I come from Madrona." (That's the area where I live in Seattle.)

"Well, no—you know what I mean."

"I think I do."

"What kind of name is Kurose?"

"That's my husband's name."

She was getting quite angry with me. Finally, I said, "Are you asking my ethnicity?"

She said, "Yes. Are you Chinese or Japanese?"

"I am Japanese and proud of it. Why is it so important to you?"

Then she said some of her friends got killed in World War II. I said, "I'm very sorry, but I don't think I'm responsible for it. I'm against war, so please don't regard me as your enemy." For many years, on December 7, they'd bring up Pearl Harbor: "Your people..." They'd want to talk to the students about it. I'd argue with them that that kind of history isn't what it's about. I always tell my students that war is the enemy, so you can't name people as the enemy.

It's changed a lot in the nineteen years I've been there. Because our busing is no longer mandatory, it's starting to get sterile again. We've lost a lot of black students. Oh, it was a challenge and hard at the beginning. I think the problem had more to do with money than color. You send these kids to a neighborhood with Porsches, Volvos, Mercedes, and mothers who are constantly at school to see to the needs of their own children. The whole lifestyle is so different from these bused kids, usually of single parents or working ones who can't participate. The PTAs there are like pink teas in beautiful homes. What working parent can go to a PTA meeting at ten o'clock in the morning?

The kids in my class were wonderful and starting to get along with each other. I said "We're not going to compete." Many of the parents in these affluent neighborhoods are so anxious for their kids to be at the top of the class. I said, "I'm sorry, in my classroom there's nobody at the top of the class, nobody in the middle, and nobody at the bottom. We work cooperatively. No grades in my class."

At first, the parents didn't like it. They love to have their Susie first in line, top in math or top reader. I said I don't give tests that way. I give them problem-solving activities where they work cooperatively. Nobody's answer is wrong. We try to justify the answer. If they say, "Four plus three equals eight," I say, "Let's see if we can justify that statement." So the children work in groups of four and think about it. Each may come up with a different answer. So they rethink it. This one little boy who had four beans and three beans had to justify the total of eight. He suddenly realized something. He then broke one bean in half and said, "Four plus two plus the two halves of the seventh bean equal eight." He *thought* it through.

When I first began teaching, I thought I had to have lots of knowledge that I could share with my students, so they could memorize all these things. That's not what education is about. We need to teach them that the planet earth is here for us to cherish and share with everybody. We have to stop this possessive approach, especially with young children. I realize as they grow up, they may have to compete. But at the low-elementary level, they need to build up their self-esteem and self-worth and, above all, learn to *think*.

I remember a letter from a college student who'd been one of my kids. "You made me interested in math and science. They have been among my favorites ever since. I know that not only does 5+6=11. So does 6+5. But the foremost part of your curriculum was peace. It has made the big difference in my life." Teaching them the skill of living on this earth in a peaceful manner is what education should be about.

It's so sad to hear teachers saying, "I can't wait to retire. I can't wait for the school year to be over. I can't wait until three-thirty when the kids will be out of my classroom." If you've lost that spirit, I don't think you should be teaching.

Some of them are burnt out because the classes are so large or because they can't deal with the anger of the kids. When busing started, most of the black kids were out in the hallway or being sent to the principal's office. I protested: this gives the wrong message. The other kids, the whites, see them in the hallways or in the principal's office and think they're all bad kids.

I said we don't need to punish kids this way. So I've been working with community people, trying to get a peace curriculum passed through the legislature, because if you can't get along with one another, what's the use of having a Ph.D.?

I have four kids at each of six tables. Every morning, I have a bouquet of flowers on each table so the students may enjoy its beauty—and learn the botanical names. In this way, they learn to spell *rhododendron, azalea, chrysanthemum*. They put a flower picture book together. On the back, they write a poem about the flowers they've come to know. In learning botany, they learn math as well—how the leaves are attached, how they are spaced, they count the petals. When the petals fall, they don't throw them away, they study them. You'll see children treasuring the stems, with the petals gone. It is not learning how to memorize, but how to see them as beautiful parts of their lives.

We grow salmon in the classroom. I take the children to the fish hatchery at the University of Washington. We see the spawning salmon. They allow us to squeeze the eggs out, which we bring back to the classroom. We have an aquarium with refrigeration. And we grow the salmon eggs. We raise salmon! [*Laughs delightedly.*] Part of our curriculum is the life cycle of a salmon. The children learn a song about these fish. We release the little fingerlings back into the fresh streams, where they can hide under the rocks and gradually finish their lives, going back into the sea. Then we all sing "Bon Voyage, Bon Voyage."

Every morning, we go outside to exercise. My bused-in children, especially, don't need to be thrown into a classroom immediately. They need to get some of that energy out. We make a big circle, we study the clouds, the motion of the sun. While they exercise, they count by fives, by tens, "higher, higher." All this time they're learning multiplication.

As we observe the clouds, they come up with these fantastic things: "Mrs. Kurose, you're talking about these cirrus clouds, but why do we see the cumulus?" They use these words not by rote, but because they connect with them what they experience at that moment. It's so exciting! I realize I'm learning so much from my students.

I encourage them to write constantly. They keep a journal and they write their thoughts. I don't say, "Spell it right," certainly not at the beginning. They do inventive spelling and their stories are so exciting. I'm pretty good now at deciphering their spelling. But they know from the beginning what they've written. They share it with the group. So the observing and the writing are relevant to their day.

They know all the phases of the moon. My students tell their parents about a waxing, gibbous moon. A number of mothers and fathers there have told me, "We didn't know what a gibbous moon was until our first graders came home and told us. We're learning astronomy from your students."

I was honored as Teacher of the Year for the Seattle area. My name was submitted by the parents. The following year, the National Science Center gave me the Presidential Award for Excellence in Science and Mathematics. There was one winner from each state.

Bush was president. It was very ironic because under him the teachers have been damned with fewer benefits, and the students with fewer services. At the Rose Garden, some of the teachers were so excited about Bush. One said, "I'm never going to wash my hands." I said, "Ughh!"

Bush came up to me, smiling: "Hi, would you like to take a picture with me?" I just couldn't help myself and said, "No, you're not my favorite president." He just looked. I don't think he was even listening. I said, "You're supposed to be our 'education president,' but you don't show it. You're allotting all this money to the military, when all these children need education." I added, "One stealth bomber would pay for the salary of hundreds of teachers. Two stealth bombers would probably supply many good school districts. You need to change your priorities."

He just stood there with his plastic smile and he said, "Okay," as he put his arms around me and had this person take a picture of us. He didn't hear a word I said.

I was thrilled to be in Washington. I was thrilled to see the White House. But I was sad because things just didn't fit. I had borrowed a dress from my friend because I didn't have any formal gown to wear. I put "Peace" buttons all the way across. I wear these buttons every day, on every garment. When my grandchildren come over, the first thing they say is, "Okay, you have them on." My students love it.

During our Curriculum Night, the parents are invited. We have to explain what we teach. I said, "I want you to know that peace is the most important part of my curriculum. I teach science and math, but if a child is not at peace with himself or herself, with the neighbors, with the community, true learning cannot take place."

On this night, one man said, "That's none of your business. I want you to teach reading, writing, and arithmetic. That's why I'm sending my kid to school, to learn the three Rs. What's all this nonsense you're handing out about atomic bombs, Sadako, or whatever?" I said, "Yes, I do tell them about Sadako and the thousand cranes because I think it's a wonderful children's story."

Sadako was a twelve-year-old girl who was an A-bomb victim and was dying of leukemia. There was a Japanese legend that if you fold a thousand paper cranes, you can have good luck and a long life. She made 650 cranes and then she died. I thought children could relate to this.

I said to this man, "Please, take this book home and read it. It's not controversial, it's not subversive." He took it but he wasn't very happy. I said, "If you have any problem, you can always call me at home. Or I'll stay after school. Or I can come to see you. I'm interested in the parents as well as the children. I work hard and I want you to know I will deal with any of your concerns."

This was in September. That was the last I heard from him—until

November. I got this call, "Mrs. Kurose, I'd like an appointment with you. Can I drop in after school?" I said, "Of course." I was nervous, had no idea what he was going to say. He said, "I want to tell you a story." I thought: Uh oh. "My son is reading so beautifully. His math is wonderful, and he treats his younger brother so nicely. He's not a mean kid anymore. And he likes to talk things out. I offered him a set of G.I. Joes, but he said to me, 'Dad, Mrs. Kurose would be very upset. That's a war toy. I would rather have a microscope.'" He was delighted. He said, "Mrs. Kurose, if you have any tax problems or whatever, I'd be happy to do your taxes for free." He was an accountant.

Another parent who came said, "Boy, were our faces red! My wife and I were yelling at each other, and our little daughter said, 'Stop, stop! You're supposed to cool off and talk things out.'" The child was in my class.

Is my teaching today better than when I was younger? Absolutely. My face gets red when I think of the first day I taught. "All right, children, let's pass out the workbook." Ridiculous. Aside from the classes I take, the children are teaching me how to discover things. You can tell a child that mixing vinegar with baking soda is going to fizz, but it won't make an impression unless they do it themselves. We do little magic things, too. I take a boiled egg and put it on top of a bottle. It won't go in no matter how we push it. We put a match inside, burn out the carbon monoxide, and pretty soon the egg plops in. I ask them why it did so. They have to think things out. How can we get it out? You try to shake it, you try to suck it, it won't come out. You blow into it and the egg pops up so dramatically. The kids go "Wow!" They see it.

Some of the teachers don't like my methods. They're very regimented and feel that my children are too free moving. One complained, "Why are you taking them outside for exercise? They get enough exercise on the bus." I said, "I'm not only doing it for my bus children, I'm doing it for myself as well. I get inspired."

I can understand some of these young teachers with families. It's a full-time job, so they lead a difficult double life. They spend so much time on paperwork, xeroxing, and dittoes. And these SATs* are so meaningless. It's an insult to the intelligence of young people. You don't need paper and pencil. You can count beans, multiply them, grow them. All this is magic and so is learning.

I have a science club from kindergarten through the fifth grade. I have a cross-grade teaching: big kids work with little kids. They love it.

The most important thing I learned was to respect children. You

---

* Scholastic Aptitude Tests.

hear lots of complaints about how young kids aren't respecting us anymore. Are we respecting them? Respect begets respect. Children are very perceptive. If you are not valuing them, they know it immediately.

I wonder if we don't really ruin kids in school, cause them to lose respect for themselves. I think the biggest crime is to have a kid sent down to the office. I see that all the time. I see them constantly getting expelled. Why would you expel a kid? Let's face the truth: somewhere along the line, we have failed in our teaching.

In our state, we just passed "Three Strikes and You're Out" legislation. Three crimes and you're incarcerated forever, or something. Won't we ever learn that punished children become punitive people? If you wallop them, that's the only thing they're going to know, so they wallop others. Treat them as human beings and they'll act that way.

Edward was eight years old. His fourteen-year-old brother was shot in a playground, a gangland situation. The mother was homeless. "Can I take him home?" I asked her. She said, "It's up to you." So I brought him home, bought him some clean clothes. I bought him three pairs of socks and three pairs of shorts. He was so proud. "Do I got to give these to my brother?" His brother was still in the hospital. I said, "No, these are for you." He thought I'd given him gold bullion. His eyes were like big marbles. "I get to keep these?" I thought I was a do-gooder, but he did more for me than I did for him. I was impressed with his sudden pride.

I said, "Now we're going to eat." He said, "We get to go to McDonald's?" I said, "No, we're going to buy a trout, with a head and tail and everything. You're going to cook it. We're going to practice science and have a great meal at the same time." We brought it home. He examined it. We washed it. I let him look at the flesh, study it, salt and pepper it, put it in the oven, and watch it change. As he saw the flesh grow firmer, he shouted excitedly, "It's changing!"

We put it on a platter. I said, "Okay, this is going to be your dinner. But let's de-bone it." So we did it together, put the skeleton to the side and he examined the bones. He kept shouting, "Wow!" He got to take the skeleton to school the next day to his great delight. I put out the goblets with milk in one, juice in the other, and water in the third. At different levels, I said, "Take your spoon and hit those." He hit the glasses and cried out, "I'm making music!"

I took him outside to look at the sky. I said, "There's Orion's belt and there's the Big Dipper and Cassiopeia." I explained it to him. Now, he always talks about that night and his discovery of the sky.

Then I said it was time to go to bed. And when he saw the bed in a room of his own, he couldn't believe it. He had never slept in a bed by himself, let alone a room of his own. The next morning, he made his bed very carefully.

When I took him to school, during the creative writing time, he said, "I got a story." He told it to me: "It's about stars that came down to Garfield to play football." Garfield High is where his brother got shot. "When the stars realized they had no hands, no eyes and no legs, they went back up to the sky and made their own formations. They made Cassiopeia, the Big Dipper, and Orion."

At our school, he's been punished, suspended. This same kid. He's got the potential. He loves learning, but we're ruining him. The pity of it is the waste. Unless we stop this punitive mentality, we're going to lose a lot of kids. We've got to teach them how to deal with their anger, but we can't do it unless we learn how to deal with our own anger.

Every time he saw me, he'd say, "Peace, Mrs. Kurose." He'd be at the playground fighting with other kids and when he saw me, he'd say, "Ooops, I forgot. Peace." And he'd stop fighting.

After he left my class, I'd see him sitting in the principal's office. I'd say, "Send him to me. I know how to deal with him." So many times, our minority kids would be sitting in that office all day. It's their punishment. I still have that story of his at school, all bound for him. But I'm afraid he's gone.

"I'm not pessimistic. I have lots of hope. I think more people are finding out about cooperative learning. Science is exciting. Math is exciting. But it means little unless it is incorporated with peace. I feel that I need to be there to be part of making the change.

Gertie Fox, 77

"I'm really 131 years old, but I've been knocked down to seventy-seven. When I go to the K-Mart, the blue light goes on and the bells ring. I'm a real bargain."

In 1966, she helped found an environmental museum in Allentown. She is active in just about every organization in the area, dealing with ecology. "My husband's illness, caring for him, takes much of my time, But I don't lessen my community work. Why give up life? It's too exciting."

I've yet to be called an old woman, though I am. Up till two years ago, I downhill skied. I skied fifty-one years straight from the time skiing was brought to this country from Germany. I started when rope tows were being used in Vermont. I kept up with the sport, took racing lessons. About eight years ago, I entered a giant slalom race run by Jean-Claude Killy up in the Poconos. I won because nobody my age was in the race.

I have two big projects: saving park land and preserving our water resources. [*She hauls out a ton of printed material.*] When I attended the Girls' Latin School in Boston—at first, girls were never judged intelligent enough to go there, but I'd been recommended by my sixth-grade teacher and stayed seven years—I always walked through the Common in the center of the city. It was the equivalent of Central Park in New York. Originally, it was where people brought their cows to graze.

Years and years ago, there was a close vote: Should it be preserved or not? I still remember those lines: "The law doth punish man or woman who steals the goose from the Common. But the law doth let the felon loose who steals the Common from the goose." I learned about Frederick Law Olmsted and how he saved parks, and I thought, What a wonderful thing to do.

I was a scared child of two immigrant parents who came to this country from Latvia, not knowing English. Here I was with the best education, and I wanted to do something to indicate my love for this land.

I got through school in 1934 at the height of the depression. I wanted to go to MIT, but there wasn't a dime for carfare, let alone school. There were no jobs. Because I was good at mathematics, I got a very bad job as night cashier in a dismal restaurant. It was between a tattoo parlor and the old Howard Burlesque.

The thing that most changed my life was something I saw in the basement of that restaurant—a dreadful thing that bothers me to this day. Why didn't I do something about it? There was a man sitting on the wet floor, peeling potatoes. He was a deaf mute. I made out the paychecks but never made one out to him. I never knew his name.

When I saw Van Gogh's *Potato Eaters* in the museum, it reminded me of this man and the horror of his sitting there day and night. He never got up, he never walked, he never left. He was a potato with those dreadful peelings all around him. That was his total life—cruelty of the highest order. I didn't report it to anyone because I was scared of losing my job. That was 1934.

At the end of that year, I went to Simmons College in Boston. I wanted to major in science. I was a student without any money, but they were generous to me. They gave me four different jobs to help pay my way.

When I finished college, I realized I was still bothered by the memory of that deaf mute, the cruelty that I did not report. I vowed I would never stand for anything like that again. If there was one thing I needed to do to explain my existence, I was going to do it.

I learned about water and realized that was where our next big shortage was going to be. It won't be oil and it won't be jobs. It's going to be worse than that, losing our water resources.

Remarkably, the first job I got along those lines was testing liquids to see whether they met standards. For instance, I tested Listerine to see if what they were claiming was true, that it killed x number of bacteria. I loved that work.

A year later, my husband, a chemical engineer, was transferred to Bethlehem to do research. For a time, I taught at the Moravian Preparatory School, mathematics, my deep love. It's beautiful.

It was my fond hope in high school to go to MIT, to learn from the wonderful things that happen there. When I was twelve, I stood in the doorway watching Norbert Wiener do mathematics. He said, "Come in, little girl." He taught me a game called Nim, which is the basis of the binary system, using only one and ten. I never knew he was going to be the inventor of cybernetics, the basis of all computers.

I need to teach children that Euclid was wrong, that the shortest distance between two points is not a straight line. The astronauts didn't go in a straight line. They would have missed the moon. [*Laughs.*] Everything moves. You can say to someone studying Euclidean geometry on the first day of school: "The basis of this course is the straight line. Okay, tell me what a line is." "It has one dimension." Blink. "How do you see it if it has no depth, no width?

You don't see it at all. When you draw it with a pencil, all you see is the result of a drawing with a pencil." Norbert Wiener taught me that mathematics is beautiful, the highest form man indulges in. I can't give that up.

I call myself an ecologist. The word *environmentalist* is too obscure. It's a different thing to everybody. For some people, it's merely picking up litter. That's not what I do. Ecology joins all these matters.

There was another influence on me. At Simmons, I was asked to be president of the Ellen Swallow Richards Science Club. It took considerable research for me to find out who she was. She lived at a time when it was thought that women were too stupid to learn science and mathematics. She applied for one of the early courses given by MIT, then a new college. They turned her down. I came across a letter in the archives: "Women don't have the capacity to go to MIT." At that point, in 1875, no women were studying science. She became a large figure in my life. I thought, I want to pattern my life after her.

She kept applying to MIT, nagging them to death. They finally let her in, but didn't have the guts to tell her she was only an auditor. She covered every course as would give her a doctorate. She was even teaching there, the first woman scientist in the country—without credentials. They turned her down on her doctorate because she was a woman. To this day, I mind that. I think MIT owes her a posthumous doctorate.

She did lots of work in water quality and mapped every source of public water in Massachusetts. We used the word *ecology*. It's from the Greek word *oikos:* home. It meant knowing every single thing that comes into the home, where it comes from, how it's used, and how you dispose of it—sewage, everything. That's what I teach children today.

[*Holds out a booklet.*] "This is the Burnside Plantation, a major piece of land I was helpful in saving. It's in the center of Bethlehem. It's all that's left of a five-hundred-acre farm of the early Moravians who came to Bethlehem. When we restore it, we'll give it to the public. And to the schoolchildren, the ones I teach, a knowledge of what early farm life was like, beginning in 1748, when the farmhouse was built. Until twenty-five years ago, the people of Bethlehem and Allentown had never heard of it.

If you speak up and the community backs you, you simply go ahead. I've protected my image by never making negative comments about anybody. I learned that from the League of Women Voters, which I've belonged to for years. You seek a consensus. If you disagree on details, they'll be ironed out in time.

I argue only if I have the facts. That's part of my credo. Don't ever say anything unless you have five different ways of backing it up. Don't ever make useless statements. You can't get up and say, "What you're doing is wrong." If you don't have the facts, just ask questions. You can make a negative statement with a question. That puts the burden of the answer on the other side.

When a developer in this area wants to build parking lots which end in polluted run-offs flowing into our precious trout stream, I get up and ask, "What are your plans for storm water drainage?" If he has no plans, he'll say, "We'll just hook on to the system you have." Around here, the system is a cornfield into which the rain is absorbed. So I say, "Your run-off will have to go to the nearest waterway." He always says, "What's the name of the waterway?" Then I know he hasn't any plan.

Then I go home and do a great deal of research. If I discover something detrimental is in the wind, I let the municipality know with a call: "Read your *Pennsylvania Bulletin*, page *x*." If there's action to take, I go to the League of Women Voters. Young people come to Burnside all the time. They've helped in putting up the entire barn. When you appeal to young people with a project that is unusual, they come in large numbers. We had more than five-hundred sign-ups in one day to help frame the barn.

I don't listen to those "Keep Young" ads. They're improper. I think I look cuter now than when I was in college. [*Giggles.*] We were so poor, we had no way of enhancing our clothes and shoes.

Another meaning to my life came when I attended the first United Nations conference on world environment, in Stockholm. I paid my way. It was grass roots in origin. The young people of Japan wanted answers for the huge Minimata disaster, when untold numbers died from mercury poisoning. Why did this happen?

I didn't know what the environmental challenge really was until delegates from the Third World nations, the majority, said: You people from the West are all wrong. It's not earth, air, fire, and water. It's disease, ignorance, and poverty. I was all prepared to talk about water quality, ecology, in terms of earth, air, water. I was stunned by their objections.

When I got home, my beliefs were shattered. I went to the library to find books on the Third World, and there weren't any. Had to send away to France. It was a revelation to a First Worlder.

It's not just earth, air, water—it's politics. I didn't know the environment in terms of the majority of the world's people. I wanted to find out who I was and what I wanted to do with the rest of my life. I realized I didn't know what I was talking about. This was June 1972.

When Paul Ehrlich got up to talk about the world population

growing too fast—you must have only two children per family—he was pushed off the stage, along with Lady Ashley. A bunch of Third World women, wearing long shawls, spread them out and walked on stage. They looked like eagles flying. It was magnificent. They said: "You have no right to tell us to have two children per family. Our two children are different from your two children. We must give birth to ten children in order to have two—eight will die. That was new to me. [*Impassioned*] They can't be limited by us.

I finally understood what was happening. We are not on the same wavelength as the Third World. We don't even know what the Third World is. At that time, I didn't know what the First World was or the Second. So how could I know the Third?

In Stockholm, I learned I wasn't big enough to be able to take world positions. But the trip fortified me to go forth with my local projects. They're all related. That's why I changed from being an environmentalist to an ecologist.

How would I like to be celebrated? I don't need to be celebrated. The creek—the wonderful, high-quality-water limestone spring in the middle of our city—has to be celebrated.

I know how I want to die. As an old lady of eighty-five, I would like to enroll at MIT, with the purpose of finally getting there. [*Laughs.*] I really want to be sitting in class, absorbing new knowledge. I want to spend my last days in a credited class. They can take me out in a body bag after that. I dream about that all the time. About ten years ago, I walked into the admissions office and asked, "Would I be able to enroll?" They said, "Certainly." So I walked out happy. [*Gives a little laugh.*]

Postscript: Gertie Fox died on January 4, 1995.

Part II

CHAPTER FOUR

The Firm

Charles A. Bane, 80
PALM BEACH, FLORIDA*

"I was born on May 1, 1913. My birthday was celebrated in Red Square, Moscow, every year.

"I grew up in Springfield, Illinois. My father was a hoisting engineer at a coal mine. My mother was an old-fashioned housewife.

"I received a scholarship at the University of Chicago, arriving at the same time Bob Hutchins did. I was one of the twenty-five freshmen who took the first course from Hutchins and Mortimer Adler: Classics of the Western World. I dropped out of school in my second year because of the depression. After a year at work, I returned. During my forth year, I was elected as a Rhodes Scholar and took a B.A. in jurisprudence at Oxford.

"It was the time of the New Deal and things were exciting at home, so I came back to Harvard Law School. I encountered such teachers as Felix Frankfurter, Thomas Reed Powell, and Edmund Morgan. A good legal foundation, I'd say. On graduation, I joined Sullivan & Cromwell, one of the largest Wall Street firms.

When World War II broke out, I joined the navy and was assigned to the Office of Strategic Services (OSS) as an aide to Bill Donovan. I served in London during the buzz-bomb period. After the invasion, I wound up at the front. It was horrible. Nobody can ever be satisfied with any kind of war experience.

When the war ended, I rejoined Sullivan & Cromwell. It was a large firm—a hundred lawyers. Impersonal. John Foster Dulles headed it, a remote man with no warmth at all. Unless you were in corporate work or securities, you really didn't find it satisfying. I was assigned to a public utilities problem and spent two and a half years on it. I was overworked, seldom seeing my family, except on Sundays. But I was anxious to get some financial security before I struck out on my own.

---

* This conversation took place in Chicago.

During my time with the OSS, I struck up a friendship with Steven Mitchell. He had a small law firm in Chicago, and I joined him there after I quit Sullivan. There were just three of us, practicing law on a catch-as-catch-can basis at times. Steve had some good connections, so all in all we did pretty well.

After I'd been in Chicago a couple of years, I was asked to become counsel to the Big Nine, an emergency crime committee. It was working on a city level at the time Estes Kefauver was conducting federal hearings. Though we may have given the syndicate some embarrassing moments, I can't pretend we really broke them up. They may still be a force to this day. I don't know.*

Steve Mitchell was about to enter politics. He was a member of the Democratic National Committee and a key figure in Adlai Stevenson's campaign for president. So I joined Isham, Lincoln & Beale in 1953.† I didn't regret it, because the work was interesting and I become a prominent member of the firm. However, it had become a narrow kind of legal practice. My own case is an example of the specialization that was to become characteristic of law practice at the end of World War II.

In 1983, I decided I'd gone as far as I could in private law practice. My children were grown up and I was relatively free. I decided to spend half my time with Isham, Lincoln & Beale and the other half in the academic world. The University of Miami Law School was a natural because it was close to Palm Beach, where we had acquired a home. It was a fifty-fifty proposition.

When I reached the age of seventy-two, I retired from Isham, Lincoln & Beale. It was mandatory. Two years after my retirement, the firm—without consulting me, of course, because I was retired partner—made a very unfortunate merger with another law firm. It was a disaster. There was no empathy, no synchronizing of the personnel. There was a scramble for positions with other law firm. Our firm ended up on the auction block—the furniture and everything else. It's typical of what happens when a firm merges with another without fully investigating the pros and cons. It had happened to several firms in New York and Boston.

The word of the firm's disaster spread even among third-year law students. Isham was not a place to try for. As a result, the firm was having trouble finding able associates. It was not a growth firm. And, in the law, you either grow or die.

It wasn't so in the old days. Many lawyers were sort of family

---

* They are.

† Robert Todd Lincoln, the president's son, was one of the founders, in 1888. He arrived in Chicago with a letter from Thomas Edison, thus securing the account of Commonwealth Edison as it was getting underway.

counselors. They had individual relationships with their clients. Sons, daughters, even maids would come to the family lawyer, just as they'd go to the family doctor.

The partnership agreement provided that the pensions would terminate on the dissolution of the firm, so I lost my pension. I felt that the dissolution of the firm was due to the grave mistake by the executive committee in not investigating the merger before it took place, so I brought a law suit against the executive committee.

I was of two minds about the suit. My daughter, who's a very good lawyer, suggested that I go ahead with it. She said, "They did wrong in entering the merger blindfolded. I think we should try to establish a breech of trust." We couldn't convince the judge that there was a trust relationship. I still think there is. I think that working partners of a firm have a duty to protect not only themselves, but to protect retirees and those who've contributed to the firm. I brought any number of clients to the firm, and the present partners—wherever they are—have gone off to various firms and have taken advantage of the clients that I brought in.

Just this morning I asked my daughter if she would Shepardize my case. It is a technique whereby you find out what happened to a particular case, whether it had been used as a precedent in later cases. We don't have the results yet, though some people have said it's a leading case in the field. That's small satisfaction to me. [*Chuckles.*]

I was represented by my daughter. We reached the federal court of appeals and the judge's decision was absolutely contrary to my assertion. So I ended up with nothing. He decided that I had taken my chances and was bound by the provisions of the partnership. I went no further. The judge is known as a free-market person, who makes a cost-benefit analysis and ignores the humanistic aspects of the matter.* That was the end of that. I was seventy-five.

Fortunately, there is a pension protection act, so the employees of Isham, Lincoln & Beale were covered, but it didn't apply to partners because they're classified as employers. I'm not bitter about it. Luckily, I had some resources, though it has made a difference in my lifestyle. It has also left my recollection of Isham, Lincoln & Beale [*a long pause*] less than pleasant. I met some fine people, some fine partners, but it has been colored by what happened after I retired.

When you're a lawyer as active as I've been, you develop a feeling that you're going to win some and lose some. The pension is merely something I've lost. [*Again, the chuckle.*] My compensation while I was at Isham, Lincoln & Beale was quite satisfactory, although I

---

* The judge, years after Bane's graduation from the University of Chicago Law School, became an honored member of its faculty.

earned every penny. It was hard work being ever-attentive to clients, being on call. No, I'm not really bitter. For one thing, it doesn't get you very far.

For a time, I was really burnt out. I really had no further interest in the law. But after a year or two, I became counsel to Cadwalader Wickersham & Taft, a New York law firm. It was a modern-day duplicate of the old Sullivan & Cromwell. I eventually shifted to a small five-man firm, more to my liking. I'm a senior person. I have the title of counsel, which means that I can go in when I like. Of course, compensation depends on how often I'm there and what business I may bring in. But it's a happy life. I still practice.

Law, like many other professions, has become specialized. To go forward, a firm might need an additional specialty. Isham, Lincoln & Beale was strong in corporate work but weak in litigation. The firm it merged with was reputedly successful in civil litigation. The thought was to put the two together, but it was so slovenly conceived.

The more mergers, the more the personal touch is lost. When I was with Steve Mitchell, we knew everything that was going on. We participated in everything at the office. When you're in a large firm, you work in your own specialty, remote from the others. There is very little warmth these days in the big corporations, a cold atmosphere: you produce or you're out. The same is true of law firms.

These days, a student comes out of law school frequently in debt up to $150,000. He's desperate. He goes to a big firm in New York or Chicago offering beginning salaries of $80,000 or $90,000. It's been up to $100,000. When you're making that kind of money, you produce or you're on your way out.

In my early days at Isham, we had two or three young lawyers. People would say, "They're not really making it, not contributing." Others would reply, "Well, it won't cost us very much to keep them on for another year or two. See if they can find themselves." That no longer happens. If the young lawyers don't produce, they're out in a year.

The bigger firms use their associates, these are the young ones, only if they are rainmakers, bring in business. The lifeblood of a firm usually is in these associates. You'd be amazed how much money a law firm makes on these young lawyers. Even if they pay them eighty, ninety thousand a year. They establish an hourly rate for their clients, so the firm is collecting three or four times what the salary is. Of course, that money goes to the partners as profits. Last year, the average income of partners at large New York law firms was a million dollars. Personally, I don't think any lawyer is worth that. [*Laughs.*]

Most law firms like to take kids just out of law school, make money on them. If they take an older man, they have to pay him more, and their profits are cut down.

Preeminent in corporate America today, reflected in law firms, is the practice of hiring people, not as employees but as temporary workers—"temps." They're often called consultants. The company doesn't have to furnish medical care or bonuses or pensions. No retirement benefits. Nothing. In many cases, they don't even withhold, so the person has to make his own estimated tax payments as an independent contractor. They have no security whatever. It's very unfair.

When my son started in the banking business in Palm Beach, he was put on a six-month consulting basis. Somewhere along the line, it was suggested he be put on as a one-month consultant. That's not very far removed from being hired day to day as a laborer. "Consultant" is just a title for someone doing an employee's work without the benefits. An "independent contractor," the law calls him [*Chuckles*].

I feel sorry for some of the young people. It's a catch-22 situation. They come out of law school with these big debts, they have to discharge them, and they get caught up in a maelstrom. Just as young doctors do. I escaped that. I didn't come out of law school owing anybody anything.

I'm not one of those who say everything was better in the old days and everything's gone to pot since. Sure, there have been great changes in law practice, but the country's changed, corporate America has changed. Law firms of the old-fashioned type could not survive today.

Lawyers who entered the practice when I did fully expected to be generalists and deal with all sorts of problems. Now young people coming out of law school are appreciative of what's happened. Many of them become tax experts, antitrust experts, securities experts. There's whole new field, environmental law, that has a strong appeal to many. The young can accomplish a great deal in these areas.

The social side is becoming very important. My daughter is married to a man who is financially secure, so she is free to devote much of her time to pro bono work. She's a legal defender in Connecticut and is in court almost every day. She's not in the traditional type of law practice, and I wouldn't want her to do that. If I had another child—I do, as a matter of fact, have a grandchild about to enter law school—I'd recommend environmental or civil rights law or something of that nature.

After I lost my case, I seemed to have lost any interest in the law. I still read cases, the *American Bar Journal*, followed the Supreme Court, but the zest wasn't there. Lately it's been revived and I feel much better.

Judith Vladek, 70
New York City

"I didn't just touch seventy, I fell over it."

She is senior partner in a thirty-member law firm. "We represent unions and individuals in employment matters, involving discrimination cases or contracts for executives or blue-collar workers. It's a wide range and exciting."

Her three children are attorneys: one, in public-interest law; another, in the Clinton administration; and the third, a partner in her firm. "I am the widow of one of the wisest labor lawyers of several decades."

I had been a typical New York semiprivileged kid. My parents were literate people who gave me a home of books and music, but no money. I worked while attending a women's city college, Hunter. It trained us to go into what were then acceptable women's fields: social work and teaching. Neither appealed to me.

During the war, I dropped out of college to work at Curtis-Wright, making airplanes. Not having advanced the war effort much with my drafting skills, I entered law school at Columbia in '45. It was inhospitable to women at the time. The dean, a proper southern gentleman, would roam the halls and, without lowering his voice, proclaim that the school would never be the same until it got rid of the women, the coloreds, and the enlisted men. He was most offended by these young men who had left Columbia, gone into the military, and come back without achieving officer's status. His snobbery was ecumenical.

There were two or three women in our class. We were a notable minority. There were two black men. One was a minister with a voice that was unbelievable. I still remember it with pleasure. The other was a wiry, tough, smart, angry young man. This was a whole new world to me.

I'd been there about two, three months, when another student came over to me and said, "You're not doing yourself any good being friends with those two. [He meant the black guys.] We've been watching you." I didn't know who the "we" were or what it meant. The school still had remnants of the white preppy establishment, who held moot court, to which one was invited for membership. Apparently I was being considered, but I was impairing my chances because of my friendship with unacceptable people.

I was largely apolitical. It was not unusual in those days for a woman to reflect the politics of whoever her young man of the moment was. I was too absorbed in trying to keep my head above water in law school and making some money on the side so I could buy clothes and stay alive.

I chose law school for all the classic reasons: to change the world. I was going to work with delinquent children, help all the underprivileged find a voice. I have since learned that teachers and social workers probably do more valuable work than lawyers. If I were to teach a learning-disabled child how to read, that would be as worthy a success as getting a woman a promotion. How does one judge the social value of these things?

I've never been politically aligned with feminist organizations, but, if I retrace my steps, I must have been an early feminist and not willing to be channeled into what was then "women's work."

I am disappointed that, in 1993, we still have a stratified work force: white males, white females, minorities. These divisions are not based on merit, but on ritual. We are still so far from home. The women I see break my heart because they represent the failure, or the very slight progress we've made.

It is no longer pin money women work for. They work for the same reasons men work: to provide for their families and for themselves. They don't get the same choice of jobs. They don't get the same chance to move up. If they are foolish enough to have children, they are no longer valuable members of the team. If they need that six or eight weeks off to deliver a child, it's as if they betrayed the employer.

Yesterday I talked to a woman who had been a superstar in a local bank. She is now in her late thirties, time is running out. When she told her supervisor she was taking maternity leave, chunks of her job were immediately taken away. Her promotional opportunity has vanished, all momentum was lost. I see this a hundred times a month. All this outrage over sexual harassment—this is as old as the plantation. The workplace is still the men's turf, and women enter at their own risk. If they're treated as if they are available, or as whores, that's because they've chosen it.

When I left law school, women could not get interviews at the major law firms. The placement officer at Columbia did not send women out. In 1970, women at Columbia had to sue one of the major law firms in New York in order to get even the *right* to be interviewed.

I was interviewed by a partner of a small commercial law firm. One of the first things he told me was that he admired my ankles. I smiled demurely and accepted the job. I would have done anything to get a job. He was smart enough to know the usefulness of young women lawyers, aside from the pay being a pittance. He sent us out to courts and administrative agencies. He sensed that a young woman appealed to the paternalism of the judges and clerks. He had one other woman lawyer. You bet he used us.

I married within my first year of practice at this office. When I became pregnant, I left. He didn't raise the point, but for me, the notion that it might be considered an impropriety was enough. It was just not acceptable to work when one was pregnant.

My husband didn't mind using my services. He was in a suite of offices with other lawyers, who asked that I not come to the office, except in the evening or over weekends. The presence of a pregnant woman would not look good to the clients.

After my first child was born, the senior partner of the firm where I'd been working called me in and asked, "How long are you planning to vegetate?" He offered me part-time work. It was a remarkable gesture at the time. It made it possible for me to continue practice even when I had a small child. When my two other children came along, I was able to get some ad hoc work. I wrote a piece on constitutional issues for the Fund for the Republic, did some work for the Civil Liberties Union, and kept fairly active while my kids were very little.

I joined my husband's firm in 1957. I was asked to work part time because he and his partner could not afford a full-time lawyer. I recently found the salary book for that period. I was listed *right there* with the secretary and the receptionist at some low hourly rate. No wonder they wanted me.

We took on many civil rights cases as volunteers, especially in the early '60s. I had prepared a case involving white ministers challenging Jim Crow at bus stations in Louisiana. They were drinking from black water fountains. When I came south, the good people working for the Freedom Riders said, "Please go away. We have enough of a jury problem without a woman lawyer adding to it."

Almost everyplace, I was looked upon as strange. Shop committees of the unions, our clients, didn't know how to deal with me. A group of tough blue-collar guys came to our office with a set of grievances. I sat them around the conference table and said, "Okay, what's the problem?" One of them raised his hand. I realized he'd never seen a woman professional except his teacher in grade school. It was always awkward, and I had to be careful not to make mistakes. I was too visible. It comes when you're the only one of a kind in a group. It's a strain.

The calls that came at night were for me. There was an assumption that I was always available in a way they never expected my husband to be. I think they see the woman as mother/caretaker and less as a remote professional. Perhaps I did extend myself in a way my husband never did.

My husband's clients rarely called him at home, unless it was a real emergency. They were always noteworthy. My favorite was the phone call he received at four o'clock in the morning. It was during a newspaper strike. My husband said, "Why the hell are you calling at this hour?" The guy says, "Are we meeting for negotiations tomorrow morning?" My husband is furious. "Why the hell are you asking me that?" The guy said, "Because I'm drunk as a pig. If we meet tomorrow, I'll go to the turkish baths; if not, I'll stay drunk."

People assumed if there was a family problem, adoption, divorce, a child in trouble, I was the lawyer to call. It was the assumption that, as a woman, I'd be more compassionate. I knew no more about adoption or matrimonial law than they did. I did one or two divorce cases, which I hated. I learned details about people's lives that I didn't want to know.

Similarly, it was assumed there were things I could not or should not do. About twenty years ago, I received a call at home one night from a distinguished corporation lawyer. "I understand you're trying an arbitration case next week." We represented the engineer's union. I said yes. "Isn't your husband available? You're going to make everybody uncomfortable and you're going to be uncomfortable."

The case involved an engineer whose supervisor gave him a very stupid instruction. The engineer, our client, told him what he could do with himself. The issue was whether a one-week suspension was a proper penalty for that little outburst. We felt it was not an unusual practice in that shop to use such language.

When I arrived at the arbitration table, I said to the assembled group—male arbitrator, my male adversary, my male client, the company representatives, all male—"I've been warned that some of you may be uncomfortable about using obscenities in my presence. To put you at ease, I would like you to know that I know the following words." I listed every four-letter word I'd ever heard.

I don't know what assignments women get these days, but I am concerned about young women today, because, like all young people, they know too little history. I'm convinced they've been misled. There's a belief on the part of many that the fight for women's rights is ancient and behind them. If they are just diligent and work hard and are good and loyal to their employers, they will have the same rights as their male counterparts. That is a damnable lie.

I see cases of thirty-five-year-old women coming to me, whether from law firms, accounting or brokerage houses, or from any other institution in our society. "What did I do that was wrong?" They blame themselves. I try to persuade them they haven't done anything wrong, that the system is still inhospitable to them. They were naive enough to believe that it was not, that things had changed.

What happened in the '70s was that women were smarter. They knew they were being mistreated, and they formed organizations. Every university had women's caucuses. That died. Women were persuaded that the fight's over. It's *just* beginning.

Why has it regressed? In large part, I blame governmental agencies. I blame Reagan, I blame Bush, I blame the conservative press for mocking women and getting away with it. Remember the propaganda campaign following World War II? During the war, women were needed to work in the defense plants. They were begged: our country needs you. As soon as the war was over and the boys came back, women's magazines carried the most outrageous pieces on the need to go back to the kitchen. The pressure was from all sources. Baking bread became the most important work they could do.

I lived through that period as a young lawyer, and it was painful. As I was striving for some kind of professional competence, every institution told me I was doing a terrible thing: neglecting my children by sending them to nursery school. Now it's happening all over again.

I still get passionately angry and it's what keeps me working. I am angry about the way American industry is treating workers. I am angry on behalf of older workers. I'm angry when I see the most solid corporations destroying their most valuable asset. In every major company today, there is a concerted effort to force workers over fifty into retirement. We're taking people who've worked thirty years for the same company and declaring them dispensable. Kleenex. You can never replace that kind of loyalty, that kind of know-how. When I deal with fifty-five-year-old men, who are unlikely to find any appropriate work for themselves again, I cry for them. I cry for a company that's stupid enough to send them away. I see this happening in every workplace, and I am angry. And when working women decide to have children, does that make them a subclass of unemployables?

How am I regarded by the young? Probably as a dinosaur. How else do the young regard people my age? We're accepted, but maybe they just tolerate us. I enjoy the company of my young partners. We frequently have lunch together. I don't think my presence inhibits them in any way. I hope it doesn't. There's a nice kind of teasing. I am called by my daughter "the last Victorian." I'm known to be a bit prissy about language and clothing style. We hired a man recently. The betting was I'd reject him out of hand because he wore an earring. I thought he was just charming, and I was delighted to have him join us.

People have told me nice things and have been nice enough not to tell me things that aren't nice. There are a lot of young professional women who tell me that I have encouraged them and that my very existence is reassuring to them. That's my value, I think. They know it can be done. I'm known in my profession with a certain level of respect and affection. Maybe it's because I've lived so long. People can see me as somebody who bumbled through, raised kids, developed a professional competence, and had a satisfying career.

To realize that I've touched seventy was absolutely devastating. [*Very long pause.*] I'm disturbed by my concern in undertaking new commitments—as if my time is limited. I never had that feeling before. I don't want to take responsibility for something that I may not be able to complete. It's a very worrisome thing. Being seventy made me angry. Being sixty-nine did not. [*Laughs.*]

Right now, I feel great. I'm meeting with clients tomorrow morning; Saturday, with a group of brilliant young men. However they perceive me, as grandmother or godmother, they want my advice, and I enjoy giving it. There's a woman in desperate straits who could not wait till Monday. I agreed to meet her in my office on Sunday. I accommodated the sound of desperation in her voice. I am full of energy. Like any other curmudgeon, I have lots of negative things to say about what's happening in my profession, but on a purely personal level, I am enjoying my work.

Things are worse in law firms today simply because women believe it's better. That's a terrible myth. Women are half the law school class today, but how many make partners? Five, ten percent at a maximum. Why are men willing to use all their work, all their energy, and not invite them as partners? Because there's a white male hierarchy. The men are at the top and feel comfortable. They use code language. They like team players and [*witheringly*] their teams are male.

It is in this man's world that I have been identified with what lawyers call "cases of first impression": cases that have made law. I was one of the early lawyers for women's class-action suits against their employers. I represented black employees in suing Revlon and Chemical Bank. They were firsts. I suppose what I get credit for is a willingness to try.

My most recent case was a loser, but there are some battles that are worth losing. We brought action against one of the old-line Philadelphia law firms, a bunch of arrogant stiff-necks. Our client was a young man who had been denied partnership. It was a bitter, long-fought trial and we won. We were reversed in the Third Circuit. The case was the first such trial *ever* in the United States. It was a very colorful, risky case. I know I was right. I ultimately lost, but I would do it again and again, and other women will do it again and again and again.

Ernest Goodman, 87

DETROIT, MICHIGAN

His law firm occupies two floors of Cadillac Tower in Detroit. There are many names on the door. From the window of his office, we see, past the nearby skyscrapers, past the Detroit River, the old and the new city.

Though each of us has a hearing aid, we have a problem in getting through at first. A slight adjustment. "Do you hear me?" I ask. "I hear you. One of my aids is going fine." [Chuckles.]

This infirmity bothers me for one reason alone. I've always loved to try jury cases. Since my hearing started to evaporate and my memory has become less secure, it's impossible for me to try a case in front of a jury. I'll say, "Judge, speak up, please. Raise your voice so I can hear you." [*Chuckles.*] It makes it impossible for me to try such a case.

I remember my first case very well. It was in 1929. I represented a young guy who was accused of murdering a friend. Frank Murphy was the judge.* He was a wonderful guy, but I was a kid just out of law school. I won the case in front of a jury. I was amazed.

My last jury case was in 1984, fifty-some years later. My hearing was becoming somewhat impaired. I didn't recognize it at first. You never do. I didn't hear what the other lawyer was saying, so I had to improvise. And I began to lose some memory. As a lawyer, you want to cite things and argue matters in the instant. You can't wait, trying to remember. I'd stop in the middle of a sentence. I'd be blocked by just forgetting a name—or even a word.

I'm still practicing law, but it hasn't the same drama as a jury case, especially a political one. I'm just phasing out now and am about to retire from active practice.

Labor law was our major interest. That was quite a while ago. Our main practice today deals with workers' injuries, disabilities, and compensation.

I got involved in labor law back in 1934. I'd been practicing for about five years and got bored with everything I was doing on behalf of businesses, small corporations. I looked around me and saw what was happening to people who were not working, selling apples on corners, starving, the depression.

Our firm, three young fellows like me, collected the accounts for all the furniture dealers in town. So many people were out of jobs

---

* He subsequently became governor of Michigan and was later appointed to the Supreme Court.

and couldn't meet the payments, so we hired bailiffs to take the furniture out of the house. I looked around and saw the horrible kind of society we were becoming, the effect it had on close friends, relatives, my father, who couldn't find work. I began to feel responsible. I never represented really ordinary people, and when I saw them struggle, I wanted to be on their side.

One day, I hear a talk by Maurice Sugar, one of the few labor lawyers in the country. In the 1910s, '20s, and early '30s, there was no labor law in the books. It was under the heading: Master and Servant. Sugar was suggesting that young lawyers could represent working people instead of those with money and power. I realized that was my choice.

Before the CIO was formed, unions had a hard time in Detroit. It was known as an open-shop town. None of the automobile industry—from General Motors and Ford down to the smallest supplier—was organized. The Manufacturers Association here headed it off every way they could: money, supplies, goon squads. Now Detroit is a strong union town but under heavy attack again.

The CIO was organized in 1935 and changed the whole character of the labor movement. John L. Lewis, who headed it up, believed in organizing the mass industry, not on a craft basis, but in the idea that workers for a single employer had something in common. I'd never experienced anything like this before, to see working people without much education, without social status, working together, to deal with employers on the basis of equality. It was an exciting moment.

I largely represented radical political organizations, including the Communist party, which was especially active in organizing unions. They were very unfashionable. That was the main attack against the labor unions: the Red issue. These were the early '30s.

It's impossible to imagine the climate, the hysteria, unless you lived here at the time. Every newspaper carried the same thing every day: Reds! The radio carried the same message whenever there was a strike. I remember the billboards put up by the NMA* in 1936—when Roosevelt ran on a program opposing big business—"Join the CIO and Build a Soviet America."

Friends of my mother would tell her: "Have you read the paper? Your son is in the CIO, and that's not good." She diffidently asked me about it. I couldn't give her a lecture on politics [*chuckles*], so I said, "Mama, do you think I'm a good boy?" She said, "Oh, you're a wonderful boy." I said, "You don't think I'd do anything bad, do you?" "No, no, of course not." I said, "Well, don't worry about that. They're all wrong." That's all I needed to say. [*Chuckles.*]

---

* National Manufacturers Association.

[He indicates a photograph on the wall: Joseph McCarthy facing Joseph Welsh.] During the McCarthy period I was besieged by people who needed legal advice. They had been approached by the FBI and were asked to identify people who were members of the Communist party: teachers, factory workers, professors. The FBI would usually visit their homes in the evening, without any announcement. The people they visited were generally labor activists, civil rights advocates. To the FBI, they were either Communists or fellow travelers. The wife would often be there, and she'd be pretty scared—especially for the kids. They'd come right down to see me, terribly upset. It meant not only their jobs but their reputation in the community, their families. They'd be named in the newspapers and on the radio, and their kids would hear about it in school and come home crying.

Reluctantly, ashamed, some would ask if informing was advisable. They didn't say it in so many words, but the meaning was clear. They were desperate. I'd say that you can't live with yourself once you do that sort of thing to your friends, people you've worked with. I would encourage them to say no.

[He indicates a celebrated Goya painting on the wall.] I needed something in my office that would give them a little courage. One day, while in Spain, I visited the Prado and saw this painting: one person with his fist in the air, facing the firing squad. Maybe it scared some of my clients. *[Laughs.]* Maybe it was to buoy up *my* spirits. I've always been in need of that.

During those years of the CIO's birth, the 1930s, I felt I was part of a grass-roots movement and it felt so good. When the United Auto Workers were fully organized and won the strike against Ford in 1941—more recognition of rights than any union had ever won—the movement began to solidify. Bureaucracy set in.

I remember one instance. A guy I'd usually see on the streets with a picket sign now had a desk at the new UAW headquarters. He looked pretty good and he felt pretty good. I said, "Things are really changing for you guys who fought to organize this union." He said, "Nothing's too good for the working man." That became a very familiar expression. I didn't realize what it would lead to. In the process of becoming a bureaucracy, you lose all the energy you had on the picket line.

With the Cold War, my work with the union came to an end. For a number of years, I had defended the left-wing leaders of the early days, who were fired by those who now ran the union. It was difficult making a living. I took on new kinds of cases.

Race was always an issue in Detroit. A black rarely got a fair trial. There were no blacks on the jury, to speak of. The police were all white. You'd get a call from the family: "My son's been arrested." They'd move him around from one precinct to another, so you couldn't find him until they were through with him and got his confession. You'd have to convince a white jury that the white policemen were lying when they said, "No, we didn't coerce anything from him. He voluntarily gave us his statement." He'd say: "No, here's what they did. They punched me in the belly, they kept a light in my face, they hit me in the back. There were two of them and I was alone." They wouldn't believe a black man against a white policeman unless you had something more.

I always looked very carefully at the confession to see if I could find one thing that contradicted what the cops said happened. I remember the guy confessed to throwing a big rock that wounded the victim. I was able to prove that a rock could not cause this type of injury. I won cases that way fairly frequently.

I had two court martial cases involving black soldiers. In the Philippines, shortly after the war, a Detroit lad shot his friend who lived in the same tent. His defense: it was an accident, the gun went off as he was cleaning it. His appointed lawyer was a Coca-Cola salesman. The trial lasted an hour. He was found guilty and sentenced to be hanged.

He wrote a letter to his father: "Dear Papa, I am in jail, waiting to be hanged. Can you do something for me?" At the request of the Civil Rights Federation, I took on the case. I filed a motion for a new trial and got the press interested. At the time, there were many such cases, and the whole system of army justice was under attack. We generated enough public interest for President Truman to grant a new trial. He was the only one who could do so.

There was a trial in the Presidio, San Francisco. We beat the murder charge, but the army, never admitting it was wrong, found him guilty of illegally carrying a gun. Even though he had spent nine months in jail waiting to be hanged, he had to serve another couple of months before he was free.

In 1950, I'd gone to Germany to represent another black G.I., who was accused of killing a young Nazi. It was a triangle, involving a German woman. He did in fact kill him. The question: Was it self-defense? The G.I. and the woman were walking along a lonely road in the dark. An attack occurred.

The case was tried in Stuttgart at a time when the United States was seeking Germany's cooperation in a possible conflict with the Soviet Union. There was a strong feeling there that no American soldier could get away with any crap against a German. Nevertheless, we beat the murder charge, though the army, of course, got him on something else.

I came back after five weeks, with no more clients. I asked George Crockett* to become my partner. He had a wife and three children and no job. I had a wife and two children and no practice. I said, "We're both in the same boat. Let's fight these bastards together. Let's be independent." As far as I know, it was the first interracial law partnership in the country. We were together sixteen years. George left to become a judge in 1966.

In the '50s, we had at least a hundred cases involving aliens, non-citizens, who were being deported for political reasons. The bigger firms wouldn't touch these cases. It would hurt their business. We and our two younger partners were barely making a living.

In the early '60s, we got involved with the civil rights movement in the South. We opened an office in Jackson, Mississippi, during the registration drive in the summer of '64. For years, much of our time was devoted to this struggle.

The Black Power movement was beginning up north, in Chicago. Younger people, just out of law school, had found a haven in the National Lawyers Guild, of which I had been president. It was the only bar association helping them in their attempt to change society.

They began to take over, and I had the feeling that I was no longer wanted by these young people. It became very obvious, even as I was handling a case against the Black Panthers in Detroit. I was the lead lawyer, pro bono. I never took a fee in these political cases. We won an acquittal. I was given a hard time by three of the young lawyers out of law school. I was really hurt and somewhat bewildered.

I went to the convention of the National Lawyers Guild, in Boulder, Colorado. It was right after the remarkable verdict in the Black Panther case. I got up to speak about something and I'll never forget the yells: "Sit down! Sit down!" I didn't know the language of that period. They didn't even let me speak. I was really shocked. At the time, I was seriously thinking of leaving the guild. If they don't want anybody over thirty... at the time, I was sixty-something.

The guild is different now. It's okay. I feel that the young members respect me and I respect them. We have a very good relationship.

The great many young lawyers today are primarily interested, as I was when I went to law school, in making a lot of money and achieving some social prestige. However, there is a surprising number of law students who want to use the law as a means of changing the society for the better—and make a living at the same time. It's the kind of a problem that exists in a competitive society.

---

* A black lawyer who had defended Communist Party leaders in the Smith Act trial in New York. The charge: advocating the violent overthrow of the government. Crockett went on to become a judge and, later, a congressman.

The issues were more clear-cut in those days than they are today. But they may be becoming clearer, thanks to the Reagan and Bush years. I've talked to law clerks, just out of school—not only at my place, anywhere—and I think there's a change beginning to take place.

As we approach the twenty-first century, I wonder, Is there no end to this kind of struggle? When I started out, I thought I would see at some time in the future a society in which I could practice gladly, an ethic of "do unto others," and so on—oh God, all the biblical phrases that speak the good life. That we could make it so. [*Sighs.*]

I realize now there is no best society. At one time, I thought socialism would bring about a decent society where people could life cooperatively rather than in constant, mean competitiveness. But I see that socialism can become different things to different people. In the Soviet Union, it became the opposite of what the vision was originally all about. If it ever appears again, and I feel it might, it will not be the end of the struggle. I think we'll always have to battle the forces of power, which will always be there. I don't envision a perfect society. Never. [*Chuckles.*]

Do I have any second thoughts, any regrets? Of course. I recently gave a commencement address at Wayne University Law School. I was in its first graduating class sixty-five years ago. I told them of changes in my way of thinking, my choices in my work. "As I look back on my sixty-five years, look ahead toward yours. Will you feel good about your life, your choices? Or will you feel: 'I should have done something else.' Try to make choices that will enable you to say, as I am saying after sixty-five years, I'm glad I made the choices I did." [*Chuckles.*]

We stare out the window toward Cadillac Square. Thirty stories below, a tiny doll-like figure is shuffling along, alone.]

That was the place, on Labor Day, where the Democratic candidates for president would open the campaign. I remember the first two appearances of Roosevelt. The crowds were so enormous, the whole square from one end to another jammed. You couldn't move. The cheers, God, those cheers. Now it's empty.

The working people have moved out to the suburbs, other cities, other states. The factories that were the heart of this city have moved elsewhere, to other countries, as well. It's a shell of the great manufacturing center it once was.

The emptiness of Cadillac Square is a metaphor for the changes that have taken place in our economy and society. See the old

County Building at the end of the square? It was built in 1898. There is a stool in front of it, so the person standing on it could exercise free speech. Trying to exercise that right, you'd get arrested as easily as not. After all the battles were over, the stool remained as a symbol: the stool on which you could stand and speak to the masses below. But there are no masses anymore. There's nobody. [*Chuckles*.]

In 1930, free speech had a hard time. Now, there's plenty of freedom of speech—if you want to address an empty square.

CHAPTER FIVE

Hold the Fort

Hold the fort
For we are coming,
Union men be strong.
Side by side,
We battle onward,
Victory will come.

—A labor song of the 30s,
based on an old Methodist hymn

Victor Reuther, 81

WASHINGTON, D.C.

It is Sophie Reuther's eightieth birthday. Relatives and close friends
are gathering at the house. Though she hasn't been feeling too well,
the occasion is festive.

"We've been married fifty-seven years. Not always a blissful
marriage, because Sophie has opinions of her own and they're good.
She was the first woman organizer of the auto workers' union and
she's had fifty-seven years of organizing me, too."

He and his brother Walter were founding members of the United
Auto Workers (UAW-CIO). Subsequently, Walter served as presi-
dent of the UAW, until he died in a plane crash.

In Victor's apartment there are multitudinous plaques, certifi-
cates, and objects d'art, mementos of long-past labor battles,
ordeals, and triumphs.

I'm a 1912 baby, January 1. Now you know why the bells ring and
the whistles blow.

My father was only eleven when he was brought over to this country from Germany. We grew up in the fields of West Virginia just
before the Great Depression. My father always wanted to be a
skilled worker, so he impressed this on his sons: You must acquire a
skill if you want to win any kind of a decent life for yourself. Each of
his sons picked out a trade and worked on it, excepting me, the

youngest of four. I got tired of digging ditches, so I became a professional hell-raiser at an early age. In college, I led demonstrations against the ROTC.

I joined my brother Walter in Detroit to see what the depression had wrought there. We walked many a picket line and went into homeless shelters, disguised as homeless ourselves. It has left a deep scar that is still with me at this late date. The problems are still with us.

Scientific progress is moving with such speed while social progress is lagging, and the great gap is upon us. Again we're seeing homelessness, but also seeing robots produce what we once saw workers being paid wages to do. There is a heavy human toll.

I get angry when I see hard-won gains given away as concessions to arrogant employers, who are even more greedy than they were in the '30s. I am embarrassed that the labor movement which once fought so hard to win these gains now appears to be the junior partner in a corporate world. So, hitting eighty-two, I want to get out and keep fighting.

I was with the rise of the CIO in the late '30s, when a new kind of labor leadership came into office. They came up through the ranks: textile workers, auto workers, chemical workers. They knew what it was to be in the shop, to be tied to the assembly line.

As time has passed and the trade-union movement has become bureaucratized, the leadership tend to look upon themselves as corporate executives. They spend so much of their time in paneled, air-conditioned offices that they have lost touch with the rank and file. They do not realize the degree of discontent in the ranks.

I think there's a spirit of change in the making now. It may not take the form of a new CIO, but I see it happening. Look at the change in the Teamsters' union. My wife and I were deeply involved in Ron Carey's campaign and the TDU.*

Inside the auto workers' union, there's a movement. At the moment, it's a little ripple on the surface, but there is deep support in the ranks. I remain very optimistic.

If I were not optimistic at my tender age. I would not undertake the chore of writing yet another book. When I announced the project, I suddenly sounded ten years younger. Ask Sophie. I have a specific task ahead that I alone must write.

I may be the sole survivor of a group that went to the Soviet Union in the '30s to help build the first automobile plant there. Later, refugees from Hitler's Germany and Austria fled to Russia.

---

* Ron Carey challenged the established hierarchy and won the presidency of the union in the early '90s. The Teamsters for a Democratic Union (TDU) has long fought for more rank-and-file power.

Many were fleeing Mussolini in Italy. Canadian and American Finns by the thousands went to Karelia, where Walter and I helped build this first factory. The Ford Motor Company was officially participating, at the request of President Roosevelt. In the end, Stalin practically liquidated the whole international community that had sprung up there. I'm one of the few still around to tell the story.

I begin my day working on the new book. I look through the mountains of raw material I've picked up from various archives—letters of survivors and so on. I'm my own secretary, my own typist. I want to keep all this very close to me. But it's not just another chapter in anti-Stalinism. I want to write about the wonderful, supportive feeling among workers across the world to help carry a good idea to fruition.

I still believe in the international solidarity of working people, but it's certainly at risk today. It's not only the ethnic strife, anti-Semitism, and ultranationalism that are surfacing, but the tragic conflict among workers, encouraged by the new corporate strategy of world competitiveness. They are not content to pit one American against another. This is everything I spent my life working toward: solidarity among workers, regardless of color, sex, ethnicity.

Was there ever such a time? Of course. That's the untold story. During the Flint sit-down strike* there was a gathering of southern workers with a scattering of blacks, who were confined to foundries and cleaning up debris, and a sprinkling of women in the cushion-sewing department (then considered women's work). You didn't have quite the ethnic mixture we had in Detroit: Poles, Yugoslavs, Swedes, Irish, and Germans.

In Flint, you had the most difficult groups to integrate—southern whites and blacks. They had been brainwashed against unionism by corporations in the South. But when confronted with the hope of shaping their own destiny through a union, you never saw such solidarity. They took their own little jalopies that represented years of savings and overturned them to make a barricade, to prevent the police from driving through. I saw some fall with eight or ten shots in the stomach. They all survived that night.

I never saw such bravery and solidarity. When they saw what was happening to their sons and fathers and brothers in the plant, the whole city of Flint turned out, broke through the police lines and came to their defense. That demonstration has stayed with me all these years and convinced me that inside each of us there is this will to be brother to brother and brother to sister.

---

* Beginning on Christmas Eve 1936, workers sat in at the Fisher body plant in Flint, Michigan. The sit-down strike ended—forty-four days later—when General Motors recognized the UAW-CIO.

This strike was forced on us suddenly because General Motors had encouraged two walkouts and precipitated the showdown before we were ready. It was a great risk for us. Thank God our leadership stuck with the rank and file. This was 1937.

Remember, the memory of the early '30s depression was still fresh in their minds and they had only a few weeks of steady paychecks under their belts. They didn't want to stand in long hiring lines all over again. Their only hope was to build a union in which they'd have a voice—the right to sit down with corporate heads and say, "These are our minimal demands covering work and wages." Democracy, if put in words ordinary people understand, has a powerful appeal. It is not enough to have a political democracy where you get to cast a vote every two years—if you bother to. You must have the democratic right every day and every hour of your working life to shape the conditions under which you work.

In the days before unions, if you wanted job security at all you had to paint the garage of the boss on the weekend or mow his lawn or bring him a pint of whiskey. You could be dismissed at whim. Once the workers tasted the power they had, they were unstoppable. Franklin Delano Roosevelt was no friend of labor when he was first elected. He had to learn the way, learn that there was a ground swell of support for workplace democracy.

It was an exhilarating experience in the '30s to feel that upsurge from below. When the great strikes got under way, it was difficult to get trained labor people to carry our message to the community. The corporations had skilled lawyers who could go to schools, churches, and neighborhoods. Let me tell you, six months after the great sit-down strike, we had difficulty getting corporate people to take the platform with our unionists, because we were telling the story of our own life experience, which related immediately to all who heard, whether it was a church audience, a black audience, or university students. Almost overnight, a whole cadre of people learned by doing. It was breathtaking.

Your voice has assumed a youthful vigor, as though it were this moment you're recounting.

It is this moment. I still go to auto worker rallies. I meet the young generation. They have stars in their eyes. They don't talk about going back to the '30s, they talk about learning from the '30s and putting it to work today. I see it, I hear it.

Some of my generation we have elevated into the middle class. We were successful in improving their living standards and winning fringe benefits for them. We can be proud of this. It was possible in those days for one spouse to earn enough to support a family in decency. Today the combined income of husband and wife is hardly adequate for medical costs and everything else.

The older generation that won these early struggles doesn't realize how much life has deteriorated for the younger ones. A lot of retirees have to be reminded from whence they came. I talk to them as I do to my grandchildren.

The younger generation has been led by today's labor leaders to believe than an adversarial approach to the corporate powers is not advisable, that you must join the big boys in being competitive—whatever the hell that means. Being competitive with the Mexicans and Brazilians isn't being competitive with the Germans and the Swedes, who get higher wages and better social benefits than we get. The younger generation has been led down the garden path by a labor leadership that saw itself in partnership with the corporate boys. They became sweethearts.

And thus unions became irrelevant. If you were serving on a jointness committee with a foreman and a superintendent, it was your task to raise hell with your fellow worker, who couldn't work as fast as someone next to him. That's hardly the role of a union spokesperson.

The word "competitiveness" is used in almost every aspect of our lives. In the matter of the nation's health, we hear of "managed competition." In TV commercials urging the young to attend school, "competition" is the spur. That's the corporation agenda. Look after numero uno. It's the reverse of solidarity. The workers in Flint didn't need Mother Jones to ask the question "Which side are you on?" Their whole life told them which side they were on. Now many unions are saying that's not our side anymore. The work force has become disoriented. It no longer understands what its agenda is. Now they learn: if you screw your fellow worker, you move up.

You don't hear the phrase "working class" much anymore in this country, but there's a working class, there's a middle class, and there's an upper class, which is small in numbers but very well provided for. Almost every political leader in modern times has used the phrase "middle class" as the one American goal. Even if you drew an hourly wage, your social status in society was a little above somebody else.* Who that other else was was never made clear. Somebody had to be beneath you if you were to become part of the middle class.

There's an irony here. We were clearly penalized by our own success. A significant portion of our membership embraced the phrase

---

* Once, when I referred to the young daughter of a garbageman as a "working-class girl," she was offended. "We are middle class," she insisted.

"middle class." They distinguished themselves from those who didn't quite make it that high. The trade union movement should have kept fresh in its mind the social goals of all society.

The younger generation's outlook is shaped by the media, which draws a blank on labor matters. It's a rare newspaper that has a labor reporter these days. I fault our labor leadership, which has done little to reach this new generation. Yet there are a lot of young people in factories and offices who have a lot of questions. Come another upheaval, they will learn as the young did in the '30s—by doing—no matter what the role of the media may be. I remain optimistic on that score.

The trade union movement has to get back to basic human issues. Homelessness that existed in the '30s is still an issue, and so is racial tension, of course. Back then, we had a feeling of progress because we were participants bringing about change. Now we are bystanders and onlookers, observing only through the media, being lectured on television. That's why the seventy-year-olds and the eighty-year-olds are important. They're boat rockers. In order to make progress, you've got to move beyond the placid waters, and the boat may get a little rocky. [*Chuckles.*]

Before the Flint strike broke out, we had to meet in small groups of five or six, secretly, in the basement of a worker's home or behind a pub, because there were Pinkerton agents hired by General Motors to spot who went to union meetings. Harry Bennett, a thug who hired other thugs to spy on workers and intimidate them, was Ford's chief of security. But once the strike was called, we didn't have halls big enough to hold those who flocked to them.

Those strikers who were sitting inside the plant had a lot of time on their hands. There were classes held in labor economics, how to write grievances, how to put out a shop newspaper. On the outside was the Women's Emergency Brigade. Genora Johnson was the catalyst.* They solicited food for the soup kitchens and cash donations. They visited homes of worried mothers and wives whose husbands and sons were sitting in.

Today, I think we're paying the price for television interrupting what once were tightly knit family groupings. Much of my early learning about labor came from my father around the dinner table. He shared his experiences with us. There isn't much of this done today. The home is no longer the center of learning.

The best way kids growing up can learn is by doing. If we can involve children at an early age in social experiences, in useful work in the community, and reward them in part with recognition, they will grow up in a way the media could never help them do.

* See the interview (next) with Genora Johnson Dollinger.

That's it: the solidarity of working people and the sense of community must be in harmony. It is as essential in the workplace as it is in the village or city. If the spirit of solidarity has been dealt a serious blow at the workplace by the corporate emphasis on competitiveness and "look after numero uno," so in our cities and villages the spirit of community has been fractured.

We have to look beyond our ethnic group, our racial group, and our age group and keep before us the multicolored tapestry of the community. We have to work at it in the workshop and where we live. Each bolsters the other.

One of the greatest contributions of the CIO, as much as improved wages and working conditions, was in helping make the nation a community—convincing Poles and Lithuanians and blacks and Hungarians in the ghettos and textile mills and workshops that they were an integral part of the nation.

When the racial riots broke out in Detroit, before the King assassination, there was not a fist swung in the factories between blacks and whites. While the riots were going on in the streets, I heard stories from black and white workers about their embracing one another. "We'll not do such stupid things," they said.*

What most distinguishes our time from the '30s is the new technology and its effect on work. We staved off this dilemma with the shorter work week, vacations with pay. We began to spread things out a bit more. That ceased when the corporate agenda took over, especially under Reagan and Bush. In recent years, we've played down the importance of sharing the benefits of the new technology. We're way behind Western European workers in these social benefits. And what happened to the idea of the four-day work week put forth so often by my brother Walter?

I remember our early contracts with the auto industry. Whenever a seniority worker was idle, no overtime was permitted. Now with widespread unemployment, some workers are putting in fifty, sixty hours a week. It's cheaper for the company than hiring more people, with benefits. There again is that pitting one worker against another, that destruction of solidarity and sense of community.

---

* In Chicago, during the 1950s, a racial incident was touched off when a black family moved into a white neighborhood, Trumbull Park. Frank Lumpkin, a black steel worker, remembers: "It was right next door to Wisconsin Steel. We had to drive in, and these people were throwing rocks at the cars. The workers in the plant were white, black, and Latino. We'd sit down and talk about this thing. There was a black worker got off the bus with his lunch bag in his hand, he started coming to the mill, and a mob got behind him. He was runnin' and the white guys in the plant saw this and they says, 'We gotta stop this.' And we did, never mind the politicians. The guys who work together know each other. That's what it's all about."

—From *The Great Divide: Second Thoughts on the American Dream*, 1988

Today, scabs, without shame, walk through picket lines and permanently replace strikers. Had any government in Western Europe proposed legislation authorizing replacement of striking workers with scabs, there would have been an immediate general strike. The population as a whole would not have tolerated it. Here, Reagan kicked it off in 1981 during the strike of the air traffic controllers. Now Caterpillar takes on the UAW and brings it to heel with this threat, and the labor movement doesn't even mobilize a demonstration. Talk about capitulation.

Yet I still have hope. When you lose hope, you bury yourself. I'm not ready for that. I have too much work to do yet. I never did find it comfortable to sit in a rocking chair complaining about my aches and pains. I think society has a lot of aches and pains. We shouldn't become obsessed with them. We've got to be pragmatic and say: There's a challenge. Let's change. Let's turn things over.

I'll never retire. I'm a gardener, too. Even the leaves I gather in my garden and turn into compost have to be turned over. [*Laughs.*]

Genora Johnson Dollinger, 80
LOS ANGELES, CALIFORNIA

*She had become something of a legend during the first sit-down
strike of 1937.*

*"I'd like very much to continue with the work I've done all my life,
but my bad health pens me in as a prisoner. I'm not too generous
about that. I chafe at the bit.*

*"My difficulties are mainly cardiac. I'm on my third pacemaker.
It's often out of function, out of rhythm, and use only half of my
heart. It takes down my spirits considerably.*

*"I would like to get out and participate in any effort, no matter
how weak I may be. I've been active in the labor movement, the civil
rights movement, the peace movement, all my life."*

I was raised in Flint, Michigan. My family were pioneers in the city
when Billy Durant was first experimenting in auto making. My
father was a good, law-abiding citizen with all the prejudices of that
day. He felt that women were not the equal of men. He was definitely middle class. He started out as a photographer for Buick, and
made enough money to have a string of photographic shops
throughout the state. He became very well-to-do. My mother,
who was from a poor family, was always for the underdog, but she
couldn't understand her daughter getting out, being a rebel.

While I was still in high school, a classmate invited me to her
home, where I met her father and her brother. Her father was a
very learned man who was something of a Eugene Debs socialist.
He became my father-in-law, a man I always loved and admired
very much. I called him Dad. I disliked my own father because he
was so bigoted and narrow.

Things got so oppressive at home that I ran away and got married. I was seventeen. In my eyes, I was just escaping prison. My
young husband got a job at Chevrolet and became an auto worker.
Flint, aside from Ford's independent work, is where the auto industry began to grow. General Motors, DuPont, corporate power. Of
course, there was no job security, no nothing.

By this time, I'd joined the Socialist Party and we were holding
pretty large meetings in the center of the town. I was becoming
very well known among the auto workers. I was not treated as just a
woman but as someone who could join the battle.

By this time, I was pretty well known by the Flint police, too, and
the company goons—and by some of the GM big shots. They tried to

stop me through my father. My uncle was vice-president of General Motors, in charge of Chevrolet production. He had given jobs to some of my cousins. My father was closely connected to GM in many ways. They cut off all his transactions, all his photographic business, all his properties.

He tried to evict us from the apartment we had rented from him. We had two little boys at the time. My mother helped me get the children fed while I was at the union headquarters. My father and I never, never got along.

When the strike broke out in Fisher Tool, we were there. The big Chevrolet compound of factories was directly across the street and we were there, too. We were right in the middle of it from the very beginning. We sat down on the twenty-eighth and twenty-ninth of December, 1936, just before New Year's Day.

General Motors had complete control of all the means of communication in the city—the newspapers, the radio. They were putting out propaganda that the Communists were taking over Flint. The women were frightened to death because we'd gone through a long depression, a slim, hard existence. They believed much of what General Motors was saying. On New Year's Eve, I saw a contingent of women coming down to the plant threatening their husbands: "You get out of that plant and be with me on New Year's Eve or I'm starting divorce against you Monday morning."

There were a couple of divorces that were played up in the press. This was a big factor to weaken the resolve of the men who were just beginning the sit-down strike. Remember, we were just a handful against the biggest industrial corporation in the world. We knew we had to make some move. Well, I decided what my purpose was: to get the women organized, women talking to women.

We put out leaflets announcing that the women were organizing, to come down and join up—and bring other women. They didn't have cars and few had telephones at that time. You had to reach them door to door. For the first time in labor history, we organized a Women's Auxiliary. A lot of people thought the name wasn't very nice, that it should have been "Ladies Auxiliary" as the wives of craft union members were called.

We did everything. Mainly, it was to get women to understand why their husbands were taking the big chance. We visited their homes, organized a nursery for the children, a first aid station with a registered nurse. They organized the kitchen that fed the strikers hundreds of meals a day. We'd just walk across the street where the men were sitting in, they'd open the window and we'd push in cartons of food. We were protected by the picket lines that were there all the time.

General Motors would start rumors that somebody's mother or father was dying and that the man should come right home. We were losing a few people that way. But as soon as the wives understood what was being done, they'd send in messages that things were all right at home, to stick in there.

We had a few friendly merchants and farmer neighbors and auto workers who had farms. They'd send in bags of potatoes and sides of beef. We had a welfare committee going around soliciting everybody for food.*

The battle began when General Motors hired some goons and ordered the Flint police to throw the workers out of Fisher Tool. They were afraid that if the sit-down continued, it would spread to the fifteen other GM plants across the country. So they started teargassing. We formed a great big picket line in front of the plant and the men turned over their own cars to make a barricade.

The police were using buckshots and rifles and tear gas and everything against us. The men were throwing back whatever they could get their hands on: nuts and bolts and hinges. Any tear-gas bomb that came over unexploded, they'd throw back into the ranks of the police.

Whenever a woman appeared, the men would courteously escort them to safety. They wanted to escort me away and I said, "Hell, no. I have as many weapons as you have. I'm staying right here." So I stayed the whole night while the battle raged. When the fight was at its height, Victor Reuther, who had been on the sound truck, encouraging the people to keep on going, came over to us and said, "The batteries are running down. We may lose this battle, but we won't lose the war." I said, "How about my getting on that truck?" Women never were on the sound car. The men thought they had to win everything. He said, "We've got nothing to lose." So I got on and tried a new tactic—an appeal to the women.

On each side of these barricades there were thousands of men and women who had come to see what was going on. Naturally, the radio, controlled by GM, made it sound like the revolution had broken out.

---

* "They'd assign roles to you. When some of the guys at headquarters wanted to tell some of the guys in the plants what was cookin', I carried the message. I was a scavenger, too.

"The merchants cooperated. There'd be apples, bushels of potatoes, crates of oranges that was beginning to spoil. Some of our members were also little farmers, they'd come up with a couple of baskets of junk.

"The soup kitchen was outside the plant. The women handled all the cooking, outside of one chef who came from New York. Mostly stews, pretty good meals. They were put in containers and hoisted up through the window. The boys in there had their own plates and cups and saucers."

—Bob Stinson, *Hard Times: An Oral History of the Great Depression*, 1970

The sound car was reaching them. On the loudspeaker, on top of the truck, I directed my remarks to the women on both sides of the barricades. I said the cops were shooting into the bellies of unarmed men and the mothers of children. I made it sound as though there were an equal number of women down there. I begged the women to break through those lines of cops and come down here and join with us.

One woman started forward and a cop grabbed her coat. She pulled right out of it and marched down to join us. After that, other women came. The police didn't want to shoot them in the back. The women poured through and that ended the battle. I was smack dab in the middle.

But that wasn't the greatest moment. The biggest victory was the strategy that involved breaking the windows of one plant as a ruse, to make the corporation feel that that was the plant we were going to pull down on strike. This decoy was Chevrolet Plant No. 9. All the plant police and city cops rushed over there.

I had the women's emergency brigade marching up and down with clubs. When the company goons started attacking the men inside, one worker with a bloody face broke a window and shouted, "They're tear-gassing us inside." We flew at the windows and broke them out.

While this fight was going on at No. 9, and up until the time they carried the men out in ambulances and took them to the hospital, the men in Plant No. 4 were busy building barricades. This was the plant GM couldn't operate without. It produced all the motors of every Chevrolet car across the country. Their best seller.

My first husband, Kermit Johnson, was the only member of the strike committee working in that plant. It employed four thousand. He had a tiny piece of scrap paper that marked out all the exits, sliding doors, gondolas, and everything. The guys from all the other Chevrolet plants came pouring into Plant No. 4 and held it in a sit-down.

So while they were carrying the guys out in ambulances at the decoy plant, No. 9, I and four lieutenants strolled down to No. 4. We came to the gate and the guys inside were yelling, "For God's sake, don't let anyone through that gate." They were throwing out the scabs and all kinds of fighting was going on inside.

We five string ourselves across that iron gate entry. The Flint police came marching up to us: "All right, out of the way. We're going in." We said, "Over our dead bodies." One of the young women said, "My father and my brother work here and nobody is going in. If you were working here, your wife would do the same thing."

The five of us women held out, stalling the police. Beating an unarmed woman was a different story in those days. We looked up and here came the emergency brigade, the Red Berets. We called ourselves that because of our red berets, red arm bands with white letters: EB. They were carrying the American flag and singing "Solidarity Forever" and "Hold the Fort." The sound car came, I hopped on it, and we organized the big picket line at the gate.

That was the single biggest victory of the labor movement. Fifteen plants across the country were on strike, but No. 4 was the plant that settled the whole business. We shut this one down for fourteen days. It was part of the forty-four-day strike in the other two Fisher body plants. It was tougher here because we had no cushions or upholstery for sitting down.

We won. Our union was recognized. GM decided to sit down with us. John L. Lewis came in and they conducted negotiations in Detroit. The guys in the plant couldn't believe it. They were struck with astonishment.* Celebration? When the guys evacuated the plant, the whole town was reveling. I was smothered in the crowds of people filling the streets, marching through the city, singing and dancing all night long. I was twenty-three.

That period was the high point of my life. It was the time of the depression, when working people had a feeling for each other. We helped each other out in times of trouble. It was a time that most people never get a chance to live through. We started to organize against hunger, poverty, sickness, everything that's hard. We were just at the point where so many of us decided we'd rather die first before we'd ever go back to being nonunion scabs. A little different from today, I'm afraid.

I was blacklisted by every employer in Flint. They wouldn't touch me with a ten-foot pole. So we moved to Detroit. I got a job at Briggs. I was fired from the one before. They caught up with me before I got in my ninety days to be eligible for seniority.

---

* "We finally got the word: THIS THING IS SETTLED. The guys in the plant didn't believe it. We had to send in three people, one after the other. When they did get it, they marched out of the plant with the flag flyin' and all that stuff.

"You'd see some guys comin' out of there with whiskers as long as Santa Claus. They made a rule they wasn't gonna shave until the strike was over. Oh, it was just like—you've gone through the Armistice delirium, haven't you? Everybody was runnin' around shakin' everybody by the hand, saying, 'Jesus, you look strange, you got a beard on, you know.' Wives kissin' their husbands. There was a lot of drunks on the street that night.

"When Mr. Knudson put his name to a piece of paper and says that General Motors recognizes UAW-CIO—until that moment we were non-people that didn't even exist. That was the big one."

—Bob Stinson, *Hard Times: An Oral History of the Great Depression*, 1970

At Briggs, I became one of the leaders of the most militant UAW local: 212. We were known as the Dead End Kids. This company still could not accept the union, so we went on strike frequently. I had taken a WPA training course in lathes and machinery, so they put me on a punch press. I thought I'd die because, by this time, I was left with one lung. I had tuberculosis at the time of the GM strike.

They offered me a job in the front office, hiring people. I said, "Of course not. The war is on and I want to do my part on the line." So I became head of the blueprint inspection department.

The girls were having a hard time with these macho foremen, who were saying horrible things to them, penalizing them at every chance. They didn't want women in the plant. In that new department, I didn't dare open my mouth for ninety days. About three days before the ninety days were up, the girls invited me to a union meeting. So I thought I'd sit in the back and not say a word.

The main speaker at the meeting was Emil Mazy, one of the original UAW organizers. Halfway through his speech, he looked out and recognized me. He said, "I don't know why you women are asking us for help. You've got one of the original UAW organizers sitting back there."

I said, "Emil, you just cooked my goose. I was just three days away from seniority." Emil said, "I want you and all these women to know that if they fire Genora, every Briggs plant in Detroit will go down." They did fire me, and eighteen thousand workers went on strike. Every Briggs plant went down. They took me back on the job.

I began to hold public speaking classes in the local, training people to get up and challenge contracts that were bad. Rank-and-file people. I became very active in our caucus. Our militant people were getting beaten up regularly. One of our best men suffered a brain concussion. Another was terribly beaten up while walking down the street with his wife. They were obviously professional jobs.

We formed an investigating committee to find out who was behind it. We suspected the Mafia and we were right. I was the only woman on that committee. When the Reuther brothers got shot and wounded—Vic lost an eye—the UAW hired a guy who had worked with the LaFollette Committee to work for them.*

Meanwhile, we're investigating on our own. One night, someone enters our bedroom with a lead pipe, clubs my husband and cracks me over the head. I wound up paralyzed down the whole side of my body. I was in the hospital for God knows how long.

---

* The committee, headed by Sen. Robert LaFollette Jr., investigated violations of the Wagner Act, which allowed workers to join unions without employer interference.

We discovered that the son of the Mafia head in Detroit had a great big contract with Briggs for all the scrap metal. You see, we were getting too close. That's when they came and did the job on us.

Now the war was over and the plants were being transferred back to civilian production. They laid off a great many women. The boys were back, you can now return to the kitchen.

Years later, in the '60s, I became active in the antiwar movement. I worked for the American Civil Liberties Union in Detroit. We had a very militant chapter. When they returned to California in 1966, I became interested in schools. I was organizing community advisory councils and appearing before boards. We played a big role in the first teachers' strike out here. There was the National Organization for Women, of course. I even signed up my granddaughter, when she was five months old.

I had to give all this up about three years ago, when my illness caught up with me. It's something you can't control. It's gotten worse and worse. I get so disgusted. At one point, my doctor suggested that I have a wheel chair. It's out in the garage. It belongs in a museum. I can't stand the thought of it. But I think that's where I'm heading, because only half my heart is functioning. I don't know anything that's okay with me right now! Oh, how I'd love to be back in action. It's been my whole life. But nature takes us all down.

It's not just *my* health, it's the health of our country that's so bad. Anybody who was at the birth of the CIO and went through all those upheavals must feel disillusioned, discouraged, and disgusted with present-day labor leadership. They think the back door to the White House is the way. Labor is in for some pretty dark days.

How can we reach the young? We've got to get a political party that addresses education, training, the needs of working people, and the four-day work week. The first UAW meeting in Milwaukee called for a thirty-hour work week with forty hours' pay. I'm pessimistic for the near future, but I think, someday, leaders will arise worthy of the American working class.

Old people, my generation, are being ripped off with a medical system that's stealing money out of their pockets left and right. The prescriptions alone, for me, run over three hundred dollars a month. How can people who receive only social security benefits pay for something like that? In a minute, I'll be taking one of those pills.

Any regrets? Second thoughts? Maybe I should have spent more time with the two young children I lost. Two wonderful kids, who were killed by a speeding taxi cab. One was ten, the other was fourteen. Sometimes you think, "Oh, my God, maybe I should have spent more time at home with them." They had such a short life. The kids in the classroom had new bikes and our kids didn't. I used to explain that we were doing it for everybody's children. They agreed with me, but they had to sacrifice a hell of a lot. Some things you can't help. I don't know. If I hadn't gone through all these experiences, I wouldn't be the same person. Other people helped make me what I am.

Sure, my body has slackened off, but my interest hasn't diminished. People who've lived through a great, great thing like that strike of 1937, people who called each other brother and sister and meant it, people who would give things to other families' kids because it was needed—when you saw that kind of loyalty to a person in the same boat as you, you can never forget, and I hope that feeling will come back one day.

I can't become cynical. I still hope we'll see a decent society, without greed, without plundering other nations, without war, and with the salvation of the earth, for crying out loud. [*Slight pause, a sigh.*] I better take that pill now.

Charles Hayes, 76
CHICAGO, ILLINOIS

"In 1983, when Harold Washington became mayor of Chicago, I took over his seat in Congress and remained there until January 3, 1993." He had previously been an official of the United Packinghouse Workers of America (UPWA-CIO).

I was the second oldest of twelve kids in the family. I was born down in Cairo, Illinois, between the Ohio and the Mississippi Rivers. The Mason-Dixon line, they said, was below that, but you couldn't tell the difference. [*Chuckles.*]

My father was a farm laborer. I started work with him at nine years old. We chopped cotton, baled hay, harvested corn. I made seventy-five cents a day. My father got paid $1.25 a day, for ten hours. A hard life, but it was challenging to me. I was determined to go to school. I graduated from grade school, all black. Me and a neighbor boy caught the freight train every day. We lived near the tracks where they switched trains. We'd hop on that train when they spliced them together, and ride to the north end of Cairo, where the train went across the Ohio. Whenever a train goes on a bridge, it slows down almost to a stop. We would leap off and roll all the way down the hill. A ten-mile trip. That's the way I got to school. [*Chuckles.*] We finally got a ride with my cousin, who was our English teacher. My mother would pay her with milk or butter.

We had algebra, geometry, English, and what they called manual training. I learned a little bit how to make furniture. I didn't think I'd be able to attend my graduation, we were so poor. Didn't even have money to pay for my robe. Didn't have a suit. My father said, "You'll just have to get your diploma on the fly." My mother was determined and, God bless her soul, she borrowed money from a relative to pay four and a half dollars for a graduation suit and some shoes. [*Chuckles.*] I'll never forget it. Thirty-five of us in the class of 1935.

It was right in the throes of the depression. I remember they used to give us flour. I'd walk seven miles to pick up a twenty-four-pound sack. And every now and then, you'd get some canned beef. It was tough, but we did everything we could to survive. That's why I get mad when I see no real commitment by Congress to create jobs for people who want to work. I should know this, because I was part of that Congress.

In the Roosevelt days, there was the WPA,* the Civilian Conservation Corps (CCC). Right after I graduated from high school, I

---

* Works Progress Administration.

went into the CCC camps. We set out trees on the banks of the Mississippi to stop erosion of the soil—not too far from Galesburg. It was an all-black camp, patterned after the armed services. The officers were white. I got $30 a month and sent $25 home. Of the $5 I kept, I still had some money left at the end of the month.

I wanted to go to college in the worst way. I had aspirations to become a doctor. It was just impossible, being black with no money. After I came out of the CCC camp, I had a job for a few months helping rebuild the tracks of the Missouri & Pacific after a devastating flood.

The first long-time job I had was with a hardwood manufacturer in Cairo. Their headquarters was in Memphis, so they really knew how to practice racism. I started out stacking lumber with older black men. Then I was moved inside the factory.

I'll never forget the time I stepped playfully on some hardwood floor that I thought was no good. The superintendent, walking through the plant, hollered, "Come here, boy!" I came over. "Don't you know you're not supposed to step on that flooring?" I said, "But I thought it was a throw-out." He said, "Let me tell you one thing and don't you ever forget it. You don't get paid to think here. I do." I never forgot it. I just said, "Uh huh."

I always had a degree of independence. I used to read quite a bit. I had read something about a union that seemed to have some jurisdiction over this kind of work. At the time it was called the Federation of Carpenters and Joiners. I wrote a letter to their headquarters in Indianapolis. I got a response. They sent an international rep and he met with me. I went to some of the older black guys who were miserably mistreated. I said, "We need some protection. You can't deal with these bosses on a one-to-one basis, because they'll fire you one at a time. But if we get together and stick together, they can't fire all of us." They agreed. I was making $7.50 a week. So about five of us sent $2.50 a piece to apply for a union charter and we got it.

Wasn't the carpenters' union lily-white?

Yeah, yeah. [*Chuckles.*] The guy they sent in was pretty decent, so we were able to form an all-black local, Local 1424. The whites at the plant had the better jobs, grading the flooring and running the saw mills. They refused to join. Of course, the company refused to recognize us, so we went on a six-week strike, all black. It worked. They recognized us, and I was elected president of the local. I was still pretty much of a kid. That was my beginning in the labor movement.

After the strike, some of the white guys saw that they weren't being treated right either. So they joined our union. This was at a time when the trades were segregated. We elected one white guy secretary-treasurer and put another on the committee with me. He and I had to negotiate our first contract in Memphis, the company's headquarters. We got on the train at Cairo, and I never saw him until we reached Memphis. We were in different cars. I was the first black guy who ever sat across the table in that company's office. There was just no way they could get around me. I was president of the Cairo local. [*Chuckles.*]

I still wanted to go back to school. I had an uncle who worked in the Chicago stockyards. He said, "Why don't you come up here? I'll find you a job in the yards and you can go to school." So my wife and I came to Chicago.

He got me a job as laborer for Wilson. We were getting seventy-five cents an hour, much more than we got in Cairo. I was working at night in the pork-boning department, hauling meat to the wagon and cleaning up. They had women boning the pork shoulders for sausage and lunch meat.

This was in 1942 and they were just organizing in the stockyards. Armour had already recognized the union, but Wilson was one of the most vicious anti-union outfits. They had a company union. Though I was a new guy with hardly any seniority, I had organizing experience. So I joined with the pro-union people immediately.

We went through two NLRB* elections and two strikes. One lasted two weeks in 1946, and there was a bigger one in 1948. Along with three other guys, I was fired for union activity. We were reinstated by the NLRB. In 1949, I was made full-time international field representative. I traveled to Kansas City, Omaha, wherever there were challenges.

The union became my life, but I still wanted to go to school, at least, learn a trade. I applied at Coyne Electrical College. I'll never forget what they told me: "We have no facilities for colored." So it was all union work from then on. I stayed all the way through, including two mergers. I had to resign my post when I entered Congress in 1983. I'm told I was the first elected union official ever to become a congressman. I served nine years and six months.

Our union was far in advance of many others in breaking down unfair practices. Male laborers were getting seventy-two cents an hour. Women, doing the same work, were getting sixty-two cents. We broke that down. White women worked in the cleaner departments, meat processing. Black women were stationed on the killing floors. We changed all that.

We realized that changing the working conditions was only part of

---

* National Labor Relations Board.

our job. We had to do something about the conditions where the workers lived, in the community. That's why I had become so active in the civil rights movement. That's why Martin Luther King came to Chicago. Talking abut crime doesn't add up to anything, unless we get at basic causes.

The closing of the stockyards in Chicago was devastating. Swift moved to Rochelle, Illinois. Wilson moved to Monmouth. They said they had to move closer to their sources of supply. The Chicago plants were getting old and outmoded. I remember, back in the '70s, when twenty thousand workers had a mass rally to save their jobs. But it was no use.

Some were able to take what was then early retirement. Some women who had worked in the yards actually put their birth dates back in order to be eligible for social security. [*Chuckles.*] They were that desperate. They'd come to me: "Look, I'm really older than I've been saying I was. You've got to help me prove it." I wrote many a letter to the social security department in Baltimore trying to straighten out ages. [*Chuckles.*] We did very well. We had a strong union.

What happened to that strength? Aside from corporate greed, the labor leadership got more interested in themselves than in those they were supposed to represent. Some of the leaders have greater allegiance to the Democratic Party than they do to their members.

I learned a lot during my tenure in Congress. Traveling around the world, comparing educational systems, it became obvious to me that, in contrast to European countries, especially Scandinavia, we're a Third World nation in that respect. We're always crying we don't have the money for education, but your mind boggles at the billions squandered on Star Wars.*

I think there's very little care as to whether or not poor kids get an education, especially African Americans. So we move toward privatization of the public school system, and you don't hear the trade union movement saying too much about it—as though there were no connection between schooling and jobs and crime.

I can see what's happening in my own community. I really feel things are going to get worse before they get better. The value of human life means nothing to some young people. My wife—she's gone to glory now—had bars put on our windows and installed an alarm system. I've made sure they're preserved. [*Chuckles.*] I don't like to go out at night. When I was in Congress, I had a guy from the sheriff's office with me all the time. He had a gun. Now I don't have that kind of security. If I go anywhere at night, I take somebody with me, even if it's my grandkid.

---

* Reagan's Strategic Defense Initiative, a program to develop and deploy a multi-billion dollar missile defense system, was popularly known as "Star Wars."

People—that is, whites—think crime is inherent to black life. I know better. I was born and bred in black areas. It's spread everywhere. Everybody who is out of a job is not lazy. Most would rather have a job than be on public assistance. The reality is that technology has eliminated a lot of jobs. But we're still fooling ourselves that things are getting better. We're still using the band-aid approach. It's not going to work.

I remember when the federal government stepped in—Roosevelt times. My daddy worked on the WPA when I was in the CCC camp. He worked on shoring up river banks and levees. He worked on highways. Today, our infrastructure is falling apart. Every major city needs rebuilding. Millions of young people would be glad to work, yet our government is not making a move in this direction.

Without work, kids are just loitering around, standing on the corner. There are so many panhandlers that I try to avoid going down the street. Yet the only talk we hear is for more prisons, sterner sentences, and more police. How long will it take us to discover that that won't cut it? You don't get at cancer with just a surgeon's knife. You get at the cause or it just spreads on and on and on.

I would really have liked to have spent two more years in Congress, but my big regret was not getting to go to college. Yet. [*Chuckles.*] One thing I know: I've had more experience at being a black than I have had at anything else. I've got seniority there. [*Laughs.*]

Marvin Miller, 72
NEW YORK CITY

*"Marvin Miller may be the single most important man
not only in baseball, perhaps in all sports."*

—*Red Barber*

*He was the executive director—the first—of the Baseball Players'
Association, 1966–1983.*

*He had been engaged in trade union work from the days of the
depression through his years as chief economist and assistant to the
president of the Steel Workers of America–CIO. In between, he had
served as a hearing officer for the War Labor Board. He quit the
union in 1965 and was considering offers from the Carnegie Foundation and Harvard University.*

*In a chance elevator encounter, he had learned that several major
league baseball players had formed a search committee: hoping to
form an association (the word* union *was never used), they were
seeking an executive director. His name had been submitted.*

*There had been previous attempts by players to organize; they
always failed because of what was considered the unique nature of
"America's leading pastime." The crowning blow was a Supreme
Court decision in 1922. A lawsuit filed by businessmen who had
hoped to form a third conference, the Federal League, charged that
major league owners were conducting a monopoly in violation of
the Sherman Anti-Trust Act. In an opinion delivered by Justice
Oliver Wendell Holmes, it was ruled that major league baseball was
not a business, but merely a series of exhibitions; it was no more
than a game. "It was an outrageous decision, worthy of* Alice in
Wonderland," *says Miller. "Owners were charging money for these
'exhibitions,' making profits hand over fist."*

*The search committee chose him as the aborning association's
director. "At the time, the owners were out to gut the pension plan,
which had been in effect since 1947. It was the players' one glory.
You could get a pension after you reached the age of 50, long after
you were out of baseball. This was one of the real reasons they were
stirring themselves to do something, to get together."*

I said there had to be a vote of all the players. I wanted to meet
everyone of them, because they had to know what they were voting
for. It was a big handicap to have the managers, coaches, and trainers included, because they, more than the players, were under the
thumb of the owners. But those were the terms.

In the spring of '66, by myself, I visited all the training camps in Arizona, California, and Florida. I stayed in motels, rented cars, found my way to the twenty training camps and met with all the players. I found they were so unlike the workers in steel or anywhere else. In industrial plants, you have a mix of youngsters and old-timers who are about to retire. Here, they were so young. I discovered how little they knew about the economic life of our country, because they had no work experience of their own.

Most of these young men had come to baseball through the minor leagues, from high school and a few from college. Almost none had any work experience outside of baseball. They had no contact with unions and yet were subject to all the antilabor propaganda that we're faced with all the time. [*Chuckles.*]

The sheer weight of that almost got me down, because they started with a tradition of brainwashing: Baseball is not an industry, baseball is not for making money, these are sportsmen who own the clubs, and they do it for the love of it. Many of the kids believed that. It had been drummed into them year after year: "You are the luckiest people on the face of the earth. You get paid for playing a game. If you make demands, the whole game will collapse, because why the hell should these sportsmen lose money? They'll just walk away from their franchises." They believed this fairy tale. [*Laughs.*]

The owners had "truth squads" preceding me into camp: the commissioner of baseball, his PR men, the two league presidents, their assistants, telling players all this crap. "A union means you'll be striking every day." "This guy, Miller, has Mafia and Teamster connections." Managers of the Durocher stripe were saying, "Get rid of this Miller guy." Just a couple of the managers were sympathetic. Gil Hodges was one of them. So the prognosis was not that great. [*Chuckles.*]

Just this morning, I was asked by a reporter why I accepted the job. I said that the players' conditions were so bad you couldn't fail to improve them. No matter how incompetent you might be at this job, given where you were starting from, anybody would be successful.

It wasn't just the dumbness of the owners but their arrogance as well. Their history was one of swatting down people, whether it was Congress trying to put them under the antitrust laws, or the courts. They always prevailed. When the players' union succeeded, they fell apart, as often happens with bullies. They had a long history in this respect.

There was the so-called reserve clause in each player's contract. It, in effect, considered the professional baseball player as a piece of property. He was drafted either as a high school or college player. The owners would make their own rules. They had the names of all these kids, chosen by the scouts as having promise. The youngster, who had never signed a piece of paper with anyone, was told he belonged to the organization that drafted him. He had no choice. No other team would make him an offer. He had two alternatives: take it or not play baseball.

The minute you signed, you became the property of that team for the rest of your natural life. The club had the option of selling you or trading you or releasing you—that is, firing you. If you refused that offer, you were forbidden from playing baseball in the major or minor leagues in the United States, Canada, Mexico, the Dominican Republic, Venezuela, Puerto Rico, or Japan.

In 1946, two wealthy Mexican businessmen planned to create a major league in Mexico. They enticed Sal Maglie, Hal Lanier, Mickey Owen, maybe seven or eight other name players. The sports writers at the time, in the pocket of the owners, labeled them contract jumpers. In fact, not one of them jumped a contract. They had one-year contracts, played out the year, and accepted the offer.

The owners said, in effect, "We own you forever." The reserve clause, right? The Mexican experiment failed after a year. The players tried to come back to their jobs. The commissioner of baseball, at the behest of the owners, barred them from baseball for life. These impudent pups had to be taught a lesson.

In 1947, one of these players filed a lawsuit, charging that this was in violation of the antitrust laws and deprived him of earning a living. He won in the federal district court and in the circuit court appeal. The owners argued that the players were well paid, but the justice said, "A well-paid slave is still a slave." The owners bought the player off and reinstated him as well as the others. In 1953, a minor league player in the New York Yankees chain filed a lawsuit. He said, "Consider my predicament. I'm the property of the Yankees. They do nothing but win pennants year after year. They've got the best players in the world and I have no chance of breaking into that lineup. My whole career will go down the drain for all my playable years. They will not trade me, insisting I'm their insurance." He lost in the Supreme Court, seven to two. All the liberal judges voted against him. That same Supreme Court declared that other sports, basketball, football, boxing, hockey, were subject to antitrust laws, but not baseball. The cheese stands alone.

In 1972, the Supreme Court decided against Curt Flood, five to three with one abstention. He had been traded by the Cardinals to the Phillies, having played for St. Louis for twelve years. I had now been with the association for six years and he had heard me say that baseball was violating the antitrust laws, no matter what the courts said. But I warned him that any suit would be risky. He decided to sue, and the association paid his legal expenses.

While this case was pending in the lower courts, we were negotiating the 1970 contract. The owners' defense against antitrust violations was that they were self-regulating. "We have a commissioner." In the pre-union days, there was no one to dispute this. They knew we'd come into court and say, "Self-regulated, your ass!" The commissioner was a creature of the owners—hired by them, fired by them, serving them. He's not responsible to the public, as he pretends; nor to the fans. He's responsible to the owners. If there's a dispute about a contract, this handpicked toady will interpret it.

They knew we were loaded for bear, with facts, figures, everything. They figured: Winning the antitrust case against Flood is more important, let's give them impartial arbitration. This became our ace in the hole.

Impartial arbitrators, in labor disputes, ever since the end of the war, have become professionals. Each side pays half his salary. Baseball never had any such thing before. It was the commissioner, like Happy Chandler, who would decide.

I found a loophole in the reserve clause. It need not make you a prisoner for life, I told the players. "If you sign a contract for '74 and if you and the club can't agree on the '75 contract by March 1, the club has the right to renew your '74 contract for one year. *One* year. I read it to mean that, having played out '75, you're free." The owners said, "Nonsense. When we renew the contract, we renew the renewal clause." They meant "into perpetuity." Could Lewis Carroll think up anything more goofy? To think that they got away with it all these years!

In order to have a test case, we needed a player who would not sign a new contract, let the club renew him for one year, play under it, and at the end of that year file a grievance saying he's free. In 1975, that's what Andy Messersmith, the pitcher, did. They renewed his '74 contract, as they had a right to do, but he didn't sign a new one and played under his renewed '74 contract. When the season ended, he announced that he was a free agent, able to deal with any team. The owner told him to fly a kite. The grievance went to arbitration and the arbitrator ruled in favor of Messersmith. He read the contract exactly as I did. That was the end of the reserve rule.

In some ways, the owners were of tremendous help. They and their toadies simply overplayed their hand. It's what happened to the crap they dished out about me being a goonsquad guy. When I walked into camp, the players would come up to me and say, "You don't look anything like I thought you'd look.* [*Laughs.*]

---

* With his gray hair, gray mustache, and quiet demeanor, he bears a resemblance to Dashiell Hammett.

I did have the help of veteran players who were hip. Jim Bouton was one. The minute the commissioner or an owner said to him, "Watch out for this guy, be careful," he said, "I knew this was our guy." The idea of a union was not a monster to them.

The first four clubs I visited in Arizona and California voted way against me. They had a big campaign, led by the Durocher types. When I got to Florida, where sixteen teams trained, you had Roberts, Bunning, Bouton, and other seasoned vets playing an important role. The vote was overwhelmingly union.

I still have my notes from those first meetings. I told the players I thought they were the most exploited people I'd ever dealt with. "Not that you have the lowest salaries, but the difference between what you get and what you're worth in a free market makes you the most exploited. A grape picker (Chavez was organizing at the time) is poverty-stricken compared to you, but the difference between what he gets and what he's worth doesn't compare to your situation."

I was exposing the whopping lie of the owners that they don't make money. I took the most recent figures in *Fortune* magazine. The total payroll figures, the total gate receipts, the TV income. It was public knowledge. I said, "I know what you've heard about unions, but you must understand that only by working together can you have any impact. Consider the player who fights back, who's a holdout. The company sends him a damn contract that is an insult. He's had a great year and they offer him a cut. You may not know this, but Jimmy Foxx, who won the triple crown, was offered a pay cut the following year. Even a Joe DiMaggio, holding out after his second and third years, probably the greatest two consecutive years any player ever had, was holding out for $35,000. He had to crawl back and take whatever Colonel Ruppert, the owner, offered him. That's the fate of an individual as skilled and valued as Joe DiMaggio. But all of you together are something else.

"There is no way to deny anything that is reasonable, because you're irreplaceable as a group. It's not that every union has a successful strike. Sometimes, it's very difficult. But, in your case, if they bring in whole teams of scabs, nobody will pay to see them."

It was a delicate situation. I didn't want to be dishonest and say there would never be a strike. I wanted to cut the crap that there would be irresponsible strikes. It was the last, last, last weapon of a union. You try everything else. You never go out on strike, I told them, unless you have tremendous support of your fellow players. A majority won't do. It had to have 90, 92, 95 percent support.

In the beginning, they were the most shy people I'd ever met. As time went by, they got more comfortable at the meetings. When we entered into negotiations, I'd ask their views. "You're my source of information. How do we know about the health and safety conditions? You're the only ones who can tell me about the nails in the fence at Pompano Beach." They were treated as adults.

We invited all the players to attend the negotiating sessions. The owners *hated* this. We'd come in with sixty or seventy players at a meeting. The owners' reps would say, "How the hell can you get anything done with so many people in the room?" [*Laughs.*] In all the years I was there, not a single owner ever attended a single negotiating session. No general managers. But the players were always there.

During a crisis, like the '72 strike or the one in '81, the owners would hold a meeting with the players, telling them of the union's outrageous demands and how reasonable the owners were. The players would sit and look at each other. They had been at these sessions and knew it wasn't like that. They know *all* of what's going on. The papers can't fool them, the owners can't fool them, because they're *there*. [*Laughs.*] The players have been the most underestimated people imaginable.

It was really the veteran players, the stars, who led the way. The younger players were remarkably quick to learn things, but the older players were even more so, in unlearning so much. The star players could not be cast aside that easily and were more able to risk the wrath of owners. Baseball fans generally side with the owners because the players make so much money today.

We live in a society in which people are taught not to look at people of great wealth, who control things, who really have the money and the power, not to question their sources. We're trained to look at lesser beings. The fan says, "Look at this guy, he makes x dollars a year. What the hell more does he want?" He thinks nothing of the fact that the owner makes fifty thousand times more and has profited from the talents of the others.

Perhaps the owner came from the shipbuilding industry, like Steinbrenner. Didn't his workers play a role in the building of his empire? Gussie Busch, without the talents of the brewmaster and brewery workers, where would he be? We are *not* taught the value of labor. We're trained to think these people are nothing. We have been taught that it's okay for the entrepreneur to make billions, because he takes a risk, doesn't he? We think nothing of the fact that the worker is risking his life, his career, his whole future. That's nothing.

The owners always claim they're losing money. My God, they're making more than ever. Before the union came in and "ruined" baseball, there were twenty baseball franchises. Now there are twenty-eight. In that time, there has been a 40 percent expansion—40 percent more jobs, more players. Two new franchises were added in 1993, at a time when big names in American industry were laying off thousands of people, closing plants. The Denver and Miami clubs—the Colorado Rockies and the Florida Marlins—paid $95 million for each franchise.*

Another reason these big boys buy clubs is the sense of power it gives them. It's a hobby that makes money at the same time.

Publicity and glamor figure in it. Charlie Finley tells this story about himself. "For all the years I've had the insurance business, not even the elevator starter knew my name. I was just a faceless millionaire. I buy the Kansas City club and suddenly everybody in America knows my name." How many people ever heard of George Steinbrenner before he bought the Yankees? But a sense of power is the big thing.

Through the past thirty years, sports writers have gibed at the owners: they don't know how to stick together, the union has licked them, they're a bunch of weaklings, they're losers. These are very opinionated, willful men of great power in other situations. To be called losers! They fume, they die over this. They want to win one.

In '81, they made a demand: Let's end free agency. [*Laughs.*] They talk themselves into it. If the players strike, they'll come back with their tails between their legs in a few days. Fifty days later, the owners caved in. Now they're at it again.

I blame the media for not explaining what a salary cap is. The owners want the union to conspire with them and agree that salaries cannot go beyond x point. The difference between what the players would get in an open market and this artificial cap would be pocketed by the owners. A couple of billion or so. The players are making no demands, merely protecting what they have already won. It's the owners who are making the demands. Yet, thanks to shallow reportage, the fan asks, "What do these players want now?"

It's not the union or the players saying, "These salaries must be this way. Every player's salary is negotiated by the owners or their general managers and the players and their agents. They're not saying, "I'll go on strike if I don't get it." The union has *nothing* to do with this. When the Boston Red Sox reached the five-million-dollar mark with Roger Clemens, it's because they felt he was worth it rather than lose him. Isn't this what the free, open market is all about?

The average baseball fan is aware of the millions a player makes, but not one in a thousand knows that the baseball owners have a gross revenue of $2 billion. It's not that the fan is intrinsically ignorant, it's that the press has never told him.

The success of the players' association may not apply to other professional sports. There are grave differences. The big difference is in the history of baseball. As they advance through the ranks, they get to

---

* At the time of this conversation in June 1994, there was talk of another strike, as the owners, who again claimed to be losing money, sought to cap players' salaries. Later, the players did strike and the 1994 season was cancelled.

know each other as minor league players. They know each other from the beginning of their careers. Contrast this with the football scab situation. Football has no minor leagues. The get them from colleges. When they wanted scabs, they went to people who worked in garages, who had semi-pro jobs. They had no association with the football players they were replacing, *none*.

In 1981, during the fifty-day strike in baseball, I got wind of the fact that the New York Mets were planning to bring in their minor league team to play out their scheduled games at Shea Stadium and that the Cleveland Indians were planning the same thing with their affiliate. Ed Kranepool, the Mets player representative, said, "Watch me." He picked up the phone and talked to a player he knew on the Tidewater team. "This is a dangerous thing. It means you're going to scab." The guy said, "Hell, no, we'll not do that. We know you guys are fighting for us." Within two hours, the wire services announced that the Tidewater team voted unanimously that they would not play at Shea Stadium. The Cleveland triple-A affiliate did the same thing. So this half-assed attempt by the owners to test the waters flopped, because the players knew one another and were familiar with the issues.

At first, George Meany* was opposed to the forming of the players' association. He was ignorant. He thought that ball players were not employees, simply independent contractors. I told him that the owners pay social security for the players, pay unemployment insurance taxes, have workmen's compensation coverage, that the players are employees as much as any steel worker or coal miner. He sat there with his mouth open. "They are? They are!" To give him credit, he took action. The AFL-CIO filed a brief with the NLRB,† urging them to take jurisdiction in baseball, for the umpires.

I've never tried to sell the players on my philosophy, that their fight is part and parcel of a bigger thing. There was a discussion of affiliating with the AFL-CIO. I told them of the advantages and disadvantages. After much pro and con discussion, they decided against it.

We have never, ever had any difficulties about race. From the earliest days, black players were in the forefront. Almost without exception, whether they were from the United States or Latin America, they had realized the owners were not their kindly benefactors and that the white players were their allies.

In all the years of the company union, from 1947, when Jackie Robinson broke in, to the '60s, there had never been a player representative who wasn't white. Jim Bunning, active in the union from the very beginning, got traded by the Phillies to the Pirates. He's a very interesting guy, a conservative and an ardent Republican. But he studied

---

* Then the president of the AFL-CIO.

† National Labor Relations Board.

everything we did. One day, he said to me, "I'll bet you think it's time we had some nonwhite players' representatives." I said, "How did you know that?" He said, "Oh, I remember things you said some years ago. I know your views." The next thing I know, when he was asked by the Pirate players to be their rep, he declined. He said, "You really got a team leader here now. I nominate Roberto Clemente." Clemente was the first black players' rep and an active one.

It's been eleven years since I've retired from that job. When they fired my immediate successor, Ken Moffatt, I was asked to come back.* I agreed to do so for a month until they chose a new head. Don Fehr has been a good one. I helped a bit with the '85 negotiations.

At the same time, I was asked to represent the minority of the Boston Red Sox stockholders, who felt they were getting a raw deal from the Yakey ownership. I thought it was amusing, I, with my union background, representing stockholders. I agreed. They *were* getting a raw deal.

Suddenly, everything fell into place. I got an award in favor of the minority owners and the two-day strike in baseball ended with a reasonable settlement. Everything was peaceful.

I began to get chest pains, but thought nothing about it and continued to play tennis and smoke. Two weeks later, I'm in bed watching the league play-offs and I have a heart attack. This was October 12, 1985. [*Chuckles.*] I and Columbus, we both discovered something.

At the hospital, an angiogram indicated some blockage. After two weeks, they gave me a clean bill of health. Everything was fine, until Thanksgiving Day of '93. It was worse than ever. They found 95 percent blockage, so I had angioplasty. They shot a balloon through my arteries, a spectacular job. Since January of this year, I've been fine.

I've had all kinds of offers in the past few years. I still see some of the players, some of the association officials, and discuss all kinds of matters. In the past three weeks, I've had about twenty interviews with reporters about the possible strike.† They call me not so much because I am *the* source, but because I'm not guarded. I don't have to be. I'm not censurable.

I still play tennis and may write another book. It'll be more in a political vein than my first book, which was a memoir of my experiences in baseball.

Even though baseball is called a team sport, the team players are great individualists. When you step into the batter's box, you are all alone. When you're on the pitching mound, you are all alone. More than in most games, it is a sport of individualists. What I am most proud of in my whole career with baseball is that I was able to educate players in the importance of acting together. That's what it's all about.

---

* The players felt that Moffatt was as much pro-owner as pro-player.

† This interview took place in July 1994.

CHAPTER SIX

Working the Land

Jessie de la Cruz, 74
FRESNO, CALIFORNIA

*She was one of the first women organizers of the Farm Workers'
Union. "I must've been almost eight when I started following the
crops. Every winter, up north. I was on the end of the row of prunes,
taking care of my younger brother and sister. They would help me
fill up the cans and put 'em in a box while the rest of the family was
picking the whole row.*

*"All farm workers I know, they're always talking: 'If I had my own
place, I'd know how to run it. I'd be there all the time. My kids would
help me.' This is one thing that all Chicano families talked about. We
worked the land all our lives, so if we ever owned a piece of land, we
knew that we could make it. That's what my grandfather kept talkin'
about, but his dream was never realized. Neither was my father's.*

*"I was given a shot in the arm by Cesar Chavez. All of the things
that I always felt like I wanted to say, I held back because of the fear
of losing a job, of being thought not a very good woman, of some kind
of fear inside me that had been instilled in me by my grandmother,
who always warned us when we did something, the police would
come. So when Cesar Chavez started talking to us and sayin'
women have to become involved, they have to speak, they're farm
workers, too, I just, oh, had a good feeling. I said, 'Boy, now.'*

*"How can I write down how I felt when I was a little child and my
grandmother used to cry with us 'cause she didn't have enough food
to give us? Because my brother was going barefooted and he was
cryin'? I can't describe when my little girl died because I didn't have
money for a doctor. Livin' out in labor camps. How can I describe
that? How can I put into writing when I'm testifying about things
that are very deep inside? About seeing all these many people that
have their little children killed in the fields through accidents? It's
things that are a feeling you can't put into words."*

When I first visited her in Fresno, she lived with her husband in a one-family dwelling. A small well-kept garden was out front. "I always looked at those flowers in other people's gardens and said, 'If I could only have my own hose and garden.' We couldn't as migrant workers. Now, as you walk onto my porch, everything you see is green. [Laughs.] I have a garden now."

Her husband died four years ago. She lives by herself in a mobile home, though her children are in constant touch with her. "It's a double trailer, with two baths, two bedrooms, dining room. Everything is compact. Real nice. A porch and a small garden out front, where I can plant anything I want. Beautiful."

I'm definitely not retired from life. Right now, there's a big fight going on in Fresno. We wanted to name a street in honor of Cesar Chavez, who did so much for all the people. The city council voted four to three against. At first they voted for it. There were complaints from some people, who were always against Cesar and the union. So they called another meeting and one councilman changed his vote from yes to no. Now the city is divided.

The growers are the ones who gathered the signatures of the business people on Ventura Boulevard. Some have just recently arrived, Arabs, who don't even know what's happening. The others are the ones who've always fought us. We have 100 percent support from the black people of West Fresno, though it was the black councilman who changed his vote. He was pressured, of course. Oh, we're going to keep on fighting. We want that street named after Cesar Chavez, to remember him by.

My health is fine, thank God. I guess keeping busy does it. Last year, I went back and worked for the union full time for about ten months. The first month I was down in Delano, cooking for seventeen volunteers. Then I was sent to Coachella Valley, about a hundred miles north of the Mexican border.

We'd get up about 2:30 in the morning, shower, and be in the office at about 3:15. We were dispatched out to different fields, telling the workers about their rights. It's the desert, about 117 degrees out in the sun. They were working without any shade, no fresh drinking water, no rest rooms, no nothing. Some of the women were pregnant, kneeling in the hot sand picking grapes. They just had a little jug by their side.

We told them there's a federal law that protects these workers and they should stand up and enforce it. We told them the wages they were getting were very low. We convinced them to walk out of the fields. They did, and they got the rest rooms. They got a table with an umbrella overhead, where they stood and packed. They got fresh drinking water. We had thousands of people out there, marching. Last summer, I get a shot of adrenaline when I'm out there, being involved in things. I have to be where the action is.

About five years ago, I suffered a mild stroke that paralyzed an optical nerve. I was seeing double for a time. I had to wear a patch on one eye one day, and a patch on the other eye the next day. But I got over that. They told me I could have surgery or wait and it might go away by itself. So I waited and am fine.

I've been as active as ever. I was president of the California Rural Legal Assistance Migrant Association, referring farm workers to lawyers who wouldn't cheat them. I'm still with the State Bar of California Access for Justice, getting funds for low-income people who can't afford a lawyer. Mostly, I talk to people, tell them about the laws and what they have to do for themselves. Whatever it is, if there's a need, I'll go.

I get up in the morning, have a cup of coffee, a piece of toast, and I'm ready to go. I haven't got a car, haven't the money for it. Somebody drops by, I get a ride or walk downtown. See what's going on, talk to friends, and whatever needs to be done, I'll do.

I live on social security, which is not very much. After paying my rent and utilities, there's about one hundred dollars left over, which I have to stretch for a whole month before I get another check.

I keep getting all these calls because they heard we didn't get the street named for Cesar. People from all walks of life are calling, not just farm workers. We'll keep on fighting, I tell them. There are some meetings coming up.

It's getting worse for the farm workers with this Republican government we have. A lot of them are hiding because they're not legally here. That's what the labor contractor wants. He hides them because he can exploit them by paying them lower wages and having them live in old barns or chicken coops.

And the pesticides. That's another thing. I've seen children that were born without spines. That's why we're boycotting grapes—the pesticides. Many of the children have died. Especially in these rural communities and these little towns around here.

More and more people are becoming aware of these pesticides. They wouldn't listen to us before, but the experts have been out there, exposing the harm. Some are being banned. Whenever I talk to anybody, I tell them about the grapes and the vineyards and the pesticides being sprayed by the tons every year. I study these things and read everything I get my hands on.

There's new leaders out there, new people from the community. Especially the Chicanos. They see how we've been rejected, wherever we go, whatever we try to do. Just the other night at the city council meeting, when somebody stood up before the microphone to talk and he couldn't speak good English, he had a translator. They always ask somebody to help them out. The whites behind us whispered, "Why don't those stupid Mexicans go back to Mexico where they belong." But we're Americans!

This anti-Mexican feeling is strong, especially here in Fresno County, where the growers try to control everything. They have the money and they figure, well, they're the boss of everything. But we're going to prove them wrong. Oh, they know me, all right. But they hardly come out this way. They go shopping in San Francisco or New York, not Fresno. Most of our business is moving out of here. Big shopping centers are being built up in the northern part, moving out of downtown.

It makes me sad to see everything that's going on, especially among our young people—drugs, jail. I wish they could open their eyes and see what society is doing to them. They put the small dope dealers in jail, sixteen-, seventeen-year-old kids. But the big fish, the ones way up who make millions, the government hardly touches.

It's the young who worry me the most. They're fighting each other, being divided. The Chicano kids are told the blacks are no good, the black kids are told the Chicano kids are no good. But among us older people, we're still together. Cesar Chavez taught us we're all in the same boat. He never saw race, he saw people.

Cesar's passing away was a big blow, but we're going to keep on going. That's one thing he always pointed out. "If anything happens to me, there always has to be somebody else." He said, "I don't want our movement to go the way the civil rights movement vanished when Martin Luther King got killed. We must go on."

We're holding up, yes. About a month ago we had a big march, five thousand people marching all the way down from King's Canyon, Ventura. Our Lady of Guadalupe was up front. Even if I don't go very much to church, I pray here at my house. I know there's a God. Otherwise we wouldn't have any rain, flowers. Look outside this trailer. What do you see? A small garden, flowers, tomato plants, whatever.

My children think the same way I do, they think the same way my husband did: the family should have roots. Remember when I told you about the cooperative we had—six families? Everybody pitched in when the big storm was coming. The day before it hit, everybody—grownups, little kids—covered all our tomato plants with little paper cups, cone-shaped. The wind was blowing so strong those cups were just torn from our hands, flying all over the place. Oh, it was hard, but everybody, without exception, put them back. We covered them gently with dirt. My little nephew, four years old, was out there running and helping. And the next day, after the storm, all the plants were there! Oh, it was so wonderful. I said, "Thank God. There is a God."

A big grower would have said, "Let the storm come. What's the difference? What the heck, we'll replant tomorrow." People like us, we don't have the money, show more respect for the land. We try the best we can to conserve the land and enjoy the trees, the fruits they bear, the flowers. Even though you don't eat the flowers, you still enjoy them. They're colorful, they smell good, they're beautiful. It makes you feel good just to have them around. You have to respect everything. Not just the land, but the animals, the people, everything.

I look at myself in the mirror and I know I'm old. But I don't feel old! Last year, they celebrated my birthday—I was seventy-three—at our union headquarters in La Paz, near Bakersfield. They had a big cake and a gift and Cesar got up and told them how old I was, and they didn't believe it. I got up and said, "When I was younger, I never said my age. Now I'm proud that I am old."

I married when I was young, and I never thought about how long I was going to live. How long am I going to be on this earth? You just live day by day. You get older and you realize there are many things you can do besides just staying home, besides feeling sorry for yourself. There's always something to do, no matter what age, as long as you can get up and walk and talk. There's always hope. We have a saying: *La esperanza muere al último.* Hope dies last. Hope for whatever you want to do. If you can't do it today, there's always tomorrow or the next year. I'm going to spend Christmas with my doctor son in Sacramento, come back and make some tamales for the rest of the family out here. And then I'll get back in action again at the Fresno city council. That's my way of enjoying life— doing something.

Merle Hansen, 74

Newman Grove, Nebraska

"I live across the field from the house where I was born. My grand-father came to this area from Norway in 1888. My great-great-grandfather homesteaded around here.

"I have four sons. My oldest is president of the Nebraska Farm-ers Union. I used to be president of the North American Farm Alliance.

"I raise mostly corn and soybeans."

I grew up in the depression and really wanted to get off the farm. We were in real poverty. All I can remember is my father and mother struggling to make land payments, pay taxes, and hang on. But I appreciate farming. It's a wonderful place to raise a family. We don't own a lock on the door. We feel secure.

I was thinking this morning about the people around here being eliminated every day. About three-fourths of these farmsteads have been torn down, farmed over. In just the decade of the '80s, one-fourth of our country's farmers have been wiped out. For the first time, there are less farmers than there were before the Civil War. In 1945, we had six million farmers in the United States. Today we have about two million.

The worst is not yet. It's predicted that four out of five of the farmers today will be eliminated. In some areas, it has already hap-pened. It's been completely corporatized. The *Wall Street Journal* says, "Let's do away with all farm programs and let the thirty-one thousand left do the farming for us." It will be like a basketball tour-nament—an elimination contest. You gamble. If you make the right decision, why, you may survive. If you don't, you're out.

We've had the illusion of happy, contented, prosperous farmers churning out abundance from the Horn of Plenty. Just like the pic-ture of the slaves as contented and happy.

There's been two Americas, run not by generous people but by greedy, selfish ones. Even back in Revolutionary times, the Conti-nental Congress at first rejected the Bill of Rights. We have to thank some farmers' uprisings, like Shays's Rebellion, where about ten people were killed. They said no, we've got to have basic rights. We can't be taxed out of our farms, out of our homes. Finally, the Conti-nental Congress set up a country for white male property holders. Women didn't have a right to vote, blacks didn't, Indians didn't. It's been a struggle all the time to expand democracy.

The farmers' battles have been a great part of this story. The populist movement, the farmers' alliances. At one time, there were two thousand locals of the alliance and a thousand newspapers and journals. When senators were elected by state legislators, who were often corrupt, these farm groups fought for direct election by the people. Teddy Roosevelt said these populists should be lined up and shot. He's the one who called Tom Paine a dirty little atheist. We're talking about the 1890s. It was the high time for the populists, especially in the Middle West and the South. In 1892, they elected as many as 146 congressmen and state senators. They had a majority in seventeen states. There was a lot of reform, including women's suffrage.

In the 1920s, the Non-Partisan League swept the Dakotas, Minnesota, and Nebraska. But they were bad years for farmers. Two-thirds of the farms and two-thirds of the banks in South Dakota went busted.

Then came the Crash of '29. In 1932, farm prices dropped to incredible lows. Hogs were selling for two cents a pound, beef for five cents, corn for ten cents a bushel, wheat for twenty-five cents a bushel.* Ever hear the story of the farmer who sold his sheep up in Sioux City, Iowa? He got a letter back from the commission company: "We got your sheep sold just fine here, but they didn't bring enough money to cover the commission. We need some more money." The farmer wrote back: "I don't have any money, but I got more sheep."

I was about thirteen. My father was active in the Farm Holiday Association. In 1928, he bought a garage in Newman Grove and was going broke. The group would meet in this garage. I'd go and liked to listen to these arguments.

One of the first actions of the association in October of '32 was to repossess a couple of trucks that the International Harvester Company had taken away from them. They just broke into the building and drove the trucks out. My dad was one of those people. The next day, they went up to a farm sale in Elgin, Nebraska. A widow woman with five children was being foreclosed. They were determined to stop the sale, so they set up a committee to do all the bidding. They were going to give this farm back to the woman free of mortgage. The total sale brought in $5.35. There were several thousand farmers that showed up. The sheriff came over and told them they couldn't do it. A

---

* "Grain was being burned. It was cheaper than coal. Corn was being burned. A county just east of here, they burned corn in their courthouse all winter, '32, '33. You couldn't hardly buy groceries for corn. It couldn't pay the transportation. In South Dakota, the county elevator listed corn as minus three cents. Minus three cents a bushel. If you wanted to sell 'em a bushel of corn, you had to pay them three cents." —Oscar Heline, an Iowa farmer, in *Hard Times: An Oral History of The Great Depression*, 1970

bunch of these big farmers grabbed him and put him in a water tank. I don't know whether it happened or not, but the farmers were in command of the situation. A lot of such stories.

They threatened to hang this judge up in Le Mars, Iowa. They stripped him and put a rope around his neck.* My dad and his cronies talked about this all the time, so it's pretty well embedded in my mind.

Roosevelt called up Milo Reno.† He said, "You got a revolution going on out there." Reno said, "Boy, I sure have." So Roosevelt went to Congress and said, "Listen, by God, you better do something because these farmers are revolting, tipping over trucks and hanging judges. You sure as hell better do something."

So it's interesting how changes are made. Some in the Roosevelt administration were sympathetic, like this guy, Tugwell.‡ They come up with the idea of parity and nonrecourse loans. It was like a minimum wage for farmers. Parity is the relationship of what farmers buy with what they sell. Today, in the '90s, parity is even lower than when we had ten-cent corn and two-cent hogs. No price at all for sheep.

A lot of the reforms took the fire out of the protest. What triggered it off in the '30s was that it hit all the farmers at the same time. One of the reasons labor has more unity than farmers is because it happens to everybody in the factory at the same time. More recently, we've had ups and downs in agriculture. In certain areas, crops have been tolerable and acceptable, but in other things, farmers have been going broke pretty bad. Remember, the tractors went to Washington in 1977.§ I was among them. It was pretty bad then, but it's gotten much worse since.

There are some farmers who are militant and try to do something about it, but there's a lot in different stages of bankruptcy who don't identify with the worst off. These early movements—the Farmers' Alliance, the Non-Partisan League, the Populists—were a much

---

* "The Judge Bradley deal came on quite unexpectedly. A group came down from Sioux City. They heard about this farm sale here and set out to stop it. Maybe a hundred or more farmers. So they went to the courthouse to interview Judge Bradley. He was belligerent and defiant. They took him out, not intending any more than talk to him. But as things went on, they took him out in the country and threatened to lynch him, which they wouldn't have done, of course.

—Orrin Kelly, in *Hard Times: An Oral History of The Great Depression,* 1970

† President of the Farm Holiday Association, the most militant of the farmers' protest groups in the '30s.

‡ A member of Roosevelt's Brain Trust and head of the Farm Security Administration.

§ Desperate farmers drove the tractors from the Midwest to Washington, D.C., to protest the government's failure to address the needs of farmers.

broader group. They had more understanding. They were pro-labor. They understood that working people and farmers had a lot in common. They had a much better social conscience than farmers do nowadays. We've been brainwashed.

These early movements were suspicious of big business. That's how we got the Sherman Anti-Trust Law—pressure from below. Teddy Roosevelt was supposed to be the big trust buster, which is a bunch of baloney. He was forced to take that position because of pressure from down below.

Today, most people's attitude toward the big global transnational corporations is that they're friendly giants. In the '30s, most people instinctively knew that big business would put you to the wall, that they were not your friend. People knew they were out for super-profits and that was it. The Cold War undressed a lot of people and stole their class consciousness.

There's been a tremendous program of divide and conquer. In the '80s, there were these extreme right-wing groups playing the phony populist game and filling people with all sorts of propaganda, confusing them. There were some frightening incidents in Kansas and Nebraska.

Do you know that today's most profitable sector in the U.S. economy is the food industry? Corporate agribusiness is even more profitable than the health business. It's more profitable than the arms industry with its $400 toilet seats. Cargill, the biggest corporate agribusiness, is in sixty countries. Conagra is in twenty-three. Absolutely multinational.

They are not only setting farm, trade, and food policies for the United States, they set them for the world. I was with Jesse Jackson when he toured Africa in 1986.* I talked with a lot of commissioners of agriculture while he was talking to heads of state. I asked the commissioner in Tanzania, "How do you set farm prices?" They had a kind of socialist economy. He said, "Oh, that's easy, the Chicago Board of Trade."

A CEO of Cargill Investor Services went to the Department of Agriculture during the Reagan-Bush years. He wrote the farm bill and the trade policies and then came back to the board of Cargill. So agribusiness's biggest gun wrote our farm bill. When Clayton Yoder left as secretary of agriculture, he joined the board of Conagra. Here he was administering a farm program he didn't believe in. He suggested that the farmers use the Board of Trade as a marketing strategy.

---

* Jackson carried a lot of rural counties in the 1988 election. In Buffalo County, Nebraska, he got 42 percent of the vote. It was amazing, but he was talking stuff that made sense to these farmers.

Of the two million farmers today, there's only about six hundred thousand who are serious farmers. They're what's left out of the six million in '45. Talk about a massive holocaust. Eighty-five to 89 percent of total farm income is from off-farm sources. In order to survive on the farm, they have to hold down a job in town.

People have to understand that the farm question is an important part of the total picture of peace and justice. A fifth part of the U.S. and world economy has to do with farm and food transactions. [*Almost shouting.*] In the last election, the farm question was hardly even mentioned. How can you deal with this?

We've got to stop pretending that we have a supply-and-demand economy when just two or three companies control over half the world's shipments of grain, 80 percent of the beef slaughter, and most of the chicken slaughter. One company has 70 percent of the soup market. Do we think for a moment that these people are interested in a free market? They play a game. I call it: "Every man for himself, he shouted, as he danced among the chickens."

We have the capacity to feed everyone in the world with a 3,000-calories-a-day diet, yet 786 million people are hungry, malnourished, or starving. It was 200 million in 1950. How successful is our food policy? [*Shouts.*] It is not. And it has practically destroyed the family farm in the United States.

The philosophy of the populists was that you can't have political democracy if you don't have economic democracy. Justice Brandeis put it plainly: "You can have democracy in this country or you can have great wealth concentrated in the hands of a few, but you can't have both." When I get a chance, I go out and talk about this thing, write about it, and preach about it.

There was a time when I was an outcast in my own neighborhood, but that is not true today. When I opposed the Vietnam War, people wrote me letters threatening to kill my cattle and saying that I was a terrible, unpatriotic person. My kids paid dearly for it. Our car was vandalized, and in school our kids were taunted and called Communists. My son was starting to wear long hair and, boy, were they out to get him. He's a football player and a pretty tough guy, but about four or five damn hoodlums caught him in town and roughed him up. Today, when he comes to Newman Grove and speaks as president of the Farmers Union, some of these very same people say he's really good.

Oh, things have changed today. I'm more respected in this community than I've ever been. I haven't changed, my neighborhood has changed—and for the better. We talk about a lot of things, about what's really hurting today. They know they're only one mistake away from being totally wiped out.

They're not always sore at the right people. This is the tragedy of America. We often chase the wrong rabbit. We have to try to convince people who their allies are and who their real enemies are.

Unfortunately, I don't get around as much as I used to. But I'm still sounding off about coalitions, about tying all the issues together. Whether we'll succeed or not, I don't know, but you've got to keep trying.

I'm active in Nebraskans for Peace and I have been for years. Some of these young people that come around are absolutely precious. They understand, they listen, they want to talk about it. And there's others who've bought the other thing. From early on, there's always been two Americas: the people who believed in slavery and those who didn't, those who believed in the women's right to vote and those who didn't. The same way with farm policy. I think we've lost a lot of that healthy dissent.

I think the most important thing for people to do now is organize grass-roots groups, where people get together and learn how to do things. It's like school, where you learn how to read and write. With these groups, you learn how to encounter people and win them over to an idea. Nebraska is about 95 percent rural, but if I could get ten active, well-organized, well-informed people in each county, I could come pretty close to running this state.

It's okay to run to Washington to convince politicians to take legislative action, but the real victories are won when we expand our ideas, learn how the process works, and organize. A lot of victories we win are lost, because we're not organized to keep them. People get cynical if they feel they can't do anything.

Whether people like it or not, they'll have to do something to defend their rights, because they're losing them. Our standard of living is skidding downhill. As our environment is deteriorating, so are our rights. What better thing can you do with your life than to try to build a more just world? When I run into my neighbors, they want to talk to me. The feeling is there.

When I was a kid, I didn't go to church on Sundays. My father would have some of his old cronies over or we'd go visit them. There were dozens and dozens of old populists in the community in those days. This was their tradition, talking it out, arguing, wonderful debates. We just don't have this core anymore. When the Farm Holiday Association sprung up in the '30s, people like that come out of the woodwork. They knew what it was about.

My father never went through fifth grade, but he used to read. I am appalled today that even in the progressive farm movement, they don't read something like *The Nation* or *The Progressive*. There's information there you don't get in the regular press. They need this desperately. You've got to put some gas in the tank if you're going to go anyplace. When they do read, it's trivial stuff or slanted the big business way. I worry about these talk radio shows, like Limbaugh's, that turn history upside down every day. We have several here in Nebraska.

In the slavery days, if the master found out his slaves knew how to read, he'd kill 'em. We desperately need truth seekers. I have a farmer friend who likes to say, "The trouble is we know so damn much that ain't true." What we're faced with is unlearning a whole bunch of stuff, and we've gotta start learning something about a new world. Yeah, I'm still preaching, you bet.

CHAPTER SEVEN

Songs My Mother Taught Me

Russell Knapp, 85

CEDAR RAPIDS, IOWA

He has a vigorous, midwestern voice, imbued with the enthusiasm of youth.

In August 1938, I started Knapp & Company: money management, stock, and business. I figured that I wasn't too bright about managing money, but the worst that could happen to me was that I'd learn how to make money with money. My goal was, of course, to succeed.

I had graduated from Coe College in 1930 and staggered around with the idea of becoming a social worker. But I went into business and it was a struggle—working for a manufacturing company, insurance, stocks and bonds. So I took the big step, to go out on my own.

What played a major role in my life was the acute nephritis I suffered from when I was nine years of age. There was no cure for it in those days. Our expert doctor told my mother there was one chance in a thousand of my surviving, that I would not live to be twenty-one. Adversity, a challenge such as this, proved valuable for me.

My parents were quality people and the church was very important to them. Methodists. My father was in real estate, one of the first in Cedar Rapids. We were quite poor in cash. Back when women didn't work, my mother was employed in the youth program of the Methodist church.

When I was about seventeen, feeling my life would be short, I had a decision to make. I could go for all the bad things in life and have a great, short time of it. Or I could do as much good as possible in that brief time left. It was a wonderful base for a whole lifetime. Religion became terribly important to me. In my college freshman year, I led the boys' club at the Presbyterian church and taught Sunday school classes.

Religion is still important to me. God first, others second, and self third. A balanced life. Coming out of a time of critical sickness, it was the trick of keeping in wonderful shape, by doing something you enjoy. My health today is magnificent.

Fifteen years ago, forty-five years of age was the oldest for competitive U.S. Lawn Association–approved tournaments. Now we're up to eighty-five. When I was seventy, I was the young kid on the lot. Now I'm the oldest of the nationally ranked in senior tennis.

I still work half time at my business. Knapp & Company became a financial group that has four or five corporations. The young people who took over have made the company a real good one. And they kept me around. I was at the office at 8:15 this morning and worked till 12:30. The last few weeks I've been awfully busy and worked much more than that. That's my goal, half-time at work. I close my door and do creative thinking.

I find in going to church I may get an idea from the minister on Sunday and let it affect me, apply it to my business. I feel it makes me a much better person. I don't understand all the Christian principles, but I find that they work.

This has all been a conscious move on my part. Money is not my real goal in life. Never has been. I've dedicated myself to support nonprofit groups. Sure, I'm on the boards of Coe College, St. Paul's Church, and St. Luke's Hospital, but it's the Knapp Foundation that most interests me. We channel out money to these places. It's hard to give away money, but we've become adept at it.

I learned finance the hard way. I learned very quickly that you've got to give your clients written reports regularly and show them whether you're making them any money or not. We gave them professional management services without charge and let them make their own decisions. Right now, we're managing about $450 million for people all over the country.

I had a hard time in 1948, '49, with the state insurance commissioner. He became very technical. He had been an unsuccessful broker himself. Fortunately, he lived only for a couple of years after, but he made my life miserable for that year and almost put me out of business. Yet that hardship was the best thing that could have happened to me. I kept the door open and worked without pay. And learned.

I took an extension course in finance. The first lesson was Benjamin Graham's *Intelligent Investor*, which became the motto of Warren Buffet, our country's wealthiest man. My whole life was influenced by Graham, who taught you what a stock ought to be worth, when to buy, when to sell.

The field is very competitive. Of the companies that started in 1938, almost every small company went broke or was merged into a larger one. We are the largest of the independent companies in Iowa. Our family owns the majority of our company. Almost all of our employees, and associates own stock. We have a source data company, software for hospitals, 313 employees.

We went into the mini-crash of 1987 with no debt. It was a frightening day. From our economic analysis, we started looking for stocks to buy. Remember, we studied market trends forty-five years ago. Our basic guide told us to make sure we had no debts. So about ten days before the October '87 crash, I paid off any indebtedness, built up some reserves, and I was ready to buy. On the downside and on the rebound, we did very well for our clients.

Joe Kennedy in '29 shorted the market and made a fortune. Think of how much he could have made in 1987. He was that smart. He was in a class by himself. As far as the '87 market went, we made an opportunity out of something disastrous. I'll never forget that day. But it proved that the world hadn't come to an end.

I'm a born optimist. I think we live in the most wonderful time in history. Recognizing many of our problems, of course. I feel very, very good as to the future outlook of our country. The next ten years will be the happiest, most prosperous that you can imagine in America, Europe, and Asia. During the last few years, we've seen some of the greatest turning points in history. We have a world free of nuclear war. The threat of communism, with which we've lived virtually our whole life, is gone.

When you look at the history, it took over a thousand years to double the standard of living. Some of my heroes feel that in the next forty years, we may be enjoying four times the standard of living we have now. One hundred fifty years ago, it took 85 percent of the people in America and Canada just to produce food. Now it takes only 3 percent. In medicine, we've learned 50 percent of it in the last twenty years. Life expectancy is greater than ever, of course.

We realize there are tragic areas of the world, Somalia, for one, where the situation is awful. We've had that type of thing always, but for the have-nots, their standard of living is a heck of a lot higher than it was. We're more conscious of people that are homeless and whatnot. We realize there are extremes, but in the last eighty-five years, the world's standard of living has quadrupled.

With the new technology, the people who are not well educated and trained, that's the type there aren't many jobs for. I think we'll see more and more effort to re-educate and retrain, to bring people back into jobs, where there are jobs.

You win a lot more ball games if you're expecting to be a winner, and your life is a heck of a lot better if you're looking at a half-full glass rather than a half-empty.

I'm a Republican and would like to be idealistic, but I always want to be completely honest, so I must say that some of my great Republican leaders aren't much different from the Democrats. Not anymore. Reagan wasn't great, but he helped build back our esteem and our muscle and our power so that Russia went broke first. [*A slight laugh.*] My wife and I respected and liked Barbara and George Bush very much as people. But again, I must say there is little difference between our two parties today.

The young people of Cedar Rapids are just wonderful, as good as they have ever been. Of course, you'll always have about 10 percent that are not great persons. But the work ethic of our young people around here is just tops. It's remarkable about these girls in our workforce today: how they can be raising babies and working virtually full time. We have twenty, twenty-two babies a year born to our employees. But, gosh, they do a wonderful job, keeping their families going and at work.

Our company's success is what the American way of life is all about. You stick your neck out, start a little business, you hire some people, first a few, then a lot, and that's the way our nation grows.

Cedar Rapids is surely one of the great cities of our country. It's partly because of our leadership. We have a foundation of one family that helped found Quaker Oats and whatnot that gave away $37 million over the last twenty years, and the Hall Foundation that's given away $45 million. They have put it back in the community. Our Cedar Rapids Symphony was written up in *Time* as one that's on the move. We have a magnificent museum of art. Our city is on the move.

We greatly admire the older people who are around here. We don't pay any attention to age. Our supper group that started about fifty years ago is down to about twelve or fourteen, but we've been friends all our lives. My contemporaries, doctors and lawyers, we eat lunch every Tuesday noon.

Of our four children, two still live in the community, a third in Virginia, and my youngest in London. She lived in Kenya for several years. We had twelve grandchildren, but one was killed in Somalia, July 12, 1993. He was a great photographer, for Reuters. He was only twenty-two. We'll have an exhibition of his photographs at our museum of art.

This mother of mine, who saved my life when I was nine, lived to be 106 and two-thirds. She died just two years ago. She lost her hearing, and she lost her eyesight, but her mind was sharp all her life. She dictated into tapes when she was 102. She published a book about her year at Drake in 1903. I still make long-range plans. I may get knocked out of the ball game, but I'm going for 110.

If I can be the fifteenth best tennis player at eighty-five, I want to be in the top ten when I'm ninety. You don't have to be number one. The main thing is to be in condition to do your very best. The balanced life, remember that.

Any regrets? There are few times in your life where you can really stand up and be counted. I remember some years ago, in our church, we had a marvelous colored doctor, Dr. Percy Harris. The chairman of the board sold him a lot in the finest residential area of Cedar Rapids. Some members of the church didn't like it. I remember at this particular meeting, there was one moment when they wanted somebody to stand up and actually say what they believed. I was one of the church leaders and for the sale. For some reason, I let somebody else do it. The majority stood up and voted for the sale. Our minister had always taught us that people are equal and not to be judged by color. [*Muses.*] Forty years ago. It was the most spectacular meeting in the history of our church. But there was that one moment, when they needed somebody in leadership to stand up. Somebody else did. It was my position to do so...Well, I don't spend much time thinking on the past.

Hazel Wolf, 95

SEATTLE, WASHINGTON

She's at the front door of her large apartment building, welcoming her guest. Small-boned, birdlike, an image of Ruth Gordon is immediately evoked. It is bitter cold, but no matter—she is at the door in a T-shirt.

In her apartment's study are a word processor, a laser printer, and a well-thumbed Rolodex, among other contemporary appurtenances. On the wall hang all sorts of plaques and certificates: Audobon Society awards (she has been secretary of the regional chapter for twenty-six years); a Wild Life Federation recognition; a cover photograph on USA Today, *with the caption "Baby Boomers Take Heart: Ninety in the '90s."*

I came here from Canada in 1923 to find a better life. There was a serious depression right after the First World War and thousands of Canadians came here for jobs. Since I was white and spoke English, I got a job and here I am.

My father, a seaman, died when I was very young and left my mother with three children to support. She had little education but lots of ideas. She worked in an overalls factory and belonged to the IWW.* She didn't believe in institutions, never voted, had no respect for judges, and wouldn't let my brother join the Boy Scouts because it was military.

I went to union meetings in Seattle with her when I was little. After World War I, they had a massacre in Everest, a lynching in Centralia, and the IWW was destroyed.†

In 1930, I wrote a radio play about the Centralia massacre. All the actors were from skid row. At rehearsal, the station manager blew his top for the swear words: "God damn," "Jesus Christ," "hell." So we had to put in "gee whiz" and "golly." The show was live, and the guys forgot the "gee whizzes" and used the swear words.

I was overtaken by the depression in the '30s. During that time I was on welfare and joined the Communist party. I belonged about thirteen years, got bored, and drifted away.

Want to know how I joined? A man was passing out a petition for unemployment insurance. It was unheard of back in those days. He

---

* International Workers of the World.

† Two towns in the state of Washington. In each instance, a vigilante posse was formed of merchants and the American Legion. They attacked IWW gatherings and killed several members.

said, "We don't expect it to pass. We're just doing this to educate people." "Who is 'we'?" I asked. "The Communist Party." So I went to a meeting, and then to a Workers Alliance demonstration that they had organized.

A woman was being evicted. The bailiffs were carrying out her furniture. We just came from the meeting and put her furniture back in. They brought it out the front door again and we put it in the back door. They finally got tired and went away.*

Fifteen years after I'd left the Party, McCarthy time, I was arrested to be deported to Canada. I was accused of trying to overthrow the government by force and violence. [*Laughs.*] When I got to jail, a woman in for something else asked me, "What are you here for?" I said, "I've been charged of trying to overthrow." I was an instant hero. I was their role model. I was in about half a day. I was trying to figure out a jigsaw puzzle and I never got to finish it. [*Laughs.*]

After fifteen years of litigation, most of it pro bono—I'd been up to the Supreme Court a number of times—the Immigration Department decided they'd had enough of me. Canada wouldn't take me. They were in sympathy with me. Also, a new legal precedent had been set: a prostitute had come from Canada; the U.S. tried to deport her, but couldn't because she had married an American. I was in the same boat, married to an American. So Canada didn't have to take me. I'm very grateful to that woman.

For twenty years, I worked as a legal secretary to John Coughlin,

---

* In 1968, I visited Mrs. Willye Jeffries in her South Side Chicago flat. She was a seventy-five-year-old wisp of a woman, African American.

"Now we had what was known as the Workers Alliance, Local 45, for which I was secretary and treasurer. We were going into relief stations, sometimes gettin' arrested two, three times a day. And puttin' people back in their homes.

"The bailiffs come and set them out. As soon as they leave, we would put them back where they came out. All we had to do was call Brother Hilton, he's about ninety-some-odd years now. Look, such and such a place, there's a family sitting out there now. Everybody passed through the neighborhood was a member of the Workers Alliance, had one person they would call. When one person came, he would have about fifty people with him.

"Well now, the landlords disconnect that stove and put that piece of pipe away. If it wasn't up to the ceiling, they'd take it, and just put the lights off. We had in the orginization some men who could do electrical work, see. We'd sneak around through the crowd, and all this nice furniture sittin' on the street, and sometimes it snowin'. It rained, but the men had tarpaulins and nothin' got ruined. Find out who owned it, see. 'If we put it back, would you stay there?' 'Yes.' 'All right, let's go.' Take that stuff right on back there. The men would connect those lights and go to the hardware store and get gas pipes and connect that stove back. Put the furniture back just like you had it, so it don't look like you been out the door."

—From *Hard Times: An Oral History of the Great Depreession*, 1970 a civil rights lawyer, who was always out front. I worked fourteen hours a day. We both starved to death. It was mostly pro bono—our clients were all broke.

I retired at sixty-seven, I get social security, $714, and a rent subsidy. I live on that easy.

What have I been doing lately? I travel quite a bit and I've been camping. I have a little tent, a sleeping bag, and a little pad. I go in the woods. I like that. You have to keep in touch with Mother Nature, it recharges your batteries. People in the cities are divorced from nature, have lost touch with their natural selves.

I have no medical coverage, so I can't get sick. I can't afford pills, so I live simply. I hate to cook, so I steam everything, mostly vegetables. I haven't bought meat in a couple of years, but I'm not a hardcore vegetarian. For breakfast, I'll have an egg, a piece of toast and a coffee. For lunch, a cheese sandwich and an apple. That keeps the doctor away. For dinner, I steam vegetables and maybe some rice in a foil. I don't make any sauces, I can't be bothered. For dessert, I have an orange because I don't have to cook it. [*Laughs.*]

If you work in the community, you don't have much time to worry about your own problems.

I don't have stress because I'm never angry. If I get mad, I'm only putting on an act. [*Laughs.*] Getting angry doesn't solve anything, and it might make a lot of enemies that you don't need to make.

Even when I was threatened with deportation, I never felt it was me they were attacking. It was Hazel Wolf out there, but not me personally. I didn't know who to get angry at, not the local people. They don't make policy. They were always kind to me. Even when they put me in jail, they did it gently. [*Laughs.*] There's somebody up there doing the hurting, but I don't know who they are, so how can I get mad at them?

A couple of years before I retired, a friend invited me to join the Audobon Society. I wasn't interested in joining a bunch of bird watchers. To get her off my back, I went on a field trip. I used to hike and canoe and swim all the time. I won several medals as a child. But I never watched birds or looked at flowers or enjoyed the scenery.

This time, I watched this little bird going up a tree, pick, pick, pick. He got to the first lateral branch, went down to the bottom of the next tree, and went up again, pick, pick, pick. It always went up. I thought: This little bird works hard for a living just like I do. Pick, pick, pick, all day long. It has a lifestyle. I have a lifestyle, too. I get up in the morning, go to work, eat my lunch, go back to work, and go home. So I saw that little bird as a creature like myself.

You feel you're like a sparrow?

Yeah. They're streetwise. I am, too. [*She scurries to her appointment book.*] I'm seeing Maria Cantwell, our congresswoman, about saving our old-growth trees. Yesterday I saw Congressman Jim McDermott about NAFTA.* I'm against it. Last night, John Coughlin and I attended a lecture on Syria. Tomorrow, I have lunch with a labor historian about the IWW. Tonight, I'm due at a monthly precinct meeting. I'm a committee officer. If I don't have a meeting, I work in my office here.

The Audobon Society doesn't have enough clout to save the planet. We've got to win the rest of the community, pay attention to their concerns. We're trying to reach poor people and people of color. We all breathe the same polluted air. But in the industrial part of the city, where the poor people live, the air is more polluted there than it is up here. It has lead and arsenic and God knows what else. There's a river flowing through with PCB's and chemicals from the industries. They fish in that river. So we're trying to clean it up. It's an environmental issue with us, a health issue with them. We can work together here.

I talk to hundreds of young people, from kindergarten up—and down. With little kids of six and seven, I say funny things. "Squirrels hide nuts and put them away to eat later and then forget where they put them. I do that all the time. Do you?" They shout, "Yeah." So I say, "You're nothing but a bunch of little squirrels." Then I tell them about eagles and spreading wings, and about forests and how they work and how we need to save them.

I make speeches about great women in the world. Rachel Carson,† of course. I talk about great women in my life. My cousin, Lois, for example. When I was five, I began to wonder if I was pretty. It was so important then. I asked Lois. She looked at me appraisingly and said, "Hazel, you look very, very intelligent." From then on, I never wanted to look pretty. I always wanted to look intelligent. So I tell the young people this story and insist that I still look intelligent.

I think people all over the world are becoming more aware. The environmental movement has caught the fancy of young people, especially city kids. They have little self-esteem because they don't think they're important. Now you see them beginning to plant trees, take out garbage, pick up litter, recycle. It makes them feel they're of some use of the community.

---

* The North American Free Trade Agreement, which is intended to promote trade between the United States, Mexico, and Canada. Since the time of this interview, the agreement has been signed by President Clinton and approved by both houses of Congress.

† An early environmentalist, the author of the enormously influential *Silent Spring*.

[*She brings out an album of photographs.*] This is a class in Decatur, Alabama. A teacher saw my picture in *USA Today* and had her class write to me. I got thirty lovely letters. I didn't know if they were written by little black hands or little white hands. I've never been to the South, so I flew down there. At the airport, I had my answer. See those children? They were really integrated, much more than in our schools up north.

I answer any of their questions. Do you still have your own teeth? Do you have a boyfriend? I say, "No, but I'm looking for one who can cook. If you find somebody like that, let me know." They think it's funny.

They want to know how it feels to be ninety. I tell them I feel like myself. Don't you all feel like yourself? Okay, there's a difference. When I was your age, I loved to play basketball and climb mountains and slide down the other side. One thing I didn't want to do was make speeches. It was scary. Now I don't want to climb mountains and play basketball. I love to make speeches. So you see, when you're ninety, you'll do what you feel like doing. In a way, I'm telling them to value old age and respect it.

Native Americans have respect for old people. I visited all the tribes in 1979, setting up conferences of environmentalists and Native Americans. Our society is set up in such a way that we don't rely on the memory of old people. It's all in computers. So they are not able to contribute when they get old, and are neglected. I'm lucky, I have five grandchildren, five great-grandchildren and a great-great-grandchild. They put up with me and I think are proud of me.

I feel hopeful. I used to worry about the nuclear war, but that seems to be put in the background for the time being. I think that we, the people of the world, are going to get together and save the planet, because it's in our genes. We're kind of a sorry species, the human. We don't run very fast, we don't swim well, we don't have good eyesight, we don't hear very well. We wouldn't have survived if we hadn't got together. "Gregarious" is the word for us.

The wolves are gregarious. So are the bees and the ants. In order to survive, they have to get together. It's in their genes. So it is in our genes. The worst punishment you can give to a human being is solitary confinement. We cleave to each other. All the great religions have as their golden core the vision of brotherhood, even though they have a very bad track record.

We ganged up in the early process of evolution to save our species. I feel hopeful we'll gang up again to save this planet through our spirituality. By the way, I'm an atheist.

If there's a gathering in my memory, I hope it's a fund-raiser for a good cause. [*Laughs.*] You could have music, but I'm not going to be listening. I really don't care whether I'm remembered or not. I'll be remembered by the people who outlive me, and when they all die, the memory of me will be gone. But we all make our imprint one way or another. So why worry? What you do when you're alive is what counts. I was born in 1898. I'm going to live till the year 2000, so I can have been in three centuries. Then I'm going.

Part III

CHAPTER EIGHT

The Muse

Jacob Lawrence, 76
SEATTLE, WASHINGTON

We're in his studio on the second floor of his frame house, where he lives with his wife, Gwen, also a painter. On the walls are some of his works in progress. On the tables are hand tools: hammer, chisel, plane, brushes. There is an impromptu, easy touch here; not at all precisely arranged. Everything he may need appears to be comfortably at hand.

He retired from teaching at the University of Washington nine years ago.

This is what my day is like. I sit here, I'm looking at my works, I'm reading, I'll go back to my drawing table, do some drawing. That's more or less it. Of course we go shopping because we have to eat. But this is my place, this is where I work.

I work constantly. I look at my tools here. I'm not a cabinetmaker, but I use them. I love to look at hand tools. They're beautiful to see, to feel. They're a symbol of working, of building. I use them that way.

The tool is an extension of the hand. The hand is a very beautiful instrument. Think of what we can do with the hand, its dexterity. It's been with us hundreds of years. You look at works of art and the tool hasn't changed. It maintains its beauty. It's like a work of sculpture. I like to pick it up, look it, turn it. I use them in my paintings as I would in a still life. To me, these tools are alive.

About a year ago, his series of panels—moments in the lives of Harriet Tubman and Frederick Douglass—were on exhibition in a number of American museums. At the Chicago Art Institute, he was a gracious guide as we strolled past each painting. It was something of a promenade: Mussorgsky's Pictures at an Exhibition *came to my mind's ear. "It is the spirit of our country. The largeness of spirit of our country. The largeness of spirits of our country. The largeness of spirits like Harriet Tubman, Frederick Douglass, John Brown, Abraham Lincoln is what made our country what it is."*

How I became an artist? In elementary school, we were given crayons, poster paint, and were encouraged to put down color. In the great 1930s, I heard stories from older people. They'd talked about heros and heroines of an earlier day. They'd talk about Marcus Garvey, John Brown, Harriet Tubman, Frederick Douglass. I'd walk the streets of Harlem and hear corner orators talk about these people. It inspired me. I realized I couldn't tell their lives in one story, so I painted a series of their lives.

It is ironic that people like myself benefited from the Great Depression. The Roosevelt administration established programs where people of all ages could receive lessons in these art centers in whatever field attracted us: dance, music, theater, painting, sculpture. It lasted about five years, a wonderful, wonderful period.

I went into one of these federal art centers as a youngster. I was about sixteen. I didn't have the means of going to college, but at these centers I was encouraged and taught by elders. Librarians, teachers, the YMCA, the church—they all took an interest in us. There was a spirit of uplift. Too bad a depression had to come along to do this, but it was wonderful for people my age, some of them now renowned. Even today, in post offices, you'll see some of their murals.*

It's too bad we don't have more of that today—government support of the arts. In schools, the first programs cut back are music, dance, the arts. If we don't realize how much these things contribute to the quality of life, we'll lose it. I see these youngsters on the street, never exposed to this experience—they've lost it, their chance at that life.

When I was growing up, everybody took an interest in us kids. The neighborhood was very tight. You'd go out on the street, you'd know just about everybody around, even if you didn't know them by name. There was a great pride in that. We were poor, but we had so much in another way: the love of the community.

If it weren't for these federal programs, I probably would have been lost and drifting like so many young people were, without any sense of belonging. I dread to think what would have happened to me. Today I go out on the street and I look at these children, twelve, thirteen years old. Where will they be five years from now? Our society today doesn't recognize what potential may be in them.

---

* On the walls of the cafeteria of Lane Technical High School in Chicago are such murals—Americans at work—courtesy of the WPA (Work Progress Administration)

What happened to me was a sense of appreciation of the human being. This feeling was developed in me, a sense of the worthiness of the person. This is what I try to get in my work. That's why I grasp the tools so much. What Walt Whitman put into words, I try to do with my tools as a painter.

I grew up in a big city, New York, with all those tall buildings. The spirit of the times encouraged an appreciation of color, of form, of texture, of just the beauty of looking at things. I heard hammering, people calling out to one another, people building. I became conscious of hearing the jackhammer, hearing a nail being driven in, hearing people walking the streets.*

I was hearing and trying to visualize these sounds. The sense of being acute to these sounds has remained with me to this day.

I haven't changed. I'm afraid our society has. Today there seems to be a lack of communication. We don't touch. There is a coldness. I don't come in contact with you, you don't with me. I just don't know what it means.

In the 1930s, there was something going on, a human kind of communication. Words meant something. Today we're ashamed to express these feelings. A few years ago, the kids in school started a program called Touch. They were looking for something. That meant there was something lacking. We didn't have to think of such a program. It was just a natural kind of thing.

The young today are timid about expressing any kind of feeling. They're afraid to bare themselves. They're afraid they might be considered soft.

How can you explain why people have become the way they are? Maybe technology running wild has something to do with it. Everything has become so mechanical. It's frustrating, the telelphone. I hesitate. You don't hear a person. It's a machine. Maybe to a young person, it is natural—to me, it is not.† I'm not averse to technology,

---

* In 1965, Jessie Binford, ninety, a colleague of Jane Addams, was reflecting on her home town, Marshalltown, Iowa, to which she returned for her last years: "Nobody walks here anymore. He jumps into his car, of course. I walk more than anyone else in this town. I'm often the only one on the street. I'd much rather get out in the evening at sunset and walk here than get into a car, with probably all the windows closed. The commonest thing I hear in this town is fear, fear of the unknown."   —*Division Street: America*, 1967

In 1970, my wife and I were walking along the street of a small South Dakota town. It was about nine o'clock at night. We were the sole pedestrians. A police car slowed down; the officer solicitously inquired: "What are you doing out at this hour? Are you lost?"

† Buckminster Fuller reflected on his grandchild: "She heard the sound of the airplane before she heard the song of the nightingale. To her, the first sound was natural, the second, unnatural."

but not, if in developing it, we lose something else. We must become aware of this other thing we're sacrificing.

Some students feel good about not coming into contact with a canvas or with paper. It's done by machine. They say: "My hand never touched it." This is a plus, the way they think. They don't feel the paper, they don't feel the canvas. It's all machine. They plug something in and they can do a portrait by computer. A student can come back that same day and bring you a portrait of yourself, without his having laid a finger on the brush, canvas, or paper. He hasn't seen you breathing, blinking, nothing like that. The air all around you is not there. There's no space. Throughout our history, these have been important factors in making a work of art.

Hammer? Chisel? Feel of the hairs of a brush? They don't want to be accused by their peers of succumbing to this human thing: touch. They'd be ashamed. Distance has become a plus to their peers and to themselves.

Maybe one day we'll live in a world of robots, a world of mechanical devices. Fortunately, I won't be alive. I feel this way more now than I did a few years ago. I feel this drawing back.

I'm retired now. I retired from teaching at the University of Washington in 1984. I loved working with the students, but you get to the point where you leave it to the younger people. I didn't retire from painting. I never will.

In school, young students want young professors. They want someone closer to their own age. That the older person may offer so much in experience doesn't matter that much to them. I've heard my students say they don't want old professors. They mean somebody forty, fifty. They turn their backs to them.

If you get to be forty, fifty, you're old. The students show their disdain. It's not always meant to be cruel, it's not always absolute, but you get it. When they say they want someone closer to their own age, they mean someone two years older. You get it in all of our advertisements, too. Insurance companies don't want to insure you. You've outlived your time. It's the attitude that we're living too long—the resources can't support us. I definitely feel this generation gap. The irony is that we have worked and contributed to the young people all of our lives.

I feel there should be more emphasis on the humanities in the home as well as in the school. The importance of the church, too. I didn't just go to church on Sunday. I went to church two or three times a week. I was taught certain values which have remained with me to this day. You don't do certain things, even though you thought you could get away with it.

When I was a youngster growing up, a person would never attack an older person, a weaker person, because of the fear of God. Now the older person is vulnerable because of something lost, a sense of morality, of ethics. How can we have that in the streets if we don't have it in the higher places? Look at our leaders, committing all sorts of crimes, then going free. Roosevelt's people weren't all saints, but there was a quality there, a feeling we don't get today.

Are we about to give up that which we have as human beings? Are we losing it little by little. What price are we paying? Maybe there are people talking and thinking the way we are right now. Maybe we can prevent this. Maybe we can mantain the quality that we might be losing.

I'm not pessimistic. I think about these things. I talk about them. I feel as long as there's one person or two people who are aware of this quality, of our capacity to think and feel, we're on pretty sound ground. I hope so.

Katherine Kuh, 89

CHICAGO, ILLINOIS

The first curator of modern art at Chicago's Art Institute; art critic of the Saturday Review of Literature; *art collector; writer. From her bed of pain (she has long suffered debilitating ills), she free associates.*

"The pain I feel is so terribly severe, but I've made up my mind not to take pain killers. My mind is dulled by them, and I'd like to think clearly to finish the book. When I'm lying down, breathing is fine. [Laughs.] I've written every word longhand, lying down with a board on my knees. The only thing I find difficulty with is remembering names. It's so frustrating."

I had no idea I was going to live this long. My main preoccupation, my delight, my life had revolved around the visual arts. Before I die, I'm trying to finish a book about this subject: What happened in my century? What have I seen? How has it changed?

The two enormous catastrophes of our century, the two world wars, totally changed art. The two creative personalities who changed art, though they had nothing to do specifically with art, were Freud and Einstein. Surrealism came out of Freud. From Einstein came the whole idea of time. Without him, there would have been no cubism.

I've been thinking about this for months: What made the first half of the twentieth century so rich, so innovative, so creative, and the art of the second half so sterile? It isn't just because I'm older. I think it has to do with the two wars.

We were in Europe when the First World War broke out. My father was a silk importer. I was a child of ten, at which point I developed polio, from which I've been lame ever since. This is a disease that is now killing me, 'cause I have a thing called post-polio syndrome. I'm very crooked because all the original paralysis comes back. The muscles and all the other parts of your body give out. All the bones are in the wrong place, driving into my lungs and preventing me from breathing. It should have killed me years ago. [*Laughs.*] It hasn't. I can hardly walk, but I'm still getting along.

One of my earliest polio memories was siting propped up at the window of a Paris hotel, watching the troops from the Battle of the Marne being brought back in taxicabs, all wounded and bloody. The front was almost at Paris. You could hear the shelling. It's a sight you'd never forget.

We believed it was the war to end all wars. We believed that out of this horror would come something new and fresh and good. That's what people believed, and the art shows it.

At first, you had the art of negation: dadaism. It was a denial of everything rational, because we were not accustomed to that scale of killing. Yet out of this chaos came the great innovative movements of the twentieth century. It grew right out of the life of our times. I don't think you can divide art and history. Without knowing about history, you might as well forget art.

Cubism bows to any form of simultaneity. You see everything at once. It was a taking things apart and then putting them together. You see a man on all sides broken up. You see a still life, and then it's put together in a new way. It had a lot to do with the idea of time, space, and immediacy. Thanks to Einstein, the artists began to see things almost clairvoyantly, in advance of their time.

I think it had to do with the war, too. When World War II ended, we almost had to close our minds to the impossible behavior of human beings. It was nearly unbearable. We began to accept the fact that human beings killing other human beings, hating others irrationally, a brutality we never before conceived of, will always be with us. Out of it came a quite sterile era in the arts—the last half of the century. Our hopelessness bred it.

One man, Picasso, with his tremendous creativity, dominated the first half of the century. The second half was dominated by a man I knew quite well, Marcel Duchamps. I admired him enormously. But he was a nihilist, especially in regard to painting. Let's face it, Duchamps, a man of profound wit and intellect, was tremendously famous or infamous [*laughs*] by the time he was in his mid-twenties, when he decided to stop painting forever. He felt it was useless. He stopped not in midstream, but very, very early. He simply reacted *against* and stopped working. By the very sterility of this thinking, he has now been rediscovered, has an enormous following. Duchamps, despite this, always kept his memory golden, don't forget that. He knew what it was all about. He knew the past. But he hated the whole idea of emotions. He wanted it all to be cerebral. And minimal. That's what we've got now. That's what art is today.

Though Duchamps preceded World War II, his influence did not affect us till later. After World War I, even though nihilism was setting in, we began to think the world could improve. Then came Hitler.

With the Second World War, American art became important. A large group of highly creative and innovative artists escaped from Europe and came here, especially men like Max Ernst and Ferdinand Leger. Their surrealism had enormous influence on young American artists, who eventually became abstract expressionists. Of these, Jackson Pollock was the one who most challenged our thinking.

I'm on a foundation that gives out fellowships to artists. I judged a show yesterday, from one until nine. I was shocked by the brutality of the work. This was so frightening. The artists were mostly untrained and were totally unable to draw a line. They just schmeer around. Some were obviously furious, technically all right, but so explicit it was painful. It had nothing to do with art but anger. I think it's going to change art, too. Out of this mess may come something, I know not what. It's kind of scary.

There is a show at a California modern museum of some sort, exclusively of conceptual art, whatever that is. The curator is very proud of it. One of her artists, the star of the show, wrote her a letter stipulating that his work is never to be seen on any wall, never to be shown. It's only to be described in the catalog. That's cerebral art. Never mind emotion.

The abstract expressionists were the opposite. They were interested in expressing their own selves at the moment of painting. Pollock was innovative in an American way, in an emotional way. I think the abstract expressionists were among the most emotional painters of this half-century. They were representing our freshness, our newness, America's feeling that anything was possible. They were highly personal. They were reflecting themselves as they worked, the immediacy of life.

Some of the European artists detested their work. Because they were highly planned in their approach, they considered this American art to be a disgusting self-indulgence. I happen to be very eclectic in taste. I loved some of the European artists. They all influenced me. I've given a lot of the stuff away—to Oberlin, the Whitney, and before it got so terrible, to the Guggenheim, to the Museum of Modern Art, and the Art Institute. Duchamps had given me a lot of Man Ray paintings. You must visit my apartment and see some of these works before I die.

Ironically, even though he influenced them, Duchamps felt contempt for what they did. He told me when he was here that he couldn't stand them. With his Old World wisdom and his sense of humor, he had little patience for the abstract expressionists. It's true, they're not very humorous. I never detected any laughs in them. They were hell-bent on what they were doing.

I think they were wonderful artists. I don't think it matters if they were self-indulgent. If you can do it, that's all that counts.

You know the only kind of art that bores me? Art that is so technically infirm, it's not worth looking at. And art that is regimented. I'm really interested in the pioneers, the innovators. The abstract impressionists were pioneers. I'm not disturbed by the stuff I see today. I wish I were disturbed. I'm bored to death.

I believe these last forty, fifty years are a period of rest. I have no idea what will emerge. I won't be around long enough to know. There is always change. Right now, I'm anti what passes for art today. We had a hundred years of creative art: the second half of the nineteenth century and the first half of the twentieth. Picasso, of course, was the quintessential spirit. That's why I'm trying like the dickens to finish this book as we enter a new century.

I graduated from Vassar in 1925. It was quite anti-Semitic and narrow in those days. I got my master's in art history at the University of Chicago. I married a Chicago businessman with whom I didn't stay very long. [*Laughs.*] I never married again because I couldn't have children. So I decided to live the way I wanted, have a professional life. The reason I don't regret dying is because I've really had a good time.

I left Chicago in 1959. My career there was a roller coaster, beginning with my gallery in 1935. I showed all the unpopular pioneers: Mondrian, Klee, Kandinsky, Leger, Picasso. I bought a Kandinsky for five dollars, at an auction long, long ago. I supported the gallery by teaching art history.

The Chicago critics hated my gallery, the *Tribune* in particular. Actually, people came and smashed my plate-glass window with a brick, so furious were they with Klee and Miró. It was done at night. They called me a Red.

After I gave up the gallery—it was definitely not in fashion—I got a state job, dealing with venereal disease. I found the prostitutes tremendously interesting people. I'd never met one before. They got quite fond of me because I would sit and talk to them and listen to their stories. Of course, I was fired. So I went back to art.

Daniel Caton Rich, the director of the Art Institute, knew all about my interests, and made me its first curator of modern art. When I acquired a de Kooning and a Jackson Pollock, after a very tough time raising the money, the *Tribune*'s art column bore the headline KUH-KUH MUST GO. While I was there, you might say that I pioneered. That's why I didn't get along with the Lake Forest trustees. These Respectables were far more dangerous than any street gang. After Dan left, I had no one to back me, so I skiddooed.

I moved to New York and became the art critic of the *Saturday Review of Literature*. I forget how long I was there—many, many years. When Norman Cousins sold it, I resigned. After I'd been there six months, the *Chicago Tribune* suggested that a write a monthly column, a roundup of art in New York. I found the old clipping and sent it back to them, with a one-sentence note: "Kuh-Kuh cannot come to your aid."

While in New York, I worked for eleven years, building up the art collection of the First National Bank of Chicago. I traveled all over the world for them. At first, I couldn't see myself working for a bank.

I didn't like bankers. [*Laughs.*] But Gaylord Freeman, the president, was wonderful. He gave me absolute freedom.

What about the Great Depression and American art? You lived through that time.

The WPA arts project was terrific. It brought millions of people to art. I think a lot of it was poor and some of it was wonderful. The idea of keeping those poor devils alive was essential. In the end, America was the richer for it.

I think museums today need a whole rethinking of their education departments. I had some idea, and a museum director said to me, "You're just as revolutionary as ever." [*Laughs.*] I said, "You'd better be, or you decay and die." A new millennium is approaching. You'd think we'd be on the verge of something great. Yet we're in this crazy moment, aren't we? I'm losing my optimism. I still fight if something is happening that enrages me.

The whole art world is so crooked now. It wasn't that crooked in my day. If I went to India or Latin America for a work, I'd always find people who talked the same language. You talked about creativity. That's not true anymore. Art has become a commodity, like stocks and bonds.

About eight years ago, a man called me and asked if I'd become an adviser to a group of businessmen. They bought art, put it in vaults, and let it increase in value. They wanted me to do the buying. I said no, I'd never deal with art in that way. He said, "We're prepared to put up large sums of money if you can buy a fine Rousseau. We'll keep it in the vault for twenty years, and when we take it out, it will be worth ten times what you paid for it, or maybe a hundred times." That's the way it's done these days. It's crazy and disgusting. But you can't fight big business, can you?

I lose my temper and I think, This is ridiculous because they're going to do it anyway. I fight very hard, but I know I won't win. [*Laughs.*] So I've learned to say it's hopeless. This is a step down for me.

I've fought my whole life through. Listen, I'm still a fighter about my health. From the age of nine until I was twenty, I wore a five-pound plaster cast. It had to be changed regularly to keep me from becoming a humpback. I had a wonderful mother who said, "You can do it." "I can't." "Yes, you can. You'll do it." I went to college at seventeen, wearing that brace. The doctors insisted that I wear it, but somehow I threw it off and I began to have a really exciting life.

I don't have many years left. No, no, no, I pray I never live to see the year 2000.

Postscript: She died January 10, 1994.

Katherine Dunham, 83

East St. Louis, Illinois

We're in the city that resembles, in its rubble, blasted buildings, long vacant, a lone silhouetted figure shuffling by, and pervasive bleakness, a bombed-out European town, shortly after World War II.

The city's populace is overwhelmingly black.

We approach a building that appears out of the mist. It stands alone, singularly stately, though in obvious need of tuck-pointing, paint, and a rehab job. It is the Katherine Dunham Center for Arts and Humanities.

Within are several large rooms, barely furnished, though rich in African and West Indian sculpture, painting, photographs, posters, and assorted artifacts.

We enter her bedroom upstairs. She is sitting up in her expansive bed, which occupies most of the room. There are scattered newspapers surrounding her: Le Monde, *the* London Sunday Times, *the* Washington Post, *and so on. A small television set flickers with occasional news dispatches.*

This conversation took place on January 20, 1993, the day Bill Clinton was inaugurated president.

I remember the stunningly beautiful and gifted dancer who introduced West Indian and African dance to the United States in the '40s and '50s. I see an elderly, somewhat weary woman whose eyes have not lost their sparkle, nor her voice its music.

She offers me a chocolate and, later, a touch of Haitian rum out of a thimble-sized cup. Several months before, she had concluded a forty-seven-day fast on behalf of the Haitian refugees.

I've been in and out of Haiti since 1935. I went there to study their dances and got mixed up in every other phase of their culture. I fell in love with Haiti. I've often asked myself: "Why do I have this feeling of longing for Haiti?" I'd been all over the West Indies and much of the world by this time, but this was the first place where I didn't think in terms of race. I went to the opening of the Senate, and here were these men in their morning coats, speaking their precise French. Here was Haiti that had won its independence from the French and sent Napoleon's army packing in 1804. Although I had been to Jamaica and Trinidad, it was in Haiti that I really felt a sense of pride.

Why is it that I dream so much of these people? Why is it that the comfort I most feel is with them? Erich Fromm, my friend, an analyst, said it's because they live with nature and understand it better than we do. I kept going back and going back to Haiti. I've been initiated there, and a lot of people think of me as a high mambo, a priestess. I didn't know whether I was doing these things for my ancestors or whether I was there as an anthropologist.

I had studied anthropology at the University of Chicago with Robert Redfield, an amazing man. He'd have been a great president for this country.

Once, I was told that I must have calling cards. I thought it was ridiculous, but Dr. Redfield said I must have them. I said, "What should I put down?" He said, "What are you?" I said, "I'm a student of dance and anthropology." So I put the two together, and my life has been pretty much governed by that since then.

I didn't realize I was a political activist until about four years ago. Dr. Joyce Ashenbrenner of Southern Illinois University had written a book, without my knowing it: *The Politics of Katherine Dunham.* [*Laughs.*] I thought, "What will she find?" It has always been my nature to do something and then think about it later.

After a few years in the West Indies, I came back to Chicago. It was during the worst part of the depression, '37, '38. John T. Frederick, head of the Illinois Writers Project, invited me to join. It was he who was responsible for my first book, *Journey to Accombong.* It was about the Maroon people of Jamaica, who had stood up against Queen Victoria and won their freedom.

On the project, I chose as a subject cults among deprived people. Nelson Algren, Jack Conroy and Frank Yerby worked with me. We were all excited about it. I visited Father Divine's temple in Harlem frequently. I think my main reason for going there so often was because you could get a good meal for twenty-five cents. [*Laughs.*]

It was so exciting that at my first performance of cult dances in Chicago in 1942 or '43, the FBI started in on me. They heard that a lot of Negroes, or whatever they were called then, were avoiding the draft by taking these foreign names. I was in my dressing room, ready to go on the stage, when they came in and asked for my paper on the subject. I told them I had no idea where a copy was—which was true. I thought the University of Chicago had a copy, but they didn't. The FBI thought I could tell them the real names of these people who were dodging the draft. I've come across this so often in conversations with the FBI, the CIA, and God knows who else.

When I performed a ballet in the opera house in Santiago, Chile, about the lynching of Emmett Till, the FBI visited me there, too. From time to time, I ran into the FBI everywhere. I had a terrible time about that.

I remember being asked about the Muslims and Elijah Mohammed. I said, "If you didn't have this hostile attitude toward us, we wouldn't be interested in these things." I don't think they ever understood. They didn't understand it in Chile when I did that ballet. The American diplomatic people there said, "Oh, please don't do this, it's unfair to us." I said, "When you stop doing this, I'll stop doing that." [*Laughs.*]

I realize I've been always speaking out. I guess my life and my art have always been entwined. If I had been a teacher in domestic science, I would have spoken out.

But in your eighties, going on a long fast—that's quite a step.

The Haitians have been treated terribly in their efforts to flee oppression. A military coup had violently overthrown its first democratically elected president, Aristide.* I woke up one morning and saw people—women, babies—being shoved and jammed around on coast guard boats. I said: "This just isn't possible." But it was.

So I started fasting the first of February in 1992, and I finished March 18. It was forty-seven days. I had cranberry juice and Evian water. I would feel tired, but I've always liked to work from bed anyway. I think it was good for me. The funny thing about it was, I was never hungry. I decided, if you're fasting it should only be for a reason that is so important to you that that's all you think about. I didn't think about food. That didn't bother me in the least.

In one letter to President Bush, I finally said, "It's the first time I feel ashamed of being an American. The other night, you spoke to the U.N. about our country leading in democracy, civil rights, and humanism. In order not to appear like a hypocrite, you should do something immediately about this Haitian refugee situation." Brent Scowcroft† answered me a long time later. It was no answer.

The Haitian refugee crisis was an outrage, but I was trying not to get angry. Over the years, I've been interested in Eastern philosophy: Buddhism, Theosophy. Just to make life easier. Don't get angry if you don't have to. But this was so outrageous that I couldn't help it. Fasting was just the thing to do, that's all.

On the eighteenth day, I went to the hospital. A Haitian doctor in St. Louis said I had to. There, I just kept on fasting. I phoned Dick Gregory to ask how fasting had affected him. He's done that quite often. He said, "I'm coming out there to fast with you." And he did. He chained himself to City Hall. [*Chuckles.*] It was really very funny.

I was very weak but didn't really notice it until the forty-fifth day. I came back here from St. Mary's Hospital and there were marches. To me, the most touching thing was to see East St. Louis and St.

---

* He has since been restored to office as president of Haiti.

† During Bush's administration, he was national security advisor.

Louis get together, holding a vigil outside this building—candles, everything. Usually, the two sides of the river never speak to each other. It was really quite wonderful. Dick Gregory made speeches—and Andrew Young. A lady friend of mine started speaking on street corners. It was exciting.

On the forty-fifth day, President Aristide and Jesse Jackson came to see me. They, of course, were hoping that I'd stop fasting. I said, "I don't know. I feel the same as I always felt." That wasn't quite true. I could feel myself slipping a little bit.

On the forty-seventh day, I stopped. People began calling me from Haiti. "We need you, and we need you alive, not dead." I began to think, "Oh, well, I guess it's all right if I stop now." My whole life essentially came down to being of some use.

Do you feel it had any political effect?

To some extent. I think there was a lot of bumping of heads to try to find out what to do. I frequently spoke to the U.N. representative to the OAS.* I honestly thought that there might be a way out without bloodshed. I felt I knew something about Haiti after more than fifty years in and out of there. I felt that the people of the military coup could be bought. I know the type very well. Give them a lot of money and send them off.

I was so shocked when my dearest friend, the traitor, allowed himself to be appointed prime minister of the present de facto government. Part of it is my fault. I originally thought he was the one who could save Haiti. I had dinner parties for him so he could meet the American diplomatic community. I see now that the State Department had always wanted this man.

As recently as this morning, I've felt I'm getting tired of politics. That's not getting anywhere. I look at television and I get a reflection of deceit. I say to my goddaughter, "Look, he just said so and so. Did you see him blush?"

Irony plays such a great role. I think you have to have an extraordinary sense of humor to live today.

Do you have second thoughts about your fast?

Oh, no. I have no regrets at all. The response has been wonderful. Little kids in school have been drawing pictures and sending letters to me. Churches have held meetings. We must have at least ten thousand followers right now.

* The Organization of American States.

And a strange thing happened. When Clinton was campaigning in St. Louis, an aide called and said that Governor Clinton was coming to East St. Louis. We made an appointment to meet here at the museum. But somebody got a hold of him for a big political meeting in the high school, and I was shoved off the edge of the cliff. No, I didn't get to talk to him. I'm planning to send him suggestions about Haiti. I know he's interested—I hope.

I saw two posters downstairs, side by side: "Have we forgotten history?" One is 1939: a boat of German Jews fleeing Hitler and being turned back. The other is 1992: the Haitian boat people.

We put our arms out to all these people who need help, but we're very selective. People ask me, "Do you think it's a matter of race, in the case of Haiti?" I say, "Certainly. If you compare the treatment of Haitians to the treatment of Cubans, you can see the difference." I watch the news, especially CNN. How many black Cubans do I see this year in those crowds? It diminishes and diminishes. Fair-skinned Cubans are royally welcomed. This goes on all the time.

The dark-skinned people are always made to feel small. My objective here in East St. Louis is to make the people feel big, feel like human beings. We've had ambassadors from African countries here, for our residents to see and meet. We've had the university bestow a degree on President Leopold Senghor of Senegal, a poet. I compare it to a soft wind blowing across the prairie. [*Chuckles.*]

How I came to settle in East St. Louis? As a small child, my mother and I passed through on our way to Alton, Illinois. Ever since, I wondered, "What is it like, the culture of these black working people?" They had jobs in those days. It has always been in my nature to look for a means. Ethel Waters used to say, "You gotta fight the devil with his own pitchfork." My whole life, I've been looking for those pitchforks.

I came here in 1965, after a tour of South America, with a proposal to the University in Carbondale to develop a mother center of Buckminster Fuller's for $450,000. He and my brother-in-law had drawn designs for it. It was a wonderful idea: six or seven satellites in other areas of the city. Unfortunately, the city fathers had other ideas. "We don't need any hip-shaking around here." That's the phrase they used. So we set up our own fund, and it's a struggle. I'm glad you got here before this house fell down.

I don't feel bitter, that's one good thing. Calling on Eastern philosophies has helped. I've learned to get satisfaction from little things. Religion interests me only insofar as it's a means of freeing man from spiritual death, whatever that is. You have to feel the vibrations of every living thing. Like this blanket made for me by some African women at Berkeley. [*She indicates the capacious blanket on the bed: colorful, intricately designed human figures in motion.*] Look at it. To me, it's alive. We have to learn to think of life, not as we do today. I feel a factor exists in this complex universe, that's greater than we are, that has made things and held them in balance. There's rhythm. Then came balance. And then came harmony.

A kind of immortality?

Absolutely. That's why I feel that I'm treading water on this whole political scene. Let it go. What I look forward to now is to free myself of the feeling that I need to reach out and help everything that's drowning. I once asked Erich Fromm why he was going to Mexico. He said, "I no longer believe in analyzing the general populace. I cannot reach everybody. I believe in analyzing the analyst. To help them reach other people."

This civilization is annihilating itself. The only thing that gives me a great feeling of optimism is that I am here, instead of slipping out some time ago. I'm about to watch new things coming in, and I'm still around to help. I feel that's why I was put in earth, so I'll do it for a while longer.

Uta Hagen, 75

NEW YORK CITY

She is an actress and has won two Tony Awards: one for her perfor-
mance in Who's Afraid of Virginia Woolf? *and the other for her work*
in The Country Girl. *She was equally celebrated as St. Joan, as Des-*
demona to Paul Robeson's Othello, and as Blanche Du Bois in A
Streetcar Named Desire. *In her younger days, after an appearance*
in "a terrible play" in Brooklyn, she was described by Alexander
Woolcott, drama critic of the New Yorker *as "the Duse of Brook-*
lyn." She has appeared in a few television plays and "once in a while
in a movie."

In Greenwich Village, the HB Playwrights Foundation,* of which
she is the artistic director, is alive with all sorts of activity: several
acting classes are in session; someone is painting a set; another is
busy at a desk, answering the constantly ringing telephone; several
are studying scripts; and a play is in rehearsal. These peripatetic,
though obviously intent, persons are all quite young.

The exception is an Englishwoman of middle age, Marjorie
Sigely. "She flew all the way from England to direct a genuine
mummers play—for nothing, by the way. These plays, dating from
the Middle Ages, involved villagers, who played all the roles. The
tradition continues to this day.

Hagen, vibrant, "full of beans," has the enthusiasm of her young
acolytes. Her appearance and demeanor belie her calendar age.

Since 1965, "we've done over one hundred productions. Our little
theater seats eighty-one. We squeeze in a hundred. It's free. People
from the community, colleagues, friends are the audience. We
haven't had an empty seat in twenty-five years. The neighborhood is
crazy about it."

Her husband, the late Herbert Berghoff, founded HB in 1945.
"He conned me into teaching, which I didn't know at the time.
[Chuckles.] *It's pretty full-time."*

When people tell me, "Isn't it a shame you're not working," I laugh
my head off. I work from ten to twelve hours a day. We have sixty
teachers, two thousand students, and are probably the least expensive theater school in the world. We used to charge three dollars a
class.

In the '50s, because of inflation, we raised the fee to five dollars.

---

* Named after her late husband, Herbert Berghoff.

After my husband died, because we were running a deficit I raised it to seven dollars.

The big gimmick in America is teaching in order to make money. People get rich of the backs of young, aspiring artists, who bankrupt themselves, borrow, and work all night long in restaurants in order to take a class. In essence, we subsidize them, but it's well worth it.

How do you survive?

My husband always called *HB* our big kibbutz. Once a year, we have spring cleaning, in which everybody participates. Me, the staff, the students, and people from the neighborhood all pitch in. The few staff people get salaries, modest; everybody else volunteers. We even get help with the printing.

We do have grants and contributions to the foundation, but the school supports itself. We own the three buildings, that's why we can manage. When we got our second building, the four-story brownstone, it was falling apart. The crazy little old lady who owned it was right out of Tennessee Williams. She had seventy-five cats, and the stench was unbelievable. The board of health got her out, and we bought it for $40,000. It's probably worth half a million now. But we worked like dogs. I take home about $200, $300 a week.

Why am I doing this? For one thing, the state of the theater in the United States has never been worse. The level of work is at best mediocre. Every little Off-Broadway house is looking to sell something. When they try out a play, they're already thinking, "Where will it be moved to?" It's not, "What does it mean to this community?" You've got to have a creative idea first. You can't say, "How will it sell?" before you even arrive at the idea. You can't use the community so you can move somewhere else—it is the death of art in the theater.

I am still fighting for the same idea they had in the village square, the idea I started with when I came into the theater as a very young child.

My father was a professor of art history at Göttingen, where I was born. It's known for its university. We came to the University of Wisconsin in 1926. My mother was a singer, and my aunt was a prominent mezzo in Germany. My father had been everything: an actor when he was seventeen, a musician, a composer, a prize pupil of Humperdinck. His one opera was such a disaster in Berlin that he decided to become an art historian. My whole background was literature and music and painting and theater.

My first job as an actress, when I turned eighteen, was playing Ophelia to Eva LeGalliene's Hamlet. It got amazingly respectful reviews. She played a very strong role in my young life. Her dream was of a repertory theater at reasonable prices. It was part of the great American tradition. Going back to Booth, the artists always had their own companies, were always in control of their own destinies. They were not run by real estate operators.

That's my bitch to young artists: Don't be slaves to realtors, producers who treat you like a piece of caca. In order to take control of your own lives, you've got to merit it, you've got to work your behind off and pursue your goal relentlessly.

The Lunts immediately come to mind. Alfred Lunt and Lynne Fontanne. As a very young actress, I was in their production of *The Seagull*. They were *fantastic*. After a show closed, they would give us all notes. On the closing night! [*Laughs*.] It was never perfect, but that was their goal. When they died, the obituaries read as though they had never done anything except drawing-room comedy. They did everything from Shakespeare and Shaw to Dürrenmatt. They were *wonderful*.

People say to me, "Nobody knows who you are anymore." I really don't care. One of the reasons I'm still full of beans is because I'm passionate about my beliefs. I'm happier in the pursuit of these goals than people who are pursuing their own belly buttons, their own success, without having a cause. They're chasing their tails.

They say, "I want to be a household name." I say, "What is that? Lysol? Toilet paper? Bounty? Those are household names." Listen to me, I'm shouting. My heart is pounding. [*Laughs heartily*.] I did a play called *Charlotta*. She was Goethe's mistress, the most important woman in his life. It bombed on Broadway. I said to Herbert, "I feel like I have a stillborn baby." He said, "Let's do it again." I toured it all over the country. Between 1982 and '83, I played it for months and months and months. I turned the play around, so it got better and better. When I returned to New York, I did it in Joe Papp's theater.* It was very exciting, jammed, standing ovations. Joe came backstage and said, "I think it's just tragic that you're not working." I was amazed. I said, "What do you think I was just doing on your stage?" He said, "Yeah, but that's for nothing." I nearly fell through the floor. If it's for nothing, it isn't work? Does your worth depend on how much money you get? He tried to laugh it off. Even Joe Papp, one of our best people.

It is as though money is the only thing that gives you a merit badge. How much money? How many awards? Awards are to me the funniest thing in American society. Everybody knows they are totally manufactured gimmicks [*pounds table*] to get more money. The Broadway season starts in the spring, so they'll cash in on the Tony

---

* The Public Theater.

awards. They can't start in the fall because they might be forgotten by the spring. They can advertise the awards because it means more business. The same with the Oscars. Every Oscar represents millions of dollars at the box office. The dumb actors stand up there and weep, "Oh, look what I got." What did you get? Nothing. [*Emotionally*] I defy the whole status quo. I think it's full of shit.

This is dangerous territory for me, I know. I won a couple of Tonys. Each time, I thought it was meaningless. I remember years ago, when Charlton Heston won the Oscar over Laurence Olivier. Doesn't that tell everything? It's nothing more than a campaign.

I got doctorates from three different colleges. After the third, I knew everything was a trade-off. At one college, they said, "You're going to give us your papers, aren't you?" Another asked, "Will you be on our board of directors, so when we audition people for the drama department…" When Nancy Hanks was head of the National Endowment for the Arts, she received nineteen honorary doctorates. She was in charge of giving out money. "If she gets an award, she may give us a grant." It is rotten.

How did I get this way? Most important were my parents. They gave me values that sustained me. They never preached. I listened to them, I watched them. I had stimulating fights with them. By the time I was seventeen, I had left home, knowing exactly what I wanted and heading for it. Sink or swim, I was going to do what I wanted to do.

As a youngster, I had enormous contempt for the movies. I don't any more. I was nineteen and married to José Ferrer. We were invited to Hollywood. Both of us did screen tests for RKO and they flipped. I thought it was dreadful. I turned down all kinds of scripts. One of them was as Esmeralda in *The Hunchback of Notre Dame*, with Charles Laughton. I told Pandro Berman, the producer, that the dialogue was terrible. "I'm used to Chekhov and Ibsen." [*Laughs.*] I was so snotty. I was just awful. People said I was a fool. "Look at the career you could have had, like Maureen O'Hara's." [*Laughs.*] I would have been suicidal.

We left Hollywood. I was never tempted again until after *Streetcar*. Suddenly, I was a hot item again. By that time, I was on every political blacklist in the country. I always say the blacklist saved me from corruption. But I don't want to be blacklisted again. [*Chuckles.*] Oh, it was horrible.

McCarthy started with me in Pittsburgh. I spoke at a rally for Henry Wallace* and I made headlines: "COMMISSAR HAGEN, RUN HER OUT OF TOWN." They printed my phone number and my hotel

---

* The Progressive Party candidate for president in 1948.

room in the newspapers. Wonderfully enough, we broke every house record. Somebody sent Claudia Cassidy* all this press stuff and, bless her heart, she was furious that they were trying to influence her.

My best friends during the McCarthy period were Republicans. They were more honest. Irene Selznick, the producer of *Streetcar*, said, "I would kill myself if I thought I was preventing you from doing what you believe in, but don't forget you're the star of this show and responsible for sixty-two other jobs, so take it easy." George Abbott said, "I got all these letters telling me not to hire you. You're a great actress, so what do I care?"

My most fruitful years were during the early McCarthy days—*Country Girl, Saint Joan,* and *Streetcar.* Broadway was uninfluenced by the hysteria, but they couldn't send me on the road.

I don't really know why I got in trouble. I have never been a conscious politician in any way. I just know that some of the people I met during those years were just about the most extraordinary group I've ever known. They were wonderful years. I was out talking, raising money for Greek war orphans, antifascist Spanish refugees. I was on the platform with Eisenhower and Mrs. Roosevelt, and suddenly I'm called a villain.

The FBI had two men, on taxpayers' salary, tailing me for two years. They said, "Who got you involved?" Fortunately, I have no memory for names. So I never had to tell a lie. I said, "There's been a woman in my house for three weeks whom I'm helping to start something for the YMCA. If you pulled my tongue out of my head, I couldn't tell you her name."

I was subpoenaed twice by the House Un-American Activities Committee. A subpoena in your hand is terrifying. My lawyers were saints. Paul Porter, the partner of Abe Fortas and Thurman Arnold, represented me for nothing. They had a 150 others they called their "conscience" cases.

The night before my first hearing in Washington, the chairman of the committee phoned to say that the hearing was called off because the guy who was going to testify against me turned out to be a perjurer. I asked, "Does that mean I can forget about it?" Paul Porter said, "Oh, no."

About three years later, I was called again. I remember I was so nervous. I remember that when I took my hands off the big table, there were pools of sweat on it. I lifted my felt skirt to wipe the sweat off. My heart was pounding.

"Did you appear in Chicago in 1948 on a Saturday in October, at noon, with Gerhardt Eisler?"

---

* Chicago's most influential drama and music critic of the time.

"No."

"We have a tape of you at that meeting."

Whooo, my heart was going wild. I said, "It couldn't have been. On Saturday, I would have played a matinee. I do two shows. It's impossible." I don't remember ever meeting Gerhardt Eisler.

Paul Porter said, "We'd like a copy of that tape." It was never mentioned again, because there was no such tape. Paul said, "I forgot to tell you. They have a number of such tactics they use to intimidate you. They'll bring up anything that they think will throw you and you'll be so rattled that you don't know what you're doing." They almost succeeded. It was the only time in my life I've ever been frightened, and I'll always hate them for that.

Have you ever had any second thoughts?

Never! Never, never, never, never. I never could follow dogma, I really couldn't. I remember when I was twelve, at a Girl Scout camp. They said, "You don't put your foot over this boundary line." I went [*taps on table in deliberate fashion, indicating footsteps "crossing the line"*]. If somebody says there's something you can't do or you must do, I immediately rebel. It has to be *my* choice. I love hot and heavy argument—I learned that from my parents—but the minute it's one way or else, forget it. That's why I could never have been a good Communist.

I'm told that the young today are more conforming. It's tragic. Youth has always been a period of rebellion. If they conform when they are young, what will they be when they're older? Fascists? The kids I know are aspiring artists and may be somewhat different.

I treat my younger students, my older ones, and my middle-aged ones as colleagues. A teacher is in big trouble when she stops listening to young people. When they begin, the have *wildly* idealistic goals. What is heartbreaking is to see them pitched into the theater as it exists and see them turn sour and mean and bitter and opportunistic by the time they're thirty. At nineteen, twenty, they're [*takes a deep breath*] like this. My job is to teach them not to lose that feeling. Call it passing the torch, if you want to.

At this moment, I feel wonderful about myself. Not last night, maybe not tomorrow. What I resent about growing old is this gradual deterioration. Your scalp gets red and it itches. You get little skin cancers, and your bladder burns. The degeneration of the body *drives me crazy*. That's the only thing that's terrible about age. My mind is alert. I don't feel spiritually any different than when I was eighteen. But the body won't always do it. I broke my knee a few years ago and got lazy, so everything started to go. But then I did tons of walking, three, four miles a day, and got back a little bit. But I'm impatient with my body.

My goddamn hearing aid has just gone on the blink. Would you like to hear about my circulation problems?

[*Laughs.*] I'm lucky in dealing with young people. They look up to me, so I don't get a sense of being ignored. About five years ago, I was in despair. I thought they were all slobs, all lazy, had no real goals, were waiting for someone else to do it for them. They came to class, sat in the back, didn't want to work, no initiative. There was a kind of cynicism, an arrogance. This was during the Reagan years, when you think about it.

In the last few years, I find a change in the attitude of the young. I've asked other teachers, and they agree with me. There seems to be a new purpose in young people. Maybe…

In the meantime, I'm teaching five classes a week, three-hour classes. I always have peripheral responsibilities, which I loathe.

What do you see ahead?

I don't know. [*Laughs.*] Tomorrow.

Postscript: We adjourned to a neighborhood bar.
I had my ritual martini. She had a Sea Breeze: "That's vodka
with grapefruit juice and a dash of cranberry juice.
Makes you feel healthy."

Milt Hinton, 83
NEW YORK CITY

He had just returned from a week's engagement at a jazz club in Berne, Switzerland: the Milt Hinton Trio. "It's in a small hotel, Thirty rooms. Each room is named after a musician. One is the Milt Hinton Room, filled with my memorabilia.

A couple of students of mine in a jazz workshop I conducted at Bernard Baruch College wrote a rap poem about me:

> *"I was born in Mississippi in the year of 1910,*
> *We moved up to Chicago and I never got back again.*
> *Now I played with Cab and Louis, with Doc and Strayhorn, too,*
> *Was friends with Clark and Dizzy, and there'll be more before I'm through.*

> *"I even jammed with Benny Goodman, with Basie, Duke, and Earl,*
> *I toured England with Bing Crosby, in the Middle East with Pearl.*
> *In 1939, I met Mona, that's my bride,*
> *And nothing's been the same ever since.*
> *We fell in love, she blew my mind, took the money,*
> *Then she went shopping, and I've been broke ever since.*
> *Now I even worked with Jackie Gleason, I played rags with Eubie Blake.*
> *I've been to the White House many times, and that's icing on the cake.*
> *I've even strolled with Freddie Keppard and Danny Barker, too.*

> *"Now I'm the oldest bass player standing, I've got shoes as old as you.*
> *But I had a wonderful time when I was in my prime.*
> *Now I'm tired, I just sit around here and play at home."* *

It works real well when I'm introducing myself to a new, young audience. I'm still an adjunct teacher at the college, once a week. I set up the syllabus and have two students teaching under me. I still

---

* References are to jazz greats Cab Calloway, Louis Armstrong, Doc Cheatham, Bill Strayhorn, Clark Terry, Dizzy Gillespie, Count Basie, Duke Ellington, Earl Hines, and Pearl Bailey.

do my occasional gigs,* then come back and chew my students out. My final exam is not written. It's a jazz concert in which everyone has to perform or write something. It's to prepare them to go out before the public.

My grandmother was a slave of Joe Davis, Jefferson Davis's father. She had thirteen children. She took the name of the overseer, not the slave owner. I came from Mississippi with her. She was my idol. From her I learned to respect people and to have some dignity.

She showed our whole family how to be independent. And how to work—the joy of working and earning anything, how when you earn it, you appreciate it more. There was no such thing as relief. I never in my life remember anybody giving us a turkey or anything. We were poor. She worked for a white family in Vicksburg, Mississippi, at $3.50 a week. But they gave her carte blanche to cook as much food as she wanted. That's how she fed our family.

This man she worked for owned a department store. She said to him: "May I have your permission to set up a stand outside your store, because in the morning people coming to work may want a cup of coffee?" She made biscuits and jelly and sold it to the black people coming to work. She made a little business out of it.

Her kids would go down to the railroad station and thumb their noses at the engineers, and these guys would throw coal at them, little black dusters. The kids would pick up the coal, take it into town, and sell it. My uncles were among these kids. That's how we lived.

My grandmother had a piano at home. I never remember asking her how she got it. My mother was the only one of her siblings who had a chance at education. She took piano lessons and became the organist at the church. Mount Heron Baptist Church.

The minister of this church, Edward Perry Jones, preached to the congregation: "There's no future for you here. Get your children out, so there will be a future for them. It's all over for you, but be sure you get your children out. Go north." The white people heard about this and ran him out of town. He came to Chicago and got a church in Evanston. My mother worked for him, while teaching piano.

Dr. Jones's sons went to school and got to be railroad porters. When the reverend died, these boys went into the "policy" business.† They couldn't do it while their father was living.

In public school, I was on the same track team with Ralph Metcalf,

---

* Musicians' slang for a paid live performance.

† The Jones brothers became the most successful and celebrated policy entrepreneurs in Chicago's black community, holding their own against the mob, which tried to muscle in. Black policy men often helped up-against-it neighbors, enabling them to "get over."

the Olympic track champion who later became a congressman.* My mother was determined that I would be a musician, so she sent me to a violin teacher, a white man. He taught everything, piano, banjo, strings. My mother was so busy making a living that she didn't have time to teach them piano. One of her students was Nat [*King*] Cole. She used to say to me, "Why can't you be nice, like Nathaniel?" He was always a nice, little quiet guy. I couldn't stand him.

This was about 1919, 1920. Black people from all over the South were migrating to Chicago because they heard there was a big strike at the stockyards, they needed unskilled labor. And black people needed jobs.† Chicago was the railroad hub of the country, and there were jobs as porters. There were more hotels than in any city: they needed bellhops and waiters. Black people were coming from Alabama, Mississippi, Tennessee, from all over the Deep South.

I studied violin, but at Wendell Phillips High School‡ I played bass horn in the band, so I could go on trips with the football team. We'd rehearse in one of the mansions of Hattie Malone.§

I was playing bass fiddle, too. It was easy to convert from the violin. It was a lucky move because all the black violin players were losing their jobs in the movie theaters. It was 1929 and Al Jolson's *Jazz Singer* was the first sound movie with music. That ended live music at the movies, the piano and the violin. All the guys I knew, the best of them, Stuff Smith and Eddie South,** were out of work.

I'm all ready to go before the public, but here's the depression and sound movies. I'd already been taking lessons at Jane Addams's Hull House every Saturday, twenty-five cents a lesson. I ran into Benny Goodman there, he was just one of the guys. I was playing good classical music, but I had no place to work.

Along comes Al Capone, opening the Cotton Club in Cicero: black musicians for white customers. Most of the kids in my class at Wendell Phillips, sixteen, seventeen years old, got a job at Al's place. They were playing trumpets and trombones and such. No violins.

I'm listening to jazz all this time, all these great bass players—Bill

---

* He was the first black political figure to publicly challenge Mayor Richard J. Daley, a gesture that set off the coalescence of Chicago's African American community that subsequently elected Harold Washington as mayor of the city.

† They became among the most militant members of the United Packinghouse Workers of America (UPWA) during the formation of the CIO in the '30s.

‡ It was renamed DuSable High School, after Chicago's first settler, a black man.

§ "She made a fortune in hair straighteners, along with Madam Walker, of course."

**Eddie South was known as "the Dark Angel of the violin."

Johnson, Pops Foster. Coming from school, there's the Grand Terrace with Earl Hines. I'm going to Louis Armstrong rehearsals, getting close, I'm so anxious to hear him. He'd say, "Get back, son, you're in the way." It wasn't till 1954 that I got to play with him. I'm now playing bass, a little jazz club on the South Side. Thirty-five, fifty cents a night, two dollars a week.

It's changed these days because there's no longer apprenticeship. When radio was king, people in small towns all over the country could hear Earl Hines and Fats Waller, the big bands. When they came to town, crowds would flock to see them, like people flock to rock stars today. Television ended all that. The visual thing came into their living room. No more surprises. They've already seen you. After World War II, all the big bands broke up.

The trombone players began to lose their jobs, too. In New Orleans, they tailgated on the back of the wagon, during funerals. No need for that in the small Chicago clubs. One trombone player was enough. Anyway, these horns were too loud for a club. They needed bass fiddles though.

I listened to those guys religiously and learned. Kids don't get a chance to do that today. When I joined Cab Calloway's band in 1935, I was the youngest guy there. I would get to observe these great musicians. I had to learn and feel my cues or I'd get thrown out. I had to learn the hard way. The only way. Today, kids come along with one song, and suddenly they're millionaires. And they don't even know music.

At first, it was very hard to get the schools to teach these young people jazz. I had a tough time to get into Hunter College here in New York. I had won all the awards, a top jazz man, but they had a classical player teaching a jazz workshop. The kids didn't get anything from him.

All of a sudden, Yale did a thing called University without Walls. They set up the Duke Ellington Fellowship and fifty musicians were told they could do something in the form of jazz music, and they were made Yale fellows. I was one of them. The students loved it! That's why I'm still doing it at Bernard Baruch College. If you're going to teach a child, you have to be able to play, exhibit to him what you mean. Don't just tell him, but show him.

Hip universities have begun bringing in jazz artists to teach master classes. It's a good sign. Jazz is recognized more abroad than it is here, because they study it. We just accept it, but it's kind of a putdown. I make an analogy when I talk to my kids. If you were to tell my wife I'm a great jazz player, she'd say to me, "Put the garbage out." I'm hers. Well, that's how we feel about jazz. It's ours. So we let other people rave about it. They appreciate it. Here at home, we leave it dormant. When you leave something dormant, it dies.

Like everything else in life, jazz is changing, but you have to understand it. When Charley Parker and bop came along, it was rejected. It was put down as too strong, too long, too this and that, too complicated. You have to be musically educated to comprehend it.

When the big bands broke up in 1950, '51, I was one of the few bass players that was able to convert to a small combination. In a small group, you have to be academically prepared to play. In the 1940's, I studied with a classical bass player, a member of the symphony. I came to understand Bach. I was eager to see his combination of chord formations, his architecture, I guess. And then we began improvising, a combination of sounds that was pleasing to the ear. Today, you get too many combinations that are not pleasing to the ear. It's not jazz, it's not music.

I don't feel too good about rock. It isn't understanding enough. It's too crude.

Jon Hendricks, one of our best jazz poets, said, "The greatest jazz poem I've ever written is the shortest: one word, 'Listen.'" If you can't listen to it, it's not good music.

It's impossible to talk about jazz without reflecting on race. When you traveled in the South in the '30s, '40s, and '50s—

They wanted to see us play, though there were rules that abused us. I played at a place once where they had a rope down the middle of a dance hall: whites danced on one side, blacks, on the other. We thought this was crazy. And it was crazy. There were absolute dangers, too.

Longview, Texas. They struck oil in the late '30s. The soil was just seeping with it, messy. It was killing the grass, making the cows sick. Black folks on the bottom as usual. The white folks got filthy rich because the oil company was paying them a mint just to drill their land. Businessmen from New York were coming down and charging these people $1,000 for those Palm Beach suits and $500 for Ingersoll watches.

Now they wanted some entertainment. "Let's bring Cab Calloway's band down here." He was a big star then. So we went down there to play. They lined up and paid $300 a piece to hit a black man. Like in those carnivals: hit a black man and he falls in the water. They were willing to pay $300 to hit Cab Calloway.

Here we are on the bandstand trying to play. They paid money to see us but they wanted to abuse us. The man who gave the dance said, "I will do my best to get you guys out of here safe, because they're getting pretty drunk."

Am I bitter? No, no. We thought it was just silly. It does kick back in crazy ways, though. There's this young white kid in New York. He studied bass with me. He loved me and I loved him. I'd bring him to my house and teach him. He'd stay over. His people didn't even know we were black. Billy Kronk is his name. He became a wonderful bass player with Tommy Dorsey's band.

So he goes on tour with Dorsey in the South. Because he always hung around with black musicians in New York, he went to some damn God-forsaken bar, where everybody was black. He was the only white guy there. Down south, when a white guy walks into a black bar, he's either crazy or he's from the police. This kid walks in smiling because he's used to us, pocket full of money, puts it on the bar to order up a drink. When they find out he's not a cop, just a damn fool, they took his money and beat the hell out of him.

So he comes to New York and tells me, "Milt, I found out I don't like all colored people." I said, "Neither do I, Bill. What's the problem?" So he told me what happened. I said to him that he made a mistake. If he'd gone to a place where there were black musicians and told them he knew Coleman Hawkins or Ben Webster or Milt Hinton, they would have welcomed him with open arms and given him anything he wanted to eat or drink. But not telling anybody who you were was inviting trouble. I gave him Red Allen's advice—the great trumpet player—"Drink hearty but stay with your party." Funny how this opposite relationship works the same way. He got beaten up like we were getting beaten up down here.

There was no resentment on the part of black jazz men toward good young white players. My God, Jack Teagarden, Bud Freeman were affectionately regarded and respected. Today, the resentment is that black jazz men aren't getting enough opportunity. There are no bands were they can go. It's far worse than yesteryear.

Chicago in the '20s and '30s saw jazz's resurgence. Everybody met on the South Side. There was a large black audience of people who'd come up from the South, who now had paying jobs as porters, redcaps, hotel waiters, stockyard workers, at steel mills. Everybody met everybody there. Black musicians couldn't listen to white musicians on the North Side, but these young white guys would come to the South Side.

Benny Goodman told me many times how he was hanging out with the great clarinet player Jimmy Noone. They'd come over and jam, and the black guy would see that the white guy was fingering his horn correctly and pick up on it, and the white was listening to the improvisations of the blacks. They exchanged knowledge and everybody got something out of it. We had all the big bands, Jimmy Lunceford and Cab and Chick Webb, Coleman Hawkins,

Claude Hopkins. Each one had about twenty-five, fifty musicians.

Now in hundreds of these hotels in New York, there's got to be three thousand kids. There won't be ten black musicians there. We've just made some inroads into Broadway shows because there have been several successful black musicals.

Today, young black musicians don't get a chance to see me because I'm playing for white audiences. They don't have the money. These big jazz parties all over the country, you don't see black musicians.

The only place you see black people hearing black musicians is on a cruise. I've just come off the *Norway*, a big ship. It's a jazz cruise. Some great name musicians are there. Thousands of jazz fans, 80 percent black. They save their money all year round for this one vacation, a week's cruise. Fifteen, twenty people from every town, they make up a few thousand. Everybody's dressed nice and enjoying it. I never saw one racial incident there.

I take my camera everywhere I go, even on the cruise. It's as much a part of me as my bass. I got interested in photography when someone gave me an Argus C3 back in the '30s. It was introduced on the market for twenty-five dollars.

When I was traveling, I noticed that every time we saw those old pictures of musicians, it was the way the photographer saw them. I said to myself, I'd like to take pictures of us as we really are. So I catch us sitting down, eating or at rehearsal. Or sleeping on a bus. Or listening to a playback. If you want to catch a man really concentrating, watch him as he's just recorded something, listening for his mistakes. You've got a fresh concept of this man.

A photographer is not allowed to shoot during a recording session, because the click might interfere. Well, I'm already there with my camera. When the conductor takes a break to make a note change, I whip out my camera and get a picture.

I never capture anybody in any embarrassing moment. Never. Now that they know my books are successful, I'm embarrassed when I take a candid shot. They see me coming and begin primping up. I don't want that. I want them as they are, natural, themselves.

There's an exhibition of my photographs traveling around the world. There's one in France right now. I never dreamed it would be like that. It's like a renaissance for me, going on eighty-four. It all came about because of a young student of mine. This kid, David Berger, was thirteen years old. I gave him a lesson. He said, "How much do I owe you?" He had five dollars. I said, "How about three dollars?" that was the sweetest thing I ever did in my life. Years later, he became the chairman of the sociology department of Temple University. He always came back to visit me. One day, he came across all these old pictures, these negatives, and started to file and index them. And that's how the book came to be.

I got a house full of youngsters all the time. It's always been that way. I remember when I was young in Chicago, some of the older musicians weren't too nice. They didn't want to show you anything. I promised myself that if I ever got to that place, I would never turn down any young guys. I'm still doing it and having a wonderful time.

I'm more active than ever these days. Today, I've got to go down and tape, learn some new music. One of the universities sent me some music that I'll play there, and I've got to practice.

Do I still practice? I've got to keep up with these kids. They want to see if I can still do it. It's the only way you can get respect from them. It ain't my style, but if you want me to play this, I'll play it. If you can notate it, I can play it.

I've been through it all. I never overdrank or overindulged, and I find I get a lot of respect out of old age. I have a prostate problem, but I understand that's par for the course. My knees hurt sometimes, but when I get to playing, I forget about all that.

Jazz has always been my life. I wouldn't have traded one day for it. I promised my wife when I first met her that I'd be scuffling with it even if I didn't make a cent. I'd never go to work in the post office. And I've been married fifty-four years to this lady. But I love Lady Jazz, too.

For some reason, bass players live a long time. We're standing up there. You don't get too much arthritis, because you're keeping your arms moving. Like symphony conductors. You're standing up, waving, exercising. Pops Foster lived till he was very old. Wellman Braude, too. Duke's bass man, Bill Johnson, the first one I ever saw, lived to be a hundred. I'm shooting for that.

Every day I'm onto something different. I plan to give a concert with the band and show some slides of all the great musicians. They should know their music history like they know their American history. Like you know about George Washington and Abe Lincoln, you should know about Duke Ellington, Jack Teagarden, Bix Biederbeck, and Louis Armstrong.

I want the young to remember me as a guy who's been through it all. Not long ago, I was in a music shop looking for some records. I heard two young kids talking. One said, 'Let's get this record. Milt Hinton is on it." The other kid says. "You got to be careful. There's two guys named Milt Hinton. There's an old guy who made records years ago, and there's a guy making records now. So you gotta see which one it was." I was standing right there, and they didn't know me from Adam. So now the guys in New York say, "Are you the old Milt Hinton or the new Milt Hinton." Well, I'm same Milt Hinton.

Chapter Nine

On the Air

Norman Corwin, 83

During the late '30s, '40s, and early '50s, radio experienced its Golden Age. As a writer, director, and producer, he created programs that were distinguished for their language as well as their content; style and substance were fused.

For me, there are two reasons to celebrate May 8, 1945. It was, of course, V-E Day. The war in Europe was over. It was also the day On a Note of Triumph was broadcast over CBS. Even now, almost fifty years later, I hear those voices. And those words. They were Norman Corwin's.

He is a member of the faculty of the University of Southern California School of Journalism.

In the late '30s, I was a publicity flak for Twentieth Century-Fox films. By a series of serendipities, I found myself as a program director at CBS. I went to a network manager with an idea for a poetry series. Instead of saying, "I don't know what kind of rating it will get," he said, "Go ahead, I like the idea." It was to be a half hour, Sunday afternoons, on the CBS network. Out of the clear, he said, "Why don't we call it *Norman Corwin's Words Without Music*"? He appealed to my sense of pride. He gave me freedom to write what I wanted.

"How would you like to take over *Columbia Workshop*?" he asked. It was the most avant-garde dramatic program on radio. He added, "Let's call it *Twenty-six By Corwin*." Well, my God, I lived like a monk all those months, did not have a date, didn't go to movies, didn't go to parties. I worked and I loved it. It was freedom. They never said, "Let's see the first thirty pages" or "This has to go under the eye of the censor. It was freedom to create. Yip Harburg, the lyricist, said, "Poor Norman, he's out of touch with everything but the world."

In contrast to television, radio enlists the imagination of your collaborator, the listener. He becomes your set designer and your casting director.* Though the singer you hear on the radio as Carmen may weigh three hundred pounds, to the listener, she's the gypsy with the rose in her teeth. In radio, there was no term like "couch potato" or "boob tube." Though there were shlocky programs, it was the ear that was poet of the senses. Imagination was the force, the spur.

Think of that wonderful little moment, brooding over something that resists immediate understanding. Bang! Just the right phrase: "I got it! I got it!" That's a moment of exhilaration. [*Gently excited.*] It's the kind of exhilaration that comes from proprietorship. You own the understanding of that word, that phrase. It's part of your lexicon, part of your experience. It's enriching.

As fan mail goes, mine was relatively small. When I got a hundred letters on a program, that was a lot. *On a Note of Triumph* brought forth an outpouring, thousands, over a period of weeks. Ratings were rarely taken in those days. My greatest reward came later, about twenty-five years later.

I was going to London. The plane left Kennedy airport at 10:00 P.M. We were in the middle of the Atlantic, most passengers were snoozing. The door of the cockpit opened and the captain walked down the aisle. He saw that I was awake. He asked if I was Norman Corwin. I said yes, to which he responded with a quote from *On a Note of Triumph*. To hear your words come back to you from a stranger in the middle of the Atlantic Ocean twenty-five years after they were broadcast was a thrill. A rare payoff, a late return.

With the '50s came McCarthy time and it all changed. There came thought control. And fear, of course. But more important, television came. The networks looked at their financial statements, and they realized that dollar for dollar, minute for minute, television was far more profitable. So radio, the medium that reflected the potential for an indigenous art, was manipulated out of existence.

It's ironic. Even the more ambitious radio programs, like *On a*

---

* For many years on the theater stage, Ruth Draper offered a one-woman program. Solo, she portrayed a variety of characters. In one of her most celebrated sketches, *Three Generations in a Domestic Relations Court,* she was a bewildered immigrant grandmother, her weary fiftyinsh daughter, and her vibrant, rebellious young granddaughter. The audience invariably gasped in astonishment as, by means of subtly moving the shawl, she was transformed from the two elder women into a vivacious seventeen-year-old girl. During one of her last years on the circuit—she was in her sixties—I asked her how she did it. "I didn't do anything," she replied. "The audience does it. I pique their imagination and they do the rest. They participate."

Note of Triumph, cost relatively little. What's $25,000? It doesn't buy the corner of a set for a TV pilot that may never get on the air.

Now there is a ghetto for serious radio. It is public radio, heard by a relatively small audience. There's no reason there shouldn't be much more, because the same inexhaustible resources of talent are still available.

Today's radio presents certain paradoxes. Call-in programs have a good premise: the listening public can express itself. However, it depends who is running the program. If the host is mean-spirited, he will attract people of like complexion, who will call in with their cloned thoughts, expressing exactly what his position is. If he doesn't like what they say, he cuts them off. I think it is one of the sources of a kind of general meanness that has crept into entertainment as well as politics.

We have moved into an era where everything is done by the numbers. Polls are taken for just about everything—for elections, for choice of margarine, for attitudes. Everything is reduced to what will turn a profit. The individual is reduced to a statistic.

Trivia has become major news. I tuned in the evening news one day. There were several serious fires in California. New York declared an emergency water shortage. A Greenpeace ship was blown up. There was some big news from the Soviet Union. But the main story on all three networks was that Coca-Cola had gone back to its old taste. It was the *Denver Post* headline the following morning.

The change that has come over our language, I'm afraid, has been one of being degraded, of its values being eroded. The influence is clearly traceable: the rise of technology, a division among professions, and the computer, which has its own language. This can be invigorating and enriching to a language, except that there is no preservative, no MSG to bring out the flavor of the language we grew up with as young people.

When I was a kid, I was intoxicated by language. I remember reading *Endymion* by John Keats, not understanding it, but being aware that this was very rich stuff, a kind of heady wine. As an infant picks up language by hearing its parents, you, unconsciously, pick up a sense of rhythm, a sense of cadence, a sense of richness. When you first meet Shakespeare, it doesn't matter that you may not understand all the words. You go to the dictionary: "What is the meaning of that?" You find out that these beautiful grace notes, these phrases and cadences, have a meaning as well. Of course, that enlarges our appreciation of our language. We don't have that today.

Fashions are set today by people in high places, celebrities, conspicuous people. Certainly when you have the language debased and cheapened by men in high office, it's going to have a trickle-down effect on the public. It's got to, just as the opposite is true. It is no accident that in the Elizabethan Age, there was not just one great poet, a supremely gifted one, Shakespeare, but there were a lot of others around: Marlowe, Ben Jonson. The age produced them. There was an ambiance of poetry and high thought. What worries me most about the younger people is the acceptance of low standards.

Television is a convenient punching bag, but it deserves its role. Our attention span has been reduced. In the early '80s, the sound bite averaged forty-two seconds. Now it's down to nine seconds. Everything has to be on the move. O. J. Simpson is selling Hertz car rentals and he doesn't sit. He runs through an airport or he drops from a crane into a car. The camera keeps moving.* Look at MTV. There's no cut longer than a second and a half.

Not only are there fewer words spoken, listening has diminished. People have been trained not to listen, because whoever is speaking is always moving. A simple head shot is a cardinal sin. It's a terrible thing to focus on a single face. To me, the human face is the greatest show on earth. It's expressive, it has character.

We are to a large extent robotized. No longer do you have a manuscript that can be preserved in the archives. In the British Museum, you can see the original manuscript of Robert Burns's "A Man's a Man for That" or Keats's "Ode on a Grecian Urn." Today, that would be printed out on a word processor and changes would be made on the machine. You would never know what was deleted and what was changed.

It's bizarre that there is a movement in opposite directions. We have enormous technological advances at an accelerated rate. You can call a corporation that has five hundred thousand accounts. You either punch it in or read your account number—there is a monitor on the other end—and it can tell you in a flash all about it. At the same time, we're descending into frightening levels of public ignorance.

It's an unorganized conspiracy. You go to a restaurant, some very expensive ones, too, and the noise is so loud, you have to shout to your companion, seated next to you. [*Mildly indignant*] You have to lean over. Why is that? We have acoustics that can easily take care of that problem. I feel it's a deliberate policy on the part of the restaurant owner. He wants the place to sound alive and busy and full of energy and vitality. And you're less likely to linger. Your table is sooner available for the next customer.

There is an element of contempt: contempt for civility, contempt for considerateness, contempt for the poor. It is again something that has trickled down from on high.

---

* Obviously, this conversation took place before the Simpson murder case broke.

I'm not a teacher by training, but I very often respond to invitations that present a challenge. That's why I came to this university. I have the illusion that I am younger than I am because I'm around young people all the time. And I very much enjoy it. For the most part, they're good students, they're eager. I have a great sympathy for them because it's very tough to land a job in this market in this age.

There's of course the usual quotient of students who don't want to be journalists. They want to be anchor persons, stars. They are outnumbered by serious students who want to acquire the skill of a journalist, who want to learn about the who, what, where, why, and the ethics of it.

I'm still writing, but not as much as I'd like to. Pro bono activity takes up a great deal of my time, as it has much of my life. There's a Latin motto: Ad astra per aspira. Reach for the stars. Unless we're aspiring to a better society, what the hell is life worth? To wallow around repeating mistakes, forgetting history?

I'm an affirmationist by instinct. I've tried to express that which was affirmative in our national consciousness. Those birds who were writing "we hold these truths" and "when in the course if human events" possessed a certain nobility of language as well as ideas. Even the knave of that period had a certain kind of dignity.

As far as the future is concerned, I refuse to believe the downward path is inescapable. Assuming that we don't blow ourselves up, we have a fair chance of coming up out of the swamp.

The term "civilization" is, in many instances, subjective. I find certain people whose country is ranked low on the scale of culture, who have high ethical standards. One of the Melanesian Islands has a parliament where the speaker says his piece with his back to the audience, because it is a tradition not to influence the audience by facial expression or gestures—just by what you're saying. To me, that is highly civilized.

As for me, I'm conscious of my age. When I catch the flu, I figure I'd better not fool around. I go to bed. But the word "retirement" doesn't belong in my lexicon. I intend to go on and do the best I can for as long as I'm able.

I think there's an improvement in our attitude toward age. For a long time, this was a youth culture, and still is, in advertising. Actually, the older group, thanks to increased life expectancy, may become a more powerful constituency. The kind of obituary I would like is short: "Norman Corwin, age 124, was killed yesterday in a duel with a jealous lover. His gun jammed."

Postscript: His father died at the age of 110. His brother, ninety, is still working at his job.

Robert St. John, 92

It is a small house, across the Potomac from Mt. Vernon, Virginia. The garden is lush and in the living room is a plentitude of paintings, sculptures, and artifacts from various societies. There are several pieces of antique furniture about.

He appears considerably younger than his calendar age. A Dapper Dan, he is slim and wears a large bow tie and neatly trimmed Van Dyke—his hallmarks. The image of George Abbott, the theater director, comes to my mind.

"When I had my ninetieth birthday, my wife suggested that I should cut down the flower and vegetable garden a little bit. I compromised. I cut down the vegetable garden by 10 percent and I increased the flower garden 20 percent. So each year, I'm more active than the one before."

To those who listened to the radio during the World War II days, his voice has a familiar ring.

I've made broadcasts from eighty-eight countries around the world. The things you see in this room are what my wife and I gathered during our travels.

World War II began on September 1, 1939. I was then thirty-seven years old. I had been city editor of the Associated Press (AP) in New York at one time. I had covered the Lindbergh kidnapping, the Roosevelt campaign, and the Starr Faithfull case.* As a twenty-three-year-old newspaper publisher and editor in Chicago, Illinois, I was beaten up by the Capone gang. I tried to drive Al Capone out of Cicero, but he drove me out. I had been left for dead in a ditch. I figured I had all the experience a reporter can have and it was time to retire.

So I quit at the age of thirty, bought a farm up in New Hampshire, was raising chickens and turnips, and doing a bit of writing. A friend, Frank Gervasi, a foreign correspondent, came home from Rome and paid me a visit. "This is wonderful, your retiring at such a young age, but you ought to cover one more story before you really quit. The war." I said, "War between whom?" This was early in 1939. He said, "You know about Hitler, Mussolini?" I said, "No. I've been living up here on the farm for six years. We don't have a radio and I haven't read a newspaper in six years. Tell me about it." He said, "I'm starting a column from Europe, much like the Washington-Merry-Go-

---

* Starr Faithfull, was a fashion model who had died under mysterious circumstances. The case became the basis of John O'Hara's 1935 novel, *Butterfield 8.*

Round.* You can work on it with me. The war is going to begin around the first of September. Meet me in Paris late in August."

I went down to the AP in New York and I said, "I understand there's going to be a war soon. How about sending me to Europe as a foreign correspondent?" They said, "Who told you there's going to be a war? We don't think so, and if there is, you're much too old to be a foreign correspondent." I was thirty-seven.

I borrowed some money from a bank, bought a couple of steamship tickets, and arrived in Paris, late August. There was a cable from Gervasi. The deal was off. He had accepted a job as an editor of *Collier's* magazine. So there I was with no job and a few hundred dollars in my pocket.

Half of everybody I talked with thought the war was nonsense. There was Chamberlain, Munich, and "Peace in our time." So I bought a couple of railroad tickets to Bucharest, for my wife and myself. I figured Paris was full of foreign correspondents and I'd have a better chance in Romania. I decided that if there wasn't a war, I'd write a book about the love affair of King Carol and Magda Lupescu.

I had to change trains in Budapest and dropped in at the AP bureau there. My God, all hell had broken loose. They were all jumping around, yelling, screaming into telephones. "Don't you know? World War II has begun. The Germans are bombing Warsaw!" I said, "Oh, my God!" They said, "You wouldn't be a newspaperman by any chance?" I said, "Former city editor of the AP in New York." They said, "For Christ's sake, take your coat off and get to work." So I had a job, I went with the Germans from Poland down to Hungary, Bulgaria, Yugoslavia.

I heard there was going to be a revolution in Yugoslavia against the pro-Nazi government. I was in Belgrade on Palm Sunday morning when the Luftwaffe bombed this undefended city. All the telephones and the radio were destroyed, so we had no way of telling the story. We were told that King Peter had fled to the south, carrying a portable radio transmitter. If we could catch up with him, we could send our dispatches back to New York. We got to Sarajevo just in time for the Nazi raid on that city. We got to an airport south of Yugoslavia just in time to see the royal entourage fly off to Egypt, with the transmitter and the country's gold supply, which is what fleeing monarchs always do.

We—that is, me, a CBS correspondent, an English journalist, and a reporter from the *Herald Tribune*—were always one day ahead of the advancing German army. We traded an automobile for a twenty-foot sardine boat and pushed off toward Greece, sailing right

---

* Drew Pearson's syndicated political column.

through the Italian fleet. On a Greek troop train, we headed for Athens, where we thought we could get some communications.

There were several thousand Greek soldiers on this train. A good share of them were killed by the Nazi planes that strafed the train. The CBS man got badly wounded, and I got a leg full of Nazi machine-gun bullets. I still have them and refuse to have them removed because they hit a nerve every now and then and remind me of things I don't want to forget.

We got to Crete in time for the big Nazi first airborne operation. We wound up in Egypt, still looking for a means of communication. I had a fistful of dispatches but no way to transmit them. We never did get to Athens because of the train attack. In Egypt, we bumped into British censorship.

Remember, this was before Pearl Harbor, so the United States was still neutral. It had worked to my advantage in Bucharest in a funny way. It was still the phony war period. There was that moment when nothing was happening. Hitler sent his entire general staff to the number one hotel in Bucharest—the Athena Palace—to plan the attack on Russia. The Nazis took over the whole hotel for their staff. The manager said, "I've got one neutral journalist who's been living here for some time. Can he have this one room?" They said okay. So I lived for several months in a hotel with the entire German General Staff.

In most European hotels, you put your shoes outside the door. During the night, the porter marks white chalk on the bottom of the shoes, polishes them, and brings them back. One night at the hotel bar, another newspaper guy and I were having a few drinks. He said, "Let's go upstairs before the porter comes up to mark the shoes." We were both a little tight. We gathered up all the shoes on the second floor and put them in front of the rooms on the fifth floor. It was almost morning before we had mixed up all the Nazi officers' boots.

The bar was open all night, so we had a few more drinks. The Germans, as you know, are very methodical. [*Claps.*] At 7:00 on the dot, they jumped out of bed. [*Claps.*] At 7:15, they all take a shower. [*Claps.*] At 7:30, they put on their shoes and go to the dining room. I decided to stand by the switchboard. At about a quarter after seven, the switchboard lit up like a Christmas tree. [*Imitates.*] "I want to talk to Herr Director!" The manager had the porter put all their shoes, maybe a hundred pairs, on the floor of the ballroom. He took great delight in ordering these Nazi officers to stand in a circle, and when he gave the signal, they scrambled to pick out their boots. It was wonderful. I figured I delayed the entire German timetable by about two hours. I claim that I am the one who really won World War II. They might have taken Moscow. [*Laughs.*]

I came back to the States in '41, as the first American war correspondent to be wounded in World War II. I quit the AP because they wouldn't allow me to publish or to lecture. The next day, the head of the NBC news department asked me if I'd go to London and be the opposite number of Edward R. Murrow of CBS. That's how I switched from being a print reporter to being a broadcaster.

When I was broadcasting from London, during the Blitz, I wasn't interested in looking for exclusive interviews with the leaders. I talked with pubkeepers, telephone operators, charwomen, and taxi drivers—the ordinary people. I thought that was where the real stories were.

I came back as head of the Washington NBC bureau. I did the D-Day stories from New York. And in announcing the Japanese surrender, I beat all the other networks by fifteen seconds. For seventy-two hours, I sat in the broadcasting booth without sleep. Kaltenborn, Vandercook, and the others came and went to restaurants and home to sleep a few hours. I waited for the flash at that machine. Five bells is to alert you that something important is coming up. When I heard that sixth bell, I announced that the war was over. The others waited for the tenth bell.

In the postwar years, the Cold War got underway and strange things were happening. On my way to the NBC office, I often dropped in at the Stork Club for a drink. It was usually in the morning, when they were cleaning up, and the bartender came on duty. The bartender and I became friends. I'd slip him nice tips and he'd tell me all the scuttlebutt that went on the night before. Bartenders have big ears. They hear all kinds of inside stuff.

One morning as I was having a drink, he leaned over and said, "I've got a big piece of news for you." He told me that the night before, the vice-president of NBC, in charge of news and special events, got a little tight and told the CBS man, "I've got three Communists on my staff and I'm going to fire all of them." The CBS man said, "I'm going to do a little firing myself."

Within a week, there was a purge of liberal broadcasters, starting with William L. Shirer, John W. Vandercook, Don Goddard, Robert St. John, and Don Hollenbeck, who committed suicide. There wasn't a Communist among us, but we were all blacklisted.

I had been very active on the lecture circuit when the McCarthy people started picketing the places where I was booked. I finally had no income at all, so I went to Switzerland. I lived there for fifteen years, from 1950 to 1965. I lived off some books I wrote. I'd come back to the United States occasionally for a lecture tour. Then they took my passport away. You can't have a resident permit in Switzerland unless you have a valid passport.

I asked the American consul in Geneva how come. He looked at a cable from Washington and said, "Because of your Communist activities." I said, "As far as I know, I've never been in the same room with a Communist." He said, "I'm not interested." So I wrote to Ruth Shipley, the horrible woman who was in charge of passports for the INS.* I bombarded her with letters, asking her what I was charged with. I got no answer. I wrote to my brother, who was a magazine editor and apolitical. He and his corporation counsel went down to Washington and saw Mrs. Shipley three times. One night, I got a phone call in Switzerland from New York. It was my brother. "I have been batting my head against a stone wall and getting nowhere. They won't tell me why they've taken your passport away. I am sick over this." The next morning I got another phone call from New York: my brother had committed suicide.

I wrote to Mrs. Shipley and said, "Now that my brother is gone, will you please tell me why?" No answer. I had written to a lot of liberal friends asking them to help me. Nobody came to my help. I guess they were scared stiff. So I decided to call on a couple of reactionaries I knew. I wrote to Senator Warren Austin, whose campaign in New Hampshire I had worked on. And to Jim Farley, whom I'd known as a political reporter. Mrs. Shipley sent them twenty-one charges against me, all of them absurd. It is known that I had been seen with suspected Communists. Guilt by association. I had associated with Bill Shirer, a suspected Communist because he had associated with me. Finally, oh God, I got my passport back.

Some of the guys I know joined the church—that is, the establishment—and went along with everything, just to get their jobs back. To Bill Shirer's credit, he never did it. Neither did I. Fortunately, Bill's book *The Rise and Fall of the Third Reich* made a lot of money, so he didn't suffer financially. I did, oh boy.

Murrow was a fine man, but I'll never forgive him for letting Shirer down. He told Bill he was let go because of his politics. My boss told John W. Vandercook, who had an evening show and was a great foreign affairs expert, that he was fired because the American public was no longer interested in that stuff. I had a fifteen-minute program every morning, and I was told they needed my time for a soap opera. Not only were you fired, but your intelligence was insulted. The joke is: most of them are gone and I'm still around.

I have retired from some things but not from others, not from life. I raised acorn squash before people had heard of it. That didn't work out very well. My chicken raising gave me a modest living till they caught a disease. I started copying antiques as a cabinetmaker. See that snuff box? It's a copy of one that goes back to colonial days.

* The U.S. Immigration and Naturalization Service.

Then I started making pieces of furniture and sold quite a few. I wasn't sitting on my tail at any time.

At ninety-two, I still have not retired. I'm as active as I've ever been in my life. I'm still writing. I still lecture. And I do a lot of physical things out here in the country.

When I had my ninetieth birthday, several hundred of my friends gathered and I made a little speech. I decided that when a person reached my age, it was incumbent upon him to give a recipe for longevity. Until the age of fifty, live dangerously. At fifty-five, stop smoking. At sixty, start courting a girl, preferably Jewish, who is sixteen years younger. At sixty-five, marry the girl (my wife, of course). At seventy-five, stop drinking anything stronger than white wine. At seventy-five, instead of riding in a small vehicle around a golf course, occasionally dismounting and taking a few whacks at an innocent little object, spend six hours a day, six days a week, two months a year, raking leaves. At eighty, because the trees grow larger and produce more leaves, increase the leaf-raking to five hours a day, three months a year. At eighty-five, begin planning how you would like to celebrate your ninetieth birthday. Continue to use a manual typewriter, resisting all propaganda about word processors or computers, and, finally, continue to harass all establishments.

I'm a great pessimist today. I don't believe in a god. If there is one, he must be looking down, shaking his head, and saying: "What a mistake I made." I think the evils of the world are intrinsic in us. I think man is a killer. We have done all these silly things like getting to the moon, but have we progressed intellectually? No. At ninety-two, I'm still not a member of any establishment, religious or political. My credo and recipe for longevity bears repeating: Continue to harass all establishments.

Charlie Andrews, 75

During television's pioneering years, Chicago was a key city. TV's preeminent critic, John Crosby, coined the phrase "TV, Chicago style." Among its first network programs were Garroway At Large; Kukla, Fran and Ollie; *and* Studs' Place. *As writer and producer, he was responsible for creating two of them.* In 1949, he won the* Look Magazine *Award as the best television writer of the year.*

If you were born in Fond Du Lac and got hooked on books and you read guys who were just a little too avant-garde to be in high school, you wanted to leave town. I read Hemingway, Saroyan, Farrell, Nelson Algren, all those guys. So I wanted to leave town and be a writer.

I worked in Milwaukee, in shoe stores and factories and stuff like that. Then I went to Chicago. Then you decided which coast you wanted to go to. Well, I ended up on the East Coast. That was the pattern you were supposed to follow, and that's what I did.

I wanted to write radio because Paul Rhymer was my idol. He wrote *Vic and Sade.* It was so charming and so funny and so low key.† The jokes had to come from character. They couldn't just be jokes. All you wanted was a chuckle, not a roar of laughter. The whole idea was that the speaker was addressing one or two people, not a huge audience.

Roosevelt, in his fireside chats, wasn't talking to America in the abstract. He was talking to a couple of farmers someplace, a couple of unemployed someplace, a couple of workers—just a couple of people. It was Dave Garroway's approach, too.

I went for radio because books take so long to write and I have no patience for that sort of thing. The most I could tackle were short stories. They work fine on radio. I was aiming at a half hour. Fifteen minutes were even better. You didn't have to make big points. You could make small, graceful little things. That's all I tried to do. Nice, quiet little things. You didn't have to play any tricks to get there.

What happened was television. At first, it was very much like radio. The original version of our show *Studs' Place* was a fifteen-minute thing. It became a half-hour show and that was fine. But then

---

* *Garroway At Large* and *Studs' Place.* I was a regular performer in the latter. My colleagues were Beverly Younger, Win Stracke, and Chet Roble.

† Among the popular radio soap operas that originated in Chicago, *Vic and Sade* was an anachronism. It was a fifteen-minute daily program, each episode independent of the others. Its humor was Lardneresque in nature.

the TV audience got big, and big money rolled in. Now you couldn't experiment anymore. You couldn't play anymore.

Garroway had one of the best radio shows, the *1160 Club*. It was mainly jazz. I'd supply Dave with little, tiny stories, not for him to read. I'd write as briefly as I could, and Dave would make something of it. He could make something charming out of any tender little thing. It was marvelous.

It was on at midnight. People weren't looking for excitement. It was quiet; it was time to go to bed. I listened to more jazz than Dave did, so I could steer him toward things. I'd say, "Hey, Dave, I heard a girl singer, Sarah Vaughan. You ought to listen to her." Dave was delighted to listen to her and fell in love with her. The two of us worked well together.

Dave was a staff announcer at NBC, and so was Hugh Downs. Their job was to do station breaks. Then Dave got his chance to do a late-night show. So did Hugh. They'd take turns filling the time. Filling the time was about all it was. Dave was developing a bunch of loyal listeners.

When television came along, they wanted to see if it could still work. They designed two shows for Garroway. This was after the war, 1946. They tried for a classic presentation, designed for a guy in a dinner jacket. Dave slouched around in unpressed clothes. It turned out to be a big mistake, and Dave was very unhappy.

He said to Ted Mills, the executive producer, "Let me bring in Charlie. He thinks the way I do. Give us a shot." They said okay. They didn't know what else to do. My thinking was to keep it as simple as possible. The studio was too small for an audience, why worry about it? At first they wanted to do it in a theater, and Dave said no. The only way I could figure out to make it work was to play to the camera. Let the camera be the audience. If the camera caught the picture of another camera, that was okay, nothing wrong with that. You could go behind the scenery, around the scenery, through the scenery. You could do anything, as long as you didn't have to worry about a big audience. One person could follow your camera: it became his eyes. They let us try it, and it worked from the first show.

Nothing came from the sky. If there was a broken chair on the set, Dave made a comment on broken chairs as he walked to the next set, which had a good chair. No canned laughter, no teleprompter. The teleprompter hadn't even been invented.

Back then, there wasn't such a fortune involved in anything. You didn't have to have it written down, you didn't have to have it approved by any committee, you didn't have to rehearse it until it was word perfect. You trusted the performers.*

---

* The storyline of *Studs' Place* was usually no more than a single page. The weekly half-hour program had no script. Among the credits was: "Dialogue by the Cast."

The business side didn't make any decisions about what went on the air. People kept pitching ideas, and then someone would say, "Yeah, that's good." If the cameraman had an idea or the guy who swept the floor, you listened and you used it if it worked. [*Chuckles.*] Well, it isn't that way now, not anymore.

It changed when daytime opened up. Up until then, there were only programs in the evening. Who is going to watch TV in the daytime? Everybody's working. The housewife has the kids, is cooking. Pat Weaver, who was the head of NBC at the time, said that people would watch in the morning. Everyone thought he was crazy. But he pushed it through and created *The Today Show.* Pat knew it would open up the whole thing. The more folksy Dave was, the more welcome he was in someone's house. I came in 1950.

Pat was looking for a certain type of guy. He didn't want a show business type, a snappy talker, a comic. He wanted an easy-going guy. He looked around and decided that Dave was the guy to be the host.

The Today Show went on the air with no sponsors at all. What happened was a huge audience response that advertisers didn't believe in, the network didn't believe in. But the people were out there and they were watching. At the end of the first week, they had bags full of mail. It was then that an old news guy, producing the business end of the show, took two guides from NBC, each with a bagfull of mail, to the advertisers.

He dumped these unopened letters on the guy's desk, hundreds and hundreds of them, and said, "Pick any letter you want. If you find one word that's derogatory, I'll pick up my mail and leave." But if they're all good, you've got to let me make my sales pitch." They were all good. Now the advertisers began to come in. More and more.

Everything was live. There was no tape. Tape hadn't even been invented. The producer and I were always on the studio floor, where the cameras were. If Dave needed anything, I was there to help him out.

One day, about six months into the show, we had a commercial for dog food. They'd put the dog food on a white cue card on a desk, because we didn't have the space for a special set. They'd have a puppy that hadn't been fed overnight. The floor manager, usually a kid getting started in the business, would stand there with the puppy for about ten seconds before the commercial went on. He'd put the dog next to the food and they'd punch up the shot of the dog happily gumming it up. Garroway would do the voice-over sell: "If you want your dog to be happy..."

This one morning, we were standing there, the food on the pristine white card, as they put the puppy down. But the dog didn't go for the food. He squatted and relieved himself. A big brown bit of relief, right next to the food. It was ten seconds before the shot came up. The kid just froze. His hands were in the air. He didn't know what to do.

The producer stepped over, rolled the dog's turd off into the palm of his hand, stepped out of the shot, and they punched it up. The dog was eating the food and everything went beautifully. When it was over, the producer walked over to the boy and said, "Son, I just want to show you the difference between a floor director and a producer. A handful of dog shit." That's the way it was. You did whatever you had to do to get the show going.

As TV got costly, you couldn't take chances anymore. I guess they were right. When you have a show that costs $100,000, if it doesn't work, that's not much in terms of television money. But when you've got a show that costs a million, you don't want to take any chances. You want it all down pat and safe.

Dave was a victim of the changes. He couldn't operate. The big shots that owned the shows didn't want guys that fooled around with the dialogue. They wanted the dialogue they had approved in advance. Spontaneity slowly, slowly disappeared. That sort of creative tension was all gone. Looking back, I don't remember a show that went down the drain because someone made a mistake. They all worked, every damn one.

It had to change. The beginnings are always fun because you're finding your way. You had the excitement of discovering things. Now there's too much money involved for that sort of stuff.

I would like to see television less stereotyped, a lot freer. It's not loose, lacks that feeling of being alive. It's cut and dried. If you listen to comedy shows today, it's a written line, an attempt at a joke, another line, another joke. If people hear laughter, they think what they heard was funny. If you took the laugh track off the big shows now, they'd be embarrassing.

The only measure they have to decide whether a show is welcomed into the home are ratings. The people that do the ratings swear that they're within 4 percent accurate. I don't know how they prove that, but I don't know how to prove they're wrong.

To a television sponsor, a million people is a total failure, even ten million, it's nothing. You gotta have million, a hundred million. Now you're talking business. More people may have seen an opera on TV than in all the history of the Met. Yet it may be peanuts in the ratings. Crazy.

We are more informed now, but I'm afraid we're not informed on the right things. I can't help but feel that the violence we experience in our daily lives is closely related to the amount of violence that young people are exposed to. Kids watching TV are exposed to something like sixty violent acts a day in their living room. Sixty of these events a day times seven days a week times 365 days a year. So violence gets to be a perfectly normal thing. Their heroes do it, and problems are resolved by a gun.

When you were a kid and went to the movies, you saw Hoot Gibson. It was always violent: the fight, the case, the shooting. The villain put his hand on his chest and fell over dead. But there was no blood. Now the camera cuts to a close-up, you see blood splattering on the wall, the open wounds. It's in your living room and quite acceptable.

I'm opposed to censorship of any kind. On the other hand, left to their own devices, the TV guys are out to make a big buck, no matter what it takes. That's what it's all about. That's the line of work I was in. If the client, the network, says the show's too slow, you've gotta speed it up, make it more exciting. How about some shooting? It's money.

I don't know what's going on. I can't imagine what's going on in the mind of an underprivileged guy. He can barely make a living. He's living in squalor up in, let's say, Harlem, the Bronx, places like that. He doesn't have enough to eat, there's rats, there's cockroaches, there's one light bulb, no refrigeration, and he's watching a program that shows a typical American family. They've got a beautiful kitchen, a huge refrigerator, a lovely sofa, pictures on the wall, rugs on the floor. This guy is saying: "That's how it is everyplace else. What made me end up here? If that's how it is, I want to get some of it." He can't do it with an honest day's work 'cause he can't find a job. How is he gonna do it? That picture is dangled in front of his eyes. He's told every time some person on TV opens his mouth, "Buy our lovely frozen vegetables, they're from Hawaii." This guy can't buy dog food. It's really frightening. What does he say to himself?

And it isn't just the guy in Harlem, it's the farmer in the Midwest who is just barely getting by. He may not be worrying about his next meal, but his wife says, "Won't we ever get a new washing machine?"

Changes may be coming with cable. The networks will be the dinosaurs when hundreds of cable outlets open up. Programs won't cost so much. Audiences will be smaller. They won't have the money to spend, so they'll have to think.

The only thing I can hope for is that eventually there will be so many stations, so many programs, that I may have a *real* choice. I'll be able to press a button and something will appear on the screen that I've been waiting for. And I won't have to sit up till four o'clock in the morning to see it.

I don't watch much television anymore. In the evening, I like to watch teams like the Chicagos and the New Yorks play basketball. Sports. A couple of shows I like. That's enough for me.

Do you feel what you have to contribute is still pertinent?

No. Nobody wants it. If you're working on a television show, you spend your whole life with your peers. You're thirty years old, you're just getting settled, you have a kid. To have lunch with me is like having lunch with your grandfather. That's no fun. And you can't make any money that way. You want to be with the guys, stand at the bars, have a drink, and toss around an idea or two that might make a buck.

Imagine walking up to an advertiser and trying to sell the kind of show we did in 1950. They'll say, "Who are the writers?" "Well, they'll make it up as they go along." "You're asking me to pay $800,000 for a show they're going to make up as they go along? Are you crazy?" So bye-bye to all that. Spontaneity? There's no way.

We all tend to talk about the good old days as if that were the right way to do it and everybody else is doing it wrong. The way they're doing it is the way it has to be done today. The shows they're doing today wouldn't have worked in our time: they're too hard, too cruel.

CHAPTER TEN

The Pitch

Charles A. Kasher, 81
NEW YORK CITY

It is talk at rapid-fire pace, at times feverish, as though he were on the back of a wagon or on a busy street corner, offering the gawking throng a once-in-a-lifetime chance at Dr. Dulcamara's Elixir of Love.

Give me a crowd and I'm one of the greatest liars in the world. I haven't had a crowd lately. [*Laughs.*] But one on one, I can't tell a lie. It's impossible for me. I was a great pitchman, but I was a lousy businessman. We had to deal with people individually. [*Chuckles.*]

My imagination blossomed when there was a big crowd. The bigger the crowd, the better I got. Don't ask me why, but I'm a compulsive truth teller with individuals. With the crowd, I'm a compulsive liar.

I made a lot of money in different businesses, but only because my intelligence overrode my inability to lie. I have a friend who hates me. Why? We were both in the film business and he had a property. He said, "When we sit with these people, tell them how sure-fire it is." I said, "I can't do that. I gotta say, 'Well, I think it's got possibilities, maybe with a little work.'" He still hates me for it.

In 1950, I remember you on a small TV screen. You talked for about half an hour. It was a pitch. There was never anything like it, before or since.

It was thirty minutes and it was a medicine pitch I had distilled down from the hour and a half that I'd use at fairs, before large crowds, year after year. It was the invention of what we now call an infomercial. We don't mention the product until the last three minutes. We'd give them humor, we'd give them entertainment, we'd give them information, we'd give them social history, and in the last minutes we'd wrap it altogether by mentioning the commercial. What you saw was a thirty-minute medicine pitch.

We drew better audiences than the features. I was selling vitamins. I told people things they were familiar with, that they understand, that they believe. Then we'd gradually, seamlessly, get them to the point where we wanted them to be. It was convincing them that nature knew best.

The vitamin story was relatively new then. I sold this product called Vigor-8. The label said: "8 vitamins, 12 minerals in Vigor 8." [*Chuckles.*] We sold five- and ten-dollar packages, which would be the equivalent of fifty or a hundred dollars now. God Almighty, did the pitch work! It was phenomenal.

I bought a lot of vitamins from drug companies, and I mixed them into wheat middlings, the discarded part, normally fed to the dogs. We mixed it up in this pretty jar with a nice-looking label. It was a powder. I trained the pitchman for all the Goldblatt and Weiboldt stores in Chicago, stores in Detroit. I had twenty pitchmen working at one time. I was quite prosperous at that point.

Before I was a medicine man, I sold hair stuff, lightweight soap. It was really a cake of hard lather. We talked about lanolin, but there was no lanolin in it. There was a lot of lanolin in our pitch. [*Chuckles.*]

In 1936, I was working with the Great Lakes Exposition in Cleveland. Sometimes ladies would come up and flirt a little bit. This looker came up and said, "If I use that, will my hair be like yours?" I said, "Of course, madam." She said, "In that case, I'll take a pass. You're loosing your hair." [*Laughs.*] Which I was. So that's when I first decided to move over to the medicine pitch.

I was a board boy on Wall Street in 1929, when the market crashed. They gave me a few extra weeks' pay and I felt rich. I went looking for jobs. There were none. The only jobs were knocking on doors, soliciting. I followed a blind ad. The guy had a box of Christmas cards. When you sold it, you gave them, free, a little box with two vials: one contained thick ink and the other, gold powder. You could write your name on the card, sprinkle the powder, hold it over anything warm—a light bulb—and it would all melt together and be embossed.

I said, "How much will you charge me for just the little embossing kits. They were cheap. I bought a gross of them. I found a spot in the Grand Central terminal where I could pitch it. I set up a folding card table in front of a milk bar. It was getting toward Christmas. I worked out a pitch and showed people how to write their names, and it went like wildfire. It cost me twenty cents a box. I sold them for fifty. I made quite a bit of money. That was my first entrepreneurial act, and I was seventeen. From that day, I never turned an honest dollar. [*Chuckles.*]

There's no special art. I was well read, had a decent voice, an articulate guy—give me a crowd and I blossomed. A guy came up to me and said, "I hear you're in the same business I am. I'm a pitchman." "What the hell is a pitchman? I don't play baseball." He explained the glory of the road, the high pitch, the low pitch, the big cars, the beautiful clothes. We went out on the road.

He was selling some stuff you put on your eyeglasses so they don't steam up when you go indoors from the cold. Naturally, he called it StayClear. Within a short time, we were broke. I had taken up selling tie forms. It's a little thing with two loops you put around your neck, you tie your tie in it, and you never have to untie forever after. We didn't make a nickel. We'd stay at the Milner Hotels, flops, a dollar a night. Sometimes we were so broke, we slept in the car, a jalopy.

We're in Columbus, Ohio. Somebody said that's a good town for pitching. Pitchmen tell each other. There's an underground telegraph, a brotherhood, held together by *Billboard* magazine. It had a column, "Pipes for Pitchmen," good fairs, bad fairs, watch out for the cops here, and so on. If you were in it long enough, everybody knew you. A marvelous brotherhood.

It's evening. We needed money for room rent, something to eat. We set up in the doorway of a store that was closed. We were pitching, he with his eyeglass polish and I with whatever. A man in the crowd, with his hair down to his shoulders, beautifully dressed, expensive Stetson, buys one of my items as soon as I get through with the pitch. He says, "Ilshay." That means "shill." He gets his money back and gave me back the goods.

Pitchmen eek-spay ig-pay Atin-lay?

Of course. His name was Jack Bentley. He was operating at Kresge's dime store on the main street. The next day, we walk by and watch this guy. He was pitching hair stuff. He was giving away free samples and getting a crowd. He took in like twenty-five dollars. We almost fainted.

He was a high pitchman—makes the long pitch. A low pitchman is just a demonstrator. We'd go listen to this guy all the time we were struggling in Columbus. He'd buy us coffee. One day, he says, [*voice hoarse*] "Hey, I blew my pipes. Think you can cover for me a couple of days?" He took me in, had my clothes pressed. We used to work in a dental frock coat that buttons up around the neck. "They'll think you're a professional." So he took me up to the hotel and rehearsed me. The next day, my first pitch was seven minutes and I took in nothing, but by the end of the day, I was making fifteen, eighteen dollars. I was getting the hang of it. He blew his pipes again and now he's stuck with me. On top of it, the Kresge manager, because we help bring traffic in the store, says, "You gotta keep this guy. We get twice as much action at the counter."

So we become partners, meaning, he takes in all the money and doles me out a few bob every now and then. [*Chuckles.*] But we got to be good friends, and I got to be a good hair worker.

We went to the Polish part of Buffalo, where I knew the store. We got mobs of guys who worked in the steel mills. I did the pitch and the manager of the store says, "Fifty cents for a shampoo? Our customers pay a dime, they buy a bar of soap." We killed them. We murdered them.

We'd do gimmicks, tricks, gaffs, the hand is quicker than the eye. We would take this chemical and put it on six, seven ordinary bars of soap and they'd turn red. We'd say, "There's lye in these bars, see?" Then we take our bar of soap and take the lanolin out of it. Anyway, we said it was lanolin. Then we'd rub it in and, see, it penetrates. We did absolutely tremendous business. We didn't even know where the stuff came from. We bought it in bulk and wrapped it ourselves in the hotel room at night.

In New York, I met the guy who invented the pitch, Al. He used to take in a thousand dollars a week, doing it in a department store. He'd give the store four hundred. We'd go regularly to his mother's for Jewish meals. There was a fraternity of pitchmen once upon a time. Now, I don't know.

When the war started, I made jewelry out of cast-off wood, waste stuff. It was so successful I sold it to Woolworth's. I made a line of toys from the same waste that I sold to Montgomery Ward. I should have made a fortune, I should have gotten rich, but I was a lousy businessman.

The real challenge was out in the open, at fairs. It was the medicine pitch, lasted an hour, an hour and a half. We attacked it from every angle. The substance is: we destroy everything we eat, we boil it, we broil it, fry it [*his speech speeds to a runaway pace*] boiled, broiled, fried, roasted, toasted, baked, burned—ah, I don't remember anymore. Anyway, the pitch was, you ate twice as much as you should and you starved to death. The best parts of the food go down the drain, the rats get big and fat and you die of heart attacks. We'd go on: Doctors don't know anything about causes. They give you medicine, treat effects. You have to treat causes. What's the cause? Malnutrition, the way you live, the way you eat. Here are the vitamins, the minerals missing from your diet. It was a powerful pitch.

At the Canadian National Exposition, I made the first thousand-dollar pitch ever known. This was '46, '47. In ten-dollar bottles.

That's about a hundred dollars today. I had so much confidence. It was a form of mass hypnosis.

I went into television in Chicago, '49, '50. Everything was live in those days. I edited down my vitamin pitch to thirty minutes. I entertain, I amuse, but at the very end, I go: "Why do you think I told you all these things? Because I love you? I don't even know you. I told you these things because there's something you can do about it, and I'm the one that will help you do it." Out comes this Vigor-8. "Go call this number now."

We bought a spot on a Baltimore station for $180. We had over three hundred calls, so we knew we had a tiger by the tail. I was scared to death of the Food and Drug Administration, so I switched to the hair pitch, my first love.

I came up with the idea of Charles Antell. My first name and my mother's maiden name, my company. It was an outgrowth of the pitch I learned in Columbus in 1930. I called in Ricky Llewellyn, who was a funny guy with a great pitch and a wonderful head of hair. When I worked medicine, he alternated with me. We didn't even have merchandise. We did it with dummies. If it worked, we'd create the product and send a postcard: "Sorry it's so late, but the demand has been so great."

We did it on a TV station in Washington. There were so many calls, the phone lines blew out. We got over three thousand orders. The pitch had a lot of innuendoes and promises that it couldn't keep, but it was relatively clean. Within a year, we were in the stores. At the end of the pitch, my boy would say, "Why order it by mail and wait two, three weeks? Go to your nearest drug store." The demand was so great, they had to carry it. Within two years, we had a factory. We were doing business in the millions. We were doing as much hair dressing as all the other companies put together. My two partners were ganging up on me, so I had them buy me out.

I went into the mail-order business, with new products. I sold a spray gun at $19.95. The original pieces cost me twenty cents. [*A friend interjects: "It was the copy Charlie wrote. Even in a catalog, it was still the master's pitch."*] It was a mammoth success, incredible, extraordinary, unheard of. The spray gun didn't work very well, though, so we refunded probably 30 percent of all the money we took in.

I got into automotive items. Our spark plug was a huge success. We became the fifth largest distributor in the world. It didn't work very well. About 20 percent complained. We refunded, of course. But we still made a bundle.

I got tired of the mail-order business and sold out all my holdings. I set off for England to become a film producer.

*After four frustrating years of almost-deals, of ideas that didn't
quite catch fire, of gamble that didn't quite pay off, of considerable
money lost, he called it a day. His one success had been as co-
producer of the film* The Ipcress File, *but it wasn't quite enough to
balance out the losses.*

I retired after I found that I couldn't get a picture off the ground in
Hollywood. I tried for four years. I was sixty-one. Aside from occasional writing, I've done nothing else. How does my day go? It does-
n't go at all. You have to push it along. [*Chuckles.*]

I had some serious surgery, a little heart business. I live in the
country with beautiful scenery. I watch television, read. I keep up
with the world as a spectator. Other than that, I really kill time. I
mean I *kill* it before it kills me. [*Laughs.*]

When I think of the pitchmen of my day, I think of jazz musicians.
When I think of what passes for the pitch today, I think of rock. Jazz
required true technique and knowledge of your instrument. Rock
requires writing shitty songs with stupid lyrics and noise. In our
day, the pitches were brilliant. You always astonished the audience.
They never knew what you were going to bring up from under the
counter. You entertained them, you made them laugh, you were a
teacher: "I'm gonna show you how you can…" Now there's a pseudo-
audience with pseudo-questions getting pseudo-answers from a
pseudo-pitchman. In those other days, the pitch had to be seamless.
On that fairground, the minute there was a break in your pitch, people would say, "What am I doing here?" You had to hold their attention against the noise of the merry-go-rounds and the carnival
barkers. There's a rich history, going back to the medicine show,
snak eoil salesmen, herb doctors who sold laxatives, elixirs.

People didn't come to hear the pitch. They came to look at the
cows and blue-ribbon hogs, to go to girlie shows, to see the two-
headed boy. You had to dissipate all these diversions and focus them
in on what you were pitching. You had to be good. It was an art form.

Naah, there are no great pitchmen anymore. When I think of Jack
Bentley, of Al, of young Rickey, of myself [*a long pause*]…yeah.

Danny Newman, 74
CHICAGO, ILLINOIS

*"Danny Newman has done more for the performing arts
in this country than any ten foundations."*
—W. McNeil Lowry, Vice President, The Ford Foundation

*His evangelical fervor overwhelms any acquaintance or passing
stranger. He is P. T. Barnum in spirit, though his manner is pure
Diaghilev. His black fedora, conservative dress, and upright pos-
ture are in striking counterpoint to his pitch. His is the singular fus-
ing of formality, hyperbole, and bonhomie.*

*From a recent press release in 1994: "Danny will celebrate sixty
years in show business and thirty years of these with the renowned
Lyric Opera Company of Chicago." (Need you ask who wrote it?)*

I call myself a press agent, never a public relations man. Never. I do
work in the performing arts, a highfalutin term. It covers ballet,
symphony, opera, as well as plain show business: the circus and
vaudeville and motion pictures and legit theater. "Press agent"
sounds old-fashioned to many people today. It has a pejorative
sound and they don't want to be identified with that. When I meet
somebody who calls himself a communications director, he's
annoyed when I say, "Oh, you're a press agent."

I began as a fourteen-year-old boy in the theater. That was 1933.
My heroes were the advance men of legit shows on tour. I thought,
"Geez, someday I'll be a real press agent like them." Eventually I
became one.

Richard Maney, the nonpareil, wrote such brilliant press releases
that the *New York Times* ran them on Sundays as though they were
written by their critic. They were eccentric and colorful.

When I came into the field, radio was not all that established. We
went for a mile to hear the first Dempsey-Tunney fight on somebody's crystal set. Print was the big thing.

As a boy of fifteen or sixteen, I was already at work, coming into
the office of Claudia Cassidy.* Legit press agents had one day of the
week to visit the critics. She was wonderfully patient with me and
would tell me stories of her friends, Alfred Lunt, Lynn Fontanne,
Laurette Taylor, Lotte Lehmann, Rosa Raisa. It was so personal.

---

* For many years, the doyenne of Chicago's drama and music critics, celebrated
for her style and toughness.

In the '40s and '50s, when I was established in Chicago, I dealt with seven daily newspapers.* I would go to all of them. I loved it.

Part of my function was to get all the papers to cover dress rehearsals. That was no small task because we were competing with crime, with accidents, all the things they needed their photographers for. Almost all the time, I succeeded. I made it an art, convincing the picture-assignment editor to cover the rehearsals.

Before the Lyric, there was the Chicago Opera Company in 1946. Also, the Metropolitan on tour and the New York City Center Opera Company. I handled all of them. At the time of the rehearsals, I had the photographers from all seven papers. By the time they were getting the pictures out of the soup, I was already at the paper, writing the captions. I wrote them all, complete. There were a lot of foreign names: Italian opera singers, whose names the picture-desk guys couldn't spell. So it was a great service to them. Of course, I began to embellish. As long as I'm writing, it might as well have a theatrical flair. There is a certain floridity of style and extravagance of phrase that I feel is expected of us because [*hams it up*] we are in the theater! We're not running a bank. I think of all of us as performers, even if we're press agents.

Once, when I handed in what was, for me, a conservative blurb, Tom Willis† was startled: "Usually when I get a release from you, trumpets are blowing. There is something not quite right about this one."

For years, my captions were sacred. They would run them exactly as I wrote them. I took great pride in that. The picture editors felt involved. This could not happen if I sent over some messenger or called them on the phone or sent out some press releases. I was *there*. Lloyd Lewis, managing editor of the *Chicago Daily News*, was an erudite and scholarly man.‡ He was asked, "Why do you give Danny Newman's attractions all that space?" He replied simply, "Danny is always there."

Today my colleagues deal mostly by fax. It has nothing at all to do with the personal one-on-one. I've been blessed with boundless and unflagging energies. Despite the years, I have retained those.

I always came to the newspaper office with eight, ten big envelopes, effulgent with photographs, bursting with releases [*gears up to carnival-barker speed*]—the annual visits of the New York Opera Company, the Metropolitan, the New York City Ballet

* The *Tribune*, the *Sun*, the *Times*, the *Daily News*, the *American*, the *Herald-Examiner*, and the *Journal of Commerce*.

† At the time, music critic of the *Chicago Tribune*.

‡ He had begun as a press agent and was, at one time or another, a sports writer, drama critic, civic historian, and playwright.

Theatre, the Art Film Festival, with French, Italian, and Russian pictures, the Oriental Theatre, Minsky's Rialto burlesque house. I was also handling in those years [*without missing a beat*] the Allied Arts Sunday concerts at Orchestra Hall; the hard-ticket, reserved-seat movies, such as John Houseman's *Julius Caesar*, Sam Goldwyn's *Porgy and Bess*, and *El Cid;* the Wild Indians shows, [*faster and faster*] hard tickets at the McVicker's and Harris Theatres, Mayor Kelly's Kelly Bowl at Soldier Field; the Goodman, the old Chicago Opera Company, and the Lyric, beginning in '54. [*Takes a short breath, very short.*] I was doing most of these things at the same time. Never had less than half a dozen attractions at one time. The '40s and '50s were the peak of this activity. Associates? What associates? I worked by myself, of course.

"*I remember the first Indian show I ever handled. About forty or fifty of them came off the day coach from an Oklahoma reservation. I met them at the train. It was a terribly dusty ride, three days. I took them over to an old hotel and got them rooms.*

"*None of them had ever been in an elevator or had ever used the telephone. They discovered they could call each other in their rooms. All night long, the switchboard operator went crazy. They were riding the elevators up and down all the time. It was their discovery of a new world.*

"*Several columnists turned it down because they thought it was a press agent's invention. I told another columnist all the details, sitting at his desk for two hours. He was so moved, he ran the story for three days.* [A long pause.] *Today, press agents would send a release about something like this, but you have to personally tell the story.*"

I would start at five in the afternoon, get home at one in the morning, because I had to go to all the papers. I often forgot to eat, I was so excited by it all the time. The next day, when those gorgeous layouts came out, it was marvelous. For years, the *Chicago Tribune* ran the entire back page on our opera dress rehearsals. I've had my front-page triumphs, too. We don't have the personal press agent push anymore, the aggressive spirit.

It was not unusual to see me in the city room in my shirt sleeves, at a typewriter, flailing away with my two fingers. Many had the impression I was an employee of the paper. I fostered that idea, that I belonged there. If you tried that today, seven security guards would escort you out. Anyway, I couldn't work their computers.

Before plane travel, they came by train. I was at the station all the time: Twentieth Century, Broadway Limited. I brought my own photographers when the papers couldn't make it. I'd rush the film holders to the picture editors. They appreciated this rush service.

One Saturday night, when we celebrated an opera singer's birthday, we brought in cake between acts and all the singers gathered in the dressing room. If I made my own pictures, I came to the paper on Sunday morning. No press agent ever came in on Sunday. I had an open field. The Monday papers always featured my birthday boy or girl.

I had to crack every part of the paper. I went to see financial editors, sports editors, fashion editors, cooking editors, columnists. I would take one of my prima donnas or actresses to a top fashion house and have her pose in their finest clothes. We'd make the fashion page. The same with her recipes. I would bring my vaudeville star to the fight gym and have her put on gloves with a famous fighter or palooka. Bang. We're on the sports page. The gym was then near the *Sun-Times*. Kup was then a sports reporter.* It was a hot day, the windows were open. The cab fare was $1.50. The driver had no change for a ten. Kup dropped some money down from the high second floor. Can you imagine that today?

Today, a public relations agency in Chicago doing similar work employs about thirty people. But not with the intensity or passion. The trend has been toward less individual involvement. Today, the city's two daily newspapers are more like other corporations, not too receptive to the personal touch. [*Disdainfully*] Media agents today...

In 1946, the Met came with Lucia di Lammermoor. It was the Chicago debut of Richard Tucker. About three minutes before curtain, I was standing at the stage door when an elderly Italian man was having a hard time trying to get past the doorman. It turns out he was the illustrious conductor of the Civic Opera during the '20s, Pietro Moranzoni. We were all sold out clean. No seats. So I said, "Maestro, you'll sit with me in the wings."

Tucker was an unknown at the time, but he was singing like Gigli or Bjoerling. The audience was stunned. Very big applause. In the final act, as Tucker sings over the grave of Lucia, sort of a double aria, the audience goes wild. Suddenly, the old maestro, who hadn't said a word till then, turns to me and says, "This tenor, he's Italian, no?" I said, "No, maestro, he's Jewish." He says, "But heeza papa and mama, they Italian Jews maybe?" I say, "No, they were born in Romania." The applause is still going on. "Ahh, heeza study in Italy." "No, maestro, he completed all his studies in Brooklyn." A long pause this time, as the applause is beginning to subside. "I don't care. Heeza the best Italian tenor I ever hear."

---

* Irving Kupcinet, Chicago's longest-tenured columnist.

Could this happen today? First of all, media people wouldn't be standing at the stage door. I doubt whether they'd know the stage manager, who gave us the chairs.

In the '60s, I took a divergence in the road. The Ford Foundation suggested I should apply some of my concepts of subscription attendance. I call it "committed attendance": people who sign contracts that they will be there for the whole season. Not these slothful, fickle, single-ticket buyers, whom I've excoriated on five continents. I don't really hate them, but I dislike them. They come to pick the raisins out of our cake. They wait four or five years until you have a big hit. They don't go regularly, they don't participate. They do nothing.

When there's a commitment, wonderful things happen. The subscriber begins to develop taste, discrimination, discernment. He begins to become a better man. Years ago, many men were dragged by their heels, against their will, by their culture-vulture wives. What has happened now? A miracle. The men have come to love it. They are often more enthusiastic than the ladies and have become the greatest boosters of not-for-profit performing arts.

You're an evangelist for culture?

Yes, that's a good word to use. I've been called the Billy Graham of subscription theater. I've also been linked by the press to Billy Sunday. Most of my young associates don't even know who Billy Sunday was. The generation gap.*

[*Softly, slowly*] Four years and four months ago, I lost my wife of forty years. Grief so overwhelmed me that I lost my drive. I closeted myself in my office for a long time. It seemed forever. In the past year or so, I've come to myself. I'm in motion again."

The Ford Foundation had me going all over the United States to teach the philosophy of subscription audiences. In 1961, there were only four theater companies in the country. Now there are between four and five hundred. It was to end the era when theater companies opened and closed like revolving doors. It wasn't that nobody came, but not enough came to keep the place open.

Under my system of committed audiences, it's not unusual for a theater to have 15,000 or 20,000 subscribers. The Globe Theatre of San Diego, one of my projects, had, at last report, 53,000. This applies to ballet, opera, symphony. In the early '60s, there were only

---

* He was the most celebrated of evangelists at the turn of the century. An ex-baseball player, he was "saved," and was as renowned for his virulent xenophobia as for his fire-eating style.

two professional ballet companies in the country. Both in New York City. Today, when I address them at a convention, it takes a big ballroom to accommodate them.

As I look back on my life—nah, I'm not an introspective person. I don't ask questions about myself. I tend not to have regrets, dwell on what I should or should not have done. I always look forward to the next project.

We all have fantasies, I know. But I really feel I've lived mine. If I had my choice, I'd like it just as it has been. It's not unusual for old fuddy-duddies to look back on their salad days and say, "Ah, those were the days." But I honestly think those *were* better days, not that we haven't done some good things since then. In general, I think we treat human beings better than we did. However, on a day-to-day basis, I'm afraid not. There's so much less emotion, less passion. As Duke Ellington's song goes, we "don't get around much anymore." It isn't so much having more imagination as having good feet.

I remember 1942. The war was on and, at the train stations, they wouldn't let anybody past the barrier, because of troop movements. I had to wait, along with a crowd of people. I was there for Jimmy Durante, who was playing that week at the Oriental. I had never met him before, so he had no idea what I looked like. Suddenly, I see him coming down the ramp, heading straight for me! He begins to pump my hand. I said, "How did you know I was the press agent who was supposed to meet you?" He said, [*imitating Durante*] "You had that worried look."

Would a performer today be able to spot a media agent that way?

No, because they don't have that worried look, you see.

Part IV

CHAPTER ELEVEN

God

Reverend William Augustus Johnson, 93
CHICAGO, ILLINOIS

A comfortable, well-appointed, Episcopalian retirement home. It is in an arbored enclave, along the lakefront, in Chicago's Hyde Park. Among its residents are professors emeriti of the University of Chicago, social workers, doctors, and several clergymen. "I'm the only Baptist here," he says.

He is in a wheelchair.

I continue my work as pastor of St. John Church–Baptist. I have been pastor here fifty-two years, came when I just turned forty. I have seen them come as babies in my arms to professors in colleges. It is predominantly African American middle-class.

I suppose I should have stopped some time ago. I was impeded by the amputation of my left foot. Circulation. It slowed me down. Recently I had a little accident that put me in the hospital for a few days.

I stumbled or blacked out and found myself lying under a car. It was my car, by the way, which I had just departed from. Voices began to yell, "Drag him out, drag him out." That wasn't very inviting. I was dragged out, part of my clothes torn. Four days in the hospital. I just can't let that stop me.

I go to church every morning and spend about five hours so as not to overstrain myself—answering the telephone, calling members, writing letters, reading church literature, trying to keep up with the times. Things are moving so swiftly these days, I have to stay up nights to catch up with them.

Yes, I'm ready to preach tomorrow morning. If my guest speaker does not come, my sermon is ready. I wait on divine inspiration, sir. I keep my eyes open, for I might find a sermon in stones or in running brooks. By Tuesday night, I must have an idea or I'm getting a little nervous. By Thursday evening, I'm searching: What did I read last week? What's in that book I laid aside? I must find it. Friday morning I have the ideas and begin to two-finger type it. And I'm ready to go.

If no thought comes to me, then I must keep puzzling. It may be something that occurred, some news item, accident, incident. I don't pick up everything, because my business is to preach the gospel, not say the news.

The great voices of yesterday are not around anymore—old-time preachers that delivered a sermon forty, fifty minutes and people listened attentively. I remember when churches were filled because there was a great voice in the pulpit.

Members of our church have become trained, educated. Their needs must be met. Not forgetting those members of your church whose academic background is limited. You must not forget this level. We had working-class, blue-collar, with limited education, more so in other years than now. Fifty years ago, there was one boy who said, "Gee, if I could only go to college." Today, I can throw an apple in any direction and hit a college graduate. I can almost hit a master's degree in any direction. Just throwing at random. Some communities remain isolated from the great push, but we can't do it.

When I first came to Chicago, I looked at the South Side, a block from where my church is now located. I never saw such a noisy place. On Sunday afternoon, it was terrible—radios going loud on those streets. I decided I wouldn't move here if somebody paid me a thousand dollars. I discovered something: the bulk of the people in Chicago are decent citizens. There's a small group, they're vociferous, they're dangerous, and they're in the minority. It crosses race lines. Once the bulk of Chicago people were Caucasian. Now it's black and white. Now they got a problem. [*Chuckles.*]

I have been described as conservative. I've been next door to trouble and stayed out of it. But I stood on the platform with Martin Luther King down at Soldier Field. I knew him as a boy. I preached for his father in 1944, '45, down in Atlanta, preaching at his home church. When he came to Chicago, I said to him, "Martin, I got a church and I got a home here. If you can use either one, let me know." That's all. I don't stand up and see if the camera catches me by his side. Did I subscribe to the civil rights movement in the '60s? Oh Lord, yes, yes, indeed.

I'm conservative in behavior but not otherwise. I walked the streets because a Caucasian friend of mine was disturbed and asked me what he could do. I said, "I don't know anything we can do now, but let's walk together." So he and I walked with Martin Luther King.

I was born August 1, 1900, Washington, D.C., twelve blocks from the United States Capitol. I experienced a call to the ministry and accepted it. I've been a pastor since 1927. I was a pastor for the Baptist church in Washington for three years.

My mother and father were both dead before I was four years old. My father was in the United States Navy for thirty-one years. He rose as high as he could, to petty officer, which means that he cooked for the captain instead of the men. He cooked on several ships, including the *Mayflower*, which used to be the president's ship. My mother was a housewife.

I was raised by my aunt, my mother's sister. She, my sister, and I lived together. She received a small pension. This money kept us out of the orphan asylum. It was my father's house.

I never, to my recollection, saw a sign that said "white" or "colored." Not at that time. Oh my dear, we can't possibly have visitors coming from abroad seeing these signs. We didn't have the hullabaloo we hear now. Was it segregated? Oh Lord, yes. If I went to the theater, I knew I had to go to the gallery, so I went up there. I went to that restaurant, I was told they were not serving, so I didn't go. I was told that if that's theirs, they want that. Let them have it. We'll build our own. So we built our own theater, where we had stage shows. Built our own, enjoyed our own, ate dinner at the nearest restaurant.

I had no intention of joining a group that's going back to Africa. I've been there in these last years and I felt very strange. I felt like a visitor. The only relationship I could see was skin color. I was comfortable, but still a stranger. This is my country. My father was thirty-one years in the navy. I think he's earned something, and this is mine.

I didn't march in Selma, but everyone knew where I stood. I said what I pleased from my pulpit, because that was mine. Sometimes I step out of the sermon, out of the pulpit onto the lectern, and say what I like. I have my own ideas, however. The church must not be used as a political platform. No politician, to my recollection, in the fifty-two years I've been here, has ever spoken from this pulpit. We have a lectern, a speaking stand, at which those things can be spoken of. The pulpit is here and the lectern is there.

When did you receive the call?

I wanted to be a lawyer like Perry Mason. A courtroom lawyer to win all the cases. That changed when I received the call to preach in nineteen hundred and twenty-five. I was twenty-five years old and married. At the time, I had a job as a driver for a wholesale cleaners, fifteen stores. One day, I heard voices inside my head. I replied as though a person said it to me. I said no. I knew it meant I'd have to stop dancing, and I'd just started to learn dancing and was enjoying it. But I was a Christian and a deacon in the church and I woke up to the fact that you don't tell God no. "Do you really want me?" I look around, nobody moves. I didn't hear them call my name. "You really mean me? I'll do it."

I jumped out of the little Ford truck, left the keys in the switch and ran. I ran practically four blocks to my pastor's house. He was outside, sweeping. He said, "What's wrong?" I said, "I've been called to preach." He said, "I know it. I've been waiting for you to find out." As I look back, I wonder what I was excited about. As if I'd been told something wonderful and I had to go tell it. Something about Jesus. That was very childlike, I guess, which isn't a bad thing either. You must be childlike in attitude, not childish, still have that sense of wonder and amazement. I had that feeling. It's difficult to explain.

One evening, it wasn't a year later, the doorbell rang. There's a woman, said, "Are you Reverend Johnson?" I didn't know what to do with that title. She said, "Our pastor has left us. Will you come around and preach Sunday morning?" I said, "I don't know anything about preaching." She said, "We know it, but come around." So I went around there Sunday morning, and they accepted it as preaching.

I'd seen the service conducted because I was a deacon. So I followed the pattern. On the third Sunday, they said, "Brother Johnson, we want you to be our pastor." I said, "I don't know anything about being pastor." They said, "We'll help you." So I became pastor, fifty-one members. A very proud pastor. I'd been in Sunday school all my life, so I started with Bible stories: the woman at the well, the story of the prodigal son. You want to hear it? You're on.

A certain man had two sons. One of them was restless, irritated. He didn't have radios, but he caught some news, some glimpse of what's happening outside, and he was being cramped. So he says, "Father, can you give me now the money which would naturally come to me when you pass?" The father gave it to him, and he went off to live in a far country.

I stop there and make a separate sermon out of it. How far did he go? By my own experience, he could go three blocks from here to the lakefront, the same mess going on down there. How far did he go? Went to the far country, got in with a bad gang, spent all the money he had, got to the point where he was willing to take any job.

He's a Jew, but he takes a job taking care of pigs. He got to the point that he was so hungry, he was about to eat the swine, but he looked up, remembering now, this is wrong. "My father's got servants and every one of them is eating and enjoying life more that I am. I'm going home. Tell my father I sinned against Heaven."

Starts home, ragged and dirty, forlorn, disillusioned, disgusted. Begins to talk to himself: "I'm going to tell Daddy I was wrong. I'm not even worthy to be his hired servant. Make me as one who deserted."

Half a dozen men sit over there and get hired for one day. Day labor, the lowest level of employment. His father was leaning over the fence—just had his breakfast, doing the morning chores—he saw a figure coming down the road. He had a slouch but it wasn't an old man's slouch. Finally he recognized something about that boy. He said, "This is my son. He was lost and he is found. Hallelujah!"

I get to shouting right here. The boy says, "Daddy, I messed up." The father interrupts him. [*Excitedly*] "Hey, get some clothes, get some shoes on, get that robe there. You kill that calf we've been keeping. Let's have a party. This is my son, was lost and is found." [*Takes a deep breath; he is weeping.*] Oh Lord. Excuse me. Have I ever been like that, like that boy, away like that? I did go away from home one Sunday. What happened? I didn't throw the money away. I might put that in the sermon, too. My own experience.

I was in Newark. I had enough to pay the railroad ticket. I had enough to pay rent one week, three dollars and a half. I had enough to feed me Friday and Saturday. Sunday, I had no money, no food. I was downtown. I sat down in the park, thinking I ain't got nothing to eat. Another Negro came and sat down by me. We chatted about this and that. I thought we had common ground. He said, "Nice to meet you." I said, "By the way, can you lend me a dime?" He reached in his pocket, handed me a dime, and looked at me with contempt. When he walked away, I promised God [*weeping*]—that I'd never put myself in a position where a man would look at me like that.

I went up to Market Street, and I could have brought a hot dog and a glass of root beer for a dime. I bought a loaf of bread and walked up to the statue of Abraham Lincoln and sat on his lap. I'd heard my aunt say, "Before you die, you might have to eat dry bread." The bread was hard to swallow. I said, "Lord, if you give me a chance to work, I'll never put myself in a position like that again. Amen."

I had nothing, not a nickel. I had a job set for Monday morning, a porter at a men's club. [*Sniffles.*] Oh boy. The man looked at me. Nobody ever looked at me like that. Nobody. I'd rather starve than borrow. I was about nineteen, some seventy-four years ago.

I have to live these sermons. Who was really the prodigal—the son or the father? I put myself in both roles. Sometimes I'm the father, sometimes the young man. How far did he go from this point to get to that bad community? That bad community may have been right at home? How far is far? How high is high?

While I was in Washington at my first church, not yet ordained, someone told me about Negro pastors building a school of their own. It became the Washington Baptist Theological Seminary. I'm the last living of the first five graduates. We studied the Bible, church history, homiletics. I was coached for nine months by an older pastor. My church invited three hundred to come and put questions to me. It went on for three solid hours on a hot Sunday. Don't ask me about fans. We used paper fans. Don't ask me about air conditioning. There was no such thing. They finally decided to ordain me. Up to this year, I carried a copy of my ordination papers in my pocket.

Several years after his pastorate in Washington, he was called to Nyack, New York. "A nice little village of two thousand." Three years later, he served at a larger church in Plainsfield, New Jersey. In 1940, he came to Chicago.

I've seen St. John Church–Baptist grow and change. It is today filled with displaced people. When I first came, most were working people in the stockyards and the steel mills. When the yards and the mills closed, some took the money they'd earned and bought homes further south. They still attend my church, coming from a distance. Oh Lord, yes. Their children and their grandchildren, too.

Where shall we put our emphasis for the end of this century? With the elderly, I think, because there are so many of them. We still do have some young parishioners. They regard me as a grandfather. Remember now, I've preached here for three generations. Children become fathers and grandfathers, too.

A woman who works at the retirement home is passing by. She pauses as he greets her. "I'm one of five generations who has attended Reverend Johnson's church. My mother and my grandfather are still members. Oh, I remember a lot of sermons. He makes it so simple. Even a child can understand."

I haven't yet prepared a Sunday sermon. There is somebody else scheduled to preach. But I must have a sermon ready, so if he stubs his toe at the front door, I'm ready. After all, I am the pastor and get paid for that.

If I was to live seven more years, I'd have spanned the whole century—but I'll be in heaven by then. I'd just like to go one Sunday morning and say, "Beloved, this is my last sermon. May the Lord be with you." Go out, get my hat, and be taken home. I can't stand the pressure of seeing people I knew as babies, grown men now, saying to me, "Pastor, why did you leave us?" None of that.

I just want to be remembered as someone who cried with you when your baby was sick, who went to the cemetery with you. I was there. I don't send somebody else unless I just can't make it in the snow with this one leg.

When am I going to retire? Aren't you too old? Are you really doing any good? I never bothered with those questions before, but I'm at the point of thinking it. The deacons suspected it, so they passed a resolution: Willie Johnson should be the pastor of this church until he's physically and mentally unable, or the Lord calls him. [*Chuckles.*] I'm here this morning. But it could be tomorrow or next week that something goes fuzzy. Until that moment, I'm supposed to stay.

My health is all right. I go every day. I couldn't do more than that at forty. I know how to bear the pressure. I know there's a storm raging. I know that dangers can come to a community, to the point that people say they can't go there. When the pressure's right, they'll go there and look and listen. A baby's cry sounds the same in the Robert Taylor Homes as it does on the Gold Coast, in that beautiful crib. A woman in pain sounds the same. Trouble and sorrow is the same on the lakefront as it is in Cabrini-Green. And decency, moral goodness and ambition is the same, there and here.

I scratched the skin and you know what I found under that brown? I found white skin and blood running. Just what I find if I scratch your skin. If I'm the same, then I must ask for the same privileges. I must also remember that if I'm the same, I must take the same responsibility.

Mayor Daley, the father, was right when he said we don't make slums. No, you don't, Mr. Daley, but you go easy on laws that prevent slums. Make it so it won't be fifty years before Robert Taylor Homes will be front washed, new door, a lamp there, and white people moving in, integrated. Maybe Chicago is changing for the better, I hope. The Lord moves in mysterious ways. I won't be here, of course.

God made man a self-conscious being with the power to choose and *select.* Man is capable of both, good and bad. Yes, we are saint and sinner. He can move from the depths of Hell to the heights of Heaven, and do it so fast it can make your head swim. He can act like an animal, but he can also move up. Hard to believe *all* the goods are in anybody.

I've never seen a totally evil person. You got to know how to meet a man. I can't meet that evil man and start: [*growling comically*] "Brother, ought to do right!" No, that's not the way. He's both, sir. Capable of walking with the stars or scrambling in the dust with the pigs. For Thou hast made us, Lord, a little lower than the angels. Amen.

Betty McCollister, 73
Iowa City, Iowa

She writes a column for the Cedar Rapids Gazette *and* The Humanist, *a bimonthly. She had written regularly for the op-ed page of the* Des Moines Register, *until it became a Gannett publication.*

I am a secular humanist. I believe in the separation of church and state. This is what I'm fighting for constantly. Among fundamentalists, it's the dirtiest word in the language. Don't think I don't get hate mail from Christians. It goes with the territory.

Really, we're very nice people. We believe it's up to human beings to use their intelligence to make the planet as good a place to live in as possible. We don't believe you can turn to the Bible and pull verses out and say: "This is what God says." Quite a few of us believe there's a transcendent dimension to life, but we don't think any religious sect should enact secular laws. Our Founding Fathers were very specific about it.

"My father was a professor of botany and retired as head of the department at the University of Iowa, where he spent most of his working life. He wrote the definitive book on myxomycetes. They're slime boils, the things you see on dead logs in wet weather.

"In 1937, I went to Swarthmore on a scholarship and didn't fit in very well. I planned to major in German and philosophy, ha, ha. So I went to Germany in 1938. I was there on 'Kristallnacht.' I walked out and saw all the broken glass. I still have the sign I brought back: Juden Verboten. *This was in Munich, November 9, the anniversary of the Beer Hall Putsch. I came back in a hurry, January of '39.*

"I was to work in New York. A guy from Iowa City who had danced with me when I was in eighth grade and he was a senior wanted to know how I'd turned out, so he looked me up and I married him." Because of her husband's job, they and their six children lived nomadically, assigned to different regions of the country. "About ten years ago, I was living in New Jersey in this horrible suburb, with overpriced, lousy schools, when I could have been living in civilization in Iowa City.

"I got into journalism accidentally and I've done straight news reporting, music criticism—I'm an amateur cellist—theater, features. I built up quite following and quite a few enemies."

Every time you write a piece criticizing Christians who want to see the government impose their ideas on everybody, you get hate mail.

This has become a passion with me. I have good memories of growing up in the Episcopal Church and they were a civilized lot, as Christians go. What I always say is, some of my best friends are Christians but I wouldn't want my daughter to marry one. Very broad-minded, right? [*Chuckles.*]

I write about Christian responsibility for the Holocaust. I write about Christians like Jerry Falwell and Pat Robertson and the Catholic bishops stepping on the First Amendment. The pope said America is going to lose its soul. [*Outraged*] The soul of America is its First Amendment. This is what makes us what we are, and if we lose it, we're just not going to be America anymore. Anyway, the soul of America is none of the pope's goddamn business. There are blistering letters saying that the *Gazette* shouldn't run my stuff anymore.

I'm fighting creationism at the grass-roots level, where they are making out like bandits, they are so successful.* The last time I wrote a piece saying creationism was not a science but a dogmatic religious doctrine that should not be taught in biology classes, I got a slew of hostile letters.

I've been told by scientists that the textbooks today are worse than the ones in use in the early '20s, before the Scopes trial. The biggest bucks are in the fundamentalist Christian states, Texas, Arkansas, California. Publishers don't give a shit whether their books are any good. Most of them are totally awful. If they can sell a biology textbook that doesn't mention evolution, they won't hesitate. That's where the profits are.

I'm worried stiff about the success of fundamentalists in getting their people on boards of education. They run stealth candidates. They don't say what they are. You're lucky if you get a turnout of 15 percent in a school board election. So if somebody can organize 8 percent of the vote, that person gets elected to the board. Pat Robertson claims that, in the last year, his people got two thousand representatives on the boards. They're very well organized and very well funded. And very successful. Creationists say theirs is the absolute truth. No scientist would ever say that. That is the biggest problem: we are a nation of scientific illiterates. So we can be easily had.

I believe absolutely in the freedom of religion, to believe any damn thing you wish. But to use the United States government to impose your ideas on the rest of us, hell, no.

Prayer in schools? It's an abomination. If God is stupid enough to think it's a real prayer, he doesn't deserve to be worshipped.

---

* A few years ago, while I was visiting an industrial city in northern Pennsylvania, a public high school class informed me that twenty-four of them were creationists, three believed in evolution, and two were uncommitted.

I'm open-minded on the subject of God's nature. My very favorite book in the Bible, in anything, is the Book of Job. It comes close to what God would have to be. He's saying it's an enormous mystery, far beyond our pitiful brains to comprehend. I certainly don't believe in Jerry Falwell's God. [*Imitates his accent.*] "I know everything what God thinks, boy. God wouldn't think nothin' without I told him he could. And what God thinks is, 'I got to have millions of dollars to spread among my people.'" No, that's a God I don't believe in. Not that crap.

I once wrote a column comparing God to King Lear. I agree with Laurence Olivier, who said Lear was a stupid old fart. He didn't have brains enough to be fooled, but the kind of guy that people pray to when it isn't real prayer at all—say, government-mandated Christian prayer—he's as dumb as Lear. "Teacher says I have to pray to You. I hope You're flattered." To me, this is blasphemous. We have been religious for at least five hundred thousand years. Neanderthals were religious. Archaeological findings tell us that. It's quite possible that we are barely beginning to penetrate something that is there and has been there all along, but we are still so primitive our brains can't grasp it. Einstein had some interesting things to say about that, and his brain was a hell of a lot better than mine. He talked about the great joy, the beauty, the something that is there but we don't know what it is. My point is I just cannot accept a God that is stupid.

Your language is quite salty.

[*Laughs.*] I read Chaucer quite a bit. I try to rattle cages. Somebody has to do it. I'm pretty much Anglo-Saxon, so I can say things about Christianity that somebody named Goldstein cannot say. If he did, he'd get a swastika on his house, at the very least. So I have a sense of mission about this.

This last spring, '93, I went to a concert in the local Episcopal church, and I looked in the prayer book. It put the idea of contrition into my mind. So I wrote my piece about Christian guilt and the Holocaust, and it appeared on Palm Sunday. [*Laughs delightedly.*] And you should have seen the letters.

If you do a great wrong, you should do what you can to make it right. Then I reread the gospels that are read during Holy Week, and all this stuff about the Jews killing Jesus is simply not to be found. None of it ever happened, and that should be publicly acknowledged. The whole thing is a fabrication. Boy, the roof fell in. Somebody wrote that the Jews have only themselves to blame, because they're so obnoxious. Several wrote in to say that the Holocaust never happened. A guy from the university wrote a very eloquent letter in response. A retired Presbyterian minister in Cedar Rapids recommended that every member of his congregation read my article. A Lutheran minister did the same thing. Same thing happened when I wrote about evolution. Yeah, I do stir things up. I plead guilty of trying to make people think.

I do try very hard to fight clean. I don't tell malicious lies. It's against my personal code of ethics. But the fundamentalists, on the contrary, have said on more than one occasion that humanists go into the second grade and tell kids that rape and incest are wonderful. It's worse than pure fantasy, it's a violation of the commandment "Though shalt not bear false witness against thy neighbor." I happen to believe in it very strongly.

I value the Bible. I think everybody should know it. I think the Bible should be taught as literature, particularly the King James version. You can't appreciate Bach, you can't look at the work of some of our greatest artists, you can't really read Chaucer unless you are familiar with the Bible. This is an important part of our heritage. As for some parts—pure propaganda. St. Paul was an emotional basket case. I can't stand the man.

Yeah, the fire is still in this old dame. [*Laughs.*] I don't mind being old. I adore being a grandmother. I have six children, fifteen grandchildren. I think they're pretty proud of what I've done with my life on the whole. I certainly have made mistakes along the line. Who hasn't?

I think today's children are terribly underprivileged compared to the way I grew up. Iowa City was a lovely place to grow up in, but today a lot of it is automobiles and overcrowdedness. We had a meadow on one side of us and the woods on the other. We could get out and be alone with nature. It was wonderful to walk to school through the snow in the winter, the flowers in the spring, through the changing leaves in the fall. We didn't have television, so we were in the outdoors a lot more.

I think television has had a really destructive influence on a lot of kids. It is so passive. You sit and you watch it. If you're reading a book, or even if you're listening to the radio, your imagination is working.

Television is overkill with news of disaster. It's pounded into you to the point where you just get numb because you can't constantly agonize over all these ghastly problems. I wonder if the kids haven't been rendered a bit numb.

The violence they're exposed to—and the grungy sex. I don't think six- and seven-year-olds should have their noses rubbed in it. They're not ready for it. As we evolved, this was never done. People went through puberty rites and had role models, because they lived in tribes. And all of a sudden, after 250 million years of evolution, four million years of human evolution, we don't have that sense of belonging, we don't have community standards. We don't have any sense of community. I think it's tough.

I was nine years old at the time of the Wall Street crash. Mother and father, they weren't totally wiped out. At least, my father kept his job, but his salary was cut and all of our savings were wiped out. I think that material things have assumed a lot more importance than they had when I was growing up, hard times and all.

I have some friends but I don't have an active social life. I have one particularly close friend. We go back to the time when I was seven and she was eight, and I see her regularly. Half of my friends are dying, getting Alzheimer's, Parkinson's, all those dreadful diseases. I'm so lucky. I just have cataracts, my hearing is going, and I had a hip replacement. [*Laughs.*] After all, these things served me well for seventy-two years. If they want to wear out now...

My immortality is in my children and grandchildren. Mozart is my God, my entrance into the sublime, and at my memorial service, they'll have wine and cheese and Mozart.

Richard McSorley, S.J., 79

*"I am the second oldest of fifteen children of a family from Philadel-
phia. I spent thirty-seven years teaching, most of them at Georgetown University, and I retired in 1985. I am now director of the
Center for Peace Studies at the university."*

I had begun teaching in the Philippine Islands, when World War II
broke out. I was a prisoner of the Japanese from December 13, 1941,
until February 23, 1945: three years and three months. When I came
back to the United States, I finished my theology studies and was
ordained a priest.

I was immediately appointed pastor of a mixed-color parish in
southern Maryland. Nobody else wanted the job. It was rural, small,
poor, though a few fairly well-off people lived there. It was quite
racist. This may sound hard to believe, but I had never heard a word
about racism, though I had a Catholic education—grade school, high
school, seminary. The only time I met a black man was on an elevator, when you say up or down.

Here, I was made a pastor of a church where the blacks sat on one
side and the whites on another. They received holy communion separately. I wondered why they did that. I was that innocent. A year
later, when I saw what it did to the souls of both people, black and
white, and to the bodies of the black, I couldn't be silent.

I started talking about segregation as a sin, and it started me to
understand that the gospel of Christ had a social meaning. It affects
all society and you have an individual responsibility. I gave my first
sermon on racism. The provincial superior in Baltimore didn't like it.
"I would have fired you like that, moved you away." But Cardinal
O'Boyle, one of the leaders for racial justice at that time, warned
him against it. I had been there four years and stayed on for four
more. I got a full education on racism there. What set me off was the
faith of the black people, especially a man named Aloysius Butler.

There was no heat in the church, just a fire stove in the middle of
the aisle. On a Sunday morning, an hour before mass, I was fiddling
with the stove and getting nowhere. The people were lined up on
both sides of the confessional box, just waiting. Nobody offered to
help me. I thought this was pretty silly, since they all made fires in
their houses. As I look back, I think the white people didn't want to
carry the firewood in front of the black people. And the black people
were reticent because they didn't want to annoy the white people.

Finally, this man, Aloysius Butler, came over and said, "Father,

I'll help you." After mass, I called him to the sacristy. If he'd do this regularly, I'd pay him a dollar an hour. He was making ninety-four cents an hour driving a truck for the naval station. He said, "No, I'm doing this for God." I turned away from him. I was so ashamed. Why am I talking this way to a Catholic man? There was nobody listening, just he and I and God. At that moment, I realized I was a racist. I would never have said that to a white Catholic.

I felt worse when I found out I had fired his wife the week before. When I had come to the church, I was told that this black woman would clean the church once a week for a couple of dollars. I said that since we had so little money, we could get volunteers to do the job. I discovered there was racism even here, too. Despite this, Mr. Butler volunteered to build the fires.

I had been visiting families who were curious about the new pastor. Though the black people were all poor, some of the whites had pretty good jobs at the nearby Patuxent Naval Air Station. It was about seventy-five miles south of Washington. A lot of them were military people. This one family, of the all-white church nearby, was fairly wealthy. They were the only two college-educated people in the area. When they asked me how I liked things around here, I spoke of the Indian community: "They're treated like Negroes and Negroes are treated the way we had treated the Indians." The woman said, "You better be careful, Father, talking that way around here, because they'll think you're a nigger lover." She put her hand over her mouth. I said, "I will be careful because I don't deserve to be a nigger lover"—and I put my hand over my mouth—"because that's the reputation Christ has." They just sat there, looking at each other. I said, "It looks like we've run out of words, so it's time for me to go."

At my car, the man leaned over and said, "Father, why don't you just put it down to the fact that we're just dumb southerners and don't know no better." He expected me to say, "Oh, forget it." but I said, "Okay, you're just dumb southerners and don't know no better."

Of course, the word got out all over town, and I was rated as a Negro lover, as opposed to a lover of white people. You can't love them both. It affected the kids, too. Children would usually be delighted if the priest would invite them to his house for cookies. They never came to my place. They wanted nothing from me. I built a basketball court, which they'd never had. I was a pretty good player, so I thought I'd teach them. They didn't even pass the ball to me. I was the enemy. When we played baseball, they put me in right field—the worst place—and I was the best player of the whole crowd. [*Laughs.*]

This was the beginning of my education about race, and it took some time for me to change my mind about war. When I was in the

Philippines, I believed all the American propaganda about the Japanese. I thought our army and navy would wipe them out just like that. During my imprisonment, of course, I thought they were all bad. When MacArthur bombed around the camp, along with the others, I'd say, "Damn them. Damn all the Japanese." I was just a patriotic boy. When we dropped the bomb on Hiroshima, I said, "Thank God, the war is over." It was an ordinary American feeling. Not the one I have now.

As Martin Luther King saw the connection between racism and war and Dan and Phil Berrigan were speaking out, I was looking at the whole thing retroactively from my prison-camp days. But I was beginning to see the connection. Dr. King and the Berrigans were risking their lives and reputation for their faith. I hadn't risked anything.

At the time, I was at Georgetown and a friend of Bobby Kennedy's. I became the tutor for his two oldest children, to keep them doing their homework, also instructing them in tennis. I was the university's coach.

When I read on the bulletin board that the Berrigans were arrested, I thought to myself, "This is bad news for me." This was 1967. They were part of the Catonsville Nine. Here I was, respectable and accepted and no longer in the doghouse. At first, when I was invited to join the Berrigan support group, I held back: "I've got a contract," the usual cop-out stuff. Anyway, it's another lost cause. But as King and the Berrigans were calling on the churches to speak out, I knew I had to answer the call.

The Kennedys knew about my change of heart pretty soon, but they said nothing about it. At the time, Bob Kennedy came out against the Vietnam War and was being pushed to run for president. When Gene McCarthy won the New Hampshire primary, I wrote Kennedy, urging him to take the step. He wrote back saying, "I've been thinking about it."

After I joined the Berrigans, I was arrested many times. At Georgetown they thought I was crazy. They were very unhappy with me. I was following King's lead in connecting racism to war. The greatest sermon I gave in my whole life was at an all-white church, St. Michael's. The subject was St. Francis Xavier. I worked like a dog on it and taped it ahead of time, because I knew I'd be misquoted.

My heart was going a mile a minute when I started. I said, "I'm sure that if Francis Xavier were talking to you now, he'd ask 'Where are the good Catholic colored people?' There was dead silence. Oh, boy. I took a deep breath and said, "I have found out that there are sixty-seven canonized black saints in heaven. They are with God in perfect beatitude. So all of you have your choice. You can either go to heaven with God and these sixty-seven black saints, or you can go to"—and I took a long pause—"wherever you want to go." I heard all kinds of gasps in the audience.

Right on the heels of that, at the chapel of Georgetown, I took off on the sinful war. I brought in Gandhi and King and the Berrigans and everybody I could think of—Thoreau, you name it. People walked out. Articles appeared in the school paper about my unpatriotic communist talk. I answered them in no uncertain terms. There was a huge controversy. The authorities didn't like it.

I've been arrested about seven times. Once, I was in the same cell with Dr. Spock. There were about 150 of us going to Congress to protest the bombing of Cambodia. There was one steel hanging bed, chained to the wall. I said, "We both can't fit in this bed. Let's take turns every couple of hours." Spock said, "You know nothing about anatomy. I'll show you how we'll do it." We never got to bed at all. We spent the whole night talking to the people in the other cells.

It was in '64, that I decided to teach nothing but war and peace at the university. I assigned all sort of books on the subject. By 1966, it had become a popular class, though the attendance was limited. Two of the top ROTC students were there, but they were warned they'd lose their commissions if they spoke out. It was that year, after we read something about Vietnam, several students said they thought the government was deceiving us. I asked the class how many thought the president was lying to us. Fourteen out of sixteen put up their hands. I never thought I'd thought I'd come to a day when I would see this. Unfortunately, the '80s were not the '60s.

Once Reagan came in, there was a cut-off of interest in social justice. The students have gone along with the government more. I've kept going, hitting away at the dangers of nuclear war. There were attacks on my courses. The student paper put my picture on the front page: THE MOST CONTROVERSIAL COURSE IN THE SCHOOL. It was the best promotion I ever had. In my last ten years of teaching, I was getting one hundred students, with three hundred trying to get in. There was great interest in the course, but student protests diminished and so did public interest.

I'm afraid that the young aren't nearly as interested in social issues as they once were. They're still strong on serving the poor, on the human needs of the homeless and the sick, on immediate needs. What's lacking today is a national cause in which all can join. The spark was out there in the '60s. It's something the young have to start themselves today, and it's harder.

From 1964 on, I've made my office the Peace Center, with much support from the university. I put out a weekly column for sixty-five mostly Catholic newspapers. I have a hefty file of crank mail, and not a very big one of positive letters.

Last winter, I went down to a large parish in Sebastian, Florida. I talked about killing and tax resistance. I discovered that the Knights of Columbus had put up a flag on the front lawn of the church, without permission. There was a huge spotlight on it, and when you came out of the rectory, it blinded you. The pastor, who was afraid of the Knights of Columbus, said he'd take it down someday. I said, "I'll do it right now." I did, and put it in my room.

I wrote a letter to the Grand Knight, listing ten reasons why a national flag should not fly on international property. Our faith is international. A national flag doesn't represent Christ, the Church, love. Isn't that what this parish is about? This flag represents the Gulf War and all the other hellish wars we've been in. And furthermore, this violates the separation of church and state. The pastor liked the letter. I sent a copy to the bishop, and he liked it, too. The parish council voted twelve to nothing—no more flag. The Knights of Columbus were furious, of course. [*Laughs.*] I asked to speak at their meeting. They refused. A committee of their members came to meet me. They said, "Let's start with a prayer." We said one prayer after another. I lost track. Their first question was, "Are you an American?" I said, "I'm an American citizen, decorated by Douglas MacArthur with a Purple Heart as a POW. Why didn't you invite me to your meeting?" They said, "They would have killed you." "What was their answer to my ten points?" The guys just sat there, and that was the end of it.

I'm seventy-nine now, so my day isn't as vigorous as it used to be. I used to engage in minor fasts on Mondays and Saturdays, on bread and water. I remember from my concentration-camp days in the Philippines that if you have all the water you want, you don't ever feel very hungry. And you can live on the bread. I had to give it up nine years ago when I had a five-way bypass and an aneurysm at the same time. I'm okay now. I get up about 7:30 and spend a half hour in prayer, have breakfast, answer a bag of mail. I have some articles to write and am working on a book. I sometimes join in demonstrations. Last week, I went down to the courthouse in Alexandria, Virginia, where Phil Berrigan was arrested.

I spent a couple of nights helping out Phil Berrigan's resistance community in Baltimore. Because of the arrests, they're short of help. It's small stuff, but it's something. Oh, I still get in trouble. It's a habit now. In 1971, I was ordered out of the Georgetown community. I said to the superior, "I don't want one penny of my salary to go to the university while the military is still here on campus." He said, "You've taken a vow of poverty. You can't decide that." I said, "I'm not deciding how we spend the money. I'm asking you not to spend the money immorally." At the time, I was still teaching and my salary would go to the Jesuit community. Every year, the community would make a fifty- or a hundred-thousand-dollar contribution to

Georgetown University. An open conflict is going on now between those who support the military on campus and those who oppose it.

The superior said, "You don't belong here. Live someplace else. You're better off independently." So I lived for ten years with the Community for Creative Non-Violence. It's in a poor, slum section of Washington. The Lutheran Church owned three houses in the neighborhood. The sympathetic pastor gave us one to start a Catholic worker house. It offers shelter and food to the homeless. We have five of them now in Washington. I go there twice a week for mass. I'm now back in Georgetown with the Jesuit community. In '81, a new superior came in. He was a pacifist.

When you reach old age, they figure you won't be around too long, so you're not that important anymore. It's clear that your opinion doesn't amount to much. "Let him say what he wants to say. It doesn't matter." But old age is still full of surprises.

I almost became Bill Clinton's Willie Horton in the last presidential election. When he was a Rhodes Scholar in England, he was at a big antiwar rally at the American embassy. He invited me the next day for a prayer service for peace. I offered the St. Francis prayer for peace. Afterward, we marched to the American Embassy with little white crosses in our hands and left them on the steps. When I got off the train in Oslo, Norway, to visit peace groups, he was the second one behind me on the step. He said, "Can I go with you?" We spent the day together.

They tried to use this against Clinton. Here I was a friend of Dan Berrigan's, a "Communist." This fellow from California, Dornan, the professional patriot, was on C-Span five nights in a row damning me as a fascist and a Communist. He was quoted seriously by the Moonie paper, the *Washington Times:* "Imagine Clinton going around with a friend of Dan Berrigan."

A reporter from that paper kept at me. "You were with Clinton in Norway. Didn't he say he was going to Russia? Didn't he say he was going to give up his citizenship?" I thought it was a joke, but this guy was serious. I said, "He didn't say anything of the sort. We were both interested in peace and were in a strange country for the first time." Then I said, "Any candidate for president of the United States would be crazy if he thought the press would say the truth about what he told them." The next day they had a front-page story with a headline: DON'T TELL THE TRUTH, JESUIT PRIEST TELLS CLINTON. Friends of mine finally advised me: "Stop talking to the press. They twist what you say any way they want."

This all happened in the early '90s, and I was in my late seventies. So I discovered it's never too late to learn.

Virginia Bowers, 71
CHICAGO, ILLINOIS

We're in the first-floor apartment of a six-flat in Uptown. The area on the city's North Side, close by the lake, was once a solid middle-class community. Throughout the years, as the burghers moved away, it has become a way station for the considerably less affluent émigrés, native and foreign: Appalachian whites, African Americans, Latinos, and Asiatic. In more recent times, upwardly mobile young couples, as well as free-floating young whites and blacks, have come on the scene. It has a transient air, as though it were still the city's port of entry.

When I came to this neighborhood in about '65 I got to manage two apartment buildings. A couple had a little baby, about nine months old. It was bitten by a rat in its crib one night. The owner said, "Stick some glass in the holes, so we can say it didn't happen." I said, "I will not do it," and was fired. I called the housing inspector for Public Aid, a black man, and that's how I got involved with JOIN.*

I became JOIN's office manager. We had a sit-in at the Public Aid office and lots of demonstrations. That's how I first met my dear black friends. JOIN sent me to Washington, D.C., to sit in on social security meetings and whatever. I went to Atlanta and met Dr. King to help plan the poor people's campaign. I met just about all the civil rights leaders. At the time, I had five kids, my husband had a job with a chemical company, and it was hard.

I'm from Blytheville, Arkansas, about sixty miles from Memphis. In my teenage years, I worked in a restaurant and learned how to run them. I worked in a liquor store for a week, but it got the best of my conscience. Guys would come in and buy the rotgut, and I knew that their children were hungry. So I quit.

I had wonderful parents. My father had only about a second-grade education, but he would sit down with my homework and tell me how to do the math. He couldn't write, but he could do it in his head. He was a cook in a restaurant.

My first husband worked on his father's farm. He wanted me to dress in silks and satins and stay home, but I could not. There was something working inside me. I was a Sunday school teacher when I

---

* JOIN (Jobs or Income Now) was a militant rights organization that was created in Uptown by members of SDS (Students for a Democratic Society) in the '60s. Rennie Davis, later one of the Conspiracy Eight, was a founding member. The actual day-to-day work was done by the tenants themselves.

was fifteen. It was Southern Baptist. But I've all the time never looked on just one religion. I believe in any of them as along as they treat you right.

I became a minister in about '85. I've always been a churchgoer, and it was just something that hit me all at once. I was sittin' here in my platform rocker, just rockin' back and forth. I was under such a heavy conviction. I had been reading the Bible a lot. I said, "Lord, talk to me. Let me know what you want me to do." I would not get a response. So I said, "Do you want me to take your word? Do you want me to preach your gospel?" When I said that, I had the warmest, hottest feeling come over me, from my head plumb down through my toes. I said, "Thank you, Lord," because I got my answer.

I was goin' to a black church with a black minister. A mixed couple, me, and another white were the only nonblack people there. Race was never discussed at home. I knew the blacks had their side of town and the whites had their side. My older brother disowned me because of my involvement with black people here in Chicago and with Dr. King. The last time I went down there, he said, "Are you still involved in that nigger business?" I said, "We're involved in any race of people that needs help." He said, "You're no sister of mine." I had one brother in Memphis, and I did not say what I was doing in Chicago. I just let that die.

One of my sisters owns a bar in Tennessee. She says, "They're not black like you got in Chicago. These are niggers we got here, because they have no respect for the white women, saying everything to 'em. I know there's a difference between blacks and niggers. These are strictly niggers."

I'm the only one in my family that feels this way. I guess I came to Chicago and got educated. I do remember one black woman back home who lived across the road from us. She took care of me and my brothers and sisters when my mother miscarried and like to died. I go sit on this woman's porch with her in the swing. If she'd keep us for the night, I'd sleep in bed with her. It never dawned on me, she's black and I'm white. I was probably twelve, somewhere around there.

I married about a month before I got out of tenth grade. When I came to Chicago, I went to Senn High School and took courses on office business machines. I worked for the Department of Transportation for the state for years. I've got a lot of education through organizing and stuff with JOIN and by working with a lot of intelligent people. I also went to Truman, the community college, up here, and I took math, English.

We'd have good times at JOIN, black and white together. The

police did not like it, especially what we call hillbillies associating with blacks. They nailed us a couple of times.

At the same times as I got into real estate management, running a thirty-five-unit, I was working with Public Aid. Little Dovie and Big Dovie, my two dearest black friends, and I started the WRDA here: Welfare Recipients Demand Action. I was in management, but I could see how they were taking poor people, old people on social security. A lot of what we call yuppies are moving in from Lincoln Park and shooing these people out. Take the condos across the street; they do not want poor people, they want professionals. They want $200,000 ones, just a couple of buildings from here. I did not like that one bit. I can't explain it, but I guess I was always for the underdog.

I had already been taking a Bible course from a correspondence school in Pasadena, California. So I got my certificate. They don't charge anybody. They just have donations from their members. I got ordained through the Calvary Grace Church from Pennsylvania. I got all my licenses—my pastor's, my minister's, and my evangelist's—for Missionary Baptist. It's not Pentecostal, the way I was raised, but that's okay.

I do believe in healing, because I've done a lot in my family. If you have a chance, go up to Grace Baptist Church up here on Broadway. Pastor Smith has a great gift of healing. He'd get out in the pulpit and say, "The Lord has told me, don't preach today. I'm to heal." Lord have mercy, let me tell you, I have seen some healing there like nobody would believe.

You see, when you're praying for the sick, the energy flows out of you into that person. They may be on drugs, alcohol, have bad spines, whatever. Would He straighten 'em out! Absolutely. One Sunday, I saw one guy with a motorcycle jacket and a big old chain around his waist. The pastor prayed for him twice—he didn't get it all the first time. This guy jumped up and tore that chain off his waist and threw it up in the pulpit. Right then, you could tell the difference. The chain had come off, the guy had changed. If the Lord hadn't been there, that chain could have hit somebody in the head, because it was a long chain.

I have healed. Me and my first husband prayed for a little girl once. She was burning up with fever. The doctor wasn't there. The minister wasn't there. They asked us. We prayed for her, laid our hands on her and the fever went away. Six years ago, my son, who's the house painter, infected his eyes with paint chips. He couldn't hardly see. So I prayed for him, laid my hands on him, and he got okay.

I preach and heal, but at the same time, if there's a school issue, you'll see me on the picket line. If it's a fight for equal housing, you'll see me on the picket line. I'm on the board of the Uptown Law Center and on the Community Rights Assembly. Jesus said the poor would be with us always and they have to have help.

I preach to whoever wants me to come to their church. I've been to a black church, to a white. My sermon's the same for both. I don't sit down and pore over a whole bunch of stuff like a lot of ministers do. I go through the Bible and get those verses that pertain to healing. Like the blind man sitting on the side of the road. He knew Jesus was there, but couldn't see him, so he just touched the hem of his garment and Jesus, of course, said, "Who touched me?" And right then, he healed the blind man. I preach what comes to me.

I'm a tutor at our local school down the street here. This year, we're starting out at first grade, all the way up to the fifth. The local school council, a group of parents, hires us and we get paid a stipend by the board of education. Its not how much education you have, but if you can do math, English, reading comprehension, have a way with children. We teach spelling, reading. We have one big room of tutors, grades one to five. We're there from 9:30 to 2:30, five days a week.

I have one girl, a third grader, who cannot read. So I teach her reading every day, five days a week. Forget math, just reading. We pronounce each syllable. Put two syllables together and you've got a word.

Some of these children need so much attention. When they come to school, you can tell whether something is bothering them or not. They're not going to do any work until you hear what their problem is. You put your arm around them. "What's wrong?" And he says, "My dad got drunk last night and he beat Mama up." So you have to loose them up a little. I say, "Okay, we'll work on that later. Let's work on this now. One plus two is what?"

Each child is different, so you have to approach that child a different way. I've got one little girl at 11:30 who's autistic. She's in third grade. I know how to approach her because I know her family. But sometimes you get so frustrated, because they can't understand and you just have to keep on, keep on, keep on. Maybe you'll have one line in reading and you'll help them with half a dozen words. Maybe they've got some of those same words in the next line, but they don't remember. Their mind is *gone*. One little boy today, he drove me bonkers. Each child is very personal to you.

Unless people take time with these children, they're lost. If you don't get your education now, what kind of life are you going to live? Are you gonna be homeless and on the street? One teacher told them that yesterday and they laughed. They thought it was very funny. Fifth graders, somewhere around ten, eleven years old.

I said, "In the future, it's not gonna be paper and pencils. It's going to be computers. So you're gonna have to learn how to operate one. You can't make a living working at McDonald's or Burger King. You want a nice car, you want a nice home, you want nice children? Where you're going now, you can't have it. You will wind up on Wilson Avenue forever."

Last year was a learning experience for me, because while I'm a mother and a grandmother, I became a great-grandmother. So I have to understand children. When I get out on the streets here, all these children are hollering at me, "Hi, Miss Virginia." Even in school, some of the little ones, these autistic kids, they'll run up and grab me. It makes you feel *good*. It really does.

I get up maybe five, six o'clock. Then I gotta make me a pot of coffee. My son usually comes by on his way to work and gets him coffee. If I'm not feeling very well, I just lay down, relax, and watch the news. Maybe I'll pick up somethin' for the kids, cookies, doughnuts. I've slowed down a little on my community meetings because of my tutoring. But now and then, I'm with a committee checking out housing violations. I'm still at it.

My health's poor. I've had two spinal operations since I last saw you. But I don't let it stop me. If I ever stopped, I'd hang it up. I just keep going every day because that is built into me. Just go, keep going. I've got to keep my brains active.

I try not to let old age bother me. Sometimes I feel like a hundred, sometimes I feel like a young girl. Some days I don't feel like going. Maybe I've hurt all night long, but I can't stop. These kids are going to be there, and I've got to go teach them to *think*. I just regret I didn't get started earlier. If I had started when I was younger, I could have gotten much more accomplished.

When I die, if I'm still a tutor, I'd like to see my little kids there, provided they know what a funeral is. Some parents won't let them go to one. And if some of the old people I've been involved with in organizing and street work, if they were there, that would be just great.

CHAPTER TWELVE

Community

Joe Begley, 75
BLACKEY, KENTUCKY

*The town is in the eastern part of the state, bordering Virginia,
yet, seemingly, a planet's distance from the bluegrass country of
thoroughbreds and mint juleps. The shacks, peeking out of the deep
"hollers," offer a pathetic foreground to the impressive Cumberlands.*

*In 1978, driving along the dirt road off Route 1, into what
appeared to be a ghost town, we asked an ambling, gaunt Lincoln-
esque figure the whereabouts of Joe Begley. "You're talkin' to 'im,"
he replied.*

*"To me, the mountains here has been kind of a wild refuge for
people. I don't think people know the history of Appalachia. They
don't know much about the history of the country, as far as that goes.
The school system has failed. It's been dead for a hundred years. It
took me fifty years to stand up and make an about-face and realize
who I was and what I am doing. What I was taught was a Mickey
Mouse world, a make-believe thing. Somewhere along the line, I
shoulda picked up on that."* *

*Joe and his wife, Gaynell (whose great-great-great- grandfather
fought at Valley Forge—"I may have left out a 'great'"), run the general store, C. B. Caudill. "That was my father-in-law, a good worker,
honest man. It's wore out two men, but it's still surviving." The store
celebrated its sixtieth anniversary in 1993.*

*On a wall in the store are two hand written signs. The first: "Don't
trust the Republicans & for that matter, don't trust the Democrats.
We need to trust ourselves & our ability to make things better. But
not them. Not now. Neither party has earned it." The second: "Compromise...HELL!"*

This country has gone to hell. I try to do with people that's in trouble here. I ministered to black and white. We've got some good little

---

* From *American Dreams: Lost and Found*, 1980.

leaders here, but we don't have any national leaders. Big industry has destroyed little people. The corruption in Washington with the banks and the railroads and big business. And the military. The last twelve years has been terrible. I'm still fighting. I'm seventy-five, but I'm more ablaze right now than I've ever been in my life. I started this in nineteen and sixty-six, when I backed the Freedom Riders and Martin Luther King. I wanted to join them, but I couldn't right then. I kept up with them and got in with all the other black people. I think discrimination against poor white people, against black people, against Indian people is still runnin' wild.

My mother was in the Presbyterian church down here and they taught me in school that black people was undesirable and poor people and Indians. It took me fifty years to stand up and say, "Hell no, this ain't the way to go, because there's too much calamity going on against little people."

I was told by my Cherokee grandma about the way her people were treated. My dad was a white man, and he tried to say that we was wrong. He wanted to keep a job, and he knew the Indians were considered like black people in this country. But she told me right.

My cousins, they didn't have much association with me and my brother because they knew we were Indian-related and they said we were savages, a little bit dangerous, and we would wind up dead or in the penitentiary. But we're still living and they went to the penitentiary and some of them's dead. So, you see, it's the attitude that you have in life.

I like to fight. Sometimes as you get older, the flame goes down, but some person comes along and says something to my taste and he's tryin' to do right and is bein' abused and my flame burns bright again and I'm on my way.

This has been more than a store for thirty years. I use it as a battlefield, because I can organize. Like in the navy, it was my ship and they couldn't throw me out. I organized in the store, and then I moved into the community.

I'd never organized anything in my whole life, and I really didn't know how to go about it. I never studied it. But I did learn the hard way, right here in the community. They helped me do that. I would drink with them, I would eat with them, I would chew fat with them, and I would fight with them. I talked to them and I let them do the talkin'. I'd let them tell me what they wanted, and if it was right, I would encourage them and go with 'em. It's a small community, everybody knows us here and we get on fine.

They wanted me to compromise on this strip-mine issue, the coal operators and big industry. Hell, I'm not gonna fight for somethin' for thirty years, take a chance on killing and being killed, and just say, "Well, I'll go your way." I don't give up stuff like that. I'm certainly not goin' to walk away from it.

I was in the navy and I've overcome fear. I've walked into hell and there's too many things I've got on my mind. The trouble with most people now is that they don't even know their own problems. But, by God, they all want to go to heaven. I've got too many things to do to worry about the hereafter or where I'm going when I'm dead. I know where I'm going right here.

I go to schools. Today I talked to sixty, seventy eight-year-old children. They come here to the store. I've got their names on the wall. I tell them that sometimes they ought to say no instead of yes. They have to hear it from somebody that stood on the line and got shot at.

We've got to educate the young people on environmental issues. All over this state, we've been beat up so badly by industry—pollution, nuclear waste. The governors are cracking down on little people to clean up all of this, but they don't seem to be doing anything about the nerve gas, about the nuclear waste in Oak Ridge, Tennessee. And these big companies, the strip miners, there's no rules and regulations on them at all.

An old man asked me once, "I'd like to know what makes you tick, Joe Begley?" I said, "People like you. You make me click." Just about every day, somebody calls from another state, "Come on out here and help us on the strip mining." I say, "I'd like to, but my ship is sinking, big hole in it. I gotta stay here and stop the leak. If you get too far from shore, you're gonna drown."

Oh, I've been shot at, I may not be able to live through all this, but after thirty years of fightin', I'll just have to keep right on. Something's come out of it. In Blackey, we've got a brand new day-care school. We've got a new water system. We're going to have natural gas. We've got a new city park. We're looking after elderly people that's been abused. We're looking after strip-mining abuses. I think we're doing a real good job, and I'm proud.

I think we've still got young people that will lead this country. That goes for my four children, too. Some are teaching school here in the colleges and high schools, and bring up all these issues. My grandson's teaching, too. I wish I was twenty years old. I'd really go at it more vigorously than I do.

I think the educational system in this country has failed, just like the legal system. I was in a community college over in Floyd County. I was raised there. This young lady student was sitting in the lobby. I knew her grandfather. She didn't know who Martin Luther King was. She never heard of Roosevelt. I've got in this store all kinds of relics and tools that old people used. The young people who come here don't know what these tools are for. They never used them. I put it on videotape so they can look at it. It keeps me young to talk to young people. It rubs off on you.

Most are from this area. They're children who've been deprived of education, deprived of recreation. They're poor people. We've got some young men in this town that was pretty tough. Undesirable people. They drank, they stole, they've done everything. We got a hold of them, we told 'em we're for 'em and we'd help any way we can. A lot of them turned around and are good workers now.

We brought the college right into the communities, so they don't have to go seventy-five miles. All these poor people that was called dumb are now book people. They're nurses, they work in doctors' offices. They're photographers. You'd be surprised. But it takes time. You don't do that overnight. If we can do it, I'm sure this nation can do it.

Blackey was a ghost town. It was a worked-out, old, deep-mining community. Back in the early '20s, there was a lot of mines here. The railroad was coming in. The town had a lot of people. Everybody was workin'. They had restaurants. They had a bank, hotels, clothing stores.

The depression, a flood, and a fire destroyed it. At one time in Blackey, when you talked to a person you really didn't know where that man was from. He might be Czechoslovakian. He might be a Filipino, he might be from Syria, Ireland, all over.

Today, there's about 125 people. That's all there are. But they come around from all over. When I walk in Blackey, I'm walking the whole nation. And I know these people. I say, "Hello, how are ya doin'?" Find out what's on his mind. All these things are important in a little community. A railroad man was in the store, watchin' people comin' in and out, buyin' potato chips or a loaf of bread and askin' questions. He said, "Boy, you got it made. You got the best job in the world." I'll agree with that.

It's just like being home, sittin' in the back yard on a nice couch. People come by, they've got problems. I've got a list of federal agencies, state agencies, the phone number of all of them. On the board, I've got 150 names with telephone numbers. If they say, "I'm in trouble, who can help me?" I say, "Call this number. Tell those sons of bitches. Talk to the horse's mouth, don't talk to me. If you can't get anywhere, maybe we both can, but you gotta set off the fire."

Facing off to some of those state legislators and the governor a couple of times, it was a challenge. I didn't go to school very much. I thought I'd went to the penitentiary when I went to school because I just couldn't react to 'em. I don't like big people with a lot of money to take advantage of a little person. I want an old person here to feel free and go into court in front of a judge, in front of a lousy, scheming, manipulating, lying lawyer and not be afraid. Old people don't want to go to court. They think that a young attorney will humiliate them. Hell, nobody can humiliate me when I'm going after somethin' good.

My one big regret is not becoming an attorney, to knock down another attorney that uses big words that we know nothing about. I would like to have been educated to the extent that I could have knocked him down, hit him like he hit me. In the last thirty years, I've learned enough that I don't have to call an attorney. I've talked to so many legal assistance people that I know pretty much what to say. But this world is so big and complicated and corrupted that some legal words and paragraphs that meant something five years ago don't mean that today. The alphabet has changed, the wording has changed, and it's changed for the worst.

Harry Caudill* was the kind of lawyer I'd have liked to be. He kept me out of the penitentiary many times, because I was fighting all the time. He encouraged me and handled so many cases of people in trouble with the big money men. He was a wonderful teacher.

We've had the worst twelve years of federal administration that any country could ever have. I believe we was gettin' to be a Third World country. This country is overabundantly rich. There's no reason that people can't have jobs. I'll tell you what's wrong: the people that own this country is big industry. And they ought to pay it. I'm talkin' about the banks, I'm talkin' about oil, I'm talkin' about railroads. They can pay off that debt tomorrow, but they won't. They just want to make a profit of billions of dollars. They can make jobs, too. So can the government, but it won't. Take health care. If these wealthy businesspeople can't pay into the government for medical care for poor people, they ought to pick up their pick and shovel and get the hell outta town.

I watch the newscasts as best I can. I'm familiar with Bosnia and the Holy Land. It looks to me like religion is gonna bury us all. It's in Russia, in China, in Ireland. We're killing each other all over the world. It's mind-boggling. But I've got to worry about a little bit closer to home. I've got to worry about what *our* destination is.

When I was fightin' the strip miners, I'd go to colleges. That's where the coal operators and the gas company sent their people to talk. Some of these community colleges and the University of Kentucky get money from them, so they won't talk about what industry's doing to people.

---

* A populist lawyer who took on some of Kentucky's most powerful companies, on behalf of the unions, miners with black-lung disease, and environmental advocates, among others. His most celebrated book is *Night Comes to the Cumberlands.*

We've got one coal operator whose performances ought to put him out of business. But he's got so much money that the governor said he was a cornerstone of Kentucky. We've got some good legislators, but they're too few and get voted down.

The pollution is coming in on us. I see the trees going. Hell, I saw the beaver go, I saw the game go, I saw the rivers go, I saw the hills go, and now I'm seeing the people go. In seventy-five years, I saw that, and we can't wait seventy-five more years for all this to change. I'm talkin' about survival.

I've just learned how to fight after seventy-five years. This has been a college. I've got a Ph.D. degree in hard knocks. One man said, "Why don't they kill that Joe Begley?" The other guy said, "That wouldn't do it, because ten thousand people will take his place and keep this battle going." I like to believe in the multiplication of things. The multiplication table is probably one of the best things that ever happened.

I want to make that hundred years of age. If I keep busy, on the go, I've got a pretty good chance. The only medicine I've taken in my life is Bayer aspirin. I've had an operation or two, like hernia or hemorrhoids, but that's caused by hard work. I've been lucky. People half my age are dying or dead. It fires me up, because there's so many younger that's dead that I know.

I enjoy battles. I've got to have a good fight to keep me going—fist fights, too. I could go further, but it would make me look bad. But you gotta pick your fights, where it means somethin'! Most of us run in fear. If you do, you might as well commit suicide and get it over with.

I was a torpedo man in World War II. That's been fifty years ago and, at the time, I thought it was great to get in a fight and kill people and get it over with. Fifty years later, I'm sweatin', my temperature is way up, I got salt water in my mouth. I still have these reactions. I think it's because I did things that I can't pay back.

I put torpedoes on those planes that kilt all those people. A Japanese ship. I remember that. I was a mechanic on the torpedo. It keeps me awake, it irritates me so bad that I can't get it right. I knew it was wrong, but I knew that I had no choice. They bombed Pearl Harbor, so we bombed the hell out of 'em. War is more than hell. It's for lunatics.

I had two sons in Vietnam, and I was against Vietnam. Our boys should never have been there. In front of me now, I've got a picture of one of my sons with a flamethrower, putting flames in a North Vietnamese foxhole. We believe in this country, we want to protect our country, but when I see this fellow here with this flamethrower, and this North Vietnamese foxhole, I say, "Wait a minute. This ain't what's it's about." If I'm not mistaken, when we were fightin' the Japanese, Ho Chi Minh was on our side. A few years later he's our enemy. What the hell were we doin' there anyway? It's this kind of fakery that gets me all fired up.

There's no way that a man can slow down. I owe it to the people in this county, and more particularly to my family and the people I live with in this community. There's no end to the battle. We're all gonna have to go in the end. I'm not prepared to go yet. I don't want to go, and I'll fight the hell out of it to the very end. The last flicker of my life will be against something that I don't think ought to be. And death, you know, is an enemy to me, and I'm gonna fight that.

Postscript: During my first visit, I had met Joe's wife,
Gaynell, who, as a young woman, had attended Berea College.
She had said, "I like poetry awfully well.
Edna St. Vincent Millay wrote one when she was eighteen:

> "'All I could see from where I stood
> Was three long mountains and a wood;
> I turned and looked another way
> And saw three islands in a bay.'

"And then it goes on to say—oh, darn! [Laughs.]

> 'A man was starving in Capri;
> He moved his eyes and looked at me.'

"You know, Millay saw over the hills to the rest of the world.
It touched me early, early, early, and made me think I was kin."

Wallace Nelson, 85,
and Juanita Nelson, 70
Deerfield, Massachusetts

They are members of Quaker community Woolman Hill, which was given to them, years ago, by Antoinette Spright, who, in the spirit of John Woolman, believed in goodwill among all people.

Their house, made of hand-me-down lumber, is atop a small hill, surrounded by greenery. Wallace built it with the help of neighbors. It is barely furnished. Aside from an ancient table radio, there is no acknowledgment of technology. Two gas lamps provide the light. There is no telephone.

The three of us are seated at a plain wooden table, obviously handmade.

WALLY: I was born in Arkansas. A poor family, very religious. My father was a Methodist minister. The most remarkable thing about my family was their sense of being reliable, of knowing what was talk and what was action. My father felt that if you said you believe a thing, the only way to demonstrate it is by trying to live it. This was my legacy.

The first thing I remember is seeing these signs: COLORED and WHITE. It was at a railroad station. The room that was marked COLORED was always dirty, disheveled. You walk across where it says WHITE and you'd see something clean and well kept. When I finally saw a streetcar, it was WHITE in front and COLORED in the rear. The line of demarcation was very clear.

Somehow, my family didn't accept this idea. We were taught that we were brothers and sisters to the whites. So I grew up believing that there was one race. I do not use the terms "multiracial" or "interracial" because there is no such existence for me.

Didn't you have certain feelings toward white people?

No. If the course of history had been turned, if the wheel, the damning wheel, had fallen upon people with dark colors, they'd behave just as stupidly as the white ones. So I didn't blame them because of their white skin. I blamed the blacks for kowtowing to this stupidity. I never have had any feeling about whites as whites.

During my early days, I ran into the idea of pacifism and nonviolence. These concepts impressed me.

JUANITA: I was born in Cleveland, in what our society calls a very poor family. My mother was the strong one. She was a woman of very firm opinions and believed in doing what she thought was right. My parents were both from Georgia. When my mother told me stories, I didn't know how she'd been able to leave Georgia alive, because she was quite a firebrand.

I went to Howard University for two years, but it was not my cup of tea. What made it bearable was meeting a woman named Pauli Murray. She was in law school, about ten years my senior. She got a group of us together under the aegis of the NAACP.* She knew about Ghandi and the fledgling CORE,† which had started in Chicago.

I had my first arrest as a freshman just before Pearl Harbor. It was 1941. Three of us coeds had gone to Washington, D.C. It was a terrible place. We tried to eat at Walgreen's and were arrested. We thought it quite a lark and were disappointed when, after three hours, the dean of women came to bail us out.

We were just about to have supper. The dean's arrival saved me, because I've never eaten when I've been in jail. I was going to eat that time. [*Laughs.*]

Though I had a scholarship at Howard, it was too difficult for my family to keep me in school. I went back home and worked on a weekly newspaper. I was nineteen. Because we tried to organize the Newspaper Guild, we all got fired. We were reinstated, but I learned some of the stuff Wally was just talking about. People are pretty much the same. This was a black newspaper, seemingly liberal, because it fought discrimination. That was its stock in trade, but its behavior was no different from a white employer's.

Juanita is wearing a button: Don't Pay War Taxes. A picture of Thoreau is on the wall. There's a poster of a soldier, with a gun and bayonet, killing another soldier: Not in Our Name with Our Money.

You two have been arrested enough times to qualify as jailbirds.

JUANITA: He's the real jailbird.

WALLY: I'm an ex-convict. My first arrest turned out to be a five-year jail sentence. It was during World War II, so called, because we've had World War II's ever since I've been born. I told the government that I had no enemies in Germany or Japan and if I did, I would not be killing them. I simply don't believe in killing. They insisted that I come and join the party, enter the armed forces. I said no. I was advised by older pacifists to ask for conscientious objector status. It turned out to be the wrong advice for me.

---

* National Association for the Advancement of Colored People.

† Congress of Racial Equality

I was sent to a conscientious objectors camp in Ohio, and I soon realized I had chosen the wrong option. I should not have registered at all. I felt I should not have anything to do with the war. After a year, I left camp. Five other buddies made the same decision.

The six of us went to Detroit and joined a community in the neighborhood, where in 1942, the riots between the whites and blacks were most fierce. We set up a little center, with a co-op store and recreational activities for the kids. There were eighteen of us, black and white, living together.

We were arrested, put into the Detroit county jail, and subsequently tried in Cleveland for leaving camp without permission. The trial had a foregone conclusion. The judge gave us five-year sentences, the highest possible. We were AWOL.* [*Laughs.*] We had told everybody we were leaving. We advertised it all over camp. I finally did thirty-three months.

While in the Cleveland county jail, awaiting removal to the federal prison, we accepted the idea of an appeal. Our lawyer told us that if we signed a statement that we were ready to serve sentence, the twelve months in county jail would count as time served. Two of us felt we couldn't sign that. We didn't *choose* to serve sentence: it was a lie. Since they were the ones who put me in jail, they'd have to make all the decisions. The two of us were left behind in the Cuyahoga County jail.

One day, we saw the sheriff walking by with a young man and young woman. We'd been here long enough to know that if the sheriff himself was the escort, this was an important visit. We wondered who they were, especially the woman. I'd been in prison now two years, and that's the closest I'd been to a woman. A friendly officer told us her name was Juanita Morrow, a reporter for a Cleveland paper. We said to him, "Tell her we have a story to tell."

JUANITA: When I met Wally, I was intrigued. He's responsible for my becoming a pacifist. I remember asking him the $64,000 question: What do you do if somebody's got a gun on you and is ready to kill you? I remember him saying he would try to deflect the gun, or whatever, but he would not play God and take somebody's life in the fear that his would be taken. It made sense to me. And I admired their spunk, his and his friend's. Also, they were just good company. That would have been in '43. Fifty years ago.

WALLY: Juanita and I do live on very little. Our income is something like five thousand dollars between us. If people in the so-called Third World could live the way we're living, they would think they

---

* Absent without leave.

were rich. But I know we're rich. Look around you. We go out here and we work. We don't worry about getting ill. We do get ill. I do more than Juanita. She's the strong one. We have a vegetable garden. That's how we make our living, selling to the farmer's market. And it provides most of our own food. We own a little truck that we need for our vegetables, and it helps us raise that five thousand.

JUANITA: After Wally and I started living together, we got involved with a group called the Peacemakers. They were old-fashioned pacifists, who felt that the only response was nonregistration for the draft. It was not just against war, but a total approach to nonviolence. To me, war is the inevitable outcome of the way we live every day.

We question the whole economic system. I'm not completely against electricity. If I could provide my own, it would be all right. But I don't want to go through the corporations that supply it. I think we could all do with a lot less.

In our workshops, I also talk about outhouse economics. We've had an outhouse for twenty years. My approach to ecology is that the simplest way is the best way. You talk about the five-gallon flush. With an outhouse, you don't even need a two-gallon flush. In most things, we're just where everybody else is. We're trying to do with less and less.

I have gone as far as a manual, portable typewriter. I'll go no further. See that fax machine over there. It was offered by our support committee, and I'm not touching it. I don't want it. We just keep demanding more things, up and up and up.

Are you for the destruction of machines? Are you or have you ever been Luddites?

JUANITA [*laugh*]: Well, sometimes I refer to myself as a Luddite. Maybe I should be like Carry Nation,* going around chopping down fax machines. We don't have electricity. We used kerosene for years, and then we finally did get gas. But at least I'm not on the line. If I want gas, I get it. If I don't, I don't get it.

WALLY: We're not deprived. We are accepting a marvelous opportunity of trying to live a life that measures up to our talk. We do a lot of talking. We say a lot of things. Talking is easy, but how are we living?

We began this whole process when we moved out of Philadelphia to New Mexico, from an eight-room house to a small adobe house. It's been a growing, exciting experience. It's not deprivation.

---

* A fiery temperance crusader, active during the last half of the nineteenth century. She was often pictured with a hatchet in her hand, as though about to attack a saloon or any liquor-dispensing establishment.

JUANITA: I left my job and, when Wally got out of prison, we started living together. That was in '48. We moved into a community right outside of Cincinnati in '50, with Ernest and Marian Bromley. We lived together for six years, all of us tax refusers. We found a way to earn our livings. I did a lot of typing of envelopes. Wally was organizing for CORE, a sort-of-paid job. With the Bromleys, we helped form the Cincinnati chapter.

I got so tired of typing, I went back to school—Ohio State—to get a degree in speech therapy. I figured I could do part-time work and something else.

We moved to Philadelphia, where we lived for eleven years. Having spent four months on Koininia Farm, an integrated cooperative in Georgia, we were experiencing all these shootings and threats. While in Philadelphia, Wally became a traveling salesperson for Ernest Morgan and the Antioch Book Plate Company. That way he could get an income with no tax taken out. We always had to find a job where no tax was deducted.

WALLY: When we first moved out of Philadelphia and went to New Mexico, we were often asked whether we were a retired couple. We laughed. It means you've retired from some job you've been doing for a million years and you've got a pension from that and an old-age pension. So you do nothing but live around, go from one senior citizen center to another, take trips. We laughed because, if we don't work—

JUANITA: —We don't eat. [*They laugh joyfully.*] We got nothing. As far as social security is concerned, I don't even use my number. I guess we'd get the lowest. We made a wee bit when I was on the paper.

WALLY: You may not even have made the minimum.

JUANITA: That settles it, that's nice. We used to say we don't want to take social security, but we've never made an absolute about it. If we were disabled, we said maybe we would. But now that's all clear. [*Laughs, a pause.*] I think we've slowed.

WALLY: Not at the same pace. Do we have the same energy as when we left Philadelphia? The answer is no. Not too long ago, we were observing that we don't go as fast as we used to.

JUANITA: On Saturday, we get up at five o'clock in the morning, because that's market day and we have to get ready to go. We sell at a farmer's market in Greenfield. Wally has to be there around seven.

---

* The Pioneer Valley War Tax Resisters.

The market opens at eight and he has to get set up. I stay behind and keep working in the garden. The market is over at 12:30. He has to pack up, and if anything is left, he has to peddle that, and maybe gets home in the middle of the afternoon. We count our money and see if we've made one hundred dollars that day. [*Laughs.*] It's hard to describe a typical day for us. From March on, it's garden, garden, garden.

WALLY: Yesterday, Saturday, I was under the thrust of getting home by two o'clock, because we had a special meeting of people who are carrying on this vigil. We've been having a vigil for eighteen months over this house in Colraine. A couple of our members* refused to pay taxes and the IRS finally took away the home. Another couple bought it at an auction.

JUANITA: We were successful in having no bids the first time, and again in '89. Wherever Wally goes, there's going to be some kind of tax resistance. We're saying it's wrong to confiscate houses to force people to pay for killing. It's bigger than just the house. There has been an injunction issued. Two state troopers came Friday, just two days ago, to warn us: "You can leave or we're going to arrest you." We already have a preconceived plan that once arrests are imminent, the Morning After Team, as we call ourselves, will not accept fines or bail, and just be there. We will not leave if they ask us to leave. So it probably means arrest. It's going to be this Thursday. Of course I'm going to vigil, and if they put me in jail, that's what they will do. [*Laughs.*]

WALLY: In 1948, the Peacemakers started war-tax resistance. It began with nonregistration, addressed to young men of draft age. We decided that older people who had any kind of job could also participate, could say no to the government in a very active way.

JUANITA: This was the one way older people could actually do something about it. We're asked all the time, with every paycheck, every year, to pay for warheads. More than half the money goes to the military. In some ways, it's almost worse to pay than to fight. You're just paying for somebody else to do it for you.

WALLY: That's what got us started. When you take a stand on non-payment, you've freed yourself from a lot of fear. Most people are frightened to death of the Internal Revenue Service, the tax collector. If you can get over that one big fear, your heart and mind are left open to consider: "How am I living? How does my living contribute to what I abhor?" You immediately begin to see a lot of things. It gets you to begin to see beyond the horizon.

JUANITA: I was arrested only once for tax refusal and was in for only one day. It happened while we were living in Philadelphia. Wally was away on a trip selling book plates. We'd been sparring with the IRS for years. We have never filed, because we have no allegiance to a government whose major business is making war. They would ask us to come and see them. We'd say, "We're not really interested. If you want to come and talk with us, that's fine. We'll tell you why, but we won't give you any information." This had gone on for some time. Finally, they were able to trace the income I had from two part-time jobs in Cincinnati. They came at an early hour in the morning, when I was still in bed, in my accustomed nudity. So I got up and put on my robe—

The story is interrupted as a neighbor appears at the door: "We want to find out if Juanita is going to jail." "Probably," she replies. Wally laughs.

JUANITA: Anyway, the reason they didn't keep me in jail long was because I didn't get dressed. I merely put on my robe. There were two officials at the door and seven guys outside, waiting. I realized they wanted me to get dressed so they could take me to jail. I decided I really didn't want to go, so why should I get dressed? So they took me in my robe. I think that's why they held me for only one day.

Randy Keeler, whose house was taken away, is the one who got us here. We had left New Mexico because we couldn't find any land that we could afford. The board of Woolman Hall has agreed that we can stay here for life. We have many visitors. Wally does a lot of peace workshops. We're active in other matters, too.

One of my passions is the subject of money. It has no reality. I hate it because of what it does to our minds. Another thing that bothers me is interest. Where does it come from? Money doesn't make money. I get a lot of flak from that.

Another thing is land. It doesn't belong to people. We didn't make it and we shouldn't own it. It would be like selling air and sunshine, which we'll eventually be doing anyway. [*Laughs.*] We can use the land, be good stewards.

I'm afraid I'm pessimistic. But, as Ammon Hennessy* once said, "I don't know if I'm going to change the world, but I'm sure as hell gonna try to see that it doesn't change me."

---

* An old-time Catholic activist who was an associate of Dorothy Day.

People ask me, "Are you still doing that?" Nobody asks me if I'm still eating or washing the dishes or looking at the stars. It's just my life: living without even talking about it. I think there are a lot of people like that, and I think that's what saves the world.

A little story about Wally. He has this great idea: I'm my brother's keeper. When he was in prison, probably Danbury, there were four men playing cards. A call came for one of them to go to court. He didn't look very fit. Wally was thinking: "I'm one of the few people whose clothes he could wear. But he doesn't bathe very often. I don't know if I should do this, but I've got to do it." While he's thinking it over, one of these guys who's playing cards and cussin' and everything unbuckles his belt, pulls off his pants and throws them at this guy. He doesn't think about being his brother's keeper or anything. He just does it. This is what I'm talking about.

What's next for you two?

WALLY: There's a book I've come across about the Mondragos Cooperative in Spain: *We Make the Road as We Travel.* You see, I don't think there is any blueprint. It's a constant. You're never going to get there, you're always on the way.

If there is a what's next, it's moving this foot before the other one and not letting it stay behind. I won't move if I don't put this foot before the other—I'm gonna stand still. Therefore, the hope is to continue to put one foot before the other and without knowing where that's leading you to. I think we're wrong to have to know. It's good to know where I'd like to go. It's good to feel that I'm headed the way I want to go. But the important thing is that you go. You may find yourself there or you may not. You turn around and you take another course. But just don't stop putting that foot before the other.

Postscript: After Juanita Nelson was jailed as a result of the Colraine vigil, she went on an extended fast. She stopped when she felt it was time to do so. It was her decision.

Raymond Koch, 84

CHICAGO, ILLINOIS

"I started my carpentry when I came to Chicago in 1950. From that time on, I worked at the trade."

I'm from a family farm outside Oregon City, Oregon, in sight of Mt. Hood. It was a homestead, so our job was to clear the land. We had eighty acres of timber. My father, who had been a tool-and-die maker, didn't like factory work. That's how the farm came about. He was never a farmer, but I became one. [*Chuckles.*]

There were eight children in the family, so you started working chores when you were six or seven, hoeing in the fields, helping with the cattle, carrying in wood. You worked for hours, but you had a job to do and you stuck with it.

We had a one-room school, so each of the eight grades took turns reciting. You marched up to the front and the teacher would take you through all the subjects: reading, writing, and arithmetic, of course. Three miles to walk to school, and three miles home.

I didn't go through any apprenticeship as a carpenter. What I had behind me was all that farm work, all those tools. In those days, the union would take you in if you said you were a carpenter. You had to get your own job, find your own contractor. My first boss had me nail down flooring. He stood around, saw how you were doing, and that was it.

I left the farm when I was sixteen, looking for an education where I could afford the tuition. My father wanted all his children to be educated. Only two of us were able to go to high school. He heard about a cooperative community down in Louisiana. He didn't like working for a boss, for wages, so he went down there. They put him to work in a saw mill. It wasn't for him because, at this colony, he had two or three bosses instead of one telling him what to do. [*Chuckles.*] He came back home in 1924, just in time to vote for Bob LaFollette.*

Someone sent him a newspaper clipping about Commonwealth College, a worker's school in Mina, Arkansas. The idea of the school was not just learning a vocation but a sense of community. It was a beautiful place, an old farm overlooking the mountains. They built their own school, buildings and all. The first work I did was to help put up the school, out of pine boards.

At Commonwealth, I was in charge of assigning work to all the students. We had about sixty students every term. We did our own

* The Progressive Party candidate for president. He polled five million votes in the 1924 election.

gardening, cooking, washing, building. We canned a lot of food. The students paid fifty dollars a quarter, so it brought in a little money.

The people who taught there had been college professors, engineers, lawyers, editors, or organizers. So the teaching you got there was broader than you would get at a traditional college. We had a library of five thousand volumes. We would read everything possible related to a subject, instead of just textbooks.

I met my wife, Chuckie, there. She came because she had written a letter to Upton Sinclair. One of his books, *The Goose Step*, was critical of our traditional colleges. He was a member of the Commonwealth board and suggested she go there.

The townspeople were somewhat critical of us because the girls wore pants and smoked cigarettes. It was in fundamentalist country, yet there were a surprising number of neighbors who were old Gene Debs supporters. We were near the Oklahoma border, where, before World War I, more votes were cast for the Socialist candidates than in some of the big cities.

When I got back from Germany in '45, I felt I had a better chance for work in Chicago. My first job was in a three-man shop: finishing, hanging doors, things I hadn't done before. Then, for a building contractor, we put up cottages, small brick houses, and some of the first ranch houses.

This was before the days of drywall: bits of Sheetrock or gypsum board in place of plaster. Carpenters made the framing in those days, the openings. Later, they'd come from a millwork place. We were still in the handsaw age. Soon, the first electric saws came out, revolutionizing carpentry. You could do all the joists, cut 'em off in thirty minutes, for the whole house. Before that, each plank would take you five minutes. The electric saw had a guard, but one time I carelessly let this blade hit my leg and I had a beautiful cut. I've known people to cut their fingers off.

Soon came a lot of other electric tools: planers, drills, gougers. We used to do that with chisels and hammers. The first nailing machine I used had a little cartridge that shot this bullet, which pushed the nail in. You'd go nailing as fast as you could move it. Now you have the staple gun. I used to file my own saws. Very few carpenters today can do that. They don't have to because the handsaw is hardly used anymore.

Building is not a matter of one trade, though the carpenter was the master craftsman because he framed out the whole thing and made the house a reality. Then came the plumber, the electrician, the glazer. Most glass is now preinstalled. Even the beams, the trusses come preformed. With the age of plastics, the work of all these craftsmen has altered.

I'm not against the technological changes. It's made my work easier. We should accept progress even if it means fewer jobs in my trade. But we should concentrate on finding jobs for everyone. If it means cutting down the work week to thirty hours, I'm for it. You can't just keep cutting wages as a means of keeping the industry going here, because you're only increasing poverty. If you throw a carpenter out of work and turn him into an unemployed, he's of no benefit to society. A shorter work week will give people more time for leisure activities. I've enjoyed my leisure since I've retired. [*Chuckles.*] That was twenty years ago.

When I was a carpenter, my wife and I started to write. Since my retirement, we've published four children's books, a history of Commonwealth, and a novel about Orval Faubus. Remember him?*

We went to Maine, hoping to write more books, but we spent all our time working on the house and raising vegetables. It was too primitive. The long cold winters, the thirty-mile trips for medical attention when my wife got sick, and the isolation were just too much.

An architect friend of mine in Chicago had a three-flat that needed remodeling. There was a lot of carpentry to be done. In exchange, we had a very nice English basement apartment, to which I added a guest room. So I became janitor, caretaker, and gardener. This fit in perfectly with my retirement, because I could not sit around and do nothing. That wasn't my style. Work to me is pleasure.

I used to worry a little about having to tell myself what I'm going to do each day, because all those past years, people laid out work for me. I knew what I was to do between 9:00 and 4:30. Now I had to tell myself what to do and when. Shall I go walking to the lake? Shall I take a swim? Shall I work in the garden? This problem soon disappeared because there was enough work to keep us busy. We got our rent knocked down to very little and were fulfilling a good function.

Social security, a fairly good carpenter's pension, plus low rent enabled us to travel. September was our month for enjoyable group tours. First we hit all over the United States, Mexico, and Canada. Since then, it's been the Mediterranean, Greece, China, Brazil. We allocate our money carefully, but not too tightly. We're going to Hawaii soon, on one of those organized tours.

We shop for food about once a week. It runs to about sixty-five dollars. As we get older, we eat out a little more often.

There's a church out here that does good deeds all over the place. I

---

* Faubus, as governor of Arkansas, was an intransigent opponent of the Civil Rights Acts in the early '60s. "He was a fellow student of mine at Commonwealth. Would you believe it?"

do carpentry for them. I don't change. That's my charity: on occasion, I do some carpentry for friends. I don't ask for union carpenters' wages, but I expect a little reward. [*Chuckles.*]

We have an independent alderman who has always fought the machine. Aside from doing some carpentry in his ward office, we pass out leaflets, put up signs, and represent our block. If there's an election coming up, we canvas our precinct. I help my wife in registering people She's registered hundreds of people in front of the Jewel Foods store.

We're proud that we helped elect Harold Washington as mayor. We worked very hard. My wife got a Distinguished Woman Award for the job as she did as a registrar. We're involved with community police, three or four of them walking the beat and meeting neighbors. We attend all meetings, but are now limiting ourselves and letting others take over.

We find that the elderly who are active are deeply appreciated and are honored by the younger people. They go out of their way to make sure that we are hearing what they say. [*Chuckles.*] There are a few people who are so filled with anger that they will curse what is happening in our ward because it's changing. One guy came over while I was handing out leaflets, and started cussing, blaming an alderman for everything wrong in the ward—for "bringing those people in." He was really advocating a kind of ethnic cleansing. We don't like it in Yugoslavia, but here he was saying "get rid of those people." Yet we find some of the young people here, just starting their families, active in wonderful ways.

What I'm doing now is a continuation of my life. I've had about four lives. Retirement is my fifth. Childhood in Oregon, Commonwealth College. Working with the children of miners in West Virginia. I took a ball, bat, and bicycle into the coal camps and organized clubs for the kids. I was down in North Carolina, during a bitter textile strike, working with the children. In St. Louis, I was helping organize the unemployed. I became educational director of the UEWA (United Electrical Workers of America), midwestern district. Four years in the army. Then came Chicago and carpentry. Now is my fifth—or is it sixth?—life. [*Chuckles.*]

I'm in the hearing-aid stage. Chuckie is in the cataract stage. I may be getting there, too. As you age, things close in a little bit for you. That's why traveling is still important, and we enjoy it. I can still climb a ladder, but I have a tendency to get a little dizzy once in a while. Chuckie has fallen down a few times, but she's still folk dancing.

I think as you get older, your telescope gets longer and you can see further back and maybe further ahead. Your personal horizons may not be as distant. What I see immediately happening around the world is quite discouraging, but I've never given up the faith that we can solve the problems when we are finally forced to tackle them. I hope it doesn't get to the point where man is extinct before we make up our minds, because that's where we're headed unless there's a turnaround. I'm philosophical enough to know that even if all the people are dead, the bugs will still be here. [*Chuckles.*] What's that saying? Think globally and act locally. We buy into that. That's why we're active on our block and in our precinct. If you don't do it, who's going to do it?

I think our marriage of sixty years has grown closer, even without children. I think we're in the hand-holding stage now. Neither one of us wants the other to fall down. [*Chuckles.*]

Postscript: He died on May 14, 1994.

Bresci Thompson, 86
NEW YORK CITY

We're in a condominium, one of the hundreds in a huge housing complex financed by the International Ladies Garment Workers Union. The residents are mostly retired teachers, social workers, and other city employees.

It is in Chelsea, a neighborhood, he says, celebrated for "poverty and creativity." Through the window, we see the fabled Chelsea Hotel, where Virgil Thomson, Thomas Wolfe, James T. Farrell, Nelson Algren, and Brendan Behan were frequent guests.

He is the doyen of the community, having lived here all his life. A slim, small-boned, tightly knit figure of graceful moves, he is a familiar to most of the residents. His air is one of constant ebullience.

The apartment is, in effect, a gallery of landscape paintings—his.

I'm a product of the Hudson Guild, a settlement house. I entered kindergarten at the age of four. We lived in a basement, in great poverty, always on the verge of being dispossessed—my parents, my three sisters, and myself. We spoke only Spanish at home, though I am South American Indian and Scottish as well as Hispanic.

My grandfather was a Thompson. He went from Scotland to Argentina to be a bridge builder. He married an Indian woman who was raised a Catholic. But they both disliked Catholicism because of what it did to her tribal culture. So we were raised nonreligious. At the age of seventeen, my father left Argentina to avoid military servitude. He worked in the silk mills of Patterson, New Jersey, a nest of Italian anarchists.

His best friend was Gaetano Bresci, who was saving money to send for his sister, a silk worker in Italy. During a strike there, the king, Umberto I, ordered the strike smashed. Gaetano's sister was killed. So he said to my father, "I'm going back home to kill the king of Italy." In 1900, he approached Umberto I with a bouquet of flowers and a gun, and he killed the king.

He was sentenced to life imprisonment. There was no capital punishment. Because of his dastardly deed, a law was passed: anybody with the name of Bresci had to change it. The name was to be erased from Italian life. My father said, "That name is going to live. If I have a girl or a boy, that name, Bresci, will be there." That's how I got this name.

When my wife, who was Irish American, and I visited Ireland, our tour guide was Miss Bressy. She said, "My parents had to change their name legally." My wife died eight years ago. We'd been married fifty-one years. She was a teacher, head of the neighborhood schools. The kids all loved her.

I was surrounded by Irish American people in the neighborhood who were loving, caring, and big-hearted. We were considered foreigners, but they shared. In Chelsea, the two words were: "poverty" and "survival." The creative spirit came from the Hudson Guild.

I learned to sketch and paint at the guild at the age of six. We lived in cold-water flats, toilets in the yard. Going to Hudson was heaven. They had electric lights, we had kerosene lamps. We didn't even have a meter for gas lights. We had no baths, not in the whole neighborhood.

My wife was a social worker for the Hudson Guild. That's where I met her. She was in the nitty-gritty of life—saw the ignorance, the drunkenness, no job, sick children. There was no welfare, no home relief. During the depression, Hudson had to cut the salaries drastically, so she became a teacher, right across the street.

[*He indicates a photograph on the mantelpiece: an attractive woman in a mantilla.*] My mother was a genius at survival. My father was well educated and poetical. He gave my sisters non–saint's names. My oldest sister was Alba, bright light. My other sister's name was Savia, the sweetest part of the flower. My third sister's name is Senda, the road to Utopia.

The tragedy came with my littlest sister, eleven months old. Her name was Libertad, liberty. It was 1918. There was an epidemic of Spanish influenza. I heard screaming in the hall when she died in my mother's arms. We had no money to bury her. My father said, "I'm going to bury her in the backyard in a macaroni box." An Italian janitor in the building befriended the undertaker, and she was buried in Potter's Field. Those things you never forget, the people, as poor as you are, helping. This sense of community.

My father worked on the waterfront and tried to organize the men because of the shake-up. The boss man would say, "You—you—you," and he'd choose from a favored claque. They shared their wages with the boss. My father objected: "I have four kids. I work as hard as that man you always pick—" He was beaten up badly and lost his job. He didn't have any definite skill, but he had a beautiful build and would get whatever hard, physical work he could find. He heated up ovens at one o'clock in the morning, so the bakers would be ready to make the bread. That was his last job. He died at the age of forty-five, of a heart attack.

I saw such misery around me as a young child that I've always been alert to these things. There has to be some way to end poverty. I saw these men as beasts of burden who had intelligence, who had heart, who loved their families.

To these people, the Hudson Guild has brought a sense of culture to the community which they might never have known. I've been with it for eighty-one years and am still active on the board. I talk to kids at the guild and visit schools, telling them what it was like in the old days: sleeping on the fire escape, going to the toilet in the yard, carrying the slop jar. These things are shocking to the kids. They had no idea.

Youth has been so maligned in the last two decades. No jobs, yet they're struggling. I look at the young who have very little money, little chance for a career; scholarships are few and far between these days. The future depends on them. People like myself, we're dying away.

They respect me, but sometimes I get irritated with some of the things they do: don't give you space walking in the street, roller skates coming at you full force, some of those bicycle riders. You can get hurt, broken hips.

There's a basic fear of some of the youth who come along in groups. A lot of the seniors hold off, away from them. Yet I've seen so many of these young people help old people cross the street. It's up to the individual. You can't label a whole group.

Chelsea is a mixture of many races and so many ages and lots of bias. There's a fear of black people coming in. We have some projects here named after Dr. Elliott, who founded the Hudson Guild. It's a mix of blacks, some poor whites, and Puerto Ricans. I speak Spanish fluently, so I understand their style—lots of music and dancing in the streets. It's not accepted by older people, because of fear in not knowing this way of life.

Here's where the Hudson Guild still plays a big role: getting people to understand each other. It was financed by the Ethical Culture Society. In fact, I got a scholarship at the Ethical Culture School, thanks to Dr. Elliott. Eighty percent of the students were wealthy kids. Dr. Elliott had to panhandle money for my lunches, car fare, and clothes.

These kids had formal dances, evening gowns, and tuxedos at the age of fourteen or fifteen. One of the pupils who spoke Spanish loaned me his tuxedo. This one girl had bid and she chose me because I was a good dancer. She said, "My parents would like to meet you." So I went to this town house. [*Gasps.*] I've never been to such a place in my life. I was greeted by servants. I met her parents and they were playing mah jongg, which was the popular game in those days. She showed me her father's trophy room. He was a horseman and a yachtsman and he had all these cups. I looked at one and it said "Exton," instead of "Eckstein." She said, "My father had to change his name because he was not accepted in the clubs as a

Jew." That was the first time I began to feel things were not that beautiful. I also knew that Jews helped Dr. Elliott in founding the Hudson Guild.

[*In recalling the moment, he had, as a matter of reflex, gracefully danced around the room, his hand extended, in the manner of a flamenco artist.*] I learned this at the Hudson Guild. They had a couple, in white gloves, who came in and picked out ten boys and girls. You put your white gloves on and were very gracious. The kids were all laughing. The woman asked me to come over. She said, "Put your arms around..." I was afraid to do that. And I was right in line with her breasts. She said, "You're so beautiful." I was about ten or eleven. [*His eyes glow.*]

Imagine what I was feeling. I didn't know what the hell to do. I never had that smell of perfume and the closeness of this woman and her breasts. That was seventy-five years ago and I'll never forget it. [*He laughs and reenacts the moment, with a touch of flamenco as well as ballroom style.*]

Did the Spanish civil war play a role in your life?

Oh, my mother was very active, on the side of the Loyalists.* My father had died. This was in 1936. There was a large grocery store, where she used to buy chorizos (Spanish sausages) and olive oil. The store insisted on buying things from the Franco regime, despite neighborhood protests. My mother organized a picket line, with the newspapers taking pictures. She wore a cross, though she resented the Catholic Church's support for Franco. Even though her lovely land was far away, it was deep in her heart. I was never involved with politics. We kept it out of the Hudson Guild because it would divide us.

The only time I had trouble was during World War II. I guess I was influenced by Dr. Elliott and my father, who said, "War is only two things: power and greed." I was a conscientious objector, but it was difficult because I had no religious background to save my goose.

At the time, I was working as a display manager at Abraham & Strauss in Brooklyn. I couldn't make a living as a painter. I wasn't that good. But I was painting with merchandise and color and fashion. I set the windows and showcases. I loved it. I was there thirty-three years.

Dr. Elliott, who had been a pacifist all his life, made a speech at the guild, supporting the war. "We have to get rid of this cancer, even if we have to bear arms." He had known many Jews, and the Jewish

* I.e., the Republicans, who were loyal to the democratic government that Francisco Franco eventually overthrew.

people were being persecuted by the Nazis. But he didn't convince me. He said, "Bresci, I admire the way you stand by your principles, but you're going to face a lot of heat." And did I!

The FBI came to the Hudson Guild and to Abraham & Strauss. They even went to some of my teachers. They asked my wife's aunt, who was living with us, if I was a Communist. They didn't ask if I was a fascist. We were fighting them, not Russia, which was on our side.

They visited Abraham & Strauss. My boss was in the First World War, had been gassed and had gotten malaria. He had a large American flag in his office, and each department had a "thermometer" to measure how many employees had bought war bonds. The only department that didn't give 100 percent was the display department, because that son of a bitch Bresci didn't buy any. The boss came through for me. He told the FBI that I was a kind and friendly person and he trusted me. I was never called.

I had a trial down at Foley Square. At the time, Lew Ayres, the movie actor, was in prison as a conscientious objector. The judge asked if I'd join the medical corps. I said yes, but I was never called.

On the whole, my life these days may be uneventful, but I'm very busy. I help older people around here. I still spread the gospel of the Hudson Guild. I take walks, go to museums, and take my two younger sisters out to an Irish pub that is lovely. The price is right, the food is good, and the people are convivial.

I don't drink, because I've seen the misery of alcohol. If the longshoremen didn't show up with their wages on Friday night, forget it. They'd be drunk with eight or nine kids waiting. I saw abuse. I saw Mrs. Flanagan with flour on her face to hide the black eye. Booze is not for me.

Dancing is for me. I'm a good ballroom dancer and they're in great demand at senior centers. We see about 80 percent women and 20 percent men. The men don't dance, they just sit there. When the women find out that I'm a dancer [*Claps hands*], that's it.

I have two girlfriends whom I met at a *thé dansant*. Real French. That's what they call it in Bay Ridge. My sweethearts were in vaudeville years and years ago, as ingenues. Now they're characters because they have silver hair. One is very cultured, but you have to be very careful with sex these days. They're widows, and you never know what their lifestyle was with their husbands. They don't know each other. [*Laughs.*] They have money from their husbands' insurance and keep themselves very well groomed. They have their hair done every week. I love beautiful women.

The songs they play at these places are from the '40s and '50s. Songs from the World War II period, big bands. It's great. You can sing the songs. Today's songs don't have the poetry.

I'm in pretty good shape, even though I never exercise. I have a normal American diet, nothing special. The only thing I have is osteoarthritis of the neck, but dancing takes care of everything.

I've been out of Abraham & Strauss for twenty-one years. I'm often called as a model and as an extra in motion pictures. I wait for calls from my agents, one for print and ad jobs, the other for films. It's strange, isn't it, that I am in this work.

There are photographs of him in various guises: a cardinal, a Russian, a widower in a nursing home, a fashion model. On the other wall is a large photograph and a long piece that appeared in the New York Times: CHELSEA, 81 YEARS OF LOVE, SURVIVAL AND ART.

There is my family, my mother of the Old World, my sisters, and there is the neighborhood. And there is one of the Hudson Guild, 1905—a penny a glass of milk. My beloved community.

Guadalupe Reyes, 75
Chicago, Illinois

*She lives in Pilsen. Years ago, it was a Bohemian neighborhood;
today, it is the city's largest Mexican community. She is recognized
in the area for her activity in neighborhood matters. The mayor
recently appointed her as a member of the Chicago Transit Authority: "I feel funny about it."*

*Of her eleven children, four daughters are community activists.
Her oldest, Mary, is executive director of the Pilsen Neighbors'
Community Council. "I lost one in 1983. That was Bobby. He was
retarded and physically handicapped. He was number six and
became the center of our lives."*

When I was a very young child, I remember my father working the
coal mines in Pittsburgh, Oklahoma, where I was born. He con-
tracted rheumatism, so we moved away from the mines to Kansas
City, where he worked on the railroad tracks. He wasn't making
enough money to support the family, so he became a migrant worker
in the fields. We, the children, worked, too. There were six of us.
Minnesota, Iowa, North Dakota...

I was about eight years old. Working in the sugar beets was very
hard. On your knees all day. Miles and miles. We'd start school in
November and leave in May, so we could go work in the fields. It was
a hard life, but I think it prepared me to be what I am today.

I left the fields when I was twenty and came to Chicago. I helped
my father and my sisters come here, too. My father was so ill, we had
to get him out. He never questioned authority. He just didn't know
how, and his English was very little. He just wanted to live and take
care of his kids because my mom died when I was eleven. He just
tried to survive with us.

I married a man who worked in the Wisconsin steel mills. We
raised this family. We lived in Hyde Park, very beautiful, but there
was land clearance coming up and they were tearing down buildings
all over the neighborhood for a new development. The landlord who
bought this building didn't care how we lived. There were no lights
in the hall, no heat, no hot water, rats, all kinds of stuff, garbage piled
up to the door.

I used to be afraid of him. I used to lock my door when he came
around and screamed. He'd ask how many kids I had. It wasn't easy to
get an apartment when you had kids, so I was afraid he'd throw us out.

The kids would get sick often, because it was so cold in the place.

My husband said, "Don't say anything, he'll throw us out." We had six kids then and I was expecting another. I came back from the hospital and I was worried. What's going to happen to this baby?

I was just running around, looking for something, when I met this new alderman, Mr. Despres.* He was going around visiting people and told me, "If you need anything, let me know." He gave me his card. I put it away. I didn't know where the power was or who could help me.

I didn't feel no support from anywhere. The nurse said, "Give this landlord a chance." My husband was scared. So I took the card and went to the alderman's office. He was out, so I explained everything to his secretary: "I've been home five days from the hospital with the baby." He said, "Go back home. We'll get some help."

In two, three hours, my house all of a sudden was full of people from the Health Department. It was a blessing. God was hearing my prayers. I was scared when all these people came in. They said, "We got a call. Did you go to the alderman's office?" "Yes, I did."

They saw the garbage at the door. They saw how cold it was. They checked the heat. That same evening, about five o'clock, we had five janitors cleaning up the garbage, cleaning the walls, putting lights on, scrubbing the floors, everything. For two years we were without heat, my kids were always sick, but after I saw this happening I realized how much power I had. All I have to do is speak up and say what was bothering me. Since that day, that's what I've been doing. That was a turning point in my life.

I found out that the landlord was just another person, that I could talk to him whichever way he wanted to talk to me. If he wanted to be angry, I could talk to him angry. I didn't have to be afraid of him. So I discovered these things and this helped me a lot in raising my family. It helped me a lot in going to the schools and talking to the principal. I always thought that teachers knew everything. Whenever they said your kids is this and this and this, I'd say okay. But after that, I would go and say, "Tell me about it. Explain." Teachers are human beings just like everybody else, and they make mistakes just like we do and they act like we do sometimes. That's why I believe all the things that's happened in my life were probably to prepare me for the life that I would live later.

We moved out of Hyde Park and landed up at a project. We had a lot of trouble there because the black people wouldn't accept us here. They would tell us to go back where we came from. I was afraid for my daughters, so we stayed there only for a year. My husband borrowed money, and we bought a little old house out there. This is where I started getting involved.

At first, the Bohemians who lived here didn't want to mix with us.

---

* See chapter 15, "Public Servant."

The ladies had their own rummage sale and would not allow us to buy or sell. They didn't want us to use these things. I started saying hello to them, sometimes with cookies, offering them one. It was something new to them, Mexican people coming into their neighborhood. They didn't want to share. They were afraid we would steal. But as we went on, I started to make friends with all of them. I included them in whatever we were doing. We would invite them, offer them our Mexican food. We became very good friends. They would look to find me, invite me to their dinners, brunches, give me presents for Christmas. I formed a parents' group and they elected me president.

What I found out is that we're all human beings and nobody is that much different than the other. There's a difference in color, but we all have feelings. We all believe in God. I think if it wasn't for Him... It's only by the grace of God. I go to church on Sundays, Bible class. I talk to my seniors about their religion and how God lives in our lives.

My father passed away in 1968. He lived with me the big part of my life, very ill all the time. My husband died in 1970. He was a very gentle person and was surprised by what I did. He would say, "If that's what you want to do, do it, but be careful."

I need to talk to you about how I felt in those days about Bobby, my retarded child. Since he was born, I always felt—and I think all parents feel this way—that we are responsible. You feel guilty, maybe you weren't resting well or eating the right food or whatever. I used to get depressed. I used to take him outside for walks, although he couldn't walk very well, trying to make up for the guilt that I felt. I used to sit in my kitchen and cry, because I would see him sitting there, a big boy, playing with nothing. He was about twelve, thirteen.

They put a brace on him, so I would sit him on the table and swing his legs, put on oil, massage them and exercise them every day, in the morning. Then I put him on a tricycle, put on little elastic bands, and push him out in the hallway. Every morning or evening, when the kids were there, they would do it. They told me he may not talk because his vocal cords have been damaged.

I feel God was with me then. I read in the paper a little article that said blowing balloons would strengthen the vocal cords, so I taught Bobby how to blow balloons. These penny balloons. He loved it because he'd blow 'em up, then stick 'em with a needle. As he grew, I bought the five-cent ones, but now he was getting too expensive. He'd break them all. I thought of buying him a beach ball, but he didn't like that because they wouldn't pop.

Bobby started to talk. I could hear sounds where he made noises. I was feeling my efforts were being rewarded. At the same time, I cannot say seriously that I made him talk. I wanted to cure him, but I knew it wouldn't happen, right? I was still trying. I felt I owed him something.

I used to call Mental Health and tell them to send somebody to help me with my son. It didn't work. I was going a little out of my mind. Finally, I decided to find out if there was other people who have the same problems.

I put a notice in the neighborhood paper, and I got about four people who had the same problems. We didn't know what we wanted to do, but I felt comfort that there were people who could talk to me. What happened was that other people joined these meetings: students from the universities taking Special Ed, community reps working with schools. Mental Health came around. Curious to ask what I was doing, I said, "We're just talking." We didn't know what else to do, right?

The students were the ones who started it. They investigated places we might take our kids, finding sources. That gave me a lot of courage. Mental Health would tell me, "Lupe, just don't get disappointed if nothing happens, if things don't work out." I said, "Whatever happens will be better than nothing." So I kept on working with these people. I had about fifty parents now that came together. We were just meeting in my house or in an office somewhere across the street or somewhere.

I went over to Dvorak Park, where they had a recreation center for the handicapped. We brought our kids there, and I kind of took over the program. I organized the people there, and we'd say we need this and this and this, and they had nothing to offer.

One day, this professor came over, from some city college, and he says, "I will help you. We'll have a school going and you will run it."* I said, "No, no, no." I got scared. What would I know about a school? My daughter Mary said, "Let's do it, Ma." I said, "But, Mary, I don't know anything about this grants or state monies." All she said was, "Let's do it."

The hardest thing was getting parents to agree to let their children come to our school. Mary and I had to go to their homes and reassure them over and over and over. We were at all the meetings, asking people if they knew any handicapped kids in the neighborhood, getting names, addresses, telephone numbers, and making follow-up visits. We decided to open the school.

We gave the school a name: Esperanza. It means "hope." I never

---

* "One day a crazy man came to our door, a professor. He was interested in handicapped children. Would we help him get public funds for a school for kids like Bobby? People warned us that this guy was weird and might pass things on to Bobby. I felt if Bobby can learn anything from him, it's a plus."

—Mary Gonzales, in *The Great Divide: Second Thoughts on the American Dream*, 1988.

lost hope that there would be something for my son. This professor and his wife were the directors. There was a staff, and Mary and I were on the board. Two of my other daughters worked as volunteers. We had to have a lot of volunteers.

We started with a little pilot program of twelve kids. What happened to me is that I began to feel better when I started to do something for my son. No longer depressed. I think all parents should experience that. We had our problems, but Esperanza grew very well and is still going. They have a workshop and a bakery where the clients bake bread.

Mary and I knew that Bobby would soon have to leave Esperanza because of his age. The Board of Education pays the school so much for his education as long as he's below twenty-one. Where will we put him? We didn't know nothing about adult workshops, so we set up a place called El Valor. It means "courage." We had some help, of course. It's a place where Bobby can stay forever.

He learned how to put things in little bags and how to fold shirts and how to do table work, and discipline, where he'd have to sit down. It was a wonderful experience for him because he was around adult people. And he earned some money.

We have seven residences now and about forty-eight clients that live there. In some cases, their parents are too old to deal with them or they've died.

Bobby was thirty-three years old when he died. This happened at El Valor. He usually had some seizure because he was an epileptic. He had a seizure there and didn't come out of it.

Bobby was the center of everything we did. If we had a party, we counted Bobby in, because he liked parties. He liked to dance. My granddaughter Anna used to take her guitar and say, "Come on, Uncle Bob, let's sing." They'd sing together. He gave us a lot of joy.

He was very funny at times. At my birthday party, Bobby wanted to give a speech. He started talking about Harold Washington and how we should vote for him. Washington was already mayor. We would clap for him and go along with it. He felt very proud and he made us laugh a lot.

For my seventy-fifth birthday about three hundred people showed up at the church. Everybody around here knows me because I'm still involved in many things. I still work at El Valor as a board member. I organized the seniors around here, make them aware of their rights and how they can stand up for themselves. We lobby for, let's say, national health care, send out letters to Springfield, Washington, everywhere.

There was a lady who was complaining about her apartment. She didn't have any lights, hot water. She says, "I've talked to the landlord and he won't do anything." I said, "You want to go with me to this meeting? Will you speak up?" Mayor Washington had a lot of meetings in the communities. She said, "I don't speak English." I told her we'll have an interpreter. She spoke up. All kinds of city people were there and an inspector came up to her and asked for her address and telephone number and came to see her the next day. And it happened: she got lights, hot water, everything.

I just came from a meeting today at the Chicago Transit Authority, the CTA. I'll be very honest with you, it has been difficult for me to be on the board. I'm one of seven. I was appointed by Mayor Daley. I have always been in the community doing things for people around me, but now I feel like I'm on the other side of the fence. I'm sitting with people I used to fight before. We had a big thing with the CTA years back because they were not hiring Hispanics. We stopped the buses. Now I'm at the same table with lawyers, all in ties. I don't feel I'm prepared. I don't know how to act. My thinking has always been fighting back. When they talk about these complicated giant contracts, I don't understand. Or the way they talk—very sophisticated. I've been there a year. I'm trying real hard. I'm talking to the other board members, asking them: How about this? What about that? I'm losing that fear, because they're just people.

I still walk around the community every day. The young people always say hello and are very respectful. But I do see a very sad future for young people. Not enough things for them to do, no jobs, drugs, AIDS. I see my grandchildren growing, and I just feel so bad that we don't know what's coming in the future.

There's only one thing I have regrets about. In regards to my father. I was told very young we had to respect mom and dad. So when he grew old and sick and diabetic, I was still obeying him. He had to follow a diet. When I tried to make him, he'd say, "Don't give me that. I don't like it." So I wouldn't give it to him. I'd say, "I can't tell my father no. I should obey him." Still, I should have...

Suppose you were elected president and were making your inaugural address. What would be your message to the country?

I would say we have forgotten how to pray. We have forgotten to let God guide us and to follow His commandments. If God wants me to do something, no matter who's in front, I have to push them out of the way to go and do what He wants me to do. A loving God doesn't mean being nice to all people. If there's someone trying to take away my rights and says he believes in God, that's not right. You need to defend your rights because God wants you to do the work that's ahead. Who am I to say no to God?

Chapter Thirteen

Health

Quentin Young, M.D., 70

He was director of medicine at the Cook County Hospital, Chicago, from 1972 to 1983. "My job was to attract young doctors to the place. They came and worked their butts off. Occupational medicine was introduced into a public hospital. The county board objected: 'It's a hospital for indigents. They don't work.' We pointed out that our wards were full of people who were victims of the workplace: lead poisoning, brain damage, injuries. Today, Cook County has the largest occupational training program in the country."

He is active in Physicians for Social Responsibility and the Medical Committee for Human Rights.

While I've had wonderful experiences in my life, nothing compares with laying hands on patients. Technically, I became a doctor in 1948, when the State of Illinois licensed me. I became a doctor in my head a decade before that, right on the heels of the depression.

Sure, there was an ideal, but a certain opportunism, too. I'd stumbled onto a profession that was mainstream, highly regarded. I saw a kind of freedom, too, that would allow me to practice medicine, with a leeway for other activity.

In the course of my years, I've been active in a number of unpopular causes, but it hasn't affected my practice. Quite the contrary. It seemed to me, I got more popular. If I had been a professor somewhere, my tenure would not have come through. If I had been in business, they could have picketed me. I think a doctor is more immune from this sort of danger than any other professional.

My class at Northwestern was overwhelmingly white male. We're talking 1944. Sons and nephews of doctors, alumni. It had the quality of a guild. Many seats were occupied by virtue of connections.

There were always four Asians in the class. It was a grant. In our class of 120 there were ten women. Now it's 50 percent. They were isolated, teased, badgered, and humiliated. I remember clinics, with a large number of students, where the professor would deliberately call on the women to examine the male genitalia of a urologic patient. Objectively, there's nothing wrong with that, but it was quite obvious he did it to prove how wrong it was for women to be in this profession. The boys tittered, of course. The humiliation was seldom overt. It was just reminding the women that they were guests in the house.

In contrast to today, we were still in the Dark Ages. What doctors did up to the middle of this century was not much different from what Hippocrates did three millennia before. We didn't have the tools.

I trained at Cook County Hospital in 1947. I often ask my students to guess the year I started, by defining the way they treated pneumonia. At the time, 50 percent of those who got it died. Seven years before I got to medical school, there were three elements in the treatment. One was to put on a canvas pneumonia jacket, which covered the person's chest and arms, to keep the heat in. Then they'd give him quinine to reduce the fever. And then they waited for the crisis, a euphemism for "Will he live or die?" It was hardly different from the way our forebears practiced for centuries.

What happened in '40? Sulfanilamide. The first chemotherapy. In '41, penicillin. In '46, streptomycin, the first drug for T.B. We finally knew we had drugs that would do something. If you look at the pharmacopeia, not of 1100 B.C. or 1100 A.D., but of 1900 A.D., you see remedies in the "eye of the newt," in a Shakespearean witch's brew.

Paradoxically, the notion of caring was stronger then than it is now. You were the comforter. The idea was that you served your community. Most of the doctors were still in general practice.

World War II was the turning point. Young doctors who served in the military saw the "benefits" of specialization. They encountered doctors of prewar European training, who had skills in eye, ear, nose, and throat, skin diseases, you name it. We had very few specialized programs in this country at the time. They saw the specialists with higher rank, better jobs, more perks.

When we demobilized in '45, '46, the young doctors came out in the tens of thousands. They had had their careers interrupted, but they had the G.I. Bill of Rights. Why go back to simplistic stuff, to general practice? A boom in specialization took place after World War II. There were more rewards.

The U.S. government, responding to the surge toward specialization, began to fund medical schools to permit full-time specialists. So we got away from groundedness in practice and we got academicians. We were responding to the wave of the future. It was the government's way of moving medicine toward the high-tech, hyperspecialized catastrophe. It was a classic example of an enlightened, well-intentioned policy that led to the health care crisis today: runaway costs and a world turned upside down. When I started it was 80 percent G.P.s. Now it's 20 percent G.P.s. Eighty percent are specialists—an ironic turnaround in the attempt to advance services to the American people.

The AMA's behavior was that of a guild.* They defined the standards. They were bound by family and brotherhood. They restricted the number of people who enjoy the guild imprimatur. They had control of the medical schools.

Up until 1911, homeopathic medicine was in stiff competition with traditional practice. It was the Flexner Report that put chiropractors in the realm of quack doctors. Until then, anybody could play.

Today, in the '90s, the AMA has, unwillingly, opened the doors for alternative medicine. Doctors had been taught to disdain chiropractors, homeopaths, osteopaths, as quaint and nonscientific, as frauds. It turns out that Americans have always, like people the world over, had alternatives to orthodox Western medicine. Hispanics relied on folk medicine. Native Americans had their highly developed medical folkways. Acupuncture came out of the East. Alternative medicine had always existed on the margins, but this season it has experienced a rejuvenation. It has become mainstream. The profession has tried to restrict its right, but the law has stepped in.

The AMA paid a huge penalty in a big federal antitrust suit for trying, in effect, to outlaw chiropracty. After a multimillion-dollar settlement, the AMA agreed that it could no longer keep chiropractors out of hospitals.

When I came onto the scene, the AMA was the absolute arbiter. There was no important health legislation that did not enjoy AMA sanction. Nothing happened if the AMA didn't want it to happen. When Lyndon Johnson was Senate majority leader, he brought out a whole series of health bills that had no hope of going anywhere. Like voters' rights and civil rights bills, they were beaten every year. Roosevelt, at the height of his popularity, had a national health insurance scheme. It went nowhere. Truman tried it. Down the tubes. The stuff didn't even get out of committee. The AMA was wired. The personal physician of just about every congressman was working for the AMA. I've had congressmen as patients and I can testify to that. Up until the middle of the '60s, the AMA called the tune.

The '60s was the beginning of a new era. Some power was coming to be shared. Medical schools expanded enormously. From seventy

* The American Medical Association.

and eighty schools, they expanded to 130. Black students, limited to two black schools, Howard and Meharry, were beginning to be admitted elsewhere. Until then, out of twelve thousand or so medical students, there were sixty blacks outside of their two schools. That battle has been far from won. Black students in medical schools, including Howard and Meharry, may be as much as 6, 7 percent. It peaked and is actually declining. Why? Blacks overwhelmingly come from poverty communities, where education at the school level is very bad. Women are doing much better. An entering class is between 40 and 50 percent.

I went to County as an intern and resident. I spent the better part of five years training in general internal medicine. I went to work in the tuberculosis hospital. Out of twelve thousand hospital beds in Chicago, four thousand were devoted to T.B., one-third of all the beds. The reason? People with T.B. didn't stay in for a week or ten days. They stayed for months, even years.

At the turn of the century, tuberculosis, the white plague, was the first or second killer in this country. But drugs came along in the '40s that would not only treat the patient but make him noncontagious. The T.B. sanatorium had a dual function: to give the patient a comfortable haven, but, more importantly, to take him out of the family, out of the workplace. With the new drugs, they didn't have to stay in the hospital very long. When I came back to County in 1972 as medical director, the tuberculosis hospital was an anomaly.

In the '90s, T.B. has made a comeback because of the large number of compromised hosts. Persons whose immune systems have been destroyed. They have become victims of a form of T.B. that isn't even pathogenic, has no specific cause. AIDS is the cause. The other reasons are the debilitating things of our age: the large number of homeless and drug users. We have a huge reservoir of people susceptible to this type of stuff, even without AIDS.

I happened to come along when pulmonary medicine as a specialty was being born. It grew out of the T.B. tradition, I had a personal decision to make. I could easily have become a pulmonary specialist by virtue of my experience. Five hours a day I'd go to the hospital, and in the afternoon I'd go to my practice.

Over a period of five years, it became clear to me that I didn't like the limitations of specialty. I liked the idea of the whole apple, treating people across the board. I was a general practitioner for adults. I took my first space in Hyde Park and have practiced there ever since. My practice is as unique as the area.

Most doctors have a practice defined by race and class. In Hyde Park, your practice has a huge racial-class variation. You have blacks of all classes. Because it's a university town, you have academicians. You have working people, unemployed. This is one of the excitements of my practice.

I make a few house calls. My three young colleagues make a lot. There was an age when the house call was central to the practice. Technology did it in. The doctor reasons that if you're sick enough to need a visit, you probably need some studies, a chest X ray, a blood test, you name it. We can't do it in the home.

The house call became the hostage and ultimately the victim of high tech. You'd say to the patient, who would describe a high fever, coughing, headache, something severe, "Go to the emergency room." There you had the equipment for a proper exam. That was the beginning of subverting the emergency room into an alternative, very costly, primary care setting.

I think the house call is on its way back. More care is being put in the home as people live longer and have a hard time getting out. They can survive in a house if they get a monthly or semimonthly house call and some health services. The doctor has to be part of that equation. Just as high tech has changed the nature of the practice, it has affected medical students. There was always a competitive air. Yet, today, the recurring note among applicants for medical school has been: I want to help people, I want to serve. They sound a lot like me in my student days. At least that's what they say to their admitting officers in the medical schools. I have no reason to believe it isn't true.

However, on the exit side, there has been a slow shift, imperceptible over the years, that became full-throated by the '70s and certainly throughout the '80s. It is a reflection of the rise of the yuppies, of the Reagan era: I'm all right, Jack, the tooth and claw, you do good by looking after your own interests.

What's happened since the '80s? The past ten years have seen a new phenomenon. We overdid the specialism. The marketplace does not apply to health care. Repeat: *the marketplace does not apply to health care.* The fact that we quadrupled the number of specialists didn't result in a competitive market with costs going down. They went up. They continue to do so, because this is a guild, a monopoly.

The profession is in a deep crisis, a funny kind. May I offer a diagnosis? There are 625,000 doctors, in excess of one to every 400 patients. Very high. Thirty years ago, it was one to 700, 800, with every advantage to the doctor, because there were far fewer. But the overflow of specialties does not lead to reduced costs, even though there are too many gastroenterologists, too many special surgeons. The price is stiffer than ever.

My profession is in a profound state of depression, a sense of loss. With all the rhetoric, the Hippocratic oath, the AMA, and "I want to serve," there was a dynamic between the profession and the public, the patients. There was a link. This goes back to the earliest reaches of the race. They set aside somebody to be the medicine man, the shaman, who deals with the gods, with weather, healing. It was embodied in one person. In modern times, there was a separation of the spiritual, the priest, from the secular, the doctor. In this millennium, the doctor was the lesser of the diad. There was probably no Western writer who didn't make fun of the doctors of his time: Shakespeare, Cervantes, Molière. They were the clowns who gave you crazy pharmacies, and they'd make you sick, sometimes kill you with bleeding. They were mocked.

But a miraculous thing took place: scientific developments by nondoctors. It was a bacteriologist who found penicillin and streptomycin. These nonphysicians created the tools that made doctors the real medicine men, the real magicians.

The crisis now is the alienation from the object of all these advances, the patient. The link, the unity with patients, was cut off. Today, patients as a group are hostile to the medical profession.

With high tech and the explosion of information came the fear of knowledge. There is so much to know that, as a specialist, you have to know more and more about less and less, until you know everything about nothing. That's a joke, buddy. But the reality is that people specialize in our high-tech society because of their fear of being unable to grasp the whole. This fractioning is very much at the root of this alienation. Technology is not fear of knowledge. It's fear of patients.

When you look at the computer, when you look at the lab sheet, you avoid the laying on of hands. If you approach a doctor-in-training today and ask him how Mrs. Smith is doing, he'll instinctively go to the computer and punch up the latest lab stuff. "Did she have a good night's sleep? Is that pain in her chest different." "Oh, I didn't check that." Distant? You bet.

The malpractice explosion is not accidental. Doctors will point to malpractice litigation as a major cause of cost inflation. They say doctors are practicing "defensive medicine." They're inclined to do tests they don't even think are necessary against the remote chance that they'll be sued by a venal lawyer or outraged patient. There's a germ of truth in that. The art of malpractice litigation has been developed by specialist lawyers who have sharp skills. They get very, very good at trading on human misery, on the alienation patients feel.

It's not a matter of the doctors' declining skills. Doctors are more skilled every year. You can't say they're making more mistakes. With their technical skills, there's less likelihood of failure than ever.

It's really just the public's expression of their animus toward the profession: the doctor who was so distant, who was arrogant, who promised too much, who charged too much, who didn't pay close attention. The malpractice reprisal is a way of getting back at him. It's just another symptom of the separation of patient from doctor.

Something as crude as the polls show it. In prestige, doctors used to be number one, just behind Supreme Court justices (in the pre–Clarence Thomas era). They were rated with the Nine Old Men. Now, they're not rated as bad as used car salesmen, but they're in that league.

I've seen a distinct shift in my professional lifetime. When I began practice, youthful, enthusiastic, I would trade my knowledge with the patient. I would try to explain this ulcer, how it was formed, or what your pneumonia is made up of, or try to describe the anatomy. The effort at patient education is au courant now, but it was offbeat in the '50s. Usually, the patient said, "You're the doctor. Don't bother me with these niceties."

The change is in the patients. They have become more sophisticated. In this instance, it's a triumph of the media. The public's interest in health matters has become insatiable. It's reflected in the explosion of "health watch" kinds of programs and in the regular press. In my own radio program* I sense a healthy skepticism on the part of my audience. And hunger for knowledge. When I have a guest who's, say, an articulate dermatologist, the call buttons light up immediately. After twelve years at this, it's clear the public wants to talk about their pains.

The media has done a magnificent job. Almost daily, we're finding out new things to do through modern technological advances. I'm not a know-nothing on technology. I just hate to see it supplant the personal touch.

The doctor's psyche has been profoundly affected. You often hear them say, "If I knew then what I know now, I wouldn't go into medicine." That would have been heresy in the past. It's not a matter of economics. Doctors make more every year in America. They're the most highly rewarded sector. Yet they're saying, "I don't want my children to go into it." I'm old enough to remember when the doctor wanted every child he had to follow in his footsteps. This change has to do with their sense of alienation, their sense of rejection. They haven't figured out why.

In America's urban emergency rooms, you see armed guards. It's not rare for those guns to be drawn. There's violence in emergency rooms, a tension. You can feel it. Those long waits, seeing a doctor you'll never see again, looking at confiscatory fees just to go through

---

* He conducts a weekly program on Chicago's public radio station.

the process. In the old days, there was a feeling that the doctor was a person who cared, who not only could help you but would. That's lost. "He'll help you if you got the bucks."

Even after World War II, patients admired doctors, who did these miraculous things. They give you a shot of white substance in your butt and a disease like gonorrhea or syphilis would disappear. It would be gone forever. That's magic, boy. Or this poor family youngster who couldn't breathe, they put him on a machine, took his heart out, fixed the valve, and he went on to a full life. That's magic beyond the Bible.

Doctors began to be revered and respected and came to think of themselves as agents of God. In the fullness of time, they began to think of themselves as God. That's a very bad state of mind, because they ain't God. Came this last decade and a half and they weren't prepared for "The Fall."

I remember when the nurse was trained to stand up whenever a doctor entered the room. She lived and functioned only by orders from the doctor. These young girls in nursing schools were almost like nuns in a convent. They lived in confinement twenty-four hours a day. They wore uniforms that were, to be generous, unique. They worked very hard on the hospital floors. They had this long period of intense servility. They were conditioned to be the doctors' handmaidens. For a long, long time, their teeth were on edge. Today they are rambunctious and wrathful. They feel, with ever more boldness, that they have the right to skills, prerogatives, and rewards commensurate with what they've learned.

They have, along with patients, begun to question the doctors. There has been a subtle shift and a granting of respect and authority. The doctors had no choice but to change. They're troubled, they're unhappy, they're angry, but they're not humble. Humility is in short supply in this profession.

The darkest development in our troubled health care system is the advent of corporate medicine. The AMA had all sorts of laws—they still exist—against corporate medicine being practiced, yet these laws have been ignored. Large conglomerates came in.

Public hospitals, which were improving until about fifteen years ago, have become the absolute dumping pit. The system has always dumped on the public sector everything that had no profits in it. Today, it has become the specific behavior called "prudent management."

A prudent manager, who has his MBA, has a patient who appears to have a heart attack in the emergency room. He has to have systems in place—all systems go—meaning, he has to train his doctors and nurses to move that person in safety, though sometimes the transfer is hurtful, even life-threatening. He has just saved his hospital ten thousand to twenty thousand dollars. That's as good as getting a gift from a wealthy donor. Increasingly, this is the way the private sector is looking at the unsponsored patient.

Until five years ago, there were free clinics, teaching hospitals. People felt they were taking charity and their pride was hurt, but damn it, they could go and get some care. Now that's gone.

The government is driven by a marketplace strategy. Applied to health, it's a form of social Darwinism. In effect, it will eliminate the "inferior"—defined as the disabled, the sick, the elderly without money.

Unlike my generation, young doctors coming out today have a dark vision. They come out fifty thousand dollars in debt. They are pushing thirty, maybe have a kid or two. They immediately become available to these corporations at a salary. They don't have the luxury of being socially concerned. We're getting to the point where the doctor is a highly paid technician.

Despite the bleak picture I paint, there are hard-working, idealistic students in all the medical schools. I saw them later, as interns at Cook County when I was there. They came, worked their butts off, and wonderful things happened. It can happen elsewhere, now and in the future.

Patients are worried and they're organizing. The elderly are forced to organize. Their numbers swell. Doctors have made sure we're going to have ever more elderly people. The Medicare system lies there, tantalizing, failing. With the elderly in the vanguard, more people are organizing for their health needs.

I envision—it's really my epiphany—a new kind of union between physicians and the objects of all their training, the patients. Something beyond "Father knows best."

The alternative vision is really frightening. An industrialized system, controlled by five or six monopolies, care allocated, excision of the unworthy or unfit, as we move toward a euthanasic society.

Florence Wald, R. N., 76

BRANFORD, CONNECTICUT

In 1957, when I was forty years old. I began the most productive chapter of my life. That's when I was appointed dean of the Yale University School of Nursing. At that time, Yale was thinking of closing the school. I had a chance for the next ten years to be in a position of power. It was something I had never thought of doing, but I came into it with a zeal and earnestness.

I am a graduate of the school, and we had an excellent education. We were being prepared as expert practitioners, with a lot of clinical work. Just as a medical student does.

World War II came along and profoundly changed medicine and nursing. Remember, we didn't have antibiotics. There were no such things as transplants. Replacing blood and fluids was something rarely done. With the war came the technology. It was as if, almost overnight, the nurses were changed into engineers. They needed to know the technicalities of all the instruments. They were learning how to transplant organs, how to do brain surgery, how to work on all the blood vessels. We were into engineering dynamics.

Did it lessen the personal touch? Very much so. My education had been essentially about the patient as a person, as a family member, as part of the society in which he lived. With the changes, the patient lost any kind of identity. He was simply part of a change in dynamics. The doctors got so involved in the technology that it was like the sorcerer's apprentice. They couldn't stop what they were doing, couldn't stop to heal the patient. He was getting sicker, not only with the illness, but with the treatment.

At the same time, this was the '60s, there was a real revolution in values. The medical and nursing disciplines have always been the most conservative and self-sufficient, not responsive to public issues. But when society began to look at civil rights, young medical and nursing students, and a few doctors, were drawn into the conflict. They went on marches to Selma and were involved in peace rallies, protesting the Vietnam War.

The Yale Medical Center was in "the Hill," the black ghetto of New Haven. Before our eyes, riots were going on and we were drawn into it. People whose houses were burned needed shelter, so we made space for them in the nursing home. We were getting involved and undergoing a change without realizing it.

Some things that are taken for granted today were unheard of at the time. If patients were critically ill and wanted to know what could be done, it was the exclusive province of the doctor. If the nurse attempted to get the doctor to face it, he'd turn on his heels.

Out of the civil rights battle, there came to be, on our campus and elsewhere, the patients' rights movement. We began to have meetings that included lawyers and chaplains as well as nurses and social workers. So from the mid-'60s on, you were getting a very different kind of physician than you had before.

Until then, nurses had suffered very badly, not being able to intercede for the patient. One wonderful day, an English physician, Dr. Cicely Saunders, came to our campus. She had been educating herself in the care of cancer patients in the last stages and was developing palliative care. She was building a hospice in London. She showed pictures of patients, before and after treatment, so we could see them overwhelmed with pain, then able to relax and be themselves. The medical students gave her a standing ovation. This was 1963.

She had given us a new avenue in the care of patients. It affected me so much. I decided, at the age of fifty, to prepare myself in developing such care here in the United States. It was an unlikely choice for the dean of a top nursing school, but Dr. Saunders's appearance strengthened my resolve to take risks. In ten years, interest in the hospice movement was so high that, in 1975, two thousand attended the first national conference in Washington.

Another offshoot of the '60s was a change in the Yale curriculum. In most of the graduate programs, nurses were trained to be administrators and teachers, but not as clinical practitioners. We were starting something new and nursing organizations at first poopooed it, but little by little it gained ascendancy and respect. It was a small but vocal faculty that turned the education around.

The only thing I still criticize about the nursing profession is that there is not enough attention to the practice. It's gotten a bit too academic. With the technological leap, the loss of the personal touch had affected them, too. But here's where the '60s revolution played a role.

As far back as the '50s, and certainly in the '60s, we were teaching nurses to stick to the issues and, instead of being passed over by the doctors, to insist on their attention. All the years past they were compliant. Why, if a doctor came in the room, the nurse stood. If you went into an elevator, you waited until after the doctor entered.

From now on, the nurse isn't there to teach the patient what to do, to *tell* the patient. Now, it's: What does the patient want? They should be able to exchange ideas and work together in order to tackle the illness. This has since become common practice.

The students I was teaching in the '50s and '60s came into their own in the '70s and '80s. With the women's movement, they went far beyond what I would have ever done myself.

For many doctors, it has been very, very hard. They have essentially been given another role to play. They have to bring the patient and the family in on sharing the facts and making decisions. They had to unlearn the old ways: doing whatever *they* thought best. The doctors have to share their knowledge.

Nurses are beginning to learn how to question. And doctors are beginning to learn that nurses have intuitive skills and that is something they need. With patients now joining in decision making, the nurse has become their advocate, helping them frame their questions in such a way that the doctors will understand.

Midwifery? It's being taught in a number of schools now. I think it's great. It's just as important to be out of the hospital in this case as it is for a patient who is terminally ill. Birth and death are both life events. Sometimes, in the hospital, a woman's progress in labor is interrupted by the medications they give to contract the muscles so that baby can be born quickly. They may have to cut the skin to get the baby out. Natural child birth doesn't require that. There's less technology.

That's why alternative medicine is on the rise. The therapeutic touch is so important, that approach would never have been recognized in school in the old days—not scientific enough.

What's going to happen in the next decade will be very interesting. More than ever, nurses are going into primary care, to help society prevent illness. Many who thought of going into medicine may choose nursing instead.

Nursing is something that appealed to me from the very beginning. I had been quite ill as a child, and my troubles were eventually solved by having my tonsils out. [*Laughs.*] So that's what drew me. It was either social work or nursing. It may have been the tonsils that led me to my choice.

I was originally a student at Yale School of Nursing. I returned as a teacher, after some time on the Rutgers faculty. When President Griswold chose me as dean, I was astonished. I didn't know what his thinking was. He had been dissatisfied with the old curriculum and wanted me to design a new one.

We were concerned that the school wouldn't survive, so the whole faculty got together and came up with a position paper for Griswold. He went for it. Our idea was to develop links between nursing and some of the other graduate programs at Yale, to expand the horizons of nursing. So it was sociology and anthropology for our students, as related to our practice.

Holistic teaching?

You could call it that. At first, nursing organizations found this heretical. We had to prove that it works. Because our school had a prestigious reputation, the nursing profession allowed it to be an exception to the rule. Now, it's pretty well accepted.

I became an army nurse toward the end of World War II, during the Battle of the Bulge. I had pacifist leanings and was distraught by all the carnage. I was sent to Fort Dix for training, and then to West Point, where I worked in the obstetrics ward for a year.

At the Columbia Presbyterian in New York, I was working on a research unit, developing all these technologic techniques. I just couldn't take it. I wasn't any good with machines. So I went back to school and studied psychiatric nursing. It was much more personal. It was a turning point for me in ways I hadn't foreseen.

I have been in retirement for some years, but my volunteer work keeps me as busy as ever. I'm quite active at the Connecticut Hospice, just outside New Haven. I was one of its founders. If some patients need extra attention that no one else is able to give, I'm down there. I'm delighted as I see the younger people find new ways we hadn't thought about.

Our team meetings at the hospice are very exciting. The chaplain, the social worker, the nurse, the doctor, the arts director, and the volunteer sit down and discuss every patient once a week. Each brings his/her own knowledge into the discussion. The chaplain, so astute, makes what seems to me a religious diagnosis, where the patient is in his spiritual world, where his strengths are, and what the family wants. Every other member of the team takes it from there, to make the patient's remaining days a time of comfort and understanding.

I have another project: trying to help nurses who've never been published. There's one, a practical nurse, who has so much to say. They have not been recognized enough. She has a book in her, somewhere. I intend to get it published.

As you get older, you speak out more and take more risks. You don't owe allegiance to any institution, you're a free agent. I'm a little gloomy at the moment. I honestly don't think we'll ever have national health service in this country. Of course, I'm in favor of it. Canadians take pride in their national health service. But my feeling here is that we're too much of a capitalist country and the haves don't feel any obligation to the have-nots.

More and more, I feel that speaking out and taking risks is a very important part of one's life. A dear friend of mine, Virginia Henderson, ninety-five, has been a role model for me. When I was dean at the School of Nursing, she did a bibliography on all the literature about nursing on a pittance. She gave us advice that was invaluable. She's had more influence on nursing than almost anybody.

What is most exhilarating to me is when young nurses come up to me and tell me I've been an inspiration to them. Of course I think of Virginia Henderson and what she has been for me. Nurses are learning to be more courageous.

I shall never forget the one moment that was so revealing. While I was at Yale, President Brewster invited all the deans to meet him for lunch at the alumni club, in the private dining room. Women were not allowed on the front steps, so I had to go through the kitchen. I thought it was a panic. The dean of the medical school said, "I'll go up the stairs with you." That was the way we solved it.

My successor, an ardent feminist, whom I watched grow, would never have tolerated it. She made Morey's—you know, the Whiffenpoof-song place—change their policy and admit women.* She's now on the board. The new generation has a backbone I didn't have. I think they're doing a fabulous job.

---

* A tavern in New Haven frequented by Yale students. It became celebrated in the song Rudy Vallee made famous.

Esther Thompson, "Over 70"
CHICAGO, ILLINOIS

A regular Saturday-morning gathering at Operation PUSH on Chicago's South Side. PUSH's founder, Rev. Jesse Jackson, is on the platform, along with Rev. Don Parsons, who will offer the sermon. A score of other clergymen and community figures are seated up there, as well.

The services have not yet begun, but a slight, elderly woman has been busy for the past hour, passing out programs, seating people, greeting strangers as well as friends, simultaneously carrying on a conversation, patting a shoulder or two. She is, obviously, the general factotum.

A few of her comments escape me; I cup my ear. "I'm deaf as a post," I say. She says, "That's all right, baby. Keep living. We all be."

I do janitorial work at Oak Forest Hospital—for over thirty years. I also work with my union—the hospital workers'. I work every day and I think every day is beautiful. My father worked at the stockyards long years ago. My mother always work. She's still living, ninety-four. Mmm hmm. My husband, he's retired. He worked in a drop-forge shop, thirty-seven years. Hard work. I've been married over forty years. When we ain't fighting, we argue. [*Chuckles.*] My children, they're all grown. I didn't have but two. One is deceased. I got eleven grandchildren, all grown. I don't baby-sit. I don't like to be bothered with no little children. I don't want nothin' to stop me from going when I want to go. My hobby? It's doing what I'm doing.

My organization, Operation PUSH, is most important. I came in when it first started, and I fell in love with it. I thought the world of everything they were doing to help better the system. The system is so wrong, there's a lot of changes should be made. We cannot always say it's just the young people. Some of the older people not right either. This is a constant battle all the time.

There's something wrong with the whole nation. Every nation is corrupted. Something needs to be done about this dope and guns and things and whatnot. You cannot expect teachers to be raising the children, too. [*Loudly.*] Parents must be involved. Everybody. This is what makes me go.

You gotta remember that a lot of the kids haven't been taught about the past. This young generation don't know what the older generation went through. They figure things just come on a silver platter, when the older people knew all about fightin' for jobs. From the younger generation, you can't expect no more because their parents are so young. So how you going to teach history when the parents hardly know history? They're tired and they ain't even old enough to be tired.

I don't have time to get tired. I can't stop. This is what makes me go. Energy. I will go whatever, if they have meetings anywhere. I go to them, whether it's here, Washington, or whatever. I ride the bus in here every week.* I don't miss no weeks.

Jesse Jackson passes by: "She's a working person's person. She never stops: she marches, she demonstrates, she fights back, always. Teenagers will be fainting, she'll still be walking. Just full of life."

Where does this energy come from?

From God, that's where it comes from. I look at people not half my age and not able to do anything. Youth is not everything. We got more sick youth than people that's not. There is something about this system. It makes people sick. We must keep fighting for these young people because, if we don't, what is going to happen to 'em?

Our conversation is constantly interrupted as people at the meeting, the young and elderly alike, recognize her: effusive greetings and frequent embraces. Says a middle-aged man: "You know what it is about her? The beauty of Esther Thompson is that she will never benefit from most of the gains we have made. She is the first and foremost person out front on the battle line, to protest, to picket, to do the unorthodox—unsystematic things that has got us this far."

A matronly woman in her Sunday best has been listening. She adds: "She's always been like an ancient landmark. The Bible says, 'Remove not thy ancient landmarks.' That's what she is. She's one of the pillars that holds the foundation of this building. She's a mother to us all."

I'm not that religious, but I believe in helping others. I'm not one to stay in church all the time. I work on Sundays because I'm off Fridays and Saturdays. I've been doing it for thirty years.

I was in the March on Washington in '63 and I was there last week.† I found it still very inspiring. You know what made me feel good about it? This time you got more young people. They want

---

* She lives in Robbins, Illinois, a predominantly African American suburb of Chicago. Its residents earn less per capita than residents of almost any other community in the state.

† She is referring to the August 1993 march, which commemorated the thirtieth anniversary of the March on Washington.

things, want to make things happen. Things got to change. [*Louder, touching a preacher's cadence.*] These kids go to school, they've been in college, there's still no jobs. We are the first to be fired off a job. Every nationality can come in and do something but us. Why not take care of these American people, these kids right here?

They cannot be walking around here with guns and things. This dope is killing our children. We don't raise no dope here. They bring it into our neighborhood. They're shipping it in here. The system allows it. If your kids get arrested with a little package of dope, they go to jail. When they bring a hundred tons in here, nobody says anything. It's very upsetting.

These kids sell it because there's no jobs for them. I'm not saying all of them would go to work, because some would not work even if you give it to 'em. Young, old, middle-aged, decrepit, some will not work. But then this is fast money. How can these kids have all these cars when you supposed to be twenty-five years old before you can get insurance? Who's signing for all these insurances and things for these kids to ride around in all these new cars? So you know it's something wrong with the system all over the world.

Why do they let this dope come from other countries? Why do they allow them to raise all that dope? They have to have some way to raise it. You going to tell me nobody don't know anything about that dope being raised in these open fields? You could pour gasoline over it and burn it. When you send bales and bales and tons and tons of dope right into America and then you goin' to tell me the people in the White House don't know nothing about it? The whole system is wrong. They need to start checking from the White House to the outhouse.

It's a double standard. When it started hitting these rich kids, then everybody got concerned. As long as it was hitting these poor people, nobody was concerned about this dope. When you got kids that are nine years old, thirteen years, killing, you're going to say there's nothing wrong? These kids out there killing for shoes and that kind of stuff. You've got gun shops all around these high schools. Don't tell me it cannot be stopped. You going to tell me parents cannot check their children's rooms? Then what do you expect the policeman to do? You must do something yourself.

I cannot actually explain why these people take dope. In my mind, I feel that a lot of times it makes them feel important. It makes them feel big for that moment. But it doesn't last, because soon it wears off and they got to go back over there again. You're not escaping.

There's no escaping these projects that you build all over in the poor neighborhood. You cannot say you built projects for the betterment of people when you put them all together like a bunch of cattle.

To stack people up on top of one another, it's too many different personalities.

The next thing about it: parents don't start with the children when they're young. You can't start when they get three years old, you have to start with the cradle. Why do you think them kids are killin' so early? [*Loudly.*] Go through their bedrooms. See what is in there. Look up under the mattress. Kids aren't supposed to go to school with knives and things. Parents must help constantly.

Why keep building all them jails? They pick up these kids for just anything and they have no money to get out. You think of the money the system has to pay to keep them there. What happens? They go right back. Start giving these people some *jobs*.

So much bad is happening. When these children have babies and babies and babies, that don't help the system, because they're too young. Babies taking care of babies. Little boys and girls are very fertile when they're young. A lot of time, all he's gotta do is touch you once and the girl is pregnant. But parents don't tell their kids that.

It hurts when you see these kids strung out here on this dope. I'd rather see 'em drunk than see 'em punching themselves with needles. Then you got too much AIDS going around, too many germs going around. So it's sad. [*Her voice rises.*] We gotta keep talking about it. But when I march for the betterment of the world, I get that feeling of inspiration.

I do have hope for them. I see a different atmosphere than I did in '63. Now they're more serious. Just ordinary people out there, all of them going for the same thing: betterment of life. I'm not saying only about America. I want to see it better for every nationality in the world.

My mother played a big role in the feeling I got. She knew that things were not right. She worked for the railroad, cleaned cars. During World War II, she was an electrician because they had nobody. When the war was over, that was all over. She went back to cleaning cars. She always knew what segregated was. We have *always* known it. The only difference about it, we was up north. At least the people in the South understood it. Everybody knew where they stood. But right here in Chicago, there was neighborhoods you could not live in.

How do the people I work with feel about me? I don't care. That's not what I'm there for. I came there to work for the patients. Not all my fellow employees are going to like me, but I could care less. They all respect me like I'm going to respect them.

I can't worry how people think. I only worry how Esther thinks, how she feels. This is me. Nobody thinks for Esther, that's the bottom line. I'll retire when I get ready. When I want to stop. I imagine that time will come, but don't you tell me when.

That's what keeps me going: that feeling of betterment for the kids who come after I'm gone. If you sit down in a corner and do nothing, you will soon deteriorate, your body. Your blood does not circulate right. You begin to get lazy and whatnot. As long as you keep going, keep energy, you be better off.

In the mornings, I take care of my husband because he's sick. I leave everything clean when I leave home. I get up about four o'clock in the morning. I start at the hospital about seven and I'm off at three. After that I get on the bus to the city, to attend meetings.

I had a massive heart attack last September but I'm doing fine now. I was in the hospital for three and a half weeks. I looked at all the people coming around—bypass, open-heart surgery, they had to have lungs. I'm lying there terrified of everything. I just passed out completely and they rushed me to the hospital.

When I came to, three days later, I was just having a fit, beating on the bed. The nurses says, "What is wrong?" All I could do was point to my throat because I thought I couldn't talk. The doctor said my blood pressure was so high, he didn't know why I didn't have a massive stroke. When I went to the doctor about three weeks ago, he told me I was in fine condition.

At the hospital, all the patients talk to me because I talk to everybody. Everybody knows me. I buy little things for them. If necessary, I get on about something they should be doing for themselves.

I've seen patients come into the ward who couldn't do anything for themselves. It's a miracle just to see these patients get better with physical therapy. It's a miracle just to look at it. By the grace of God, it's not me in one of them chairs. You get more young people in chairs today.

The only regret I have is that things haven't changed for black and white. I have a serious problem with that hatred. If you cut your arm, it runs red blood. Cut mine, it goes red blood. We got all the same thing in our body regardless of color. Nobody been able to prove there is a separate heaven or hell. If they can prove it, then you got something.

When you die, if they don't throw dirt on your face, then they bury you in a vault. One thing about life, it don't stay with nobody. We don't live forever, because if we did, we'd all be dead.

I believe there is a hereafter, but I don't know what it is. I'd like the hereafter to be a better world. It cannot be no worse than what it is here. I think we should treat everybody right, because we don't know where we're going. They must realize that they must die if nobody don't kill 'em. You do die. The Lord didn't put us here to stay forever. Honestly, people need to get together and think about it.

Ted Cox, 82

PALM SPRINGS, CALIFORNIA

He lives in a house by himself. "I've been a widower for six years, after thirty-six years with the same woman. I get lonely sometimes, but, still, I like the solitude."

I live on social security and about three or four thousand dollars of my limited savings, which is not a hell of a lot. But I do live a simple life without having to be tight or stingy. I do all my own cooking because I like it. My social needs are met by almost daily meetings at 6:00 A.M. with my AA group.

I am still an alcoholic, because we feel we never get over it, even though I haven't had a drink in forty-three years. Whatever this fucking disease is, nobody can find out why it is that if I took one drink, I'd probably be on my way to my death or a wet brain. You don't get over it any more than you get over diabetes.

Most of my life I was a newspaperman. I started out at fifteen, still in high school, in Wadsworth, Ohio, a small town near Akron. After having hounded the editor's office in Akron and Cleveland for ages, I was lucky to get a scoop on a big murder story in Wadsworth, and was given a job on the *Akron Times-Press*. I was then transferred to the *Cleveland Press*, the mother newspaper of the Scripps-Howard chain. I was nineteen.

I was with the *Press* for quite a number of years. Then came a stint with the Washington bureau of the United Press, and then the war. After my army discharge in 1946, I wound up in Chicago as the editor of a labor paper. After a year, I was fired, probably because of my drinking.

I drank daily, though I never got drunk. I was a maintenance drinker. I needed a couple double-headers at 6:30 in the morning, when I got up: bourbon and water, just to straighten myself out. I was too nervous, too frightened. I wouldn't admit to these fears. I was far too macho, so I couldn't be afraid of anything. It was much later that I realized the nervousness was not only the need to replenish the booze in myself, but to anesthetize myself against a lot of hidden fears.

Around ten in the morning, I'd need to go out for another shot or two, and two to three for lunch. There were the afternoon and early evening thirsts and a couple to put myself to sleep at night. That's what I mean by "maintenance drinking."

I couldn't get another job in Chicago, though I had a hell of a good record as a reporter and as an editor. I have a feeling my breath had something to do with it, even though the *Chicago Daily News* was about 90 percent populated with alcoholics, AA or nonrecovering. Drinking was fashionable among newspaper reporters at the time.

I moved in with a very nice girl I'd met at the labor paper. She subsequently became my wife. But I had no feeling of permanence, because at that time I was at the bottom. She moved in with me when I fell off the kitchen stool with D.T.'s.

I tried pretty hard to get work, but I simply couldn't. So I just daily went to the bar and talked to other alcoholics early in the morning. I would go home, do some writing, and hate myself.

I finally got a job with a lighting fixture company. I was a pretty good worker and visualized myself as someday being czar of the industry. Why I felt that, I don't know, because I was still drinking. Years later, I did become managing director of the American Home Lighting Institute. I wasn't the czar but I was a big shot.

But let's go back to 1949. One morning I was so disgusted with myself that I cut myself off after one drink, went home, and called AA. I was so blurry, I could hardly make out the letters in the phone book. They sent two guys out to call on me.

I had a wonderful five-month honeymoon. I was doing a pretty good writing job and felt that I really deserved a drink. What the hell, I was healthy again and wasn't really an alcoholic anyhow. So I went out and had a shot. I said: God damn, I'm not an alcoholic. It seemed to work.

It took me about three weeks before I was up on the twelfth floor of the Plaza Hotel in New York, so terrified I'd jump. So scared, without any drink in me on that Sunday morning, I didn't have the guts to jump. I was going to commit suicide because my life was over. I just couldn't stand myself or anybody else. That was in 1950-something. I did have a job then, in public relations. I'd just hosted a big cocktail party for one of my clients, a paint company.

I was walking the streets about eight o'clock that Sunday morning and you couldn't get a drink. I walked and walked and walked, waiting for the joints to open. I was waiting for twelve o'clock. They didn't open till one, so I kept on walking. At that point I got over my jitters and didn't need a drink, but I thought I did. So I got my fix, my last shot. It was 1951. It took me two and a half years, off and on AA, to achieve permanent sobriety.

In the meantime, Joe McCarthy was flying high. My days with the labor paper came into play and I was fired by the public relations firm. They'd been visited by the FBI. I was executive vice-president by then. I always rose rapidly. I had been visited by some prick from the Naturalization Bureau. Everybody was trying to get in the act. That was in '55.

It was assumed that I would answer all the questions of this fucking gumshoe who called on me. I didn't. In fact, I delivered him a lecture. Anyhow, they dragged me into court, so I got publicity I didn't really need. The FBI boys visited the president of the company and I got fired. He suggested that I get the hell out of Chicago and go to California. He warned me that I'd get thrown out of the Public Relations Society, which was slightly to the right of Colonel McCormick's *Chicago Tribune*. He was supposed to be a liberal, this guy. I called him a fucking coward and told him I'd one day become president of the society, a job he coveted. Subsequently, I did become its president.

I formed my own public relations company and was doing quite well, despite the political climate. In 1956, one of my clients, the American Home Lighting Institute, invited me to become its managing director. I held that job until 1972, when I was sixty years old.

I had become absolutely fed up in a meaningless job. I felt I was doing nothing worthwhile and became more and more disenchanted. I arranged to sell my firm in 1968. I took three years to gradually retire. I had already had two heart attacks by that time. In 1972, I moved to Palm Springs. I had some savings and bought this condominium.

Most of the time, I've been so busy here that I was tempted to move back to the rat race in Chicago and New York, but I've stayed on. I keep in touch with things as much as I can. My big regret is the limitation of energy that I have.

I'm very active with AA out here, the oldest member. I make just about every daily meeting at six in the morning. We experience a kind of fellowship that can't be defined. It's important to all of us, especially those who may be in a depression.

I'm still writing, beginning at seven in the morning. I often write pieces for a monthly, *The Human Quest*. It was formerly *The Churchman*. It's about a hundred years old, one of the oldest religious magazines in the country. It's a liberal religious journal. I'm a contributing editor.

My first book was called *Through a Black Hole*. It's a kind of social science-fiction work. It's a speculation concerning world crisis, a black hole, worse than the depression of the '30s. I use a heart attack as the metaphor. I've seen so many people change after a severe attack, so I suggest a change toward a new world, based on cooperation rather than competition.

It's the same theme of my second book, *Rising from the Bottom*—how alcoholism, hitting bottom, and AA change people. Again, a metaphor about getting so tired of getting sick and tired, you join AA. You don't get in to get out of the rain. You get in because you're so desperate there's no other place to go. It's a "twelve-step" program for America and the world. It's fairly obvious we're hitting bottom now, worldwide. There's a bare possibility that the crisis might change human beings and, therefore, some institutions. For better or for worse.

I'm talking about the AA steps, written in 1935 by a couple of alcoholics, a New York stockbroker and an Akron surgeon. With the help of some drunken newspaperman. I apply the twelve steps to humanity. Primarily, it's getting out of the black hole of denial, to recognize that our life is unmanageable and to help each other help ourselves.

I usually get up about 4:30. I get out on the patio, stark naked, regardless of how cold it might be, and go through stretching exercises, a kind of yoga of my own. I jump in the pool and do about ten to fifteen lengths, get dressed, and am ready for the daily AA meeting.

I return, cook my breakfast, and write in my daily journal. I use the written word to analyze my problems and whatever hopes I may have. Then I read and rest a bit. I have to, since I've had quite a bit of heart trouble in the past year. I have an occasional lunch with a friend of mine, usually have supper by myself, and go to bed early. That's about it. And keep away from television.

Once a week, I lead a creative-writers group. I enjoy that very much. There's some pretty good talent out here. Sometimes, I write letters to the editor—about some goddamn stupidity of the people who own the United States and other countries. I'm about to dash one off on Haiti and our shafting of Aristide. I can't wait until I get that one off my chest.

Speaking of heart attacks, I've got to take some lasix now. It's a diuretic. Time out.

[*A half hour later, we resume our conversation.*]

According to the best medical authority money can buy, you are now talking to a ghost. I was fifty when I had my first attack. They put me in the hospital. It was great, the first time I was free from the office that demanded twelve hours of my day. I was a damn workaholic, too. I loved that first attack. It was at the time of the Cuban missile crisis, and I was lecturing sixteen doctors and nurses in my room. I counted them. My room was always full.

In 1975, I took a stress test and flunked it badly. The cardiologist told me to go home immediately and not lift a fork until they got me on the table for open-heart surgery. At the time, I had a hard-on against the medical establishment generally. I had been reading a lot and had even attended a few seminars on holistic healing. On the day I got this sentence, surgery or death, I felt I was going to die. It was the deepest depression of my life.

I told the cardiologist that, though I agreed with his diagnosis, I wasn't going to have surgery. I was going to give holistic health a try. He said, "I certainly do not recommend it." I said, "You don't have to. I'm going to do it anyhow."

That night, I called another AA guy, who was in an outfit called the International Cooperation Council, a world organization. I told him I'd join him at their annual meeting in Anaheim. He said, "Hey, what the hell's the matter with you?" I said, "Oh, nothing." He said, "You're a fucking liar. There's something wrong."

I went down there and got a load of lectures on holistic health. I got in a program with a medical center in Los Angeles: a strict diet of no cholesterol, no fat, no salt, no sugar. I walked three to five miles every morning. It was a diet that is now felt to be almost too strict. I was on it for three years and, to some extent, am still on it. It's a modified Pritikin diet. I formed new tastes in food and new habits in eating. I do my own cooking and work out different soups. I'm damn good at it.

Aside from diet and exercise, there are affirmations. I am not a religious person, but spiritual, yes. I meditate twice daily. In the morning and afternoon, I relax the body and let the mind go blank. I do this for about twenty minutes. I say, "Thank you, God, for healing my heart. My powerful new heart pumps cleansing blood through every vessel of my body and brain and pumps it out through my bladder and bowel." It sounds pretty silly, but it works for me. I'm still alive, right?

I'm working myself back up again after these several congestive heart failures I've had. For a time, I had been pumping 15 percent, practically nothing. A lot of people just go on the couch. For some reason or other, whether it's the affirmations or I'm just a stubborn son of a bitch, I said, "If I'm going to die, I'm going to die doing something." So I came home, jumped right in the pool, made two lengths and got out. Now I've worked myself up to ten and more.

My health is pretty good now, except for my limited energy. I'm really only good for two, three hours a day of work. I have a girlfriend who reminds me. She's a kid of seventy-two, which is practically jailbait at my age. She visits me about nine days a month. She's an artist and writes occasionally. We help each other. We enjoy each other's company and have a good sex relationship. The quantity has gone down a bit, but the quality has improved at the age of eighty-one.

I never did care much for the Palm Springs social life. I turned down so many invitations that I don't get invited anymore, which is all right with me. The AA meeting itself is an association with people, a very intimate one. It's one to one. I meet a lot of newcomers who are shaking it out for the first time. I sponsor two or three.

Sometimes, of all things, I go to a small Catholic chapel here. I've never been a fan of the Vatican and never will be. I'm accepted here because the young priest is a very enlightened guy on all social issues and is trying to work out changes in a trying world.

It's a fairly active life I have, after all. But since I had this bad year, the doctors don't want me to drive too much because it's quite tiring. I've been in Emergency four times with something called a TIA: transient incident something. It's a one-day stroke. I recovered and, lo and behold, I had my first accident five months ago after sixty-five years of driving without one. The car was wrecked. I was hurt a little, but without those straps, I probably would have been killed.

I know this sounds crappy, but my greatest regret—until I was in AA—was that I was unable to give or receive love. I never said it to my wife or any of my girlfriends. I thought it was a sissy word. I didn't want to get involved, even in my marriage, because I thought it might lead to kids, a house in the suburbs, and a mortgage—and I wouldn't be able to save the world. I even used the fact that most of the great men had lousy marriages. Abe Lincoln, for instance.

I was very detached. I didn't realize this was a form of cruelty to those that loved me, especially my wife. I was unable to love, because I was afraid of it. That was my curse. My blessing now is that I hug people when I go out. And I'm learning to listen instead of shooting my mouth off.

I did adopt my first wife's daughter when she was five. We remained fairly close, even after her mother divorced me. She got hooked up with a slugger from the old Teamsters union, a Mafia guy. One time, she showed me a bullet hole in the kitchen wall where he shot past her. He slugged her a few times. She left him, he came back, she saw no way out, so she OD'd. That was the end of that. My only child.

I love young people for their spirit, but many of them seem so shallow, so obsessed with self. This self-involvement leads them to one drug or another, alcohol, TV, or whatever addiction it is to avoid the realities of life. I try to help them, but I don't know. The difference between then and now is that work doesn't mean that much. I had a social connection with the people I worked with. I don't see that today. Strangely enough, the kids here love me. Rather than being a big-shot old fart, they see me as fairly open. I think it's my vulnerability they detect, my fears.

I'm not really afraid of death. We wouldn't be alive if we didn't have some instinctive fears, but on a conscious level I don't fear it. I know that judging from my general health and age, it might come any minute. I can even accept certain chest pains or whatever the hell it might be as the beginning. Then there's a little fear. My great fear is being hopeless and helpless and useless. I've been through that and I hope to hell I'll never go through that again. If I have to, I'll meet it when it comes.

I've made all the arrangements to throw my body in a box and no funeral, because that's for the living. Cremation, I suppose. Although I haven't asked anybody to do it. I assume my AA friends will have a memorial service. I hope they will speak of me as a continuing force in their life because of the ideas I share with them, and the help that they gave me. And that's about it.

CHAPTER FOURTEEN

The "Other"

Olga Companioni, 72

"It's 'companion' with an i." She is petite, silver-haired, and quite voluble.

She was in Chicago for a board meeting of the National Inter-Faith Network. "I got involved when my younger son died of AIDS. He was thirty-four for two weeks only. He told me, 'Mother, I've had the most wonderful thirty years because I have lived to the fullest.'" He was gay.

Her husband was an accountant. She is, too.

I am trying to keep the dream of my son alive. A son that died three years ago. I am the mother of another son, an orthopedic surgeon. The two best sons in the world, one in heaven, the other on earth. When Raul left, he gave me a torch to carry on.

When we came here from Cuba, George was eight and Raul was four. It was a new start for us. When my husband died, George was finishing college and Raul was in a Jesuit high school in Tampa. I had to start all over again. Always God has been on my side. I have seen Him through the valley of tears. He has helped me with His rod and His staff.

Raul was the very best student. He first went to Wharton, at University of Pennsylvania, and then got his degree at Harvard Business School. He was on the dean's list.

When Raul was eighteen, a year after my husband died, he took the great step to tell me he was gay. I couldn't ever believe it. I was devastated. I wanted to die. Why? Because for him, not for me. I worry about him.

It wasn't that you were overwhelmed by sin?

[*Her voice rises.*] No, no, no. Not about that. It was his happiness. When I was in turmoil, I went to see a priest. He didn't say much. He put on a tape of this Jesuit, very progressive. Father McNeill. In this tape, he talked about living in this environment and [*very emotional*] this is the same as any other. Good people. He showed me a new vision. I have learned a lot.

In the wall of this priest's office, there was hanging, that I always remember, Jesus Christ in the shroud. When I got out of that place, I got so much peace in my heart. It was incredible! It was something like instantaneous. It was a combination of the tape and Jesus Himself. Even my daughter-in-law, she couldn't believe the change that I experienced.

I went directly to Raul and we embrace. He didn't have to tell me anything. [*Chokes up.*] We embrace in the most wonderful embrace ever could be. It will last forever.

Since then, Raul taught me all the time. He was very educated. Anything that would come in the papers, in any place, parents of lesbians and gays, they have pamphlets and he would be sending them to me. He wanted to live free, and he was a better person to accept himself and to be free.

He wanted me to know his friends. He had so many. As a result, I belong to Dignity, Tampa Bay.* He was so popular, a wonderful swimmer, took part in the Gay Olympics. When he finished Harvard, he became a broker and he enjoyed that very much. He contributed a lot of money for AIDS.†

I'm praying for a change in the Church. That's what I'm praying for. The Church is negative about AIDS. Father McNeill was kicked out of the Church. I think with time something can be reached. But now I get very angry.

In the St. Petersburg Times *(June 20, 1993), there appeared a lengthy profile of Olga Companioni, written by Anne V. Hull. A passage from it: "Olga has kept her passion for religion.... She is a Roman Catholic who has decided not to abandon her faith in the Church, despite its conservative stance on AIDS education and gay and lesbian issues. She has decided to stay and fight. 'What impresses me most about Olga,' says Sister Catherine Cahill, administrator at the Franciscan Center, 'is her faithfulness to the Church. She has a tremendous sense of* we are the Church. The Church is not some group of people passing down laws. The Church is us.'"

When this article came out, the young priest at Sacred Heart, at mass, recommends everybody to read it. So that is happening at my Church.

---

* An organization of gay and lesbian Catholics, family members, and friends. It has no sanction from the Church.

† The obituary in the *New York Times* described him as a philanthropist involved in gay causes.

What about your fellow parishioners?

There are very many that are positive. Others, they—I say hello, they're not there. It's another friend I have lost. She didn't want to come to my house because I was doing an abomination, you know. She's not even a Catholic, she's a fundamentalist. That's even worse. I wish her the best. I keep most of my friends. That woman is the exception. I pray for her.

In general, of my group, they're positive. One wrote to me: "Let's talk, over a cup of coffee." So I talk to her about all these problems and you know that she finished by giving me a hug. In my family, there is understanding. The ones that didn't, at least they see things better now.

I think in general there is a split in the Church. There is also a macho feeling in the Latino community, and I would like to educate more people to challenge that. There was a survey, I have it someplace. Catholics supported in Tampa the ordinance for gay rights. Seventy percent were in favor.

I never questioned the Church before. I still go to mass because my relationship is with my God. Besides I know very many understanding priests in the Catholic Church.

I have lost something. When my son told me about his homosexuality, I said "Why didn't you tell me before? We would have helped you." Here he had to go through hell until his acceptance of himself. In high school, he even went to see a psychiatrist because he wanted to [*dramatically*] get rid of *that*. Some solution! The psychiatrist told him, "Raul, you have to accept yourself." That's exactly what he didn't want to do. He didn't go back because that was not the solution he wanted. He thought it was a sin. He was a devout Catholic, but getting very angry with the Church.

There was a gay rights ordinance in Tampa and an attempt to repeal it. Who was in that fight to repeal? This family association and the bishop. He said it should be repealed. I said no, he is wrong. God is for all, without exception. That was in the newspapers. Oh, my faith is so deep. I pray for changes in the Church, and when I have to speak out, I do. I say again and again, God is for all.

The more I know about homosexuality, the more I am convinced it's nothing you choose. It is something you are born. [*Excitedly.*] And why? Because it comes in your genes. It is nothing he chose.

I wrote a letter to the bishop. I said exactly what I felt about it, and I made the example of my son. To open their minds to love, compassion, and understanding. He knows that I disagree with him. It was a very nice response, and he even gave me some pamphlets to read. But I think it comes from the Vatican, the trouble.

I think the pope has to think a little bit more. There are many things to be changed in the Catholic Church and I am for that. I truly believe in women's ordination. And the marriage of priests, too. They are so lonely, they need a companion. For the people that want to be like that, alone, okay, do it. For the other ones? Why? So many good priests that we have now, they have to leave the Church if they get a wife. And the same is with gaiety. I am for all those changes.

For me, my faith is the main thing in my life. I pray for the conversion of the Church like I pray for the conversion of Russia. To be more open, to be more human, to understand our race, to live in this world. I am not for abortion, because life is so precious. But sometimes when you think about it—[*long pause*]—but I'm not for that at this moment.

I have learned a lot since Raul got sick. My mind has widened, yes, yes. It is beyond beyond. It's my beginning as an activist. I must tell you about something special, this experience I had with Raul.

He was in the hospital and it was Gay Pride Week. For the first time, the Empire State Building was illuminated in lavender. Raul wanted to see it in that light. It meant so much to him. The night before I was to visit him, I saw the Empire State lighted. So I stayed till nine o'clock at night, because early you cannot see the light. I asked for a wheel chair to bring Raul to the sixteenth floor to see it. I wrap him because we have to go through halls very cold. On the sixteenth floor is the observatory where you could see the Empire State.

He and me, what a beautiful and moving and wonderful experience. When he saw it, he started crying. I thought, "Oh, he's devastated with the disease," and I say, "Raul, don't cry. You will be up and you will be doing the same as you have done till now." At first, he didn't answer me. Then he said—and what a lesson he gave me—"Mother, when you see somebody cry, don't do anything. Don't try to make a touch. Just, wait. That's all you do." He said, "I'm not crying of suffering, pain, agony. I'm crying of joy to see something lighted for what I've worked so hard in my life." [*Restrains a sob.*] I told my son: "Take it. Part of that light is yours. You deserve it. But let me tell you, my son, I will try to keep it lighted." [*Crying.*] He game me his torch and that is what I am doing.

We had a small service two days after he died. Only his good friends were there. The second service was a big one. That was the first time that I talk in public. Never in my life have I done so before. I had always been very talkative, but not in public. So I prepare something simple about my son, my feelings and the feelings of his friends. I read a letter from a friend of his, many years, a woman. The other was a client, to diversify. The other one was a nurse. So whatever they said, I put in my speech and then my thoughts. You know, his spirit was in that place. I had a standing ovation.

My other son, George, he said, "Mother, please, not too long. The shorter, the better." [*Laughs.*] Well, I broke him, he was crying. He told me when I was finished. "Mother, I can't believe it. Not only were you wonderful, but you spoke English perfectly, without an accident." [*Laughs.*] I never dreamed I could do that.

Even with the loss of my son, life is so wonderful that you cannot throw it away. You have to be delighted with that and live everything to the fullest. It's a crime not to do it, because it is a gift from God.

Last week I received a letter from a stranger, and he said I am his inspiration. He address me, "Olga." I now talk in a lot of places. I am now very known in the gay community.

While my son was in the hospital, I marched in the New York Gay Pride parade and I made him so happy.

I went to Washington for the big march of '93. There were parents like me, people from PFLAG, Parents and Friends of Lesbians and Gays. I wore the two medals Raul won in the Gay Olympic games. All his life he was a competitive swimmer and lately a very avid tennis player. He was going to go to the other games, but his dream never came true.

I am very welcome with many young people. I danced with my son at a gay club and he was so proud to be with me. I was so proud to be with him. And the people with their eyes wide open. I have been with him on Fire Island and his friends all treat me like a queen. [*Emotionally*] I have those memories forever.

My life is so busy now, you couldn't believe it. I start my day with mass every day. Last January, a son of a friend of mine died of AIDS and I was in the mass as a Eucharist administrator, a help to the priest. I belong to the new wave of ministries, and I know bishops who are very open. Something is going on and I'm in what's going on.

I have touched some priests, once even a bishop. He told me his brother was gay. In a symposium in Detroit, he said he changed his attitude "because of this lady over there." He pointed to me. He said that, thanks to me, he got together with his brother and they are in union. I see changes taking place and there will be more. There is no other way.

Not every day is the same. Usually I go to mass at seven o'clock in the morning. Saturday, no, it's eight. I always give thanks to God and Jesus. First, for giving His life for all of us. Second, for being so wise to let me have His body, every day, to reassure me, to give me strength. A living God.

After that, I come home, and then go for a walk. I walk every day one mile and a half, then I have my breakfast. I go twice a week for exercise. And then—Francis House.

It is a shelter mainly for the people infected with HIV. There I have so many friends. They are clients and very young. The first thing Sister Anne did was to give me the books, because I am an accountant. She said, "I need help." I balance the books and give it to the treasurer. I do it very quick because I take all the work home. When I came back from New York after Raul died, I saw this was the place for me.

I'm retired from regular work for money, but I work now more than ever before. It's a work that gives me so much satisfaction. It is my calling, yes, yes. Many of my wonderful young friends are dead at this moment, but at least I know I have done something for them, for their parents.

My son lives through me and in me. Maybe he lives in that young boy who wrote me that letter from St. Petersburg. He sent me some poems, one dedicated to his mother he never met. When I went to speak, he was there—AIDS, HIV-infected. Yes, maybe Raul's spirit is alive in this boy, too.

Harry Hay, 81

LOS ANGELES, CALIFORNIA

He is one of the most celebrated and outspoken elders of America's gay community. At six feet four, he cuts an imposing presence. "I was born on Easter Sunday and the Titanic went down the following Thursday. Two Titanics can't exist in the world at one time. When one shows up, the other has to go down."

I have always been trying to find out who I was. I knew I wasn't what my parents said I was. I knew that I didn't resonate to what the teachers said about me. The people around me weren't making any sense, they weren't telling me who I was. I finally decided that I was going to find out for myself. So this has been my life: to find out if there were others like me.

"*My father was born in New Zealand and came here in 1879. He graduated as a mining engineer and went to South Africa. My mother was born at an army fort on the Arizona frontier when it was still Indian territory. Her father was a young lieutenant, whose first assignment was to go out into the hills and find Geronimo. He brought Geronimo in exactly ten days after my mother was born.*

"*My grandfather was an idealist who believed deeply in what he was doing. He was told by his commanding officer that they were to promise Geronimo that he and his people could live in peace on their properties. When they found Geronimo, they made that promise to him. But when they brought him in, there was a new commander, General Nelson Miles, who believed the only good Indian was a dead Indian. He said, 'Geronimo is not going back with his people. I'm sending him to Florida.' My grandfather and the others of the expedition said, 'But we gave him our word.' Miles said, 'You don't give a gentleman's word to a savage.'*

"*After the Spanish-American War, my grandfather resigned from the army and became a professor of military science and mathematics and engineering at the University of Nevada. In 1906, at the time of the San Francisco earthquake, Cecil Rhodes invited him to come to South Africa as a consultant engineer. My mother and father met in South Africa. Later, my father became the general manager for the Anaconda Copper Company in Chile. During his work in London he shared offices with another engineer, named Herbert Hoover.*

"*When, in 1928, my mother suggested that I try for an appoint-*

ment to West Point, my grandfather wrote to me: 'I will not allow any blood of mine to have anything to do with the United States Army. As far as I'm concerned, it's a sea of corruption. It doesn't keep its word. It no longer has any honor.' He was a man who was true to his word. So was my father's father and so was my father. It is my legacy: I'm also a man of my word."

My parents wanted me to grow up an all-American boy. My father wanted me to be a football player. I was about ten when my father came home one day with a pair of boxing gloves. He wanted me to learn to box and take care of myself, because I was growing up a big sissy.

I was pretty. I had curly hair. The boys always called me a sissy in school. I was eight years old. They'd fight with me, and I didn't want to fight. They always liked rough and tumble, and I didn't like rough and tumble.

When I put on the pair of gloves, my father wanted me to hit him. I couldn't. It was as though there was a glass wall between me and him. It was not my nature to hit. I couldn't get him to understand. My brother, four years younger than I am, tore the gloves off my hands and he and my father got into a real scrap and had a wonderful time, but this was not for me.

I was beginning to recognize that there's something I don't like here. I don't like to compete. It's not only the macho aspect. I want to celebrate with people, to share with them, not to compete with them. This is still true of me at eighty-one.

I had more friends among the girls than among the boys, but they were also pushy and I didn't like that either. When I was about eight, the boys said I threw the ball like a girl. So I asked the girls. They said, "You don't throw the ball like a girl. You don't throw like a boy either. You throw it like a sissy."

From the boys' point of view, sissy and girl were the same thing. So I was neither one nor the other. As I said many years later, if I had used the sense I was born with, I would have recognized that I was free, because I wasn't caught by the constraints of either one. Silly old me, I didn't figure that out yet.

I suppose I was unhappy, so I retreated into the world of books. I read every damn book that was in the library. I went through the children's section from *A* to *Z* about three times. That grew tiresome, so I went to the adult section. Remember, I'm about nine. The love-story parts in the adult books were dull, so I skimmed through and sought out the action, the adventure, various places.

This was about 1920. The Los Angeles library had those wonderful nineteenth-century books with steel engravings in them and tissue over the front. When I got to Alexander Dumas, there were slightly erotic frontispieces. But I sensed that the very amorous pictures were not on the shelves. They were in the glass case behind the librarian's desk, locked. What's in those books that makes them too hard to get at? A nine-year-old boy is not about to be told by the librarian what's in the closed case. Something has been removed from the eyes of children, hasn't it? I'm thinking to myself, "If the book on the shelf has a naked woman in it, [*whispers*] the one up there has to be a naked *man* and I want very much to see this naked man."

And what was it?

Calm down, calm down. We're only at chapter one. [*Chuckles.*] No adult, obviously, is going to get me in that glass case. Consequently, I have to figure out a way.

It was just after World War I and we're in the flapper stage, with all sorts of liberating things happening to women. Next to the library was a place that gave marcels, a brand new way of waving hair. The librarian had long, stringy, gray hair. I suggested that she'd look great with a marcel. She said [*imitating a high, woman's voice*], "I would love to go there, but I can't because the library stays open till six and they close at four-thirty." So I said that I work in a grocery store, deliver, make change, cash checks, and could pinch hit for her. We didn't have child labor laws yet.

Doing all this work? Of course. I'm bright. Don't forget, all little fairies are bright. And I'm an eleven-year-old fairy. I was in fourth grade at eight. The others were ten, eleven. I said to the librarian, "Miss Longly, let me check out books in your presence for a week and you'll see that I'll handle things just the way you want me to. Then, maybe next Wednesday afternoon, you can make an appointment."

I checked out books for a week, had people pay fines when they were overdue, and made notes in her account book. She was satisfied. "I think you can handle it by yourself. I made an appointment for next Wednesday afternoon."

The moment she's gone, I find the key in the lower left-hand drawer and take down the book. It's the most disappointing thing you've ever seen in your life. It's full of naked *women*. I thought I was going to get a naked *man!* Now that I've got this case open, what else have they got up there? There was a book of poetry about grass, by a man named Whitman, and I wasn't interested in grass. But right at the other end was a book by a man named Edward Carpenter. It had been published in England in 1921 and the pages in it weren't cut. I sliced them open. This was very interesting because he was talking about men who were friends and lovers of other men. He talked about

Alexander of Macedon and Michelangelo and Shakespeare. They're all dead, but suddenly I realize he's talking about me. I'm not the only one of my kind in the world. I'm not so peculiar.

Until that moment, I thought I was the only one. And hiding it because I'd get beat up by the other kids, and my father wanted me to be the way he was, so I couldn't let him know either. But he knew. When he brought home the boxing gloves, he knew what he had on his hands. He couldn't miss it.

My mother had a different take. [*Chuckles.*] She had fallen madly in love with the Edwardian English culture. She liked the little suits that small boys wore in the private schools, Little Lord Fauntleroy-style. So she had me dressed up like that: curls, Buster Brown hat, white collars, short velvet pants. I looked like a sissy. My mother dressed me for the part.

When I read through the pages of the Carpenter book, I see a word: "homosexual." I don't know what it means. I'd never seen the encyclopedia and it isn't there either. But I know it's me. The word "homosexual" doesn't appear in an American dictionary until about 1938. It wasn't in any American encyclopedia until after the Second World War.

What about fairy?

Oh, everybody used that. "Queer." I didn't begin to hear that until I'm about twenty-eight.

From the moment I came across the Carpenter book, I started fantasizing, having dreams about another boy who was just like me. It wa a recurring dream I had for years. I was standing on a hillside just before dawn. There's a boy—I still see him—he's reaching out his hand to me. I catch his hand; we go to the top of the hill and watch the sunrise. I'll never have to come back, because we'll have each other. That was my dream for years and years and years and years. And then suddenly, one day, I met him. And it turns out *I* was the boy on the hillside and I was to catch *his* hand. [*He gently indicates his companion, John, who has been seated nearby, during this conversation.*] We're going on thirty-one years.

I even imagined visiting Carpenter, because we were both alive. He did visit Walt Whitman and was a socialist, too. In his preface, he talked of our kind serving among the Indians as shamans.

I don't like the words that are being used today to describe us. I'm now speaking of us as the "third gender." The younger generation loves it. I use it now quite a bit. You're a first-gender man. I'm a third-gender man. I like the phrase because it involves responsibility, too. I believe we are reinventing ourselves. We had been obliterated by every organized religion you can think of for the last two thousand years and we have been almost wiped out. We didn't have a language, we didn't have a way of recognizing each other, and no way of reaching out to each other until I started this thing in 1950. I'm trying to discover how to open up my world, and in doing that I open up yours.

"The closet" is a term that was invented in the '70s. The phrase we had always used was "putting on the mask." We automatically all wore the mask. That was our protection, because until 1975 we were illegal in the state of California. Illinois was the first state to change the law, in 1961. We all said, "Oh, one of these days, we'll go to Chicago."

I was always a very tall kid. At thirteen, I was six feet three. When I reached that age, my father said, "It's high time you learn how to work for yourself." What did he mean by that? I earned every cent I ever had, beginning with that grocery store. He never gave me an allowance. I earned it. I guess he meant heavy work, "work as a man." And it was summertime, so it was okay.

He sent me to his brother, who was raising alfalfa in Nevada. Everybody looked at me and assumed I had the strength of a six-foot-three man. They think I'm eighteen. Of course, I'm not up to it. My musculature is all wrong. But my father sent me here and, by God, I'm going to do it. I'm not going to be found wanting.

For the first two weeks of pitching hay, I hang onto the chains of the wagon to pull me from shock to shock. On the other side is a wonderful old Indian who comes over and pitches all my shocks so the wagon can keep going. These shocks were about 250 pounds. [*Chuckles.*] I stick a hay fork in it and it falls apart. I'm getting nowhere. All of a sudden, at the end of the second week, I put a fork in it, lifted the whole damn thing up and it all hung together. With my ungainly body, I pitched 250 pounds of wet hay onto the wagon.

They were a particular group of men who did this work. They traveled through Nevada, Idaho, and Montana in the summertime. In the spring and fall, they worked in the mines of Utah and Colorado. They were members of the IWW, called Wobblies.* They decided to educate me, passing me little pamphlets—*Value, Price, and Profits*, that sort of thing. They slipped me Edward Bellamy's *Looking Backward*, a novel about a worker's utopia. They'd insist, "You read this at night and we'll question you in the morning." They told me about the great strikes they took part in. So here's Herbert Hoover's associate's son studying with the IWW. [*Chuckles.*]

---

* The International Workers of the World was an organization of migratory workers, self-educated and labor-conscious, who believed in One Big Union. They were especially strong in the Southwest and Northwest, but their strength declined precipitously after World War I.

My mother was a Catholic. So I had instruction and Sunday
school. A priest, who was a friend of the family, thought I'd make a
good Jesuit. So I was studying Aquinas in the wintertime and Marx
in the summer. My sexual education began at this point, too.

On Saturday night, the guys would get their pay, hop in the truck,
and head for a town known as Poison Junction because of the bootleg
you got there. They'd get all liquored up and go to the cathouse to
get their rocks off. I'd go with them because I had already been
introduced to rotgut liquor and knew how to handle it by the time I
was thirteen. But the cathouse was awful. It was embarrassing for
her and me. I got out of there as soon as I could.

From then on, I always managed to stay outside. But somebody
would always notice this, and on the way home I'd get these long,
liquored lectures about "those morphodites, who are always looking
for nice kids like you." They didn't know the word "homosexual,"
either. They knew the words "pervert" and "god damn hairy fairy."
I'd listen, and after he got sick over the side of the truck, I'd clean
him up. Boy, I'm picking up their manners pretty fast. I'm not shy
and gangly anymore, but I know I have to hide who I am.

I'm now accepted as a good worker. At the end of the following
summer, they tip me off on an easier way to get back home. I've been
taking the bus, train, bus, train. They give me an old union card to
get me a job on a tramp steamer. Unload at different ports and jump
ship at San Pedro. It won't cost me a cent and it's easy work.

We dock at Monterey, a couple of stops before I jump ship. It's
about nine at night. The guys head for the nearest speakeasy and
then the cathouse. Back on board, a voice came to me out of the dark-
ness: "I notice you didn't go into the cathouse tonight with the rest
of the guys." All of a sudden this voice became a person. He was a
perfectly copper-colored handsome man of about twenty-five. He
had curly hair and blue eyes. A regular seaman, he had come from
Mombasa, a port on the East African coast. His name was Matt.

He said, "We'll unload tomorrow night at Santa Barbara, and
when they go to the cathouse, maybe you'd like to walk on the beach
instead." I said I'd like that very much. So about 8:30 the next night,
we were walking along and our hands were close, swinging. I was
terrified that if I caught his hand and I'm wrong, he'll not only hit me
but disgrace me in front of everybody else on the ship. All of a sudden, I take the chance, grab his hand. He twisted it up behind, brings
me around into his arms, and kisses me. I knew I found exactly what
I was looking for, waiting for. It was absolutely wonderful. We made
love on the sand dunes. I was fourteen, and I was in Ninth Heaven.

That was what?—over sixty-five years ago. Your first love, you
never forget that. I can still see him. All of a sudden, I knew what

love was all about, what all the books I had read were about. He was so gentle and so kind to me. He gave the loveliest gift that a new boy finding out who he is has ever received.

He said to me, "We have a brotherhood everywhere in the world. In some places, we are respected. In some places, we are persecuted just like we are here. But this is not everywhere." He said, "Someday you will be traveling to a strange land and you won't understand a word that is being said. The smell will be strange and the sounds will be strange. All of a sudden, you will be in a white square. Because you are tall, you will stand over the heads of many people, and across the square, you will see a pair of eyes open and glow at you. In that moment of the eye lock, you are home and you're safe and you're free. He has been waiting for you and you have been waiting for him."

Can you tell that suddenly whether the person is gay?

The moment you lock eyes with a person. Remember, heteros don't look each other in the eye. There's always that veil that comes down. I don't think it's fear. Plato says, "The eyes are the windows of the soul." You, a hetero, have no intention of allowing anybody else to read your soul. This man gave me the knowledge that we are a brotherhood, that I can find my people elsewhere in the world, and that is what the eye lock will do. He told me where the cruising grounds were in Denver, in San Francisco, in Washington, D.C.

Oh, I must tell you of the scare I gave Matt. He thought I was about twenty. When I told him I was fourteen, he nearly had a hemorrhage because he could have been put in jail for thirty years. I said to this man who won my heart, "I would give my life before I would say a word that would in any way distress you." I promised to leave school at the end of the year and join him in Panama. Of course, I never heard from him, but I never forgot him and cried about him for years. But I was learning who I am.

In 1950, when I founded the Mattachine Society, we were interested in finding out who we are were as a separate people. We had to reinvent ourselves. Your society had infected us into believing that we are perverts and degenerates. We were heteros with nasty habits. We'd have to be corrected. For generations, we've had this rotten image of ourselves. I never did. I'm Goddamned if I'm gonna have a low opinion of myself. This has been my struggle all my life.

What I needed to do was to find a word that described ourselves as we wanted to be looked at. Not the way you wanted to see us: "homosexual." All you had to do was mention that word and every cop on the corner would tell you who was a dirty pervert, who was probably perverted by the choir master and now goes around perverting all the little kids. I didn't need that. Remember, "homosexual" had just made it to the dictionary. For six months, we looked up all the prefixes and suffixes in Greek and Latin we could find. We finally came up with a word we liked: "homophile," lover of same.

Shortly after the Kinsey report came out, we sent out a manifesto, a call to form a new underground society. We would go to jail before we would reveal any information about it. We had been suffering from blackmail by the police for year. The moment a person was listed as homosexual, his name appeared on the front page of the newspaper. The moment that happened, you lost your job, you lost your insurance, you lost your credit. Police would say, "You'll be on the front page, unless..." Not just police, anybody. So the Mattachine Society came into being.

For years, I'd been collecting folk music. In reading through the histories of the early centuries, from, say, the ninth century to the thirteenth, dissenters used to sing of their struggles and pass on the latest news through folk music. I was invited to teach a course in its history at the Southern California Labor School. It was, naturally, left wing. Later, during the worst of the witch-hunt days, a couple of stool pigeons on the schools' board testified against me.

When I was subpoenaed to appear before the House Un-American Activities Committee, I went to a civil liberties lawyer I'd known for years. We were close friends. I told him they'll probably ask about the Mattachine Society. "They'll know by now that I founded it." He asked, "What's that?" "It's for gay people." He froze. "I won't handle that at all." He gave me a list of other attorneys. Everyone said no. They were handling political people, but homosexuals, no. At the end of the five-week search, I was almost catatonic I was so frightened. Finally, one guy said, "I'm really too busy, but I can see your hands underneath the counter are just about pulling the leg off the desk. We'll do something. Can you come here at five o'clock tomorrow morning?"

We rehearsed from five to seven-thirty every morning and put in twelve-hour stints over the weekend. Different approaches to all the trick questions they'd ask. He wanted me to emphasize my family background. On my mother's side, I'm a fifteenth-generation American, going back to 1608, Jamestown, and to cousins at Plymouth Rock. One of my ancestors owned the farm that is now Trinity Church in New York. I go there every year just to pat the pews. My lawyer thought that at least it would put them off in their questioning.

I was grilled by Frank Tavener, the committee's lawyer. A huge man. He's sitting behind this big, long oak desk, his gut underneath it. I told him my father was a partner of Herbert Hoover and all the jazz—all the West Point graduates in my family, the Mayflower Compact, on and on. Finally, he said, "Fascinating. But are you a member of the Communist Party?" I said, "No." At that moment, he realized he'd asked the wrong question. If he'd said, "Are you or have you ever been…?" But he didn't. He'd shot his wad.

At this point, he gets livid, red and purple. As he jumps up, this great oak table, with his gut coming up underneath it, starts to tilt. The stenotypist is right in that tight corner with all those bundles of files and papers. As the table goes over, suddenly the whole place has rolls of paper unraveling all around and rolling about. Half the committee is on the floor, trying to find which page is which. The more they unwrap them, the more they roll. It's a wonderful clown show.

By this time, the whole courtroom is in hysterics, laughing themselves sick, screaming, yelling. When the chairman gets it all quieted down, someone in the back stifles a laugh and it starts all over again. There's pandemonium for at least five minutes.

Finally, the chairman says, "I think the committee understands the tenor of this witness's testimony. We've gotten the most we can out of him, so I suggest he be excused." My lawyer is wiping his brow: "How we got through that, the Goddess is with us."

I had been sitting through this beautifully. As I go down to the bailiff to sign myself out, I discover that my hands, which I had been holding quietly in my lap, were locked. The bailiff had to call two other attendants to help pull them apart. I was absolutely terrified, but I lived through it.

How the Mattachine Society got its name? While at the labor school doing research on medieval and Renaissance music, I found out about early peasant revolts and men becoming monks in order to avoid going on the Crusades; I learned of forbidden ritual dances, of the wearing of masks and women's clothes, of Societies Joyeur and the Societies Madachien. One of the homosexual guys in my class—there were several—said, "Why don't we call ourselves the Madachien? We have to be masked in public just as they were. And we want to be political in our way."

At the beginning, our society was left of center. It changed later on, when newer apolitical people joined and took over. We were the first to challenge a homosexual arrest. In 1952, one of our members was entrapped and jailed. An old labor lawyer who had fought the good fight most of his life for losing causes took the case. "I don't know anything about homosexuality. You guys will have to teach me, and I'll handle it."

At this time, we're still not fighting for our rights. That comes later. All we're asking for is our dignity. We've got to reinvent ourselves as a separate people with a message, but we still don't know what the message is. The only place we'll find it is in our experience and our imagination. We're beginning to develop a language. It was so exciting, our membership jumped by leaps and bounds. In California, we had five thousand people by 1953.

In May of '53, 150 showed up at our convention, and it was the first time some of these people encountered 149 others like themselves. It was like Gideon's army. All of a sudden they said we don't have to do this underground stuff anymore. "We can have club meetings just like the Democratic clubs." I said, "You don't know what you're into, babies." The witch hunt was at its worst. My name was still hot. And, bang, I was kicked upstairs because I was an embarrassment. For me, the dream was dead. I wanted no part of a middle-class compromising crowd. I knew it was suicidal, too. The five thousand went down to five hundred.

A new Mattachine Society was formed, went great guns for a while, and sputtered out. I'd say, at this point, it's about two generations back.

At my suggestion, some guys put out the first openly gay magazine in the country. January 1953. It's going well, but in 1954 the post office slams down on it as being prurient and illegal. We take it to the Supreme Court, the Roth case, and the Court decides our stuff has educational and artistic merit and should be permitted the use of the mails. We win. *Lady Chatterly's Lover* and Henry Miller got in ahead of us. Two heteros. But we fought the case.

I'm out of the picture for a while, but I come back in the '60s. We're part of the civil rights movement, of course. In 1966, we set up a North American Homophile Organizational Committee (NAHOC). We picked Armed Services Day, May 20. It was the struggle to make gays eligible for the armed services. I'm not the slightest bit interested in building up our armed forces. It's really a nonissue. Gays have been in the military all along, for Christ's sake. The fight is for first-class citizenship.

When the kid is asked to fill out the draft questionnaire: "What is your sexual orientation?," we tell him to write across it: "None of your goddamn business." If everybody did that, the army would be stymied because they wouldn't know who they were getting. This was long before Stonewall.*

Up until Stonewall in '69, we had been talking about ourselves as

---

* A gay bar in Greenwich Village in the '60s. The New York City police had been harassing the patrons of Stonewall as well as other such places for years. It was a matter of course. One day in 1969, the patrons and other gays of the community retaliated. The city—the country—was astonished. So were gays everywhere. So were the police. That moment is considered revolutionary for homosexuals. Gay Pride Week, held each year in a different city, is a commemoration of that moment.

individuals; "I." With Stonewall, it became "we." I thought it was great. We formed a gay liberation front in Southern California within weeks of Stonewall. Kids come up to me and say, "You started the Mattachine Society. Tell us about it." Here I am with gray hair down to my waist and the kids weren't supposed to trust anyone over thirty.

Beginning in 1979, I started a group called the Radical Fairies. We're in Australia, in Africa, in England. There are ten of us in Canada.

What's your program?

Ahhh, that's not for you to ask. We are the fairies who always loved being fairies. We're the sissies who always loved being sissies. We love being different. We don't have to be the same as you. It has always been assumed that we're a variation of you. We're not. We're quite different.

We have self-discovery workshops all over the country. So many of our people are still ashamed, still have that image of themselves that they inherited from the schools and churches. When they hear about us, they're at first terrified, but now they're coming along, even if secretly, quite excited. They like that phrase "third gender" more and more.

How long will you continue this work?

How do I know? My health isn't as good as it was. When I go, I'd like to be remembered as a guy with an idea or two that may have been useful for my people. I'm talking about the people I've been looking for all my life. [*Suddenly angry.*] You people, you heteros, kept me away from my family!

Are you sore at me because I'm a hetero?

The heteros are the enemy. And then there are nongays. We elevate you to that—almost as good as us, but not quite. It means you're not the enemy.

Oh, thank you. The use of the word "fairy" by heterosexuals is a put-down, denigrating, yet you proudly call on it.

That's right. I don't like "fag." Faggots are something you can break over your knee or burn in a fire. You can control it. A fairy can't be controlled by you. When we use the word "fairy," you are uncomfortable. We like it that way.

Having reached a certain age, do you sense something lost in today's young?

Like some of our older ones, a lot of these kids have been taught to loathe themselves, so they drink or go to a psychiatrist. What I'm saying is, "It's a gift to be gay." I watch young eyes open and glow. This happens with young fairies when they come to our gatherings. Often they come forward and say, "Thank you for inviting me. I found my life." One of the greatest pleasures I have is, when I travel around the country, a young man will come up to me on the street and say, "Can I have a hug?" [*He stifles an oncoming sob.*] He'll whisper in my ear, "Thank you for my life." Every time, every time, it wipes me out. For me, that's the greatest gift of all.

Valerie Taylor, 79

Tucson, Arizona

"Hold on a minute while I get over onto this couch. I'm feeling fine but my left leg is behaving badly. I ran into this knee business. It has worse days, and yesterday was one of them."

We're having a long-distance phone conversation.

"When I fell and broke my right shoulder—I had already fallen a few times—I thought, 'Well, I'm a klutz.' Oh, I always have been. Everybody has always reproached me for being clumsy. I'm in therapy now, and I've progressed to the point where they let me walk on a little walker."

I live by myself. I have half a little concrete block house. The people who own it formerly owned the gay club here. For the last three months I've been getting along very badly. But I said no, I won't go into a nursing home. Some acquaintance came in to take care of me. She was here about two hours a day and I was totally alone the rest of the time. For three months I've been lying in bed, reading and eating junk food.

I get along on social security, but something wonderful is happening right now. They knew I was laying out like two hundred dollars a week for somebody to keep house. And what do you know? They remembered I was the one who started the fund for Jeannett Foster, the poet. We called it the Sisterhood Fund, to keep her in her nursing home, because she had no money. It's bad to be in a nursing home anyway, but when you're broke, it's worse. So some of my friends have set up a fund for me, the Valerie Taylor Fund. They sent out letters to five hundred feminist bookstores and whatever gay and lesbian publications they could find—even *The Advocate*, the big one. They send the money to the Antigone bookstore in Tucson, and every week they forward me a bunch of checks.

Somebody began this whole thing by saying a little bombastically that I'm one of the great national treasures. [*Chuckles.*] Thirteen published novels and a half a book of poetry—Jeannett's being the other half, of course.

I've been writing since I was eight years old. I'm practically eighty now, short, gray-haired, have a spinal curvature and a great-grandson. I'm known for writing nonpornographic lesbian fiction. When I started back in the '50s, I wanted to read about people who just didn't jump in and out of bed every other page. But real people with homes and families.

I was born in Aurora, Illinois. Used to be a nice little town. Now it's a bedroom suburb of Chicago. In 1939, I married a man who turned out to be an alcoholic no good bum. I left him after fourteen years and supported three children. I lost one son three years ago. He was an alcoholic and died of it.

I used to work in the office all day, and then I'd go home and write "true confession" stories for *MacFadden's*. This was before I knew anything about lesbians.

In those days, if you didn't get child support, nobody did anything about it. We had some strange meals with lots of rice, but we never missed a meal. Nor did I ever consider giving up my kids. One son has been married three times and has three children by two of his wives. The other one is still single and lives here in Tucson. I have five beautiful grandchildren.

I've always said I was bisexual. I was about thirty-six when I realized what a woman could mean to me. That was about eight years into my marriage. The failure was not because of that.

I never hid my lesbianism, but I didn't make a thing out of it either. In those days, you'd lose your job if you ever came out of the closet. I'm talking about the '50s and '60s in Chicago.

Nobody ever paid any attention to me. I was just a proofreader and copy editor at Henry Regnery.* Half the staff at that time was gay. Henry didn't know it. I don't think he'd ever heard of such a thing.

One of the women at Regnery always treated me like everyone else—courteously. After I quit, she invited me for a Sunday-night supper. "My lover and I have been wanting to know you better for a long time." She was afraid to reveal herself while we were at work.

At age twenty-two, I belonged to the American Socialist Party. I'm an old-fashioned Gene Debs admirer. There aren't many of us around. I was always in the peace movement and the Women's International League for Peace and Freedom. The ones Mr. Reagan called a bunch of communist dupes. I've always spoken out.

My grandchildren are quite yuppie, and they're not at all interested in political issues. They're sweet girls. Oh, they're quite aware of my lesbianism. One of them told her teacher at the university that her grandmother was a noted lesbian author. She said it with great pride. It turned out that the teacher owned some of my books. Trish was very pleased about it. Gay people have a lot of acceptability they never used to have.

I never had much trouble. I was not a bar person and the bars were being persecuted all the time. Chicago cops had a lovely system. You'd be sitting there having a quiet beer, the jukebox going. A guy would go into the men's room and leave a joint on the window sill. Pretty soon another man, also in plain clothes, would go into the

* A conservative Chicago publishing house.

men's room, come out with the joint, making little cries of happy surprise. So everybody there was arrested.

There were not many lesbian bars. Some were syndicate-owned.* I was always up front. If you try to conceal things, they usually come out worse. We didn't have the underground network that the men had. If you were a gay man and said you're moving to Mobile or wherever, everybody would rush up with numbers to call.

There weren't many of us out in the open, although people always watched. In 1931, I was in Dallas, wandering around, looking in bookstores. I saw a copy of a gay magazine in the window, so I went in and said to the boy behind the counter—a kid no more than eighteen—"Do you carry *The Ladder*?" It was the only big lesbian magazine those days. He said, "No, but would you like to meet some girls?" There was a sort of unwritten code. He figured: She looks like a real nice dyke. I was about forty-five at the time.

In Chicago, you didn't need a code. We had the *Tribune* of Colonel McGooseneck.† The *Trib* put all the gay bar addresses on the front page. A complete listing. If cops nailed some patrons, the *Trib* would print not only your name and address but where you worked—just in case your employer happened to miss it.

Finally the Mattachine Society was formed. It was a gay man's and lesbian's group. I was one of the founders and national board members. For a time, I was the only woman on the board. I edited the newsletter, which you could carry in your pocket. It told you what your rights were. In every monthly issue, we'd expose a member of the vice squad, the undercover police.

There was a cop named John Small who was very handsome and worked the pub washrooms. It was a bum kind of entrapment. We published a picture of him, along with a description. He was furious because his cover was blown.

Lesbians don't go cruising as much as gay males. They're more discreet. There was a lot of loneliness. Part of it was due to the old "fem and butch" mystique. If there were two women, one was fem and one was butch. We had no model except straight marriage, of course. Then

---

* In 1933, shortly after Prohibition was repealed, a schoolmate and I traversed a number of Chicago bars, sampling the suddenly legal brew. With luck, the house would "pop" after the second drink—that is, offer one for free. Once, we wandered into a bar frequented exclusively by women; we were the only males present. The bartender was friendly enough, though the house did not "pop." My friend, who fancied himself a ladies man, tried to cut in on a couple dancing to the jukebox. One was a stunning blonde, very feminine; her partner bore a remarkable resemblance to Alexander Woolcott. My friend was rebuffed out of hand. We departed, somewhat bemused.

† A nickname coined by Nelson Algren in reference to Colonel Robert Rutherford McCormick, publisher of the *Chicago Tribune*.

the sexual revolution came along and we had to find a new stereotype: Just be yourself. In those days, even if you were with friends at a bar, strangers would come up to you and ask if you were fem or butch.

I knew fems who used to turn their paychecks over to their butches and get lunch money back—just like straight women and men. When the straight people began to act sensibly, we didn't have anybody to copy. And a good thing, too.

In the '60s, I'd get letters from Jesus, Kansas, or Podunk. She thought she was the only lesbian in town. She'd ask, "How do I meet women? Is there an accepted way?" The stereotyped answer was: get a copy of *The Well of Loneliness*, sit in the coffee shop at Walgreen's, and read until someone comes along and asks what you're reading. If she's heard of the book, she's probably looking for somebody, too. That was the only lesbian book a lot of people had heard of.* I read it when I was very young—not a particularly good book.

There's more power in the gay movement these days. Look at the March on Washington last year. More than a million took part. There's always a backlash, but there is more tolerance today. It was very frightening in the '50s, during McCarthy time. There were ultraconservative gays, who were more than making up for being gay and hoping nobody would know. There was no networking or cooperation, all very closeted. Around '69, '70, there was something called the "lavender network." They wouldn't have anything to do with men. You couldn't have a husband, a son, a male friend. At the first Gay and Lesbian Pride Week gathering, in '71, '72, I spoke out: "We have to work together, gay men and gay women, because our interests are the same." Somebody threw an egg at me. Missed, luckily. They were very angry. They said: "Don't ever come to our headquarters again." They're no longer in existence. There's always a lunatic fringe in every good cause.

When I joined the Chicago Peace Council, they said I'd never get gay rights recognized by that bunch. Some of the council big shots were very stuffy. I was introduced not as a gay but as a member of the Women's International League. I don't know how they knew I was lesbian, but two young gays there approached me, wanting to know how they could tell their parents.

When Betty Friedan started her women's group that became

---

* Another of the Chicago bars my classmate and I patronized in '33 was McGovern's Liberty Inn. He had succeeded in making a date with the barmaid, June, whose helmet hair style gave her the startling appearance of Louise Brooks. To compound my frustration (I had made a feeble pass at her, too), she said something to me that I interpreted as denigratory. For some reason that I fail to understand even now, so many years later, I blurted out, "Have you ever read *The Well of Loneliness*?" I had no idea whether or not she had heard of the book. She simply said, "I think I'm being insulted."

NOW, she didn't want any lesbian members. That's why I never joined NOW. She said they'd take over. Perhaps they would, because they're used to being political and have a tendency toward leadership. There are some lesbians who wouldn't be caught dead at a political rally. But if you come out for one good cause, you're more open to others. If you're for peace, you're probably for civil rights.

I think more and more older women are coming out. What have we got to lose? I knew some wonderful old lesbians when I was younger. They were free and easy about things. Out here in Tucson, we have a very good upper- and middle-class gay group called Wingspan. I can't afford to join it.

Until this shoulder and leg trouble, I was very active. I joined the Quakers in helping the homeless. This is a money-oriented town with a lot of poor people in it. They come here to keep warm in the winter. The streets are full of panhandlers and well-heeled tourists. They play big golf tournaments here. It's a very bad town for poor people. It has no Medicaid. This is a town of nursing homes and retirement communities.

About twenty-seven miles away, we have a little place called Green Valley. Overpriced retirement stuff. You see a billboard with a couple in their golden years playing golf. It's a very fine town for geriatric doctors, who have something to sell to old folks with money.

I talk to kids in high school and they always come up with this question: "Do you think it's fair to take social security, 'cause there isn't gonna be any left when I get there?" My answer is: "Yeah, I don't think it's fair. But just what are you going to do with your old grandmother? You can either let her starve or put her on social security. Or you can take her out and shoot her, so you'll be sure to have some money yourself when you're older." The kids look shocked. Especially the Hispanic kids, who are very grandparents-oriented. Tucson is about 30 percent Chicano. I find the Chicanos are, as a rule, kinder, more courteous, and more civilized than most Anglos.

I think I'm religious, but I'm not sure by whose definition. I have a tendency to think of God as female. We have a darling old Quaker gentleman who always referred to God as he, she, or it. If you go to a black church, you'll find that God and Christ and the Apostles are black.

I came from a very advanced family. My father's two grandmothers were feminists—tiny, spunky women. My great grandmother Hoad marched in the first suffrage parade in Elgin, Illinois, with my father strapped to her back.

My country grandpa, my mother's father, was a follower of Bob Ingersoll, the old agnostic. They'd sit at the table and he'd say, "Have some more gravy on those potatoes. Those are God's own, plenty of it." Somebody at the table would say, "You talk a lot about God and you're an atheist." And Grandpa'd say, "No, no, I'm an agnostic. You can't prove or disprove Him. I'll tell you one thing, if there is a God, He's a lot better than you goddamn Christians make him out to be." That's the way he felt: the religious people didn't do God credit.

His wife, my mother's mother, was a camp-meeting Methodist, right down to never baking pie on Sunday. Yet they loved each other and lived together fifty years.

Some things are very much the same now as then. Family relationships don't really change that much, although I have an unmarried twenty-seven-year-old friend who just had a baby. She's a lesbian and doesn't have a regular lover. A lot of lesbians have babies. You can get artificial insemination. In some cases, my lesbian friends have chosen a father for the baby. Usually, a good guy who will not intrude upon them, but who will hold himself responsible. I'm in favor of it. If a woman wants a baby, why shouldn't she have one?

What changed a great deal is the attitude toward age. When my grandmother, the camp-meeting Methodist, was forty years old, she stopped wearing hats. She wore a bonnet. At forty, she was too old to wear a hat. It was just before the turn of the century.

After Grandpa died, she came and lived with us. She was about seventy-six. We got her into colored clothes. She'd been wearing black and gray all these years, little old bunched-up black dresses. My sister took her out and bought her a straw hat, like a pie plate, the style in 1928. It had a little wreath of pink flowers around it. Grandma fell in love with that hat. She insisted on going to church so she'd have some place to wear it. She took a whole new lease on life and lived to be eighty-four. She made a splash. The idea of who's old and who isn't has changed.

Yet you can't escape the infirmities of age. You have no idea how hard it is when you can't walk. I have to hire someone to shampoo my hair. You sponge yourself with wet washcloths. You reach for something and the shelf is too high. I don't know whether I'll get well or not.

My morale's pretty good, but you've noticed it, haven't you—your friends dropped all along the way? You're surprised how many have gone on ahead. The Quakers have had a lot of memorial services lately.

I've started a new book—which is what I'm doing now—called *Waiting to Die*. It's about staying at home and taking care of myself. It will probably be my last book. I'll die before I go into a retirement home, I'll tell you that. I've done volunteer work in some of those homes and they're terrible. Even the good ones, so called. You leave behind everything that was yours. They expect you to become a nothing, and that's what you become. I'd just as soon be on my own and then die and be done with it. Independent, you gotta be.

Part V

Chapter Fifteen

Public Servant

Congressman Henry B. Gonzalez, 76
House Office Building, Washington, D.C., 8:00 a.m.

"I try to get to the office shortly after seven. I don't look upon it as work but as some kind of mission. I don't go anywhere in the evening. I don't go to any social functions in Washington. I work here, go to my apartment, have a sandwich, go to the gym, and come back here. Midnight is the best time to work, no interruptions."

On his door is a plaque: "This office belongs to the people of the 20th District of Texas, San Antonio." "I set up that plaque when I first came here. Many of our chosen representatives, even on the local level, had forgotten where they came from. I thought this plaque was a good reminder."

This committee* had become the laughingstock of the House. I felt the time had come to change things by just following the rules, being fair, and never forgetting that these marble halls belong to the people. One of the first things I did was to stop this habit lobbyists had of paying a hundred dollars for individuals to come at 5:00 a.m. and stand in front of the hearing room. When they opened the door, these paid agents would rush in, get a chair, and save it for the lobbyists, who wouldn't show up until ten. Pretty soon all you had in the room were lobbyists, signaling each other. Ordinary citizens couldn't get in.

One morning, I ordered the sergeant-at-arms to open the doors, remove everyone who was seated there, and make space for the citizens lined up in the hall. I said to the lobbyists: "You guys live in Washington, get tremendous salaries, and take it for granted that you have access. When a little citizen comes from two thousand miles away, he is intimidated. This must stop." I remember the looks I got, daggers. If looks could kill...[*Laughs.*] But it worked.

There was a grass-roots group. Some had hitchhiked from Arkansas. Some were black, some were just poor. They lined up after the hearing to shake my hand. To me, that was the greatest

---

* The Banking and Finance Committee.

thing. It was to remind my colleagues why we were here.

If the people are not informed, if the issues are clouded by public relations firms, there's no accountability. We reflect some of the worst corrupting features of England in 1832, when agents would take bids from the rich heirs who wanted to go to Parliament. The guy who put up the most money got the job.

Today you may have no lords of the manor, but you have PR consultants. They're jobbers just as they were in England. The Reform Act of 1832 put a stop to that practice, but we have it here now. They advertise: Hire us and we'll show you what it takes to win. I call them public office jobbers.

I notice another plaque on the wall: "To Congressman Henry. Though we've had fights, you're the voice now." It is signed by Maury Maverick.* "A maverick is what they've been calling me. That's a badge of honor."

The physical exertion is much more than it was twenty years ago. Good health is necessary to discharge the job, and I've been lucky. I have no diminution of energy with a multiplicity of issues beyond banking. That's the way it's always been. I discovered this the first day I was sworn in as city councilman in 1953. Forty years in public office.

At the first council meeting, I raised my hand. The mayor asks, "What is it?" "I have a question to ask the finance director." My colleague kicked me under the table. I asked my question and the finance director said, "That's a good question. That's the issue under discussion." The mayor approved my recommendation. I could tell they didn't like it, and I discovered why. My colleague said, "We're new here. Why did you butt in? Anyway, the people wouldn't understand what this is all about." So I said, "What were you and me before we were sworn in? We're people. Are we smarter now than before we were sworn in?"

This made me think of the transformation when people get power. You start thinking there's something special about you. I must be smarter than the others because look where I am. If this other guy is so smart, why wasn't he elected? The funny thing is, once people have power, they deny it, deny responsibility.

Campaigning becomes more costly each year. Today any election for a House seat is as expensive as it use to be for the Senate. Where does that money come from? I've never been a fund-raiser. It's a self-imposed limitation. The old truism is as true today as it was a thousand years ago: He who pays the piper calls the tune. If a guy gives you five thousand dollars, he assumes he has a moral right to

---

* An independent-minded San Antonio lawyer who had served as a congressman from the district now represented by Gonzalez.

expect you to be accessible to him. It's what I call preferential accessibility. The individual confuses getting elected with doing his job. It is merely a license to do a job.

When World War II ended, I worked as a juvenile officer in San Antonio. That was the number one issue. Headlines: JUVENILE CRIME. RAMPANT INCREASE. 450%. That was 1945. I didn't know what to expect. I came from a different background. I didn't fool around with girls, didn't know how to dance, never had a date. The first girl I really dated, I married—my wife of fifty-two years.

It was the first time I realized that here in the world were eleven-year-olds who hadn't been to school, who were just out on the streets. I couldn't imagine that kind of world. A year and a half later, I was made chief juvenile probation officer. A reporter wrote a feature story: "Henry Gonzalez is the first Latino American to head a public office in Bexar County in the twentieth century." I couldn't believe it. How could this be in a county that was never less than 39 percent Mexican American?

At that time, there was a clear line between the Americanos—the Anglos—and the others. There was strict segregation. That's why I quit the office two years later. I wanted to hire a black case worker and the judge said, "You're in Texas, Henry. The day hasn't come where you could have a nigger working in here on an equal basis." He was a pretty good old fellow but he was a product of those years. I said, "Judge, we don't have any facilities for black children." I was the first one to use the word "black."

In San Antonio, blacks have never been more than 8 percent of the total population, unlike Dallas or Houston. So later, when I filibustered the race bills in the state senate, they couldn't understand. Those bills were part of the mass resistance that came out of the Confederate states in 1957. I tied the senate up for more than thirty hours. It was the only legislative body in any of the Confederate states in which this kit of laws was even debated. Of the sixteen bills, I killed fourteen of them. [*Laughs.*]

The old boys, these old nestors, were rigid and all that, but they had integrity. The Texas senate was the birthplace of unlimited debate. When they recognized me, not knowing that I was going to hold the floor, they respected the tradition. When I went into ten hours, they started getting nervous. When I went into twenty, they couldn't believe it. Just standing up on your feet, talking, you get a charley horse. Usually when these old boys get ready to filibuster, they equipped themselves with cushions. I had nothing. I just held forth.

This was May of '57, just before Little Rock.* During that fili-

---

* Arkansas Gov. Orval Faubus was defying the *Brown v. Board of Education* decision integrating public schools. (See reference to Faubus in Raymond Koch's reflections, above, in "Community.")

buster, I never strayed from the subject. I didn't read recipe books. I summoned forth all the philosophers, all the reading, and anchored on the Constitution.

When I first got on the floor, they thought, This guy must have a heavy black constituency, must be doing it for political reasons.

Funny thing is, the silly city council of San Antonio, in 1954, right after the Supreme Court decision, decided to pass segregatory ordinances "because these Negroes are going to force themselves into our swimming pools." It was eight to one. I was the dissenter. "Henry, you're crazy." Some of them were Mexican Americans.

Remember, we're a very pluralistic group. You have everything from the dark-complexioned, whom the old-line Texan calls "Messicans," to the blue-eyed ones called "Spanish." That's why I don't like the word "Hispanic." The only thing the dark-complexioned Mexican American didn't have against him were the Jim Crow laws. But in practice, he was treated the same as blacks: he was excluded.

In my family, I'm lighter complexioned. At the old San Pedro swimming pool, we'd go during the summer. I took my little brother with me and two neighborhood buddies. One was Anglo—I hate those words—and the other was really dark. A lifeguard comes up. I can still see him, a giant. "Hey, y'all get out." He pointed to my brother, Joaquin, and little George. My brother starts getting out, he's shivering, it's cold. I hollered, "Stay here." My brother, three years younger than me, starts crying. I tried to drag him back in the water. The guard said, "I told you we don't want Messicans around here." To me, he said, "Y'all right. Y'all are Spanish." So I said the heck with it and we got out. It was 1927 and I was eleven years old.

It's difficult to generalize about Mexican people. There's the human desire to be liked, to be accepted. Some of our so-called leaders wanted so much to be acceptable to whites. When I came home after the filibuster, my severest critics were these Mexican American "leaders." "Está loco. Nos quiere poner con el negro." (He's crazy. He wants to put us with the Negro.) But the mass of our people understood the sting of injustice.

We had restrictive covenants, even in San Antonio. I led the fight to do away with them. These people were for me, but they weren't a presence. The English-language papers didn't report anything that happened here. When that feature story appeared about me being the first Latino American to head public office—that's when I realized we'd been brought up wrong. We'd have to get into the middle of things and fight for what was rightfully ours.

Our so-called leaders tried to discourage me. "Henry, do you want to commit suicide." I said, "I wasn't born in City Hall. My mother didn't breastfeed me in the State House. I was happy before I held public office and I'll be happy after I leave. And I'll be happy doing it, if I'm doing what I want to do. It's a challenge, and it gives me full pay."

I worked for the Public Housing Authority in San Antonio. I defended the priest who was the first advocate of public housing. The entrenched interests, the house builders, hired hoodlums to break up our meetings and threw rocks at the priest. I headed the defense. All the time, our leaders were hollering "Don't make waves."

I didn't know whether I'd be elected again, after my vote in the city council. A police sergeant was the White Citizens Council organizer in the city's police department. He was hollering: "That damn Gonzalez, he's nothing but a chili-eating, nigger-loving Messican, who oughta go back where he came from." I'd tell the reporter I was guilty on all counts. The guy gets madder than heck. My wife starts getting these phone calls: "Hey, you expecting your nigger-loving husband for supper? Don't, he'll be dead." I got a call from a Jewish lawyer in town who was disturbed by the guy's anti-Semitic outbursts. The same people who show their prejudice toward one group usually reveal it toward others. Soon afterward, he was bounced.

I never had a desire for a job at the expense of being quiet, so as not to offend someone. My appeal was to the average citizen, who goes to work, pays his taxes, wants to be with his family. He hopes that if he puts his trust in you, you'll do the right thing. If that person doesn't like my speaking out a certain way, he has the right to vote me out of office.

I spoke out against the Contras in Nicaragua when President Reagan called them "freedom fighters." On the House floor, I called them thugs. It's hard to believe we had a president who told the people that Herlingen, Texas, was on the path of imminent invasion by the Sandinistas. That's how insane it was. Imagine calling the Contras the moral equivalent of our Founding Fathers. I've never heard a grosser abuse of words and such an insult to our intelligence. And nobody laughed. The Contras were nothing but thugs who used American taxpayers' funds.

The Republicans started shouting at me during my speech. That's when I went back to the mike and said, "If this be treason, make the most of it." They were coming up to the microphone, one after the other, to damn the Sandinistas. By the time I got up, I had all the information about these guys, paid for by us, blowing up docks, public buildings, killing women and kids. How could they be freedom fighters?

How come you've been elected seventeen times?

My district happened to be a pluralistic one. I've been assailed for being a spender because I've voted for education bills and was coauthor of the 1964 Title VII—the War Against Poverty. How could I be against these programs in a district that has the second-lowest per capita family income in Texas? That's why I have no use for the idea of the New Democrats. What kind of business is that? To me, it's just Republican Lite.

You always have opposition when you take stands like this. My last challenger was a young Mexican American Republican. [*Chuckles.*] He raised more money than I did. It's hard to explain to most people. How can you be head of the Banking Committee and not have a good campaign fund? In the first place, I may not want one. I never have fund-raisers outside my district. The last I'd have is one in Washington. Never.

How did I get this way? My mother was a devout Catholic. My father, too, but church on Sunday was left to the women. On abortion, a nonissue made into an issue, the priest jumps all over me. I tell him, "Do you think we politicians can pass a law to make people virtuous when you have obviously failed? What are you going to do with an eighteen-year-old woman who self-aborts? Put her in jail?"

I believe in the religious doctrine against abortion. It's personal. But as a legislator, I have no right to impose my belief on anyone else. The history of mankind tells us that politicians cannot mandate righteousness.

They get mad, they shout at me, but finally they pay no attention. So another "issue" arises: prayer in schools. Get God back into the classroom. Today it's gays in the military. Not long ago, it was busing. Before that, a constitutional amendment prohibiting burning of the flag. Oh, my God. My stand is simple: I'm against hysteria, just for sanity.

My constituents are a devout people. They ask me about these matters. I explain and most often they accept my limitations. Sometimes, they may misinterpret my stand as advocating abortion or advocating homosexuality. At all times, I tell them I'm simply advocating the rights of people. But when a basic need comes, a bread-and-butter issue, I'm there and they know it.

At seventy-six, my adrenaline supply is still adequate. More than that, I still believe in accountability first and foremost to myself. I'm not doing anything heroic, but I have to live with myself. If I were to pussyfoot out of fear—that was what victimized my mother. [*Mock-moans*] "Vas hacer que los Americanos se enojen contigo." (You're going to get the Americans mad at you.)

She had gone through the horrible experience of seeing my father lined up against the wall to be shot. Raiding troops had invaded a mining town in Mexico, and all they did was pillage. It was just before the Mexican Revolution, turmoil and disorder. There were groups not necessarily imbued with revolutionary fervor. One of these bandits got drunk and was about to shoot my father.

A woman, Juana Lopez, a real revolutionary, happened to ride by with her troops. "Turn that man loose." She remembered that my father, who had been a *jefe político*,* had saved her husband and son from getting shot by the *Federales* about two years before. Juana Lopez suggested to my father that we go to the capital, Durango. I hadn't been born yet, though my father told me of walking all the way. My mother had gone ahead to Monterey. When my father joined her there, it was under siege by Pancho Villa's soldiers. So they took a train to Laredo and kept riding until they reached San Antonio. When their money ran out three months later, they moved into the house where I was born.

My father was a conservative in the true sense of the word, a careful man, but liberal in his thinking. My mother was very religious. That's why I never ridicule anyone's religious belief, no matter how superstitious it seems to be. I saw how it guided my mother, and what a pillar of strength it was for her to have such faith.

The pastor of our parish had a pulpit up on high. At mass, he'd look down upon us and say: "Aquí estan barracho e llenos de tamales. Vayanse al diablo!" ("You're here full of tamales and beer, and drunk.) "¡Vayanse al diablo! (You can go to hell.")

At confessional, he'd say, "Don't dare lie, because if you do, a serpent will come out of your mouth." So at confessional, I deliberately lied just to see what kind of snake came out. When no snake came out, I wasn't too surprised. He was just trying to scare people.

My younger brother, Joaquin, the doctor, is conservative. My other brothers, engineers, businessmen, doctors are all conservative. Of my four children, only one was interested in my campaign. They all tend to be more cautious than I am.

I often ask myself: Why am I this way? Books maybe. Why, as a boy, did I pick up one of my father's books, printed in Spanish over a hundred years ago? Old leather binding. It was written by an old intellectual who became a revolutionary. You didn't understand much of it, but through the years, as you grow older, you begin to make out what it's about. I was also drawn to the writings of an old monk, a teacher and philosopher. Three months ago, I finished an English translation of his aphorisms. [*I remark on the two volumes of Thomas Paine on his desk.*] I have had a natural kinship with Tom Paine from the very first time I came across his writings.

My father was authoritarian in his behavior, in the old tradition. My brothers were scared stiff of him and docile. I questioned him

* Political boss.

often, asking, "Why?" At school, they'd punish you if you spoke Spanish. At home, they'd get after you if you spoke English. [*Laughs.*] The struggle was always to identify.

My teacher said, "You were born here. You're an American." At eight, this was a great discovery for me. So, at the supper table with my cousins while my nanny was frying the beans, I told them what the teacher said. There was an outburst of laughter. My cousin Perfecto said, "You think you're a gringo, ha, ha, ha." My nanny says, "What is this?" I told her, "The teacher said that every person born in this country is an American." She went back to the stove and said in Spanish, "I guess I've heard everything. A poco si un gato nace en el horno, es pan." (If a cat's born in an oven, that makes him bread.) [*Laughs.*] They laughed me out of the supper table.

There was one time when that fear made me do something I regret. It was the only time, but it was enough for me to never forget.

It was in 1964. Vietnam. The so-called Gulf of Tonkin resolution. In those days, you seldom had a recorded vote. It was easy going. They used to call it the Tuesday and Thursday Club, because you had no work other than on those days. They rang the bell, calling for a forum. It was the resolution affirming our support for the president at this time of emergency. The day before, the headline was: U.S. SHIP ATTACKED.

I looked at the resolution and it said, in plain English, "Mr. President, do what you want to do." This was a back-door declaration of war. The president was authorized to do anything he wanted. Here's Lyndon Johnson, friend and neighbor from Texas.

Everybody was voting aye for LBJ's resolution, Republicans and Democrats. I just couldn't bring myself to vote for it. But how could I be the only one to vote against it?

At that point, the two swinging doors burst open and in came Adam Clayton Powell. "What are we voting on?" "How does the gentleman from New York vote?" "Well, present." So there were no "no" votes. The Speaker addressed me, "Does the gentleman from Texas want to be recorded or not?" At that moment, out of fear of being the only one, I voted aye. As soon as I said it, I regretted it. And have ever since. I'll always remember this one instance I failed myself. I felt we were let down by me. I felt it keenly then, and I feel it keenly to this day.

I came out in the lobby and Sarah McClendon said, "You were the last one. You seemed hesitant." I said, "I should have voted no, because it's a back-door declaration of war." It turned out I was right. Since then, I've never tried to do violence to what I believe in. I no longer have the fear of being a minority of one.

Sophie Masloff, 76

Pittsburgh, Pennsylvania

*We are in a high-rise apartment in Squirrel Hill, a neighborhood of
the middle-class elderly, the great majority of them widows.*
She had served as mayor of Pittsburgh until a week ago.

I have been working for sixty years without a single day off. I have
been retired for about a week, and I know that this is not for me. I
am going to be out there as soon as the weather breaks.

I was the first female mayor of this city, first Jewish mayor, and
first grandmother mayor. Prior to that, I was the first female president of the Pittsburgh City Council. Before that, I worked in the
Court of Common Pleas and I held all kinds of jobs: investigator,
assistant city clerk, read briefs, set up cases for trial, helped pick
juries. Name it, I did it.

I am a first-generation American, with only a high school education. My mother was born in Romania. She came here with four children, whom she raised by herself. She'd never spoken a word of
English. It was Yiddish only. My father died when I was two.

As a very young child, I used to come downtown to pay the bills
for my mother: taxes, hot water bills, things of that sort. I was
maybe ten years old and would walk from office to office in the
City/County Building and the courthouse. I decided that this is
what I would like to do with my life.

I was a little girl with lots of energy and a terrific amount of ambition. My mother wasn't well and I was the chief support, though I
was the youngest of the four children. I got a job during the depression right after I graduated high school at sixteen. I still did most of
the work at home and volunteered, in my spare time, at Democratic
headquarters.

It's been a thoroughly satisfying life and I intend to continue. I'm not
going to stop. I've accepted a teaching job at a college for women in
Pittsburgh. There've been other offers I've accepted. In addition, I'll
be a watchful citizen of Pittsburgh, a watchdog. I know every nook and
cranny of this city. This last Sunday, one of the columnists wrote of my
being down to earth, a street person. This is what I've always been.

Unfortunately, there's a belief that it's a world for young people.
But sometimes they are anxious to make change just for the sake of
change. That's one of the reasons I didn't run for another term. I felt
in my heart I still could have done the job and probably won. A lot
has to be said for experience, but I realized what the mood of the
people was: give the young a chance.

I became mayor six years ago, when, as president of the city council, I succeeded Richard Caliquiri, who, unfortunately, died while in office. We were great friends and had conferred very often. I finished out the two remaining years of his term and ran for a full term against five men, all of whom had more money, more education. That was 1988. I was elected by a majority. I went into the campaign with everything I had to give, though there were many difficulties. Pittsburgh is basically a labor town, blue-collar, ethnic. Many believed that politics was no place for women. It was also an unfortunate time for a strong Democratic city. We got very little help from the Republican president. It was a struggle all the way, but I'm really proud of what we accomplished.

I was seventy-two when I ran for the full term. I have aging freckles, I have gray hair, all those things, but I flaunted them. I was proud of them. I stood up everywhere I went and said, "I am not a senior citizen. I am of a privileged group who have lived all our lives in Pittsburgh and have a lot to contribute." I didn't turn down a function. I went the circuit seven days a week.

All four of my young opponents brought up my age all the time. It was the only flaw they could find in my campaign. The issue underneath it all was dangerous ground and they hesitated using it, but it came up all the time. "What would happen if she died?" I faced the issue squarely. "Yes, I am seventy-two years old. Everybody dies sometime. Young people die, too. Sure, I'm old, but I'll do the job for you."

I hate the term "senior citizen." [*Angrily.*] It's generic. It groups us all together as people who are out of commission. What also annoyed me from the very beginning of my public life were the interviews that always began, "How old are you?" They never asked the men their age, but they persisted in asking me. They never missed. When I ran for council, whoever chaired the meeting never failed to ask, whenever I got up to speak, "Mrs. Masloff, how old are you?" As though that were the important issue. Everyone in the audience knew my age.

I went along with the gag. Often, I headed it off before they had a chance to ask me. I stood up and said, "Ladies and gentlemen, the people opposing me don't have the benefit of my experience." Then, I'd firmly state my age.

Knock on wood, I'm blessed with good health. I come from strong immigrant stock. We were brought up with the work ethic. A day like this [*it is a wintry, blizzardy day*] would never have kept me at home. My mother believed that, dead or alive, you went to work every day.

My first job was as a bookkeeper in the wholesale egg business. I was sixteen. Every night, when I volunteered at the Democratic headquarters, I met all the local leaders. Some, like Dave Lawrence,* years later became my greatest friends. Politics fascinated me and I wanted to be part of it.

I loved working but I've never sacrificed my home or my family. My husband died three years ago. I have a daughter and two grandchildren. I stayed with them all these years. It seems that a female is expected to do two jobs good. Not the men, of course. At the time, I believed that's what I *had* to do and I did it.

I ran four times for council and led the ticket every time. I got a good women's vote, a good one in the African American community, and a big one among the elderly. Pittsburgh has a large aging population. They had been neglected for many years and one of my priorities was in the matter of recreation centers for the old, free lunches, fighting age discrimination.

Are you looked upon as a "character"?

Absolutely. I didn't want to be considered a stodgy old lady, so I went along with the young people. I kidded with them, I joked around all the time. I accepted this nonsense, that is, I pretended to because I didn't want to appear set in my ways. It was deliberate. It wasn't that I was an oddball. I knew I wasn't. I was a "character" because I pitched in on everything that had to be done, no matter how foolish it was. If it meant looking foolish, okay. The cartoonists in Pittsburgh had a field day with me, and they all agree they're going to miss me.

[*She indicates a framed cartoon on the wall: It is indubitably Sophie, with her hallmark hairdo, a well-puffed bouffant, her oversized glasses, and those earrings.*] The cartoonist gave that to me. He is one of my best friends. I didn't mind being a cartoon figure. Many times I'd see one in the paper that I thought was unusually funny. I'd call up and compliment them, even though they were making fun of me. I'd say, "I love it." I meant to be part of the city, going to ball games, cheering for the Pirates and the Steelers, even if it was perceived as being foolish. Sense of humor had to be part of my makeup. I didn't take myself too seriously, but I took my job seriously.

I'm sure there are many women my age who have the energy to do these things. Somehow, they're put down by young people, by institutions. They don't stand up. They're intimidated by this idea that young people know everything.

We, the old, are either helpless or we have too much money. This

---

* At various times, mayor of Pittsburgh and, later, governor of Pennsylvania. At all times, a Democratic Party powerbroker.

thing about social security. The money you get from that is certainly not anything to keep anybody in luxury. Somehow, the young perceive it as taking something away from them, although it's only a pittance.

The older folks have not fought back as they should have. We treat age as though it were a disease. What's wrong with age freckles? What's wrong with spots? Young people have skin ailments, too. What's wrong with it? I have them. I don't cover them up.

I'll just keep doing what I've always done. There are a lot of unfulfilled things. I would have hoped to help my mother, who had a hard life, to make her life in the later years easier. That's a personal thing. As far as the city is concerned, I've been distressed about crime. I wanted to build a new stadium, a new baseball field. Well, money was tight and time was running out. But I still have that sense of what I might have done.

I don't know whether I'll be called upon by the new mayor. He's young and intelligent. I don't want to cramp his style or upstage him. I think maybe he's fearful that will happen. I do expect to be in touch with him when I feel something is wrong.

When I left office, I insisted that there be no farewell banquets, that nothing be named, no halls, no senior citizen homes, nothing, named for me. I'm practical enough to know that once you leave, in two weeks you're forgotten. I accept that. If anybody remembers me, fine. If not, I accept that.

John Kenneth Galbraith, 85

CAMBRIDGE, MASSACHUSETTS

Who's Who in America refers to him as a retired economist. It may be misleading: his trenchant commentary on "private affluence and public squalor" (a phrase coined in his most celebrated work, The Affluent Society, *1958) has never been more relevant.*

The only thing I fear more than anything else is having two or three vacant hours. This I can't stand. I do a lot of my reading not for the sake of information, but because it is a bridge over idleness. Idleness is the one thing I can't live with.

I've made one concession to great age: to know there are some things I can ignore. I'll leave Cambodia to somebody else. I have not yet sorted out the particular anxieties of the countries that used to be part of the Soviet Union. I'm not persuaded that I know all of Mr. Yeltsin's problems, as we speak. By the time this appears, they may appear in a very different form. These are matters which, once upon a time, would have given me quite a bad conscience.

I feel obliged to know what's happening to the economy of the United States. I feel deeply associated with the problems of Europe, Japan. I still have a strong commitment to India and the poor countries of the world.*

The Affluent Society is the book that rescued me from obscurity, in 1958. This is something that still impresses me. We have a comfortable number of Americans with a fairly high standard of private living and yet we have this ferocious resistance to things that would improve our public standard of living. As you travel around, it is this contrast that catches your attention.

We just came back this morning from Washington. It's a city of wonderful public design and public monuments. And expensive shops. Yet we can't miss the squalor with which the other half of the city lives. We have these enormously expensive television programs—nobody in the world can compete with us economically in morally depraved TV—yet we are reluctant to spend money on public schools. What I identified in 1958 as private affluence and public squalor is unfortunately true today.

I'm deeply accustomed to giving advice that is not heard. That shouldn't keep anybody from doing it, because even unwelcome advice can cause a certain amount of public annoyance. Even if you don't succeed in reform, you do succeed in making enough people

---

* He was U.S. ambassador to India from 1961 to 1963.

angry to make it worthwhile. Even if I don't expect that identifying something wrong, something insane, is a solution, I'm prepared to irritate for its own sake.

There are some things important enough to get you actively involved to stubbornly stay with it. I put in ten years of my life in organizing opposition to the Vietnam War. At first, on the inside, and then, on the outside. I first became concerned with our Indochina involvement when I was in the State Department.* It wasn't until years later that I stepped out. It was an issue so large, one had to reflect on the people who, for no good purpose, were getting killed.

In 1961, Kennedy sent me to Vietnam to report on the situation there. He knew that I didn't have an open mind in this matter, that I was already against it. The *Pentagon Papers* tells of my effort in this regard. I carried on an inside effort through the Kennedy years and into the Johnson years. In the mid-'60s, I, along with some others, realizing we weren't getting anywhere inside the administration, decided to step out and take it to the public. That broke off a lifelong friendship I had with Lyndon Johnson. He had expected his old friends to stay with him, but we felt there was a larger issue here. It's lovely to *seem* to be working from the inside, but when you're not getting anywhere, it's no longer time to simply be annoying and amusing. [*His voice assumes a sudden fervor, a tone of indignation.*] I still feel very strongly about that issue.

I felt the same way about the great myth in World War II: the effectiveness of strategic bombing. I went to Europe on that investigative mission with George Ball, the day after Roosevelt died. FDR recognized the great principle that air generals were not inclined to minimize their accomplishments. That was the most wonderfully controversial thing I've ever been associated with.

We discovered on the survey that U.S. strategic bombing of German industry had not seriously damaged their war effort. Many lives were devoted and lost to the bombing of German industry. But the war was still won on the ground and by tactical air forces. This came as a major shock to the air force. I enjoyed every moment of it.

It happened in Korea, too. We had full control of the air, but we still had to fight it on the ground. We saw it again in Vietnam. We had full control of air, and we still lost it on the ground. You were challenging an accepted doctrine, and the responding anger, I must confess, I found delightful.

You not only enjoy the challenge, but there's something spiritually rewarding. There is something personally satisfying about being disagreeable by advancing the truth. One of the advantages of

---

* In 1946 he was the director of the Office of Economic Security.

old age is that you can't be dismissed as a young squirt. You can be dismissed as well by being called a nice old boy, but you can't be dismissed when you're regarded as a nasty old boy.

I particularly enjoyed attacking big government—in a discriminating way—during the Reagan years. My old friend Ronald Reagan and I were fellow founders of Americans for Democratic Action, an undeniably liberal bunch. He became the greatest proponent of big government that we ever had. He oversaw the enormous expansion of the peacetime military establishment, which for some reason is exempt from the charge of being governmental. "Big government" is anything—except the military. In those years, I enjoyed attacking big government by pointing out that the military had become our leading example of it.

When it came to a whole range of matters, from social security to housing, from education to aid to states and cities, government was the instrument of civilization. The common charge of "big government" comes largely from people who are looking for a moral reason to avoid taxes.

There's an irony to all this. One of the reasons that liberals in our time have been reduced in power and, in some degree, marginalized, is that government, through social security, through public services, through one benefit or another, has made a very large number of people comfortable, happy, and conservative. When we look at the great authority, the great power of conservatives in our day, those of us who still call ourselves liberal must say we did it to ourselves.

Senator Robert Dole, a charming and intelligent man, is conducting a crusade against big government. Bob Dole of Kansas would not be in office today if weren't for our farm program and agricultural price supports. Whenever he attacks government, perhaps someone should suggest he further his case by enthusiastically opposing support prices for wheat. Reagan's hometown, Dixon, Illinois, was saved by the New Deal. More people should know about our history.

My generation was the first to get the picture of the affirmative role of government. In the autumn of 1934, I was moving from Berkeley to Harvard. I stopped off in Washington. It was a wonderful moment in history. Because I was an economist, and there was a great shortage of us, I was put on the payroll the next day. In those easygoing days, nobody asked if I was a citizen. I wasn't. I was a Canadian. I wasn't even a voter, but they felt I, along with many other young people, could be of some use.

These were the most depressing times economically. Long bread lines, total despair, a devastated South, destitute farmers. Even the conservative American Farm Bureau Federation said the farmers were on the verge of revolt. Militant farm groups were springing up everywhere. The government stepped in. One is always influenced by one's own experience. Even since then, I've had no doubts that government can play a strongly affirmative role in our lives.

In the spring of 1941, I was put in charge of organizing wartime price controls. There had been a huge increase in prices during World War I—a doubling—that left us with fear of inflation. I was there until the middle of 1943. It was a watershed in my life. I went in as a young, unknown economist and came out of it with a national reputation, for good or evil.

Unlike World War I and Vietnam, there is no memory of inflation associated with World War II. Price controls always showed huge public support. There was a strong objection to people who tried to circumvent controls. There was a black market, but it was small. There was a great deal of obliquy attached to illegal behavior. We greatly feared we'd hold prices and see a decline in quality. It didn't happen. Another thing was the mood of the country. The war, unlike Vietnam, had almost unanimous support from the people. There was a great horizontal expansion in production, but little vertical increase in prices. It was simply the result of a strong government policy of price control.

Would this work today? With the Cold War ended and the Soviet Union dissolved, aren't the free market advocates triumphant?

I don't think so. I don't see the free market evangelists as dominant in our time. It is simply headline stuff with a certain simple appeal. What we will be seeing is the triumph of a mixed economy. It's the only way: an admixture of public effort and market response. It is neither a free economy nor socialism: it is a fusion of the state and the market. There is a large affirmative role for the state as opposed to the luxurious levels of private consumption.

I see these countries that once had comprehensive socialism making their way back to a mixed economy, not to capitalism. To talk of a free market without restraint is nonsense. Nobody doubts that the market can produce good restaurants and good clothing and good entertainment, but where is the role for social welfare? For housing? For education? We would be in terrible shape, far worse than could be imagined, if we didn't have a public sector.

There is an easy, short-run view taken by a large part of our community, a dim view of the urgency of those who depend on the public sector. You find enormous newspaper lineage devoted to crime in the cities. If you're comfortably well-off, you can have security guards, who now outnumber policemen in the aggregate. Or you can move to peaceful suburbs. So it is possible for the comfortable to contract out of the social order.

The rest of us, I hope, are left with a strong desire to see a better balance between our social responsibility and our private consumption. And I'm going to continue to talk about that. In a democratic society, there's no alternative to public persuasion. Even if you don't persuade, you can at least annoy. I still subscribe to the old *St. Louis Post-Dispatch* credo: "Comfort the afflicted and afflict the comfortable."

Fantasy: At eighty-five, you are elected president of the United States...

Since I was born in Canada, there would have to be a constitutional revision to allow me to become president. I'm in favor of that. My fantasy would be twofold: One, the prospect that the next generation will move on to the same sort of enjoyments that you and I have. Two, to help the poor people of the world achieve some form of tolerable living. I assume you'll vote for me.

Postscript: Kitty, his wife, was sitting by, quietly listening. In response to the question "How long will your husband continue in this spirit?," she answered with a laugh: "Indefinitely."

Judge Abraham Lincoln Marovitz, 88

CHICAGO, ILLINOIS

He is senior judge of the U.S. district courts. His current duties are ceremonial in nature: swearing in new citizens and conducting marriages. "I have performed over five hundred marriages for friends of mine. I swore in the late Mayor Daley, first, as county clerk in 1950, and then six times as mayor. I swore in young Mayor Daley, and, God willing, may swear him in again." On occasion, at the request of a colleague, he presides over nonjury trials.

He is the most durable of the city's figures, celebrated, aside from his judicial life, for his friendships with celebrities in politics and entertainment.

As you walk through the corridor leading to his chambers, you encounter Abraham Lincoln in varied phases of his life: Young Mr. Lincoln on a horse; the woodchopper; the presidential Lincoln conferring with General Grant; the contemplative president; the statesman enthroned in the Lincoln Memorial.

"When my mother came to this country, she heard a lecture on Lincoln. She saw his picture with a beard. His name was Abraham, father of the flock. He was shot in the temple, the man said. She thought that meant the synagogue, so she vowed to name one of her sons after the great Jew, Abraham Lincoln."

On the walls of his chambers is an awesome gallery of photographs, all inscribed, ranging from Harry Truman to Frank Sinatra, from Bishop Sheen to Jimmy Durante, and a plenitude of plaques, awards, facsimiles of editorials, and other encomia. The centerpiece is a double portrait of his mother and father.

Several weeks ago, at the Kent College of Law, a night school he had attended long, long ago, the Abraham Lincoln Marovitz Courtroom was dedicated. In his keynote speech, Justice John Paul Stevens of the U.S. Supreme Court said, "I have always been impressed by my good friend's uncanny ability to settle cases. He has been honored by both the Daughters of the American Revolution and the Independent Voters of Illinois. He could always see both sides of a difficult issue."

I've learned from that wonderful mother of mine that you've got to learn how to disagree without being disagreeable. That's held me in good stead all my life. After forty-five years on the bench, I'm still trying to settle cases. To me, it's a satisfying experience to meet people who come in here troubled and bitter and send them away shaking hands.

When I go to bed at night, I put on my pajamas, sit in my contour chairs, and take a little personal inventory. Who did I offend today? Maybe some lawyer who didn't appreciate my sense of humor. I apologize the next day on the telephone. Then I think, "Who did I help today?" Some night I can't think of a goddamn thing I did for anybody. It's like I pissed the day away.

In the old days, there was a better rapport between lawyers and antagonists. When I was an assistant state's attorney, I could vigorously prosecute my case against a guy I knew very well, but I never personalized it. In my court, I don't think 5 percent of the cases went to trial. I would say to a litigant, "This is what I would do if I were in your place." I don't ask anybody to do something I wouldn't do myself. While I wasn't too smart, I was streetwise.

I was thirteen when I was hired for an after-school job at a fancy haberdashery downtown, at three dollars a week. When I reported for work on Monday, the nice little woman who hired me said, "What is your religion?" When I told her, she said, "I'm awfully sorry. I don't make rules here, but we don't employ Jewish people." I wanted to break every window in the place. For a lousy three dollars a week!

During high school I worked for Western Union, delivering wires on roller skates. Four to twelve, six days a week, every other Sunday. A kid gave me a ticket to see Al Jolson, who was playing in town, but it was on the Sunday I was supposed to work. The boss said okay, I could work on Saturday, and then changed his mind. I said, "I quit." He said, "You're fired."

I got a job as office boy at this wonderful old law firm at $10 a week. I had just finished high school. My boss suggested I attend Kent for law school. In those days, all you needed was a high school diploma. The tuition was $120 a year. I didn't have 120 cents. He made out a personal check to Kent and raised my salary to $12. I was to pay him back at $2 a week, but he never got around to collecting it. I got my law degree in 1925. I was nineteen.

I had to wait two years to take the bar. This is no con: I don't know how the hell I passed it. They had all these Phi Beta Kappas and Coifs, the type of kids who, years later, worked for me as law clerks. When I passed the bar, all the stenographers at the firm wrote this thing for me:

> Out of an internationally known firm of legal lights,
> Arose a lad, a lad of wills minus mights.
> Through hours of strenuous study he passed the bar,
> Let's pray no misdemeanors his reputation will mar.
> Here's hoping to M, M, A & P's mailing list*

---

* Mayer, Meyer, Austrian and Platt.

Will some day be added Abe Marovitz.
Let superior and federal courts beware
When attorney A. L. Marovitz takes to the air.
And let all lawyers pray and hide their clients.

As soon as I joined the firm, my boss would always introduce me to anybody who came in, "Meet my little friend, Abe." I was a ghetto exhibit. He was general counsel for the Democratic Party and personal attorney for the Republican state's attorney, Bob Crowe.*

In 1927, he invited me to sit with him and Governor Al Smith at the Dempsey-Tunney fight. I had just gotten my license. When we came back to the office, he asked me if I'd like to be assistant state's attorney. I said I'd love it. It was $203 a month. I called up my mother, who had just gotten a telephone in her little candy store. "Ma, we're rich!" My new job pays me fifty dollars a week!" In my neighborhood, you'd have to be a thief or a bootlegger to make that kind of money.

I was the youngest assistant state's attorney ever appointed. I was twenty-one. I served for six years. I was fired because I sent a hoodlum to jail and I wasn't supposed to do it.

I was prosecuting Teets Battaglia, a young mob member who shot a copper named Marty Joyce. I sent him to the penitentiary. I didn't know the fix was in. John Swanson, the Reform candidate who beat Crowe in the election, was the new state's attorney. The mob had him in their pocket in six months. A special delivery letter from Swanson was waiting for me at home. I was fired. It was my birthday. What a present. I thought it was the end of the world for me.

I decided to open up my own law firm as a criminal lawyer. My boss, my guardian angel, gave me a piece of advice which I've never forgotten. He said, "Abe, you be a high-priced, high-class criminal lawyer. Don't ever meet your clients in bookie joints, nightclubs, or hotel rooms. Meet 'em in your office." I made more money in four months than I thought I'd ever make in all of my life.

I'm sure some of the mob boys were your clients...?

I represented Murray Humphrey.† One of the worst was the guy who shook down the movie industry.

How come you never were contaminated?

---

* Robert E. Crowe had been the chief prosecutor of the Leopold and Loeb case. The defense attorney was Clarence Darrow. It was the case of two young members of Chicago's affluent community who, for a thrill, killed a boy of an equally prominent family. It was the cause célèbre of the early '20s.

† A mob big shot, nicknamed "the Camel" by the late Chicago police reporter Ray Brennan.

I remember what my mother said to my brothers and me from the time we were kids: "You're leaving here with your self-respect. Make sure you come home with it." Money was never my God. In 1949, when I was first inducted as a judge of the superior court, my pal, Joe E. Lewis* flew in for the ceremony from New York. He came in half stiff. "I suppose now that you're a judge, you can't be going to Las Vegas and shooting a little craps with me." I was a young bachelor then, and I'm an old bachelor now. Judge Fisher got up and gave me a lecture about having more dignity now that I'm a judge. "You can't be chasing girls."

I was in private practice from 1932 to 1949. In between, I did a wartime stint in the Marine Corps. In 1938, I was elected to the state senate, where I served for twelve years. While there, my interest was in civil rights and social welfare work.†

I don't con myself. I didn't lend any genius to the bench. I don't have a college education. I'm not a great scholar. I know my limitations. Joe E. Lewis said it best. He was the first guy to take a glass of Scotch onto the nightclub floor—before my friends Sinatra and Dean Martin did. Joe would say, "I'm not a big drinker, but I put away a lot of little ones." I can't do big things. I don't have that kind of brain. What the good Lord took away up here, hopefully, he gave me a little extra in the heart department.

I was a great believer in probation when I was chief justice of the criminal court, the largest in the country. Instead of sending first offenders, especially young black lads, to some institution where they'd get sexually abused by the older guys, I'd give them another chance. There was a prosecutor who had dreams of being governor. He was determined to expose me for being too lenient. He urged my impeachment. I showed the bar association that out of the eighteen cases he cited, all first offenders, seventeen were black.

I could never try a criminal case today. The judge has so little discretion. He's bound to follow the rules that Congress has passed, many of whom have never tried a case in their lives. They tell us what kind of sentences we have to give. There are so many disproportionate sentences. There was an article in the paper today about a kid who stole a slab of ham and was given a five-year sentence, while a big shot was given probation. Thanks to the sentencing guidelines, whatever the hell they are, black kids are the ones who usually get the short end of the stick.

In '58, when I was chief justice, that governor-hopeful had three guys in the courtroom objecting to everything I did, just for the

---

* A nightclub comic, known for his raffish ways as well as for his nimble wit.

† He has received a number of awards from civil rights groups and social service agencies for legislation he sponsored.

record. He went down to the legislature and got them to pass a real Draconian law: a mandatory sentence of ten years minimum for selling narcotics, no matter what it was—marijuana, anything. Even for kids who were first offenders. The judges under my supervision went along with them. They played along with the public hysteria. The lawyers took a lot of changes of venue to my court. I'd find their clients guilty of possession. The would-be governor thought he'd outsmart me. He took the possession count on. All he indicted them for was sale. So I held, as a matter of law, that possession is inherent in the indictment: you can't sell something you don't possess. So I'd find them guilty of possession only. He was fit to be tied.

One day, the courtroom was absolutely jammed. I couldn't get through the hallway. My bailiff told me some old guy in the bullpen, who looks like he's ninety, was charged with killing his wife. Some neighborhood lawyer he had hired pled him guilty of murder. I called the family up front and told everybody else to stay the hell out of the way.

The son says, "My dad is the finest man who ever lived. My mother was incurably ill of cancer. She used to plead with us and the doctor to put her out of her misery. My dad would work all day and stay up with her all night. Finally, he smothered her and took enough pills to kill himself. My sister and I rushed him to the hospital and saved his life. Could you show some mercy?"

I ordered a presentence investigation and found out the guy had a wonderful work record and everybody spoke highly of him. The old, white-bearded German doctor testified that she had about a month to live and was suffering terribly. So I just turned to the lawyer and said, "Withdraw his plea of guilty, sign a jury waiver, and I'll make whatever decision I think is fair." You know that no jury in the world would find this man guilty of murder. In those days, the state's attorney had a right to ask for a jury. One of the three young prosecutors was the would-be governor's errand boy. He refused to waive. The other two were more intelligent. They signed jury waivers. I found him not guilty, of course. It made headline news. The same happened with those seventeen black kids I put on probation. The papers weren't too kind.

Back in the '50s, during McCarthy time, you appeared at a ceremony honoring a woman named Pearl Hart. She was notorious in conservative circles for having taken unpopular stands on many issues of the day—for example, the Red Scare. I was astonished to see you striding down the aisle, mounting the platform, and paying her tribute.

I remembered her as a good public defender in the days when I was a young assistant state's attorney. She was a kind person who salvaged kids. Many public defenders were incompetent political appointees. She was different. Where, in a serious crime, I thought a kid might need serious counseling, I'd suggested Pearl because I had a lot of respect for her. I may not have subscribed to her beliefs, whether they were considered Communist or not, but I knew her as a kind, gentle woman who reached out to these lost kids. I didn't care what her label was.

I remember this FBI guy who was investigating me when I was up for federal judgeship. This was years later. He was asking me about a lot of things. About going to nightclubs...He had to make a character report on me. I was active in the National Lawyers Guild, which was supposed to have some Communist influences. I may have had some leftist ideas myself. I've always considered myself a liberal-thinking guy. He asked me about that association. I told him that I have no apologies for that. I may not agree with everything they may say, but I have a strong feeling for individual rights and the right to say your piece. Then he asked me about Pearl Bailey, and my speaking—

Pearl Hart.

Pearl Hart. Pearl Bailey is my friend, too. I've got a picture of her right up there. See it? I said to the guy, "I don't know if Pearl Hart is a member of the Party. She may have sympathies that way, but I know she's a very decent woman. She's befriended a lot of kids who didn't have a friend in the world, and made a difference in their lives.

I sent away for a copy of my file under the Freedom of Information Act. A lot of it was deleted, blacked out. I have to tell you honestly that a lot of guys in my office didn't share my feelings about her. It never deterred me from showing my affection for her. At the little restaurant across from the old Criminal Court Building, I'd buy her a cup of coffee, she'd buy me one. Things were more personal in those days.

I always do things on a very personal basis. I remember testifying for Joe Fusco, who was a bootlegger during the war. He belonged to the so-called mob, but he wasn't a pistol-carrying guy. He was going in business with a nice, charitable guy in this town, forming a liquor company. He'd give me a check for the Boys' Club or whatever I was interested in. The liquor commission didn't want to give him a license because of his associations. I testified on his behalf. So did Bishop Sheen. I told the judge that I had represented him at one time and knew he was a bootlegger. But he didn't shoot or muscle anybody. What he did was illegal, like gambling. I have no apologies to make for that. I said to the judge, "If you're looking for a gelding, you got the wrong guy. I've done a lot of things that may be unorthodox, but no one's ever questioned my integrity.

Maybe I judge people differently than most people do. I'd like to know what they are on the inside. I'm sure there are a few skeletons in my closet. [*He indicates a brass bust of Lincoln on the nearby pedestal.*] That was sent to me by a black man I sent to the penitentiary for life. He shot a policeman. During the trial, he made an etching of me, while I thought he was just making notes to his lawyer. As I sentenced him, I said, "You've got a lot of talent. Maybe some day, if you let time serve you instead of just serving time…About seven years later, his sister asked me if I could get a stand for him at the Hyde Park Art Fair, to sell some of his pictures.

My mother's favorite poem ends something like this: "As you close your eyes and slumber tonight, do you think a guy will say/ You've earned one more tomorrow by something you did today?" Between you and me, I'm trying to get my house in order, so when I kick the bucket, I'll have everything filed: for Kent College, the Public Library, and the Chicago Historical Society.

Leon "Len" Despres, 85
Chicago, Illinois

"I'm a lawyer and we have a small office, four of us. As an indepen-
dent practitioner, I don't have to retire. Nobody is compelling me to
follow the rules of the house, so I'm actively practicing law. I engage
in other activities, too, but law is my profession. I'm at it all day
long. That's my work, and that's what drives me."

I was elected to the Chicago City Council as alderman of the Fifth
Ward. It was the same day that Mayor Daley, the father, was elected
mayor in 1955. I remained an alderman for twenty years, while
Daley was mayor. I retired in '75 and he died a year later. My career
in the city council was virtually identical to his.

He was somewhat unsure of himself at the beginning and
retained some vestiges of modesty, but after a while he became very
authoritarian, completely satisfied that his judgment was correct. It
became a problem to push measures that he didn't rubber stamp
with his approval.

When I entered the council, there were seven aldermen who were
not Daley creatures. Some were Republican, I was an independent.
At the next election, there were only three of us. In certain issues,
during those following years, I was the lone voice. You couldn't get
Republicans interested in the matter of racial equality. During my
third year-long term, help came from some very good black aldermen and a couple of good white ones.

Were there attempts to humiliate me? [*Amused*] I should say
there were. I was attacked with the utmost vituperation. Daley, as
mayor and party chairman, told every alderman under his domina-
tion what to do. He simply assigned certain ones to go after me.
When I raised the issue of anti–African American policies, he would
assign the African Americans he owned to attack me. To show their
loyalty to him, they really poured it on. It was really something. I
just let them go ahead, I never tried to argue—there was no point to
it. I simply went ahead and pursued the policy I had in mind. The
worse the attacks on me, the greater my support on the outside.

The city council rules limited your speaking time to ten minutes. I
never got close to ten. If I introduced a controversial measure, my
time would expire in less than two minutes. Daley would simply signal an alderman, usually his floor leader, to step up behind me and
say, "Point of order." Immediately, the mayor would cut off my
microphone. So I had to learn to make my point in a minute or a

minute and a half. An involuntary sound bite. It was marvelous training.

My ward included Hyde Park, which had a long tradition of liberalism, and Woodlawn, which was almost entirely black. One of my predecessors was Paul Douglas, the United States senator. The University of Chicago administration never took part in my campaigns, but the faculty, for the most part, provided great support.

The support of the African Americans was harder to earn. I had a good civil rights record from the very beginning. I'd marched, I had picketed, had a perfect record on paper, but a white person has to prove himself or herself by actions. By my second term, after demonstrating I could take the fire, I got wonderful African American support.

The press was really my salvation, because the reporters were friendly to me. They saw what was happening and were sympathetic. Daley had a publicity machine going that created the impression that he was an ideal mayor. He was very able in many ways, but the reporters saw that he was not perfect. They saw that I made points that needed to be emphasized. It took a little time to win the approval of the editorial boards, but I finally did.

In 1960, television came into the city council, and what a difference it made. People could see what was happening. I remember the first time the council hearings were on television. It was an issue about a new police superintendent. The next day, in an elevator, I heard one man say to another, "Did you see that last night? Just one man and they were all ganging up on him."

At sixty-eight, I decided not to run again. I thought twenty years as an alderman was long enough. Although there were thousands of signatures on petitions urging me to run, I thought I should carry my enthusiasm to other activities. Do I miss being an alderman? Of course. It's very exciting to be on the council floor and fight against the odds. But it was time to branch out and do battle in the private do-good sector.

I was seventy-one when Jane Byrne, who beat the machine candidate as mayor, asked me to be her parliamentarian. The assignment lasted for nine years because Harold Washington, who succeeded her as mayor, asked me to continue. I sat next to the mayor, in contrast to the old days. Byrne lacked experience and turned to me constantly for rulings. I had to be on my toes all the time.

With Jane Byrne, there was never much opposition, never any unpleasantness. I just had to keep things going. Under Harold Washington, things were much more exciting. He himself was very skilled in parliamentary law, having been in the Illinois senate and in Congress. He probably knew it better than I did. Still, he needed me because he was so preoccupied with his tasks. I had to keep things floating. He had stiff, horrendous opposition.

Oh yes. I'm still in the battle. It's part of my personality, my life. I love this city, and I resent it being kicked around by those who have clout. At this moment, I'm with a group fighting the closing of the Municipal Reference Library. It's a shameful act. The place is a gem. The current mayor has cut the budget so much that it's fatal to the library. It'll be closed, destroyed.* He supports giving seventy-five million in public funds to the Bears for a new stadium. Cutting four-hundred thousand dollars from the library budget was another matter. It's a question of priority, isn't it?

You have to be sure not to spread yourself too thin. Occasionally, people asked me to lend my name only. I can't do that. I have to be it. I'm on the boards of Friends of the Parks—we have to preserve them from destruction—and of Business and Professional People in the Public Interest. We fight for fair housing and against excessive utility rates.

For the past five years, he has headed Friends of WFMT, a fine arts radio station in Chicago which is world renowned for its programs, notably performances of the Chicago Symphony Orchestra. "Our committee has been ridiculed by the local public television station, which owns WFMT by a freak series of circumstances. Our group is composed of musicians, members of the academic community, artists, businesspeople, community groups. In our opinion, the board of the ownership has gutted the station and, in effect, almost destroyed it.

"We filed lawsuits and really engaged in a great campaign. [Chuckles.] They ignored us, though we frequently asked to appear and make our presentation. These are simply VIPs who give assent to whatever the management decides. So we just crashed a board meeting and proceeded to make our point, much to their astonishment. And mine. This was at the very end of their lunch.

"I was eighty at the time. Attempts at humiliation don't stop me. I've been thrown out of better places than that. [Laughs.] Once I was thrown out of town. I was representing a labor union in Indiana. A group of men stopped our car and told us to leave town immediately. That's the closest I've come to being ridden out of town. [Chuckles.]

I have been a lawyer now for sixty-four years and I enjoy it. I enjoy the substance, I enjoy the technique, and I even enjoy what may be humdrum to others: drafting wills, handling real estate deals—not

---

* In fact, it was subsequently closed.

the most exciting parts of law. What's remarkable is that I still attract clients.

Half my work is in labor law. We represent unions, engage in collective bargaining, reinstating improperly discharged workers, recovering pensions unjustly denied. We have some current cases aimed at forcing the state to provide better protection for tubercular persons, filing suits to compel hearings on child labor in the fast-food places. We're representing the faculty of a dental school that was closed. We only take cases that interest us.

The power elite never employed us. We never have represented anybody on the employer's side. We're always against a big utility or a big harvester company, or a big union, too. [*Laughs.*]

The first five years of my practice I worked for a big law firm and I was miserable. I used to have nightmares that I was still working there. It was good training for me, but I found the atmosphere unpleasant.

There's been a big change in the practice of law: the size of the firms, new technology, and a decline in civility. My first job after law school, in '29, was with the second-largest law firm in Chicago. I was asked, "How do you like working in a factory?" It had thirty-two lawyers. Today it would be hardly more than a boutique. That same law firm has 250. One Chicago law firm, if you count its branches, has close to a thousand. These law firms are like big corporate businesses, and they're managed that way.

With the growth of technology, you have faxes and word processors and computers. You can marshal a huge amount of evidence, statements of witnesses, affidavits, data about prospective jurors in no time. These are advantages that smaller firms find hard to overcome.

We used to have to rely on stenographic service, drudgery, recopying of old documents. We had to have typists all day long, now we can photocopy. We have instant communication by fax or by overnight delivery. All make the practice of law much easier than it was. In that way, it's more enjoyable and far less difficult than it used to be. As for civility, I'm afraid that the traditions of courtesy and courtliness have declined. If the emphasis is so much on the business of the practice, there is no time for some of the old traditions of honor. How can you be friendly to a firm with four hundred lawyers? [*Chuckles.*] You have a brusqueness that didn't exist before.

In the big firms, there are elaborate pension and retirement arrangements as they turn the old partners out. They put them *out*—of counsel, on pension—but keep the business they attract. In the past, senior partners held on for a long time. Now these big firms with managerial techniques monitor the amount of work a lawyer does. They have nonlawyers who do this. Older partners are shunted off the pension system and come in one or two days a week.

They merge with other firms, and lawyers are detached by the dozens. We thought that Isham, Lincoln & Beale would last forever. Abe Lincoln's son was a member. They lost a major client to another firm and dissolved. It was like the Rock of Gibraltar turning into a molten mass. It was nothing. It really broke some of the old partners. I know one, a broken man.

There are firms practicing today and something will happen and they'll say, "We're closing." The office is still magnificent, but it's disappeared. That was unheard before. There were the inevitable fights in law firms, but nothing like the mergers, the sell-offs, the dissolutions that you have today.

But I do find some changes for the better. Certainly there are young people who are totally oriented to big money-making in big firms. They buck for the partner, they play political games, they kill themselves working all hours. But there are lots of young people who do work on the other side, who do pro bono work more than ever. Some of the big firms permit younger members to do this because they know if they don't, they may lose some of their most promising associates. There was very little pro bono work in the old days. When I started, if a lawyer had been interested in pro bono cases, they would have thought he was nuts.

Our firm of four is an anachronism but very enjoyable because my associates and I have established a personal reputation and we appeal to the very people who are turned away by the huge corporations. They're attracted by the feeling that they can trust us.

I feel I have much greater ability and better judgment than I ever had. I think this vitality I have is genetic. My grandfather lived to eighty-seven and his father lived to be ninety-nine. He claimed 103.

I get up weekdays at five in the morning. I dress as rapidly as I can, take the number 6 bus downtown. I take the same bus home. Often, I'm the only white. Sometimes, I'm recognized by the other passengers. I get an inordinate amount of recognition in the street from African Americans. I get it from whites, too, but not the same way. The black people remember my days on the city council. It's a very warm feeling.

I can't think of a better reward. That's what gives an excitement to my life, engaging in these struggles. It keeps you going. Remember Antaeus, the mythical figure whose strength was derived from standing on Mother Earth? Hercules beat him by holding him up in the air. If you're in touch with what is going on, feet on the earth, you do keep up your excitement much longer. I've been called a boat rocker. If a big utility that's overcharging calls me a troublemaker, that's great, isn't it? [*Laughs delightedly.*]

Do I ever think of quitting, retiring? Nooo. Yet we can't bet on mortality. I know that some day the choice will be made. I look at my old files and sometimes I prune them because if I don't, who will? I would never want to cease battling. I just have to. But I have to choose my fights, that's all. I have to feel that I'm doing things that are worthwhile and may, hopefully, have an effect. You want to have the feeling that you've accomplished something and that some things are better because you were around.

CHAPTER 16

Law and Order

Charles Lenz, 74
PITTSBURGH, PENNSYLVANIA

We're at the headquarters of the Allegheny County Homicide Division. It's a busy place; detectives wandering in and out, heading for the telephones, which ring constantly.

Above his desk are photographs of olden times; long obsolete patrol cars and paddy wagons; turn-of-the-century group portraits; and a portrait of himself in younger days.

There is an air of conviviality, verbal horseplay. The younger men good-naturedly rib him. "They say I investigated the Lincoln assassination and that I still have some of the evidence from the Crucifixion, the mallet and the nails.[Laughs.] *There is good camaraderie here.*"

He has the appearance of a benign grandfather in tip-top shape.

I went on the police force in 1950. I walked the beat in one of the real tough sections of Pittsburgh, the Hill. At that time, it was called the Boardwalk because there was more activity after midnight than during the day—bars, nightclubs. It was a mixture of black and white. I walked that beat for four, five years, and then patrolled by car. I had pretty near the whole area.

In 1956, I went to the city homicide den and been there for approximately twenty-three years. I went to Allegheny County homicide in 1979.

When I was in uniform up on the Hill and a homicide occurred, the detectives would ask for help from the people there. Your best source was the snitch, now known as an informant. I had quite a few of them, black and white. Mostly black. The detectives would come to me for information from one of my snitches. I got to like that kind of work and the next thing you know, the homicide unit asked if I'd like to come down as a plainclothes officer. So I've been homicide for about thirty-eight years.

I don't know if you'd call that a promotion. You were still getting patrolman's wages. To get a promotion, you had to be a good friend of the ward chairman. It had a lot to do with how much you contributed to political campaigns.

Back then, people knew you and respected the uniform. You got along real fine with those people. Your beat was your cup of tea. Nothing went on there that you didn't know about. When you had good rapport with people, most of them black. If a crime was committed, all I had to do was go down, get a couple of my informants and they'd say, "The person you want is so-and-so."

Every once in a while, violence would crop up. It was part of life. You didn't have the problems you have today. You never had these drive-by shootings. You never had these car-jackings. You didn't have young kids going to school with guns. They still respected their parents, who've lost control. Drugs and gangs. In '56, you had more cuttings and stabbings, as opposed to guns.

You had no trouble finding out who committed this particular crime, because people were not afraid to tell the police. They had respect for them. Now you have to go to court, and their attorneys have access to all your reports, and all your confidential informants have to spend days and hours in court and then worry about what may happen to them once they leave the protection of the police.

Back then, if the individual committed a crime, there was no problem about "I have to warn you about your rights." The Miranda decision came in the mid-'60s. That changed everything as far as police work was concerned. Back then, cases were adjudicated right at your lower courts. You didn't tie courts up with all this protection of the criminal. Either you committed it or you didn't.

Usually you had no problem. You arrested a person, said, "Did you stab him?" "Yeah, I stabbed him," or "No, I didn't stab him." There wasn't such a thing as "I got to tell you not to tell me." The Miranda decision: the protection of the so-called criminal and forgetting about the victim.

Back in the old days, you could take an individual in to the station, whether you knew for sure it was him or not, and question him. It was no problem to bring a witness, says, "Yeah, that's him," or "Nah, ain't him." You can't do that no more. You got to put him in a lineup.

It's made it tougher. You have to keep up with all the changes and the intricate parts of the law. You've got to have mandatory training now. You've got to go to academies for ethnic intimidation, being able to relate to the minorities. Back then, you'd say, "I don't want to hear it."

Ethnic intimidation just recently came into being. We're getting some of these classes in the academy: how to relate to minorities without calling them names—nigger or spic or stuff like that. I can adjust to that. What I can't adjust to is when you have a person you've arrested and you charge him with a certain crime and you have evidence pertaining to the case, including eyewitnesses, and you're getting ready to take this individual to trial, here some jail-house lawyer who has access to all the law books says, "Hey, they made an illegal arrest on you." Based on this particular law they found back in some old ancient book. That's frustrating when you have to go to court and say, "What do you mean we made an illegal arrest here? The man admitted to it." Yeah, they say, but you didn't do this, you didn't do that. Technicalities is what it amounts to.

These ethnic classes are pretty new. It's the first time I ever had it. I had no problems before. I felt people are human beings, you address them as human beings, not simply because they committed a crime. These are things I had never done before that I felt was irrational. I knew things from working in the streets. I didn't have to go through no ethnic intimidation class.

It's hard especially if you're from the old school. These youngsters nowadays, or these criminal elements, that watch TV, say, "Wait a minute, ain't you supposed to tell me that I have a right to have a lawyer, that I don't have to talk to you? I seen that on so-and-so's program." That's when it gets really frustrating. [*Laughs.*] If they watch television, particularly these gang members, they see these police stories. They watch to see what procedures the police have to go through. They pay attention to that, especially if they're gonna commit a crime. I know they watch cop shows and they learn.

We had a drive-by shooting here not too long ago. To show how smart they're getting: they took their coats and turned them wrong-side out, put their guns down their sleeves, and fired out of the sleeves through the window of the car. The shells stayed inside the sleeves. They knew that the police could confiscate the spent casings and perhaps get prints off them. Perhaps connect that with another shooting. Where'd they learn that?

Drive-by shootings just came in, and it's out of control. Particularly in minority areas. The majority of drive-by shootings are done by blacks. They care not who they hit or what damage they cause.

We just had a drive-by shooting about two weeks ago. We were out processing the scene. The individual survived, fortunately. There was a bunch of boys in the apartment where he lived. We went in and asked, "You fellows see anything?" "No, we didn't see anything." "Is this a friend of yours?" "Yeah, he's a friend of mine." I said, "Don't you know who did it?" One of them said, "Wait a minute. That's your job." That's the general attitude. These youngsters ain't no more than sixteen years old.

A lot of times I think, "Oh, the hell with it. I'm too old for this." I get thoroughly disgusted. I know this fellow that was shot knows who shot him. I know these kids know. If they don't care, why the hell should I care? I put all this time in. For what?

Yet I still get the enthusiasm if we go out on good homicide cases. At one time, I hated to get out in the middle of the night. You're awakened out of bed, it's cold, you say to yourself, "Why am I doing this? I'm able to get three pensions." But I love the work. [*Laughs.*] I've been doing it forty-four years. When you get a good homicide case, regardless—it's nice. It gets my adrenaline pumping.

What is a good homicide case?

I hate to say it, because it's that ethnic intimidation again. White murder cases, not the blacks. [*Laughs.*] It's so much more pleasant to go into a white neighborhood where you can knock on the door and people say, "Come on in." "Did you see or hear anything?" "Yes, here the other night. I heard this or that." You knock on a black person's door: "I didn't hear nothin'. I don't want no police in here. I don't want people seein' police coming in." They have to live with these people. They know that the people who've done the shooting are vicious. Their life is in jeopardy. As soon as they see a detective going into the black person's home, they say, "Uh-oh, she's talking to the police." If, twenty minutes later, we go down and grab a guy, they'll say, "I seen them police go in so-and-so's house. She had to tell them who done this job." You got to take into consideration that these people are scared. In the white, it's the opposite.

When you're talking to white people, you get more respect. They don't have to be too concerned about their life being in danger most of the time. It could be a person shot, strangled, stabbed and you have little to work on, but you interview people and eventually you might come up with a suspect. But with the others, it's harder, because it's their way of life. If you look in the statistics, you find there's more blacks killing blacks. My adrenaline doesn't pump much there.

When you knock on a black's door and say, "I have a subpoena. This individual is going to trial and you're required to be there," this puts such a fright into these people, they'll say to themselves, "Why did I ever get involved? Why did I ever talk to these people?" You can't blame them. God Almighty, some of these gangs.

Narcotics is different. They have their informants. I don't know if they have to be exposed. Ours have to be exposed in a subsequent trial.

Our narcotics people know who most of the suppliers are. Catching them is another thing. When you see a fifteen-year-old boy wearing $150 tennis shoes, designer jeans, and he has no source of income and lives in a blighted area, you've got a good idea that he's involved in some sort of drug activity.

So how do you get the informant to talk? The narcotics guy will say, "Hey, man, you're facing twenty years, but we can take care of you, lower it somewhat. Give us your supplier." So they set 'em up, make a buy, and it works out quite well.

Homicide work is still the same, but you've got to adjust to the new laws. You've got to be real careful how you prepare your cases. Make sure you're within the guidelines. If you don't, you have a ton of paperwork going down the drain.

I'm used to the old way. I'm used to saying, "Hey, you committed a crime, that's it. We're charging you with it whether you want to tell us how you did it or not." But now you've got to work until you get some sort of evidence that's going to hold up in court, before you make an arrest. You may *know* who committed the crime, but if you don't have the evidence, there's no use even taking them to court. Before, you didn't have all these guidelines to follow.

I watch these younger guys here working and I see myself in them. They still have that gung-ho attitude. They want to get going instead of taking it easy, working around, getting your evidence and things you need.

In those days, you worked your case regardless of how long it took, until you solved it. There was no such thing as you put in eight hours a day and go home. You stayed on that case. I could do twenty-four hours, go home, shave, clean up, and come back again. Maybe only sleep an hour of two. You can't do that at this present date because your mind has to be clear at all times. Because you're preparing a case for the criminal court. If you're tired, the paperwork will kill you. There's always tons of it.

I'll tell you where the new guidelines, bad as they are, make you look good. When you're sitting on that hot seat in court and testifying in front of a jury, they'll say, "He done his job." It feels good to know you prepared your case well.

I've never enjoyed homicide work so much as I have since I came to Allegheny County. The city got so bad that you no sooner finished one case, you had another one. And you're dealing with a different type of clientele: the whites. In the city, the caseloads were sixty, seventy cases. Here, the caseload is twenty-four, twenty-five. It gives you enough time to do your paperwork and prepare your case for trial.

We don't have any black homicide detectives in the county. We had four or five in the city. Very nice people to work with. There wasn't so much racial tension then. You didn't have the militants, so you had more respect.

I was fifty-nine when I left the city. I'd have had six more years to go, then I'd have had to retire. Retirement age was sixty-five. In the county, there's no retirement age. The guys here call me Pops. When we go in restaurants, they'll say, "Give my dad some prune juice and mother's oats. Make sure he's got soft scrambled eggs." I take a pretty good beating along that line, but I still have their respect.

I think my wife is getting a little concerned since these police have been getting shot at. This was unheard of ten years ago. You'd get it once in a while, but now it's getting more prevalent. I said, "Look, I was four years in the service, in combat. I've been shot at five or six times. Once, a guy missed my head by six inches—from six feet away. What's that tell you?" She said, "Somebody's looking out for you, and I keep praying for you every time I go to church. But you're not as young as you used to be and your reactions aren't as good." Ahh, my fellow colleagues will tell ya that I go right out with them and there's a few little tricks that I pass on to them.

I'm not looking forward to retirement, not really. Even when I'm on vacation, I strap my gun on and carry my handcuffs. I'm so used to it. When I walk out of the house, all the time.

At one time, I'd go home, empty my gun, put it on the shelf and leave it. Now I take that gun everywhere. Like one time I went downtown, going to a money machine. I parked across the street, I carried my gun in my belt. I walked over to the machine and just instinct told me—I seen two young kids, black, standing across the street watching me. I thought to myself, "They're going to try and take me." So I got the money and I seen them start across the street toward me, so I opened my jacket up and exposed the gun. They turned right around and took off.

I can retire any time I want to, but I enjoy this work too much. And I enjoy the fellas I work with. I look forward to coming here. Just to get out of my house. [*Laughs.*]

I cannot say I really regretted anything. I led a pretty good life. I joined the police force when you were only making twenty-eight hundred a year, and I stayed all the way through and watched it grow to a professional well-paying job. I cannot complain there.

I would like to be remembered as one of the best and longest homicide detectives in the country. And I would like to be in the Policemen's Hall of Fame as the oldest active homicide detective.

Erskine Moore, 72

CHICAGO, ILLINOIS

It is a middle-class African American community on the city's far South Side: bungalows and neatly kept front lawns. The block is something of an arbor: overhanging trees, flowered gardens, rich in greenery.

A score of family photographs adorn the living room: his wife, a public school principal; his daughter, a lawyer; his parents; old friends; and himself as a Chicago police captain. A guitar is posed on an easy chair.

He has been retired from the police force since 1983. He had become a patrolman in 1950 and rose through the ranks. He was, for a time, district commander.

"I joined the National Guard at fifteen. In those days, they didn't check. During the depression, it was a good way to make a few extra dollars. I was in for three years and was eighteen when the war broke out. I was in the old Eighth Illinois Infantry—segregated, of course. It didn't hurt our pride because this unit had a combat history second to none.

"My father, who'd been in World War I, learned to read and write in the army. My mother, who had finished eighth grade, read the stuff to him, during an extension course he took, and he committed it to memory. He was one of the most brilliant men I had ever known. He became an engineer for the Edison company.

"We were well trained and combat-ready to go overseas, but we were converted into labor units: quartermasters, truck drivers, stevedores. It wasn't until the white kids, with a few months training, came back as quadruple amputees, that we were reconverted to infantrymen. I ended up as a bayonet instructor at Camp Livingstone and was so bitter, I never went to town, not even to a dance."

He recounts his combat experiences in the Philippines and the Dutch Indies, the humiliations, his defiance, and his pride in his division's heroism. "Many of us were good athletes. I was a boxer. I hit a racist, now and then. It quieted him.

"I had been in almost six years. I was twenty-four when I got out in 1946. I had promised my father I'd go back to school and get a degree, but I loafed around with the guys and had menial jobs, waiting on tables, boiler-factory labor, and finally went to work for Edison, through my father's drag. I stayed in shape all the time."

In 1950, I took a police examination and passed. I became a patrolman and walked the beat on the West Side. It was mostly white in those days. The people were friendly. Mostly middle-class. The problem was with the hard-hat type who was barely making it. The others didn't want you around socially, but were intelligent enough not to be rude. Hell, I wasn't trying to marry the guy's daughter, just to give them service and get the hell out.

It all changed when the blacks started moving in. The working-class Italians, who had been there for years, didn't want to move, but when the panic peddlers forced them to get out, they blamed the blacks. This was before the projects sprang up. The neighborhood had mostly two-story, two-flat houses, and when the blacks came, the young whites would firebomb the homes, even with policemen watching. We had to put one man in front and one in back. My partner was a young Italian.

He told me about a sergeant's exam coming up. We studied for it together. Lo and behold, never dreaming I'd get the job, I ended up passing the exam with a relatively high score. This was in 1961.

I was assigned to the Tenth District on the South Side. It was a nice place to work because there was very little crime. It was mostly white, but as the blacks started to move east, the panic peddlers came out again, and the whites fled. I know all of them regretted it, because they left a lot of good lakefront property. But it was the thing to do. Otherwise, they'd be accused of being a lover of blacks.

My job as a patrol sergeant was to ride the car, monitor calls, see that the men responded. There were two white old-timers working for me. One was a real cutie. He'd come at me with a fake southern accent: "How y'all today?" He kept at me every day. Finally, I had enough. "You've been trying to insult me for a long time. Next time you do that, I'm going to kick your ass from here across the room." [*Assuming a whine*] "I didn't mean nothin'." I had no more problems. When I passed the lieutenant's exam, he became my sergeant. He was shady, but I always tried to keep him in front of me, because I know what he really thought.

I found out something: as a police officer, I could take abuse from some people and not get upset. Know why? The guy who was giving me a hard time knew I could end this when I got ready. Now and then, a little wild woman would scratch and push me. I'd simply grab her hand and restrain her. She expected me to do that. [*Chuckles.*]

I had just become a sergeant. It was in Englewood, which was becoming wholly black. There was a disturbance in an old-time English basement. Two white officers came with me. We heard all this screaming, "SOB" and all the four-letter words you could think of. We pushed through the door and there was a little black fellow sitting in the middle of the room, like Buddha. He's hitting the telephone and cursing a hot blue streak. He's talking to a recorded message, but he thinks somebody's listening. He's drunk as hell. He sees these two white officers and says, "Oh, y'all, boss, s'cuse me. I'm just a poor old nigger trying to make it. Forgive me." Then he sees me. "What *you* want, you? You got all that gold wrapped around your damn head. Let me hear you give an order. You Uncle Tom, SOB. If these white gentlemens told you to do something with me, you'd do it."

When we got outside, one of the officers said to me, "Aren't you mad? I was afraid for that guy for a while." I said, "No. He had three things going for him. Any one of them missing, I'd have smacked him around. He was little, no threat. He was drunk, no threat. He was black. But if any one of those elements had been missing, I'd have kicked his ass." They said nothing. [*Lets out a rich laugh.*]

In the '60s, they were trying to integrate the beaches and it became quite a problem. White kids would come out and riot, and the police let them get away with it. Finally, Jim Hackett stepped in. He had been a white naval officer who didn't have much use for blacks, but he went down the line with the law. He took no crap from anybody. "We're going to clean this up." And he did.

While working there, I met Jim Rocheford,* who was taking over the task force unit on the West Side. He had me transferred to his group. We did a good job. We worked mostly on felonies. Undercover. We used to put on old clothes, raggedy. Guys with small features would dress up as women, ready for any rapist. I used to sit down on the curb in a bum's outfit, with a wine bottle. These strong-arm guys would come up behind you, attack you, and roll you. We'd pound lumps on them and take 'em on in. We were white and black, all mixed up. We worked beautifully together.

When the captain's exam came along, I made up my mind to pass it. I spent a minimum of ten hours a day in that basement. I went from 205 pounds to 235 pounds in a month and a half, because all I was doing was eating, taking a shower, and studying. My wife would bring sandwiches down to me. Out of two hundred and some who took the test, I was number twelve or thirteen. I told my wife, "I'm not the smartest guy on this job, nor am I near to being the best police officer, but nobody is going to beat me on this examination."

After I passed, a deputy chief said, "Erskine, I'm glad you made it. They're taking care of you fellows now. They took care of the Irish first, and then a few Poles. Now it's your turn." I said, "Why, you rotten SOB, the only clout I got is between my ears." I thought the guy was going to congratulate me for my effort. I was really crushed.

As a captain, I became watch commander. There were three watches in one district. I had the day watch. The district comman-

---

* He subsequently became superintendent. "A brilliant guy."

der is in charge of the entire station. It was a quiet area—burglaries and family disturbances.

I became district commander of one of the highest-crime areas of the city. Abject poverty, narcotics, all the awful stuff. That district has a history of hustlers going back to the late 1800s. Policy played a big role. These guys were looked on as heroes. They were not like drug addicts, killing people, that sort of thing. The police treated them like they were princes, because they were paying off. So-called ministers were involved, too.

I was foolish enough to try to preach to the people about the wrongdoing. I had forgotten my attitude as a young fellow, thinking that hustling isn't bad because I know these guys personally and they're all right. All I could think about is this so-called easy money destroying the community, destroying the kids' values, making 'em think there's nothing else. Once you leave that eighteen-square block, there's a big world outside, and being a policy runner, a hustler, is not a marketable skill.

Several of these phony ministers got together because I was costing them money. They were being paid off by the gamblers, for interceding on their behalf. I was now district commander, and the white ones who preceded me all winked at this. I said, "This community can't afford these parasites."

Within a few weeks, I was called in and was told I was going back to the rank of captain, "for the good of the service." Bilandic was mayor at the time.* The crazy part of it was that *crime was going down* in the district. I assigned some of my men in plain clothes, all black guys, to work the projects. They reported directly to me. Two of the guys† had been in trouble with the administration because they were active in the Afro-American Patrolmen's League, a militant group. But they were real good policemen. The people in the projects trusted them. Within a year, they made sixty-two felony arrests and solved three murders, one of which was two years old. Finally, I integrated the unit and these guys walked through the project, getting respect. They couldn't solve all the social ills that make crime, but they were catching criminals and running them out. I thought, because of this success, it could be extended to other areas. But instead I was demoted.

It wasn't just the ministers. There was an incident. Several Afro patrolmen of the tactical unit, in plain clothes, were stopped by some white officers and a scuffle ensued. A 10-1, a riot call, was put in. I

---

* He succeeded to the mayoralty when the elder Mayor Daley died. He was defeated in the following election by Jane Byrne, who ran on an antimachine platform.

† Renault Robinson and Howard Saffold.

got a call at home about one o'clock in the morning. When I got down there, I said, "This is stupid, policemen fighting policemen." I wanted all of them to keep some self-respect, so I would talk to one group, then the other. It was the biggest mistake I made in my life. I should have brought them all in together and said, "This crap has got to stop."

Everything was going fine, I thought, until there was shouting in the lobby. A black officer had struck a white officer, who he said had done something to him. I locked up the black officer for assault. A series of lawsuits were filed. It made the papers, of course.

I was called in by Rocheford, who was now superintendent of police. "You let me down. You vacillated instead of making a strong decision." I became indignant, but he was right. "Now I've got to answer for all this." He put some stuff in the paper and said, "You're still my friend and I respect you. I think you're an excellent policeman and you'll keep your job."

But as soon as he was replaced as superintendent by O'Grady, it was open season. I was busted back to captain, "for the good of the service." The men who worked for me thought I was stupid to fight the system.

When Jane Byrne was elected mayor, she booted out O'Grady and made Joe DiLeonardi superintendent. Joe D. offered me the job as director of the Beat Representative Division. It was a community-relations type of thing. You had the rank of district commander, but you worked with civilians instead of officers. I wasn't crazy about that job. It was mostly women I dealt with. But I found out that many of them knew their stuff far better than I ever would. It was the easiest job I ever had in my life. I stayed there until I retired in 1984. That was nine years ago.

Years ago, a police officer, especially in a minority community, was looked up to because his job was a little better than the other guy's. Now, he's just another worker. You've got blacks—the advertised ones, athletes, rock stars—making millions. They are few, but they, along with the pushers and pimps, are the ones who make the headlines.

White police officers were only looked upon with respect by the poor, lower-middle-class communities. In the minds of the upper middle class and the wealthy, they were just servants whose only function was to cart away the social garbage, period.

We've always had shake-ups in the department. And when they got a little prestige, they abused it. You had white officers abusing minorities, beating the hell out of them, locking people up for no reason at all. You had black officers who were even worse. They were like overseers in the South.

But I do say that most officers I ran into, black and white, even the crazy-talkers, were professionals. Most of these men do an honest job. Who are the police? They're a cross section of our lower-middle-class society and they bring to their job what they grew up with. The intelligent ones can keep that feeling in check.

Sometimes communication is difficult between well-meaning whites and well-meaning blacks. The black will sometimes unburden himself on the white just because this person isn't listening, and accuse him with a blanket statement. The white fellow, because he feels guilty, will get overly patronized. So they can't talk to each other, and end up laying it on the line.

Young black officers today fall into two categories. The progressive young black, who has honed it and knows where he's going, makes a wonderful officer. But most of them get discouraged after a while, and if they have a better education, go into other fields. There was a time when they couldn't even make sergeant. Then you've got the slick, hip type of black kid who comes up. He's friends with the gangbangers, with the dope addicts, and may have snorted a little himself. He's deadly. He'll sell anything, including himself. Money is the only thing that means anything to him.

When I was commander of the district, I told all the young fellows, white and black, "I don't want any money, any envelopes passed in here. If I catch you, you're going to jail." We caught two of these bums and put 'em away. A bum is a bum, white or black. Thank God, we caught most of them before they even hit the street.

I think things are a little better now. Police who are brutal or dishonest stand out more now because the public is far more sophisticated than it used to be.

What makes me mad is to see some ministers, some politicians, paying tribute to gangbangers. Meet the president. Hi, hell. A guy who's been selling dope, robbing, the cock of the walk, getting fear from all the kids of the neighborhood—he has the brain of a peanut. That's why he drops out of school. He doesn't have the courage to stay and learn. He establishes his own set of values, and young kids, out of fear, follow him. Here's a guy, forty years old, with no marketable skills. How the hell is he gonna stop selling dope? No way. When I see this fool being given status, it infuriates me. Let him prove he's changed. In the Scriptures, James says, "I'll show you my faith through my works." Show me what you've done.

Because of the fear of crime, I see this country swinging all the way to the right. I see all these rotten right-wingers jumping up and yelling, "Family values." There's a truth in it. But it's the way they use it that it is phony and hypocritical.

When I was a young policemen on the West Side, fighting these gangs, the Cobras and the Vice Lords, they'd see the front end of my car and get moving because they knew I took care of business. We had the respect of most people of the community. You telling me they don't have family values?

I guess I'm becoming more of a stoic than anything else. To worry over things you have no control over causes the pain to be greater. I don't cry easily, but the things I saw…I'd drive down my district—projects, crowded, close living. I'd see young girls, fourteen, fifteen years old, on drugs, trying to pick up cars on the street. I'd have an unmarked car, I'd ride around, talk to them, let 'em out. Just to see what was on their minds. Nowhere to turn, nowhere to go. Working for slick pimps, selling out their community. Some white officer, from another neighborhood, who does not identify with you, he thinks you're not even human, thinks that's your way of life. [*Holds back a sudden sob.*] Sometimes I'd sit in my office and break out in tears, man. I couldn't take it.

Sometimes, things happen inside me, I hate to admit. There was a black woman coming in crying, distraught. A punk beat her up and car-jacked her. She was a hard-working woman. For three days I drove around with a pistol on my seat. I prayed he would car-jack me, because I would have blown his butt away. It could have been a different kid. These are the kind of things that happen to me occasionally, and I don't like that in me. This is why I sometimes think God knows who to give power to.

Since my retirement, people ask me, "Don't you miss it?" I say, "Yes, I do. I miss the aggravation, the political influence, and the B.S. that goes on." All in all, it was a good experience. It paid for my house and it made me respect people more than I used to. I'd go to community meetings with people from the projects and listen to them express themselves. Maybe they didn't speak good English, but some were absolutely brilliant. They were natural born leaders. It was really an awakening in my late age.

It took me back to the time I was in the service. I saw guys who could hardly read or write and who were so much more competent than I was in many areas. At times you get complacent and forget to respect people for what they can bring into a situation. It made me love my people much more.

There was a time I'd walk out of church when the gospel singing gets started. All that loud yelling. I didn't realize what it was doing for these people emotionally and spiritually, how they needed it. Now I can sit there and understand. It may not be good music in some cases, but I like to see people enjoy themselves and be refreshed.

I used to think this was the kind of thing that was holding us back, because I associated it with those phony preachers. I used to tell the guys, "There are five *P*s that destroyed our community, under the heading "Parasite." They are preachers, politicians, pimps, pushers, and prostitutes." Today, I would eliminate "preachers." When I referred to the phonies, I was not talking about the many who minister and lay down their lives.

Today, I'm a deacon in a Baptist church where they shout occasionally. I couldn't handle gospel singing at first. I remember when Thomas A. Dorsey started it.* I always associated it with low-down blues. But now, I see how they uplift people's spirits. It's never too late to learn, even about your own people.

My mother played a big role in whatever little knowledge I have of the Scriptures. But I'm not religious in a traditional way. It's not my main interest. I'm trying to learn, write a little, read, listen to classical music, watch a TV documentary. I can't handle talk shows or soap operas. I've lived one. I cook, drive my wife to work. My health is not great. Old men's problems. Prostate troubles. Losing weight. Trying to keep from being depressed.

My big interest is learning the guitar. I've always wanted to play an instrument. My mother wanted to give me piano lessons, but in those days, only softies played piano. So I played the bugle in the Boy Scout drum and bugle corps. I always loved music. Just this last Christmas, it happened.

I bought a cheap guitar and played a couple of chords from a book. All of a sudden, I liked it. It was for me. I found I could play ice-cream-melody-type chords—you know, the background "Blue Moon" kind of stuff. They gave me a guitar at my retirement party. Mayor Harold Washington showed up. I pick up some chord books and pluck away. After a few beers, who cares?

[*He picks up the guitar and tentatively works at it.*] I try, naturally, spirituals. [*He offers a recitative as he plucks away.*]

> Way down yonder in the middle of the field,
> Angels are working at the chariot wheels.
> I ain't particular about working at the wheel,
> But I just want to see the way that chariot feel.
> Oh, let me ride, let me ride, let me ride into Zion, O Lord.
>
> I got a mother in the holy promised land.
> I ain't gonna stop till I shake her hand.
> I ain't too particular about the shaking of her hand,
> But I just want to get into the promised land.
> Oh, let me ride, let me ride, let me ride.

* Professor Dorsey is considered the father of gospel music. Before he was "saved," he was known as Georgia Tom, accompanist of the blues singer Ma Rainey.

Alice McGrath, 76
VENTURA, CALIFORNIA

"I've hit the big seven-six. Last year, when I hit seventy-five, there was a party in my very conservative community. Everybody was there: bankers, progressives, Chicanos, old friends, the whole bunch. The newspapers were saying how wonderful I am. I've decided that forty, fifty years after you do something, you're forgiven for it."

Stylish and slim, she is in a short skirt and boots, and wears her hair in a Clara Bow bob. Her perky appearance conceals a bustling kind of efficiency. She immediately takes charge of all the necessary details. She is the classic factotum.

I've dealt myself into everything that I've ever done. About fifty-some years ago, when I was about twenty-three, I volunteered at the CIO because my ambition was to be a labor organizer. I just thought that would be a wonderful way to live my life. I had no background for it. I just invented the idea.

Suddenly I got pleurisy. It was in the days before antibiotics, when they put you in the hospital and hoped you'd live. When I got home, a CIO lawyer working on the Sleepy Lagoon case asked me to help him summarize the day's testimony. As I read it, I became so enraged, so appalled by the hatred of this judge for the defendants, his insulting of the defense attorneys, his helping the prosecutor, that I decided to go down and sit in at the trial. It was even worse than what I read.

The Sleepy Lagoon case was a famous rotten trial in Los Angeles during World War II. Twenty-two Mexican American boys were charged with conspiracy to commit murder. It was one of the most racist trials in the history of jurisprudence. I dealt myself into the defense committee.

They were charged with conspiring to start a fight at a party. They did crash it. Not unusual. In the morning, a young Mexican national was found dead. Cause of death was never established. He may have been hit by a car, fallen down and hit his head on a rock, anything. In the six-thousand pages of testimony, not one person saw any one of the twenty-two defendants near this man. Not all of them were even there.

The newspapers were sensationally racist. The Hearst press, in particular, talked of gang violence. The gangs of 1940, '41, were pussycats. They didn't have cars, they didn't have guns. But the climate was viciously anti-Mexican. They were labeled zoot-suiters, pachucos, the kids who wore drapes. Zoot suits were popular among blacks, too, and sharp kids all over. When the papers talked of pachucos, everybody knew who they meant. They'd say, "See? We never use racial slurs."

It was clear to everyone in the courthouse that they'd be convicted. The animosity on the faces of the jurors was so brazen. The defendants were crowded to one side and not allowed to talk to their lawyers. The first few weeks they couldn't get haircuts or change of clothes. The sheriff testified before the grand jury that because of their Indian heritage, "The Mexicans all fight unfair and have no respect for the sanctity of life."

Of the twenty-two, five were acquitted, five were found guilty of assault, none were found guilty of second-degree murder, and three were found guilty of first-degree murder. It didn't make any sense, because anybody who is in on a conspiracy is equally guilty.

As the defense committee was preparing an appeal to reverse the convictions, the so-called zoot-suit riots took place. They should have been called the servicemen's riots. No one knows how the first incident started. We do know that some Anglo sailors went into the barrio, the Mexican neighborhood, and tried to pick up some girls. They got into a fight. The sailors went back to their base in San Diego, a hundred miles away, and came back to Los Angeles with busloads of their buddies. They began to systematically beat up the zoot-suiters. It was Mexican neighborhoods they chose. They beat up the Chicano kids in drapes and cut their hair. The newspaper headline read: NAVY DECLARES WAR ON ZOOT-SUITERS. They showed pictures of kids having their hair forcibly cut and their clothes ripped off. This was considered by readers to be hot stuff.

So that was the climate when I was drafted as executive secretary of the Sleepy Lagoon Defense Committee. I said, "I've never done this before." Carey McWilliams, who was chairman,* said, "Now you will." So in the course of eighteen months, I acquired skills in organizing and speaking. And expressing my feelings. This was the beginning of my education.

In October 1944, the Second District Court of Appeals unanimously overturned the convictions and set aside the sentences. They found the trial unfair in every respect. Even though the defendants were vindicated, they were condemned by the press and some were marked for life. The appeals court reversal was a tiny story in the press; few read it.

---

* He had been California's Commissioner of Housing and Immigration during the administration of Governor Culbert Olson. *Factories in the Field* was his landmark book on the conditions of migrant farm workers.

Years later, Luis Valdez wrote a successful musical, Zoot Suit, *based upon the Sleepy Lagoon case. Alice was the heroine. "But I know I'm just one of many people who did that job. Never mind that 'angel of mercy' tag that someone laid on me."*

The Sleepy Lagoon case and the zoot-suit riots were the two events that most shaped my life. Carey McWilliams was my great teacher. I had always been uncomfortable in a passive role and now became convinced that activity was the answer to how one should live.

When I look back on young Alice, I'm pleased with her for what she did, but this was long enough ago. I'm such a different person now. I've gotten much more feisty as I've become older. I was uncertain then about my opinions, so I became more rigid in clinging to them. But as you grow older, the more easy you become with your opinions, the more flexible you are.

After the war, I did odd kinds of projects. I would organize a birthday party for W. E. B. Du Bois. I would organize a recall for a fascist city councilman. I would do several jobs at the same time. Even in high school I began to sense that I belonged out there, out in the world, *doing* something.

Along the line, I married, had two children, divorced, and married Tom McGrath, the poet. During the McCarthy days, he lost his job, teaching poetry at Cal State. They were rough years, but, surprisingly, it was not the '50s but the '60s that was the quietest political time in my life.

I had been working almost exclusively with issues of justice involving race. When the black people and the Chicanos were saying, "We don't need you, white lady," I said, "Okay, I won't be here." And when the children who thought burning a bank or taking off their bras was somehow going to improve the condition of the poor people of the world, I knew this was not for me. I knew enough to realize that these self-indulgent acts of anger were not the way to organize people for social justice.

The young people who went down south were really serious. Some got killed. I can't equate them with those kids in Santa Barbara burning the Bank of America. The kids who went to the South had principles, these did not. The more romantic you are, the more quickly you're disillusioned.

In the '70s came a lot of activity. The success of the play *Zoot Suit* brought out a lot of interest among the students, especially the young Chicanos. They discovered that the real Alice was alive, so I was invited to colleges and schools. I have become more active than ever. I think I've speeded up a little bit. At seventy-six, my hands are older than I am. An arthritic stiffness. But I have as much energy as ever.

In 1984, I took what I thought was a self-indulgent trip to Nicaragua. Someone said, "You don't know Nicaragua unless you go there." So I went with a group. I was appalled at the difference between what I read in our daily press and what I saw. It was really something to see what they had done in a few years, although some of what they did was incompetent—lack of experience, pressures from the U.S., all kinds of reasons. I came back saying, "Not enough people are going to Nicaragua. There is no way to convey what is happening there. You've got to be there." I said, "You need a delegations' coordinator and here I am." I began to take lots of groups down. I would call them political tourists.

I was their guide, everything. I was doing all the donkey work—getting the tickets, getting them on the bus, doing all the little things. I began to take what I called "focus interest" groups. I organized a group of doctors and took them to hospitals and clinics. I would take academics to cultural events, schools. I'd give them a dab of this, a dab of that. We'd see poets, writers, and what have you.

Aging astonishes me. I never thought I'd be so active at age seventy-six, meeting new people, having new experiences, feeling useful, and feeling lucky because of my good health. I haven't done much about watching my diet. I eat like a horse. But I feel marvelous. I like the work I do and I feel good about being an old lady.

Most of my friends are young people, that is, in their forties. The very young—unless it's in a class, a formal setting—I don't have much to say to them. I think they're frighteningly ignorant. They have no sense of history. What's worse, they don't think it matters. "Way back then" is a phrase that keeps coming up. They can't imagine fifty years ago. They can't imagine five years ago.

Language has changed. The word "liberal," when I was young, meant somebody who was scared of his shadow. Today, it means somebody of the extreme left. The *L* word of '80s is what the *C* word—*C* for Communist—was in the '50s. You talk about a "radical right" today. That's a phrase we never would have used in the '30s and '40s. "Radical" always referred to the Left beyond liberalism. We're one of the few developed countries where you can't be a declared socialist and sit down to dinner with people of substance.

For most young people I speak to, my life is a glamorous experience. They look upon my life as a performance, not as a connection. In our society these days, there are stars and bit players. If you're a bit player, you aspire to be a star, but don't really expect it to happen. But the fact is that the bit players are the mass that makes any movement go.

I think that conversation has been altered. To sit down and talk about anything that is outside your immediate concern is very rare these days. The TV sound bite pretty much sums everything up.

I happen to be having a wonderful life, but I think, for our country, it's the worst period I've ever lived through. Worse than the depression, worse than McCarthy. During the hard times of the '30s, we were poor, but there was a sense of community. The McCarthy days were terrible, but I never felt any meanness about the people I encountered. Today, we live in a mean-spirited time.

There's a rise in overt racism. People talk about undocumented immigrants as though they weren't persons. There's another word not said: "undocumented *persons*." "Illegal aliens" is the headline. The grotesque difference in the treatment of Cubans and Haitians. Cubans are accepted and given haven. Haitians are sent away. If it isn't race, what is it? Walled communities are now in fashion: Keep "them" out. We're sick and tired of the homeless, the poor, the blacks. We've done enough for them. There was a time when it was considered vulgar to be overly racist. Now it's accepted and pervasive.

So when I get mad about things and say something, it's the Sleepy Lagoon case all over again. It's Nicaragua. I connect these opposite ends of my life. People say to me, "You're doing this for reasons of your own." You bet I am. I get a kick out of what I'm doing. The juices flow. Everybody does things for reasons of their own. I make these commitments as long as my health and circumstances allow. I live a middle-class life at home. I have a nice little house on a hill, with a wonderful view of the ocean, and I'm comfortable. I learned to swim when I was sixty-five years old. I swim five nights a week at a club. After I swim, I sit in the jacuzzi and visit with the people there, none of whom are poor. When I tell them what I'm doing, they think it's just marvelous. But until I talked to them, they thought Central America was a country.

After fifty years, I've been forgiven for Sleepy Lagoon. Now, my jacuzzi friends say it was so marvelous what I did. So I tell them about our embargo against Cuba now, how we're keeping medical aid from Cuban children. They look at me blankly and say how marvelous it is to do what I'm doing.

I've been lucky, but I have regrets, of course. I don't think it's possible to be an activist and a mother and not have strong regrets. Guilt. Our society doesn't allow this. I don't know if I'd have done things any differently. Fortunately, I'm on good terms with my two children. I regret that I didn't go to college. I would have liked to do that in spite of the fact that I have met in my life some big, dumbbell Ph.D.'s.

I'm not religious. I have enough problems trying to understand things I can touch and feel and see, without trying to figure out infinity.

If I were given another shot, I think I would have become a lawyer. I don't think I was good enough in science to become a doctor. I don't have the skill to be a poet, although I've had two poems published. I know I couldn't be a ballet dancer. But I think I could have gone to law school, and the range of possibilities are just tremendous. All the way from the most selfish kind of money-grubbing lawyer to the dedicated one who works with the down-and-out. Yes, next time I'll come back as a lawyer. If it were possible to organize labor again, I might come back as a CIO organizer.

When I was very young, I had an absolutely clear idea of how I would spend my life as an old lady: I would be in an old folks' home making trouble.

Addendum: In 1994, a trial remarkably reminiscent of the Sleepy Lagoon case was conducted in Southern California. Six young Mexicans were being tried for the murder of a young white man. Their families "had migrated together—from a village of farmers and artisans transformed into a small mobile army of gardeners, janitors and housekeepers—to the affluent beachtown of San Clemente."* At the local high school, there was great resentment of the influx of their children by the progeny of their employers.

There was a confrontation after a football game, one evening in October 1993. The Anglo teenagers admitted they had driven "too fast" with their headlights off toward a gathering of their Mexican schoolmates. Reports of witnesses were confusing and highly contradictory. The sheriff admitted that the young man's death was "a fluke."

The local media, especially the Orange County Register, *carried tales of "premeditated murder." The* Los Angeles Times *reflected on the sudden deluge "of violent urban-style crime in the quiet coastal haven.*

"The defendants were arraigned for murder. The two youngest, minors, face prison terms of fifteen years to life, a statutory minimum. The two court-appointed defense attorneys inexplicably waived the right to a jury trial despite the judge's Draconic reputation. Neither could understand Spanish or directly communicate with their clients or families."

Alice McGrath sees this as a replay of the Sleepy Lagoon case. "All the fundamental elements—the grotesquely slanted press coverage, the assumption of collective guilt, the biased judge, the hysteria, is the same as in 1943." She reflects on one major difference: "The community atmosphere is far worse. It's meaner than it's ever been in my life. The anti-immigrant baiting has never been greater.

---

* From "Behind the Orange Curtain" by Mike Davis (*The Nation*, October 31, 1994).

During the Sleepy Lagoon case, the hysteria was mainly in the Hearst papers. People in general were indifferent. Today, the community is wholly caught up in this hatred and fear of Mexicans. This case has become the symbol of middle-class vengeance."

At seventy-seven, she has become an outspoken advocate of the defendants and speaks out publicly about it whenever she can.

Eldred (Bob Schneider), 80

SAN FRANCISCO, CALIFORNIA

We're at Union Station in Chicago. A few moments ago, he disembarked from the train. It is a stopover: he's returning home after a visit to the East Coast, where he had attended a reunion at Wesleyan University. He was in the class of '35.

He has long, flowing gray locks, bound in a ponytail. He constantly draws the attention of fellow passengers, without half trying.

I had first met him fifty-three years ago when he bore a resemblance to the young Robert Redford. I've subsequently run into him every ten years or so.

I was active with an antiwar society called the Livermore Action Group, in Oakland. I was the only one with an answering machine, so I became the office. If I said, "This is Bob," they wouldn't know who they were talking to because there are hundreds of Bobs. So I used my middle name, Eldred. About two years ago, I decided to make it official. All my legal stuff, my driver's license, my social security, everything, is now Eldred. Social Security couldn't handle a single name, so they called me Eldred Eldred.

Our group was concerned about the Livermore Lab making nuclear weapons. Many of the members were University of California people and were very disturbed when I got up at a meeting and suggested some civil disobedience. There had been a major civil disobedience action planned at the Diablo Canyon Nuclear plant in San Luis Obispo so we had some training in it. My little group decided to go to Livermore. They had never seen anything like it before. They kept pushing us back, we kept entering the road. Finally, we spent the night in jail at Santa Rita.

I was the only one who had been arrested before. The judge said, "If you agree not to come back for a year, I'll throw the case out of court." In deference to the others, I said okay.

When the Diablo Canyon thing came off, it was the biggest civil disobedience action in California. About nineteen hundred people were arrested. We were all bedded down in a big gymnasium. We took this occasion to sign up 250 names for the next visit to Livermore. So we did it again. They put us in circus tents as jail quarters. About fourteen hundred were arrested.

At Livermore, we blocked the road to have a real effect, not just symbolic, to stop the action. At the Trident submarine base up in Bangor, Washington, it was all symbolic. They just go over the fence and plant a tree or something. I was in favor of blocking the entrance, but I went along with the local people.

I've been arrested, oh, let's see…I stopped counting after a hundred. When I got out of the service in November 1945, I was about thirty-three. My wife was pregnant at the time, so we stayed in California and I took the job here, with the Veteran's Administration.

The VA, at the time, was in effect run by the American Legion. I had become active in the American Veteran's Committee, a progressive counterpart of the Legion. I had formed a chapter there, which didn't sit well with my boss, a fervent Legionnaire. To get rid of me, he eliminated the position. [*Chuckles.*]

I went back to school under the G.I. Bill, got teaching credentials, and had a short, brilliant career as a teacher. It was a high school in San Leandro, some history and English. The principal of the school wasn't in the war, but he prided himself on running a tight ship. I couldn't stand that, so I refused to send any of the kids to his office when they misbehaved. Of course, the students took advantage of me. My classroom was never in what we call decent order.

The principal asked me to resign and I did, since I was having marital trouble anyway. One month after I resigned, all these rough, tough, nasty kids that caused my dismissal circulated a petition and the principal asked me to come back. [*Laughs.*]

Meanwhile, I'd gotten a job that was exactly right for me at KPFA, the Pacifica station in San Francisco. I was selling subscriptions and working on a commission. Pretty soon, I was making more than the manager [*laughing*], because I did what I wanted to do, what I believed in, and was very good at it. Those three years were among the most thrilling years of my life.

I decided we ought to organize KPFA, to make it more democratic. They had a self-perpetuating board of directors. I was fired and refused to leave the premises, so they had me arrested. That was my very first arrest. I learned the technique of nonviolent resistance from KPFA. The manager who had me fired was a conscientious objector.

When I'm arrested, I don't resist in any way. I always cooperate with the police. A policeman is an ordinary guy who doesn't give a damn about the issue. He says, "If I have to carry you, I'll probably get a bad back out of it." He's right. A good friend of mine, Father Bill O'Donnell in Berkeley, sees eye to eye with me on this. We've been together a lot. He's the only person who's been arrested more times than I have. He holds the record.

At first, I'd go limp, because it delayed their doing what they wanted to do. That made good sense, but when I had a talk with a California highway patrolman and told him about an injury I'd received, he said, "How about the injuries we receive? If we carry people, we suffer—back, hernia." I can see how they feel. What began the talk was that one of the guys twisted both my arms so they were swollen from lack of circulation. I wanted to file charges, but it would be hard to prove, and if I got any money, I'd put it back in the cause anyway.

When a policeman places me under arrest, I tell him, "I'll cooperate, please don't tighten those handcuffs." Usually they're very good about it.

I'm often flat broke, but I was able to take this trip east because I won a two-thousand-dollar lawsuit against a landlord who violated the codes in refusing to provide heat. Here comes this notice of the reunion. My older brother in Florida is very sick and it may be my last chance to see him. My grandson in Connecticut has gotten married and I haven't seen his new bride. So I was able to accomplish all three missions in one shot.

At the reunion I wore a suit and tie, looked quite presentable. I have a wonderful tie that was given to me on my seventy-fifth birthday.

During this time, now, I've been soliciting signatures for Mordecai Vanunu, who has been in solitary for six and a half years in Israel. [*During our conversation, he persuaded a couple of waiting travelers to sign.*] Vanunu, an Israeli army veteran, was working in a plant that makes nuclear weapons. He didn't like the idea, so he took pictures and gave them to the London *Times*, which ran a big story. Meanwhile, the Mossad, the FBI of Israel, arranged to have him kidnapped. They had a secret trial and found him guilty of treason. He was sentenced to fifteen years of solitary confinement, of which he's served seven years.

I usually carry a placard around my neck: "Vanunu, Six and a Half Years, Solitary Prison in Israel." I wore it on the train. When anybody asks about it, I hand them a leaflet. Of the ten people I approached, eight signed it. Not a bad percentage, though not much considering the hundreds on the train. [*Laughs.*]

I decided to wear the placard at the reunion dinner. I was sitting in the very front row and all the distinguished guests on the platform saw it. They couldn't miss it. Do I dare go up on that stage and talk about Vanunu? This was my chance. When they got through with their awards, I climbed up, approached the chairwoman and said, "May I make a fifteen-second announcement?" To my astonishment, she said yes. I didn't have to grab the microphone as I once did during a Reagan speech. I was just dumbfounded.

I made a very brief announcement, as succinct as possible, about Vanunu. As I turned to leave the stage, I—on some sudden impulse—went back to the mike. I said, "You know, I didn't expect to be permitted to do this. I thought the chairwoman was going to say, 'We have the program planned. Please don't interfere.' Instead she said yes. This, to me, is an example of why this is the greatest university in the world." [*Laughs.*] Of course, I got vociferous applause. Really, in all my four years at Wesleyan, this was my greatest fulfillment.

We all sang the college song. During the next hour, more than seventy of my fellow alumni signed the petition. All through that day and the next, people would come up to me, ask me questions, and sign. I'd have gotten more, but I was off mike and it was faulty, anyway. An older man came up to me and said, "I couldn't hear very well. Tell me, was the man you talked about a Wesleyan graduate?" [*Laughs.*] My whole vision of these people changed.

You didn't demean them—

No. I didn't analyze it. It was a spontaneous act. [*As he laughs, there is a hint of a sob. He is close to tears.*] I believe with all my heart that people, I don't care who they are...

I don't know how this feeling I have came about. I had a very warm, loving mother, who had a rough time, but, it's sad to say, devoted all her life to her children. She just cradled me up to her last days.

I was born in a little town in upper New York and went to a rural, one-room school. A good woman taught all the grades. I think the Depression had a lot to do with my feeling about the system, how unworkable the damn thing is. What we had didn't make sense.

My father was a good bricklayer who was out of work for six years. His brother enticed him to go to Florida to make a fortune in the so-called land boom. When we got down, it was all over. My father didn't make a dime and had to sell his Model-T Ford to get back to Philadelphia. My mother had a tiny, little job which brought us enough to eat. My grandmother had no money, but let us live rent-free in her house.

After high school, I ran groceries for people. One of the customers was a Methodist bishop. He said he had just the college for me, Wesleyan. I'd saved enough money to get started, barely. He drove me up there and got me a job at the college store.

Then came the war. I would have been an active opponent of any war by this time, even if it seemed a good one. I'm convinced nonviolent resistance is more powerful than any other force. You need people trained in it, of course. Czechoslovakians recently performed what amounted to nonviolent resistance and took over. [*Laughs.*] I spent three weeks in Nicaragua, picking coffee. As much as I admired the Sandinistas, I think violence even for a good cause reaps violence. Although if I'd been there, I'd probably have been part of it. I can't make a judgment on it.

I was an ensign in the navy for three and a half years. A sixty-day wonder. I decided to go into torpedo boats and got a Silver Star for saving two boats that ran aground. It was at dawn and Japanese shells were falling everywhere. My executive officer was for going back and getting help, but I ignored his order because I knew we'd hit a sandbar. I was a pretty good boat handler. I was summoned for a summary court-martial for disobeying orders. But he wasn't a bad guy. All charges were dropped, and he was the one who nominated me for the Silver Star.

You're always getting in trouble, aren't you?

I don't consider it trouble. I consider it the natural order of things. The time I started a taxicab cooperative in Berkeley, I had nothing strange in mind. There was a strong cooperative movement at the time. I was straight, short hair and all the rest. I would hire anybody who could pass police permit procedure. I hired some real doozies. I had up to seven cabs. These guys said, "Let's go psychedelic." I said, "My God, what's happening here?" The stripes on the cars were of all colors, some painted very artistically. Peace symbols and everything.

It didn't prosper because the kids weren't very responsible. There was dope smoking and all that stuff. The big mistake was not getting people who believed in what I believed. I took anybody.

My domestic life is what may pass for normal these days. I've been divorced twice, have one child by my first marriage and four by the second.

My oldest daughter is my problem child. She's become involved with a religious cult called The Way. She went through Haight-Ashbury and actually wanted me to take LSD and do all that stuff. I was cool to her. I can't say I was really a decent father. I should have paid more attention to her.

I have a son who's in Argentina. He went in the Peace Corps and got interested in South America. He's married to a Scotch girl and they have three children. He's in medicine and his wife is a teacher. They get by. He respects very much what I do, but he doesn't think anything will change.

My third child is a boy who teaches school. He's a homosexual but not a prominent advocate. He looks very favorably at what I do.

My fourth is my dream child. She's an M.D. in Stamford, Connecticut. She's married to a dentist who thinks I'm just great.

They're the ones I just visited, and I'm still glowing from the royal reception.

The fifth, my oldest boy, is in computers. He and his wife are so gracious when I visit them. Except for my oldest daughter, I'd say I've done pretty well as a father. I have eight grandkids. They all seem to be proud of their hippie grandfather.

None of my kids smoke. I was once a heavy, heavy smoker. Kicking the habit was one of the biggest things in my life. I actually tried to start an organization called Smokers Anonymous.

I have good health because I believe in something and I'm active. I had a stroke about two years ago, so I cut way down on cheese and meats and am a semivegetarian.

I recently met a woman who has renewed that part of my life. I had stopped using yoga and she persuaded me to resume it. She has made it vital for me to get in better shape. She's a chiropractor. She believes in the same things I do. I had a little twist in my back. So I called her. We went out for a beer and ended up in my bed. She thinks I'm the greatest lover she ever had. She's about forty-five. She thinks she might be pregnant. The odds are, of course, against it, but I hope she is.

One of the issues I got hooked on is capital punishment. I spent a month out on San Quentin before Robert Harris was executed. He had committed a brutal murder. He was considered retarded. Alcoholic parents, regularly beaten as a kid. If society wanted to set up a system for producing a killer, they would have done exactly what they did with him.

We blocked the entrance just before he was executed, but they sent the cars around to the other entrance. Surprisingly, we were not arrested. That's the only blotch on my record. [Laughs.]

My most famous arrest was at the Chilean consulate, after Allende was killed. I went in with a list of people who had disappeared and I said I wanted to know where they were. They kicked me out. Next time, I got in through the back door and was arrested. I was taken to court, acted as my own attorney. It was great. What happened was, at the time we were picketing the consulate, an FBI man approached us. I had my tape recorder going. We were outside. We weren't blocking anything. When I was in the office, it was during office hours. The FBI man said, "I guess you guys are legal."

At the trial, they wouldn't let me use the tape recorder. But I could read what was on it. I called the FBI guy as my witness. I said, "Is this what you said?" He said yes. That was it. After he testified, he walked over to the prosecutor, I guess to apologize. [Laughs.]

I got six black people on the jury. It turned out that three of the black women were the most reactionary. [Chuckles.] But three men—one a college professor and one a bridge tender, a union man—held out for me. It was a hung jury. I had no knowledge of the law. I just reacted.

I was arrested just two weeks ago at Levi's—the jeans. Bill O'Donnell said some women are coming up from San Antonio who work at the Levi's plant. It's closing and the company's moving to Mexico. The women are protesting the loss of their jobs. Bill said, "El-dread"—he always calls me that—"do you want to come over and get arrested?" I said, "I don't *want* to get arrested, but I'm willing to risk arrest." So we sat with the women in the doorway of Levi's and were pulled in. The case is pending. I also have a court date at Livermore. On Good Friday, we were arrested there, blocking the entrance.

Let's see, I've been arrested about ten times in San Francisco, twenty times at Livermore, fifteen times at the Concord Naval Weapons Station. During the peace walk to Washington, I was arrested at Fort Ord. In Washington, I was arrested at the Pentagon. We were arrested for parading in front of the White House without a permit. A wonderful judge decided we didn't need a permit, so the rule was changed.

Many of the police in California know me. At Livermore, they say, "Hi, Eldred, how're ya doin'? What number is it? Have you broken the record yet?" [*Laughs.*] They're friendly. If we're arrested on the main highway, oh boy, the California Highway Patrol are mean—I mean, real mean. They're trained that anybody who violates the law is a bad person.

I find it easy to approach people. I was on a train to Washington to join some guys who were fasting on the Capitol steps. It was at the time Congress was debating aid to the Contras. A friend and I went on Amtrak. We asked the conductor if we could pass out leaflets. We showed it to him and promised not to disturb anyone who was reading or busy in any way. Only if someone looks at us, we'll hand him a leaflet. The conductor said it sounds okay to him.

At Salt Lake City, they changed crews. The new conductor said no soap. We told him we had clearance from the other man and persisted. He had us arrested at Helper, Idaho. They took us to a nice jail. We immediately found a woman attorney in the area who was part of the movement and a friend of the judge. He dropped the case. The police, who were nice, apologized for false arrest.

On the next train, the new conductor said, "If you pass around that stuff, we'll put you off and you'll never ride Amtrak again." We wanted to get to Washington, so we said okay. I don't believe in getting arrested for something meaningless. Three hours later, another conductor came up to us and said, "I apologize. I happen to know the attorney who took your case. I'm for you, and if you want to pass out leaflets, it's okay with me."

You know what all this tells me? There's no rule of thumb when it comes to the American people. They're really great, if they get the chance. If they hear the side they never get to hear. Right now, they're living in a dream world. They don't know what's going on.

Coming back from Washington, there was a whole bunch of high school kids who'd been on a tour of Congress. I had put on the Vanunu sign. Out of about a hundred, two kids came up to ask about it. The girl I said, "There's somebody else who would like to see your leaflet. May I show it to them?" Even this one kid makes what I do worthwhile. If Vanunu knows that somebody like me is working for him and he feels better, if that's the only purpose, it's worth it.

There's another group of young people who have a spirit of openness. About 90 percent of that Livermore Action Group were under thirty. Maybe they're a minority, but there they are.

Ever hear of a group called Elders for Survival? I belong to that. Thirty of us went to Nicaragua. They're active in the capital punishment fight, stopping nukes, environment. I think this kind of activity prolongs their lives. It's helped me, I know. When people ask me what my job is, I say, "I'm a social engineer, self-employed." Does this stuff give me hope? Absolutely.

CHAPTER SEVENTEEN

Whistle Blowers

Admiral Gene LaRocque, 74
WASHINGTON, D.C.

A retired rear admiral of the U.S. Navy, he is director of the Center for Defense Information. "We keep an eye on Pentagon spending. We're a group of retired military officers, trying to hold down the growing influence of the military and industry, so that citizens can have a bigger say.

"We collect information, we analyze it, we publish it. We aim it toward Congress and other decision makers: preachers, teachers, journalists. I have a council of over one hundred senior military officers. At least five hundred other retired officers support the center.

"We're respected because we don't resort to ad hominem attacks. We raise money from small foundations and individuals. We take no government money, no military-industrial money. So we're free to do as we think best. The Pentagon, generally, is unhappy with us because we tend to challenge what they're doing."

He had worked in the Pentagon and lectured in the war colleges. "At one time, I was assistant director for strategic plans, the best damn job you can get. I could have done anything from then on—three stars, four stars. I'm surprised they made me an admiral. I didn't want to be one."

I loved the navy. I still do. It's a chance for adventure, and you persuade yourself that you're doing something good for the nation. I love to command ships, or any unit. I've been in charge of things all my life. I was in charge of the altar boys when I was ten years old. I was in charge of a Scout group in town. I was commander of my first ship when I was twenty-seven.

It had 180 men on it—a destroyer escort, the USS *Solar*, which blew up and sank. After a court inquiry by the navy, I was congratulated on the way I handled the incident. They assigned me to command a brand new ship in the Pacific, the USS *Major*. From then on, I was always in command of ships.

I've been a war planner much of my life. After seven years in war colleges, I was with the Joint Chiefs of Staff in the Pentagon for another seven. The more I studied war, the more I became convinced it was a very stupid way for human beings to settle differences.

What we've developed in my lifetime is a form of sophisticated savagery. We now kill people without ever seeing them, so we never hear the groans and the shrieks, the horrible sounds that occur on the battlefield. It is killing done by remote control. This, I suggest, is very dangerous for us, because it has become that easy to snuff out life and not realize what you're doing. This nation, or any nation, can fall into the easy trap of killing people without due cause.

On the battlefield, you shoot the other fellow or he shoots you. The soldier is trapped in the course of saving his own life. Now you push a button thousands of miles away, send in cruise missiles or ICBMs, or hundreds of rockets at one time, or drop bombs from planes. Since it's all done by remote control, there's no feeling of remorse.

We went off to Iraq and killed lots of people over there, lots of men, women, children. We don't know exactly how many thousands. It did not affect us in any way because we didn't see any of the killing. The same thing was true in Panama. There's not an American I know that has any idea how many Panamanians we killed. The same things was true with Grenada. We just went in and didn't even ask how many people we killed. The Pentagon controls the news. Then we come home in triumph.

Considering your honorable often-decorated naval career, what caused these disturbing reflections?

There were several factors. One was the military-industrial complex Eisenhower warned us about. The other was my concern about nuclear war. The actual precipitant was my inability to command the situation in Vietnam. I initially supported that war because my government said we should be in it. I volunteered to go while I was captain of a guided-missile cruiser. I was forty-five. Instead of sending me to Vietnam, they promoted me to admiral. A few years later, I was put in charge of a group of admirals and generals to decide what we should do in Vietnam. It was 1968.

I became convinced after my visit to Vietnam, meeting with all the people, watching the horror, studying the war, that there was nothing we could do except pull out. For about four years, I did my best to persuade the Pentagon and our government, then under

Richard Nixon, to stop the war. Frustrated, feeling I could influence no one, I set out to form the Center for Defense Information.

I was still gung-ho until I was forty-five. It was then I became a dissenter. A journalist once asked me how I became an admiral. I said, "It's very simple. I did everything my bosses asked me to do." Then I began to realize that a lot of things our government was doing were not acceptable. I think it's tragic for people to grow older and not be willing to challenge whatever it is that's happening.

I've traveled a good bit around the world, and I've learned that every country has something special, whether it's their mountains or their rivers or their economic system or their health care. They all see themselves as the center of the universe. I've been to about 110 countries and I've learned something from every one. I realize that the United States is very provincial.

As you grow a little older, you have the opportunity to read more, to learn more about the history of people on this planet and to recognize that we're just passing through a phase. And that this is an opportunity to make life better or make it worse. You can change the course of human events if you recognize that in the past it has been done by one individual or ten or a group. There's so much suffering in the world, so much inequality, so much fear. When you look at things from afar, you can see that we have plenty of food in the world, if it's distributed properly; there's plenty of air, if we don't pollute it; the streams are wonderful to use for fresh water, if we don't turn them into sewers. It takes a little maturity to put all these pieces together.

When you're young, you may be obstreperous and opposed to something about which you probably know very little. It's more of a gut reaction. As you get older, with all of your life experience, there ought to be this impetus to bring about change. Unfortunately, I find a lot of my old friends are really sticks-in-the-mud. They don't want to change anything, because it makes them feel uncomfortable. It would be easier for me, too, if I didn't take on a lot of the challenges.

On occasion, I see them, but they don't understand what I'm doing. Some of them are civil in our discourse, and some of them just plain hate my guts. They question my motivation. They figure I have something to gain from this. In a sense, I do. It's the satisfaction in seeing people's lives improve. My big goal is to avoid war. I don't care where it occurs, which parties, who starts it, but it must be avoided. It's always the small people, individuals who had nothing to do with starting the wars, who are killed and maimed and whose lives are ruined.

After every war in history, little old men have sat down at a conference and settled the issues. I'd like to see little old men, little old women, or young men and young women, sit down before we go to war and try to solve these issues.

That's why I may be soon going off to Belgrade to see those folks. They're very unpopular right now. They may be the adversaries, but those are the people with whom you want to talk and try to resolve the differences.* The Serbian ambassador was in town about a month ago and asked me to visit his country. They want their side of the story explained. He came to me because of the nature of the work I've done and, I suspect, because I've been speaking out and have not alienated many parts of the establishment. My contacts have been good with the administrations of the last twenty years, both Republican and Democrat. Perhaps they've merely tolerated me, but they've listened to what I've had to say. What I propose in many cases may be radical, but not strident. Most importantly, our center has the facts.

We're a nonprofit group of retired senior military officers who monitor military affairs all over the world. We support a strong, adequate military establishment for the defense of the United States, but discourage military intervention by our country anywhere else in the world.

We have gone everywhere in the world to fight. We're a country that was born in war, the American Revolution. We couldn't wait till 1812 to go to war against the British. We declared war against Mexico in 1846. Then we fought among ourselves for five years, the Civil War. We fought the Indians until Custer was killed at Little Big Horn. In 1898, we declared war on Spain. Then we fought in World War I, World War II, Korea, Vietnam, everywhere outside our country. With the exception of the War of 1812 and the war between the states, it's been somewhere else.

It's been a glorious adventure, fighting someplace else. With powerful forces, we always win, because we pick our adversaries carefully. We made one mistake: Vietnam. We lost. That has influenced us ever since. Still, we send our troops overseas, with flags waving, bands playing. They come back and parades take place, for those that are living. Those that are injured go to veterans' hospitals.

The horrors of war are never really told, so we keep breeding generations of new warriors. We have in the United States today twenty-nine million living veterans. We're spending thirty-five billion dollars a year for veterans. I certainly don't begrudge money for veterans, but the more we go to war, the more veterans we create, the more the cost for future generations. So, in addition to being horrible for those in battle, it's a great waste of our resources, which are not inexhaustible. We chew up oil and everything else that cannot be replaced.

---

* This conversation took place in early February 1993.

We were the only nation in World War II that survived without having our homeland attacked. After the war, the United States was booming. Germany, France, Russia, all of Europe, Japan devastated, China in a shambles. We were the big shots, the most powerful nation on earth, running the world for forty years.

The only thorn in our side was the Soviet Union. We fell into the bad habit of preparing for war again. Our whole lives were built around it. We developed this wartime economy, the military-industrial complex. We still feel comfortable going to war because it doesn't really touch us. We go to war for pride and profit and prestige. If we think we're being insulted, we use our military force to show them, as we did in Iraq. These habits have to be broken. I don't see enough support in the United States to do so.

We still have a lot of young people believing everything they're told. Just as we did in our time. We believed we were the only good nation in the world and whatever action we took was right. I lecture in colleges and high schools, and I'm astonished at the disinterest in the affairs of the world: a disinterest in anything that may relate to anybody else's future. It's unlike the situation when I was in school.

I don't want to be an old curmudgeon who suggests that us old guys had a better world. We didn't. But, each year as I lecture to five hundred high school students, the pick of the crop from all over the country, it's obvious their attention is not on anything beyond their daily personal lives.

The '60s was a healthy, cathartic time for the nation, and the young were among the most fervent. I remember a big antiwar march on Congress. It was a Saturday, and I went down there in civilian clothes. I saw Wayne Morse* marching all by himself. The young marchers were showing their respect for him by giving him room. I stepped off the curb and joined him. We went up the hill and spent some time together. It was strictly against regulations. We were not allowed to participate in any demonstrations. I was still on active duty, but it was an emotional thing. That must have been in '71, just before I retired. I retired when I was fifty-three and immediately set up the center.

I was in one or two other such marches, but I never got arrested. I counsel against being arrested. I believe in the laws, and if I don't like them, I want to change them. It's our country and Mr. Clinton works for me. He's on my payroll and I'm entitled to ask him to do things. I insist. He's also entitled to my respect as my employee.

* While serving as U.S. senator from Oregon, he was one of the only two who voted against President Johnson's Tonkin Gulf resolution. The other dissenter was Ernst Gruening, senator from Alaska. They were right. President Johnson's appeal for war powers was based on a lie.

There's a need for equilibrium in our society. Keeping the boat on a level keel. That's why I'm a little concerned about rocking the boat just for the sake of rocking it. If the boat is leaning too far one way, as ours certainly is now, let's set it right. I value balance in every aspect of our life. We have two levels at the center: retired senior officers and young analysts. I notice that the older ones, the military men, are the more revolutionary, more adventurous. Our younger people tend to follow a set pattern. It astonishes me.

When you're older, you can be just as strong and vigorous, but it's a matter of keeping in touch with the world. Many of my old colleagues concentrate on golf, have gone to retirement colonies to live. It takes an effort to stay informed.

I've just come from a trip around the world: Cambodia, Cyprus, Syria, Israel. El Salvador, climbing the mountains. I'm headed off to Okinawa on a fact-finding mission. I may be going to Iraq to find out how it is these days. One has to be willing to do things, even if the general public, at the time, feels it is not the thing to do. I've been invited to go back to Cuba, and I'm accepting. I spent an afternoon last time with Ramon Castro, Fidel's brother. He's a fine guy. I think the embargo on Cuba is atrocious. I'd lift that embargo immediately. I'm opposed to embargoes in general, because they hurt the innocent people.

No one person has influenced me in thinking the way I do. My own war experiences were enough. The seven years at the war colleges allowed me to read and study a good deal—history, biography. Colleges ought to be a place where you teach people to question rather than just learn. The war colleges, strangely enough, taught me that. And when you participate in combat, you really learn what war is about. I spent four years on the front lines in World War II. Then, the Korean War and my Vietnam experience.

I learned that much of military history is just a pack of lies. They make up stories to cover the mistakes that are made, to make their actions sound heroic. There's damn little heroism in war. It opens up your mind to question a lot of other history as well. It is, at best, an inexact science. It's storytelling.

Perhaps my parents played a role. They were rather liberal. My father was a small merchant in Kankakee, Illinois. My mother was always outspoken. We were Democrats in a town that was overwhelmingly Republican, so we were always fighting uphill. I may have had early socialist leanings, because I always felt there ought to be a better distribution of the earth's bounty.

The navy is sort of a socialist society. We have free medical care for our whole lives. The military is the beneficiary of socialized medicine. It works very well: we have wonderful doctors, wonderful hospitals. It costs the taxpayers money, but I've always felt that the whole nation should have "socialized medicine"—somewhat like the navy.

The whole issue of the military can be summed up in one word: budget. Spending. It determines the direction of this nation. If you spend money on weapons, you simply don't have it to spend on other things. If you use your resources in wasteful expenditure that produces nothing—what do tanks produce?—the nation won't be strong. A strong political, social, and economic system, as well as an adequate military, makes for the security of a nation. We try to do what's best for the country, not what's best for the military above all else.

The key time for me was '68, just before the Tet offensive. I was an assistant director of strategic plans for the navy, working with the Joint Chiefs of Staff. Mr. Nitze, the secretary of navy, called me in and said, "Mr. McNamara would like you and your generals and admirals to appraise the situation in Vietnam. We're not interested in recriminations. Just tell us what we should do." After nine months of study, examining every possible avenue, we concluded the only action to take was to pull out. There was no way to win, because we didn't know what it was we wanted to win. There was no purpose to it.

Afterward, Mr. McNamara came into my office for briefings. On occasion, he'd say, "Now that's the kind of information I need to make decisions on what to do." And then he resigned. I was told by a four-star admiral, vice-chief of naval operations, "You can keep fighting and publish this report and ruin you career." It was top secret. I had no way to break the regulations, so I didn't publish it. I decided I'd get outside and fight it. I retired and set up the center. I made contact with Ramsay Clark and others for advice. We were even going to sue the commander in chief of the Pacific for bombing Cambodia, on the basis of what we found in the Uniform Code of Military Justice. We didn't have to. The war ended.

My fervor and dissent has increased as I've gotten older. When I was younger, I tended to be almost reverential toward older people and the establishment. But as you get older, you realize that whether it be a justice of the Supreme Court or the president of the United States, he's just a human being subject to human foibles. And that we individuals can speak out. We must. After all, we pay their salaries. They're our servants.

Philip Clay Roettinger, 79

SAN MIGUEL ALLENDE, MEXICO

He is six feet five, pencil thin, vigorous, and ebullient.

He is a successful painter who lives in San Miguel Allende, in Central Mexico. His subjects are primarily Mexican country people. "I have become quite friendly with all of them." His work has been exhibited in art galleries in Texas, California, and New Mexico.

He is a member of the Association of National Security Alumni: ex-CIA operatives who are whistle blowers. "Patriotism is a strange kind of affliction. [Laughs.] I'm a patriot and I want to see my country do right. I have a great love for the Latin American people, and I hate to see them taken advantage of by my country. I'm surprised at the change in myself. It's the best 180-degree turn I ever made. It happened just about the time I was touching seventy."

As a kid, I was apolitical. My father was a county judge in a small Ohio town, north of Cincinnati. He was so honest and fair that the Republican party refused to support him for reelection. Very, very conservative. We didn't mention FDR in our house. Oh Lord, no. [*Laughs.*] Naturally, I shared his philosophy until I got away from home.

I never had any ambition. I went to college, Ohio Wesleyan, because it was the thing to do. I graduated during the depression and you took any job you could get. I was a window dresser in a department store. I pumped gas at a gas station in the black section of Cincinnati. The only white guy in the area. I was there the night Schmeling knocked out Joe Louis. They were really mad. I thought I'd never live through that night. But not a one ever threatened me. Before World War II, I took up competitive shooting with both rifle and pistol and won all sorts of trophies and medals. Actually, I held the record for the .45 pistol for a number of years. The captain of the Marine Corps pistol team took an interest in me because I was beating the marines at their own game. They brag a lot about their team. He said, "If you enlist in the marines, I'll see that you're assigned to our team. We travel to various countries." I thought this was great—my God, getting paid to shoot! So I got a commission and served all through World War II and afterward.

In 1950, just before the Korean War started, I was recruited by the CIA. My wife and I and our two kids lived in a little apartment in Alexandria, Virginia. One night, a knock came on my door. A nattily dressed fellow who looked like an FBI man said, "I'd like to come in." I said, "You'd better identify yourself." He said, "I want to discuss something with you that is very important for the security of our country." I invited him in. He was a little guy, so I thought I could handle him all right. He said, "You've been highly recommended to my organization for an operation we're planning."

"What organization are you with?"

"I can't divulge that at this point."

"What is this operation I'm supposed to help you out with?"

"Oh, we can't discuss that." [*Laughs.*] "Actually, I'd like you to come down to the office to meet my chief."

"Who's that?"

"Oh, I can't tell you his name."

This whetted my curiosity because life was pretty dull in those days. He said, "I want you to meet me at a building down at the reflecting pool of the Lincoln Memorial."

So I went down and met his chief, a very studious, professorial-looking guy in a sports jacket. He said, "You've been recommended very highly and if you're interested we can proceed with the examination of your background." He still didn't give me any name or tell me anything about it. I never did find out who he was, never saw him again.

I forgot all about it and along came the Korean War. It must have been in June of 1950, I got the word that I was cleared and to report for duty. Then I knew I was with the CIA. I'd never heard of the CIA before. I didn't know what the hell it was. I went on duty in January of '51. They found out I was pretty good at lecturing, so they put me to training young recruits for the CIA. I was put in charge of one of the branches. I got word in 1954 that we're planning to overthrow the government of Guatemala. A fellow came to my office and said, "We're planning to overthrow a government." Simple as that.

Was that the exact language used?

Oh yeah. He said, "It seems necessary, and we think you'd be a great help to us."

Did he give any reasons?

No, no, no. You didn't have to do that. [*Laughs heartily.*] I said, "That sounds interesting. I'll do it." So I transferred to the Latin American operational branch and began to study the plans. They sent me to Miami, where the headquarters of the operation was: the Marine Corps air station in Opa Locka, Florida. All highly secret. Nobody knew anything about it.

I didn't give any thought to it because they explained to me that it was a rotten government, bad, Communist influenced. I said okay. I made a couple of trips to Central America, and finally he had it all set, ready to go.

Several of us went to Tegucigalpa, Honduras, and set up a station to recruit dissident Guatemalans who had fled the country, to become a "contra" force. We didn't use the word in those days.

It all came together like clockwork. Boy, it worked fine. We had a radio station. We had aircraft that dropped leaflets over Guatemala, saying the president was a Communist, a bad guy, all that sort of thing. Actually, he was the best president they ever had or ever will have. He was legally elected.

The Guatemalans had a revolution a number of years before, had overthrown a dictator we had supported for years. Juan Jose Arevelo was their first elected president, a professor, a fine man. Then Jacobo Arbenz was elected. He's the one we overthrew. Of course we said he was a Communist. But that wasn't the problem.

He had a program of agrarian reform. He didn't have anybody he could trust to carry out these plans. The only people that had any kind of organization was the Communist party. It was small, but the guys were smart and good. They said, "Look, we're not interested in setting up a Communist government, but we know what you want to do and we'll work with you."

Arbenz had a program of land distribution. There was a tremendous amount of unused land in Guatemala. He planned to expropriate it and turn it over to the poor people, the Indians up in the mountains. The trouble is part of the land he confiscated belonged to the United Fruit Company.

Sullivan & Cromwell was the law firm that represented the United Fruit Company. Two of its big shots were John Foster Dulles and his brother, Allen. [*Laughs.*] They went to see Eisenhower. Ike was a fine man, but he wasn't very bright. They didn't tell him anything about Arbenz's land reform plans. They said he was a Communist, which he never was. Eisenhower said, "He's got to go." So that's how the thing started. [*Laughs.*]

It was a classic operation. We've never had one since that worked so well. We had psychological warfare, told a lot of lies about Arbenz, airplanes and the leaflets. We had a guy in his government who worked for us. We were paying him and gave him the idea that he would take over. He didn't. We had our own guy, Castillo Armas, a colonel in the army. We actually installed him. It was our second coup. The first was in Iran, when we overthrew Mossadegh, also legally elected. I had nothing to do with that one.

I didn't give it much thought. It wasn't a matter of overthrowing communism or anything like that. It was simply a job to do. I did the best I could and did it very well.

We had a little group in Tegucigalpa. We worked there until we got word that Guatemala requested an inspection team to go down and investigate. It was either the OAS or the U.N. I forget which. When we had word of that, we got the hell out of there. We got into our little plane and flew to Nicaragua. We finished the operation in Managua, because Somoza, the old man, would do anything we wanted.

Armas was with us in Nicaragua, sort of in hiding. I was alone in the office and this little guy, the future president, kept coming in and bothering me. "Look, I want to get going. I want to get up there." I got so damn tired of him, I said, "Go ahead." [*Laughs.*] So I was responsible for getting him up there and getting him the hell out of my office. We put him on a plane and sent him up there to become president. [*Laughs.*] It was the neatest coup we ever pulled.

The guy inside the government who betrayed Arbenz got mad when we chose Castillo Armas. He was becoming a pain in the ass. John Puerefoy, who played a major part in the operation, pulled a .45 automatic on this guy and told him, in effect, to get lost. Puerefoy wound up in the Far East. He was killed in an automobile accident when he drove his Thunderbird off a bridge or something.

Armas, the fellow we put in, was subsequently assassinated. One of his guards shot him in the back while he was at the dinner table. My friend at the embassy called up and said, "They shot our boy." [*Laughs.*] I said, "What do we do now?" He said, "Well, there's this other guy that wanted to be picked." Not the one Puerefoy pulled the gun on. Anyway, this fellow became our new boy.

When it was all over, I got a commendation and the choice to serve wherever I wanted. So I chose Mexico City. I liked it there. It was at the end of the '60s, and I was beginning to have doubts about the CIA. I could never see anything worthwhile in what we were doing. In Mexico City, we were doing some pretty absurd things.

One of the goofiest things happened when we were covering the Soviet embassy. We observed everybody that went through the door. We were going through the door. We had this photo coverage from across the street. As we were going through this enormous stack of pictures, one of the guys shouts, "Hey, here's an American!" The other guys got excited. I said, "You damn fools, that's the whiskey salesman. He comes to our embassy, too."

I began to think, "What the hell are we doing? We're in a friendly country. They do whatever we ask them. How silly can we get? I had an opportunity to go into business, so I resigned. I think they were really glad, because I was constantly being critical. As far as they were concerned, it was good riddance. [*Laughs.*]

I became quite successful in business. I built two companies. One was an arms factory. We sold to arms dealers all over Mexico. Every little town had one. When I realized that the president of Mexico was getting upset about all these guns, I swung most of the work to the other company, machining for automotive plants. It was the luckiest thing I ever did, because they closed my arms factory. The other one did very well. I sold it, made a lot of money, and decided to devote my life to my true love, painting, with my new wife. I moved to San Miguel Allende and started my career as an artist.

It was in the late '70s, early '80s, that Nicaragua began to occupy my thoughts. I was getting pretty hot and bothered. My wife said, "You really don't know what's going on there? Why don't you go down and find out?" So I went to Nicaragua without really knowing anybody.

I arrived at the airport in Managua in the middle of the night. At a little motel, I ran into a group of about six Americans on an investigative tour. None of them could speak Spanish, their translator took sick, so I volunteered. What the hell, I didn't know where I was going anyway.

We met with various people. The first was a right-winger, bitterly opposed to the Sandinistas. He gave us a whole lot of junk I'd heard so many times before when I was with the CIA. I spotted him as a phony immediately. Anyway, I was with the group for a few days. When they finished up and left, I asked the driver if he'd work for me.

I'd heard these wild tales about how you couldn't move around, because the Sandinistas tightly controlled everything. He said, "What are you talking about? You can go anyplace you want to." So we drove all around the place, the coast, swimming, and I never did see a military patrol or checkpoint. Then we drove up north and I said, "Let's go to where the Contra country is."

That's when we ran into the first checkpoint. It was a rough road going up into the mountains. There was an army officer. I said, "I guess we can't go any further." He said, "You can go, but I must warn you that there was a Contra attack there last night. They've withdrawn, but we think they're still around. Be careful." So we went ahead and visited a farm cooperative sponsored by the Sandinistas, the one that had been attacked the day before.

The Contras had burned the warehouse down to the ground, attacked the place, and killed several little kids. At that point, I'd been there for a couple of weeks and had seen enough. I said, "Rudy, get me back to Managua. I'm going to fly to Washington, D.C. I'm mad."

During the time I was in Managua, I was told about a guy, David McMichael, who'd had a background similar to mine. He had been a CIA officer, whom Reagan sent down to Latin America to document the transfer of arms from the Sandinistas to the rebels in El Salvador. McMichael found that there weren't any such transfers. The Sandinistas didn't have enough arms for themselves. When he reported this to Robert Casey, he was told that was not what the president wanted to hear. It was suggested he modify is report. He refused and quit the CIA.

I got in touch with McMichael. At first, he was suspicious of me, but he checked me out and decided I was okay. In Washington, he introduced me to Charlie Clement, one of the most wonderful human beings I've ever met. Meeting him was the turning point of my life. What was happening to me was gradual—and then, *bam*, it really changed.

Charlie was in the air force during the Vietnam War. He saw what we were doing there, and he decided he would no longer be part of it. He just quit. They got him back to the States and put him in a loony bin in San Antonio. He was given injections of all sorts, to make him "sane" again. [*Laughs.*] Maury Maverick, a San Antonio lawyer, got him out.

When Charlie was released, he decided to become a doctor. He attended medical school, got his license, worked with the farm workers in California, and then went into the mountains of El Salvador with a pack on his back. With the most primitive equipment he treated the besieged peasants, who were constantly under attack by the death squads our government supported. These people came to love this man. I was about seventy when I met him. It was the high-water mark of my life. I've never been the same.

I just got back from Guatemala the other day. I also went with an investigative group to the refugee camps in southern Mexico, where the Guatemalan Indians had fled. The horrible problem is that we supply so many arms to the government, which is run by the army. Ever since we overthrew Arbenz, they've had a military dictatorship. Many thousands of Guatemalans have been killed since then.

I addressed the students at the University of Guatemala. These kids were just open-mouthed listening to the history of their country. They didn't even know about it. They were appalled. A few knew about it, very few. The Arbenz government had been overthrown before they were born.

I'm still on the go. I went to Baghdad after we destroyed the place. I thought, my God, these people would want to shoot me. Oh no, they were some of the friendliest people I've ever met. They don't hold it against me personally, but they sure don't like Mr. Bush, I'll tell you that. In every place I've ever been, the people think Americans are wonderful, but they just can't stand our government.

The first thing I would do would be to stop all military aid to anybody. I don't believe in military assistance. I believe we should destroy our nuclear weapons and insist that everybody else do the same. Think of what we could do with all the money we've been spending on the military. Think of what we could produce for our-selves and the rest of the world.

When I was young, I never dreamed I would talk this way. Every-thing has fallen into place for me. I have one son and two daughters, and they support me 100 percent. My first wife thinks I'm crazy. That's possible, too. [*Laughs.*] My cousins and uncles think, "Oh, my God, this guy's gone 'round the bend."

One thing I know for certain: I'm going to remain active until they put me in a box. When I get home, I paint, relax more than anything else. I don't even think about departing this life. I don't give a thought to it. I don't care about being remembered, though it would be nice. [*Laughs.*] But I don't worry about it.

Stetson Kennedy, 77

BULUTHAHATCHEE, FLORIDA, NEAR JACKSONVILLE

Once upon a time, I was told about the pheasant chick that comes out of the egg, running. That's my story. I remember when I was a child my mother offered me ten cents if I could sit still in a chair for one minute. I usually didn't finish out the minute, always running from point A to point B. It's been pretty much like that my whole life.

If I had been born later on, teachers and parents would have had me on whatever that dope is for hyperactive kids. [Chuckles.] If I hadn't had nervous energy, I don't know what I would have run on. As a result, I've been working overtime on all these injustices, which are so bountiful out there. It keeps a fellow busy.

In high school, when I first started writing things about lynching, my neighbors would say, "Must you write about such things?" [*Chuckles.*] I felt I *had* to write about such things.

I was born into the Great Depression of the 1930s. That's when I came of age. Down here in the sticks, we reflected to it as "Root Hog or Die."

My father had been a farm boy, one of eleven brothers, on a cotton plantation up in Bullock County, Georgia. He had moved to Jacksonville, married my mother, and began as a retail furniture man, but he always had his roots in the soil. Wanted to go back to the soil all his life.

They were saying he was too good a man to be in the business. When people were unemployed, he would carry their accounts: a dollar down and a dollar a week. He was something of a one-man social service. A young couple, just married, would come in wanting a house full of furniture, with a dollar down as payment. He would start them off with a bed or a refrigerator or what have you. He was a good-hearted guy. He would always say such things as "No boy will ever amount to anything who doesn't carry a pocketknife."

In those days, this whole country was made up of Archie Bunkers. It wasn't just a southern thing. It was a way of looking down at not only blacks but Hispanics and Asians, and in some cases, Jews. My family was very much par for the course.

At Robert E. Lee High School, my classmates started asking, "What's got into Stet?" I never answered them back. When you ask me that question now, my response is, "Don't ask what got into me. Ask what got into white America for embracing a thing like apartheid and everything that went with it for over a hundred years." What kind of answer can you give?

I was a close friend of Richard Wright.* I spent some years with him in Paris. We were real buddies there, both southerners. He just happened to be black and I happened to be white. We didn't notice it.

Richard had just written *Black Boy*.† I said to my publisher, Doubleday, "I think I'll write a book called *White Boy*. After all, my grandfather, on the maternal side, was an officer in the Confederate Army and I had uncles who were [*sighs*] high-ranking members of the Ku Klux Klan. I once peeked into Uncle Brady's closet, and there was the rope.

It wasn't just the South. The whole of America was getting racism and, above all, antiblackism. It was in the air we breathed. It was in our mothers' milk. It wasn't just racial in those days, it was all manner of injustice. I was born into that kind of society and I didn't like the looks of it and I decided to cross swords with it.

It wasn't any one thing that set me off. When I get around to finishing my autobiography, I'm calling it *Dissident at Large*. Wherever I went in the world—I had about eight years overseas—I saw the same quantity of injustice. The nature of it changed from boundary to boundary, but the stuff is everywhere. It always bugged me and I guess it always will. So that's what I spent my life doing.

Do you think the innate decency of your old man may have played a role?

He served as chairman of the board of deacons at the First Baptist Church in Jacksonville for decades. To the best of my knowledge, he's the only Christian who really tithed. He gave one tenth of his income to the church. I suspect not a great many people have done it, though they urged it. That tells you a little something about him.

I remember sitting in my grandmother's lap when she was humming little things like, "Jeff Davis rides a big white horse, Abe Lincoln rides a mule, [*half singing*] Davis is our president, Lincoln is a fool."

I remember reading want ads in the *Florida Times Union*, voted by journalists back in the '30s as America's worst newspaper: "Neat colored girl wanted for maid. No Yankee talker need apply." [*Laughs*.] When Marian Anderson came to Jacksonville for a concert, the paper's critic started off by saying, "Marian sang well last night."

I grew up very much as a nature boy, without many neighbors, eyeballing all the rest of the swamp critters around me. My father would say I had to go to Sunday school. I'd say, "The great outdoors

---

* Novelist, short story writer, and essayist. In the 1930s, Wright's *Native Son* was the most celebrated novel by an African American. He expatriated in the '40s and lived in France until his death in 1960.

† An autobiography.

is my tabernacle." He wouldn't buy that. [*Chuckles.*] I felt like I was more a member of that society than the human.

I consider them fellow travelers on the planet. That led me to writing nature poetry and, as a child, to playing Robin Hood. We stole from the rich and gave to the poor. In junior high school, I stole green plums from the neighbors and gave them to us poor boys. I got a stomach ache from picking them too soon. At the time, I was thinking I might be a zoologist or a forest ranger.

Before long, I was keeping white rats and rabbits in cages and watched to see what overcrowding did to them in terms of emotional and physical health. Looking around me at the human society, I decided we were all pen-raised people. We were suffering from all the various neuroses and psychoses and diseases that came from overcrowding.

I can't help but feel that most of mankind's problems came when we abdicated the natural habitat and started creating our own idea of a habitat, such as inner cities, which are unfit for roaches, rats, and alley cats, much less people. My father said our problem began when we stopped getting food out of the soil and out of a brown paper bag instead. He was that kind of an agrarian, a back-to-nature man.

All schools, all institutions, all of life was totally segregated, including the etiquette of race relations. It was all dictated by written and unwritten codes. The only physical eye contact I had with blacks was at the service station or with a black yardman pushing a wheelbarrow or, if the family could afford it, a black maid who lived in the adjunct outhouse sort of thing. No black children anywhere in sight.

As soon as you could learn to read, you had to know about lynching and ethnic cleansings. You didn't have to discover these things, they were inescapable. Lynching was commonplace. Good old Florida was always neck and neck with good old Mississippi and South Carolina.

After thinking in junior high that I was going to be a zoologist, I switched signals and decided that our species is in the worst shape of all and no less an animal than the caged rabbits and rats. I'd say we're the only wild animal on the planet. I've been looking through this prism ever since.

I graduated into Roosevelt and the New Deal and was much impressed. He was the first president of whom I really had any awareness. I was working as a collector for my father's furniture accounts, visiting these poor whites and poor blacks, collecting a dollar a week. If they were spending it on something else, my orders were to go through the door and haul off the stove, even if it was hot, haul off the bed, even if it was hot with people. That was the kind of world it was.

Our economic system was as flat on its face as the former Soviet republics are today. There was great awareness of this everywhere in the country. We were taking a critical look at society. Nobody has done that since the '30s. We've had half a century go by and nobody's been that frank in looking at what's going on.

I was a student at the University of Florida in Gainsville. Like those customers at my father's store, I went ahead and got married, without a job. When I heard about the WPA Writers Project, I sent for an application. I recall question number seven: "Have you ever lived by the pen?" I said no. Otherwise, you'd have to take a pauper's oath to qualify. You had to swear you had no job, no money, no property, no prospects. I was eminently qualified on all four counts and got the job.

I was a junior interviewer, pay, $37.50 every two weeks. A black woman, Zora Neale Hurston, who came on board a year later, got the same salary. She was first class as a folklorist and anthropologist. She had studied with Franz Boas at Columbia. She had already published two books, the only published author on the project. But she was very glad to get that $37.50 every two weeks. By then, I'd become the editor of the Florida guide book* also in charge of folklore, oral history, and ethnic studies. I was, in effect, Zora's boss. I was twenty-two.

We all worked in the field, keeping good hours, often at night, jumping around. It was a natural sequel to my collecting days, seeing the poor white and black culture from the inside. I was hearing speech that was unique and on its way out. I recall one time, pre-WPA, when I was dating a girl. We pulled into a lovers' lane when she said, "I ain't never done nothin' but catch hell since I was hatched." So I said to myself I'd better stop what I'm doing and take notes. [*Laughs.*]

"We weren't really pioneering oral history in these days. We weren't sure what to call it." The seeds of Stetson Kennedy's book Palmetto Country *were planted during his WPA days. "I had collected material from black and white field workers, as well as my own findings, which had not been published." The book was part of the American Folkways series, edited by Erskine Caldwell.*

We had something called the Negro unit of the project. They, includ-

---

* The WPA (Works Progress Administration) published a guide to each state. They are still the most all-encompassing of such works, rich in state history, lore, places of interest, and means of transportation.

ing Zora Neale Hurston, were housed separately in a soup kitchen in the black ghetto. We had no physical contact whatsoever, except when they sent over a messenger boy to pick up the checks. The black unit communicated by mail. Not only did we do no office work together, but there was no traveling together. We sent Zora ahead to identify informants. I called them "ambulatory repositories," richly endowed in lore. We'd follow up with a machine and record. Once in a while, Zora and I would land together in, say, a turpentine camp.

I got the bright idea of—instead of spending all this money, eighteen cents a gallon, we'd bring Zora to Jacksonville and record that world of lore in her head. I may have the only surviving tapes of Zora's voice. She sang as well as talked.

World War II came along and I had a back injury, which kept me out of service. All my classmates were overseas. They didn't have much feeling about fascism, but they were over there fighting it. I was what they called a premature antifascist.

I established a chapter of the American Students Union on the Florida State campus. We did things like picket scrap iron shipments to Japan. We weren't coed, so we'd go all the way to Talahassee, to FSU, and get the girls to pull off their Japanese silk panties and stockings and throw them in a bonfire. On camera. [*Laughs.*]

My classmates, over there, were being shot at in a big way, so I thought the least I could do was infiltrate the Ku Klux Klan, our home-grown fascists. Everybody was talking against the Klan, from the pulpit, in editorials, but nobody had any hard evidence you could take into court. I thought, "If I don't do it, who will?"

I had been working for the CIO, writing in rank-and-file language about the poll tax and the blacks' right to vote. That took me to Atlanta. I decided to establish a separate identity. I became John Perkins. It became my nom de Klan. The Anti-Defamation League set me up with some papers as a traveling salesman selling encyclopedias.

I established contact with Eugene Talmadge, who has served as governor of Georgia. Quite racist. Somehow, I'd gotten in good with him. So I went to Birmingham and applied for a job with the *Southern Outlook*, a Klan organ.

"What kind of references? Who can speak for you?"

"Well, you might try Gene Talmadge."

To my surprise and scare, he reached for the phone and called him. I kept watching his face to see whether I should start running. He hung up, smiling. "Gene says you're all right, Perkins." From then on, Perkins was busy collecting the stuff, and Kennedy was busy making use of it.

It was difficult and dangerous. I certainly couldn't let lawmen know what I was doing. About a third of the membership at Klan headquarters were cops. You could see police uniforms and the khaki deputy clothes sticking out under the robes. Plus a number of prosecutors and judges.

The hit squad was made up entirely of five Atlanta detectives. This was during the latter half of the '40s. I immediately went to the FBI—Hoover's, of course—and told them I was inside the Klan. At the next meeting, the Grand Dragon gets up and says, "I had a little call from the FBI and they warned me that the Klan had been infiltrated and I'd better watch my step. You can't ask for better cooperation than that."

They were trying to catch me, and I was trying not to be caught. I don't know if they suspected me, but they got close enough. At one meeting, the Grand Dragon ordered the guards to lock all the doors. "Well, we finally caught the rascal. He's the bald-headed bastard right out there tonight." I looked around over my shoulder and there were about seven other bald heads in the Klavern,* besides me. It was just a bluff. He did that often.

There was a radio program called *Superman Versus the Grand Dragon* We had all the kids in America knowing all the Klan passwords. The Dragon would think up a new one and I would expose it the following week. Ridicule is a very effective weapon.

I arranged with Drew Pearson to broadcast, nationwide, every Sunday, "Minutes of the Klan's Last Meeting." I would give him the names of judges, politicians, businessmen, policemen, deputies, who had been attending the last meeting. Once broadcast, these people never showed up at a meeting again. It cut down membership and recruitment as well as attendance.

I was scared all the time. I even worried while I was asleep. It was a decade of infiltration.

I remember some union organizers getting beat up by the Klan. One guy, organizing for the textiles, Horace White, weighed about three hundred pounds. They beat the hell out of him. On his hospital bed, he said to me, "For God's sake, be careful. They're the meanest, lowest-down SOBs on the face of the earth and they'll kill you."

Eventually, I went to Governor Ellis Arnall, who had succeeded the Talmadge regime. I drafted a legal action to revoke the Klan's corporate charter. He liked the idea. The headlines in the *Atlanta Constitution* said: ARNALL DECLARES WAR ON CLAN. I was put on the Georgia Bureau of Investigation payroll for a spell. No one else on the GBI knew what was going on. Too many of them were Klansmen. We did revoke the Klan's charter. Of course, we got racist governors after Arnall and they promptly issued new charters. So that's history, and life.

---

* I.e., a local chapter of the KKK.

During my infiltration time, the Klan organized a subsidiary called the Columbians, a brown-shirt Nazi thing. The memberships were interlocking. I was the seventeenth to join the Columbians. Ralph McGill of the *Atlanta Constitution* called them the juvenile delinquents of the Klan. Their job was to use dynamite. I got enough evidence and we went to court. When Stetson Kennedy was called as a witness, the Klansmen in the courtroom jumped up and hollered, "It's Perkins!" [*Laughs.*] In the witness room, one of them pulled a knife and was going to cut my throat. One of the older Klansmen grabbed him and said, "Okay, cut his throat, but not on the fifth floor of the courthouse." That's how close I came. *

I went on a lecture tour, stayed in the Village in New York and at the Hull House in Chicago. I had become friends with Woody Guthrie, Pete Seeger, Alan Lomax, and John Henry Faulk. And the witch-hunt thing was getting pretty hot. My own track record, I'm sure, did not endear me to the FBI or "Tail Gunner" Joe.

I was speaking one time in Philadelphia, Independence Square. It was on behalf of the Hollywood Ten† and the witch hunt was at its most hysterical. The American Legion threatened to tear us apart if we spoke. The federal court, at the last minute, ruled that we had the right.

On the platform with me was Francis Fisher Kane, eighty-one years old, a Philadelphia blueblood and former U.S. district attorney. He preceded me past this mob and said we must gird up our loins and not fall back. He got hit on the head. I got hit. They wadded up newspapers, lit them into fiery cannonballs, and flung them at us. They tore the platforms out from under us and we got away in police cars. What I remember most is Francis Fisher Kane.

In 1950, Claude Pepper, who carried the ball in Congress for the New Deal, was running against George Smathers, who was a front man for the Dupont interests. Smathers called him "Red Pepper" and spread photographs of him coming out of a black church. Smathers didn't say "segregation," he said "southern tradition." He beat Pepper in the primaries.

"Decades later, Bush pointed his finger and used the 'L word.' It replaced the 'C word.'‡ It shows where we've gone. The art of prefabbing thought and defining words has rendered the American people incapable of independent thought.

"I think a lot of our trouble comes from the tyranny of words. Other

---

* Kennedy's book *Southern Exposure* recounts his experiences with the Klan.

† Ten screenwriters who were called before the House Un-American Activities Committee as "unfriendly witnesses."

‡ *L* for Liberal; *C* for Communist. Our bête noire changed with the end of the Cold War.

people with special interests are creating our concepts for us. In our corporate society, who owns the mass media? Imagine TV anchors casually referring to women, minorities, labor, old people, gays as 'special interests'! Talk about the tyranny of words. Even the use of words like 'people' and 'mankind' as distinguished from all those other living things out there gets us into a great deal of trouble. We're quite possibly not all that superior. I'll admit we're pretty bright monkeys, but even so, it seems to me that, far from having risen above the world of nature, we've fallen below it. It's the so-called 'human depravity.' Not only our physical faculties have degenerated, but our behavioral patterns are all screwed up, shot to hell.

"*It's not a question of our going back to nature, becoming feral wildmen again. It's a question of raising ourselves back. We're the ones who backslid in Mother Nature's family.*"

I announced as an independent write-in candidate in the general election against Smathers, and campaigned as a color-blind candidate on the platform of total equality. None of the Florida radio stations would carry my programs. During the last ten days of the election, the FCC made them do it.

When I went to vote in my precinct, there was a mob waiting. They'd been there all day. I don't know where they got the liquor on election day. They were armed with broken beer bottles. Two deputies pulled me out of the voting booth and hauled me off to jail. The younger deputy kept saying, "Let's take him down the back road." We finally made it to the jail.

It was only two years later that Harry Moore was killed. He was executive director of Florida's NAACP, just as Medgar Evers was, in Mississippi. It was a life-risking occupation. Moore was active in voter registration. I knew him well. When he announced my candidacy, he called a black voters meeting in Ocala. They unanimously endorsed my candidacy.

He had just registered seventy-five thousand and a substantial black vote was ready. The official report was 817 for Kennedy. [*Laughs.*] I ran into Moore later on and he winked at me. "We know better than that, don't we?"

Harry Moore continued his work. The Klan warned him many times, but it didn't work. Even his mother tried to get him to quit his job. His answer was, "All progress comes through sacrifice."

On Christmas Night, on his twenty-fifth wedding anniversary, a bomb went off in his house at ten o'clock. It turned out that the Klan had floorplans of his home. The FBI went through all the motions of investgating, but no one was ever arrested, no one indicted, no one convicted.

That was forty-two years ago. I've been intermittently on the case ever since. The reason why I was *almost* killed and he was *actually* killed is that I was white and he was black. If the shoe had been on the other foot, Harry Moore would still be on the Stetson Kennedy assassination.

I'm still trying to keep the case alive and open. I have appealed to anyone having new informaton to come forward. A woman recently called me and I promptly taped her statement that her husband boasted of having had a hand in the Moore assassination. I sent it to Governor Chiles's house and he did reopen the case. The Florida commission concluded that there was no evidence and no cover-up.

The history of my life is regularly visiting the FBI with information of this sort. It started way back before World War II. I've been to see them in Jacksonville, Atlanta, Washington, New York, and got no ear at all. [*Sighs deeply.*]

Once, it came out on the floor of the Klavern that Brother Ben Culpepper was a night watchman at the arsenal on the outskirts of Atlanta. The question asked: "Why can't we come out there and rough him up some night and steal some of those machine guns in preparation for the race war?" Brother Culpepper said, "No reason at all. Just please don't rough me up too much." [*Chuckles.*]

I went straight to the FBI. There was no interest. They followed me out to the elevator and asked if I knew something about Martin Luther King and some of these other black agitators, saying they were the real menace. A few weeks later, I found out that Brother Culpepper was promoted.

Do I feel dispirited at times? I remember a silver-haired lady who'd given her whole life to the battle for justice. She asked me, "Was it all in vain?" I don't remember how I answered her.

In 1952, I testified before the United Nations in Geneva as a witness on forced labor in the United States. I arrived with a one-way ticket and eight dollars in my pocket. I didn't have an overcoat. Someone loaned me an oversized one at the airport. I traveled all over Europe and North Africa. I'd written a Jim Crow guide, a catalog of all the segregation laws in the country. Jean Paul Sartre liked it and had it published. It took me eight years to get back to this country.

I've always lived on the razor's edge. [*Chuckles.*] I remember recording a tale about a folk hero, Kerosene Charlie. He started to go around the world with twenty-five cents in his pocket and when he got back, he still had a dime left. I can't help but feel he was my prototype.

A reporter who interviewed me thirty years ago revisited me recently. She was obliged to write about an old-time militant who has mellowed. I contend mellowing is for wine, not for me. As we border on the twenty-first century, it is no time for anyone to mellow. There's just too much at stake out there, including our endangered species and the planet itself.

I think of Myles Horton* and what he said before he died. "They think they've got us defanged and declawed. Never." He was never "mellowed." I'd like to think I won't be either. I'm resolved that my last words will be the most militant.

There was an old black man living down the road here. He was close to a hundred and lived in an abandoned automobile. Every morning at sunup, he'd jump out, grab a hoe, and start chopping. I asked him what's the big idea. Shouldn't he, at his advanced age, be getting his rest? He says, "Oh, if I didn't do that, this old body of mine would think I was through with it, and that would be the end of me." I hope my energy lasts as long as his did.

---

* Founder of the Highlander Folk School in Tennessee. It is an adult education center, attended by labor organizers, civil rights activists and volunteers, white and black, northerners and southerners. It gained notoriety when it was attacked by Alabama governor George Wallace as the subversive school that Martin Luther King Jr. attended.

John Gofman, M.D., 76

San Francisco, California

Codiscoverer of uranium-233. He has written several books and published numerous papers on the subject of nuclear power.

I'm just a labaholic. I always liked the idea of working in a laboratory. If somebody locked me up in a lab and just sent food in, I'd stay there forever.

Even though I was doing well at Western Reserve Medical School—this was during the depression—I felt the need for more chemistry. So I took a leave of absence from med school in Cleveland and went to the University of California in Berkeley. It was in physical chemistry, my major interest. The giants in the field were here, and I was scared to death. I felt I didn't know anything.

A new graduate student would go around and ask any professor if there was a problem he could work on. I chose Glen Seaborg,* who was working on artificial radioactive activity. I thought this would be useful in medicine when I got back to Western Reserve.

Seaborg assigned me to find out if a substance known as proto-actinium-233 existed. I proved that it did exist and how to measure it. We published a paper in the journal *Physical Review*. Then I figured since it emitted the radiation we called beta particles, it must be decaying into uranium-233. I started to search for any decay of uranium-233, because we didn't know if it would last seconds or minutes or thousands of years. It turned out it lasts 125,000 years. This was 1940.

The teaching assistantship paid $65 a month. I had just married, so after paying the rent, $35, we had $30 to live on. There was no job for the summer. Seaborg tried to raise $100, so I could stay and work on the problem. He failed. Our discovery of uranium-233 was, afterward, hailed as a development worth fifty quadrillion dollars, if nuclear energy went ahead.

We bummed a ride back to Cleveland and stayed with our parents until the fall, when my teaching assistantship resumed. In that short time, things had changed. Scientists were considering work on the possibilities of a bomb, because, after fission was discovered in 1939, there was concern the Germans would beat us to it. This was '40, '41. I'm back in Berkeley and we got some money.

"In nature, there are three kinds of uranium. U-38 constitutes about 99.3 percent of the uranium you dig out of the ground. It will

---

* Winner of the 1951 Nobel Prize in chemistry.

not undergo fission with slow-moving neutrons. U-235 would split apart with slow neutrons. This fission is what makes our nuclear reactors and bombs possible—the one dropped on Hiroshima, for example. What makes our discovery a key is that element 90, thorium, with neutrons added, creates uranium-233. So not only is the world's uranium supply available for nuclear power or bombs, so is thorium's. Furthermore, with uranium-233, fission can occur with slow or fast neutrons. That's how come it was regarded as a fifty-quadrillion-dollar discovery.

"Enrico Fermi, at the University of Chicago, proved with his reactor that plutonium, element 94, could be produced. The nice thing about plutonium is that it's easier to separate it from uranium than to separate uranium isotopes from each other.

"In those days, there was not enough plutonium to see. We could only track it by its radioactivity. So we set aside our uranium-233 and I became the fourth chemist in the world to work with plutonium."

The Manhattan Project began in '41, '42. Before Oppenheimer went to Los Alamos, he expressed interest in my measurement data on the fissioning of uranium and plutonium. When General Groves became the head of the project, everything changed overnight. Before, when we wanted something, we had to wait six months, because the war was on. The moment the Manhattan Project came into being, we had Triple-A priority. We could take things right off the trains.

The Hanford, Washington, site was chosen for reactor work in isolation. Oak Ridge, Tennessee, was chosen as the intermediary site for uranium separation. Oppenheimer chose Los Alamos, New Mexico, for the fabrication of the bomb itself. He invited all of us in the Berkeley chemistry group to go with him.

We were very dedicated workers in those days. Oppie said, "We won't guarantee you'll have any contact with the outside world for the duration of the war." Because my wife was in medical school at the time, I elected to stay in Berkeley.

Two months later, Oppenheimer came to see me in Berkeley. He brought Joe Kennedy with him. Joe, head chemist at the Los Alamos lab, was the most brilliant chemist I ever met. You'd go out to radio shops, get him parts, he'd put it together and make it work. His hands were golden. He died at age thirty-eight, of cancer of the stomach. It may have been from radiation, we can't be sure.

Oppenheimer said, "We need half a milligram of plutonium." The world's supply at that point was one-twentieth of a milligram. Today, we're worried about where we'll put fifty tons of plutonium. I said, "You'll have lots of it from Oak Ridge in about nine months." He said,

"We need it now for some special measurements. It will make a big difference on whether or not we can make the bomb." Joe Kennedy had told him that I'd worked out a way of separating plutonium from uranium, and from all the garbage that gets produced. I had worked something out with little test tubes and beakers on a lab bench.

If we were going to make a half milligram of plutonium before the reactors produced it, we'd have to use the Berkeley cyclotron. We'd have to bombard a ton of uranium, running the cyclotron for six, seven weeks. Oppie said he had already worked it out with Ernest Lawrence,* the new head of the Berkeley labs. Seaborg had gone off to work on plutonium in Chicago.

We ran the cyclotron for seven weeks, day and night. Then we let it cool off, because there's a lot of short-lived radioactivity after such a bombardment, very dangerous. But since time was of the essence, we let it cool for only a few weeks instead of months. Working around the clock, we ended up—after using a ton of uranium—with about a quarter of a teaspoon of liquid plutonium. It turned out we had 1.2 milligrams. Oppie was elated. "You can keep two-tenths of a milligram to play around with. We'll take the one milligram." They took it down to Los Alamos and got the measurements they wanted. It seems I'm now the fair-haired boy in the atomic energy arena.

In 1942, I was twenty-four. I took the war very seriously. I wasn't questioning anything. I *did* have one question. I asked Arthur Wahl, a fine chemist who shared the lab with me, "Suppose the bomb is made. How will people live in the area with all that radioactivity around?" He said, "If a bomb goes off, it's going to send this material up into the stratosphere and is never coming back." The idea of fall-out hadn't occurred yet. It turned out later that *all* of it came back.

For me, the excitement had already worn off. I went back to med school—the University of California Medical School in San Francisco.† During the war years, I had established a lot of capital for the work I'd done. I had all sorts of offers from the Mayo Clinic. Oregon, Washington University in St. Louis, others. I accepted an assistant professorship at Berkeley in Medial Physics, a new field.

I wanted to do something with either cancer or heart disease. I chose to work with large molecules because I had had some ideas about cholesterol. This was 1948. The terms "good cholesterol" and "bad cholesterol" came out of our work. I'm still equivocal about good cholesterol, but there's no doubt about the bad being bad.‡

---

* Winner of the 1939 Nobel Prize in physics, for his invention of the cyclotron.

† He won the Gold-headed Cane Award as the student who most exhibited the attributes of a true physician.

‡ The American Heart Association awarded him the Lyman Duff Lectureship, their highest award. "I'm now, it seems, a fair-haired boy in heart-disease work."

Just last year, in 1993, the Heart Association Arterial Sclerosis Council chose me as honored guest speaker. I said I didn't want to simply engage in recollections. I had a lot of data I hadn't yet analyzed. I worked my butt off for three months and represented it at the meeting. It was good to get back in that field a little.

By 1954, I was a full professor of medical physics at Berkeley. What happened? I hadn't done much radiation work at all, but that year Ernest Lawrence and Edward Teller had established the Livermore branch of the Berkeley labs. In 1952, they decided to speed up work on the hydrogen bomb. Teller was unhappy with the rate at which Los Alamos was moving. He wanted it faster.

At about that time, I lectured to a group of physicists about my work in heart disease. Lawrence was in the audience. I went over it lightly. When I finished, Lawrence stood up and said, "I don't get it." The others hadn't said a word. About ten days later, he pokes his head in the door of my lab and asks me to explain my lecture further: "Tell me more." Finally, with the enthusiasm of a little kid, he shouts, "I got it!"

He asks me if there is anything I need in furthering my heart-disease work. I need an ultracentirufe; it separates proteins from molecules. It costs about $16,000. Today it would cost $150,000. The business manager of his Berkeley lab says it's not in the budget. Lawrence said, "I didn't ask you about the budget. Get John an ultracentrifuge. That's an order." That's the kind of guy he was. From that time on, he'd bring prominent guests to see our work. He was so enthusiastic, he'd take over and tell them all about it.

One day, in late '51, he calls me into his office. "I'm worried about those guys at Livermore. They're so intense in work on the hydrogen bomb. I don't like dangerous things done in the lab." He asks me to visit Livermore, "roam around and if you don't like anything you see, tell them to shape up, because you represent me. I'd feel a lot more comfortable about their heath out there." So I organized the Industrial Medical Department at Livermore.

What happened during those years was crucial. Their major work was in weapons research. I helped them with some of their considerations for the Pacific tests, but I still wasn't doing anything on radiation. I was arranging the examinations of the lab guys who were coming back from the Marshall Islands, but I was not yet questioning. In 1957, after three years at Livermore, I came back to Berkeley.

I was very stupid in those days. In 1955, '56, people like Linus Pauling were saying that the bomb fallout would cause all this trouble. I thought, "We're not sure. If you're not sure, don't stand in the way of progress." I could not have thought anything more stupid in my life.

The big moment in my life happened while I was giving a health lecture to nuclear engineers. In the middle of my talk, it hit me! What the hell am I saying? If you don't know whether low doses are safe or not, going ahead is exactly wrong. At that moment I changed my position entirely.

I was going ahead with my heart-disease work. Comes 1962. The Russians break the agreement between Khrushchev and Eisenhower on the moratorium on atmospheric testing. JFK, now in office, tells the labs to go ahead, to show the Russians we'll not be second best in nuclear weapons. The Livermore lab goes gung-ho. Many nuclear bombs, different sizes, different types, are tested in the atmosphere. They put on a big show in the Pacific, in the Nevada test site, which causes fallout all over the United States.

I get a call from John Foster, head of the Livermore lab. It's Teller, behind the scenes, who calls the shots. Foster says, "We have a strange request." The Atomic Energy Commission would like to set up a biological medical unit here. I said that we have eighteen, nineteen laboratories already. Why another one? He explained: from the Nevada testing site, we had released so much radioactivity in the state of Utah that the milk was three times the safe level. The problem was "solved" by the Federal Radiation Council, the group that was supposed to set the standards. They suddenly discovered that three times as much as what had been previously considered safe was still safe. They raised the tolerance level, it was a fraud.

I told him, "If you're gonna explode bombs in the atmosphere and the winds blow, the materials are gonna go deposit somewhere. I don't see how having biologists and medical people in the lab is going to solve the problem. This is just to help the Atomic Energy Commission get off the hot seat."

He agreed that fallout was the problem. He promised me a new building with great facilities and that I could bring in any scientists I wanted.

"I don't trust the AEC," I said.

"I don't either," he said. "If you see anything you don't like, we won't let the AEC stifle you. We'll back you all the way." My mission was to evaluate all the aspects of bomb testing.

I insisted on a letter from Clark Kerr, then president of the University of California, that if I didn't like anything here, I could have my full professorship back. The letter was written. The university regents agreed, as well.

I went to Washington to sign the papers. Glen Seaborg, my former mentor, was now the chairman of the Atomic Energy Commission. Kennedy had appointed him in '61. I told the commissioners that I wasn't sure about accepting this job. "If any of your programs are bad for public health, I will publicly say so. I will not tolerate any interference by documents stamped 'secret.' If you have any doubts, get someone else for the job." Seaborg said, "Jack, all we want is the truth." In retrospect, if there was one thing they didn't want, it was the truth.

They built us a brand new building. I had the loveliest office and special laboratories for myself. I had 125 people. I was working, happy, teaching a little. Some of the work on cancer and chromosomes was getting exciting. I asked to be excused as the associate director so I could work at the lab more.

There was another program at Livermore: Plowshares. It was Teller's favorite project: to move mountains, diagram canals, and divert rivers with nuclear explosives. They were to go to Panama or Colombia and build new canals with hydrogen bombs. They planned to use 315 megaton bombs in a row to excavate the land. Each bomb had one hundred times the explosive force of the one that fell on Hiroshima. When Foster told me about it, I said, "Are you serious?" He said, "It's Teller's baby. We want you to evaluate its health effects." I put people to work on it, but at a director's meeting, I called it biological insanity. It did not endear me to Teller.

Plowshares was canceled, not for reasons of health. The government was promoting the nonproliferation pact, and this project could be misinterpreted. In any event, my open criticism of it made Teller less enamored of me than ever. It was about this time that rumors began about me as the enemy within.

I further aggravated some people in 1969. I was invited to give a lecture for nuclear engineers on any subject I chose. My talk was "Low-dose Radiation, Cancer, and Chromosomes." My calculation was this: If everybody in the country were to get the radiation dose that was permissible under the existing standards, there would be sixteen thousand extra fatal cancers per year. I offered one further caveat: If there is an official safe dose of radiation, we'd have to reduce that number, because we must assume there is no safe dose. The moon shots were going off at the time, so the speech got no notice.

About a week later, the new head of the Livermore lab, Michael May, said, "Jack, I've got some flak from Washington. They're upset with the talk you gave." I said, "I didn't give away any secrets. I gave a calculation." "They're upset because they didn't know about the talk in advance. They were blindsided by the reporters." Would I mind, in future talks, sending a copy in advance. I said sure, I had no reason to withhold it.

I had an invitation from the American Association for the Advancement of Science to take part in a symposium on nuclear power. I suggested Arthur Tamplin, head of one of my divisions, who was quite familiar with it. He gave an advance copy of the speech to May.

Three days later, Tamplin comes in mad as hell. He threw the manuscript on my desk. "Look at this." The entire guts of the talk was penciled out. They left in the prepositions and the conjunctions. May had told him that if he persisted in giving the talk as outlined, he couldn't identify himself as a member of the Livermore lab, he couldn't use lab secretaries to type his manuscripts, and would have to pay his own travel expenses.

I told May this was in violation of everything agreed to when I came to Livermore. I was going to call the guy at the Triple-A 5 and tell him that he was censoring Tamplin and that I now consider Livermore to be a scientific whorehouse. I did call the association guy, who was scared to death. May stormed out and didn't talk to me for months. He backed off. Tamplin made a few minor changes and his speech went off as scheduled: critical of nuclear power.

Meanwhile, I had accepted an invitation from the Muskie Committee on Atomic Energy matters. At this time, I testified that our calculation showed that it might be closer to thirty-two thousand extra deaths a year rather than sixteen thousand.

Now the AEC went into high gear to get us. "Gofman's an incompetent," they told the reporters right after the Muskie testimony. For the last seven years, they had given me three and a half million a year and a new building and, suddenly, I was incompetent.

Chet Holifield, a congressman from California, was the new chairman of the Joint Committee on Atomic Energy. He sent word that he wanted to see Tamplin and me. He led off, "Just what the hell do you two think you're doing?"

"What do you mean?"

"You're getting all the little old ladies in tennis shoes up in arms about our program. Why the hell are you doing this?"

One of his aides whispered, "These are two highly respected scientists."

"I don't give a good goddamn who they are. They're interfering with our nuclear energy program."

I said, "Mr. Holifield. Our job is to find the health effects of radiation. We've worked on it, and this is our information." He said, "Listen, I've been told that if we give people a hundred times the amount of the radiation dose we allow, nobody will be hurt."

"Who told you that?"

"The Atomic Energy Commission, that's who. Guys like you have tried to interfere with our program before. We got them and we'll get you."

Those were his parting words.

It turned out that their expert authority was a physicist who had been dealing with data of the early '20s on people painting luminous radium dials. There were women in factories who were getting horrible bone cancer. He was saying that at a thousand rads nobody would be hurt. It was absurd, a horrible misanalysis of data. He told this to the AEC and they *loved* it. It was the answer they wanted. They didn't give a damn whether it was true or not.

From there on out, things got rougher and rougher. In early '70, I wrote Seaborg a letter. I remember him as the man who shared credit with me, his student, as codiscoverer of uranium-233. I thought he'd still have some respect for me. I warned him of some of his people and the dangers to public health and of his promise to seek out the truth.

He didn't back us. He just melted away. He didn't say anything nasty about us. He didn't have to. His underlings did the job. The atomic electricity industry was not too friendly either. One of their guys told a reporter. "Gofman's just been released from a mental institution." She said, "Oh, that's very interesting. I'll write it up in the *Village Voice*. [*Laughs.*] The guy spent the next half hour pleading with her not to put it in. The press was generally fair to Tamplin and me.

The battle was just heating up. I was still working at Livermore, had twelve people on cancer, chromosomes, and radiation. One day, the associate director told me that the AEC ordered them to take away my research money: $250,000. The lab, at first, refused. They said my work was first class. A year later, the AEC renewed its demand. I didn't fight it. I was thinking about those twelve people who would lose their jobs if I insisted on keeping my program going. It was a big mistake. I should have raised holy hell and taken it up with the university at the highest level. I said, "Let's kill the program." We did that day. It was a good program and the public would have benefited. We had already published some things in the *British Cancer Journal*. This was 1972.

I thought this would be of real interest to the National Cancer Institute at Bethesda. I was pretty sure they'd come up with $250,000 a year. The director sounded enthusiastic. He said, "Your program is exactly what we need. Would you be willing to cooperate with the Yale people on this work?" I said I'd love to. We talked for several hours. He'd let me know in three weeks. It looked very good.

About eight weeks later. I sent a nice note off to the director, understanding that there might be the usual delays in this matter. But I had to decide pretty soon about moving all our gear out of Livermore. I got a letter back from a third-echelon deputy. "Many thanks for your inquiry. The work you are proposing is not in the main line of our interest, but if you have any other ideas, please let us know." I never heard from the director.

I can guess what happened. I think people within his shop said, "Look, this character Gofman is giving the Atomic Energy Commission fits. What the hell do we need him for? He's trouble."

I applied for grants everywhere, the National Heart Association among them. I got nowhere. I had a good name in the field, so what? I no longer had any funds for research. So I resumed teaching again at Berkeley in the Division of Medical Physics.

After a couple of years, I decided to take an early retirement. I'm now a professor emeritus of molecular and cell biology. I serve on university committees. I give some lectures. The Department of Medical Physics no longer exists.

I became active in the anti–nuclear power movement. The power people were constantly putting me down because my work was harmful to them. If they couldn't sell the idea of safe doses, they weren't going to last forever. I talked at rallies and meetings all over the country and abroad. I wrote a book called *Poisoned Power*, which became sort of a bible for the antinuclear movement. I published a little collection of talks, *Irrevy: An Irreverent Illustrated View of Nuclear Power*.

There is one organization that may be worse than the AEC. It's the Veteran's Administration. There are so many cases of all these servicemen who've been out in the Pacific and flown through all these atomic clouds. They developed leukemia and cancers.

Orville Kelly had been on the Bikini Islands in connection with the Pacific tests. He developed lymphoma. He wrote me, "I've been through appeals to the VA and got nowhere." He had his records. I wrote a detailed report on him to the VA and they rejected it. [*Angrily.*] Orville Kelly was the first guy to get money. His wife benefited from it when he died.

Another woman, Shirley Donahue, wrote me. She had two young children. Her husband had been a lieutenant colonel in the air force. They used to fly right through the clouds to collect samples of the air. These guys got a hell of a dose. Shirley's husband had an accumulated dose of seventy-five rads, whole body radiation. He developed leukemia. My calculations show that it was due to his experience on the job and nothing else. His case was refused. We went through it three times. He was dead. Shirley is finally getting a pension from the VA.*

---

* "As you enter John Smitherman's house in Mulberry, Tennessee, he calls out to you. You immediately see a large, handsome face. Simultaneously, you see that he is legless. It is his left hand, resting on the arm of his automated wheelchair,

The next thing was the Karen Silkwood case. They needed someone to testify at the trial on the hazards of plutonium. I had written
an article for the *Journal of the American Medical Association.*
Silkwood, you remember, was killed in an auto accident. "Will you
help serve as a witness?" I met with Gerry Spence, the Silkwood
lawyer, the night before I was to testify. He said, "Watch the jury.
They'll tell you when you've made your point."

Kerr-McGee, the company being sued, had a bevy of lawyers,
about a dozen pin-stripes. One of their lawyers asked, "Could you
explain how it is we get such different answers from illustrious committees?" He goes on to name them. He made the mistake of giving
me an open-ended opportunity to talk. I talked about an hour, and
the guy was speechless. He couldn't stop me because he had asked
the question. The jury was lapping it up. We won the case. Her family was awarded ten and a half million dollars. The Supreme Court
sent it back, and they finally settled for $1.4 million.

I entered a case on behalf of the downwinders in Utah. Most of the
winds were blowing in that direction from the Nevada tests. The
government was saying, "No problem. It's not going to hurt you."
Cases of cancer, leukemia, started coming up. They agreed to have
twenty-four people represent the twelve hundred who claimed
injury. I testified in that case. We beat them. The government was
furious, especially when the judge cited my book as one of the three
definitive works on the subject: *Radiation and Human Health.*
They *hated* it. We won the case, but it was reversed by the Supreme
Court on the grounds of discretionary function. If somebody like the

---

that draws your reluctant attention. It is at least five times normal size; roughly
ridged, corrugated, grayish; it resembles an elephant's trunk.

"There was 42,000 veterans that participated in Operation Crossroads; 27,000
of 'em is dead. That was in the Marshall Islands and the Bikini atoll. We were
advised there would be nothin' harmful. Just a lot of excitement and a lot of fun.

"We were circlin' around the USS *Mount McKinley* when the bomb exploded.
We were standin' in shorts. I had a T-shirt on, just like this. The brass stayed
under cover the whole time. They wore heavy clothing. They were protected all
the time....All of a sudden, we saw this huge ball of fire come from the bottom
and go up. We felt the heat, we felt the shock wave...

"Comin' back from Washington, D.C., I tried to go to the VA hospital to see a
doctor. They refused to admit me because I wasn't there on a scheduled appointment. At a private hospital, they found cancer of the colon and liver, terminal.
I've been fighting with the VA to gain service connection out of this whole thing.
They have turned me down for the sixth time.

"They admit I was exposed to radiation, but not enough to create a problem.
Three doctors on my behalf said I was exposed anywhere from 1,000 to 1,800
rads.'"   —From *"The Good War": An Oral History of World War II,* 1984

John Smitherman died on September 11, 1983, a few months after my visit. His
widow, Rose, had been denied any compensation by the Veteran's Administration for years. Recently, I have been informed, she is receiving something.

president decides a crisis exists and he doesn't go through the necessary things, say, to protect people, he could say, "I used my discretion for the good of the country." This could be extended to anybody in the government who was supposed to monitor the doses. You couldn't sue them because of their discretionary function. It meant you could get no relief from the government at all in the law courts.

That's when I quit. I decided to write a book on radiation and human health. Somebody has to do it and it might as well be me. If it isn't done we'll build up a bunch of lies in textbooks and have the whole thing whitewashed. So I said, "No more law suits, no more rallies, no more lectures, I'm going to work on research"—and I'm still doing it.

It's hard to work in science when you discover there's very little you can trust. There's a group called the Radiation Effects Research Foundation in Japan. It was once called the Atom Bomb Casualty Committee, to evaluate the effects on Hiroshima. It was cosponsored by the Japanese Ministry of Health and the U.S. Atomic Energy Commission. It never occurred to me to question them.

They came to the conclusion that there are fewer neutrons in the mixture of radiation than we thought. They were going to assign new doses to people. They can make data look like anything they want. I was appalled. They were shuffling the whole deck with nobody watching. It was the clearest-cut violation of the cardinal rules of medical research. I wrote to the commission's chairman: "Dr. Shigematsu, you cannot do this. It violates all the rules." They had pulled out fifteen thousand records. It was an open invitation to fudge the data. He replied, "I appreciate your concern. It's valid. Just trust us." The reason we have rules is that nobody has to say "trust us."

How does it happen that most of these reports came out favorable to the nuclear industry? If we allow things to go on unchallenged, here's what's going to happen. Ten million, a hundred million, or a billion people are going to suffer from cancer and genetic diseases because the lies will become the truth concerning radiation and health. How many colleagues have I convinced? One in a hundred, perhaps. If I had unlimited access to Treasury bills, I could have reversed it overnight. It all depends who has the money as to what scientists think. The people at the Livermore lab saw what happened to me. Do you think any of them speak out? The cards are stacked.

Radiation will be regarded as harmless. It may even be good for you, because we've proved it harmless. You don't have to worry about waste, because we can put it out in landfills. So for a hundred years, lies will be truth and truth will be lies. The cost will be the multimillions who will suffer from vicious diseases.

Last year, in Stockholm, I was given an award by the Right Livelihood Foundation. I shared it with a courageous Russian journalist, Alla Yaroshinskaya, who blew the whistle on the lies his government was telling about Chernobyl.

I proposed in that award talk that if you want the truth, 10 percent of the money that the government provides for health research should go to grass-roots citizens' groups, who will pick their own scientists. The ordinary person, the layman, needs to say, "We'll support the scientists who dedicate their lives trying to ascertain the truth."

They should have full access to all the data and their job is to blow the whistle on Chernobyl, Hiroshima, Three Mile Island, or whatever. If you don't do this, the price you will pay will be biomedical unknowledge. Truth will become falsehood, and falsehood, truth.

The nuclear power movement is worldwide. You couldn't have told the difference between capitalist and Communist countries. I'm talking about nuclear power, not just bombs. I'm still speaking against it, writing against it, and blowing the whistle.

CHAPTER EIGHTEEN

Letters to the Editor

Henry "Hank" Oettinger, 80
CHICAGO, ILLINOIS

I was born way up in northern Wisconsin, a place that was devastated by the lumber barons. It was said, back in the old, old days, that a squirrel could go from upper Michigan, across Wisconsin, into Minnesota, without once touching the ground, the forests were that widespread. When the lumber industry did its job; the land was left with stumps and rocks, hardly fit for any kind of agriculture. Hardly fit for anything. It became remindful of Appalachia.

By 1920, the only business, the only income, was tourism. Oh sure, they'd cut a few trees for the paper mills, but it was so bad by the time Roosevelt's New Deal came in, 91 percent of the population of Forest County was on relief. The saying in those days was: There was $4.85 in circulation; some bastard would it off to Sears & Roebuck, and they'd wait for the tourists to come again.

I was a descendant of the failed forty-eighters, the German liberals who fled their homeland in the mid-nineteenth century and came and settled in Wisconsin. They were the ones responsible for Wisconsin's liberal tradition all the years up to Joe McCarthy. They provided the socialist mayors in Milwaukee and the antiwar congressmen.

"I marched in the Armistice Day parade in 1918. I was six years old. Those were beautiful, Decoration Day and Armistice Day. Civil War veterans, the old boys, were still around. Some in wheelchairs. I was the high school orator, so I'd give the Gettysburg Address. As a kid, I was patriotic as hell."

My radicalism was caused by poverty, mostly. It was just grinding poverty up there, and when the depression came, it was like a city ghetto today. Fishing and hunting was the only salvation. The game wardens were very understanding. They never prevented any poor family from having a deer or arrested them when it meant their livelihood. Old Bob LaFollette became our political saint. When I was twelve years old, I distributed literature for Bob's presidential campaign in 1924. He got over five million votes, which was a hell of number at the time, for a third party.

I became a printer's devil up in Crandon before they had a linotype. I did everything. While in my senior year of high school, I helped run the press, set up type, and wrote news. The next year, I moved on to Waukesha and then caught on as an apprentice in Milwaukee. I worked there until about late 1931. That's when the depression hit town.

I got laid off for about three years. They told me my job was waiting for me as soon as business picked up. I finished high school in 1930 and dreamed of going to college, but the tuition was, as I remember, seventy-five dollars. We didn't have that kind of money. I spent those three idle years in the Waukesha Public Library. That's my alma mater.

That's about the time I started writing letters to the editor, perhaps my greatest claim to fame. The first important letter I wrote was to the *Milwaukee Journal*, quoting Bishop Sheil of Chicago, who said we are all spiritual Semites. The anti-Semitism up there in 1939 was as bad as anything I've seen. Then the war started.

The most recent letter I've written also has a religious tinge. The governor of Mississippi says that we are a Christian nation. As an atheist, I'll agree with him when Donald Trump, Ross Perot, and all the other billionaires sell what they have and give it to the poor, when they admit that it's harder for a rich man to get into heaven than for a camel to go through the eye of a needle. Or if they condemn the practice of the last twelve years of getting poor people to hate poor people, getting people to hate blacks, hate the homeless, hate themselves. Or if they would convince Americans to love their neighbor. Then I'd say we're a Christian nation, but not now. I sent that one in yesterday.

I got active in the union movement and never, never have enjoyed life so much. The Wagner Act comes along, insuring that we can organize. John L. Lewis breaks away from the AFL.* The printers union joined the CIO. Now what would a printer, of a tightly exclusive craft union, know about organizing big auto plants and steel plants and factories? Many of the most active and hippest organizers for the CIO were Communists. So I joined the Party in 1940 and quit in 1946, because I didn't care about the idea of strictly following a line. It was amicable.

After the war, the CIO kicked out all the radicals, especially the

* The American Federation of Labor.

Communists. A few years later, people were asking, "Why doesn't labor organize?" If they hadn't booted out some of their best organizers, labor might not be in the sad shape it is.

Eighteen years ago, I was automated out of the printing business. I'm one of those many automatees. I get a very small pension, nothing like we expected when we pioneered in union pensions. So it's close to the bone.

"Remember, the printers had a great tradition as the aristocrats of labor. Jacob Bronowski said, 'The democracy of the intellect comes from the printed book. The happy passion of the printer sits on the page as powerful as knowledge.'

"Print shops were always connected with cathedrals, and to this day they are called chapels. The new kid who had to clean up and do all the dirty work was called either an imp or a devil. I was fourteen when I became a printer's devil. I learned to set type by hand, under the old cases, as they were called. In two years came the linotype.

"Today the linotype is out, and with the new automation, most of the printers, myself included, are out.

"In the early days, there were occupational hazards: fumes from the metal pots, benzyne to wash type. The Typographical Union, the oldest in America, set up a home in Colorado for the old and sick members. We also had the highest pension in the country and, by far, the highest strike benefits. We were highly paid, highly respected, and, seemingly, secure. Along came automation and the union busting of Reagan. Together, it was devastating.

"I was at it for forty-six years. I was what in those days was called a swift, the highest level of typographer. I could go to any city in the country and get work.

"I could set five characters a second. That was big stuff. Now with phototype, you can set something like fifteen hundred a second! Good-bye, linotype jobs. It's all computer-run.

"In 1960, our union membership was 120,000. Now there are less than half that. This, of course, affected our pensions. All these years, I had looked forward to a respectable union pension. With the old guys put out of work, the $300, $400 a month pension I had expected turned out to be $125.

"I wasn't as badly off as some of the others. With my social security, I at least squeeze by. But those comparatively young men of forty-five, fifty, they have kids in college, mortgages. Imagine the feelings of high-class craftsmen no longer needed. I was sixty-two when I got laid off. Right now, I could go down to any shop and set type exactly as I did before—if there were a linotype to set in on. But it's gone.

"The Tribune *used to have sixty-five linotype operators in the day shift, about forty on the second shift, and maybe twenty on the lobster shift, between midnight and eight. Now, here comes two o'clock, Chicago time, closing time at the New York stock market, and one goofy line comes out of New York, with all the fractions* [makes a rackety machine sound], *ten thousand words a second. It goes all over the country and doesn't require one single goddamn operator.*

"I'm no Luddite. You can't stop progress. But you can't tell me there's no way that the workers who are replaced can't share in the saving of all that money? It was their skills and muscle and pride that kept all this going all these years.

"I had such joy in my work. There's no greater feeling in the world for a man than to know that his work is helpful and worthy of praise. Now our great tradition, our skills, have been turned into binary numbers.

"Today the composing room of a newspaper is as silent as a tomb. Have you been over to the city desk of any of the papers recently? It used to be so wild and romantic. Now, it's dead. Like the composing room.

"In the days of hand-setting type, there was a written legend on top of the case: 'To justify the line is to justify the time.' There was a pride in putting spaces to make it absolutely full. That was justifying the line. Then you lift the whole and place it perfectly. That's justifying the time. What a beautiful credo for the printer: 'Do good work.'

"Today, the sloppiness is unbelievable. There are no real proof-readers anymore. You find one-syllable words divided. The other day, I saw quotation marks with a period at the end of one line and the end quote mark on the next. Why, a printer would have committed suicide if he had been caught doing that."

I live alone. I was divorced in the '50s. I married the daughter of a hack Republican politician who was in real estate. It was like Othello sneaking away with Desdemona. He disinherited her the week we got married. We have one son, a doctor in Grand Rapids.

During these intervening years, from the '50s on, I've been kept hopping in the civil rights movement. My gosh, I've been busy. I've lost track of the demonstrations I've been in. You name it, I've been in it.

My first demonstration was in 1932, a hunger march. It was a straggling little bunch, about seventy-five of us at most, marching along the streets of Milwaukee on a very cold day. Both the *Milwaukee Sentinel* and the *Journal* redbaited the hell out of us. In fiery editorials, they accused us of trying to overthrow the government. Oh, boy. This was just before the New Deal came in gave us some hope.

If there's something I want to complain about, I sit down and write a letter to the editor. I have no hesitation, no trouble, no writer's block. One of my favorites was in regard to Sammy Davis Jr. Here he was pictured on the front page of all the papers, hugging Richard Nixon when he was president. I sent the letter all over. *LIFE* magazine, two Chicago papers, and the *Milwaukee Journal* picked it up.

Let's see if I have it here. [*He shuffles through a stack of clippings, then reads.*] "I never really cared for the humor of Sammy Davis Jr. I always laughed, though, so my friends wouldn't think I was anti-Semitic." He had just converted to Judaism. "But now I give up after seeing him hug old Richard Nixon. That's too much like Eliza hugging Simon Legree."

The biggest negative response I ever got was for my letters praising Harold Washington when he ran for mayor. I wrote a letter condemning the slurs and insults constantly aimed at him. People came up to me on the street: "You want that goddamn black bastard to get in?" I was wearing a blue Washington button and a cab came along as I was crossing the street and deliberately sideswiped me. He missed by an inch of knocking me down and yelled, "You motherfuckin' nigger lover." A week later, I'm in the Greyhound washroom. A huge young black man approaches, the kind you're scared of. His face is blank. He sees my button, smiles, and stands next to me, doing what he has to do.

I'm proud of the letter I wrote on Shakespeare's 400th birthday, 1964. I said that William Harvey is given credit for discovering the circulation of blood. The honor should go to old Will. There's proof in *Julius Caesar*, where Brutus says, "You are my true and honorable wife, as dear to me as are the ruddy drops that visit my sad heart." *Julius Caesar* first appeared in 1599 and Harvey didn't start his lectures until 1616, seventeen years later. So I figure old Harvey attended a performance of Shakespeare at the Globe Theatre.

Ever since, when I see an article about William Harvey in some old newspaper, I shoot off a letter. Never has anybody come up with any reason why I might not be right. I made the *Tribune* with that letter.

Most of my letters are aimed at what I feel is an injustice. I worked at the *Waukesha Freeman* back in the '30s. It was the most hidebound Republican county in the state. I set up the editorials on the linotype, and every once in a while I'd write a letter to the editor challenging one. He would print it and attack me editorially. And I would set up the editorial condemning me. [*Laughs.*] He and I were good friends.

The glory days were in the '60s, when Chicago had four newspapers and the underground press. Sometimes I'd have three, four letters the same week. [*Whispering, confidentially.*] I have caused some controversies, too. The latest happened when I wrote a letter to the *Tribune*.

I was so sick and tired of bums like Rush Limbaugh and cheap comics always going to town on Ted Kennedy. Just joke after joke. No one ever mentioned his work on legislation. He's probably the most progressive senator we've got today. All they could talk about was his helling around. Well, that letter caused an uproar. [*Laughs delightedly.*]

Oh, I've gotten some vicious responses. The *Milwaukee Journal* used to put people's addresses at the end of letters. After the one on anti-Semitism, I got two death threats signed with a swastika. My mother said, "Henry, please stop it, I don't want you killed." Believe it or not, my last death threat came during Bush's oil war. [*Becomes highly indignant.*] I was absolutely opposed to it. I got a couple of threats on the telephone.

I've had letters published in perhaps 75 percent of the major newspapers in the country. If something happened, say, in California, I'd write to the *San Francisco Chronicle* or the *L.A. Times*. In fifty-five years, I've written, I'd guess, about fifteen hundred letters. I used to subscribe to all sorts of publications, *The Nation*, the *New Statesman*, the *New Yorker* when it was fifteen cents, beautiful days. I cut it out when inflation reduced my tiny pension to nothing. I go to the library quite often.

I don't go out at nights much anymore, because I got mugged two or three times. It's hell when a guy has to stay in his house. But maybe it saves my liver and also my money.

I've been drinking since Prohibition was repealed, mostly beer. The other day, a friend and I were trying to figure out how much beer I had consumed since December 1933. I figured out I'd drunk enough to build the North Branch of the Chicago River. He thought it would be, bottled, enough to fill two trains of eighty cars.

During the '60s, I associated with a lot of young people. I think I was the only old geezer the kids really trusted. I was with them in all the demonstrations. I got tear-gassed with them in Lincoln Park in '68.

I've been called a bleeding heart. [*Excitedly*] What the hell is a bleeding heart? I thought maybe it referred to those pictures of the sacred heart of Jesus. What's wrong with that? If anybody isn't a Schwarzenegger or a Rambo, he's a wimp. I prefer Mr. Rogers any day.

I get up quite early and turn on the radio for so-called news. It's really entertainment. I no longer watch TV because it's repeat and repeat of the same trivia. I've been a sucker for newspapers all my life. I read and it's there and I can go back and study it some more for its inconsistencies. You can't do that on TV.

My anger hasn't diminished a bit as I get older. But I sure need that humor to go along with it. I figure I'm only going to live until the year 2008. It'll make me ninety-six. You know why? I figure the Cubs will win the World Series in 2008 because that will be a hundred years since they last won it.

I'm getting up in years and I want to do as much as I can in what little time there's left. I'd feel useless unless I have some effect on the life around me. It keeps me thinking. I have something to do in my life. Otherwise, what would I do? I've had a compulsion for so many years to try to right matters, but, boy, it's getting tough now. I'm telling you, there's such a right-wing swing in this country. I can't imagine my life without these letters. It would be so bland.

The kids in the '60s were one of our best generations, even though they may have backslid into temperance. They drink wine or something, no more shots and beer. But they fought against racism, against the stupid Vietnam War; they kicked out a war president.

One day, while marching with kids on the campus of the University of Wisconsin, I saw a sign: "Ask not what you can do for your country, ask what you can do for mankind." I said there's my generation. The hell with Kennedy's. Remember what Gary Wills said about Kennedy's call about what you can do for your country? He called it a beautiful prescription for totalitarianism. I agree with him.

Not many of my old friends are left. I'm the senior citizen in almost every place I go. In my apartment building, which has many old people, they're thrilled when they see my name.

Oh yeah, I've got a letter coming up about all these layoffs. All of a sudden, a big corporation will announce, "We're getting rid of eight hundred thousand people." You see it almost every day in the paper.

There is only one more thing I want to do as the time is running out. I want to win the lottery, buy three ships, man them with American Indians, and send them over to discover Italy.

Part VI

CHAPTER NINETEEN

Legacy

Sophia Mumford, 94
AMENIA, NEW YORK

Miles of hills, greenery, and dwindling roads set it a world apart from the Big City. "We have always lived in this simple, unrecon- structed house. We did almost nothing to it. The house was there, we liked it, and that was the end of it."

She is the widow of Lewis Mumford, one of this century's most illustrious American men of letters: architecture critic, city plan- ner, culture critic, sociologist, educator. "We were married for sixty- nine years. In that time, you form yourself. But the principal thing is that I've tried all my life to be me."

She is seated in a well-worn armchair; a walker is nearby. The furniture is "old time," sturdy. Though there are several whatnots scattered about the room, there is no sense of disorder, nor cramped- ness. On the contrary, an air of roominess, and something to spare, pervades.

I never thought about being remembered. Over the years, until I was about seventy, I honestly thought of myself as a second-rate person. I didn't have the oomph. I wasn't the sort of woman men made a pass at. Men never did. [*Chuckles.*] Not when I was young and not when I was old. They accepted me, as a friend. I was treated nicely, but I wasn't a sex object ever. And that was a black mark.

I'd never got all A's in school. When we were young, George Bernard Shaw was all the fashion. We read Shaw's play religiously. A great many of the young women I knew read his prefaces and could discuss them intelligently. I didn't have the brain for that. I could do his plays very well and understand them, but I couldn't think abstractly, and for a long time that troubled me.

It wasn't until in the '70s, up in Cambridge, something happened that made me think maybe I was all right, that people wanted me for myself. Someone who had won the Nobel Prize in biology, he and his wife were giving a big dinner party. She called to remind me and I said, "We can't, because Lewis has to be in New York." She said, "What about you? Why don't you come?" It had never occurred to me that anybody would want me without Lewis. I stammered something and she said, "Certainly you'll come. I'll call so and so and he'll bring you out." Suddenly I thought maybe it isn't only Lewis, maybe they want me for myself.

Lewis worked at home, I was at home, and we talked all the time. I was a very ignorant and uneducated girl when I married him. But over the years, wisdom did pass from one to the other. I would have denied that if it weren't for an item in my diaries I came across the other day. We had been talking during breakfast, when, on his way to his room, he stopped and said, "No one is ever going to know the amount of intellectual stimulation you gave me." That was the accolade.

It began in 1918 with our meeting on our magazine, *The Dial*. I was eighteen and accidentally got a job as stenographer. It was probably the best journal of arts and literature that America has produced. There I was, an absolutely ignorant girl without any education, in with these highfalutin young men, who still quoted Greek verse to one another. Ezra Pound, James Joyce, everybody of that set was published in *The Dial*.

It was very exciting. I was taken up by a world that I'd never known existed. It was also fun because I was the only female with five or six very elegant young men working around the office. I grew into the job and learned a lot that I would not have known had I a conventional education.

My family was very poor, and it was decided that I would take a three-year commercial course that would qualify me as a bookkeeper and stenographer. My education ended when I was sixteen. Mumford came along and, in a little while, I realized we were drawn to one another. After reviewing some books, he had become associate editor of *The Dial*.

In those days, you called each other by your last name: Mr. So-and-So, Miss So-and-So. After about six months, the managing editor said, "Don't you think, Miss Wittenberg, it's time we used first names?" To me, that was a moment of glory. It meant I had been accepted. I was part of the group.

It means something if you call someone by the first name. It means you know that person and want them as your friend or intimate. This is not so today. A young man telephoned me the other day, a stranger. He wanted a bit of information, purely impersonal. After two seconds, he said, "May I call you Sophie?" I was shocked. [*Laughs.*] When my daughter was fifteen, I answered the phone and it was one of her friends. I said, "This is Mrs. Mumford." Afterwards, she berated me soundly.

"That was so off-putting."

"What should I have said?"

"You should have said you were Sophie."

"But I didn't know who I was talking to."

"That's got nothing to do with it. It's just being friendly."

If human relationships have any value, they have to have quality. You have to learn about a person before you know what his quality is. But if you start right off the bat as if he were a personal friend of long standing, where do you go from there?

Living with Lewis had its amusing difficulties. As I was sinking myself into the creative world, he became, for a time, more interested in regional planning than in architecture. I found it very dull with the new friends he was bringing in. Gradually, I began to see what it was all about and acquired an interest in the environment. Lewis never ceased to be interested in everything.

He loved New York, but saw the city, a living entity, grotesquely denying the value of human life. He was pointing this out back in the '40s.

From 1926 on, we spent four months of the year up here in the country. With our second child, we came to live here year round. At the time, he was art critic of the *New Yorker*. It became as important a part of his life as architecture. But all he studied and wrote about always led to the human aspect. He studied theology, philosophy, English, aside from architecture, art, and city planning. He read and reread Melville, and more and more, he saw the human dilemma and the choice you had to make in life. Nothing was outside the field of his humanistic vision.

He feared from the very beginning that if man didn't put himself in the center, he would be forced into the shadows by the sheer push of technology. He foresaw what is happening today.

Lewis spoke out against Vietnam when it was a very unpopular thing to do in the literary world. It took me a while to catch on to what was happening in Vietnam. At that moment, my own personal life, something in the family, was so absorbing that I didn't pay any attention to public affairs. I was amazed when I later learned that much of the country was against the war. I had to catch up on that. Lewis was president of the Academy of Arts and Letters and was to make a welcoming speech one morning. He had a bad cold and a high fever. He said, "I'll leave immediately after the speech, go home, and go to bed. You stay and get the repercussions of it."

In his speech, he said, "No man worth his salt who pretends to be a writer should write a word until he has first spoken out against what we're doing in Vietnam." There was a fury in the audience. People who had welcomed us with open arms in the morning refused to speak to me, walked right by me.

This was in the early '60s. As the years went on, and we met the young people who were given awards that day, one and all said it was an extra honor for them because of his speech. They were all against the Vietnam War. It was the older people in those early years who didn't want to be bothered with it.

Lewis never hesitated. He always lived by his principles. He just couldn't have done anything else. Nor could I. In essentials, we were alike. I didn't know the phrase, acquisitive society, but I had no interest in the acquisition of things. Neither did he. As we went along, we discovered there was never any discussion necessary here. He never accepted a job just for the money. It had to feed some interest of his own. He would cheerfully say no to a grand job, because there was something closer to his heart that he preferred doing.

I think the ruin of civilization is being speeded up by the pressures on people to buy things they don't need. I'm rabid on the subject of advertising and television. I think it's absolutely loathsome. In the past, by and large, people bought what they needed. They worked hard in order to get the necessities of life. Today, you're urged to spend money to buy unnecessaries. Don't get me on the soap box now. [*Chuckles.*]

Do they enjoy what they're doing or do they do it because it's the only thing to do? I read that one of the new ways of keeping a family together is to go to a shopping mall on Saturday or Sunday. What have they gained? To acquire something they may not need?

As work-saving things were manufactured, work itself became denigrated. You do it only when you can't get a machine to do it. I see the value of a dish-washing machine. I also see its stupidity. When you have a lot of dishes to be done, a lot of people to attend to, it's excellent. But for, say, two people, it's simpler to wash dishes by hand. The machine doesn't save you any money, doesn't save you any time.

At home, I did the washing, he did the drying. I asked him once, "Would you like us to have a dish-washing machine so you wouldn't have to dry the dishes?" He said, "Certainly not. It makes a hell of noise. I like to dry the dishes as you wash them. We always have a good time talking."

In the days of a neighborhood store, you knew the people who ran the store. They knew you. You knew your neighbors in the street.* For a housewife, shopping was a social event. People need one

---

* Jessie Binford, Jane Addams's Hull House colleague, during the last years of her life, reflected on her return to her hometown in Iowa: "Nobody walks here anymore. He jumps into the car, of course. I walk more than anyone else in town. I'd much rather get out in the evening at sunset and walk than get into the car with probably all windows closed. My sister gets into the car and drives to the grocery store, a block away, instead of walking."

—From *Division Street: America,* 1967

another, to enjoy one another on occasion. At a modern shopping mall, they're alien to each other, customers and clerks.

In the old days, people worked too hard. Working people of little means had too heavy a burden. Slowly, ideas of unions came along, work conditions improved, life began to offer something beyond mere subsistence. People began to have wider horizons. But they had no spirituality to guide them as to what life was all about. Was it just to acquire what the rich had, as advertised? Why *do* anything, when a machine can do it? Work itself was denigrated. Why were we created? We're even letting the mechanistic feeling creep into child education. For the first few years, it's important for the child to be central, to be given room to be himself. Now we give them computers when they can barely manage their fingers. Right from the start, we teach them that machines are there to serve them, instead of developing themselves. It's changed the conception of the human being as somebody capable of growth within. Everything now comes from the outside.

Just yesterday, I was looking at the catalog of a nearby college. I couldn't believe the courses they were offering. How to use a computer. How to make a good investment. How to get a good job. How to, how to. There was hardly one course to make the inner man grow. If you suggest that a course in ancient history may play a role in a person's growth, they laugh at you. What relevance does it have to our life today?

When Lewis came into my life, conversation, good conversation, became part of our natural selves. It wasn't just talk, it was an exciting back and forth. Now, weeks go by and there's just nobody to talk to, except for the occasional telephone call, where you simply chatter, but no ideas. We read poetry out loud. We read novels. During the day, Lewis worked intensively and I had plenty to do around the house. But evenings, after the dishes were done, we both read.

Sometimes I get depressed, very, without anyone like Lewis around. It doesn't last, I'm sensible. But it's not a pleasant life, when you're used to talking about everything—I mean, I read a poem and Lewis would immediately say something about it. Here, there's nobody, just nobody at all whom I can...

I think this glorification of old age is a great mistake. I resent this whole trend toward increasing the span of life. It used to be three score and ten and you were through. Allow for the fact that people live longer now, okay. Set it at eighty. From eighty on, you're living on borrowed time. Older people become nonproductive, sad, ill, increasingly self-absorbed because they haven't the energy to go out and do more. Why go on?

When Lewis was ill, I myself wanted to—I would very gladly, if we could have done it with dignity—just take whatever simple means to get out of it. We lived full, enjoyable, creative lives while we were able to, and what was left was diminution, downhill all the way.

But I didn't know how Lewis felt about this. We had never discussed it. He felt the human body had its own purpose and that was that. Since I didn't know how he he'd feel about taking a pill and departing, I couldn't do it. For the first couple of years after Lewis's death, I furiously resented being old. I felt there was no sense of my being here and watching a beautiful dream go into the dust.

But then people began paying attention to me. I developed a circle of younger people who came to me and feel they got something from me. They wanted to know about life in the '20s, the Golden Age to them. I told them what it was like, and they listened.

Now I'm content to stay on. I wouldn't go now. But what about people who don't have those memories to go on? Living day to day without joy. Shouldn't they be permitted to go without any social stigma?

How can one judge the importance, or lack of it, of another's life?

I waver. It's my heart speaking. It's Lewis, those last years, his living half the way—I so resented it. He got obstreperous, incontinent—and I had always so respected him. He was so worthy of admiration and respect. And he had lived with such dignity. To him, and to me, to live a dignified life was what it was all about. There's a phrase from *The Brothers Karamazov* that I've always treasured. Old Father Sosima says to the brothers, "Every day, every hour, every minute, walk about yourself and see that your image is a seemly one." That's what I mean by dignity.

Would I like to see the year 2000? No. Sometimes I think I'd like to come back in three hundred years and see whether we had destroyed the machine or whether we had become robots. Humanoids. I can't see celebrating the year 2000, because I don't expect anything of it. When we celebrated the end of World War I, we did believe we were building a new world. New art forms were coming in, new approaches. It was a period of hope. Of course, it was blasted very quickly. But I did at least see that.

I've always had trouble celebrating events or holidays. I was nine years old when they decided that Lincoln's birthday would be a holiday. I remember thinking, even as this little kid, "Why is this the day I should be sad about Lincoln? I could think about him some other day." That feeling has stayed with me always.

I resented it when certain friends thought they had to call me each year on the day of my son's death. To offer sympathy. I might not even have remembered that was the day. I might have been grieving two days before or after. [*Aggravated*] I want to mourn on my own time. I don't want to mourn when somebody says it's time to mourn. Rejoicing is different. You can rejoice with other people. But when I'm sad, I want to do it on my own.

What made it easier for me with Lewis, as with the death of our son, Geddes, is that I've always felt that life and death were continuums of the same thing. When death came, I couldn't go to pieces over it. I wept. I was sad, but I couldn't go yowling about, the way some people do, getting hysterical. Death has to happen, and I've always accepted that.

What is so sad about my son is that he died so young. He was killed in the Second World War when he was nineteen. And now there's nobody left. His sister is dead, his father is dead. When I'm dead, there will be nobody who knew my son to carry his essence on. Those of us who remember him will be gone. That's the only time in which immortality, or the lack of it, troubles me.

I don't know the nature of the universe, so I can't say this or that is going to happen. I can, as an optimist, hope that those I loved, I will connect with. I feel that way about my mother, too. I don't feel that way about my father, whom I loved more than I loved my mother. He was self-sufficient. He got from life what he gave to life. A rare soul. My mother, who tried to be good, was hard inside and never quite got the return she wanted. Nobody loved her as much as she wanted to be loved. I have a feeling that I must have contact with her eventually. She needs me.

I'm afraid of one thing. I want my death to be dignified. My fear is that something will cause me to live past the point where my life has value. I don't want to live on. I won't go to a doctor now except for minor things that can be immediately remedied. But corrective things, no. From now on, if life says it's leaving, I'm not doing anything about it. If I get a bad pain and it's diagnosed as cancer, then I won't wait, I'll go. I'm ready, because I feel I've had a good life.

Margot Jacoby, 95

NEW YORK CITY

Her home is on the Upper West Side. She lives alone and is obviously mistress of her domain, an expansive, old-fashioned, high-ceilinged apartment. She is in perpetual motion as she offers her guest small cakes, strong coffee, and even stronger opinions. Her demeanor is that of a tough little bird flying 'round and about, with much to be done and so little time to do it.

We were very important people in Berlin. My husband was a celebrated copyright lawyer. Our milieu was the world of art: actors, singers, painters, writers. Berlin, in those days before Hitler, was the most intellectually stimulating, the most ma-a-arvelous city in the whole of Europe. We were wealthy, spoiled. I had a cook, a house maid, a personal servant, a governess. I came from a well-off family and married into a well-off family. When we fled, we were penniless.

I shipped out my husband and son to Palestine in 1936. There was no other way. I had great connections. I stayed to take care of our office in Berlin. You know something? In my opinion, women are much tougher than men. I, for example, am not easily intimidated.

I left in 1938, just a few days before "Crystal Night," when they destroyed all the property of the Jews. A Swiss banker friend of mine said, "When are you leaving?" I said, "Maybe in a month." He said, "No, you are leaving the day after tomorrow." Outside of Germany, people knew better than we in Germany.

I was a singer, a good one. I had a big contract for an opera house in Kiel. Salome. When Hitler came to power in '33, it was the end of my German career. In small script, at the very end of the contract, was written: "Are you of pure Aryan blood?" I tore it up into pieces and threw it away.

I had a sister in America. She was an actress who had come here in 1921. She loved it and was very successful. I sometimes saw her on television. She's dead.*

My husband had a lot of money coming from clients, over a hundred thousand marks. I engaged a lawyer, who was also out of work, to get the money. I have never seen such a stupid man. Every letter he wrote, I wrote again. Horrible. I had a hard time, but I did collect some.

I first came to America as a tourist, in 1938. In 1945, I came to stay. Of course, I saw it with European eyes. In '38, I felt I was on the

---

* Her sister had a principal role in the play and subsequent film, *Tomorrow the World*. After the war came, she was no longer hired because of her German accent.

moon, a different planet from Europe. I couldn't believe such a thing existed. It was terribly vulgar. Ugh. I had some special experiences impossible in Europe.

I was almost raped by a taxi driver in Niagara Falls. In a Pullman to Chicago, I was in a lower bed. Suddenly a man entered in pajamas and, before I knew it, he was under my covers. He put his hand on my mouth and said, "Don't scream. I will do nothing that you do not want me to do." With all my force, I took his hand and shouted, "Get out! Get out!" He went out as if nothing had happened.

Couldn't this have happened in Germany, too?

Never! Never! Never, my dear.

Under Hitler?

Never. No, no, no.

My husband and I were separated by the war. He refused to stay in Palestine because he could find no work. German Jews were taboo. The Zionists only helped Eastern Jews. They figured that we had always looked down on them, and whatever they did was right. He went to America and I didn't see him for seven years.

When the war was over in 1945, my son and I landed in Philadelphia. We had crossed the Atlantic on a Spanish freighter. There were six refugees and Spanish sailors. It took four months. It was horrible! They put us in the hole with the others. I would not go down there. By force, I occupied two cabins on the upper deck, one for me and the other for my son. He was nineteen. I told the captain that my husband had paid enough for the passage and I'd pay him for the cabin afterward, but I will by no means be down *there*. You had to be tough.

I hardly recognized my husband. For seven years, he lived in New York a beggar—no money, no food, in a furnished room. He was a poor broken man. Fortunately, I knew people who could help. After my long experience, I found all that counts is who you know: pull, connections. People of power, of money. That's what decides your fate. Toughness alone doesn't help.

I never in my life mixed with another class of people. I am not an equalitarian. I am, if you want to call me that, an elitist. People of certain culture, people of quality who are at least as intelligent as I am. I never mixed with people I considered inferior.

Whom do you consider inferior?

[*Without losing a beat.*] Stupid people. Not poor, not at all. That doesn't make a difference. Stupid people who are rich, I hate them the most. I associated with people of moral quality, of ethics, of honesty. You will agree they are difficult to find in America.

What changed most was the appearance and behavior of the black people. In 1938, you never found a black person in a restaurant. In a bus, they were sitting in the back. It was de facto segregation. They would never dare to be fresh or aggressive or openly hostile. In '45, it all changed.

Apart from the color of their skin, they were dressed like parrots, in different colors: red, green, yellow. They had found something to straighten their hair. They were more like white people than they had been in '38. They were less restrained, enormously aggressive.

I don't want to live with them. I have nothing against them. It is not the color of their skin. It is the social difference. If I have one black person that is educated and has good manners and is intelligent, I don't even see that the person is black. I don't like white people either that I consider inferior. I keep away from them.

The main change I saw in America, my dear, is the quality of life. Especially the services. In 1938, on the table in the cafeteria were rolls, as many as you want. Relish. You bought a cup of coffee for a nickel. You could eat six rolls. My husband took me for my first meal, and we had seven courses for ninety-five cents. Nobody had to go hungry. In 1945, I can't believe the prices!

Oh yes, my dear, I saw homeless people in 1938. In Chicago. I was invited by rich people I had met on the boat for dinner. As we passed Michigan Boulevard, I saw something dark, lying in an entrance to a building. I recognized people lying like sardines. Everyone had a newspaper covering them. They were rolled in it like sausages to keep warm. It was icy in Chicago, March 1938. I said to my host, "What is this?" He said, "Don't look."

[*Sighs deeply.*] In becoming old, I have not become more compassionate. Today, I believe that 10 percent of humans are good people and 90 percent are swine. That is unfortunate for me, at ninety-five, to feel that way. When I was young, I believed that everybody was born a good, decent, wonderful creature. This idyllic attitude I have completely changed because of my experiences in America.

I am by nature optimistic and have known marvelous people in my life. But 90 percent are dishonest, exploiters, liars. They betray you. I'm very pessimistic today. There is so much fraud, even with these homeless people. I know you are not responsible for your fate. But I think capitalism in America is not what capitalism should be. The form in this country is totally perverse, criminal. I believe capitalism should be mixed with socialism. You have that in France, Germany, and in England. Here, it is cruel. It is hypocrisy.

The so-called freedom in America is only used here in a fraudulent way. It is not good that you can be free to marry, make five children, pack your luggage, go to another state, take another name, marry again, and don't ever take care what happened to your family. This is promiscuity and total disregard for responsibility.

Isn't this true to some extent of other countries, too?

No-o-o-o. Never. In Europe, it starts, my dear, from the day you are born to the day you die. Authorities always know where you are. You are forever registered. When I once said this, an American flew in my face. He said I was defending a police state. It is not true. If you have nothing to fear, why do you do you fear the police?*

Four times my pocketbook was stolen. Four times I had burglars. In one case it was the building custodian. There were people I trusted and found out they exploited me. May I tell you of one, my dear?

My husband had been a delegate to the United Nations. He represented the American Jewish Congress. After he died, I was invited to join a South Pacific something. There I became friends with an Indian diplomat and his wife. One day, he said he was in a fix and needed fifteen hundred dollars in cash. He gave me a check. A few days later, he asked for another fifteen hundred dollars. He was still in a fix. So again I gave him the cash. This was Monday. On Tuesday, his first check bounced. So did the second. Three months later, I called his niece who worked for the United Nations and said if I don't get the money in twenty-four hours, I'll have her uncle deported. That's how I got my money back. So I don't trust Indians anymore. I do have two friends in this building who are Indians, the doormen. I like them more than any other.

If you are an old woman, alone, you are really a victim of everybody. An old woman alone is really uninteresting to a lot of friends. The moment my husband died, every other woman was afraid I would steal hers. So they all abandoned me. I was relatively young, sixty. But I was young in spirit and I was a *looker.*

I don't like old people. I don't like withered flowers.

You're not withered.

[*Amused.*] I'm more than withered. I'm dead. I see myself as a caricature. [*Pauses.*] I don't like myself since I became old. I don't dislike myself, but I dislike my infirmities: my crooked hands, my sightless eyes. I live like a recluse. I see nobody.

---

* This is a startling paraphrase of the late Mayor Daley's reply to complaints about Chicago police surveillance in the '60s.

How do you explain your spirit, your fervor?

My doctors can't explain it either. I worked all the time. I made
something of a hobby into a business: antique buttons. I became an
expert. [*She brings out an impressive display of Roman heads, of
blue stones in silver settings, of miniature works of art in the shape
of buttons.*] These buttons were worn only by men in the early nineteenth century.

I love men. I can't say I dislike women, it is just career women I
hate. I hate the feminists. Argh. And how.

The button business is an artistic outlet. I was a designer of men's
jewelry. Not a career, a small business. I like independence, but I
don't like women who, in my opinion, destroy men, who emasculate
them. They think they are equal, they take their jobs. They want to
be soldiers. Argh. I have nothing against a creative woman, be it a
painter, a writer, a musician. But I don't like a woman as a conductor.
I don't want to see her on the podium. It is stupid, but I can't help it.
I still say the destiny of a woman is to be a woman, to be a mother, to
make life for her husband pleasurable, to make his life as a breadwinner easier. Sometimes she has to be a breadwinner, but she can
still be a homemaker.

And this rape business. Most of the time the women are the ones
who provoke it. I know it's not always like that. I became the rape
victim of a taxi driver. But often it is the woman. I don't believe in
date rape. I think the woman is the seducer of the man.

You believe Eve led Adam...

Absolutely. Oh, I am not a fundamentalist. I'm not religious at all.
I'm agnostic. I hate religious institutions, but I believe in nature and
I adore spires. I'm for abortion, of course. I hate these people with
fifteen children.

I became antifeminist in America, because of their terrible emphasis on sex. I know that sex rules the world, but to have it open on the
table, argh. Marlene Dietrich, she was pathological as far as sex was
concerned. And she was German. She was a woman. You see?

Please do not get the impression that I am antiwoman or antiblack
or antipoor. Not at all. I respect phyical work, the worker I have seen
in Detroit. I wouldn't mind taking that man to the opera. I am not condescending when I say they are the most important people. I am
really a socialist. I love working people if they are real workers.

I think every second person on welfare is involved in fraud. I have
nothing against a black who is an honest, good worker. There is
fraud everywhere. Blue Cross, Blue Shield. The scandals are simply
unbelievable. Corrupt on the highest and the lowest levels.

The system corrupts us all?

No, I am not corrupt. I tell you why: I had a Prussian education. Prussia was a country for law and order. I speak now before 1914. Our civil-servant system was an absolute model for honesty, reliability. All that was finished when Hitler came to power. No cheating on taxes. You were a responsible, obedient citizen. That's why the Germans in this country all are very prosperous.

Did they ever question authority?

It didn't exist. I got a driver's license here and in Berlin. Here, in 1960, the man who tested me said, "Put a twenty-dollar bill on the seat and I'll pass you." This is typical. In Germany, never.

If you never questioned authority, might that not have led to totalitarianism?

It may. There were many things that led to Hitler, but I don't mean to speak about that. It's too much to tackle. Authority under the Kaiser was good authority. They didn't punish you without reason. If you ever got in conflict with the law, you were never frightened. You knew the law was impartial and just. You were never punished for anything you hadn't done.

Our culture was so much higher than here. When my husband came out of the war in 1919—he was four years at the front—he made an awful lot of money. After he took out a big life insurance policy, he said, "Now I want to live." We lived like kings. Fantastic. We were all the time around the world, traveling. It was a high life, but not foolish, not like here.

What is high life in America? You drink yourself dead, yes? The typical successful businessman, what does he do in America? What is fun for the average American rich man? It is not even wine, women, and song. Where is the song? The Germans love music, opera, concerts, theater. He drinks good beer.

What about those George Grosz cartoons of the German bourgoisie/ Wasn't the high life he portrayed coarse, gross?

No. Consider the average American and his obsession with sex. He doesn't even know what sex is. He is boring, childish. When I visited my sister in Hollywood, I saw it all. Too much.

The Germans today are disagreeable, awful, arrogant, lazy. I was back there and I don't recognize these people. I am so foreign there.

Before 1914, we did have a social anti-Semitism. As a Jew, you could not become a civil servant unless you were baptized. Then came the world war. My husband never allowed us to talk about it. He had lost all his friends. But he was on the best of terms with all the officers.

Today, I keep away from everything. I have seen enough. I have enjoyed enough. I just want to be left alone. I was always interested in politics, but more in culture. I kept away from people who I saw on the street forming a group. I ran. I am not a joiner. I am really a great individualist.

As you get older, the only joy in life is to make other people happy, to give. I give away things I love best. I help people whom I like, but there are very few left because all my friends are dead. I would help a stranger, but I'd have to be convinced he's worth it. I am today very suspicious of people. When I was young, whenever I met somebody, I assumed he was decent and honest. I was totally mistaken. They are all crooks and liars.

I have lost my faith in humanity. I give only for animals. I love all animals, except cockroaches. No, I don't like the animal rights advocates. They're like the feminists—noisy, screaming, disgusting. I have nothing against homosexuals. To me, they can do what they want. But to hang a sign: "Hi, I'm gay and proud of it." I could take a gun and shoot them. I think it's so disgusting. Don't boast.

I am not a conservative in the way of the religious people or these Republicans, whom I don't like. Or the bourgeoisie, whom I hate. I'm rather left. Don't you think if your intellect is rather broad, you are sooner a leftist than a rightist?

I think the Vietnam War was horrible, horrible, horrible. It was a crime. We didn't have the slightest reason to be there. That we are the number one supreme nation that could help the world is something preposterous. We get information that is distorted. There is no other population as gullible as Americans. You can tell them anything and they'll believe it.

[*A long sigh.*] It's too bad I don't have the faith I had once upon a time when I was young.

If you had your life to live over again, is there something you might have done differently?

[*A long, long pause.*] I might not have married my husband. He was superior in intellect, witty, generous, the very best. But I was too young, too inexperienced. I didn't really make him happy. We were very different in temperament. He was one of those introverted men who you couldn't get close to. There was a glass wall between him and me. He met me when he came from the war and I was still in school. I was like a timid little girl whom he could order. He was a tyrant, but an awful nice tyrant. I was in awe of him. My son said to me one day, "He was nuts about you." I know in his distant way he loved me. It only came out when he was about to lose me in Hitler time. He was fighting to keep me, but he was helpless and that was when I was no longer the schoolgirl. When I put him on the boat, that was the one time I could do something for him. It was too late.

When my husband died, I knew I had loved him dearly. In spite of all this lack of closenes, his death was the biggest blow I ever got in my life. I'm still grieving. It was thirty years ago.

I live for my son, who is my whole life. He was a professor of medieval literature. He is more than perfect in three languages. When Nixon took away all those educational subsidies, his department closed and he has been without work for a year and a half. He works as a translator and lives on social security. He is sixty-seven. I will leave him whatever comes from the sale of this apartment. It is worth a lot of money. He is my reason to live.

I do still have energy, but with all my energy I can do very little. If you are mostly blind, you are condemned to nothing. The only thing I can do is listen to music.

Carolyn Peery, 99
CLEVELAND, OHIO.

"Oh yes, I remember when the Titanic *went down. It was so sad. I was living in Kansas City. There was hardly a dry eye anywhere, although people were not personally aquainted with them. Only rich people could travel overseas at that time."*

She lives in an apartment with one of her seven sons and his wife. There is a touch of elegance in her appearance, yet of indubitable hospitality, as we are seated on a davenport. Her soft carpet slippers enclose tiny feet.

She has gathered a couple of the albums of old photographs and, from time to time during our conversation, she refers to them.

Here's a picture of my mother-in-law. She was born into slavery. She was six years old when freedom was declared. She remembered when the slaves had to leave their cabin doors open. That came to mind when I remarked to my grandmother one day, "You leave the door open and it's so cold." She said, "Well, for most of my life, we had to leave the doors open so that we could hear when the mis'tress or master called." My mother-in-law remembered seeing the slaves get behind the door, jumping up and down, saying "God bless Mr. Lincoln. God bless Mr. Lincoln."

My grandmother, my father's mother, didn't know exactly how old she was, a little past a hundred when she died. *There's* a picture of her first husband, a giant, seven feet something. He always wanted to run away from slavery and go into a circus because of his height. My gandmother used to tell me how he'd come home in the evenings and lie down in the mud, cover himself, and stay there the whole night, because he thought that bleached out whiter. He was very light-complected. He did run away by the underground. He joined the circus and I guess *this* was the act. [*She refers to a photograph of a tiny woman, a midget, in the company of a huge man wearing a fancy hussar uniform with a white-feathered helmet.*]

He gave a command performance before Queen Victoria. She gave them a beautiful medal. As the years went by, he had amassed quite a bit of property, and he told my grandmother he deeded it all to her. On the way back, he died in some mysterious way. I remember when she went to New Jersey and claimed the property that he'd left her. Nothing came of it.

My grandmother drove a covered wagon from Kentucky to Kansas. She had five children with her, and her mother, who was an

Indian. At the time, the schools in Kansas were integrated. It wasn't until after that they were segregated. My father was the first African American to graduate from high school in Junction City. He was obsessed with the idea of going to college. So he took every penny Grandma could scrape together, plus the few dollars he made working in the fields, and went to Fisk University. He got a teaching degree. Years later, I myself went to a small Baptist college in Des Moines, Iowa. A white school. I was one of the two black students there. I don't think that I learned anything I didn't know. [*Laughs.*] You would think it was a thousand miles below Mississippi, the segregation was so bad. Restaurants, hotels were forbidden to us. I couldn't eat in the college dining room. Nineteen-thirteen. It was worse than the South, because you knew what to expect there. But up here, it was so startling and blatant. Most of the girls' parents were ministers, devout church people. We had our graduation picture taken in our white blouses and black skirts. The photographer said to me, "You are a little darker, I want you up front here where more light shines on you." Some time later, I visited a girl in our dormitory who had the picture on her dresser. She had cut out a piece of leather, like a shield, wrote the class and year, and pasted it right over my face. [*Laughs.*] It was so convenient.

It doesn't hurt me now, because I think how ignorant and insensitive some people can be. It shows how nice they were to your face and behind your back, hypocritical.

I've been so many denominations. My father's parents were Methodists, but somehow he became Baptist. My mother's parents were Seventh Day Adventists, but my first job as a teacher was in a Congregational school. [*Laughs.*] My children were all baptized Episcopalian. [*Laughs.*] I better explain. My husband, a railway clerk, was transferred to different places. We went to a Minnesota town where we were the only African Americans. My mother, who lived with us, said, "I'm not going to be a heathen. I got to find a church." An Episcopalian minister came to our house and we became Episcopalians the next day.

While I was still attending college in Des Moines, my uncle built a hotel for black people, who couldn't stay anywhere else, except a private home. He had my mother operate it. We met all kinds of influential African Americans who passed through. One day, Dr. Clarence Pickens came by. He was one of the founders of the NAACP. I had just graduated and I asked him if he knew of any openings as a teacher. I wanted to teach in an all-black school. He told me about the American Missionary Association.

They recommended Athens, Georgia. In my way from Des Moines by train, there was a layover of three hours in St. Louis. I remembered Madame Walker,* who had stayed with my uncle when she visited Des Moines. The bright idea came to me to visit her. She and her husband were so gracious, when neither knew me from any other wandering young woman. Mr. Walker sent a young man down to pick up a ticket for me. The young man helped me as I was struggling with my baggage. In those days, chivalry prevailed. It was not yet "all aboard" time, so he sat down with me. Two bewildered-looking white conductors came by, looking from side to side, until they spied me. They asked me for my ticket, which I gave them with a smile. They said to the young man, "You said this ticket was for a white woman." He said, "I was not asked about color." Thanks to Madame Walker's husband, I had a comfortable night's ride in a lovely parlor car instead of a rickety Jim Crow vehicle. We fooled them that time.

After a short time teaching in Athens, which I enjoyed, I heard of an opening in Mound Bayou, Mississippi. It was established after the Civil War. It's still there and all-black. It flourished at one time, when they had the cotton gin. When they brought in the cotton-picking machines, it went down. Oh, it was so inspiring to teach there.

When we were little kids in Albany, Missouri, the railroad station was the most interesting place in town. The train ran right through the middle of the city, and we'd wave at the engineers. At the station was the telegraph, and to hear that tick-tick-tick-tick-tick-tick was interesting. But at Mound Bayou, I'd see black people doing the very same thing. It was just mind-boggling. The station agent was black! The telegrapher, the postmaster, everybody was black! And the principal of the school was a very educated man. It was so exciting. [*She indicates a photo in the album.*] That was an old house built by the freed slaves. The principal lived in it. He could have had a brick house, but he wanted to live as the others lived. Just like I wanted to live in an all-black community. [*Laughs.*]

Oh, the students were so eager to learn. They were eager to do anything for the school, even the little chores. It was that feeling of wanting to become somebody. From the time of the freed slaves, that was their motto. "You must learn." My grandmother would always say, "Do you have some lessons now?" It was the attitude of all the black people I came in contact with: aspiring to be educated.

I taught there in 1916 and 1919. Some of my students became artists, librarians, teachers, funeral embalmers, a comptroller at

---

* One of the most famous and respected of African American female entrepreneurs. Her cosmetic products for black women were renowned and her corporation highly successful. She was admired for her generous contributions to African American colleges, especially her scholarships for young women.

Fisk. I was there for two years, two more years in St. Joseph, Missouri. In many places, married women couldn't teach. You said yes to your heart and no to your profession.

I took child care courses and became something of a practical nurse. My career didn't seem to be on the rosy side at all. My husband, who was brilliant, just couldn't get his feet on the ground. He easily passed the railway mail clerk exam, but met with such discrimination when we moved to Minnesota in 1925 that he was always in a fight. [*Laughs.*] He wouldn't step back at all.

He was away from home constantly. Things deteriorated, so he finally left home, divorced, and married a much younger woman. They moved to Los Angeles, and I was left with seven boys. Along came World War II and three of my kids were in it. When the Korean War came along, my fourth said, "Mama, I'm not gonna fight in this one. They've done nothing to me. I'm not going." I said, "Ross, I don't want to see you go but they will put you in prison." Well, he went to camp, but when they sounded reveille, he wouldn't get up. They wanted to know what was the matter and he just said, "I'm not going to war, that's all. They didn't do anything to me." They thought he was insane. I think he must have acted sort of. [*Chuckles.*] They kept him there for a year, free to roam about. Finally, they gave him three hundred dollars and said, "You get the so-and-so out of here." [*Laughs.*]

By this time, his brothers had already been home from World War II and told of the discrimination they saw and how fruitless war was. They were leaning to the left.

I'd never given much thought to politics. My sons educated me. [*Laughs.*] I didn't know the first thing about communism or socialism. We were Republicans. If you were a Democrat, a black person would have been tarred and feathered. Of course, with Roosevelt, black people turned Democrats.

My husband—I kept in touch with him—went out to California and became dyed-in-the-wool Republican. He actually wasn't conservative, but he was a politician and twice ran for the legislature. He just wanted to be a big fish in a little pond and couldn't as a black Democrat.

In the meantime, a wonderful thing happened to me. The English teacher of my third son, Alvin, said he gave a brilliant talk on Disraeli and that he ranked right along with two of her other pupils, Eric Severaid and Harry Reasoner. Somehow, she invited me to a state convention of a group she thought I'd be interested in. It was the Women's International League for Peace and Freedom. What drew me to them was their attitude toward war. I still had three sons in the service.

It just seemed to open up doors for me. It seemed like I'd been blocked before and that a big heavy load had been lifted. It was liberating. I was in my early fifties and almost at once secretary of our chapter. One thing just led to another. A woman professor at the university was resigning as chairman of the Civil Rights Committee of the state PTA. She recommended me for the job. They were just beginning this fight. It was the late '40s.

Black people didn't have any jobs as clerks in the big stores. The three largest were afraid that if they hired blacks, they'd lose their trade. We worked for two years, going to all the stores. One of the big ones said, "If you get ten thousand signatures that they will patronize our store with black clerks, we'll have something to work on." We got ten thousand signatures easily.

It was a new experience. I never dreamed I'd do any of this. One day, one of the stores called and said, "We need two clerks here, one for greeting cards and one for the sewing department." This man from the Urban League called me—he and I were the two African Americans in there—and said, "The impossible just might happen. It's up to you and me to prepare the girls for this work." We had them ready. Shortly afterwards, I came by to see how things were going. The manager said he just stands back and listens to the cash register. [*Laughs.*] When it got out that two black girls were working in this store, all these ten thousand people came running in.

Joining the Women's International League, it just opened up a new life. It made me more aware of politics, too. I volunteered in the wards, as a Republican, of course. Most black people weren't interested in politics because there was nothing in it for them. But one woman, Mrs. Rush, was a real politician. She organized the precinct and always took me along. At the time, I didn't know a thing about politics.

When I was a little kid, Teddy Roosevelt and McKinley came through Junction City. I was just in first grade and marched the long way to the depot. They would come out and stand on the back platform of the train and give their speeches. We had little flags and we went waving them and were called up on the platform and sang "My Country 'Tis of Thee." I didn't know anything but Republicanism.

The big Republican state convention was coming up and she invited me to a caucus. I had no idea what that was. When they named the delegates at large, Mrs. Rush was excluded. She got up and said, "For fifty years, I have been in the Republican Party and I have made waves. This is embarrassing. I belong to the National Organization of Colored Women's Clubs, fifty thousand members. When I tell them how long I've worked for the Republican Party, they'll ask, 'What office do you hold?' Now you have refused to send me as a delegate at large." Her husband got up and said, "She works and works so hard, but when something significant comes along. I've got to go inside my pocket." [*Laughs.*]

We were on the convention floor when they read out the names. I said, "They didn't call your name!" She said, "Hush, we'll get thrown out." Oh, I began to boil. I think that's the only time I ever had high blood pressure. I went up to the chairman and said, "I always heard that politics was dirty and now I see it." I saw Senator Judd over there and I jumped all over him for voting year after year against the Fair Employment Bill whenever it was introduced. I squabbled with him for a long time. [*Laughs.*] I had never spoken that way before.

[*Free associating, she, on occasion, juxtaposes years and events.*]

During the depression, I told my mother, "Mamma, we're going to vote for Roosevelt." She said, "What? Vote for the Democratic party?" She began to cry. "I'm not going to vote for somebody who kept my mother and father in slavery." I said, "Times have changed. Roosevelt is somebody who's working for the people. My mother didn't vote that time, but when Roosevelt came in and said everybody of a certain age should have a $30 a month pension, well, I don't think she ever had $30 of her own in her life. [*Laughs.*] It changed me completely from Republican to Democrat. My eyes were opened.

Even then, I didn't really begin to question. I was looking at it from the perspective of just two parties. I think maybe then the Cold War had started and the witch hunt. It affected our family. My boys had experienced such racism in the army and navy, they came home ready to throw the Republican and Democratic parties out.

In 1948, my kids fell into the Progressive party, and they were then dubbed "Communists." From then on, there was turmoil. My kids always spoke out and got in trouble. The FBI were on their trail constantly. The neighbors became afraid and shied away from our family. The white neighbors didn't seem to shy away as much as the black.

Up to this time, I was getting sort of recognized. I was called upon by schools to make talks. When the Communist scare came along, I was no longer invited. It was in all the papers. The Peery boys were headlines, hostile. They were in the news as subversives. They were the oldest boys.

My two little ones had gone down to apply for work, which was scarce. A truck would come by to pick them up to do some work on a farm. They were waiting in the park in downtown Minneapolis, where transients used to gather all the time. My boys were lying under a tree, waiting for trucks and shielding themselves from the sun. The police came along and hit them on the feet. They thought they were black transients. The kids didn't know what happened. "We're waiting to go to work." The police thought they were smart alecks and began jerking them around. The kids protested, and one of the cops hit one of the boys across the neck with a billy club and made an awful scar there. He socked the cop and ran. [*Laughs.*] The cop says, "I'll shoot," but he just outran him. I didn't know a thing about it except that he turned up here with this terrible scar. I should have taken him to a doctor but I didn't have my wits about me. The other one, they put in jail, but I went down right away and got him out.

My boys played a role in my education because their time of existence was so different from mine. They were active. I would try to quell them down. They'd listen, but once you're stamped subversive, you had no privileges whatever. They were turbulent times.

I was still active in the Women's International League. I got a little flak from a few members, the more conservative ones, but not from most. I still belong and am probably the oldest living member.

It's pitiful, after all these years, there's nothing but wars. If we aren't in war one way, we're in it another way. I used to hear my aunt reading about the Spanish-American War. It didn't last long. Then came World War I, World War II, Korea, and now it's just about everywhere. And we're in it one way or another.

I feel there's been a distinct improvement in race relations. When I came along, there were hospitals you couldn't get into. I remember this dentist turning me away in a very rude manner. Come to find out later he was a Hitler type. There's still racial tension, but that comes because black people will stand up. The law is behind them and then you had nothing to back you up. But it's something you've got to keep working at. I believe there is a foundation for a better world, but we still have a ways to go.

Most of those I knew are not around. Hardly any. But you know what? [*Perkily*] I find that young people are interested in old folks. We have a shirttail relation, a beautiful young person who's an attorney now. I remember when she was born. I ran into her two years ago and she writes me regularly.

Oh, I'm still interested in the outside world, but I have to stay home. [*Laughs.*] I've had cataract operations from which I'm just recovering. And this everlasting postnasal drip, that's the worst thing. I don't know how many operations I've had. I still read all kinds of books. I still attend church, a Baptist one. It hasn't played much of a role in my life, though I had been a Sunday school teacher.

I'm in an adult Sunday school class now and I tend to speak out. I have trouble with forgiveness. I want to be forgiving, but I can't. I sweep it under the rug. I just don't see how people can be forgiving of those who tried to kill them. I find it hard to be that. [*Laughs.*] I really want to be forgiving, but deep down...

I find it a bit difficult to forgive my former husband, because of things that he did. But since Christmas I said to myself, "I'm not going to have anything but love in my room." I started thinking, "Get thee behind me, Satan." Maybe that's the first step.

I've begun to feel rather optimistic with the Palestinians and the Jewish shaking hands. If you can't forgive, you have to pretend that you forgive. You have to, in order to go on. Where would the black people be if they hated every white person on earth because of slavery, because of the injustices done? I suppose we're among the most forgiving people, because we've known white people who were not racist.

A young man I know can't stand white people. He says so all the time. He's kind of a loner, off to himself. He has two good friends and they're both white. [*Chuckles.*]

That's it. Oh, I have a book full of regrets. There were things I did when I didn't know any better. For instance, my marriage. Had I looked through the glass darkly, I would have seen something and that would have changed all the other things. But my kids say, especially my oldest, "Mama, if you didn't do it, I wouldn't have been me!" [*Chuckles.*] I'd like to be remembered as a loving mother. That's it. I guess they'll be celebrating my hundredth birthday soon. I'd just as soon have a good dinner. [*Laughs.*]

Postscript: Her hundredth birthday was
celebrated shortly after this conversation, her son Nelson
told me they did have a good dinner.

Helen Nearing, 90

HARBORSIDE, MAINE

In 1969, I visited her and her late husband, Scott Nearing.

As I remember that time and place: "Along the coast of Maine, heading toward Harborside, the waves of the ocean slash against the rocks. It is a twisting, turning, dirt road; a howling distance from the small New England towns where alien hallmarks are now familiar: McDonald's, Kentucky Fried Chicken, Dunkin' Donuts, Holiday Inn, and car dealerships.

"He is ninety-five. His leathery, lined face reflects rivers, roads, valleys, storms, and blows from fellow men, over all of which he has prevailed. (For most of his long life, he has been a dissenter, pronouncing opinions that have, in large part, been unfashionable to prevailing thought. It has cost him dearly in the academic world.) He has written fifty books.

*"She is seventy-seven. She moves with the grace and lissomeness of a young girl. They have become folk heroes among the back-to-nature young and advocates of health food fare."**

The following is the result of a long-distance telephone conversation in 1993.

People still stream up here. I thought when Scott died, they would stop; but they're still coming. They all seem to get something. So it's a nice job I have in my old age: welcome people, show them around, talk to them.

I'm a woman who still feels she's a girl. I'm fleet on my feet, read a lot, play music a lot, have many friends. I think I've had a very lucky life. I've traveled all over the world, met wonderful people, and am still leading an active life at ninety.

I'm looking out at the salt water right now. In Vermont, we had seven hundred acres and Scott gave it away to the town. They never even thanked us. They though it was a tax dodge, ha, ha, ha.

Anyway, they considered us un-American. Reluctantly, they accepted it. Here we have 140 acres and most of it has been turned over to young people to homestead. They paid what we paid for it. I have four acres left and it's just enough for me. A little garden, a little house, a lot of water and trees around me. Beautiful isolation, which is what I like. Scott died ten years ago, on just about reaching his hundredth birthday. I've lived these last ten years by myself and by preference. If I can't live with Scott, I'd rather live alone. A lot of

---

* From *American Dreams: Lost and Found,* 1980.

kids come up and flex their muscles. "What can we do to help?" And they do help. They'd heard of us through Scott's lectures and our books together.

Scott was always a dissenter. His political and economics books are still sanctioned. They're still thought of as heretical. We had to publish them ourselves. Our sweet books paid for the bitter books. Our sweet books are the maple sugar books, our gardening book, and *Living the Good Life*. They're not dangerous.

The book that came out last year is *Loving and Leaving the Good Life*. It describes Scott's delicate and dedicated going. He decided at the age of one hundred, that was enough. He wasn't sick. He didn't have any aches or pains or anything. His body was tired and he said, "That's enough." He stopped eating. He fasted for a month and a half. I aided and abetted him and he got no food. Three weeks after he reached one hundred, he left. That is exactly what I will do when I get looser in the head or body.

I'm afraid I've got to go on a while yet. I've still got something to do. To grow myself, to wind up my life, and, on my way, to help as many people as I can.

I get up early and have an orange or an apple for breakfast. Then I write. There's a balcony open to the sun on the east and one open to the sunset on the west. I write on these balconies in the morning. I'm working on book now: *Aging Well and Dying Well*.

People come in the afternoon. They may have heard of us, and they just turn around the corner. I never know who will be here. A couple from Scotland dropped by this afternoon. From ten to twenty people a day drop in. They want to see if the life here is real, if the house and the garden are real, and how I'm getting along. They're really concerned and most are darling people. They all seem to get something.

It was Scott, of course, who most influenced me. I was twenty-four and he was forty-five when we met. I had the good sense to recognize his integrity and greatness, so I latched on to him.

He was in trouble because he stood up for certain issues. Authorities didn't like his point of view, so they ousted him. He had been the most popular teacher at the University of Pennsylvania. He had the biggest classes in economics and sociology. They kicked him out because he was against child labor in factories and mines. That is not a radical position today, but it was then. Sixty years later, the university gave him a honorary degree—but no back pay. [*Chuckles*.]

Scott was more of a political person than I was. I went along with everything, but I never would have initiated it. I never went to college. Within two weeks of graduating high school, I was in Europe, studying the violin. I was not interested in politics.

Of course, I was anti the Vietnam War. Anti any war. I think all wars we've had were commercial. They had nothing to do with ideals. Oh, I'm still active politically in small ways. I went to Cuba this March as the member of a peace group. I've signed up to go again. We went wherever we wanted to go, saw whatever we wanted to see, talked to whomever we wanted. Our government is strangling them with the embargo. They're just people who want to be treated like anybody else. Thanks to us, they're living at bottom level. What the U.S. is doing is disgraceful and psychopathic, just to keep a macho political stance. I still contribute to causes that write to me.

I was born into a vegetarian family so I had a good-health upbringing. My parents were exceptional, I was lucky in that, too. But they were disturbed when I went off with Scott. He was twenty-one years older than I, and a Communist. It was not a great choice in their mind. Scott was a vegetarian, too. Otherwise, I wouldn't have tied up with him. It required that certain way of living for someone to be attractive to me. Perhaps that's why I've always enjoyed good health.

Do you suffer infirmities now and then?

No-o-o! I've never been sick. [*Chuckles.*] Scott had no ailments. We have never had arthritis or any of these things that old people have. We never went to doctors. I just tripped in the garden today—scraped my leg and had to put a Band-Aid on. That's about it as far as infirmities go.

It's not so much diet as spirit. I believe in continuity: that we existed before and will afterward. I believe in reincarnation. At least, some form of it. I'm easy about it, though. I'm perfectly satisfied if it is not so. I do believe in the beneficence of life and that it has a purpose. I don't have to have a priest to tell me that. I don't have to have a religion.

I believe in loving nature and wanting to live in a beautiful place. I was born in New York City, but you can have it. I don't care if I never go back. I like living in the country.

I get up about six o'clock. Then I tend to the mail. Book orders come in. I sell quite a lot. Then I do writing of my own. Then it's lunchtime, and people start streaming in. At about six in the evening, I have a big salad. I read in the evenings.

I read and reread the classics. I would rather be like the Brontë sisters, who had twelve to twenty-four books in the house. I listen to music on the radio. I have it tuned to NPR only.* I still have no television. The only time I looked at television deliberately was at my neighbors: to see Nixon resign.

---

* National Public Radio.

I had an older brother and younger sister who were not at all attuned to the life of my parents. They were just suburban Americans living suburban lives. They wanted to like the neighbors next door, and I was never interested in the neighbors next door.

My neighbors here are young and congenial. This is a very simple part of Maine. It's undeveloped, not too many people around. About three cars a day go by. Most of these young are fairly well-to-do. They've had everything and it's not satisfied them. They want to live a simpler life.

Technology suggests an altogether different life. That's something I will never touch. Can you imagine Thoreau or Tolstoy talking into a word processor? Scott and I both wrote by hand and then I typed it. I turn to the typewriter in order to get it to the printer. I had an electric typewriter and gave it away. I like to pound a typewriter. I'm a bit Luddite, yes.

I grow my own food. Vegetables and fruit. I don't eat animals. Bernard Shaw was asked why he was a vegetarian. He said, "Why should I explain the normal way I eat? You should explain why you eat carcasses."

There are not so many old friends left when you get into your nineties. But I don't mind if I don't meet any more people. I've met enough in my life. And I've got enough thoughts in my head and enough books and about four hundred classical records: Bach, Beethoven, Brahms, Bartók. And even Joan Baez.

If you hear that I go tomorrow, if I fell downstairs and cracked my head, you'll know I went happily and I've had a very good life. And I've got very interested to know what's on the other side. What goes on out there? I'm curious. I think there's more than just a void out there. If there's nothing, then it's a good rest. If there's something, well, I'm willing to tackle another job. Another lifetime, another job. It's been very interesting to be a woman. Maybe I'll be a man next time.

I've made a date with Scott to meet him again. I made a date with him to be my daughter. I thought I could bring him up better. It would be good for him to be a woman for a while. Scott thought in those terms, too. He was awake and alive to all sorts of possibilities.

When I go, I want no fuss. No commemoration or wake or celebration. Just breathing is interesting. Just the fact that we've got this curious body we have to lug along with us and you keep it going by breathing in and out. That's interesting, isn't it? The trees all around us, and the animals are doing it, too. And I'd like to help them. So it's natural that I say no to those who seek to pollute the world. They make breathing so much more difficult.

I'm just arranging to give this house and land, the whole place, to all, and trust that will keep it going after I'm gone. It's not going into the real estate market. It will be maintained more or less as it is. I'm calling it the Good Life Center.

Regrets? I wish I had played the violin a little longer and a little better. But then I would have been a professional, and I might never have met Scott. I asked Scott if he had ever regretted any of his decisions in life, knowing how his career was in ruins. He said quite seriously: No, he probably would have acted even stronger if he had the chance again. But in his personal life, he'd have learned more about being kinder to people and understanding them more. As to losing his career, I sensed no bitterness in him at all, nor any regrets. Had he behaved and been more discreet, as most of his colleagues had suggested, he'd have been just a college professor. Whereas, now, he reached many more people.

As for growing old, aging, it's a wonderful process. It's a mellowing and a growing and a completion. It's a thrill. Turning point in my life? There were no points, no angles. It was all in a circle, things naturally following after each other. I don't feel I had any great decisions to make. My very being followed along in a very beautiful curve, so it's now rounding into a complete circle.

I have no fear of dying, none at all. I don't know what it is to be afraid. It'll all go on with me or without me. While I'm here, I'd like to help: hoping that some day, instead of learning to kill, we'll learn to behave decently. Scott had a good phrase: "Do the best you can in the place where you are."

CHAPTER TWENTY

At the Home

Millie Beck, 74
SAN FRANCISCO, CALIFORNIA

She and her older brother, Gregory Bergmann, 85, are visiting Chicago as delegates to a convention of the embattled elderly. He is a bantam game-cock, who has been in labor battles since his young manhood. He had worked as a circulation manager for William Randolph Hearst's San Fancisco Examiner; *as a porter; as a union organizer; as a labor journalist. He was an ad hoc participant in the San Francisco general strike of 1934.*

As he recounts his life's trials, much of it having to do with family sorrows as well as his David and Goliath battles with "the big boys," there is a constant: his capacity to bounce back.

He is continually on the move, a graceful one, in the hotel room, seeking and finding one thing or another: an old newspaper clipping, a manuscript, a live battery for my nonfunctioning tape recorder. He succeeds in all three quests.

She has been listening to his account with considerable interest, as though hearing it for the first time. She has an air of equanimity, in contrast to her brother, and is more amply proportioned. Her pride in him is manifest. "Gregory has been a big influence on me in my life. We talk to each other two or three times during the day, seven days a week."*

I was born in San Francisco. I joined the Marine Corps in 1943, during World War II. I was twenty-six at the time. I wasn't that gung-ho, but I felt that in the military service you did what you were told, and it didn't bother me at all. I met my husband at depot supply while I was in the corps. We had three children. He died in 1972. I was working as a bookkeeper.

When I was sixty-five, I moved into a federal housing project in Antioch, California, about sixty miles from San Francisco. You have

---

* 1993 was the year of the visit. Gregory Bergmann died in 1994.

to be sixty-two years of age or older. It's low-income subsidized housing, which means you pay one-third of your income in rent. It's racially mixed.

Each project has a tenants association. It's required. At the time, the man who was president of our association was charging people a dollar for cheese, two dollars for butter, that sort of thing. According to the federal government, you can't charge for any products. He was charging people for traveling back and forth. The tenants were getting rather angry and asked me if I would run for president. I was reluctant, but I thought, "Well, I'll try it."

This man did not conduct hearings in a democratic way. If you raised your hand to vote, he would say, "Hey, Sadie, what do you got your hand up for? I didn't want you to vote that way." And they wouldn't vote. So I contacted the Antioch Committee on Aging and asked them to oversee the election. I won seventy-four to eight. He was very downfallen. He thought he'd win.

How I got this way? Gregory, of course, is a great influence on our family. He's the oldest. There's Dan, there's Ray, and I'm the baby girl, eleven years younger than Gregory. We were all a union family, except for Dan, who is a millionaire. He is against unions, always was. For the first year, I went to parochial school; but it was too much money for our family, so I went to the public schools.

When I got out of the service, I worked at the Fairmont Hotel, as the front-desk clerk, as cashier, and as night auditor. It was during the war, when they had women at the front desk.

After my husband's death, I followed my son to Alaska and lived there for three years. I just took care of the three grandchildren. I came back here to do bookkeeping again. It was the only profession I really knew.

At sixty-four, ten years after I retired, I became active in the project. What annoyed me was that every time I went down to our community center and told these women about Ronald Reagan, they'd say, "Oh, no, Ronnie wouldn't do that to us." There had to be something I could do to wake them up. I'd go house to house. I keep going all the time. When old people have their mind set, it's impossible. I started writing letters to the editor. I think they published about eighty-five in the *Antioch Ledger*.

I wanted an "over sixty" clinic, because I found that doctors weren't treating their elderly patients right. They would give them a pill and say, "This should do you. You're getting old and that's all you can expect. Go home." The pill would be something like a valium to tranquilize them. I got angry. I decided we should have a clinic for elderly people, where, if you're dizzy, they don't just say it's because you're old. We raised $450,000 and we have that clinic.

We didn't like what Kaiser, one of the largest HMOs* in California, was doing. They'd say, "Have a pill, go home." My son said, "Don't talk to a doctor or a nurse. Go where the money is." So I called Kaiser's marketing rep and said, "The Antioch Committee on Aging does not appreciate what you're doing to the older people of this country. I want to see the number of people you have on your computer printout who are over sixty-five in this county." "Oh, we can't do that." I said, "Will you come to our meeting?" They came and said, "You've read our brochure." We got mad and said, "We don't want your (may I say the word?) damn brochure. We want service for the elderly, not just a pill. And you're sending them to other parts of the county, when they have no transportation." So we made them set up a transportation unit.

Somebody said to me: [*mocks horrified voice*] "How could you do that? It's a big company." I said, "What's the difference? You pay into it, don't ya? You ought to get something out of it." Now their social service worker and a marketing rep come to every one of our meetings. The only way you can get something done is to go out and tackle it.

A lady came to see me one day and said, "My doctor went to Los Angeles and the new one charged ninety dollars for what the old one charged forty dollars." I said, "Why didn't you tell the doctor, 'Hey, you can't do this.'" She said, "Oh, I can't. He's a doctor!" I said, "What the hell, he's in practice to make money, and he's taking your money. Tell him you're not satisfied with his service." "Oh, I can't do that." Oh God, that just irritates me. She said, "*You* speak up. I can't." So that's when I got that "over sixty" clinic.

People are just so timid. You have to realize with many of these old women, all their lives their husbands made the decisions for them. When their husbands died, a lot of them didn't even know how to make out a check. Part of our health program helps people with all this.

I'm working now for a two-hundred-bed convalescent hospital. Our county has two such hospitals that are for-profit. They're either Missouri- or Arkansas-based. They charge over three thousand dollars a month. They won't take Medicaid cases, maybe one or two. I heard about three people who've died because they couldn't get in. We've been talking about this for three years. One day, I said, "This is enough talking. Let's do something."

Now we have a task force of twenty-two people: an architect, nurses, doctors. We have two hospitals involved and the head of our county health services. They all come to every one of our meetings.

---

* Health maintenance organizations.

We figure, in '94 or '95, we'll get federal and maybe state money to build this.

Yeah, I guess people look up to me. Just the other day, somebody said, "Ask Millie." I said, "What do you mean, ask Millie?" "Well, you've got clout." "I have no more clout than the man in the moon. I'm just not afraid to ask."

This is the whole point with older people. They're so afraid. Five years ago, there was an old woman down the hall from me. She's rushing around.

"Where are you going?" I said.

"I have to go to work," she said.

"You work?"

"I have to go and clean houses because, after rent, I don't have enough to keep my car."

I said, "What do you get?"

"Well, my husband was a farmer, so we don't get much social security."

"Why don't you get SSI?"* I said.

"Oh, I couldn't do that. I might lose my social security."

I said, "I'll go with you. I don't have a car, so we'll go in yours."

"No, no, no," she said. "I'll lose my social security."

I convinced her to go and she got her SSI. You have to constantly nudge them. They are so afraid of authority—any authority at all.

One day we were having a bingo game, one of the main activities of the elderly. One of the ladies came upstairs. She was nervous. "Mildred, you have to come down, there's a policeman here." I asked him, "What do you want?" He said something about gambling, a complaint. We went back and forth on it. After he left, somebody says, "Weren't you afraid to talk to the policeman?" I said, "What for? What were we doing wrong?"

I don't challenge authority in a personal way. When I call up the head of a utility, I don't holler at him. I say, "Hey, rates are going up too fast." He says one thing and another. He knows me. Same thing when I go to the city council to complain. I have all the facts, but I never embarrass anyone personally. They're just people with jobs.

If I wake up at five o'clock in the morning on a day where I'm calling somebody at the planning commission, I lay in bed thinking, "How am I going to say this?" I don't want it to sound like I'm challenging him. I try to put things in such a way that he doesn't have to step down. To let him save face. I find it easier that way to get what you want. It has to be that way.

There aren't too many people who will speak out. They are afraid

---

* Supplemental security income.

of losing what they have. Fear. I hate to see that come up in the elderly. They're scared to death. They'll sit in their apartments with their curtains all drawn. They withdraw within themselves. Sometimes they resent what I do. Don't make waves.

I'm not going to stop. Somebody asked me the other day, "What are you going to do when the convalescent hospital starts?" I said, "Don't worry. I'll think of something else."

I visited a friend of mine at a local hospital, and all the time there was hollering and yelling. Four to a room. One woman was dying, moaning all the time. I think these people should be allowed to die in dignity. We need a soundproof wing for those people that holler, so they can yell as loud as they need. Everybody says, "How about the costs?" I said, "Don't worry about the cost. We'll get it when the time comes. It's the need now."

It takes a lot of people to make something go. Because I speak up more doesn't mean that it works just because of me. You have to have everybody involved.

Frances Freeborn Pauley, 88

ATLANTA, GEORGIA

A soft, southern accent, reminiscent of "quality people" in a Flannery O'Connor short story.

"Freeborn is my middle name. It was spelled different ways back in the family. My mother's and father's family were early settlers in Ohio, which was then the Western Reserve. I have stories of their coming in on covered wagons. My great-grandfather was a doctor in the Civil War. My father had a men's clothing store in this little bitty town, Wadsworth, Ohio. It burned down one Saturday night, so my uncle asked Papa to join the seed business. That's how we came to Atlanta. Ever since 1908, I've lived in this vicinity.

"Neither my mother nor my father were prejudiced people. I remember mother thinking it was ridiculous for black people to go to the back door when the front door was closest."

She lives in a retirement home in Atlanta. "I have two rooms and eat one meal a day in the dining room. They do some of your housekeeping so it's a very easy life."

I'm just a fat old lady. I'm thankful I can still maneuver to some extent, but I regret I can't be as active as I've always been.

What is my day like? It's simply facing the problems of old age. My chief problem is that I'm losing my eyesight and I love and love and love to read. And I like to try to write. To take away reading and writing…it's hard not to be depressed. I felt like I'd just as soon be dead.

I still have peripheral vision, so I can still walk and look out the window and see the colored leaves. So I won't go just plain blind, as you would if you had glaucoma or something like that.

Just daily living gets to be a little more of a problem because you've got to remember where you've put things out or else you can't find them because you can't see where they are. So you're always doing something like hunting for your shoes. It seems to take me ten times as long just to do something like get dressed and make up my bed. Just to look after myself is great, great effort. So far, I'm able to do it, my finances as well. I don't know how long it will last, but I'm thankful I still can.

Sometimes I have lots of telephone calls because of the kinds of work I've done in the past. I've worked with a lot of poor people who would call me and tell me their problems. Then I would try to think of something I could do about it.

When Vernon Jordan* was a youngster, he and I used to work

---

* At one time, executive director of the National Urban League.

together a lot on civil rights. Somebody would say, "Let's do something about this. It's terrible." One day Vernon said, "Ask Frances. She'll do something even if it's wrong." [*Laughs.*]

I don't get as many calls as I used to, but I'll get them. Someone will say, "I'm being evicted. What can I do?" I'll try to figure out something. I try to at least find somebody that can help them.

In my younger days, I was director of the Georgia Council on Human Relations. From about '60 to '68. People around the state know me: just poor people hither and yonder.

At the moment I work with an agency, the Open Door Community. It's an old apartment house where homeless people live and are fed. Black and white. That's my main interest: the homeless. I can't do so much as make a pot of soup, but one thing I can do is be friends. Aside from a cup of soup, they need somebody that cares about them.

I still speak occasionally for various groups. Last week, CALC (Clergy and Laity Concerned) asked me to speak at their annual meeting. The twelve homeless people who run the Open Door were waiting for me in the parking lot and escorted me to make this talk. It was a wonderful feeling.

They feed people on Sunday morning and have their church service in the afternoon. It's informal, more religious than a church. I always try to be there. When you've been there, you feel like God was there. These people really believe in loving their neighbor, feeding the hungry. They really believe in the teachings of Jesus. You don't hear that very much when you're among some church people.

I'm very religious but I don't affiliate with any church. I've seen organized religion do too many cruel things. When you go to Open Door, you know Jesus was there. The backyard is free. They don't allow the police in to arrest homeless people. At night, the yard is simply spaced with bodies, wrapped in blankets, sleeping on the ground. Last Sunday somebody preached a little service about Jesus hanging around here. I thought to myself, if you're looking for Jesus, you *will* find him in our backyard.

One of the beautiful things about homeless people is their caring for each other. A man died in the yard—we knew him slightly—and we were all grieving. At the memorial service the next Sunday, one of his homeless friends drew a circle on the ground and he said, "Johnny used to draw a circle just like this and say, 'Come on, fellas, throw in your change.' We'd throw in whatever change we had, scoop it up, go across the street, get a bottle and share it." So with that, this little group stood around the circle and threw in red roses.

I got married in 1930, during the Depression. My husband was a landscape architect and his business went to zero. So I was concerned about people that didn't have anything to eat. I appreciated the government stepping in, the WPA and the PWA,* because that's how we ate. The government specified there must be a landscape architect to lay out the site planning for a new courthouse or school building or maybe a park. We got paid a little bit more than the guy that was planting the trees. Not much, but it was money to eat.

I heard about this new government program of free lunches at school. The first thing I did was call a meeting. I didn't have any better sense. I didn't go and see the school superintendent. I just telephoned all the school principals in the county to please come to a meeting. Within six weeks, why, we had hot-lunch programs going on in all the schools. See, you can cut through the red tape if you just go ahead and do it. Don't wait to make all the plans and check with all the people, because somebody along the way will stop you. Anybody can do it. I don't think people realize how much power they have, but you have to use it.

If a homeless poor person off the street, with two or three other people and maybe a black preacher, goes into a politician's office, the first thing you know, the politician is really listening because he probably thinks they have a lot bigger following than they really do. I think everybody's voice is important.

This doesn't mean there aren't voices in the wilderness crying out and nobody pays them any mind. Maybe they just didn't get to the right place at the right time. Maybe that's what some of us are supposed to do: guide people to the right place at the right time.

My daughter just spent the weekend with me. She lives in another state. I worry because I usually forget things. She said, "Mama, I want to tell you one thing. Deaf, yes, you are. Blind, yes, you are. But, Mama, you're not senile." [*A light laugh.*]

There are two hundred in the building where I live. The problem with a lot of old people is that they don't use their minds. They just listen to the soap operas. It's like everything else: use it or lose it. I think it's as true of your mind as it is of your arm. Don't you?

The exercise I take and believe greatly in is Tai Chi. Chinese. You use your mind here, too. It takes more concentration than anything I've ever tried to do. It's wonderful. You've got to concentrate on how that arm is moving.

Today I'll have lunch in the dining room with the rest. I was going to a play but canceled it. I love plays and discussions about them at our city's repertory theater. The last play I saw was about Clarence Thomas and Anita Hill. It was good.

I sure was upset about Thomas's appointment because I know so

---

* The Public Works Administration. It was headed by Harold Ickes, Roosevelt's secretary of the interior.

many wonderful black judges who could have been appointed. [*Indignantly.*] And then for them to appoint *him*. I admire her for trying to stop it. I just wish she had succeeded.

When I was a little girl, I didn't have any black friends. The kids I played with in the neighborhood were white. When my family first moved here from Ohio, my mother wasn't used to black help: the nurse, the maid, the cook. Paying them a pittance. My mother didn't think it was right to have somebody work for nothing all day long.

I remember the neighbors criticized her because she had somebody for an eight-hour day. If they came in and cooked breakfast, they left after lunch. If they cooked dinner at night, they came in the middle of the day. She believed black people were people and should be treated the same way as whites. I don't remember much conversation about it. That was just the way it was. In the depression, it bothered me that white people could get free medical attention and a lot of free things, where the black people couldn't.

I was a young housewife, but I couldn't stand to do nothing but tend my two babies. So I organized a clinic for poor people, black and white. I always had some project, and I guess I was a pretty good organizer.

Did I get in trouble? Sure. One time I was down in southern Georgia working for the Council on Human Relations. I had driven a carload of black people down to the courthouse in this little town. Some white people saw me. It was unheard of for a white woman. This white man came with a gun and said, "I'm going to kill you." That sort of a problem. [*Laughs.*] This was in the '60s, when the blacks were trying to register to vote.

I had alerted the FBI to the fact that we were going to register. Sometimes the FBI would be there to protect us, sometimes it wasn't. A black man once said to me, "I'll just tell you the truth, ma'am. It's a heap better when they ain't here."

Anyway, that day I went across to the FBI and I said, "See that man over there? You see he has a gun. Well, he just threatened to kill me." He said, "What did he tell you to do?" I said, "He told me to leave town." So the FBI man says, "Well, I think if I were you, I'd leave town." He didn't approach the guy at all.

So I left town. There wasn't anything else I could do. I was not brought up to be afraid of things. That was one thing I thank my parents for. But this time I was scared. You'd be crazy not to be. What little training I had in acting sometimes helped me. I've always been able to play the part. You can't *act* scared. You lose it if you do. When I got to the edge of town, I got in a phone booth and called the governor. I told him what happened. I said, "You promised that if I went in, you'd give me backing, that you approved of what I was doing.

We've got to have some help down here or somebody's gonna get killed. They threatened to kill me, and I'm worried about the leader." (The young black man who was at the head of the group.) He said, "All right, I'll send people." Within an hour, the state patrol was there. Nobody got killed that day and they did register.

One time I had a meeting with some of Dr. King's cohorts. We had registration plans for Albany, Georgia. A black woman was with me, and we were riding down the road. I realized that the police were following. Oh, they always followed me. I said to her, "I'm going to pull out, and I want you to get out because I don't want you involved." So she got out and I moved on ahead. A little way down, the police stopped me, arrested me, and took me to jail. I just stood there while they were trying to decide what to charge me with.

I knew the jails were full of civil rights people. I thought, "Oh, my God, they're going to put me off somewhere and nobody will ever find me. About that time, the press came along. It may have been Pat Watters of the *Atlanta Journal*. I said, "Call Atlanta, get me a good lawyer, but do not call my family." I didn't want to scare them, and I knew I'd get out anyway. Somebody came down from the mayor's office and says, "The mayor says charge Mrs. Pauley with a traffic violation and let her go."

That little black woman I dropped off had the courage to go to the mayor's office to tell I'd been arrested. Let me tell you something: unless you had been there, it's hard to realize how much courage it took. I don't remember her name, but that's what she did.

I went back to the motel and sat down on my bed. I was shaken. "What am I gonna do? Shall I leave or what?" Then I said, "No, I cannot leave. I'm not through." So I went downtown and told the Albany chief of police that I hadn't quite finished what I was doing in town and although a few people had suggested I leave town, I had decided to stay. And walked out. He just sat there with his mouth open and didn't say anything.

It was very hot in southern Georgia in the summertime. So I often drove at night. If I got somewhere, I'd be so drenched, I'd have to change my clothes before I could go and be decent. I had several frights driving nights, because often the police followed me. Today when I see a policeman, I'm still scared of him. I don't any more trust the police than...

You sound like a black person.

Well, they *know*. Funny you should say I sound black. Margaret Mead used to come down here and stay with a mutual friend. I was invited to a dinner party because she wanted to discuss civil rights at an armchair level. I had a couple of drinks and we got into a heated discussion. I believed in public schools and Margaret Mead believed in private schools. It was a really hot argument. Martinis do that, you know. After I left, she said to her host, "Now that fat woman who sat over there, she's not really white, is she?"

Some of the young people at Emory University, close by, often ask me to come and talk. They know about me. Recently, a guy from Pakistan came by to pick me up, to take me to a meeting. Some of the old ladies were sitting around in the lobby and saw me leaving with this kid, wearing his native Pakistani tunic. I heard one say to the other, "Frances would go out with anyone." [*Laughs.*]

They look at you strangely, though fondly?

Not too fondly, though I think I've converted a few. Of course, to reach anybody, you've got to care about them. Some of the guests at the retirement are great, some lousy. Just like any group. They don't understand me and I have a hard time understanding them. Quite a few are ministers' wives. I don't have much in common with a minister's wife.

They're very prejudiced against the homeless. One said to me, "I'd scrub floors before I'd beg for food." I looked at her, eighty years old and all dressed up. I said, "I wouldn't hire you to scrub floors. I don't think you'd do a good job. What would you do if you couldn't find a job scrubbing floors?" She just looked at me, mouth open. [*Laughs.*]

Do I have hope for our species? [*Laughs softly, sighs.*] Maybe the young people may save us, because I sense a lot of them are waking up. I see them more interested in the community than the past generation of young. But I'm an incurable optimist. What did that Chicano woman tell you? Hope dies last?* That's wonderful. That's it.

---

* "With us, there's a saying: *La esperanza muere al último.* Hope dies last. You can't lose hope. If you lose hope, that's losing everthing."
—Jessie De La Cruz, in *American Dreams: Lost and Found,* 1980

Bessie Doenges, 93

We're in her apartment at a senior citizen's center. The electric fan gives forth a pleasant breeze on this hot day. She is relaxing on the divan, her tiny feet casually plopped onto the nearby end table. "Someone described me as petite. I can describe everybody else, but not myself. Maybe I don't want to look at myself. I'm just kidding."

She writes a regular column for a neighborhood weekly, The Westsider. *"I write about old age and how terrible it is."*

I can't seem to remember what happened yesterday, but I can remember what happened in 1912, things like that. I was eleven when the *Titanic* sank. They let the women and children into the lifeboats, as they themselves drowned. See, there is some goodness in people. I remember the suffragettes. And the writers, Galsworthy and H. G. Wells. We read him a great deal.

I was born in Canada, 1901. The Boer War was on, and there've been wars ever since. If we keep having them, we'll blow ourselves off the earth. Don't you think so? My mother and father were in church and the minister said, "All able-bodied men should go fight the Boers." My mother said she threw her arms around my father to keep him from going. She kept a diary. They all kept diaries. My ancestors were Tories who fled to Canada. They made the wrong turn. My great-great-grandfather's best friend was Benedict Arnold. Can you imagine?

What's my day like? I wake up in the morning and I think, "I'm glad to be alive." So I roll over on my stomach and feel just great. I look up to see what time it is and I go back to sleep. Finally, I get up and do a little dance on account of my arthritis. It helps. Then I stagger out to the kitchen and get this wonderful oatmeal. We used to call it porridge. I just pour hot water on the flakes. Get the coffee. Just pour water on that. I bring it back very carefully to this table. Then I get the *Times*, which a dear friend puts outside the door. And I read the obituaries. And I think things could be worse. In fact, it's damn good. I got through the night, by golly, and I'm likely to live through this day. One day is as good as a hundred days, when you reach this age.

I have a hundred things wrong with me. I could start at my head and go right on down. I smoked until 1958. When the doctor told me to stop, I said, "You're asking me to cut off my leg." He said, "Which leg?" So I stopped.

You're a salty one.

Oui, oui.

I take my time getting dressed, go downstairs and get my ticket for lunch. I've sat at the same table for eighteen years. We know each other thoroughly. Then I take my cane and try to get to the Strawberry Fields in Central Park. I ask someone to help me across the street and I've never been refused yet. They all come through, every single one. When you're ninety-two and five-sixths, you can get away with murder.

At the Strawberry Fields, I sit there. It's marvelous. It's like a beautiful picture: trees, a young man playing the violin. People have staked out claims. If I sit down at a certain place and the woman who always sits there comes along, I immediately get up, bow, and take another seat. You own that seat and it gives you a feeling of security, which you want very much when you're older.

Then I come home, take a little nap. Then I read and write this stuff for *The Westsider.* At six o'clock, the real evening starts. I have a scotch and soda and watch TV. I watch the news, and then *Jeopardy* comes on and *Wheel of Fortune.* Maybe you're too refined to watch it, but by this time I've had the drink and anything looks good to me.

Then it's eight o'clock and I fight sleep, damn it all. I fight it with everything I've got! I don't want to go to bed, life's too short. Actually, I sleep twelve hours or maybe fourteen. Sleep is my last lover. I don't want it, but there you have it. By nine o'clock, I've given in and fall into a delightful sleep. I accept it with grace. What else can I do? I wake up in the light of the morning. Yeah! Yah-hoo!

I always wanted to write when I came to New York. I used to get stuff in the *Times,* this was 1920. I wrote in the Hearst papers and got more money for verse than I get now. I never told anybody about it. I was writing brochures for a Protestant welfare group and got twenty-five dollars a month.

I grew up in a writing atmosphere. My father was a writer and a judge in New Brunswick. He had a story in the *Saturday Evening Post,* the same issue with Scott Fitzgerald. He wrote for Scribner's. High class. Then he suddenly stopped.

I came to New York to help my husband with his small printing business. I tried to write the great American novel. Well, I wrote it, but I couldn't sell it. I gave up writing and typed reports for a large insurance company. I was fifty-three and said I was forty-two. They were already funny about age.

About thirteen years ago, when I was eighty, I started writing again. A teacher at a senior club set me off. Almost at once, I began to sell to the "Metropolitan Diary" in the *Times*. At first, they only gave a bottle of champagne. Then the editor said, "We pay starving poets twenty dollars. Are you a starving poet?" I said, "I certainly am." So I got twenty bucks and my name in the papers. It's a family curse: we write and never get to the top. Then the great *New York Times* stopped paying. They didn't want any professionals for the section, they wanted sort of like "Letters to the Editor" stuff. I got something in Newsday's *Viewpoint* and they paid me 150 bucks. Wow!

I have something published in *The Westsider* every week. Fifty-two pieces a year when you're ninety-two and five-sixths—I've got scrapbooks here if you want to look through them. Verse, prose. I'm eight weeks ahead now.

What do I think of my contemporaries here? I like them. We have so much in common: surviving and trying to get something out of life. So we listen to each other's oft-told tales, because we probably do the same thing ourselves. We cannot help but like them, because we have common memories. They are really *us:* we're all one person.

I have a motto: "Judge not, lest ye be judged," and "Let him who is without sin cast the first stone." I believe that because man is prone to sin, and anyway, it's none of my business. I refuse to judge. My husband and I never judged each other. We were married forty-four years. He died in 1971 and I still wake up with his name on my lips. Writing about him makes me feel good.

I discovered things about him that I hadn't realized before. For instance, he had a way of thinking about animals and birds as if they're people. There was a swan up in Pelham Bay Park. He used to bring it food. Sometimes he even gave him our lunch. I didn't think much of that. I wrote about this: *The Wayward Swan.*

I think the young today are much more honest than we were. They see things as they are. I would not want to be young now. They're having a hell of a time. I feel I've been lucky in life. In the depression, my husband's business, my goodness. Terrible. We slept in the park because we had no money for rent. He said, "I'm gonna sell the dump. I'm a burden to you." I wouldn't let him. I still had a job. We'd sleep in the park, what'd it matter? I let him do the worrying for both of us. No, I don't judge the young. They're having an unhappy time.

What are your thoughts as you read the news today?

Simply terrible. People starving to death. Do you have a right to be happy when you read about a Bosnian child as you have your morning toast? Do you know how many pills I take for everything? Six, seven times or so. One for emphysema; something I call "dipsydoo-dle," for circulation; for blood pressure; for my heart; for diverticulosis—which makes me sick. I cut it out.

Scientifically, the world has gone beautifully. It's very exciting. You see a young woman walk along the street with something in her ear. She's talking to someone on the telephone. It's exciting to be alive, but I don't have a great deal of hope for the world. I think we're going to blow ourselves up. We could have *everything*, everybody. We're going to make it so we don't have to do donkey work: press a button. We can enjoy music, art, gardening, all the fine things. And have time to be friends. But we're going to throw it all away. I think we're no damn good.

What is it about the human race?

Our jungle heritage. [*Chuckles, self-deprecatingly.*] I have the nerve to make any statement. It's such a complex, dark problem. A lot of stuff I write is about the supernatural. I don't know why that is.

Do you believe in the supernatural?

I don't know. I really don't care one way or the other. Yes, I do care. I don't want to die. How would I like to be remembered? I don't want to be celebrated, just forget it. Take all my writings that are left and make a big bonfire out of them. I'm going to be cremated, and I don't want to linger if there's something the matter with me. I've got a will to that effect.

I must be independent. I wouldn't want to live with relatives, have them boss me around and be a burden. That's why I went to my wonderful doctor of forty years. I told her my feet are going to sleep. She said, "Bang them on the floor."

Listen, I get out on the street with my cane and all of a sudden, I've lost my balance, I can't take a step, I holler, "Help, help." Immediately, a crowd will come and they'll want to help me home. But I get my balance back and I walk.

No one has ever failed to help you, yet you say these same people will blow themselves up—

There seems to be something in man, an altruistic something, away from the self, toward others. That is the hope of the world. But with all the wars I've seen, all the unhappiness, I don't think the world will survive. I sure *hope* it does.

I'm a Baptist and Methodist, but I haven't been to church for many years. I notice that people my age who have religion can face death better than the ones who don't. They'll say, "The Lord is watching over me and he'll take care of me. If he wants me to die, that'll be great. I'll die with His name on my lips. Oh, my blessed savior." I can't do that.

I envy them and I don't. They think they're going to heaven. I don't know about the hereafter. I think the soul survives, perhaps. Yeah, I think there's something in people that may survive. I just plain don't know. I don't laugh at people who believe in the supernatural. They may be right! I wouldn't say either way.

I'm an agnostic, I guess. Then again, maybe I'm not. I don't want to influence anybody one way or the other. I don't want to offend anybody, hurt them. 'Cause, listen, words can hurt. Oh, boy. I had a stepmother, a very beautiful woman of a very fine family. Somehow she hated us. I had a cancer on my nose when I was a baby. They had to cut through the nose to get it out. I was so sensitive about it as a child. They'd call out to me, "Split nose." My stepmother called me "an ugly little hussy," "a fiend out of hell." She said, "I hated you from the minute I set my eyes on you."

I used to run away a lot and was something of a problem child. Look at it from her point of view: she was a beautiful woman, thirty-one years old when she married my father. Here are these three kids dumped on her. She had been married to a planter from India, and there were all sorts of clippings about him and his lovely Canadian bride. You've got to think about that. I did judge her for years, but now I don't know.

Maybe that's why you're so lively. You don't carry that extra vengeance and self-righteousness.

I've got enough faults without that.

We look through her scrapbook. There are scores of her columns, "Bessie Writes" and some Times' *"Metropolitan Diary" pieces.*

Here's one I wrote in the '80s. [*She reads.*] "Entering the park, I stared at a chestnut tree that I fell into, or it fell into me, and I got to be it." I have a hundred things like that.

I wrote about my friend Jack. He sent me a note that's stuck on my Frigidaire. "Life, a hop, a skip, and a jump, and it's over." He died a week later.

Here's another: "My nephew said, 'Some birds just sing in the springtime. After that they only call.' I tried a little jig on my ninety-two-year-old feet. 'It's true all right,' I agreed. Everything sings in the springtime. The primal shout, when they all start singing at once. Aren't the birds telling us something? Something about survival, about hope, something about love, would you say? What else does it do? What else? It dares you not to believe in God."

T. S. Eliot was right when he wrote, "April is the cruelest month, breeding lilacs out of the dead land, mixing memory and desire." That's how I headed one of my things. "Imprisoned in the city on a rainy Sunday, in a fifth-floor walk-up. Hard for two to live in peace. You prefer the sanctuary of the empty streets. I didn't blame you, but you came back too soon, bringing me a bunch of purple lilacs, backyard lilacs, back home lilacs. Thrust them in my arms with love abundant, giving us a chance to start all over." I think I'll add another line. "Sixty years gone by, but I still see you standing there and smiling. With the lilacs in your arms. Yes, yes, April is the cruelest month."

In her office, the director of the center reads from a letter to the editor of The Westsider: *"In the last few issues, Bessie has become sublime. Her pieces have always been good, but suddenly they constrict the throat and make the breath catch. She's sharing herself in such an immediate and personal way now. She's offering herself with total unselfconsciousness and yet full consciousness. What a gift she's given us. Thank you, Bessie."*

In the manner of a tour guide, Bessie introduces me to some of her fellow residents as we pass through.

PORTLY MAN: *I'm blessed by the Almighty, if there is such a thing. I say to myself, "I don't know everything, therefore this is one of the things I don't know." I'm eighty-nine and I was in the clothing business. I'm interested in something I know nothing about. The fact that I'm looking is the important thing. Seeking is more important than the end.*

WOMAN: *You've heard of my son. He translated* The Dead Sea Scrolls Uncovered.

PORTLY MAN: *I'm not interested in anything that's dead.*

THIN MAN: *Do you understand German? I'm a free thinker. Die Gedanken sind Frei.*

STUDS TERKEL: *I have to scram, but I enjoyed meeting you.*

PORTLY MAN: *That's what life is about, passing the time of the day.*

MUSCULAR MAN: *Not passing, filling. I'm a body builder, eighty-one years old. I've become known for that. I'm the oldest guy doing this.*

PORTLY WOMAN: *I sang Brunhilde in Germany, and I sang Kundry in Parsifal at La Scala. Without an agent. Are you interested in music? The story of my life is unbelievable.*

We're on the patio of a restaurant, watching the passing parade on the crowded city street.

I eat up their faces. They all look beautiful, and the reason is that they are alive. Everything alive is beautiful. Even murderers. Whatever good there is in them is still alive. The alive part, call it the soul, call it what you will. I choose not to see the other part. It's not my affair.

[*She laughs at something she sees. Or is it something she thought?*]

You've got to have humor to get through life. It's the one best thing, so help me. Maybe I'm laughing so I won't burst out crying. Who knows? Listen, I figure, since I got to be this age, I've got it made. No matter what terrible thing may happen, I'm still ahead of the game.